CHILDREN'S ILLUSTRATIONS FOR THE STORY OF THE FRENCH PORTAGES

In each case the child's undirected first attempt appears at the left, his directed drawing at the right.

Learning and Teaching History in the Middle Grades

By

MARY G. KELTY

*Formerly Supervisor of History and the Social Studies
in the Training Department and Instructor
in the Teaching of History, State Teachers College
Oshkosh, Wisconsin*

GINN AND COMPANY

BOSTON · NEW YORK · CHICAGO · LONDON · ATLANTA · DALLAS · COLUMBUS · SAN FRANCISCO

The Athenæum Press
GINN AND COMPANY · PRO-
PRIETORS · BOSTON · U.S.A.

To the Memory of
THEODORE C. LUTZ
*Whose Faith in Education
opened up a New World*

NOTE TO THE TEACHER

Because of the length of this book it has been necessary to set many of the tests at the end of each story and unit in a style different from that which the teacher would use for the children. To save space, the tests have been printed in run-on style with the right responses checked (see pages 121, 152, 280, 322, 517, 522).

In administering the tests to children, however, a different arrangement of the responses is desirable. Instead of the run-on style, experience has shown the value of arranging the materials with the choices printed in list form, with the break in the sentence made at the beginning of the dependent clause or phrase, and with the connecting word or words repeated each time.

The following are examples of the manner in which these materials would be arranged for presentation to children.

A. Travel is good for people   (Part Two, p. 121)
   ___ because it helps them to spend their money.
   ___ because they learn many new ideas.
   ___ because they have a good time while traveling.
   ___ because they do not have to work when traveling.

B. The Aztecs were the Indians   (Part Two, p. 152)
   ___ who helped Cortez's soldiers to fight.
   ___ who lived in and around the city of Mexico.
   ___ who lived on islands in the Gulf.

C. Washington chose four men to be cabinet officers   (Part Three, p. 280)
   ___ so that they might give him their advice.
   ___ so that they would not have so much to do.
   ___ so that they might win votes for him.
   ___ so that he might have a guard.

D. General Taylor's expedition showed   (Part Three, p. 322)
   ___ that the Americans had more courage than the Mexicans.
   ___ that the Mexicans would not fight for their country.
   ___ that it is almost impossible to march an army far across sandy
        deserts.
   ___ that it is easy to conquer a people as scattered as the Mexicans.

E. The greatest thing which Hammurapi did was   (Part Four, p. 517)
   ___ to make good laws for business.
   ___ to force everyone to obey the laws.
   ___ to classify the laws in a code.

v

F. Phoenicia was governed   (Part Four, p. 522)
      --- by kings.
      --- by wealthy families.
      --- by all the people.
      --- by the priests.

Children's careless placing of the check mark which indicates the right answer has long been a source of difficulty. The children often complain that they "meant" the check to be placed before a given item, when in fact it may be placed between two items or nearer a wrong item. To prevent this situation from arising, teachers will find it helpful in hectographing, mimeographing, or printing the tests to place a small base line (---) in front of every item. All the illustrations above have such a line for this purpose. Children may then be directed to make their check marks directly upon the lines.

CONTENTS

PART ONE. THE PSYCHOLOGICAL AND SOCIAL FOUNDATIONS

PART TWO. LEARNING AND TEACHING EARLY AMERICAN HISTORY

PART THREE. LEARNING AND TEACHING LATER AMERICAN HISTORY

PART FOUR. LEARNING AND TEACHING THE BEGINNINGS OF CIVILIZATION

LEARNING AND TEACHING HISTORY
IN THE MIDDLE GRADES

PART ONE. THE PSYCHOLOGICAL
AND SOCIAL FOUNDATIONS

The importance of the social sciences in the school curriculum, and their contributions to the thinking of the adult population, have been very generally recognized within the last few years. In theory, at least, they have been accorded a key position as the "core of the curriculum." The public has become convinced of the crucial necessity of greater social intelligence and good will among the members of a democratic state.

There is, indeed, danger that too much may be expected from the mere introduction of new social-science materials and new methods into the schools. The movement needs to be protected against the extreme claims of its overenthusiastic followers. The fact is inescapable that the school operates as an instrumentality of society, and that as such its aims, purposes, and values must reflect the aims, purposes, and values of the highest-grade life from which it proceeds. Teachers are only units of the social group; they unconsciously absorb society's sense of values. Even the children live in the social order, as well as in the schools; and if there is too much variance in the respective points of view and weights assigned, it is the school, not society, that will seem impracticable, visionary, or reactionary, as the case may be.

Nevertheless, the school is unquestionably one of the chief agencies through which more desirable adjustments can be made and a better social order evolved — provided it is not too far divorced from reality. And the social sciences can play a responsible part in bringing about such changes.[1]

The social sciences of the public schools include history, economics, sociology, political science, civics courses (variously named), and certain phases of geography and anthropology, whether in isolation or integration. Moreover, increasing efforts are being made to bring out clearly the social implications of *all* the school subjects, and of all the activities which go to make up school life.[2] For this reason many educators reject the term *social studies* and prefer instead the less inclusive term *social sciences*.

[1] For an invaluable statement of the change in the teacher's own viewpoint see Charles E. Merriam's *Civic Education in the United States* (Part VI of the Report of the Commission on the Social Studies of the American Historical Association, Charles Scribner's Sons, 1934).

[2] A good résumé of objectives is given by W. S. Monroe and Ruth Streitz in *Directing Learning in the Elementary School*, pp. 271 ff. (Doubleday, Doran and Company, Inc., 1932); and by R. E. Swindler in Part III of his *Social Studies Instruction in the Secondary Schools* (Prentice-Hall, 1933).

3

The Objectives to be Achieved

Before such specific matters are considered as materials to be included in the curriculum, methods of instruction to be used, and gradation of activities to be utilized, it is desirable to clarify the general point of view, or "frame of reference." To what end are efforts to be directed? What kind of "good life" is to be envisioned and for whom?

The Social Sciences as a Whole

Modern school systems usually attack the problem by making an intensive study of the general objectives of education and of the objectives of elementary education. They then decide which of these objectives social-science instruction as a whole can carry on, which of these objectives each subject can contribute, and the objectives which can be achieved by each subject at the different school levels.

Two points of view are usually combined: that of the scientific study of social needs and that of the specifications for "the good life" as laid down by philosophy, educational sociology, ethics, and aesthetics.

After such a study the school either formulates its own statements of the objectives or adopts a formulation with which it is in sympathy. By the time that stage is reached, the entire teaching force is acquainted with the "frame of reference" within which their efforts are to be confined. A clear and intimate knowledge of the objectives to be attained *serves as a guide in the processes of selection of materials and in instruction* and as a *standard for evaluating the results obtained.*

A recent study has examined the foregoing questions from the point of view of the social sciences as a whole. Charles A. Beard's *A Charter for the Social Sciences in the Schools*,[1] together with the criticisms of it which other scholars have made, should be studied carefully by every teacher who is charged with the responsibility of directing social-science experiences anywhere in the public schools, from the kindergarten up through the college.

Another less satisfactory volume is the *Conclusions and Recommendations* of the same commission. The reports, however, are in such broad outlines that teachers have had difficulty in applying their findings to specific problems. The task as outlined looms gigantic in proportions. How much of it can the schools hope to achieve? In what directions can they most intelligently apply their efforts? Such questions have not been answered.

[1] Part I of the Report of the Commission on the Social Studies of the American Historical Association (Charles Scribner's Sons, 1932). See also the criticisms by David Snedden, "Social Studies for What?" in *School and Society*, XXXVI: 358–362 (1932); by C. H. Judd, "Programs of Social Studies for the Schools of the United States," in *Elementary School Journal*, XXXIII: 17–24 (1932); and by M. E. Haggerty, "The Low Visibility of Educational Issues," in *School and Society*, XLI: 273–283 (1935).

History

Experts in all fields have long recognized that each of the disciplines has its own values to contribute, its own ways of viewing problems and materials, its own methods of work, and its own generalizations. The integrationists also have recognized these distinctive values and have brought all of them to bear on the solution of their problems.

Probably the best recent analyses of the values inherent in each of the social sciences for the achieving of the general pattern laid out in the *Charter for the Social Sciences* are the following two volumes: Beard's *The Nature of the Social Sciences*[1] and Bowman's *Geography in Relation to the Social Sciences*.[2] A more succinct summary of the general objectives of history is stated by W. G. Kimmel in *Instruction in the Social Studies*.[3]

The concern of the present volume is with a limited field, and space requirements preclude a detailed résumé of the findings in regard to history on all levels. In general, however, the objectives concern themselves with two main categories: the development of rich and well-integrated personalities and the development of socially efficient citizens.[4] These general concepts can be resolved into the elements of (1) equipment of practical knowledge; (2) inspiration of social ideals; (3) methods of work; (4) insight into processes; and (5) skills. Older attempts to distinguish between attitudes, interests, and understandings have proved confusing rather than illuminating.

History on the Middle-Grade Level

Most of the writings on the objectives of history treat the subject in general and with the high-school pupil in mind; they assume that a definite point of view has been established by their findings with due regard to the demands of social needs and of scholarship. Too little attention has been given to the interests, capacities, and mental development of the children at different levels, although any results achieved must be conditioned by such critical factors.

The primary-grade level has probably been more successful than any of the others in achieving a differentiation based on development; "socialization of children" seems to have been generally accepted as its major objective. Perhaps this very success on the primary level offers an explanation of the lack of success on the middle-grade level; teachers

[1] Part VII of the Report of the Commission on the Social Studies of the American Historical Association (Charles Scribner's Sons, 1934).

[2] Part V of the same report.

[3] Bulletin No. 17 (1932) United States Department of the Interior, Office of Education, pp. 5–12. A summary of social-science objectives may also be found in Fancler and Crawford's *Teaching the Social Studies*, Chap. II (published by C. C. Crawford, University of Southern California, Los Angeles, 1932). For a discussion of patriotism as an objective see Bessie L. Pierce's *Public Opinion and the Teaching of History* (Alfred A. Knopf, Inc., 1926).

[4] See Harold Rugg's *Culture and Education in America*, Part VI (Harcourt, Brace and Company, Inc., 1931).

there have attempted to continue exactly the same objectives and the same techniques, oblivious of the fact that the child's entire outlook on the world has been changed by his mastery of the reading process. This new situation which has arisen the middle-grade teachers are likely either (1) to ignore, thus continuing the primary objectives and technique or (2) to overestimate, and in consequence to throw children immediately and entirely upon their own resources, thus attempting to reach at one bound the full objectives of maturity. This break occurs at about the beginning of the fourth grade. What is urgently needed, therefore, is an analysis of objectives and technique suited to the capacities, as well as the interests, of children entering the fourth grade, and during the immediately succeeding period.

The evidence of psychological experiments [1] goes to show that powers of apprehending relationships, such as comparison and contrast, evaluation, analysis, judgment and reasoning, abstraction and generalization, pass through stages of development. Not to recognize this fact substitutes wishful thinking for an attainable program. Many teachers who have not studied the developmental process try to make speed too quickly. They put materials before children and subject children to experiences with which their capacities and interests do not enable them to cope. For example, such comprehensive problems as the following are in actual use:

To Know [name of city] Present and Past (Grade 4)
To Understand the Dependence of [name of city] upon the Other Regions of the United States (Grade 4)
To Discover the Relationship between [name of city] and Distant Lands (Grade 4)
How People Live in the United States (Grade 5)
Immigration into the United States (Grade 5)
In What Ways are the People of the United States and Europe Interrelated? (Grade 5B)
Round and Round the World (Grade 4)

The high point of absurdity was reached in a recent exhibit accompanying a meeting of the Department of Superintendence when among splendid examples of really worth-while projects appeared one on the whole problem of the "New Deal." A poster accompanying it showed a farmer plowing under every third row of cotton. *This exercise was the work of children in Grade 4B!* That children of the ages of eight or nine are completely unprepared to grasp the implications of such a problem is too evident for comment. When the results obtained from such studies are discouraging, teachers are likely to conclude that any social-science materials are too difficult for middle-grade children.

[1] See "The Processes of Learning History in Middle Childhood," *The Historical Outlook*, XXIV: 445–456 (December, 1933); and *The Social Studies*, XXV: 21–31 (January, 1934).

On the other hand, teachers who have not studied the problem of development in comprehension may pitch the experiences at a level appropriate to the lower-middle grades, but may never advance beyond it. For example, one of the goals of middle-grade social science may well be "the ability to comprehend a coherent narrative of successive events in a unit movement." Such an ability may be developed adequately by the end of the fourth grade, but all too often the later experiences of the fifth grade, the sixth, the junior high school, and even the senior high school are devoted to supplying *more* materials of the *same* type, the only differences being quantitative. Such a conception of objectives is stultifying in the extreme, just as the examples quoted on page 6 are confusing in the extreme.

It should be frankly stated that the objectives of history instruction have not been and probably cannot be established by a strictly scientific method. Subjective weighing of values must enter into the process. But the differentiation of objectives according to the mental development of children can be guided by the constantly growing volume of laboratory studies.

The conclusion must be that the *general* objectives of history will be developed so far as possible at all levels of the educative process, but that *in addition* each level should set up its own objectives in terms of the mental development of children at that age level.

A possible statement of such special objectives of history in the middle grades may include the development of the following desirable changes in children :

1. *A lasting interest in history.* To be determined by children's withdrawal of history materials for voluntary reading and by their own statements of choice of subjects.
2. *The ability "to comprehend a coherent narrative of successive events in a unit movement."* To be developed by the retelling of parts of the story after reading several different accounts, by exercises in sequence in time, and by practice in making outlines and summaries.
3. *Ability to visualize clearly the overt aspects of the historical scene.* To be developed through the use of pictures and models and construction.
4. *Understanding of vocabulary terms and of large movements as a whole.* To be developed by direct experience, by discussion of meanings, by associations set up through cards containing terms on one side and meanings on the other, by tests of comprehension, and by putting before children materials that are coherently organized.
5. *Information as to the most important persons, places, and dates in history.* To be developed by presentation in a meaningful setting, by drill, and by testing.
6. *The ability to use books.* To be developed by giving practice in looking up words in the index, in knowing under what word to look, in ascertaining what the book contains and how it is organized from the table of contents, in making use of chapter and topic headings.

7. *Skills in picture and map interpretation and in making maps.* To be developed by noticing costumes, buildings, and other social institutions in pictures, by tracing routes, and by reading and applying the keys of maps.

8. *Simple reasoning processes in history.* To be developed by easy and direct exercises in descriptive and constructive imagination, comparison and contrast, cause and effect, evaluation, synthesis and analysis, drawing inferences, and making and applying generalizations. See the tabulation on pages 82–91.

The first objective will probably be accepted by most readers. The second may require explanation, especially for administrators or persons who have not been in intimate contact with young children. They are likely to take such an ability for granted.

It may seem that children would naturally think in coherent, continuous trains of ideas, but an examination of the evidence contradicts this easy belief. Piaget [1] found that child narrative proceeded by juxtaposition; and its order was disconnected, with little regard for either time or cause. Without practice in narrative, coherence of thought did not develop markedly before the age of eleven. Other studies also show that small children have little conception of sequence and continuity.

It is true that narrative, or the arranging of ideas in coherent sequences, "is not a profound achievement of analytical thinking"; but such arranging or following of the general outline and trend of action is a first step toward coherent grouping of ideas. Thus one of the simplest types of associative thinking lays the groundwork for analytical thinking.[2]

The third objective, the fourth, sixth, and seventh are also generally accepted. The fifth is decried by many progressive extremists, and the eighth can be carried out only so far as children's development allows them to go.

Individual differences will make themselves apparent in the attainment of these objectives. Some children will not have achieved any of them even by the end of the middle-grade period. Others will be far advanced along the first seven of the objectives by the end of the fourth grade and will be making satisfactory progress toward the realization of the eighth. Progress in all eight abilities is possible, however, throughout life.

[1] Jean Piaget, *The Child's Conception of Physical Causality*, pp. 254, 281, and *Judgment and Reasoning of the Child*, p. 55. Harcourt, Brace and Company, Inc., 1930, 1928.

[2] The importance of continuity in historical thinking may perhaps be presented negatively by the results of a study of double promotions. The breaking up of the continuity of progress by rapid acceleration was found by the experimenter to have a more unfavorable effect on the pupils' grades in history and geography than in any other school subjects. See Harry E. Elder's *A Study of Rapid Acceleration in the Elementary School* (unpublished master's thesis, University of Chicago, 1925).

The Question of Historical-mindedness

Probably no phrase is used in the literature of history teaching more often than "historical-mindedness," and probably few are as vague in connotation. Two definitions will therefore be helpful in clarifying meanings:

Historical-mindedness in the public is not a matter of gazing backward; it is the intellectual habit of thinking about present affairs in the light of the past from which they developed. It is an intellectual perspective which comes from seeing situations in their setting, an emotional equilibrium which comes from getting outside one's own limited experience. Without an understanding of how familiar ideas and institutions have grown up through adjustment to changing conditions, personal ideas and loyalties are apt to become dogmatic and emotional; and without an understanding of the foundations upon which modern society is built, personal action is apt to be made with unsound haste or with a sense of futility.

Historical-mindedness, far from making people conservative and irresponsive to change, might presumably make them less resistant to facing the facts of change and more aware of the soundness of adjusting to them. It might enable them to see that society is not static, that a cross-section of any civilization, including our own, shows a part in a process of development. It might lead to a realization of the possible range of values, qualities, and choices, and of the importance of choosing consciously and wisely.[1]

Historical-mindedness is the mental attitude of the historian in search for truth. It is the attitude which recognizes things as becoming, which sees in past and present continuity, growth, evolution. It is the attitude of mind required for weighing historical evidence and determining its value; which insists on knowing whether a document or relic be genuine; which inquires as to who said such-and-such, what opportunities he had for knowing, what ability he had for relating, what motives caused him to record the tale. In short, historical-mindedness is a frame of mind characterized by inquisitiveness, open-mindedness, eagerness to know the truth, no matter what it be.[2]

It has been generally agreed that the development of historical-mindedness and a sense of evidence requires powers of comparison, evaluation, analysis, synthesis, cause-and-effect reasoning, and generalizing far beyond the average child in the middle grades. Such an objective belongs rather to the secondary level.

However, certain teachers, Henry Johnson in particular, have shown through their own work that even very young children can begin to appreciate what constitutes evidence and the need for evidence. For that reason a few very simple exercises of that sort have been included in Parts Two, Three, and Four of this volume. After the children have once been introduced to the general idea, the more advanced among them will be able to discover many specific applications.

[1] Quoted by Conyers Read in "A Broadcasting Venture in Mass Education," *Social Studies,* XXXVI: 299–300 (May, 1935).
[2] Howard C. Hill, "History for History's Sake," *Historical Outlook,* XII: 311 (1921).

References to Historical-mindedness and Sense of Evidence

Pages in Part Two. 117, 136, 144, 148, 151, 163, 164, 170, 181, 185, 192, 196, 215, 227, 232, 247, 255, 260, 266, 269.

Pages in Part Three. 279, 317, 326, 358, 361, 363, 368, 373, 398, 444, 449, 456, 457, 458, 467.

Pages in Part Four. 484, 495, 499, 500, 503, 517, 525, 527, 538, 544, 548, 553, 565, 570, 576.

The Social-Science Program

There is a good deal of unanimity among school groups as to the objectives to be attained through the social sciences. They may differ as to the nature of the social order to be hoped for, but from extreme radical to extreme conservative they are in substantial agreement as to the development of the individual and the good citizen. Their writings on the subject show striking similarities. In their programs, however, great differences exist.[1]

The social-science curriculum may be thought of as a process of constantly widening the child's horizons, both in space and in time, of enlarging and enriching his experiences, of helping to integrate his personality, and of increasing improvement in his social relations.

Among the schools of thought there is uniformity in practice on the primary-grade level.[2] They agree that the life and the experiences of the primary grades should center about the interests of the child as a member of his own social groups, — the family, the school, the community, — though some systems are much more consistent and thoroughgoing as to the degree in which they apply their beliefs. Notably, some continue the general theme of living in the community from the first grade through the third; some, only through the first and second, introducing in the third the study of life in other lands. In general the overt aspects of community life and the simpler community relationships furnish the materials.[3]

In spite of such minor differences, the statement holds true that nowhere else in the public-school system have educators agreed among themselves on their program as they have in the primary grades. Integration is the rule, and separate subjects hardly exist.

Integration or Subject Units the Issue

After the child has achieved a degree of mastery of the reading process and is consequently enabled to begin to work more independently,

[1] The best general survey of the situation in the United States is given in the Fourteenth Yearbook of the Department of Superintendence of the National Education Association, *The Social Studies Curriculum* (1936).

[2] Even as to "planning in advance," long a moot question. See Harold Rugg's *Culture and Education in America*, pp. 297–303.

[3] Fannie W. Dunn, "The Environment as a Primary Source of Materials of Instruction," Eighth Yearbook of the Department of Supervisors and Directors of Instruction, National Education Association, pp. 14–42 (1935).

he passes out of the primary grades into the middle grades. There all is chaos so far as regards any generally-agreed-upon plan.

Some schools choose to continue the same sort of activities that were used in the primary grades, basing instruction almost entirely on direct experience. Others seek to advance beyond the overt aspects of community life and the simplest community relationships. In them the middle grades do not continue on the same line as the primary, in which attention was concentrated almost entirely upon the immediate environment. They continue to draw upon the child's experience in his environment, but they go beyond what his eyes see in space by colorful descriptions of how other people live, and they go beyond his own experience in time by simple narratives of how the present civilization came about. Not much emphasis is laid upon cause-and-effect relationship or upon reasoning as a process, but a full and rich store of acquaintance with the worlds of space and time is developed, with contemporary life used as a method of approach. Upon such a basis the upper grades can go far in studying actual social-science relationships. They can then reason about social problems, because they are already in possession of the needed basic concepts.

A crucial point on which the two schools of thought differ is their utilization of direct versus vicarious experience. The first depends very largely on direct experience, throughout the middle grades as well as the primary. The second seeks to build, *upon the direct experiences which have already been supplied*, an understanding of broader relationships and a larger world than the unaided senses can detect.[1]

On the junior-high-school level the first school of thought provides integrated or fusion courses. The second school of thought is ready also to accept integrated units as *part* of its program, because it feels that the subject-units view of the world which was provided by the middle grades has supplied the children with *something to integrate*.[2]

The arguments for and against fusion have been reviewed so often that there is little point in repeating them here.[3] Probably one reason why the field seems so hopelessly confused and divided over the matter is the fact that truth lies on both sides. Integration is, without question, valuable as a means of synthesizing many different points of view and of bringing them to focus on socially crucial problems. And, on the other hand, many of those points of view and generalizations are developed, and the specialists maintain can best be developed,

[1] For discussion of direct versus vicarious experience see Charles E. Merriam's *Civic Education in the United States* and Harold Rugg's *Culture and Education in America*, pp. 312–320.

[2] See also the discussion on reasoning, pp. 79–94.

[3] See Howard Wilson's *The Fusion of Social Studies in Junior High Schools* (Harvard University Press, 1933). John Dewey, in *The Way Out of Educational Confusion* (Harvard University Press, 1931), pp. 36–37, also recognizes the possibility of activity organization or subject organization as equally good.

through the subjects as such. These disciplines also make possible a continuity of viewing affairs, and a coherence and systematization of thought[1] between units as well as within units.

Recent developments on the junior-high-school and the junior-college level suggest that perhaps a higher synthesis is already taking place. The warring elements may be brought together, and the values inherent in both programs may possibly be achieved. Already they are very close together in actual content, although not in vertical arrangement of the content.

An Evolving Pattern

The evolving pattern may be represented diagrammatically as follows, though a diagram is always an imperfect medium for representing flexible and complex elements in a situation.

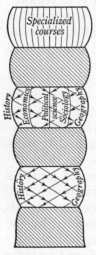

Senior College and Graduate: separation[2]

Junior College: integration (partly)

Senior High: subject units

Junior High: integration (chiefly)

Middle Grades: subject units

Primary Grades: integration

The weakness of this diagram is that it would make it appear that no "subjects" at all are or can be included on the junior-high or junior-college level, which is far from the case. Likewise it uses only the crudest design of interlacing lines to show the interrelations constantly brought into play in the program of subject units.

The underlying idea, however, is clear. In the primary grades the child exhausts the educative values of the overt phases of community living which he is fitted at the time to comprehend. Then the complex of world realities is broken up into strands of time and place, and he follows them through separately until he has a new fund of understandings of time and space on which to build. This process extends throughout the middle grades, with interrelationships constantly stressed. His world, both present and past, is *described* to him in a vivid, intelligible series of pictures, organized about the major cue concepts and generalizations of the subjects.

By the time the junior-high-school level has been reached the child's fund of understandings and information has again reached the point where it is desirable to stop and weave them together into a higher integration, organized about present problems or forces. And so on throughout the period of formal schooling.

[1] Howard Wilson, *The Fusion of Social Studies in Junior High Schools*, p. 97.
[2] Integration to be effected by the individual himself.

The Place of History in the Social-Science Program

History is by no means the only social science valuable for middle-grade children. The contribution of geography has long been recognized. Civics (as an attitude of responsibility and co-operation, an understanding of group undertakings, and a habit of participation rather than as a study of mechanics of government) is included in the program of activities of all progressive schools. And materials from other social sciences, such as anthropology, are being included as fast as experts in each field make them available for young children. The inclusion of other materials in the program, however, does not detract from the value of history in explaining "how things came to be what they are." Its viewpoints on continuity and change are invaluable.

The place of history in the *program of "subjects"* is clear, though many problems yet demand experimental study,— for example, the point at which instruction should be introduced, whether American history or world history should be introduced first, and in what respects the field pursued in the upper grades should differ from the treatment in the middle grades. But practice throughout the country gives pragmatic sanction to a program continuous from the fourth grade onward.

The task of the curriculum-maker is so to arrange the materials of the "seamless web" of all the social sciences as to differentiate at different levels of maturity and yet to effect an integration of the whole. Criteria for such differentiation and integration are (1) the necessities of scholarship, (2) the realities of society, and (3) the limitations of the teaching and learning process at the various grade levels.

The history curriculum of the elementary school should therefore include an introduction to the development of the institutions of civilization and a more specific examination of the rise and growth of the national culture. Each teacher in every school system should be acquainted not only with the program for her own grade but with the entire program throughout all levels, so that she may be conscious of the integrated plan and of the part that she and her work play in it.

The *integrated program* now being pursued in some middle grades presents other problems, but the question is not whether history is to be included in such programs. Holders of such widely opposed points of view as Harold Rugg and Rolla M. Tryon speak on this point as follows:

Our new plan of assembling the material of economic, social, and political life in one integrated course does not minimize the importance of history. On the contrary, although "history" does not appear in the daily program as a separate subject, it really has a larger place in the curriculum than ever before. A tremendous volume of historical material is utilized by the students. Thus "more history" is the slogan of the new course.[1]

[1] Harold Rugg in *Teacher's Guide for an Introduction to Problems of American Culture*, p. 46 (Ginn and Company, 1932).

In discussing the program of integration Tryon says:

While there are cases wherein a subject other than history is made the core subject, the prevailing tendency seems to be in the direction of using history as the core.[1]

Principles of Selection of Materials

In no respect is it more apparent that the general "frame of reference" is a conditioning factor than in the selection of materials to be included in the social-science program. Since, obviously, not all the content of history can be included, there must be selection. And selection must be made with reference to some point of view, and in keeping with certain openly-agreed-upon principles, or it will be made in response to (perhaps unconscious) prejudices and feelings of value.

Beard summarizes the following as the consensus of opinion of the Commission on the Social Studies of the American Historical Association[2]:

1. The program should present an accurate picture of the total situation (of the present; comprehension of contemporary life).
2. The portrayal of movements and changes should convey *a strong sense of development in time.*
3. A beginning is made with simple observation widening into deeper knowledge and thought.

Beard assumes as a matter of course that the materials so selected shall meet the demands of scholarship. The first point above shows the agreement of the commission with those persons who would have the curriculum concerned with contemporary life and social needs, but the second principle states clearly that contemporary life cannot be understood without a background in history.

One of the greatest problems to be faced by teachers of the social sciences is the belief held by some educators that the social sciences should concern themselves only with current issues. The fallacy of this point of view is pointed out by the commission as follows:

There is no assurance that the problems discussed today with such assiduity will be the problems before the country when the children now in the grades have reached the age of maturity. History is in a large measure a record of unexpected crises — at all events of crises not generally foreseen or at best dimly foreshadowed. . . . Burning questions of the hour may be ashes tomorrow.[3]

Anyone who will compare the books of civic instruction of, let us say, 1875 with the problems which a child trained in them confronted in mature years between 1890 and 1930 can readily see that by no possible effort of mind could

[1] R. M. Tryon, "The Place of History in a Program of Integration," *The Elementary School Journal*, XXXIV: 667–675 (1934).

[2] *The Nature of the Social Sciences*, pp. 189–191.

[3] C. A. Beard, *A Charter for the Social Sciences in the Schools*, p. 42.

the teachers of 1875 have fitted the child for dealing precisely with many of the difficult issues that later perplexed him.[1]

Besides being temporary in its nature a list of problems [selected for present consideration in the schools] will be partial, one-sided, and perhaps trivial in spots.[2] While some of the problems of democracy must find a place in the social studies program, they cannot form the entire substance of it. . . . Furthermore a wide knowledge of facts and a discipline in thinking are the prerequisites to a fruitful consideration of controversial questions.[3]

The same principle is often stated in this form — only *functional* material should be chosen, that is, material which has a direct value in developing attitudes, understandings, and appreciations. All schools of thought agree as to the desirability of this criterion. A passing of the belief in wholesale transfer of training strongly reinforces the necessity of this functional emphasis.

Many difficulties, however, beset the path of the curriculum-maker who attempts to build his entire curriculum around such a concept. Activity analysis has furnished many isolated themes,[4] but it is itself largely a subjective process. Moreover, it is extraordinarily difficult for any person to trace and record fully and accurately all the bases he himself uses in the solution of problems for which his school life did not and could not prepare him specifically. No group — the fusionists or the advocates "of subjects" — has a monopoly on functionality; each is trying to achieve it, and each is still far from the goal.

A possible solution is to examine carefully the various movements and forces selected by competent social philosophers, historians, and geographers as fundamental to the development of American life and institutions, and to select those which have a bearing on the problems of society as determined by investigations and stated by "frontier thinkers." The relationships, broadly considered, would necessitate inclusion of all the great forces in American history, each at its appropriate level of learning, and would necessarily consider both the present and the past.[5]

Further principles of selection should be stated with reference not only to the needs of society and the demands of scholarship but also with reference to the learner. Three considerations which are usually quoted need special attention:

1. Interest   2. Difficulty   3. Relative values

One of the most extensive studies of children's reading interests, that made by Uhl,[6] showed that their primary interest was in *action*.

[1] C. A. Beard, *A Charter for the Social Sciences in the Schools*, p. 95.

[2] Ibid. p. 43.   [3] Ibid. p. 46.

[4] See Howard Wilson's *The Fusion of Social Studies in Junior High Schools*, pp. 113–143.

[5] See John Dewey's *Democracy and Education*, p. 250 (The Macmillan Company, 1916).

[6] Willis Uhl, *Scientific Determination of the Elementary School Course in Reading*. University of Wisconsin Studies in the Social Sciences and History, No. 4. 1921. See also L. M.

Therefore the field of history selected to present first to young children should be a field in which stirring stories of action predominate.

Piaget[1] noticed a "systematic interest" in industry, machines, and adult handicrafts on the part of children generally, although girls were slightly inferior to boys in this respect. Such an interest is valuable for school purposes and should be capitalized.

Even the subject of war should not be omitted entirely, though certain organizations so recommend for propaganda purposes. A true representation of war as it is may perhaps carry its own moral; at any rate it must be included in its broad, general outlines if anything like a true picture of our social development is to be presented.

Freeman[2] suggested beginning with a simple historical narrative,—a series of events occurring in time sequence. He believed that the history of one country constitutes a thread easier to follow than that of all the world. Probably under the current practice of weaving materials into units this consideration bears less force than formerly; nevertheless, it is a factor to take into account in attempting to decide the difficult question of whether to begin with American history or with world history in the fourth grade.

The question of difficulty has never been adequately investigated. There is little to suggest that one topic is more difficult *per se* than others, except phases so far removed from little children's experiences that they have no background for interpretation; for example, the tariff, banking, money, constitutional development. With most other topics, difficulty is a factor of the method of presentation.

A further qualification should perhaps be made in pointing out the difficulty of *dissociating* one's ideas of the present from one's concept of the past. The more remote the period and the more unlike the life of the present, the more difficult the material will probably be.

Relative values in very simple matters — dates, places, the names of persons — can be and have been determined[3] with some degree of success by scientific methods. The relative values of such important matters as movements and forces, however, must be determined by the "frame of reference." Selection of these is conditioned by the same factors as operated in the choice of objectives.

Using much the same principles of selection, however, workers arrive at very different conclusions. Some choose integrated materials; others, subject units. Of those who choose subject units, such as

Terman and Margaret Lima's *Children's Reading*, Revised Edition (D. Appleton-Century Company, Inc., 1926); and Franklin Bobbitt's "The Wider Vision" in *Home and School Guide* (The New Wonder, Vol. XI, G. T. Shumann and Co., Chicago, 1932).

[1] Jean Piaget, *The Child's Conception of Physical Causality*, pp. 195, 226.

[2] F. N. Freeman, *Psychology of the Common Branches*, pp. 150–152 (Houghton Mifflin Company, 1916).

[3] See W. H. Burton's *The Supervision of Elementary Subjects*, pp. 365–367 (D. Appleton-Century Company, Inc., 1929).

history, some believe that the facts point to beginning with American history and then advancing to world history, while others draw the opposite conclusion.[1] In the lack of objective evidence as to the superiority of the one plan over the other, the following conclusions may be summarized:

In favor of placing American history[2] first may be cited the following facts

1. The materials are, on the whole, closer to children's experiences; they hear about them, read about them in newspapers, and see them on the motion-picture screen to a greater degree than the materials concerning other countries.
2. There are more reading materials available, especially for smaller children.
3. American history begins with a series of stirring action stories, and investigations have shown that children are most attracted by the quality of action.
4. It requires less dissociation from the present than does such a remote period as prehistoric time.

In favor of placing world history first are the following values

1. This is the logical order.
2. It develops the world point of view from the very beginning of the study of history.

The question is one which is capable of determination by scientific investigations, but to date such investigations have not been made.

The Problem of the History of the Local Community

One of the favorite subjects of the social sciences, especially in sections of the country where local pride is strong, has long been the history of the local community.

Undoubtedly such a topic has value. A study of the local community can be given concreteness and reality because it deals with localities and names which the children already know. Through it they can be brought to realize that history deals with actual occurrences. As such, local history serves as an excellent introduction to the larger story of the nation or the world.

On the other hand are certain insistent difficulties which cannot be ignored. The most serious of these is the problem of materials. In the great majority of cases the materials are not available in any form which can be used either by the teacher or by the children. To assemble the data, for even one community, is the life work of a trained historian. When the average teacher attempts the task, the result is a pitifully inadequate collection of undiscriminating tradition and unimpor-

[1] See Hannah Lindahl's "History in the Intermediate Grades," in *Elementary School Journal*, XXXII: 257–265 (December, 1931).

[2] This is the course recommended by the *Conclusions and Recommendations* of the Commission on the Social Studies of the American Historical Association, pp. 59–60.

tant facts. Even the most charitable point of view can find little of educational value among such ill-advised symposiums.

In the comparatively few communities for which adequate histories have been assembled by expert workers the materials are, almost without exception, on an adult level. The teacher must tell the story orally to the children. Moreover, much of the history concerns itself necessarily with minutiae which are not worth the while of the person who desires only a general view. In a few cases the materials of the local histories have been rewritten for children, suffering somewhat in accuracy in the process, but even in such cases not enough is available to provide for a wide reading program.

A second difficulty is the teacher herself. Because of the mobility of the American population a great number of teachers are working in communities to which they are strangers. They remain there for a few years and then move on. Thus they do not even know the local traditions. And, as already stated, practically none of them have had the long and arduous historical training necessary to collect and evaluate materials.

The criterion which should be kept constantly in mind is that of *relative value*. Without question, local history would be of some value at any level, — first grade, fourth grade, eighth grade, senior high school, or senior college. The critical point is whether such materials are of *more* value than the broader views of life which might be given in the same time with the same effort and considering the same degree of maturity of the children.

A possible conclusion is that the local history of the community can be presented with profit, provided that accurate materials are accessible. Since in most cases it will depend largely on oral presentation, it had better be included at a grade level where oral presentation is a chief method used, — for example, in the third grade. After that time, when the power of independent silent reading has been developed, the principle of relative value would suggest other materials as preferable.

Local history might also be included in the school program again at a higher level, when it is desirable to furnish some training in collecting and evaluating documentary evidence, — for example, to a limited degree in the senior high school and to a much greater degree in the upper levels of the college.

State History[1]

The problem of state history is somewhat different. It is much farther away from the experiences of young children, and therefore its contribution toward concreteness and reality must be less.

[1] See R. M. Tryon's "The Teaching of Local and State History," Sixth Yearbook of the National Council for the Social Studies, pp. 132–143 (1936).

As to its materials, the same difficulties in the training of teachers remain. State histories, written by trained historians, are much more likely to be available than histories of local communities. They are not any more likely, however, to be suitable for reading by young children, and on the whole they contain an even larger proportion of detail of little interest or importance for the general reader. Local pride should not blind the curriculum-maker to the principle of relative values.

Moreover, in most of the state histories the events of greatest importance are those which were felt far outside the state boundaries, — for example, the French or Spanish explorations in general, Indian wars, the westward movement, the influence of industrialization, the struggle over slavery. It would seem, then, that the children could profit more by studying those large movements in their fuller setting, — for example, the settling of the country as a whole, — the teacher taking care to make the local applications. At points where the individual state made a notable contribution there might well be wide reading and reports, with as many activities as the teacher considers desirable to stress state contributions to the national life, or important state influences not satisfactorily covered by a general view of the national life.

Principles of Organization

Many different methods of organization have been applied to history materials: the chronological, the counter-chronological, the biographical, the topical, the problem-project, the contract, the unit-of-understanding, and the unit-of-work (activity).[1]

While it would be interesting to review the history of each of these plans, only a few of them are in wide use at the present time. In schools which offer "subjects" the chief methods are the unit-of-understanding and the contract. In schools offering integrated courses the chief methods are the unit-of-work (activity) and the unit-of-understanding. There is substantial agreement among all of them that materials should be organized as intensive studies of a few carefully selected topics rather than as hurried encyclopedic surveys of an entire field.

The Unit in the " Subject " Plan

It is unfortunate that the word *unit* has been applied to so many different plans of organization. Its use, therefore, does not indicate with any clarity the particular plan or philosophy which the user contemplates.

[1] See "Organizing the Social Sciences," in R. M. Tryon's *The Social Sciences as School Subjects*, Part XI of the Report of the Commission on the Social Studies of the American Historical Association, pp. 429–529.

According to the authority who has done most to popularize the unit plan, Professor Henry C. Morrison, a unit is "a comprehensive and significant aspect of the environment or of an organized science . . . which being learned results in an adaptation of personality."

"In terms of subjects, a unit is a significant body of interrelated subject matter focused on a central core of thought or an interpretation, capable of being learned as a whole by pupils."[1] It must follow a generalized theme and must be composed of materials which can be comprehended, as opposed to materials which no developmental unity ties together.

Perhaps one way of clarifying thinking on the matter is to show what a unit is *not*.

A unit is not an aggregation of materials placed side by side because they describe events which happened to take place at approximately the same time. Such events are discontinuous and noncumulative; they are not bound together by close relationships. To treat one after another such diverse subjects as the Centennial Exposition, the railroad strike of 1877, the invention of the telephone, the Chinese Exclusion Act, and the gift of the Statue of Liberty because they occurred at about the same time is to ignore completely the fact that *thinking* must be in connected, continuous trends. No child could do anything with such materials as the above except attempt to memorize them.

Neither is a unit the same as a *topic*, or a thread or phase of historical development considered from its beginnings to its end. Such a topic necessarily excludes close relationships to other movements which vitally affected it, and therefore cannot itself be fully understood. For example, if the topic of slavery is to be traced from its beginnings in 1619 to its results in our present national life, it becomes hopelessly entangled with the growth of the industrial system from 1812 on, with the tariff of the period shortly following, with the growth of sectionalism, with the development of the humanitarian movement, etc. What is to be done in each case with children who know nothing about the subjects in question? Go back and explain the whole tariff movement in order to throw light on the problem? Trace the whole history of the industrial revolution in order to ascertain its effect on slavery? From these examples it can be seen that a purely topical treatment for young children is thoroughly impracticable.

Biography stories cannot constitute a good history program for middle-grade children, because they are disconnected and discontinuous; they do not build up a cumulative picture of a force or movement. A middle-grade history program in terms of biography moves directly counter to the modern tendency to organize materials in all subjects in terms of relationships.

[1] Henry C. Morrison, *The Practice of Teaching in the Secondary Schools*, Revised Edition, pp. 24, 200–214 (The University of Chicago Press, 1931).

In 1909 the published report of the Committee of Eight gave voice to the opinion that children were more interested in persons than in events, and that therefore the appropriate subject of historical study for the middle grades was biography. This opinion was not based on scientific evidence; in 1909 opinion could not be so based, for the scientific study of education was then in its infancy. When the investigator today examines the heterogeneous collections of materials in the history texts and courses of study of the decade before 1909, assembled as they were without coherence or cumulative effect, he does not wonder that the committee members, in despair of finding any unifying principle that children could understand, decided that biography was the only thread which could tie the unwieldy mass together.

But that was a great many years ago. As early as 1915 Henry Johnson pointed out the unsatisfactory results secured from grouping events about men. He suggested instead, in the interests of proportion and continuity, that men be grouped about events.

In 1923 Miss Marion G. Clark,[1] who was also dissatisfied with the results obtained by the biographical method, made an experimental study of children's understanding of continuity and change. She found that even fourth-grade children could appreciate change and development, and she therefore concluded that a continuous narrative based on action was better suited to them than were merely biographical stories.

Gradually practice in the field changed. Texts discarded the biographical in favor of the topical and then of the unit organization, to conform with test findings and the opinions of experts.[2] And still one finds echoes of the thirty-year-old Committee of Eight opinion in recently published books, stated as dogmatically and with as little supporting evidence as if a scientific technique were unknown even yet. "Books must necessarily be biographical or semibiographical in character in order to gratify the developing interests of the pupils in the personal side of history," says one writer,[3] who then proceeds to set up a biographical curriculum for the grades. Another[4] quotes biography as the chief subject of study for the middle grades, though he admits that units are better for the upper grades. This positive statement is made by a third[5]: "The study of progress, however logically the events

[1] See *The Historical Outlook*, XIV: 147–150 (1923).

[2] Maude E. Doane, *Practices in History in Grade V* (unpublished master's thesis, The University of Chicago, 1932).

[3] H. G. Wheat, *Psychology of the Elementary School*, pp. 345, 358 (Silver Burdett and Company, 1931).

[4] C. C. Schmidt, *Teaching and Learning the Common Branches*, p. 289 (D. Appleton-Century Company, Inc., 1929).

[5] Paul Klapper, *The Teaching of History*, p. 5 (D. Appleton-Century Company, Inc., 1926); see also the recommendation of R. O. Hughes in the Sixth Yearbook of the National Council for the Social Studies, p. 203 (1936).

may be grouped, is never as real and as concrete to a child as the study of a real person." A close examination of the investigations in the field of the social studies offers no support to such a statement; in fact, it points to the exactly opposite conclusion.

A teacher [1] whose children have been trained on the unit basis, and who administers tests at the end of each unit, recently related to the writer a curious difficulty which the children encountered in their attempt to arrange certain lists of events and lists of persons in time order. They had little difficulty with the events, but they reported that when they came to the lists of names they "had to stop and think first what event each man was connected with, and that was harder." This teacher's experience seems to indicate that if children have been trained in handling units, and if their reading materials have been arranged in units, they find less difficulty in following a unit movement than in tracing an event through the various biographies of great men.

The point of this discussion is *not* that biography has no place in the teaching of history. Its values are recognized by the most exacting critics. The point is that the *biographical method of organization* is not the best method for middle-grade children.

What is to be attempted, then, is to trace the development of great *movements or forces* within clearly defined limits. Each such movement or *unit* constitutes a "significant phase" of the development of our civilization which, because of its interrelationships, can be *understood* rather than memorized. For example, "Voyaging and Exploring" is not a unit, because there is no essential continuity or interrelationship between all voyages or all explorations. They constitute disconnected elements; the child cannot follow through the relationships, because there are none. Neither is "Heroes of Everyday Work" a unit, and for the same reason. There is no deep underlying connection between the elements which make up the unit, and therefore no connection can be traced and understood by the child. Such broad general topics as "Our Country" are ridiculous as units.

The essence of the unit, then, is its coherence, its continuity and cumulativeness, its embracing of the necessary relationships which enable a student to trace a movement or force. It must be capable of being *understood*.

Each unit is treated intensively and with a wealth of detail in order to provide, as fully as may be, for vicarious experience. The details are not themselves to be remembered, but they provide the color, the vividness, the lifelikeness that enable a child imaginatively to live through the experience described. Other things being equal, therefore, a *longer story including the details* which make for lifelikeness is easier for the child to read and comprehend than a short story which

[1] Mrs. Laverne Glennon of the Wilmette, Illinois, public schools.

gives only a skeleton summary of action. A fifteen-page story of Magellan's adventures can be experienced vicariously; a single page can only be memorized.[1]

Teachers and administrators should give particular attention, in their choice of a course of study and a text, to the manner in which the period since the Civil War is treated. That period should without question be treated in the same unitary, connected manner as the earlier history. Many texts break down at this point and present only disconnected biographies instead of coherent, connected units dealing with the supremely important social and industrial and economic topics which affect the child's everyday existence.

Following is an illustration of material in history organized in what is undoubtedly a unit, since it meets all the tests described above.[2]

The treatment of "The Industrialization of America" may begin with the invention of spinning machinery, which produced thread in such quantities that weaving machines were devised also, that these were so hard to manipulate that power was applied to them, that the processes were then so effective that a great demand arose for raw cotton, that the extension of cotton fields demanded a rapid method of cleaning (hence the cotton-gin), that the quantity production of cloth led to the invention of the sewing-machine, and that all these machines led to the factory system and the rapid growth of cities.

Such an organization leads naturally from one step to the next, and an understanding attitude is possible toward the whole. The relations indicated are not the only relations possible with such materials, and they run the risk of oversimplification; but they are coherent and cumulative.

The stories of such events should be arranged in stages of learning that are each easy enough to be mastered without discouragement, interesting enough to furnish an incentive for going on, and not so long that they constitute a tax on the child's ability to follow the relationships involved.

The Contract

The word *contract* refers more to the formal set-up of materials than to the principles of organization itself. A topic, a presidential administration, a biography, or a unit might furnish the materials which are then divided into levels of assignment and arranged for individual progress. A contract "method of work" has distinguishing characteristics,[3] but in general the principles laid down for the unit may apply also to the contract as a method of organization.

[1] Substantiated by an unpublished investigation made by Professor Wilbur Beauchamp of the University of Chicago.

[2] For an excellent discussion of the unit and the project see Howard Wilson's *The Fusion of Social Studies in Junior High Schools*, pp. 147–153.

[3] See H. L. Miller's *Creative Learning and Teaching* (Charles Scribner's Sons, 1927).

The Unit in the Plan of Integration

The materials most widely used in the junior high schools offering integrated social sciences are probably Harold Rugg's series of textbooks. His units are of the "units of work" type, most of which are themselves made up of "units of understanding." He recognizes the necessity of preserving the chronological development and of organizing "broad strands" through which the interrelationships within the era are maintained. Some of his divisions are units of history, and certain others, units of geography. They are integrated to no greater degree than is the case with modern textbooks in subject units. They are groupings together of materials from subjects. As such there is decided similarity between subject-unit treatment and integrated treatment,[1] except in the principle of continuity from one unit to the next.

The units of work commonly used in the middle grades of schools operating on the plan of integration have generally followed the topical plan; that is, they have selected one thread and have followed it down through the ages, such as

A Study of Boats [2]	Aeronautics
How Man Has Made Records	Astronomy
The Telling of Time	The Story of Lighting
The Building of Roads	The Story of Communication
Bridges	Travel on Land, on Sea, and in the Air
The School Bank	Children and Architecture

That such topics are more "lifelike" or "natural" than such a unit of history as "The Greeks Gave the World the Ideal of Freedom" is only an expression of opinion. They can no more be called "real-life situations" than the latter. The usual argument is that in real life one is confronted by problems, not by subjects. Surely in real life one may be confronted by the *fact* of a particular bridge, or boat, or road, or he may have to make a record. But to trace the development of transportation from the beginning of time to the present is no more a "real-life situation" than to try to find out "How the United States Became a Great Industrial Nation." Such topics are valuable. If they are not already in the program of separate subjects, they should be inserted in it. They can easily be treated within existing units.

The topical method is not new; it was given a very thorough try-out in this country after 1880.[3] That it was superior to the organization by presidential administrations is clear; but it failed to show the interrelationships between the topics, and thus presented history as

[1] See Howard Wilson's *Fusion of the Social Sciences in the Junior High School*, pp. 164–165.

[2] See the Teachers Lesson-Unit Series, Teachers College, Columbia University; Waddell, Seeds, and White, *Major Units in the Social Studies for the Intermediate Grades* (The John Day Company, Inc., 1932).

[3] See R. M. Tryon's *The Social Sciences as School Subjects*, pp. 481–492.

an artificial bundle of separate threads, with no connecting tissues to hold them together. It passed from the scene.

When used as a method of organization for middle-grade children the deficiencies of the topical organization come into clear view.[1] Such children have no foundation of general understanding of nations and peoples upon which to build. When, therefore, they find in their study of time-keeping that a people called the Greeks made certain advances, they can have little understanding of why this advance was made. They do not see the progress as a resultant of all the forces at work; it becomes fortuitous and more or less accidental. Likewise, in the study of road-making they find that a people called the Romans made wonderful progress, and they are *told* that roads were needed to keep the Roman Empire together. But without an extensive study of Roman life and institutions they cannot see that the advances made were a resultant of all Roman social organization.

The very interrelationships and functionality upon which the activity movement is postulated are lost sight of. In striving to achieve integration only a new kind of isolation is achieved.

The advocates of this type of material are fond of comparing it with the tedious accounts of political movements and detailed campaigns of wars in the older histories. The comparison should rather be made with the products of the "new" history concept,[2] which reflects human effort throughout the ages along all lines, artistic, scientific, economic and social, as well as political. For example, Greek life is treated in the "new" history as the whole manifestation of Greek genius, stressing the permanent contributions in the arts, science, and philosophy, rather than as only a succession of wars among city-states.

Finally, the organization of an integrated course in terms of such topics as those listed above ("Boats," "Records," etc.) entirely loses sight of the relationship *between units*. John Dewey has criticized severely the extremes of the activity movement which do not provide for continuity and coherence and cumulativeness of development.[3] Any single unit can attain its highest value only when it is related to other units, all together synthesizing an understanding of the world and our institutions. An "integrated" program, on the contrary, may consist of a series of disconnected topics. Is this not as bad as the disconnected nature of materials within a single unit (a characteristic of the separate subjects of the last century), as a protest against which the whole integration movement was launched?

[1] See E. H. Reeder's "Social Studies — or Geography and History?" in *Education*, LII: 258 (1932); W. C. Bagley's "Is Subject-Matter Obsolete?" in *Educational Administration and Supervision*, XXI: 401–412 (September, 1935).

[2] See James Harvey Robinson's *New History* (The Macmillan Company, 1912).

[3] In "The Need of a Philosophy of Education," *The New Era*, XXV: 214 (November, 1934, London).

The Emphasis upon Comprehension

Certain critics some years ago pointed out the futility of memorizing facts,[1] without being able to offer constructive suggestions as to any better method of considering problems. At present some believe that direct experience in the immediate environment is the only method of "real" learning. Apparently they do not recognize the limited understanding of the world which must result from such a philosophy. All schools of thought agree that direct experience is the basis upon which understandings and interpretations must rest; but they differ in the degree of realism with which they face the problem of how and when the child is to be led beyond all possible boundaries of his own experience, in both time and space.

The question is how to utilize direct experience as a basis for learning, and at the same time how to present materials of wider scope without falling back upon the utterly inadequate resource of memorization.[2] Not going beyond direct experience is a comparatively easy matter, but ensuring comprehension of problems rather than memorizing necessitates an understanding of the complex thought-processes involved in learning.

Comprehension is a comprehensive term. The comprehension of a child three years of age differs from that of a boy of ten, or fifteen. The scholar's comprehension of his specialty grows constantly with his years of study.

The teacher, then, must analyze the stages,[3] so that she may be able to adjust the experiences of the curriculum to the capacities of the learner. If she tries to pull him ahead too fast, confusion and attitudes of dislike result. If she provides opportunities for only the simpler and lower stages of direct experience, the child is deprived of his opportunities to develop. Both these extremes can be found in school practices today,— perhaps the former more markedly among teachers eager to be progressive but with an insufficient knowledge of psychology, and the latter among conservatives whose conception of the difference between middle grades, junior high school, and senior high school is that the higher levels have *more* of each subject but more of the same kind.

For this reason the list of objectives on pages 7 and 8 begins with such a simple purpose as the development of "ability to comprehend a

---

[1] See the table of subject failures in Bagley and Kyte's *California Curriculum Study*, Chap. XIX (University of California, Berkeley, 1926).

[2] For a good discussion of direct versus vicarious experience see Charles E. Merriam's *Civic Education in the United States*, pp. 159–162. A very helpful analysis of the "hierarchy of symbolism" is given in H. L. Hollingworth's *Educational Psychology*, pp. 209–210 (D. Appleton-Century Company, Inc., 1933.

[3] An excellent statement of stages in terms of requirements of science is given by Isaiah Bowman on pages 20–21, 30, and 119 of *Geography in Relation to the Social Sciences*.

coherent narrative of successive events in a unit movement." Some theorists, especially those far removed from daily contact with young children, inveigh against such a purpose. From their writings one might gain the impression that the comprehension of a series of events was pernicious, to be discountenanced under all conditions.

Of course, nothing could be farther from the truth. Orderly, systematic thinking is needed in every field of human endeavor. The trouble is that the theorist who has had little experience with young children takes this ability for granted and wishes to begin building upon it. Primary and lower-middle-grade teachers, however, know that it is an ability which must be acquired, and experimental evidence[1] supports their view.

Comprehension of a train of thought and the ability to retell it are, then, legitimate objectives for younger children. The chief difficulty in this connection is that teachers may encourage children to remain on this relatively low plane by making no other demands upon them and by providing them with no opportunities for other kinds of thinking.

As soon as a given child has mastered the comparatively simple process of following a coherent line of thought, he should be given exercise in the so-called higher thought-processes, such as reasoning. (See pages 79–94 for a detailed discussion of how opportunities for reasoning may be provided for young children.)

Even though the problem of objectives may have been clarified, children's comprehension still remains largely dependent on the selection and organization of materials of instruction. Purely chronological materials defy comprehension; they can only be memorized. For example, if on one page such diverse matters as the Election of 1876, the Centennial Exposition, the Invention of the Telephone, and the Withdrawal of the Troops from the South are treated successively in a few lines each, memorization is the only method of treatment possible, and frequent reviews are necessary if any residuum of learning is to remain after an interval of time.

On the other hand, a unit organization of the industrial revolution such as that illustrated above on page 23 leads naturally and logically from one step to the next. The child can see the relationship between successive topics and therefore can *understand* instead of being forced to rely on memorization.

It follows that middle-grade history materials must be something other than abbreviated editions of upper-grade texts, which include about the same number and range of topics but with shorter discussions of each. Long ago Henry Johnson pointed out the fallacy of assuming that the way to make a subject easy was to say little about it.

---

[1] Jean Piaget, *Judgment and Reasoning of the Child*, p. 19; and *The Language and Thought of the Child*, p. 95 (Harcourt, Brace and Company, Inc., 1928, 1926).

In middle-grade materials there must be rigid exclusion of subjects for which children's experiences form no basis of understanding, such as the tariff, currency and banking, constitutional development, etc. Not only must the subjects included be fewer, but each one should be treated with a wealth of stirring incident and colorful detail. Such characteristics awaken interest, help to identify the self with the character, and thus provide for vicarious experience.

The crucial role which the *understanding of vocabulary* plays in comprehension in general cannot be too greatly emphasized. An entire section is later devoted to this problem (see pages 60–64).

Gradation of objectives, and wise selection and organization of materials, however, are not the only desiderata. Comprehension, even with such an organization as outlined above, and with rigid control of vocabulary, is still dependent on direct experience.

The technique described in this book makes specific provision for experience as follows:

Conversational Approach (pp. 40–41), in which the tie-up with life situations or previous experience is suggested, motivates the desire to investigate.

Creative Activities (pp. 69–77) provide for trips, interviews, and investigations in the community and for manipulation of materials in the classroom.

Specific discussion of *Application to Present-Day Conditions* (pp. 77–79) points out direct connections of the past with the present, which would very probably escape the child's attention unless pointed out.

Discussion (pp. 57–64) of the theme, including an opportunity for explanation of specific vocabulary terms, helps to apply what is already known and thus to clear up serious causes of misapprehension, while *Exercises in Reasoning* (pp. 79–94) demand that a passive attitude of retelling be abandoned and active consideration of the theme be substituted for it.

Even such matters as the way in which the *Reading and Study* (pp. 41–57) are carried on and the *Drill* and *Testing* (pp. 94–108) managed can tend to increase comprehension.

Exercises in Organization (pp. 104–105) help the child to discover that there are thought patterns in writing and that he can learn to follow the various patterns used by different authors.

Very different mental attitudes result from learning carried on according to the points of view mentioned above, as compared with the attitudes which result from the retelling of the story as the only stage of comprehension contemplated.

Comprehension is thus seen to be intimately connected with the *interpretation* of historic facts. It goes back of the facts themselves to the *meaning* of the facts. A learner may begin with the statements that Louisiana was purchased in 1803, Florida in 1819, Texas annexed in 1845, Oregon added in 1846, and the Mexican Cession made in 1848. To get the full meaning of the Westward Movement, however, he must go back of these facts to such interpretations as the influence of the frontier upon the democratic spirit and the value of free land as a preventive of social revolution.

That so little progress has been made on the interpretation level as opposed to the fact level, throughout the country as a whole, is undoubtedly due to the inadequate preparation of teachers in the subject matter of history. Little improvement can be hoped for until teachers are much better equipped in subject-matter and until all college and university courses concern themselves with the implications and generalizations of their subjects as well as with minutiae.

Emotional Attitudes and the Learning Process

Even though the objectives be of the most approved type and though the curriculum content be selected and organized according to the wisest principles known, the success of the social-studies program is not assured. Educators have recently begun to recognize the fundamental importance of emotional factors in the developmental process. If a child feels antagonism toward the teacher, if he is unhappy among his associates,[1] if the activities in which he is expected to engage are of negligible interest to him, satisfactory results cannot be hoped for no matter how high his I.Q., how hard he studies, or how good his "marks."

This emotional coloring is a product of all the factors which, together, make up the life of the school,— the teacher, the children, the classroom, the playground, the principal, the supervisors, the gymnasium, the auditorium, the equipment, the clubs and organizations, the curriculum, the methods, the home background, and the relations with the community. If the resultant of all these forces is a general feeling of physical vigor, buoyancy, and confidence, it conditions the child's attitude toward everything he attempts. He expects the activities to be interesting because they usually have been; he expects to succeed because he has succeeded in the past; and he is happy with the other children and the teacher because the circumstances amid which he spends his hours of school-living are satisfying. The influence on the integration of his personality is immeasurable.[2]

---

[1] See Charles E. Merriam's *Civic Education in the United States*, Chap. XII, "Teacher and Taught"; S. L. Pressey's *Psychology and the New Education*, pp. 114–122, 146–173 (Harper & Brothers, 1933).

[2] See page 51 for suggestions as to the teacher's obtaining help in the diagnosis of emotional disturbances.

Among these forces one of the most powerful is the relation exist-ing between teacher and pupil. The least that can be hoped for is a feeling of mutual respect and consideration; at best they like one another as individuals, irrespective of professional relationships. No gushing sentimentality is desired by children, but no domineering. The straightforward man-to-man attitude of co-workers is the most adequate expression of democracy in school life. The teacher who allows herself to entertain a feeling of dislike for the troublesome child, instead of regarding his aberrations as a problem to be solved, falls far short in her professional point of view.

No less influential in coloring the emotional tone of the school is the attitude of the children toward one another. If the school mechan-ism of rewards, marks, and prizes or the extreme application of com-parative measurements divides the children into warring ability groups, or if it sets every child's hand against his neighbor in emulation and rivalry, there can be little happiness or satisfaction.[1] The nervous ten-sion is too acute and the feeling of insecurity too great.

With the removal of rivalry, tension eases. Co-operation and helpfulness apply not only in the "regular" work of the school but also in managing the club and program activities and in solving many of the problems of living together. Under such conditions each child may feel that he is a responsible member of the group, sometimes following, sometimes leading, and not merely an object of dictation.

The activities engaged in, whether pleasurable or otherwise, strongly influence the attitude toward the school as a whole, and the social-science program may be a constructive force in this direction. Much physical activity is called into play, both in the community at large and in the manipulation of materials in the schoolroom. The class reading and study can be strongly motivated by the action interest and by the feeling of the worth-whileness of the materials from the point of view of social welfare. The recreational reading for hours of leisure helps to reflect a glow of interest back upon the class activities. Even the type of measurement and the diagnosis of difficulties can be a help or a hindrance. They may, for example, aim at principles or emphasize details, and it may be possible to prepare for them intelli-gently or they may depend upon the whim of the teacher.

If the foregoing possibilities for favorable emotional tone are utilized, the child becomes an active and co-operative member of a dynamic society rather than a passive and dominated unit in a mass.[2]

[1] See Benjamin Brenner's *Effect of Immediate and Delayed Praise and Blame upon Learning and Recall* (Teachers College Contributions to Education, No. 620, Columbia University, 1934).

[2] Will French, "Developing a Social Studies Philosophy," *Progressive Education*, XII: 233–238 (1935); James W. Welsh, "The Development of Morale in the Elementary School," *Educational Method*, XIII: 28–35 (October, 1933).

A Warning about the Problem of Interest

Certain holdovers from an earlier regime are blocking the efforts of conscientious teachers. That the presence of a motivating stimulus is necessary to learning is well understood. This motivating factor is often spoken of as "want" or "need." Many teachers have interpreted the need of a stimulus as implying that they must furnish children with exciting situations in order to arouse interest, or that they must provide unusual objects or activities. Modern dynamic psychology, however, holds that any activity for which an individual is specially fitted is likely to be performed with spontaneity and zest and to furnish its own drive. Ideas themselves elicit responses. Such a belief sounds like an echo of Herbert Spencer's dictum: "At each age the intellectual action which a child likes is a healthful one for it"; and it is in agreement with Bertrand Russell's statement: "Disgust is proof of premature presentation of matter in indigestible form."

The child possesses naturally an eager curiosity which pries into all varieties of human relations, and a "will to power" which grows with successful application. He is attracted by *action* either in the concrete or in stories, as Uhl's study[1] shows. History, if presented in a form easy enough for him to understand and to master, appeals naturally to this intense curiosity or desire for mental manipulation. Artificial stimuli need not be added.

Since pupils of middle-grade age have an almost unlimited curiosity, the teacher need only to "set the stage" or "condition the behavior," and the desired responses will arise spontaneously. "This spontaneous wish to learn which every normal child possesses should be the driving force in education." It remains for the teacher to see that the conditioning activities are suited to the capacity of the learner.

Early followers of the progressive movement maintained that activities must follow the lead of the child's spontaneous interests and choices. Experience, however, showed the ephemeral nature of many of those interests. The point of view generally accepted now is that any worth-while lead and purpose may be followed which the child embraces as his own.[2]

The Technique of Learning and Teaching: the Foundations of Technique

On the same level of importance with the objectives and the curriculum, and second only to the whole emotional atmosphere, is the technique of learning and teaching, which are obverse aspects of the same process.

[1] Willis Uhl, *Scientific Determination of the Elementary School Course in Reading.*
[2] See S. L. Pressey's *Psychology and the New Education*, pp. 91–98.

The distinguished geographer Isaiah Bowman defines technique as follows:

"A technique is a system of orderly or rational procedure and notation." [1] Its purpose is "to focus the attention upon selected objectives," [2] and "it provides schedules of categories of inquiry that guard against the overlooking of data." [3] "Perhaps the greatest danger is the substitution of purely technical procedure for creative thinking. . . . Rigorous method has its place but so too has the untrammeled moment." [3] An adequate technique must provide for both.

Subject-matter experts and extreme radicals are equally scornful of technique. Their attitude has been influenced partly by the history of "methods" in American education, partly by the failure of education to make use of the scientific findings of experimental psychology, and partly by their own ignorance of the psychological foundations that can be utilized.

Extremists are likely to feel that the adoption of a technique cramps the individuality of the teacher and limits her initiative. Bowman's definition given above should help to remove such apprehensions. In fact, a good technique utilizes every possible variety of experience and every resource that a teacher has at her command. It limits her only in regard to the order in which the experiences are presented; and this order depends upon a study of how children learn most effectively.

The Dismal History of "Methods" in the Social Sciences

A critic can hardly refrain from skepticism when he surveys the history of methods in the social sciences. Within the professional lifetime of teachers still active in the schools a bewildering array of methods has appeared, and they have been in use in quick succession,— chronological method, topical method, biographical method, lecture method, type-study method, source method, supervised-study method, socialized method, problem method, project method, counter-chronological method, unit method, contract method, activity method, — to say nothing of "lessons," such as drill lessons, review lessons, inductive lessons, deductive lessons, picture-study lessons, map-study lessons, story-telling lessons, and appreciation lessons. Some of these are methods of organization only; many are methods of both organization and presentation. Each has its day and passes from the stage to give way to the next.

During the period of ascendancy of each method conscientious teachers have felt that they must teach every day's lesson in every subject according to the principles of the method fashionable at the moment. Their invariable experience has been that it seems to work well with certain kinds of materials or at certain stages in the learning

---

[1] In *Geography in Relation to the Social Sciences*, p. 98.
[2] Ibid. p. 111.   [3] Ibid. p. 112.

process and that it secures certain values, but that it breaks down with other kinds of material, that it does not apply equally well to all stages of the learning process, and that by its exclusive use many values are lost.

For example, the chronological method did give children some sense of time and enabled them to see, to a certain extent, how events taking place at the same time impinge upon one another; but it did not enable them to follow the coherent development of any specific movement. The topical method did provide for the following of coherent strands, but it made very difficult the ascertaining of interrelationship between strands. The biographical method pointed out the controlling and sometimes dominating influence supplied by individuals, but it lost sight of movements and economic controls. The lecture method, at best, provided for broad interpretations, but it called for little activity and hence little except passive repetition on the part of the learner.

The type-study method so organized materials that certain significant problems were brought sharply into focus, but others were neglected, and the interconnections were slighted. The source method supplied color, but it was intolerably expensive in time and effort. The supervised-study method provided help in fixing good study habits, but it neglected other activities. The socialized method helped to break up the formality and lifelessness of recitation periods, but it was inapplicable to independent study. The problem method helped to force reactions, but it was applicable to few situations actually found in the social sciences. The project method supplied a needed emphasis on activities, but it concerned itself too little with the social value of the content. The counterchronological method suggested a valuable type of approach, but it broke down as a method of organization and presentation of a first view for young children.

The unit method, as described by the authority who did more to popularize it than anyone else,[1] made a splendid contribution to the understanding of history, but it refused to be influenced by the contributions of progressive education toward the diversifying of activities, and it paid too little attention to the social value of the content of the units. The contract method did provide for individual differences, but in a rigid, formalistic manner, with undue emphasis on grades and marks. The activity method provided needed emphasis on emotional urge, on physical movement and manipulation, but it gave not enough attention to cumulative development in the child's thought or to interrelations between the activities.

The various "lessons" mentioned above are clearly applicable only to limited phases of learning.

[1] Henry C. Morrison, *The Practice of Teaching in the Secondary School.*

About the time that teachers have been reaching these conclusions with regard to any specific method, another method has been advocated by some influential educator, some well-publicized school system, or some highly respected experimental center. In order to be considered up-to-date and progressive, the teachers then have felt the necessity of dropping the old and going over to the new — lock, stock, and barrel.

After a few years the process is repeated again, and so *ad infinitum*. Little wonder that the evolutionist surveys the prospect with dismay and concludes that methods are ephemeral and useless products!

The critical point in this "dismal history" is that there has been in each case so little attempt to analyze the values and the failures of a particular method. Its protagonists have made extravagant claims for it; its opponents have ridiculed and rejected it *in toto*. There has been little dispassionate weighing by scientific methods as to what is valuable and should be retained and what is irrelevant or ineffective and should be replaced,— what is effective at one stage of the learning process and what should be substituted for it at others.

Consequently there has been little orderly, systematic, cumulative progression, little building upon the experiences and mistakes of the past, — in short, little evolution. If the whole cultural inheritance had been transmitted in the same bungling, shortsighted manner, it is hard to envisage the kind of world in which we should be living today.

Needed: a New Integration and a Higher Synthesis

What is needed is very clear. It is, first, a more profound study of the learning process; second, an appraisal of the values (if any) of all known methods in relation to some stage of the learning process; and, third, an integration of the established values into a higher synthesis.

Knowledge about these three matters exists in different degrees. A great many studies have been made about certain aspects of learning, many of which are applicable to the social-science field. These can be utilized, but gaps still exist which will have to be filled up by referring to a consensus of expert opinion.

The values and shortcomings of the various methods have been reviewed exhaustively in the professional literature of the last quarter of a century. The best that can be done by an individual worker is to assemble the points brought out in the various discussions and to weigh them. In so doing he will, of course, be influenced by the points of view that he has developed from a lifetime of direct experience in working with all the methods enumerated.

In attempting to integrate these various values into a technique which is a higher synthesis the chief problem for the present is to integrate the best features of the Morrison unit-of-understanding procedure with the activity-unit-of-work plan. Professor Morrison's procedure is itself an integration of many but not all the methods enumerated above. It has made an enduring contribution to American education and has stamped its impress on procedures throughout the country. But, at its lower levels, it has manifested the weakness of refusing to accept the values of variety in experiencing which has been the great contribution of the activity movement. On the other hand, the activity plan, while it has introduced a flexibility and an adaptation to interest which are invaluable in the freeing of the American child from domination, has nevertheless manifested a lack of concern for continuity and development in experience which has greatly impaired its usefulness.

The following pages are devoted to a discussion of an integrated technique which seeks to bring together the two sets of values. The "steps" of the Morrison plan have been abolished, as tending to formalize and mechanize instruction. Many teachers who have attempted to follow it religiously have become hopelessly entangled in the machinery. Its terminology also has been dropped, as needlessly confusing. From the activity program the elements of application to everyday life, of child purposing, of interrelationships of materials from many fields within a unit, and of variety of activities have been retained; but the main outlines of the unit have been planned in advance, and there is continuity and developmental coherence between units.

Moreover, the plan projected combines periods of individual-study-and-progress with group work.[1] It recognizes the fact of individual differences in reading and in reasoning as well as difference in talent and in tastes. Therefore reading is carried on as an independent activity by all children who have achieved a mastery of the reading process; and creative activities are suggested to discover and develop the special abilities of the gifted child as well as of the "manual-minded." Drill work and remedial work are directly conditioned by the specific difficulties of individuals.

On the other hand, years of observation of school systems which have devoted themselves exclusively to plans of individual progress have demonstrated clearly the social shortcomings of their programs. Children have had insufficient opportunity for co-operative enterprises. Some of the systems themselves have recognized this difficulty and have broken their school day into two parts, one for individual work and one for group work.

The plan to be developed in the following pages combines independent work with group work at different stages of the learning process without any disruption of the entire school organization. For a time

[1] See Leonard Power's "Co-operative Group Plan and the Individual," *Educational Method*, XIV: 240–247 (February, 1935).

all children pool their efforts, their resources, and their suggestions. Then the group breaks up into its elements, and each pursues his special difficulty or interest, only to come together again to appraise results. Thus the group and the individual constantly supplement one another's interests.

One suffers no illusions as to the finality of the form suggested. Improvements will continue to be made as long as there is life in the educational system. But such improvements can be stabilized, and progress can be made much more direct and unwavering, if the method of evolution is followed rather than that of revolution.

Outlines of an Integrated Technique

Students of the various methods that have been used in the social sciences will recognize in the following description an integration of the conversational method, the inductive method, the supervised-study method, the story-telling or lecture method, combined group-and-individual progress, the discussion method, the deductive method, picture-study and map-study "lessons," appreciation "lessons," the project method, the activity program, map-making "lessons," the problem method, the unit method, drill "lessons," test "lessons," organization "lessons," and "recitations." Each is fitted into the technique at the point where it seems to have a real contribution to make to the effectiveness of learning.

How the Teacher Prepares for her Work

Naturally the primary preparation for the teacher is a fully adequate knowledge of the subject matter to be taught, not only on the fact level but also on the interpretation level. In addition she must have a comprehensive knowledge of present-day institutions and world problems and an understanding of child nature and development. With such equipment she is enabled to establish objectives intelligently, to choose materials for attaining the objectives, and to tie up the classroom situations constantly with real-life situations. The inadequacies and shortcomings of most of our teaching of the social sciences may be attributed directly to the fact that not enough teachers are thus prepared.

The teacher who has this equipment can do much planning in advance before she is faced daily with the multitudinous tasks of institutional management.

Among these tasks which can be planned in advance, first in importance is the selection of the units of understanding or units of work, without which the school program becomes chaos and the child's systematic development is seriously impaired. The subdivision of these units into manageable blocks should also be planned in general outline, though the details may well be left for adjustment to the abilities and interests of a particular group.

Next comes the task of collecting an ample supply of reading materials for the children. These may include two or three parallel texts, books for extensive reading, and a list of books for recreational reading. The first two categories should also be scrutinized as to their suitability for the independent readers or for the lower-ability groups.

In the comparatively few schools which have adequate libraries this task is the simple one of removing the books from the general reading room to the classroom. In most systems, however, the teacher's energy and initiative are taxed to the utmost to collect enough books of the right kind. The slender resources of the school library must usually be supplemented by ransacking the principal's office, the superintendent's office, and any other places where stray copies of books may have become impounded.

The co-operation of the city library is also needed, and arrangements may be made for withdrawing for classroom use all the books for the first unit. Arrangements for children's library cards should also be made.

In certain rural or village schools where no city library is available, the assistance of the state library commission and the traveling-library service must be sought.[1]

If the book selected as a basic text does not contain suitable study-guide questions, the teacher may wish to make out such lists of questions in advance, while she has more leisure than during crowded school days.

Another matter which must be anticipated is the problem of general equipment,— maps (both wall maps and outline maps), globes, pictures, slides, the lantern (the teacher may even need to learn the method of its operation), and all sorts of construction-equipment which may be planned with the assistance of the art teacher and the manual-training teacher, with the principal's advice and concurrence.

In most cases a schedule of planning for some years ahead is necessary in order to build up an equipment that even approaches adequacy. In the meantime, however, the teacher should make quite sure that she is utilizing to the full every bit of equipment that is available. In how many cases one hears principals eloquently testifying as to boxes of lantern slides lying unused in the offices, of expensive maps buried in one room and used nowhere else, and of public libraries vainly offering co-operation!

If the teacher's educational philosophy recognizes the function of drill in fixing certain invariable associations, she needs to select from

---

[1] See Lucile F. Fargo's *The Superintendent Makes a Discovery* (pamphlet of the Library Extension Board, The American Library Association, 520 N. Michigan Ave., Chicago).

each unit the few items which form the legitimate subjects of drill. The assistance of scientific studies may be called in at this point. Drill cards may also be made in advance.

If objective tests are ever to meet the merited criticisms which have been heaped upon them, they must be very carefully and thoughtfully drawn up, with due regard to the testing of reasoning as well as of memory. Such tests are not likely to be made in the hurry of the hours after school closes each day. To be sure, only preliminary forms can be made in advance, and actual use will doubtless reveal many instances in which changes should be made. But hurriedly constructed tests thrown together on the spur of the moment would doubtless suffer from many more deficiencies.

With all these tasks completed in advance the teacher's time and energies are freed for what are, after all, her main functions, — the *directing and assisting of learning* and *creative teaching*. The *teacher* remains a more potent factor than any *method* or *technique* that she may use.

Mechanics to be Completed in the First Days of School

Beginning with the first day the teacher meets the new group of children, her major concern throughout the year is with the children's learning.

In order best to direct and assist such learning she needs exact and detailed knowledge about each child. Most school systems recognize this fact, and many of them have for each child a dossier in which his case history is kept from the day he enters kindergarten until his graduation.

For the benefit of teachers who do not have such assistance in studying their children the following suggestions are made.

It is helpful to know each child's I.Q. as determined by an intelligence test, and to scan the previous teacher's marks. The day of "determinism" has long gone by, and no one now advocates grouping children with reference to their intelligence alone. Nevertheless the I.Q. is useful as an indication of what may be expected.

Since comprehension in history is so largely dependent upon reading ability, a good standardized reading test should be given. On the basis of these three kinds of data — the intelligence test, the standardized reading test, and the previous teacher's marks — the teacher can make a study of the group and decide, tentatively, which members will probably be able to work independently under proper direction and which will need much more specific help from the beginning. She classifies them, for her own guidance, as "Independent Readers" and "Lower Group."

The results of years of experience have made many workers in the field of education exceedingly skeptical as to the social and emotional effects of homogeneous grouping and separation into classes meeting in different rooms on such a basis.[1] The independent readers and the lower group may therefore remain in the same classroom, and they may be members of the same class. The sole reason for dividing them is to be able to give needed guidance in reading and study to the lower group during the reading periods and at the same time to develop the independence of the more advanced readers in comprehension, reasoning, and planning of activities, as fast and as far as their ability warrants.

During much of the time the two groups form one unit, — during the conversational approach and the discussion, all through the general-activity period and the drill games, though qualitative differences will show throughout. Only during the period of reading and study, the preparation for drill, and the testing does the class function as individuals.[2]

For ease in managing the reading program, however, it is advantageous to seat the lower group in a compact body, preferably at one side of the room.

As a last preliminary it is helpful to give a pretest over the entire field to be studied. A list of such tests is given on page 107. The results obtained at this time from the use of Form A may be compared with the results obtained from the use of Form B of the same test at the end of the year, as a measure of progress.

A clear picture of the classroom, with the children ready to attack the first unit, shows the more advanced readers seated at one side of the room. Plainly posted is their list of readings, with exact page references. Each child has his own text at his desk. The other texts are placed on a bookshelf easily accessible; the list for extensive reading is close at hand. The titles for recreational reading are posted, perhaps near the door, where children may examine them at their leisure.

The pictures and the drill cards are in assigned places, and certain suggestions for activities are posted.

At the other side of the room sits the lower group, with their texts at their desks. By such an arrangement the teacher is enabled to supervise their activities much more closely than those of the other group.

As the study progresses through the first few stories the two groups become accustomed to the great range of activities included, and evolve an order of work.

All these preliminaries are completed within a few days after the opening of school.

[1] See Parl West's *A Study of Ability Grouping in the Elementary School* (Teachers College Contributions to Education, No. 588, Bureau of Publications, Columbia University, 1933); J. W. Tilton's "The Feasibility of Ability Grouping" in *Journal of Educational Research,* XXVIII: 30–35 (September, 1934); Ninth Yearbook of the Department of Superintendence of the National Education Association (1931); Thirty-fifth Yearbook of the National Society for the Study of Education (1936), Part I.

[2] See the detailed discussion of each of these activities, pages 41–57, 94–98, 98–108.

The Conversational Approach

In approaching a new unit of work the teacher's major problem is to insure a favorable emotional attitude toward the question on the part of as many children as possible. If the curriculum material has been well chosen, and if the children's previous experiences (if any) with that kind of material have been pleasurable, the task is easy. Activities for which children are fitted and ideas which they comprehend "furnish their own drive."[1]

Interest is awakened and children are convinced that the new unit is worth while by means of an easy, informal, give-and-take conversation which precedes study. With older children in the middle grades and with all children in the upper grades the pointing out of direct connections with present-day problems and current events is one of the most successful lines of attack[2]. Experiments[3] have shown, however, that young children in the lower middle grades get little out of a study of current events and present-day problems. They do not possess the needed foundations in understanding which are laid by geography and history.

With younger children in the fourth and fifth grades, then, the most profitable line of approach is the pointing out of bases of understanding which may be supplied by their own direct experiences and observations in life.[4] Their pooling of experiences and interchange of views not only assist understanding but furnish a most valuable form of social co-operation. The inexperienced or inexpert teacher is at first blind to the opportunities afforded and is likely to believe that children have never lived through or observed any experience that can be utilized. Conscientious application of the principle, however, soon deepens her insight. At intervals it may be necessary to *supply* the actual experience needed as a foundation, either in the classroom or in the community, if there is reason to believe that most children have not had it.[5]

In addition the period of conversational approach facilitates a direct tie-up with what has gone before, so that the continuity of development may be clearly seen. Such an exercise does not aim at review for the sake of review, but it selects out of the previous fields of knowledge those factors which lead directly and coherently into

---

[1] For a psychological analysis of this stage in learning see *The Social Studies*, XXV : 21–22 (January, 1934).

[2] Taubeneck, Misner, and Beatty, "History Begins with the Present," *Progressive Education*, XI : 82–87 (1934). This is the counterchronological approach.

[3] M. G. Kelty and N. E. Moore, "An Experimental Study of the Teaching of Current Events in the Middle Grades," *Elementary School Journal*, XXXII : 417–425 (February, 1932).

[4] See examples in the conversational approach on pages 122, 414, 479.

[5] See pages 131, 332, for examples.

the new unit. To be avoided at all costs is the mere accumulation of disjointed facts, which the child can only memorize.

A third function of the preliminary conversational activity is to suggest what the new problem is, and perhaps to forecast the probable lines of solution. At times reading a map indicates what may be expected, and helps to focus attention upon the main outlines to be followed.

In psychological terms, this exercise furnishes the desired mind-set or, in older terminology, recognizes the principle of apperception. The principle, though known for years, has been more honored in the breach than in the observance. In terms of the stimulus-response theory, the conversational approach shows the need and furnishes the initial stimulus. It is also a unique application, in terms of social-science materials, of the pretest idea.

Throughout, the activity is group activity, and progress toward understanding is achieved by the children during this period as members of social groups.[1]

By the time the conversational approach has been completed, if well carried out, the children are predisposed to an active favorable attitude toward the new unit, the connections have been firmly established, and the independent readers are now ready for individual work. Even the members of the lower group are ready to put forth much more effort because of a favorable emotional tone.

Reading and Study

So far the group has worked as a whole. The members differ so greatly, however, in both rate and comprehension in reading[2] that they can no longer proceed profitably under uniform conditions. For example, not only do the reading tests show a wide range of ability, but Professor Freeman has found that the standard deviation increases greatly from the ages of nine to twelve, the age of most of the children in the middle grades.

For these reasons the class, as already described (pp. 38–39), is divided now into two groups: independent readers and lower-ability group. They are still members of the same class, they sit in the same classroom, and they carry on their activities at the same time. A picture of the classroom situation has been given on page 39.

In the literature on the subject of ability grouping, teachers usually are warned that children are not to know that they are in a lower-ability group. Naturally the term will never be used in their hearing,

---

[1] See W. A. Brownell and Howard Easley's "General Conditions Affecting Teaching and Learning," *Review of Educational Research*, III : 338–339 (October, 1933).

[2] For a psychological analysis of the reading process see *The Social Studies*, XXV : 23–25 (January, 1935).

but the assumption that children are not keen enough to know in which group they are working underestimates their intelligence. A more realistic attitude is to face the situation and to proceed in a matter-of-fact way, putting the whole procedure on the basis of need. Such-and-such children need help and guidance in reading; therefore the teacher gives them special direction until they can read well by themselves. The point of emphasis is that no stigma is to be attached to the group which the teacher helps.

In the plan under consideration the facts, first, that upper and lower groups work together during most of the stages of learning except the reading-and-study stage and, second, that they are not isolated in separate rooms or class periods, help to preserve the feeling of group solidarity. Moreover, the groupings are different for different subjects. And yet, at the same time, the inescapable facts of individual differences in reading ability are faced squarely, and treatment is provided accordingly.

The teacher of a fourth grade just beginning the reading of history is likely to fall into one or the other of two errors. She may conclude that the children's ability in silent reading is still very weak, that they are still little more than babies, and she may therefore expect very little of them and fail to develop independence on the part of the more able members. Such a teacher needs particularly to study how the upper-group instruction is managed.

On the other hand, the teacher may conclude that fourth-grade children are now able to read independently, and she may give them no more guidance than the direction, "Open your books and read the story beginning on page 27." Such a teacher needs to study the discussions, for the teacher's guidance, of the reading of the upper group, and her responsibility in teaching the lower-ability groups *how* to read history materials.[1] She needs especially to realize that she must use her silent-reading technique in the history class.

The Procedure for the Independent Readers

Basic text.[2] The picture of the classroom, with its seating arrangement, its book lists, and its book supplies (see page 39) should be clearly visualized before reading about the procedure followed.

As soon as the conversational approach has been completed (which may take from perhaps five to perhaps twenty minutes), the independent readers immediately begin reading from their text, which they have at their desks.

[1] See *Better Reading Instruction*, Research Bulletin No. 5, Vol. XIII, National Education Association (November, 1935).

[2] See Tyler Kepner's "The Influences of Textbooks upon Method," Fifth Yearbook of the National Council for the Social Studies, pp. 143–172 (1935); Miriam A. Compton's *An Evaluation of History Texts: a Check List* (McKinley Publishing Company, 1932).

Years of experience have pointed to the practical value of using a basic text.[1] It serves as a frame of organization, enabling the child to keep before him in tangible form the development of the line of thought being pursued. He does not see this so easily if he has read from many books but possesses no backbone or framework to which to tie the additional ideas gained from wide reading.

In the discussion, and the testing also, it is helpful for the group to be provided with at least a minimum of common background. If necessary the following study directions for textbook reading are written on the board, to make sure that every child in the upper group knows what to do during the period while he is working independently and while the teacher is working with the lower group.

1. Read the entire story through to find out what happened.
2. Then test your understanding of the story by asking yourself the questions printed at the end of the story. [If the text used does not supply adequate questions, the teacher will find it necessary to write study-guide questions on the board or to supply mimeographed or hectographed copies.]
3. If you cannot answer some of the questions, turn back in the story and read again the part which tells the answer.

The tendency of children to identify the self with objects which are the center of interest [2] makes possible a degree of vicarious experience through reading. The child "loses himself in the story." For the time being he is not freckled-faced, tow-headed Johnnie Jones, who always has trouble in adding numbers; he is swarthy-faced Magellan on the quarter-deck of the *Victoria*, bearing on his broad shoulders the responsibility for the lives of three hundred men. Through such identification the child educates himself through experience as he reads.

The first study direction given, to read the entire story through,[3] thus aims directly at the second objective as given on page 7. The other directions help in clarifying meanings by each child's appraising his own comprehension of the story. Particularly important is the selecting of the main phases and the subordination of supporting detail, however spectacular. As a practical matter, this assistance can be facilitated by printed study-guide questions in the text. And, finally, the teacher's deep understanding of subject matter is directly tested by her ability to appraise the study questions furnished by the text or to formulate her own.

Many factors need to be considered, however. If the questions in the text are very numerous, they necessarily test details rather than

[1] E. W. Dolch, "Goals in Intermediate Reading," *Elementary School Journal*, XXXV: 682–690 (May, 1935).

[2] Louise B. Wright, "Value of a Motivated Assignment: an Experiment in Directed Study," *University of Pittsburgh School of Education Journal*, V: 64–67 (December, 1929).

[3] H. L. Hollingworth, *Mental Growth and Decline*. D. Appleton-Century Company, 1927.

important phases, and their use is a hindrance rather than a help. In such cases it is necessary for the teacher to devise better questions.

The problem of the placement of the questions has received much study. An inconclusive experiment [1] some years ago suggested that the study questions should be placed first. However, studies in the field of reading have pointed out that the nature of the reading is fundamentally affected by the direction as to what to find. Since a main objective in history is to develop the independent ability to comprehend a coherent narrative of successive events, that type and placement of study questions should be used which will directly function in developing such an ability. Preliminary focusing of attention on specific phases may inhibit it.

Numbers of experiments [2] have showed the advantage to be gained by the pupil's reciting to himself after reading rather than continuing to reread indefinitely without testing himself. Too strong condemnation cannot be given to the practice of requiring children to write the answers to all the study-guide questions in a notebook. Under such circumstances the tendency is to reduce learning to an automatic copying; the knowledge is folded away with the notebook, and the pupil feels comfortably that he has learned when in fact he has done nothing but write. A reaction to the stimulus of reading is strongly to be desired, but the reaction should be mental and not merely physical manipulation. *Understanding* is the objective.

The teacher will discover many types of shortcomings in the reading processes even of the "independent" readers. Some have a tendency to repeat the words of the book. Some read rapidly but inaccurately. Some complain that they did know the answers to the study-guide questions once, but have forgotten them by the time the discussion period comes. These difficulties, however, can be overcome by patience and firmness in rejecting unsatisfactory answers in the discussion period throughout the years of middle-grade social-science experience. Overcoming them is one of the great values to be derived from such experience.

As time goes on and pupils become more familiar with the kind of understanding which is stressed, some of them will spend much less time than formerly on the study of their own text. These are the readers who have had a tendency to memorize everything printed. Others will spend much more time than formerly; these are the readers who have had a tendency to skim through material rapidly without much comprehension of the ideas involved.

[1] John N. Washburn, "The Use of Questions in Social Science Materials," *Journal of Educational Psychology*, XX: 321 (May, 1929).
[2] Arthur I. Gates, *Psychology for Students of Education*, Revised Edition, p. 336 (The Macmillan Company, 1930); S. L. Pressey, *Psychology and the New Education*, p. 408.

Parallel texts. When the independent readers have completed the analytical and intensive study of their own text, they are ready for the next exercise. This is reading from parallel texts which are readily accessible on the bookshelves. After each child finishes his own text he goes quietly to the shelves, selects another, returns to his seat, and reads this second version of the same story. He may read two or three such versions during the time allotted.

After finishing the parallel texts, it is helpful for the reader to return once more to the study-guide questions in his own book. The wider reading should have made the answering of them once more an easy matter. It is not necessary or desirable to use different study-guide questions for every book.

The values of reading from parallel texts are obvious. First, the reader gains the advantage of looking at the subject as a whole from different points of view, sometimes from conflicting points of view. The resulting comparisons are valuable in developing an attitude of judgment. Second, the reading from several sources makes impossible that bane of all social-science instruction, — word-memory. If a child has read only a single text, he can, and all too often does, carry on his thinking in the vocabulary of the one author he has read. But it is impossible for him to carry in mind the varying methods of expression of different authors. Even if he would rather memorize than think, he cannot do so. He is forced, rather, to follow the thread of the story and to carry on his thinking in his own natural vocabulary.

Following is a list of texts used in the units described in Parts II, III, and IV of this book. Books used less than five times during a year's work are not included. Neither are texts included which compress each account into a brief paragraph or two.

TEXTS USED IN PART TWO (EARLY AMERICAN HISTORY)

Title of Book	Times Used
KELTY. *Beginnings of the American People and Nation*	48
BARKER, DODD, WEBB. *Our Nation Begins*	41
BURNHAM and JACK. *Beginnings of Our Country*	41
BEARD and BAGLEY. *First Book in American History*	31
CLARK-GORDY. *First Three Hundred Years in America* (hard)	26
NIDA. *Following Columbus*	26
SMALLIDGE and PAXSON. *Builders of Our Nation* (hard)	24
WOODBURN and MORAN. *Finders and Founders of the New World*	23
KNOWLTON and GILL. *When We Were Colonies* (hard)	17
KNOWLTON and WHEELER. *Our Past in Western Europe*	17
SMALLIDGE and PAXSON. *Finding America*	15
CLARK-GORDY. *Westward toward America*	14
McGUIRE and PHILLIPS. *Adventuring in Young America*	12
NIDA. *Following the Frontier*	7
WOODBURN and MORAN. *Makers of America*	6

TEXTS USED IN PART THREE (LATER AMERICAN HISTORY)

Title of Book	Times Used
KELTY. *Growth of the American People and Nation*	85
BURNHAM and JACK. *Growth of Our Country*	52
BARKER, DODD, WEBB. *Our Nation Grows Up*	49
BEARD and BAGLEY. *First Book in American History*	44
CLARK. *Westward to the Pacific*	43
SMALLIDGE and PAXSON. *Builders of Our Nation*	35
HALLECK and FRANTZ. *Makers of Our Nation*	32
WOODBURN and MORAN. *Makers of America*	31
McGUIRE and PHILLIPS. *Building Our Country*	30
NIDA. *Following the Frontier*	18
McGUIRE and PHILLIPS. *Adventuring in Young America*	7

TEXTS USED IN PART FOUR (THE BEGINNINGS OF CIVILIZATION)

Easy:

KELTY. *How Our Civilization Began*	39
CLARK-GORDY. *Westward toward America*	36
BEEBY. *America's Roots in the Past*	25
CHAPMAN. *Stories of the Ancient Peoples*	21
KNOWLTON and GERSON. *Our Beginnings in the Past*	21
CLARK-GORDY. *Early Story of Mankind*	19
CORKE. *A Book of Ancient Peoples*	18
KNOWLTON and WHEELER. *Our Past in Western Europe*	15
CHAPMAN. *Stories of Our European Forefathers*	14

More difficult:

HALLECK and FRANTZ. *Our Nation's Heritage*	34
NIDA. *Dawn of American History*	34
BARKER, DUNCALF, BACON. *Old Europe and Our Nation*	33
COULOMB, McKINLEY, WHITE. *What Europe Gave to America*	33
HARDING. *Old World Background to American History*	33
WICKHAM and PHILLIPS. *America's Heritage from the Long Ago*	33
BURNHAM. *Our Beginnings in Europe and America*	32
WOODBURN and HILL. *Historic Background of our United States*	30
GORDY. *American Beginnings in Europe*	29
HAWLEY. *Adventures in Old World History*	29
VOLLINTINE. *American People and Their Old World Ancestors*	29
GREENWOOD. *Our Heritage from the Old World*	28
SOUTHWORTH. *What the Old World Gave the New*	28
BEARD and BAGLEY. *Our Old World Background*	27
NIVER. *Old World Steps to American History*	27
BOURNE and BENTON. *Introductory American History*	26
HALL. *Our Ancestors in Europe*	25
TAPPAN. *Our European Ancestors*	24
SHERWOOD. *Our Country's Beginnings*	23
HORNE and BUCKS. *Europe, the Mother of America*	15
MARSHALL. *Story of Human Progress*	5

Extensive Reading

After the child has read the whole story from several different textbooks he begins to find that he is gaining few new ideas, except perhaps in unimportant details. There is much repetition of the general line of thought, and the child's interest consequently lags.

It is then time to turn to a different kind of material, designated in the book lists [1] which follow as "Extensive Reading." Books of this kind break up the movement under consideration into its component elements. Some view it from one angle; some from others. For example, certain of the books in the list on pages 48–49 are collections of brief biographies. Some are geographical in emphasis. Others are mainly social histories. One is an elementary political science. All together they throw much additional light on the subject from many points of view and greatly broaden and deepen understanding by pointing out interrelationships, especially with geography.

Naturally no child in the group will be able to read all these books; but enough material is included to stretch to the fullest the abilities of even the brightest child. The readers are given definitely to understand that they are not expected to remember everything which they read. With the good foundation of understanding already laid by the study of the texts they can well be encouraged to forget details. The feeling of meaning will remain.

For children in fourth and fifth grades it probably will be economical in time and effort to give specific page references to these extensive reading materials. Sixth-grade children, however, if they have had the training suggested for the fourth and fifth grades, should be able to locate for themselves the pages dealing with the subject about which they wish to read.

Under the old formal bookkeeping view of education, teachers felt that the child should not be given anything to do unless they could test him on his accomplishment. All sorts of devices have been suggested for testing extensive reading: cards of reading reports, book reports both oral and written, check lists of various sorts, etc. None of them have been completely satisfactory and many of them have had unfortunate results in the piling up of accumulations of pages supposedly read.

In the plan under consideration here the teacher frankly makes no attempt to test consistently all the extensive reading. Opportunities are provided [2] for those who have read items they regard as particularly interesting to tell the group about them. And the inspiration as well as the material for many of the creative activities [3] will come from these books.

Following is a list of extensive readings used in the units described in Parts Two, Three, and Four. Books used less than five times during a year's work are not included.

[1] For examples see pages 48–49, 116, 304–305, 481–482, etc.
[2] In the discussion period; see pages 59–60.
[3] See pages 69–77.

EXTENSIVE READINGS USED IN PART TWO (EARLY AMERICAN HISTORY)

Title of Book	Times Used
SOUTHWORTH. *Builders of Our Country*, I	27
MONTGOMERY. *Beginner's American History*	26
PERRY and PRICE. *American History*, I	25
FOOTE and SKINNER. *Explorers and Founders of America*	23
COE. *Founders of Our Country*	21
TAPPAN. *American Hero Stories*	20
BEEBY. *Community Life Today and in Colonial Times*	17
CHANDLER and CHITWOOD. *Makers of American History*	14
FIELD. *Finding the New World*	13
SHAW. *Discoverers and Explorers*	11
VAN LOON. *Short History of Discovery*	11
COE. *Makers of the Nation*	9
DAVIDSON. *Founders and Builders of Our Nation*	9
VOLLINTINE. *Making of America*	9
INGRAHAM. *Story of Democracy*	8
FARIS. *Real Stories of the Geography Makers*	7
PRATT. *Exploration and Discovery*	7
SOUTHWORTH. *Builders of Our Country*, II	7
TAPPAN. *European Hero Stories*	7
FOOTE. *Makers and Defenders of America*	6
JONES. *Geography by Discovery*	6
LAWLER. *Story of Columbus and Magellan*	6
HAZARD and DUTTON. *Indians and Pioneers*	5
TAPPAN. *Letters from Colonial Children*	5

EXTENSIVE READINGS USED IN PART THREE (LATER AMERICAN HISTORY)

GORDY. *Leaders in Making America*	31
EVANS. *America First*	25
SOUTHWORTH. *Builders of Our Country*, II	20
COE. *Makers of the Nation*	19
UHRBROCK and OWENS. *Famous Americans*	17
CHANDLER and CHITWOOD. *Makers of American History*	16
FOOTE and SKINNER. *Makers and Defenders of America*	16
BURNHAM. *Hero Tales from History*	15
MONTGOMERY. *Beginners' American History*	14
LEFFERTS. *American Leaders*, II	14
VOLLINTINE. *The Making of America*	14
FARIS. *Where Our History Was Made*, II	13
BROOKS. *Story of Cotton*	11
DAVIDSON. *Founders and Builders of Our Nation*	11
FARIS. *Real Stories from Our History*	10
SANFORD and OWEN. *Modern Americans*	10
TAPPAN. *Heroes of Progress*	10
BEEBY. *How the World Grows Smaller*	9
McFEE. *Stories of American Inventions*	9
PARKMAN. *Conquests of Invention*	9
LEFFERTS. *American Leaders*, I	8
TURPIN. *Cotton*	8
EGGLESTON. *Stories of American Life and Adventure*	7
FORMAN. *Stories of Useful Inventions*	7
HART. *Romance of the Civil War*	6

Title of Book	Times Used
LARGE. *Everyday Wonders*	6
BARROWS and PARKER. *United States and Canada*	5
FAIRBANKS. *Western United States*	5
TAPPAN. *Travelers and Traveling*	5

EXTENSIVE READINGS USED IN PART FOUR
(THE BEGINNINGS OF CIVILIZATION)

Easy:

HILLYER. *Child's History of the World*	31
COFFMAN. *Child's Story of the Human Race*	28
CORKE. *The World's Family*	17
HODGDON. *The Enchanted Past*	14
BEST. *Glorious Greece and Imperial Rome*	11
TERRY. *History Stories of Other Lands*, I	10
WADDELL and BUSH. *How We Have Conquered Distance*	8
WELLS. *How the Present Came from the Past*, I	7
SCHWARTZ. *From Then Till Now*	6
BEST. *Egypt and Her Neighbors*	5
BEST. *Nations of Western Europe*	5
ERLEIGH. *In the Beginning*	5
WELLS. *How the Present Came from the Past*, II	5

More difficult:

VAN LOON. *Story of Mankind*	27
HARTMAN. *The World We Live In*	23
O'NEILL. *World's Story*	17
HARDING. *Story of the Middle Ages*	13
NIDA. *Man Conquers the World with Science*	12
BURNHAM. *Hero Tales from History*	10
KUMMER. *First Days of History*	10
LANSING. *Man's Long Climb*	9
POWER. *Great People of the Past*	9
HAAREN and POLAND. *Famous Men of the Middle Ages*	7
ILIN. *Black on White*	7
RICHMOND. *Egypt, Greece, and Rome*	7
HAAREN and POLAND. *Famous Men of Rome*	6
HOLBROOK. *Cave, Mound, and Lake Dwellers*	6
KUMMER. *First Days of Knowledge*	6
KUMMER. *First Days of Man*	6
MARSHALL. *Readings in the Story of Human Progress*	6
Story of Writing (American Council on Education)	6
BAIKIE. *Ancient Times*	5
GUERBER. *Story of the Greeks*	5
GUERBER. *Story of the Romans*	5
HAAREN and POLAND. *Famous Men of Greece*	5
INGRAHAM. *Story of Democracy*	5
MACGREGOR. *Story of Greece*	5
MILLS. *Book of the Ancient World*	5
Story of Our Calendar (American Council on Education)	5
Story of Numbers (American Council on Education)	5
Story of Weights and Measures (American Council on Education)	5
Telling Time (American Council on Education)	5
WEBSTER. *World's Messengers*	5

Recreational Reading

All the materials mentioned so far are designed for use in the school-room. There is, however, another type of reading which possesses such great values for the building up of interest in history that it warrants separate mention. This is the type listed hereinafter as Reading for Recreation.[1] It is to be used at home or in the free reading periods in the library.

Some of these books are fiction. Some are based on history, with the action centered about a fictitious boy or girl. Some are picture books. Readings of this kind may well be kept in the school library rather than in the classroom, but the teacher or some of the children may from time to time show the new copies, point out some of the most attractive pictures, read an exciting anecdote, or give a brief book review in order to arouse interest. No attempt is made in any way to test such recreational reading.

It is to be remembered that a "lasting interest in history" is one of the objectives adopted (see page 7). Recreational reading is an invaluable means toward attaining this objective. Whether or not it is attained, however, is largely dependent upon the kind of books supplied for this purpose. If the teacher attempts to substitute ordinary text-book materials, materials which require intensive study, materials which are too advanced for the abilities of the group for which they are intended, or if she insists on testing the results, she will probably defeat her own purpose.[2]

A Problem in Poorly Equipped Schools

The teacher in poorly equipped schools finds that she faces a dual problem. The lower-ability group is probably very poor indeed in its reading comprehension, because of the poverty of its opportunities, and it needs a great deal of help and direction. But during the long period when she is helping these children to read, the more advanced group has exhausted the meager reading materials and has nothing to do.

In anticipation of this difficulty, before each subunit is begun, the teacher prepares the available pictures, a suggestive list of creative activities, a set of questions on application to present-day conditions, reasoning exercises, and drill cards for fixing the desired associations. When each child has finished all the reading available, he turns to these lists and finds ample outlet for his energies and talents until the group is ready to proceed once more as a whole.

[1] For examples see pages 116, 304–305, 481–482.

[2] For methods of stimulating wide reading see W. G. Kimmel's *The Management of the Reading Program in the Social Studies*, pp. 29–31 (McKinley Publishing Company, 1929); also W. S. Gray and B. E. Leary's *What Makes a Book Readable* (The University of Chicago Press, 1935).

As time goes on and the children become familiar with the wide range of activities included in the technique, they know how to prepare themselves for what is to come almost as well as the teacher does. What is going to happen next is no longer the teacher's secret.

The Procedure of the Lower Group

While the independent readers have been occupying themselves with these matters, how has the lower group been occupying itself?

What to do about the children who have difficulty in reading has long been a serious question. With the increase in effectiveness of the compulsory-attendance laws, the decrease in child labor, and the influx of increasing numbers from the least-favored social and economic strata, the problem has assumed gigantic and alarming proportions.

With the deep-seated economic forces which condition such differences the teacher as a professional worker cannot cope. To a certain extent she can influence the whole emotional atmosphere of the school so that the underprivileged child may at least find happiness and security in his school living.[1] To a smaller degree she can determine curriculum content which is suited to the peculiar needs of such children.

But one thing she *can* do. She can adjust technique to the requirements of the situation. And in most systems she can adjust the theoretical "standards of attainment" to the realities of child differences.

Every possible assistance [2] should be sought from the physician, the psychologist, the psychiatrist, the social worker. The teacher should feel perfectly free to bring her most stubborn cases to the attention of the principal and to advise with him as to where help could probably be found. Giving such advice is a main function of the principal. Not until every resource of the community has been exhausted should the few really "problem children" be given up and an entirely new curriculum set up for them.

Most of the children in the typical lower group, however, are probably not such stubborn and obscure problem cases. They are problems mainly because they have not yet learned to read.

In the upper grades the problem is somewhat simplified by the fact that even the lower-group children probably can read materials written for children two or three grades lower than their own. For example, a child enrolled in the seventh grade will probably be able to read a topic as treated in a fourth-grade book. The teacher who is accustomed to facing facts begins, then, with the child *wherever he is* and helps him to grow as far as he can. It is sometimes true that after the seventh-

---

[1] Roy F. Street, "Factors Related to Maladjustment in School," *Elementary School Journal*, XXXIV: 676–680 (May, 1934).

[2] See S. L. Pressey's *Psychology and the New Education*, Chaps. 3, 5, 6, 8, 13, 16 (Harper & Brothers, 1933).

grade child has read and thoroughly comprehended a given topic in a fourth-grade book, he can turn to the same topic in his own book and get something out of the reading, while he could have done nothing at all with it if attacked directly in the first place.

In the middle grades no such solution can be applied. A fourth-grade child cannot turn to a history book written on a first-grade level, for there are no such books, nor could there be.

The administrator is tempted to select the line of least resistance and to decide that instruction in factual materials demanding a mastery of reading ought to be delayed until the upper grades or junior high school. The experience of decades, however, proves that waiting does not solve the problem. It merely postpones the solution until conditions are worse than ever and possibilities of improvement are even smaller.

It must be recognized clearly that the *ideas* presented in good modern courses of study and the best of the modern textbooks in history do not present difficulties to most of the group. Experiments in oral instruction show this conclusively. Neither is the problem one of interest, as the construction and art activities show. The difficulty is a *reading* difficulty and can be overcome only by helping children *to learn to read.* The teacher in the middle grades must therefore be an expert in the teaching of reading, as well as in the subject to be taught.[1]

How can children in the lower-ability group be helped to learn to read? One avenue of approach has already been discussed at length: the conditioning of the whole emotional tone of school life. A more immediate stimulus is supplied in the period of conversational approach, during which the new subject is presented in as interesting a light as possible and children are influenced to feel that it is worth while. The amount of effort that they are willing to put forth is a vital factor in the whole situation, and interest directly affects effort. Direct experience is also brought to bear on the new unit,— during the conversational approach.

Oral Story Helps Bridge the Gap from Oral Instruction to Silent Reading

The teacher faces frankly the fact that the lower-group children cannot yet get thought independently from the printed page. Therefore, as soon as the conversational approach has been finished and the independent readers have begun to read their texts, she turns her attention to the lower group, who are seated in a compact body at one side of the room.

She knows that for the time being she must furnish them with a crutch. Or, to change the figure, she must help them to bridge the

[1] See Arthur I. Gates's *The Improvement of Reading,* Revised Edition (The Macmillan Company, 1935); Gerald A. Yoakum's "The Improvement of Reading in the Middle Grades," *Education,* LVI: 1–6 (September, 1935); Marion Monroe's *Children Who Cannot Read* (The University of Chicago Press, 1935).

gap from the predominantly oral type of instruction to which they have been accustomed in the primary grades to the silent reading of the middle grades.

Her procedure is first to tell the children orally the main outlines of the new story, stripping it down to its essentials but including a few colorful details to strengthen the motivation. Only such names of persons and places as are absolutely essential are included, and these are written on the board. Children practice the pronunciations of the more difficult words. New terms are avoided, and the whole story is told in an informal, even colloquial, manner, to ensure so far as possible that these lower-group children understand *what it is all about.*

In terms of psychology, the teacher attempts to assist the children to become acquainted with the vague undifferentiated whole before making any attempt to break it up for analysis.

Thus, before the members of the lower group turn to their books at all, they know the main outlines of the story, and they are acquainted with the principal names which they will encounter. They approach the reading, then, with a feeling of confidence that they will be able to understand the thought. Very different from the old attitude of indifference or expectation of failure!

It is interesting to note that in many European schools where foreign languages are taught so successfully the teachers make use of this same principle. They first tell a new story to the children in their own tongue, or choose a story that is already well known. Then they tell the same story in the new language which is being studied.

The Teacher Takes Charge of Directed Silent Reading

Needless to say, the text chosen should be one in which the vocabulary has been most carefully controlled. The story should be long enough to include many colorful details and to explain at length the meaning of new vocabulary terms which are introduced. The vocabulary being the same, a longer story is easier to understand than a short summary.[1]

The short skeleton summary makes vicarious experiencing quite impossible; memorization is all that is left to the pupil. It is probable, therefore, that the text which is the best to use as basic for the independent readers is also the best for the lower group in the fourth grade.

Upon finishing the telling of the oral story to this group, and while the independent readers are directing their own efforts, the teacher seats herself near the lower group and proceeds to direct their reading of the history story in exactly the same manner as she would in a period of silent reading.

For example, she states, "The first two paragraphs tell us why

[1] See the reference to Beauchamp's study in footnote 1 on page 23.

Marco's father and uncle wanted to go to China. What was their reason?" The children read to find the answer; if some are quite unable to find the reason stated, others assist them by pointing out the specific passage which gives it. The answer is then stated orally. Thus the reading of even the poorest readers is reinforced, and they have the first point clearly in mind before trying to proceed. Through this procedure members of the lower group are enabled, perhaps for the first time, to know the satisfaction of "giving the answer," of measuring up to the demands laid upon them, and of not falling behind the others with whom they are associated.

In fact, as time goes on, it usually becomes possible at intervals to shift one or two children, who are showing marked improvement, from the lower group to the group of independent readers. By the end of the middle-grade period only the most obscure and stubborn psychological cases are left of the original lower group.[1]

Progress is slow, however, and the teacher often becomes discouraged. An understanding of the psychology of reading will enable her to analyze her own processes and to recognize just what she is aiming at. She must be familiar with the different kinds of reading possible and with the fact that the particular way in which one reads given materials depends upon one's purpose.

She obviously cannot spend all her time every day working with the lower group. There are many other pressing duties. She will therefore be able to read with them only the story as given in the textbook. It is quite likely that, in consequence, many or perhaps most of the children in this group will read only the one book.

A few, however, may progress a little faster than the others, and the most skillful or the most conscientious may wish to have books at their own ability level which they may take home with them. For such children a list of "Other Books" is suggested in the stories composing the units which constitute Parts Two, Three, and Four of this book.

The following list of "Other Books" for the lower group does not contain any which are used less than five times during a year's work.

OTHER BOOKS FOR THE LOWER GROUP USED IN PART TWO
(EARLY AMERICAN HISTORY)

Title of Book	Times Used
WILSON. *A History Reader*	18
DAVIS. *Stories of the United States*	15
WAYLAND. *History Stories for Primary Grades*	15
BLAISDELL and BALL. *American History for Little Folks*	12
DODGE. *Stories of American History*	11
BLAISDELL and BALL. *Child's Book of American History*	10
LUCIA. *Stories of American Discoverers for Little Americans*	10

[1] Elizabeth B. Bigelow, "'Improvement in Reading as Shown by Standard Tests," *Educational Method*, XIII : 258–263 (February, 1934).

Title of Book	Times Used
PRATT. *Stories of Colonial Children*	10
BLAISDELL and BALL. *Short Stories from American History*	8
PRATT. *Beginners' Book*	6
BLAISDELL and BALL. *American History Story Book*	5
WELSH. *Colonial Days*	5

OTHER BOOKS FOR THE LOWER GROUP USED IN PART THREE
(LATER AMERICAN HISTORY)

DAVIS. *Stories of the United States*	9
EGGLESTON. *Stories of Great Americans*	7
WAYLAND. *History Stories for Primary Grades*	7
CHAMBERLAIN. *How We Travel*	6
EVERETT and REED. *When They Were Boys*	6
FAIRGRIEVE and YOUNG. *The World*	6
ALLEN. *How and Where We Live*	5
BALDWIN. *Fifty Famous People*	5
CARROLL. *Around the World*, III	5
CHAMBERLAIN. *How We Are Clothed*	5
TAPPAN. *American History Stories for Very Young Readers*	5

OTHER BOOKS FOR THE LOWER GROUP USED IN PART FOUR
(THE BEGINNINGS OF CIVILIZATION)

TERRY. *History Stories of Other Lands*, I	5
TERRY. *History Stories of Other Lands*, II	5

Other Means of Learning Available for Lower Group

In the above discussion the difficulty which lower-ability-group children have in obtaining meaning from the printed page has been recognized by providing oral story-telling (see pages 52–53) and very closely supervised reading periods (see pages 53–54).

Other avenues toward comprehending meanings are also available and are possibly even more effective with lower-group children than with upper groups. Such are picture-and-map study (pp. 64–69), oral discussion (pp. 57–64), and activities (pp. 69–77), such as a construction, manipulation, actual experience, dramatization, drawing, carving, etc.

Through such approaches these children gain meanings which strongly reinforce the vague and nebulous ideas they are likely to obtain through reading alone. This fact should point out a fallacy much too common in the reasoning of teachers as revealed by their practice. Many teachers feel that because lower-group children read slowly and poorly they should spend all their time in improving their mastery of the reading process.

Therefore, while the upper-group members are viewing pictures and carrying on other interesting activities, the members of the lower group are kept at a constant grind of reading. Such a practice overlooks two principles: first, that concepts may be built up more readily by *varying* the methods of presentation (reading, pictures, map-making, construction, dramatization, etc.), and, second, that great importance should be attached to giving children opportunities to do what they *like* to do. It is only human to enjoy doing what one can do well, and lower-group children may excel in many forms of manipulation. Therefore physical activities of many kinds should be utilized. They are not only means of clarifying ideas; they are spurs to both interest and effort in acquiring social-science understandings.

The Question of Workbooks

Since workbooks have come to be utilized in so many fields, the question often arises as to whether they are helpful in acquiring understanding of middle-grade history.

Obviously, if the teacher is very poorly prepared, the more the teaching can be taken out of her hands and the more the child is enabled to guide and direct his own progress, the better. An instrument which opens up new vistas to the poorly prepared teacher, and which furnishes the child with specific, definite, and workable directions is doubtless a help in more effective learning.

However, general lines of policy should not be laid down on the postulation that the teaching will be bad. Other conditions being favorable, should a workbook be used? If so, what is its function?

The specific function of the workbook is to furnish opportunities for practice in skills and for application of general principles to specifics. It can profitably guide a child's procedure in the aspects of study which he can attack as an individual, but it has little to offer for the wide range of activities which should properly be group enterprises.

In the first place, it is generally agreed that the amount of written work called for in the lower middle grades should be kept at a minimum. Many workbooks violate this principle. Moreover, the continued utilization of the history periods, day after day, for individual silent reading and for individual practice and testing exercises in a workbook can become as deadly and monotonous as the old question-and-answer recitation. There is little of socializing or inspirational value in such practices.

To what extent workbooks should be used in the middle grades, then, depends immediately upon the objectives to be attained. Of those given on pages 7 and 8 it seems clear that the first can be developed much better through active group co-operation than through a workbook. The development of the second could be assisted by workbook numbering exercises in time sequence, but outlining and summarizing at this level can be carried on only with the assistance of the teacher; and the most valuable means of all, discussion, does not lend itself to workbook technique. The third and fourth can be tested through a workbook, but, for development of understanding, dynamic and resourceful teacher-participation with immediate reactions is needed. The fifth can be tested by a workbook but not developed to any great extent. The sixth can be applied as written directions, but actual doing under watchful supervision is more helpful. The seventh can be tested, but again the valuable *teaching* aspects cannot be included. The same can be said of the eighth.

The conclusion, then, seems to be that a printed set of test exercises or drill exercises may be helpful for the individual aspects of study, but that it must be supplemented by a generous amount of group activity. The function of the *teacher* and the *group* in developing meanings and understandings must not be lost sight of.[1]

The Discussion

It will be recalled that the basic step toward comprehension, which is capable of attainment in the lower middle grades, is the developing of the "ability to comprehend a coherent narrative of successive events." That this ability is not a natural possession of children has already been shown (see page 8).

The first means toward developing it are the study-guide questions already referred to (pp. 43–44). The particular function of these questions is to help the child to appraise his own comprehension of the story read. However, until he learns how the teacher uses these questions in the discussion period, it is likely that he will have little understanding of how he may utilize them by himself in his history-reading period. His own intention to remember becomes a factor in his success [2] when he learns what is to be done with these questions.

As already pointed out, whether or not the study-guide questions can be utilized in developing the ability to follow the thread of the story depends upon the type of questions used. If there is a long list centering attention on unimportant details, they are worse than useless, for they direct attention away from the continuity of the story. If, however, they are well chosen and are few in number, each of them covers an important phase of the story and directs attention toward significant aspects.

A little child cannot be expected, at first, to follow an entire story in systematic fashion in his thinking, but he can begin by following the thought centering around one comprehensive question at a time.

Therefore the suggestion is given that the first exercise after the reading, with the objective of developing the ability to think in sequen-

---

[1] See E. B. Wesley's "Workbooks in the Social Studies," *Historical Outlook*, XXII: 151–153 (April, 1931).

[2] S. L. Pressey, *Psychology and the New Education*, pp. 415–416.

tial trains, should be the oral answering of the study-guide questions. The children of the upper group, at least, from the very beginning will be forced to answer in their own words, because they have read many different versions of the story. The influence which such social participation has upon retention is generally recognized by psychologists.[1]

One can almost feel the wave of horror that will sweep over many teachers when they read the suggestion given above. "Why, that is going back to the old question-and-answer recitation!" they will exclaim. It has been the theorist, however, or the administrator very far removed from children, who has made teachers feel that the answering of well-chosen questions is a crime. The purpose of such thinkers has indeed been laudable, — to break down the deadening monotony of recitations consisting invariably of nothing but detailed and unimportant questions and answers, and to attempt to substitute more active and penetrating thought exercises.

However, the theorists have commonly overlooked the fact that the ability to find and give a comprehensive answer to a comprehensive question constitutes a stage in learning. They take this ability for granted and wish to begin here and to build upon this ability. Any third-grade or fourth-grade teacher, however, knows, as stated above, that children have to be trained in this ability, just as they have to be trained in the interpretation of maps.

The fatal weaknesses of the old question-and-answer procedure were *that the questions were poorly chosen and petty, that children used the words of the book, that this procedure was continued in classes long after the corresponding learning stage had been passed,*[2] *and that no other procedures were used to call forth general activity and reasoning.*

Therefore again the suggestion is boldly put forth that the first exercise following the reading be the oral answering of the study-guide questions. Such oral expression itself is a means of clarifying one's ideas.

During the discussion period a unique opportunity occurs to discover misapprehensions and half-understandings which it is vital to clear up before attempting to proceed.[3] The wrong answers given by children should not be dismissed by merely turning the same question over to another child who gives the right answer. The wrong answer often furnishes the clue to blocks in thinking.[4]

---

[1] S. L. Pressey, *Psychology and the New Education*, pp. 413–415.

[2] That is, as soon as it becomes evident that the members of a group can and do habitually test their own reading satisfactorily by answering the study-guide questions to themselves, the oral answering of the questions in class may be dispensed with. This stage is not likely to be reached by many of the children during the middle-grade period.

[3] See J. M. McCallister's "Reading Difficulties in Studying Content-Subjects," *Elementary School Journal*, XXXI: 191–201 (November, 1930).

[4] Sometimes a blackboard sketch or illustration will help. See R. E. Fildes's "Blackboards and their Use," *Elementary School Journal*, XXXV: 760–767 (June, 1935).

Written responses can never be so illuminating as those given orally. In the lower-middle grades a child's mastery of written expression is so limited that his written forms cannot give so accurate a picture of his thinking as his own extended oral account of a comprehensive phase of the story gives. But teachers who have large classes feel all too great a temptation to ask the children to write the answers in a notebook and then consider that "the lesson has been learned."

Some of the difficulties which are unfolded during the discussion are as follows. Even the independent readers have little idea how to separate the important thread of the story from the supporting details, and to give only the main thread. With the teacher's help during the discussion period, however, they soon begin to learn.

Moreover, the children's standards of comprehension which they set for themselves in testing their own silent reading are very superficial, until the teacher's firmness in insisting on clarity and completeness of statement have altered such standards. At first children are complacent; they satisfy themselves too easily. Later, as a result of training, they become more exacting with themselves. They accept responsibility for testing their own learning.

A special problem is presented by the child who reads rapidly but inaccurately. He is likely to pride himself on his speed and to skim many books, turning restlessly from one to another. His bad habits should be revealed to him, and he should be kept at one book, if necessary, until he has achieved an adequate understanding. An opposite problem is the child who dawdles but who can do better. Possibly keeping track of his own test scores may spur him on.

The members of the lower group also are asked to answer the questions. Some of them, as a result of the teacher's direction of their reading, are able to do as well as some of the upper group. Others are aided by hearing the answers given by other children in language which they can understand. Oral repetition reinforces the ideas.

After the answers have been given satisfactorily, there is opportunity for children who have been particularly impressed by new viewpoints encountered in their extensive reading to give these materials to the class. They are encouraged to remember the name of the books in which they found the statements. If challenged, they should be able to locate the reference. In time they also begin to note differing and even conflicting points of view among the authors read.

Some teachers encourage children to record questions which occurred to them as they read, and for which they found no answers in the texts. These are later taken up for class discussion. Others present questions worded very differently from the questions in any of the books, in order to ascertain whether children have really been following the thought or whether they are bound to a certain wording or phraseology. Comparisons and contrasts are often pointed out, the reasons for actions stated, old principles applied to new settings, the geographical relationships made explicit, generalizations formulated, etc.

The discussion period applies a rigorous test of the teacher's knowledge of the subject matter and of the materials in the reading lists. It is not uncommon for children to report the most preposterous versions of what they have read, and for the teacher and the group to allow such statements to pass unchallenged because she and they do not know whether or not the statements are true. Nothing could do more to violate the very objectives sought.

The free-and-easy informality of this period, with its give and take of opinion, can do much to break any feeling of tension, to develop a genuinely social attitude on the part of the children toward one another and toward the teacher, and, in short, to socialize the entire procedure.[1]

The Special Vocabulary of History

The discussion period also offers an opportunity for the *teaching* (as opposed to the testing) of the special vocabulary of history terms.

That each subject has its own special vocabulary is a truism. Geometry speaks in terms of angles, corollaries, congruence, etc. Geography speaks of isotherms, latitude, longitude, regions, etc. Art speaks of tones, values, and composition.

That understanding involves comprehension of the terms used has been made clear by an abundance of investigations from Hall's initial study in 1890[2] to the elaborate investigation by the Commission on the Social Studies of the American Historical Association.[3]

It is equally obvious that comprehension is a matter of levels; one's comprehension of any term will probably deepen and broaden throughout his lifetime.[4] Not all the connotations and implications will come at once; growth is in the direction of adding one definite meaning to other definite meanings. Any such vague thinking as that expressed by the common "I-know-but-I-can't-express-it" attitude should be viewed with suspicion.

The teacher can perhaps best understand the child's situation, when he begins to read a new field of content, by remembering her own more or less recent experiences in beginning to study psychology. How con-

---

[1] See J. Wayne Wrightstone's "Analyzing and Measuring Democracy in the Class Room," *The Nation's Schools*, XI: 31–35 (May, 1933); J. Wayne Wrightstone's "Measuring Teacher Conduct of Class Discussion," *Elementary School Journal*, XXXIV: 455–460 (February, 1934).

[2] See Kelley and Krey's *Tests and Measurements in the Social Sciences*, pp. 227–228 (Part IV of the Report of the Commission, Charles Scribner's Sons, 1934).

[3] Ibid. pp. 1–53 and Appendix.

[4] G. C. Schweisinger's *Social-Ethical Significance of Vocabulary*. Teachers College Contributions to Education, No. 211. Bureau of Publications, Columbia University, 1926.

fused her thinking was, at first, by the discussion in terms of bonds, neural connections, mind-set, redintegrative substitution!

The special terms should be introduced gradually and with abundant illustrations and applications. But that a knowledge of them indicates a measure of understanding seems to have been established[1] statistically.

Special Vocabulary Lists

Obviously the teacher must have guidance in selecting the items which compose the special vocabularies. And about the selecting of such items many controversies have raged.

The most inclusive list, covering all the social sciences, appears as Appendix II to Kelley and Krey's *Tests and Measurements in the Social Sciences* (107 pages). This list is subject to two grave limitations from the point of view of the teacher of little children. Not only is it so long that it is unusable in its present form, but it has purposely excluded all items naming material or objective things. The purpose, of course, was to focus attention upon relationships; but that purpose assumes that children will, through some undescribed process, associate definite and accurate meanings with the names of all objects, whether they have ever seen them or ever will see them. Such an assumption is open to question; teachers of little children will reject it. Meaning may be read into such terms as the years go by, or it may not. The teacher of middle-grade children would prefer to focus attention directly upon any such doubtful terms, whether they denote relationships or whether they name objects. Experience of various kinds is needed, even to associate clear concepts with the names of objects.

Moreover, the results of the tests given on the list named above [2] must also be interpreted with a full understanding of the conditions under which the testing took place. The questions were distributed on the random sampling principle. *There was no assurance that children had ever had any opportunity to learn the meaning of the terms;* in fact, the courses of study in many places would make it quite clear that many of the children had never even been exposed to content which would make such understanding likely.

Therefore, from the results gathered no conclusions can be drawn as to whether children at a given age level *can understand* such terms. The measurement applies only to what exists under present conditions. *If the tests had been given only to children who had had intimate contact with content using the terms, and if the teaching had been according to the best-known practices,* then it would be fair to conclude that only one thing was being measured, that is, children's *understanding or ability to understand* (not their lack of opportunity to understand). The edu-

[1] See the *Historical Outlook*, XXIII : 7–21 (January, 1932).
[2] Kelley and Krey's *Tests and Measurements in the Social Sciences.*

cational field cannot advance very far so long as it measures what ought to be done by what is being done.

Other more specialized lists have drawn up vocabularies of the various subjects. One list has even attempted to draw up a special vocabulary of American history on the middle-grade level.[1] It is this list which forms the basis of the vocabulary studies in the units which follow (Parts Two and Three). Here again, however, it is clear that the terms chosen depend entirely on the content selected, and the content in turn depends on the objectives set up. To appraise the list, then, it is necessary to judge it in terms of the discussion of content (pp. 10–17) and the discussion of objectives (pp. 4–8).

Other controversies rage about the lists in separate subjects. One criticism [2] is that words in one subject list may be found in another subject list also, and specifically that most history words are contained in lists for economics, political science, and sociology. The second part of the criticism, of course, has no validity for the elementary-school teacher, whose children have been studying history, and therefore wrestling with the special vocabulary of history, for years before they begin any consideration of political science, economics, and sociology as such.

The first part of the criticism must be viewed with reference to the function of the vocabulary lists. If they are designed to serve merely as categories of terms, — "watertight compartments" whose logical structure would be marred by any interrelationships, — the criticism is valid. If, however, their function is to assist the teacher in ensuring that children *learn to understand* the terms, it is of no importance, for example, that the same word occurs in both geography and history lists. The history teacher ascertains whether or not children understand the meaning of *trade route*. If they have already learned the term in a geographic setting, nothing more need be done. Surely no harm has been wrought by finding out! Indeed, viewing the meaning from different angles must help that steady growth in comprehension so much to be desired.

Even such a differentiated list as the *Basic Vocabulary in American History for the Middle Grades*,[2] however, is still unusable by the teacher. To become functional, it must be broken up into small groups of words which are directly connected with a given unit of subject matter. The child can easily learn the meaning of four or five words a week on the average if he meets them in an appropriate context and if appropriate learning exercises are provided (see examples of such groups on pages 116, 119, 276, 480, 481, and following).

[1] See the *Journal of Educational Research*, XXIV: 335–349 (December, 1931).
[2] E. B. Wesley, "Some Criticisms of Word Lists with Particular Reference to History," *The Social Studies*, XXV: 79–82 (February, 1935).

Developing the Meaning of Terms

The initial task of making clear the meaning of such terms is largely conditioned by the textbook. In reading the text, understanding ought not to be complicated by unnecessary vocabulary difficulties introduced through the author's attempt to achieve style. On the other hand, terms which are basic to thinking in history should be included systematically and consistently, a few at a time. Some of them the textbook itself, if well made according to modern standards, will explain before it introduces the term.[1] In such cases the psychological order of development is to explain clearly the setting or combination of circumstances out of which the need rises, thus developing the *concept* first. Then, when the idea has been made clear, the name is presented.

Obviously, however, an entire vocabulary list cannot be introduced in this manner or the text would become intolerably cumbersome. The teacher also must aid. She soon finds that the words may be brought into four categories for convenience in treatment:

1. Those whose meaning can be grasped from the context (for example, *mutiny*).
2. Those for which a few additional words of explanation are needed (for example, *admiral*. The text may make it clear that the admiral is a naval officer but may indicate nothing as to his comparative rank).
3. Those whose significance falls so far outside children's direct observation that they can best be grasped by a dramatic representation (for example, *secession*).
4. Those for an understanding of which direct experiences must be *supplied* (for example, *representation*). This task does not loom so large when it is remembered that only a few new words are introduced each week.[2]

The period of discussion is the time when the teacher may well direct attention toward these new terms.[3] The children have already finished their reading and thus have had the opportunity to get the meaning directly from the context if possible. But if hazy or incorrect ideas have been associated with the terms, now is the time to ascertain the fact.

It cannot be emphasized too strongly that a dictionary definition is not desired. For the child to give the meaning in his own words is infinitely preferable.

Many teachers are strongly opposed to anything that savors of repetition in any form. They assume that if a child has once been cor-

---

[1] For example, see the following study showing that children prefer reading materials which contain explanations: A. D. Mandeville, *Children's Interests in Two Types of Reading Material Used in Geography* (unpublished master's thesis, The University of Chicago, 1930).

[2] An excellent discussion of "hierarchies of symbolism" is given in H. L. Hollingworth's *Educational Psychology*, pp. 209–210.

[3] Except those for which the supplying of a direct experience is needed. Such terms should be introduced with the accompanying experiences during the period of conversational approach.

rected on the meaning of a word, or has once been told the meaning, he will remember the right idea rather than the wrong one. They forget how many times they themselves have looked up words in the dictionary and within a week have forgotten what they found out!

To assist in the correct association of ideas, association cards [1] may be made by the teacher with the children's assistance or by the children themselves. These cards bear on one side the term, and on the other side not a synonym but a phrase or clause statement of the meaning of the term which fits the present level of the child's development. The cards are made accessible to the children during their period of reading and study, so that they may concentrate on their own difficulties.

When the testing period comes,[2] the test on the item should not be couched in the same phraseology as the drill card. What is desired is to appraise understanding, not word memory.

Multisensory Aids: the Visual and Auditory Appeals

When young children begin to read history, one of the great tasks confronting them is the correct visualizing of the scenes presented through the words of the book. It is probably as difficult for them to *dissociate* the environment by which they have always been surrounded from the historical scenes described as it is to construct the proper new images.

To assist in the forming of clear-cut, definite imagery, illustrative materials are indispensable, — pictures, charts, graphs, drawings, maps. Investigations [3] have shown that pictures are "an invaluable means of getting certain kinds of experience of a concrete sort," — still pictures if a situation is to be analyzed, and motion pictures if development or motion is to be shown. They point out also the superiority of classroom over auditorium use. That pictures help little in developing the ability to give explanations or generalizations [4] does not detract from their usefulness in their own sphere.

From such investigations the teacher learns what may legitimately be expected from the use of illustrative materials, and what their limi-

---

[1] See examples on pages 118, 280, 484. The Thorndike-Century Junior Dictionary, Winston's Simplified Dictionary, and the Merriam-Webster Dictionary for Boys and Girls will be of great assistance in making the cards.   [2] See pages 101–102.

[3] F. N. Freeman, *Visual Education*, p. 70 (The University of Chicago Press, 1924); Thirteenth Yearbook of Department of Elementary School Principals of the National Education Association, chap. vii (1934); Varney C. Arnspiger, *Measuring the Effectiveness of Sound Pictures as Teaching Aids* (Teachers College Contributions to Education, No. 565, Columbia University, 1933); W. W. Charters, *Motion Pictures and Youth: a Summary* (The Macmillan Company, 1935); Frances Consitt, *Value of Films in History Teaching* (G. Bell and Sons, London, 1931).

[4] Ben D. Wood and F. N. Freeman, *Motion Pictures in the Classroom.* Houghton Mifflin Company, 1929.

tations are. Knowlton and Tilton's experiments [1] should be read by any overenthusiastic worker who believes that the use of the motion picture will solve all the problems of learning in the field of social science.

Although recognizing the limitations, the progressive teacher nevertheless leans heavily upon illustrative materials as one of her invaluable aids.[2] Many matters about which she needs guidance must wait for further investigation, — for example, the question of *when* the pictures should be used, that is, at what stage of the learning process. Although evidence is lacking, one might conclude that if the new unit is completely divorced from the experience of children (for example, in beginning the story of prehistoric life on as low a level as fourth grade), the pictures might well be shown before the reading. If, however, the subject be not too remote, a good practice may be to afford opportunity for the children to form the habit of visualizing for themselves the scenes about which they read, and soon afterwards to correct wrong ideas or to supply deficiencies by presenting pictures for study.

Probably the most common error in the use of pictures is the practice of putting before children a large number of illustrations of varying degrees of excellence and taking it for granted that the children will scrutinize them in an analytical manner and see in each one all the values which it was intended to give. Thoughtful and experienced teachers, however, know that no assumption could be farther from the truth. The children, in such cases, usually run through the pictures aimlessly and idly and do not see what is there.[3]

They need to be *taught* what to look for in a picture, just as they need to be taught to read. At first the teacher will question, direct, and suggest what to look for, much as she would in a silent-reading period. And, as in reading, as soon as the children have developed the ability and formed the habit of looking at pictures analytically, the directing of the process by the teacher may be discontinued.

The practice of using lanterns and slides [4] and stereopticons has doubtless contributed much toward a more active attitude on the part of both teacher and pupils. The admirable use of children's own graphs, drawings, summaries, and outlines in slide form cannot be too highly

---

[1] Daniel C. Knowlton and J. Warren Tilton, *Motion Pictures in History Teaching* (Yale University Press, 1929) ; Knowlton and Tilton, "Auditorium versus Classroom Showing of Motion Pictures in History Teaching," *Journal of Educational Psychology*, XXIII : 663–670 (December, 1932).

[2] Henry Johnson's discussion on "Making the Past Real," chapters viii to x in his *Teaching of History*, though written many years ago, still remains one of the best expositions of the subject (The Macmillan Company).

[3] Gladys Hoppes, *Ability of Pupils to Read Pictures for Geographical Purposes*. Unpublished master's thesis, The University of Chicago, 1930.

[4] See H. E. Brown and Joy Bird's *Motion Pictures and Lantern Slides for Elementary Visual Education* (Bureau of Publications, Teachers College, Columbia University, 1931).

commended.[1] John Dewey [2] pointed out long ago that children see more vividly if they are later to do something with the ideas gained, which suggests that the pictures be immediately associated with the general activities.

Administrators, supervisors, and teachers, however, have little cause to feel that the visual-education movement is making satisfactory progress. Investigations have shown pointedly that, though the values of illustrative material are everywhere given lip service, equipment in the majority of schools is woefully inadequate.[3] In fact, in many schools throughout the country it is absolutely nonexistent (aside from a few totally inadequate maps).

Under such conditions teachers have attempted to remedy the situation by making their own collections of pictures, largely from advertising matter. While the motive is laudable and the collecting shows admirable initiative, the pictures thus collected are often fearful and wonderful to behold. An Indian maiden immaculately groomed, with a feather in her hair, kneels daintly before a stream in such a landscape as never was on earth or in the sky. Whether many of such pictures do not do more damage than good in helping to visualize accurately is an open question. On the other hand, some of the pictures in advertising materials are of a high standard of excellence.[4]

About the only resources left for many teachers are the pictures in the classroom textbooks. Even these may be so hastily thrown together, so trivial, so downright inaccurate, that they may only attract the attention for a moment by the fact that they are colored, but serve little purpose in reinforcing the printed descriptions.

Assuming that the pictures are serviceable, however, the teacher misses a great opportunity if she neglects to draw from them all the lessons that they are capable of teaching. As stated above, she cannot rest assured that the children will see these values for themselves. A free, informal conversational period may be held, during which the children point out the significant features which they can discover, and the teacher questions them as to phases which they do not notice, — costumes, characteristics of building, modes of travel, decorations, indica-

[1] Annette Glick, "The Use of Visual Aids in Teaching the Social Studies Past and Present," Fifth Yearbook of the National Council for the Social Studies, pp. 123–142 (1935); Annette Glick, "Making History Real: A Guide to Material for Vitalizing and Visualizing History," Historical Outlook, XVII: 382–385; XVIII: 29–37, 64–82 (December, 1926, to February, 1927); Thirteenth Yearbook of Department of Elementary School Principals of the National Education Association, chap. vi (1934).

[2] How We Think, p. 38 (D. C. Heath and Company, 1910).

[3] J. W. Baldwin, "Use of Equipment in Teaching the Social Studies — Past and Present," Fifth Yearbook of the National Council for the Social Studies, pp. 106–122 (1935).

[4] See A List of Free and Low Cost Educational Materials for Elementary Grades (Peabody College for Teachers, Nashville, Tennessee, 1933); Rowena Hansen's Help for Teachers, United States Office of Education, Washington, D.C.).

tions of peculiar customs, etc.[1] All these factors are needed for activities which are being carried on.

Picture materials are suggested for every subunit in Parts Two, Three, and Four of the organization of history which follows (see pages 117, 278, 507–508 for examples).

Interpretation of maps is another ability [2] which needs specific training and development. The map equipment of many schools is pitifully inadequate, and the teacher finds those in the textbook her only resource. She often does not recognize the fact that children see in a map even less than they see in a picture. And how seldom does she give specific exercises to assist them in discovering how to tell land bodies from water bodies, how to trace routes marked differently, how to use the keys and the scale of miles, and how to determine in what direction specific routes are going.

All these matters take time, and the teacher often feels under such pressure to "cover the ground" that she neglects to lay a solid foundation in skills upon which understanding partly depends. The attempt to make haste results in vagueness and haziness; a few of the brightest children teach themselves, and the rest remain untaught.

Upon first beginning map work, experience suggests the value of using sand-table models; in such models the difference between land and water bodies is clearly distinguishable even to beginning fourth-graders. After the relationships have been clearly presented on the sand table, it is relatively easy to see the same things on a flat map.

History wall maps for middle-grade children should be as simple as possible. The more crowded with names and data, the more difficult they are to follow. And yet the value of wall maps, supplementing the small maps in the texts, is evident for the localizing of events.

Outline maps also are of considerable utility, especially in the testing of place relationships [3] which have supposedly been learned during the period of reading and study. Such maps are easier for younger children to use if they show water bodies in color or land bodies by shading.

Picture maps also have a contribution to offer, especially in the awakening of interest. Their deficiencies as to true space representations can easily be offset by supplementing with the use of other types of maps, such as political maps, physical maps, etc.

---

[1] An excellent list of illustrations classified by countries and covering all periods of history is offered in Historical Leaflet No. 82, *A List of Illustrations for Use in History Teaching in Schools*, issued by the Illustrations Committee of the English Historical Association, Russell Square, London, W.C.I.

[2] Mary T. Thorp, "Studies of the Ability of Pupils in Grades Four to Eight to Use Geographic Tools," Thirty-second Yearbook of the National Society for the Study of Education, pp. 494–506 (1933); George F. Howe, "A Study of the Ability of Elementary School Pupils to Read Maps," ibid. 486–492.

[3] For examples see pages 138, 294, 527.

The use of maps of different scales and sizes and types helps to prevent children's associating a given place with a given map to such an extent that they are unable to find it if a different map is used. Locating in the text map, and then on a wall map, political or physical, is an excellent exercise.

A globe is a necessary piece of equipment, especially for use during the period of exploration and discovery, when the true forms of the continents were being unfolded. Whenever it *is* needed, no kind of map can take its place.

In addition to pictures and maps, graphs [1] are of value in presenting certain relationships of size or value or in abstracting other aspects for separate consideration. They help particularly in quantitative phases of comparisons. Investigations [2] indicate that circular graphs are easier to follow than line graphs, though practice seems to use the bar graph more frequently. Superior fourth-grade children and average children above that age level can read simple types of graphs.

Cartoons, however interesting and significant to upper-grade children, have little meaning for pupils in the middle grades, probably because the pupils' powers of abstraction are incompletely developed.[3]

The radio doubtless possesses potentialities as yet unutilized. As an instrument of adult education it seems to be coming into its own, as well as in such significant aspects of school education as music appreciation. For social science on the middle-grade level, however, in spite of children's undoubted interest in radio's dramatic presentations, it must be regarded at present as a more or less incidental or accidental supplement rather than as a permanent educational instrument [4] whose use can be planned in advance.

School systems which desire to utilize the great possibilities of multi-sensory aids [5] must necessarily provide equipment and space for stor-

[1] Harper and Otto, "An Evaluation of Graphic Instruction Materials," Thirteenth Yearbook of the Department of Elementary School Principals of the National Education Association, pp. 228–237 (1934); Kathryn C. Thomas, "Ability of Children to Interpret Graphs," Thirty-second Yearbook of the National Society for the Study of Education, pp. 492–494 (1933).

[2] C. O. Mathews, *Grade Placement of Curriculum Materials in the Social Studies.* Bureau of Publications, Teachers College, Columbia University, 1926.

[3] L. F. Shaffer, *Children's Interpretation of Cartoons.* Teachers College Contributions to Education, Bureau of Publications, Columbia University, 1930.

[4] See Yearbooks of the Institute for Education by Radio (Ohio State University, 1931); Thirteenth Yearbook of the Department of Elementary School Principals of the National Education Association, chap. ix (1934); Florence C. Fox's "Children's Preferences in Radio Programs" (Circular No. 17, United States Office of Education, 1930); Sidonie Gruenberg's *Radio and Children* (Radio Institute of the Audible Arts, New York, 1935); Cline M. Koon's "The Technique of Teaching with Radio," *Elementary School Journal,* XXXIV: 106–110 (October, 1933).

[5] For a summary of research as to the effectiveness of different kinds of aids, see Thirteenth Yearbook of the Department of Elementary School Principals of the National Education Association, chap. x (1934); for general suggestions see "Materials of Instruction," Eighth Yearbook of the Department of Supervisors and Directors of Instruction of the National Education Association (1935).

age : filing cabinets, lanterns, slides, motion-picture machines and reels, together with shelf and closet space. Studies of equipment give suggestions for minimum standards (see "Equipment," pp. 113–114).

On the other hand, there is a constant complaint from principals and supervisors that teachers do not use even the small amount of equipment which is available, and that expensive maps, lanterns, slides, stereopticons, etc. remain untouched in the storerooms. To remedy such a situation requires a definite program of planning and classification of resources, in which teachers, principals, and supervisors may co-operate.[1]

The assistance of the music teacher should be enlisted in the attempt to provide multisensory aids. The music of a given period or a given people is a reflection of the genius or soul of the people, and the sympathetic listener can often gain from it an appreciation of the culture under consideration. Suggestions for the inclusion of music in the program are given at intervals in the lessons composing Parts Two, Three, and Four of the organization of history which follows.

General Activities[2]: Creative Education

Thanks to the lessons impressed upon the field of education by the project method and later by the movement for activities, it is no longer necessary to argue with teachers that the development of the whole child cannot be achieved through reading and discussion alone. While those are vital and indispensable parts of the educative process, they should be supplemented by physical activity as a needed means of reaction and for achieving integration of personality. It cannot be too often reiterated, however, that the whole emotional atmosphere in which school life is lived is more important in the integration of personality than the use of any particular kind of activities.[3]

In the early years of the project movement many teachers went to extremes. They considered physical manipulation the only type of exercise needed, and they confused aimless or trivial movements with purposeful activity. Therefore the thinking involved was often crude in the extreme. The problem method helped to restore the balance and to recognize mental activity as one of the highest and most needed forms.

[1] See Ella Gross's "Making Aids Available Within the School," Thirteenth Yearbook of the Department of Elementary School Principals of the National Education Association, pp. 171–174 (1934) ; H. J. Van Westrunen's "Administration and Management of Materials," Eighth Yearbook of Department of Supervisors and Directors of Instruction of the National Education Association, pp. 118–128 (1935).

[2] W. H. Kilpatrick, "The Essentials of the Activity Movement," Progressive Education, XI : 346–359 (October, 1934) ; Gustin and Hayes, Activities in the Public Schools (University of North Carolina Press, 1934).

[3] See "The Social Studies Laboratory for Grades Four, Five, and Six in the Co-operative Group Plan," Educational Method, X : 34–44 (October, 1930).

Today there is no disagreement between the proponents of the activity program and the proponents of subject-unit programs as to the *use* of activities, either in number or in kind. They both utilize equally all types. The point on which they do not agree is the core of organization, as summarized above (pp. 24–25).

Creative Activities

The movement toward creative education helped to broaden the whole program of activities, both in subject units and in the program of integration. It emphasized strongly the purposes back of physical and mental manipulation. In particular it aimed to discover special interests and talents and to furnish a congenial setting in which they might grow. The movement was strengthened by Terman's findings, "The direction of later achievement is likely to be foreshadowed by early preoccupation of interest," and by Thorndike's discovery that there is considerable continuity in the main fields of interest from childhood to maturity. It is to the advantage, then, both of the individual and of society, that such choices and talents be discovered early.

During the first years of the creative-education movement a serious mistake was made. It was assumed that the mental content which expressed itself through various forms of the creative act exists naturally in children's minds. Children were invited to "create" when they had no particular desire and no materials upon which to draw. For example, a child who knows only that Magellan circumnavigated the globe feels no urge to celebrate the feat in a poem. A child who knows only that Walter Raleigh was executed by an ungrateful government feels no poignancy in the situation, which makes him wish to dramatize Raleigh's powerful story. The mistake was the old mistake of trying to make bricks without straw. Creative expression was introduced too early in the learning process.

In the plan presented hereinafter in this book, activities of the creative type are not attempted until the children's interest has been aroused (conversational approach) and until they have read widely (reading and study), have talked over the implications of the story (discussion), have seen the pictures and maps, and have listened to the music of the period (multisensory aids). Having undergone these various forms of experience, they are at last in possession of a stock of ideas, they are permeated with the spirit of the achievement, and they are ready to express their feelings on the subject.[1] Creative imagination is ripe to function.

If a school system is organized on the activity plan, the general and creative activities can be developed at whatever time the children are

---

[1] Helpful suggestions may be found in the Fifth Yearbook of the Department of Classroom Teachers of the National Education Association, chaps. ii and v (1930).

ready for them. In schools organized on the subject-unit plan there should be early in the year a meeting of the grade or home-room teachers together with the principal and the supervisors of art, music, physical education, manual training, and home economics, and with the special teachers and supervisors (if any) of history, geography, and language. The curriculum can then be worked out as a joint product; each discipline has an invaluable contribution to make from its own point of view, and the work of all is enriched by tying them together. Especially is the work in the social sciences connected constantly with art and language. Only by such means can all the points of view be fully vitalized.[1]

Another factor of great importance, especially in the case of children markedly gifted in some direction, is the voluntary project, which may be engaged in alone or by groups.[2] For such projects the teacher at first furnishes suggestions; she also makes available the needed materials. The child alone or the group then carries on the chosen activity at home, or before or after school, or in free time. The teacher gives help if asked to do so. The fact that there is no assigned home work in the plan under consideration makes it possible for children to have time to devote to their special interests. In fact, the only "home work" consists of recreational reading and voluntary projects, except in the case of children who themselves choose to perfect various exercises at home or to make up deficiencies.

Recognition of the result is a factor of considerable weight in children's desire to spend time and energy on voluntary projects. In many cases the result can be utilized in a projected pageant, a dramatization, the museum, or a demonstration in the classroom. The children may vote to select the best of such contributions for inclusion in the school museum.

It is of great importance that both individual and group projects be included among the creative activities. Some children do excellent work by themselves but cannot fit in happily with teammates. Others are valued members of groups but lean too heavily on leaders for inspiration and initiative. Both types need the well-rounded experiences of working sometimes as co-operating members and sometimes as individuals. Unless the teacher feels keenly the importance of this matter, they are likely to follow naturally their own line of choice and to engage exclusively in one field. They need to experiment with both.[3]

Another puzzling question is whether or not certain children should be discouraged from following exclusively a single line of interest. For

[1] A good summary of principles is given in chapter xi of Bagley and MacDonald's *Standard Practices in Teaching* (The Macmillan Company, 1932), and in J. Cayce Morrison's "Trends in Educational Method," *Educational Method*, XIII: 129–137 (December, 1933).

[2] See J. Edgar Dransfield's *Administration of Enrichment to Superior Children in the Typical Classroom* (Teachers College Contributions to Education, No. 558. Columbia University, 1933).

[3] See F. N. Freeman, "An Analysis of the Basis of the Activity Curriculum," *Elementary School Journal*, XXXV: 655–661 (May, 1935).

example, should the child who always wants to construct be encouraged sometimes to do imaginative writing? Or should the child who always wishes to dramatize sometimes be encouraged to design a stage set instead? No general rule can be laid down. Doubtless in the great majority of cases diversification is desirable. And yet the teacher must hesitate to interfere with the development of the budding poet or musician. In this problem, as in so many others, the solution is a completely individual matter.

Again, the project method has quite changed the point of view of the average teacher with regard to standards of attainment and appraisal. The older point of view was that the product should reach a high degree of technical excellence; and to achieve it, especially for exhibition purposes, the teacher often felt the temptation of putting on the finishing touches herself. The modern point of view is that the children, or the group, are the arbiters; they set up their own standards in terms of the purpose for which each product is intended, and a child's own pleasure and satisfaction in his work are criteria of predominating importance.

Another great value is secured in that when children begin to create they usually find that although they have read many details in their stories and have looked at a great many pictures, their concepts and imagery are still vague. They therefore go back to their sources to collect additional materials or to remedy deficiencies. Thus drawing, construction, and dramatization reinforce reading and observation, with the best possible "drive" — the child's own feeling of his inadequacy.

In the beginning the teacher will probably be obliged to supply long lists of suggestions in regard to possible activities.[1] As children try out these media and become familiar with the range of possible forms of expression, they develop in originality and initiative. They begin to see possibilities on their own account and to make choices out of the many ideas which come to them unaided.

Following is a tabulation of the variety of forms of expression used in the units composing Parts Two, Three, and Four of this book. It is not possible or desirable for any one class to complete them all. Nor is it necessary or desirable for every individual in a group to participate in every form that is selected. Some members may well work on one activity, and others on other activities, presenting their products before the group. But taken as a whole the suggestions which are given provide reaction members of the learning cycle, they allow for bodily expression as well as mental activity, they provide for group as well as individual planning, they discover and foster special abilities, and they help to provide a harmonious emotional atmosphere, thus making happy and normal development possible and furnishing powerful motivation.

[1] An inclusive list is found in H. E. Wilson's "Things to Do in the Social Science Classroom," *The Historical Outlook*, XX: 218 (1929).

A TABULATION OF THE ACTIVITIES USED IN PART TWO

Activity	Found on Pages
Drawing and painting	
Imaginative pictures	124, 154, 219
Diagrams and plans	184, 190, 194, 201, 227, 259
Drawing from copies	135, 150, 159, 170, 248, 253, 259
Posters	180
Designing	117, 150
Mottoes	234
Picture maps	187
Map-drawing	124, 126, 127, 135, 151, 154, 159, 170, 180, 191, 194, 198, 205, 214, 219, 223, 231, 235, 238, 250, 253, 257, 262
Time charts	117, 137, 144, 147, 151, 154, 159, 163, 170, 187, 191, 194, 198, 205, 219, 223, 238, 250, 253, 262, 265, 268
Construction	
Sand-table modeling	117, 119, 120, 127, 166–167, 187, 190, 212, 216, 221, 222, 224, 226, 236, 238, 250, 253, 256, 262
Historical models	120, 124, 184, 214
Scenes	117, 129
Stage settings	159
Clay-modeling	129, 227
Soap-carving	222, 250
Making motion pictures	246, 250, 253, 257, 259, 262, 265, 268
Making graphs	129, 133, 144, 187, 205, 226, 227, 259
Estimating costs, distances	197, 205, 227
Dramatization	
Reading dramatizations	135, 143, 147, 163, 170, 180, 184, 187, 190, 194, 197, 201, 205, 219, 222, 231, 235, 238, 246, 250, 253, 256, 259, 265, 268
Informal dramatizations	120, 129, 150, 163, 170, 180, 205, 219, 238, 268
Formal dramatizations	176
Pageant	274
Trips, interviews, and investigations	120, 124, 132, 150, 167, 201, 205, 214, 219, 231, 234, 253, 259
Demonstrations	124, 131, 132, 154, 201, 246, 250, 259, 262, 265, 268
Collecting : uses of	132, 144, 147, 150, 151, 170, 180, 191, 214, 259
Sewing	163, 184, 201, 205, 222, 234
Use of advertising	148, 150
Planning activities	154, 176, 194, 197, 234, 265
Writing	
Letters	129, 132, 135, 205, 231, 246
Lists	135, 144, 155, 180, 184, 188, 191, 219, 232, 244
Diaries	147, 167
Poems	147, 201, 219
Documents	117, 194, 231, 238, 265
Newspaper articles	234
Composing music	167, 201
Singing and listening to music	117, 120, 129, 143, 150, 154, 184, 194, 197, 200, 205, 214, 222, 226, 246, 249
Oral reports	
Imaginative speeches	120, 124, 136, 159, 163, 190, 222, 246, 253, 257, 268
On children's experiences	115, 118, 120, 122, 126, 131, 132, 136, 151, 160, 163, 167, 170, 180, 184, 188, 190, 191, 194, 195, 197, 198, 201, 205, 214, 219, 223, 227, 229, 231, 232, 235, 244, 246, 250, 262, 265, 268
On readings	117, 120, 126, 129, 132, 133, 144, 147, 148, 154, 163, 167, 170, 180, 184, 187, 188, 191, 194, 198, 201, 205, 214, 219, 222, 223, 227, 231, 235, 238, 246, 250, 253, 254, 259, 260, 262, 265, 268
On pictures	151, 191, 214
Reciting poetry	144, 194
Teacher reading to children	124, 129, 151, 194, 205, 214, 222, 231, 234, 238, 250, 259, 262, 265
Of travelers	117, 147, 151, 227, 238, 259, 262
Making tabulations	156, 164, 168, 171, 189, 192, 207

A TABULATION OF THE ACTIVITIES USED IN PART THREE

Activity	Found on Pages
Drawing and painting	
Imaginative pictures	283, 306, 315, 348, 371, 392, 402, 444, 456
Diagrams and plans	339, 352, 366, 431, 464
Posters	292, 306, 334, 421
Designing	301, 339, 361, 401, 444
Mottoes	292
Picture maps	292, 460
Map-drawing	283, 292, 301, 306, 315, 320, 325, 360, 371, 444, 456
Time charts	278, 283, 292, 300, 311, 315, 320, 339, 361, 366, 371, 380, 402, 412, 441, 444, 448, 453, 458, 460, 465
Construction	[453, 456, 460
Sand-table modeling	283, 298, 299, 320, 325, 375, 379, 380, 402, 431, 441, 444,
Historical models	300, 306, 311, 320, 375, 392
Scenes	315
Stage settings	278
Clay-modeling	283
Soap-carving	301, 401
Making motion pictures	325
Making graphs	278, 306, 311, 315, 339, 343, 344, 360, 361, 392, 416, 426, 453, 464
Estimating : costs, distance, etc.	278, 279, 283, 307, 315, 348, 352, 393, 394, 431, 450
Newspaper clippings	278, 411
Dramatization	
Reading dramatizations	292, 301, 306, 320, 325, 339, 348, 361, 366, 371, 375, 380, 389, 397, 453
Informal dramatizations	283, 292, 320, 351, 366, 371, 388, 397, 464
Formal dramatizations	439, 441
Pageants, programs	439, 469, 477
Puppet shows	278
Trips, interviews, and investi-gations	283, 311, 315, 325, 335, 339, 343, 347, 351, 352, 371, 402, 411, 412, 416, 421, 426, 431, 448, 460
Demonstrations	279, 306, 311, 332, 334, 335, 339, 343, 344, 348, 352, 388, 402, 411, 414, 416, 421, 426, 431, 460
Collecting : uses of	278, 283, 287, 306, 311, 315, 320, 339, 343, 348, 361, 371, 375, 392, 396, 397, 421, 431, 456, 464
Sewing	278
Use of advertising	396, 416, 448
Writing	
Letters	287, 301, 361, 448
Lists	320, 335, 344, 361, 388, 421, 426, 431, 446
Diaries	278, 392, 469
Poems	315, 348
Documents	380, 392
Newspaper articles	361, 371, 444, 456
Composing music	315
Singing and listening to music	278, 292, 301, 306, 315, 320, 324, 334, 347, 351, 360, 370, 375, 392, 396, 401, 411, 425, 444, 448, 452, 460, 464
Dancing	371
Oral reports	
Imaginative speeches	292, 371, 426
On children's experiences	275, 276, 278, 279, 288, 292, 293, 301, 303, 306, 307, 309, 311, 316, 332, 333, 335, 339, 343, 344, 345, 348, 352, 361, 366, 371, 376, 389, 392, 393, 397, 401, 402, 412, 416, 417, 420, 421, 423, 426, 429, 431, 432, 439, 455, 469
On readings	278, 279, 283, 287, 288, 292, 293, 301, 302, 306, 307, 311, 316, 320, 325, 326, 335, 339, 343, 347, 348, 352, 360, 361, 366, 371, 372, 376, 380, 388, 389, 392, 393, 397, 401, 402, 403, 411, 412, 416, 417, 421, 426, 431, 432, 441, 444, 445, 448, 449, 453, 454, 456, 458, 460, 462, 464, 465
On pictures	279, 287, 325, 339, 360, 371, 392, 416, 421, 431, 441
Radio broadcasts	306
Teacher reading to children	283, 292, 301, 306, 311, 315, 320, 325, 335, 343, 361, 375, 380, 388, 389, 392, 397, 401, 411, 426, 431, 444, 453, 456, 465, 469
Of travelers, etc.	278, 283, 287, 301, 311, 315, 320, 325, 348, 375, 380, 389, 392, 397, 402, 411, 416, 426, 431, 444, 448, 453, 460, 464
Actual performance	278, 315, 332, 336, 343, 347, 348, 361, 371, 392, 421
Making tabulations	278, 366

A TABULATION OF ACTIVITIES USED IN PART FOUR

Activity	Found on Pages
Drawing and painting	
Imaginative pictures	488, 498, 509, 524, 532, 569, 591, 597, 620, 645
Diagrams, plans, tables	488, 547, 564, 575, 581, 592, 629, 637, 641
Drawing from copies	482, 508, 515, 569, 607, 611, 615, 645
Designing	493, 514, 515, 520, 537, 542, 591, 597, 602, 603, 615, 620, 633, 641, 645
Mottoes	569, 597
Picture maps	591
Map-drawing	488, 508, 515, 520, 524, 536, 542, 551, 559, 569, 575, 581, 591, 603, 607
Time charts	482, 483, 488, 493, 498, 508, 515, 520, 524, 542, 551, 564, 569, 591, 597, 602, 607, 620
Construction	
Sand-table modeling	482, 508, 514, 519, 524, 530, 532, 537, 542, 547, 551, 559, 602
Historical models	508, 509, 515, 520, 524, 547, 552, 564, 575, 597, 602, 611, 633
Scenes	514, 515, 519, 520, 524, 527, 591, 607, 615, 637
Stage settings	645
Clay-modeling	483, 514, 537, 575, 645
Soap-carving	508, 509, 514, 542, 547, 559, 616
Making motion pictures	483, 493
Making graphs	488, 497, 520, 591
Estimating costs, distance	598, 634
Dramatization	
Reading dramatizations	532, 533, 611, 633
Informal dramatizations	483, 508, 515, 520, 532, 533, 537, 542, 551, 559, 569, 575, 581, 592, 607, 611, 620, 629, 638, 645
Formal dramatizations	633, 637, 641, 645, 650
Pageant	560, 564, 569, 575, 581
Trips, investigations, interviews	482, 483, 488, 492, 493, 497, 498, 508, 514, 515, 547, 569, 576, 597, 620, 633, 641, 645
Demonstrations and experiments	483, 488, 491, 492, 493, 498, 508, 509, 515, 520, 547, 564, 575, 607, 611, 615, 634, 650
Collections : uses of	483, 488, 508, 524, 532, 537, 564, 575, 576, 602, 616, 620, 633, 638, 641, 645
Sewing	520, 532, 564, 591, 597, 602, 616, 633
Planning activities	607, 620, 634, 637, 645, 650
Dancing and games	488, 537, 547
Writing	
Letters	602, 645
Lists	483, 488, 493, 509, 511, 537, 543, 547, 564, 569, 575, 581, 599, 602, 613, 629, 631, 634, 643, 646
Diaries	537
Poems	508, 525, 542, 591
Documents	525, 611, 620, 629, 645
Composing music	542, 591
Listening to music and singing	482, 492, 497, 508, 514, 524, 530, 541, 546, 551, 559, 569, 575, 580, 591, 597, 602, 607, 615, 633, 641, 645, 650
Oral Reports	
Imaginative speeches	542, 551, 564
On children's experiences	479, 483, 484, 485, 488, 489, 493, 496, 498, 499, 509, 510, 514, 515, 520, 525, 537, 538, 547, 552, 560, 564, 565, 576, 579, 581, 592, 598, 603, 607, 611, 612, 616, 620, 629, 634, 638, 641, 642, 645, 646
On readings	483, 488, 489, 493, 498, 509, 510, 515, 520, 524, 525, 532, 533, 537, 538, 542, 547, 548, 549, 551, 552, 559, 560, 564, 565, 569, 575, 576, 577, 581, 592, 597, 598, 603, 607, 611, 612, 616, 620, 621, 629, 633, 634, 637, 638, 641, 645, 646, 650
Teacher reading to children	482, 483, 488, 497, 498, 509, 515, 520, 525, 533, 542, 547, 551, 559, 564, 575, 581, 591, 597, 603, 616, 620, 633, 634, 641
Of travelers	508, 524, 547, 575, 581, 645
Making tabulations	651

To attempt any detailed discussion of the activities listed above would require several volumes. Teachers who desire help or suggestions will find the following references of assistance.

On Drawing and Painting

ALICE C. RODEWALD. *A Fifth-Grade Experiment in the Social Studies*. Ethical Culture Branch School, New York City.

E. H. REEDER. "Lessons in Our Schools, No. IV: A Lesson in History," *Teachers College Record*, XXXI: 115–120 (November, 1929).

On Construction, Clay-Modeling, Soap-Carving

A. ADELE RUDOLPH. "Elementary Industrial Arts and Leisure-Time Interests," *Educational Method*, XIV: 318–323 (March, 1935).

On Making Maps

E. W. CRAWFORD. "Pupil-Made Maps," Thirteenth Yearbook of the Department of Elementary School Principals, pp. 219–227. National Education Association, 1934.

On Making Graphs

KATHRYN C. THOMAS. "Ability of Children to Interpret Graphs," Thirty-second Yearbook of the National Society for the Study of Education, pp. 492–494 (1933).

MARGUERITE SCHWARZMAN. "The Neurath Pictorial Statistics." *Progressive Education*, XI: 211–213 (1934).

On Dramatization

HELEN CAMPBELL. "Informality in Dramatization," *Educational Method*, XIII: 35–41 (October, 1933).

ELEANOR HUBBARD. *The Teaching of History through Dramatic Presentation*. Benjamin H. Sanborn & Company. 1935.

On Pageantry

V. E. STONE. "A Pageant Produced by Small Players," *The Historical Outlook*, XXI: 27–29 (January, 1930).

On Trips, Investigations, Interviews

MARY HARDEN. "Going Places and Seeing Things," *Educational Method*, XIV: 324–331 (March, 1935).

RUPERT PETERS. "Free Services Offered Children by Museums and Art Galleries," *Elementary School Journal*, XXXV: 32–41, 123–130 (September, October, 1934).

HAROLD S. SLOAN. "Seeing Social Problems First Hand," *The Social Studies*, XXVII: 22–27 (January, 1936).

MARION E. MILLER. "The Museum and the Schools," *Progressive Education*, VII: 287–394 (December, 1930).

Thirteenth Yearbook of the Department of Elementary School Principals of the National Education Association, chap. v (1934).

On Collecting

M. T. WHITELEY. "Children's Interest in Collecting," *Journal of Educational Psychology*, XX: 249–261 (April, 1929).

PAUL A. WITTY and HARVEY C. LEHMAN. "Further Studies of Children's Interest in Collecting," *Journal of Educational Psychology*, XXI: 112 (February, 1930).

On Writing

CAROLINE H. GARBE. "An Experiment in Correlating English Composition with the Content Subjects," *Elementary School Journal*, XXXI: 96–110 (October, 1930).

STELLA SUFINSKY. "Self-Expression — Creative Work," *Educational Method*, XIII: 76–81 (November, 1933).

On Composing Music

SATIS COLEMAN. "The Progress of the Movement for Creative Music," *Progressive Education*, X: 27 (1933).

On Correlation of History and Oral Language

ELIZABETH HALL. "Reading and the Social Studies," *Minnesota Journal of Education*, XI: 176–178 (January, 1931).

Application to Present-Day Conditions

On pages 14 and 15 was considered the inadvisability of attempting to frame a social-science program solely in terms of current issues. The point of view was presented that current issues cannot dictate the organization of the program but nevertheless must be seriously considered. The degree to which they can be included must be determined with reference to the capacities of children at the various age levels. Moreover, a background of principles, of viewpoints and generalizations, and of types of thinking peculiar to the various disciplines is needed also.

For these reasons it was suggested that the primary grades concern themselves chiefly with the overt aspects of community life, while the middle grades attempt to build upon that foundation an acquaintance with the main aspects of the world of space (geography) and time (history). After such foundations have been laid, children are then ready, in the junior high school, to consider the deeper interrelationships as well as the problems presented by living in the present-day world.

In the discovery of the worlds of space and time, relationships of the simpler types are continually pointed out; and the child can understand them the better because he has obtained (or is obtaining) a view of the world as the home of man and an understanding of man's great adventure on the earth. He is in possession of basic viewpoints in terms of which comparisons and contrasts take on new meanings.

If the teacher makes a practice of continually pointing out the relationship of the events and movements which are under consideration to present-day institutions, conditions, and problems, much of the pressure will be removed which now forces the construction of the curriculum in terms of what are called functional or lifelike wholes entirely removed from the setting which produced them and the forces of which they are the product (for example, the history of transportation, of time-telling, of building houses, of medicine, etc.).

For the teacher to point out the applications of subject-matter units to present-day conditions involves, on her part, first, an adequate mastery of the fundamental meanings of the subject on an interpretation level rather than on a fact level; second, an understanding of world problems at the present time. Without the first she cannot discern the underlying forces or trends which may be connected with present conditions; she is likely to become lost in a morass of details and to teach only isolated facts. Without the second she is completely at sea. No connection can be pointed out between the past and the present by one who does not know what the problems of the present are.

Any teacher of the social sciences, then, whether in the fourth grade or in the senior high school, must be a constant student of world affairs. She must realize that time to read newspapers, periodicals, and recent books is as necessary to her teaching as time to correct papers and to plan lessons. Travel, attending lectures, and listening to worth-while series over the radio help to broaden her point of view and to deepen her understanding.

There can be no question, however, that the average teachers in American schools today need help in the pointing out of such relationships. Most of them are young; they have had no experience in public affairs; their own education has only begun; and they have a multiplicity of duties to perform in connection with their daily work. Any realistic view of the situation recognizes that they must be given assistance.

To meet this very real need, each of the subunits treated hereinafter in Parts Two, Three, and Four gives a list of suggestions headed "Application to Present-Day Conditions."[1] In many cases the sources of the answers are indicated also.

The fortunate teachers who do not need such help will, of course, disregard the suggestions. Others will use them in part only, to be adjusted to the demands of the local situation and to the varying needs of the times. No such ready-made lists can ever take the place of a dynamic, interested teacher, and no such suggestions planned in advance can hope to deal with "spot news." However, teachers in the lower middle grades have comparatively little occasion to refer to the details of "spot news," as investigations[2] have shown that lower-middle-grade children at present do not possess sufficient foundation of knowledge of the world to profit by much current-events reading. But even young children profit from focusing attention on institutions and conditions of the environment with which they are familiar, and older children, even beginning with those in the fifth grades, are increasingly interested in the news of the world.

[1] See examples on pages 117, 278–279, 483–484, etc.
[2] See footnote 3 on page 40.

Educators should face the facts of the conditions as they exist. For a generation teachers have been exhorted to "tie up the classroom instruction with real-life situations." That more has not been accomplished is not due to the unwillingness of teachers. It is because the teachers have needed help and help was not forthcoming. For this reason the exercises headed "Application to Present-Day Conditions" are consistently given in every subunit hereinafter.

Exercises in Reasoning[1]

In no respect have teachers been served more poorly by the disagreement among schools of psychology than in regard to the whole problem of reasoning.

When the old faculty psychology was in vogue, the reasoning faculty was generally assumed to be a function of adolescence. Middle-grade children were supposed to be capable only of memorizing.[2] Belief in transfer led to methodical and systematic training in memorizing and to almost total neglect of reasoning at this level.

With the coming of the specificity theory, method and system vanished. Strong support was supplied for the belief that only current issues were worth consideration, since identical elements were not likely to be found in other fields. Reasoning suffered. The vehement insistence of some psychologists that a certain amount of transfer takes place furnished little guidance to teachers because of the inability of the experts to agree on the form.

The period of confusion led to laboratory experiments whose results showed conclusively that even very young children can and do reason. Without scrutinizing carefully the conditions under which the experiments had taken place, enthusiasts thereupon proceeded to set up for the middle grades social-science programs of such complicated subjects as those listed on page 6.

What they failed to notice in the investigations was the fact that children can and do reason cogently *in regard to matters with which they have had direct experience.* In apprehending relationships among objects not clearly present to the senses, children do poorly until about ten or eleven years of age, and adequate comparisons and generalizations are not made until the twelve-year age level [3] with materials of this sort.

From these facts, however, two completely different sets of conclu-

[1] For a review of the psychological evidence in regard to reasoning see the *Historical Outlook*, XXIV: 447–450 (December, 1933), and *The Social Studies*, XXV: 27–28 (January, 1934). For sex differences in reasoning see J. A. Fitzgerald and W. W. Ludeman's "Sex Differences in History Ability," *Peabody Journal of Education*, VI: 175–181 (November, 1928).

[2] For a curious recrudescence of this point of view see Luella Cole's *Psychology of Elementary School Subjects*, pp. 78–81 (Farrar & Rinehart, Inc., 1934).

[3] See the reference to the *Historical Outlook* in footnote 1, above.

sions have been drawn. One school of thought maintains that the social-science program for children throughout the entire period of the middle grades (ages perhaps eight to twelve) should be limited to phases for which direct experience can be supplied. Obviously, this program very strictly limits the range of activities and does not develop the power of gaining meanings through reading. It places little value upon vicarious experience.

A Workable Philosophy

The other school of thought maintains that the experience in overt aspects of community life furnished in the primary grades can and does supply a rich fund of direct experiences upon which a broader program for the middle grades can be soundly built; that the broader program can in many cases supply real-life experiences sufficiently like those constituting the social-science program to ensure understanding; and that vicarious experience can take the place of direct experience in cases where the latter cannot be furnished, provided that the former series of direct experiences has furnished materials which constitute large enough elements of the new ideas to be gained vicariously.[1]

The second of these two theories seems a broader and more inclusive philosophy upon which to build a social-science program for the middle grades. However, it involves a very careful analysis of the various processes classed together under the general caption "reasoning." The scientific investigations already referred to have made clear (1) that certain of these processes in vague, undifferentiated form are engaged in, to a degree, even by very young children; (2) that enormous individual differences in the refinement of these processes occur among children of a given chronological age or in a given grade; and (3) that the abilities are strengthened and improved by specific practice.

Until the contrary is proved, the point of view will be accepted that the development of reasoning in history will not transfer to other fields, except in the form of generalizations, unless the fields possess many identical elements. Practice in reasoning in history develops reasoning with historical materials. Since so many of our present-day problems are only current history and are rooted in past history, this qualifying and limiting statement still leaves a vast field in which reasoning thus developed can operate.

Moreover, it is recognized clearly that possession of a body of facts about history does not necessarily lead to reasoning.[2] Fact exercises are

---

[1] For a discussion of direct versus vicarious experience in preparation for citizenship see Charles E. Merriam's *Civic Education in the United States*; also Harold Rugg's *Culture and Education in America*, pp. 312–320.

[2] Ralph W. Tyler, "Measuring the Ability to Infer," *Educational Research Bulletin*, IX: 475–480 (November, 1930); Joseph C. Dewey, "The Acquisition of Facts as a Measure of Reading Comprehension," *Elementary School Journal*, XXXV: 346–348 (January, 1935).

not enough. It is necessary that "reasoning" be broken up into its elements, that practice in reasoning of a very simple type be constantly supplied to exercise and strengthen the growing powers in each one of these elements, and that provision be supplied for the progress of the gifted children of a group far in advance of the standards of expectation applied to the others.

Thus the teacher makes a conscious effort to *force* a mental reaction on the part of the children. When one recalls the ceaseless activity, both mental and physical, engaged in by young children, it seems strange that teachers should be compelled to think about *forcing* reactions. And yet it is true that children in many cases have been so repressed, or so drilled into habits of merely reproducing what they have memorized, that by the time they enter the fourth grade they no longer exhibit a desire to react in original ways. Under such circumstances it becomes the teacher's task to *force* a thoughtful reaction as opposed to a memorized reproduction. In happier situations it is the teacher's task to *encourage* original reactions.

Specific Examples of Exercises in Reasoning

To assist teachers in making an analysis of reasoning, the following tabulation has been prepared (pp. 82–91). On the pages referred to in the tables are given specific exercises in the different types of reasoning, based on the specific materials with which the children have been concerning themselves. These are the types which teachers often refer to vaguely as "thought questions."[1] Obviously, in conducting the exercises the teacher makes no reference to such terms as "generalizations"[2] or "inferences." Equally obviously, there will be enormous differences in the performance of different children in the same group. There can be no one standard to which all must have attained before they can "pass" from the grade. Growth differs in rate as well as quality. But that children can and do profit from opportunities for developing their powers of reasoning in general is shown by such investigations as Helseth's.[3]

The questions and exercises are classified according to the mental reaction needed in answering or solving them. The reaction, however, in order to qualify as real reasoning, must be a genuine and original reaction of the children themselves. If the text prints a generalization concerning a certain historical matter, the children's repeating of that statement does not constitute a process of generalizing, for the comparison, abstraction, and conclusion have not been done by the children themselves.

[1] See W. S. Monroe and Ruth Streitz's *Directing Learning in the Elementary School*, pp. 271–322 (Doubleday, Doran and Company, Inc., 1932).

[2] Neal Billings, *A Determination of Generalizations Basic to the Social Sciences* (Warwick & York, 1930), and Will French, "Six Slants on the Social Studies," *School Executives Magazine*, LII, No. 6 (February, 1933).

[3] I. O. Helseth, *Children's Thinking*. Teachers College Contributions to Education, No. 209. Bureau of Publications, Columbia University, 1926.

TABULATION OF EXERCISES AND TESTS IN UNDERSTANDING, JUDGMENT AND REASONING, AND SKILLS USED IN PART TWO: "LEARNING AND TEACHING EARLY AMERICAN HISTORY"

B = Kelty's *The Beginnings of the American People and Nation* (a textbook which carries into effect the principles outlined here)
L = Kelty's *Learning and Teaching History in the Middle Grades*

Exercises and Tests in	Unit One	Unit Two	Unit Three	Unit Four	Unit Five
I. Understanding: Of persons	B18, 50, 58, 71 L118, 130, 133, 136	B88, 99, 114, 125, 133, 144, 154, 163, 172, 182 L173–174	B201, 260, 275, 289, 318, 326 L195, 209	B345, 354, 368, 385, 398, 417, 429, 438, 445 L240	B466, 498, 509, 518, 531, 539, 546 L271
Of places	B18, 37–38, 50, 71 L117, 118, 121, 126, 130, 136, 138, 139	B88, 99, 114, 125, 133, 144, 155, 163, 172, 182 L152, 171–173	B201, 209, 226, 239, 251, 260, 275, 289, 318, 326 L207	B337, 355, 368, 385, 391, 398, 417, 438, 445, 450 L239–240	B477, 498, 509, 518, 531, 539 L269–270
Of time	B18, 50 L118, 120, 121, 126, 127, 129, 130, 131, 137, 138–139	B88, 99, 133 L144, 145, 147, 149, 151, 152, 154, 159, 161, 163, 164, 167, 172, 173	B201, 209, 275, 289, 326 L180, 181, 187, 191, 194, 198, 205, 207, 208, 209	B368, 385, 398, 450 L219, 221, 223, 238, 240–242	B466, 477, 498, 539, 546 L250, 253, 262, 263, 265, 268
Of vocabulary meanings	B18, 28, 37–38, 50, 58, 71 L116, 119, 121, 124, 126, 128, 130, 132, 133, 135, 136, 139	B88, 99, 114, 125, 133, 144, 155, 163, 172, 182 L143, 145, 147, 150, 151, 152, 153, 158, 159, 160, 162, 164, 165, 166, 167, 168, 169, 174–175	B201, 209, 226, 239, 252, 260, 275, 289, 308, 318, 326 L178, 179, 181, 184, 185, 187, 188, 190, 191, 193, 195, 197, 198, 200, 202, 203, 204, 206, 210, 211	B337, 345, 355, 368, 385, 391, 398, 406, 417, 429, 438, 450 L213, 214, 215, 216, 217, 220, 222, 223, 225, 226, 228, 230, 231, 234, 235, 239, 242, 243	B466, 477, 498, 509, 518, 531, 539, 546 L245, 247, 249, 251, 253, 254, 256, 258, 260, 261, 263, 264, 266, 267, 270, 271, 272
II. Judgment and reasoning: Sequence in thought (*See also* Organization)	B18, 27, 36–37, 49, 57, 71 L116, 119, 121, 124, 128, 132, 135	B87, 98, 113, 124, 132–133, 143–144, 154, 172, 182 L143, 145, 147, 150, 152, 153, 158, 159, 162, 165, 166, 169	B200, 209, 226, 239, 251, 260, 275, 289, 308, 318, 326 L178, 179, 184, 187, 190, 193, 197, 200, 203, 204	B337, 345, 354, 368, 385, 391, 398, 406, 416–417, 429, 438, 445, 449 L213, 214, 216, 217, 222, 225, 226, 230, 233, 234, 237	B465–466, 476–477, 497, 509, 517–518, 531, 539, 546 L245, 248, 249, 253, 256, 258, 261, 264, 267

Exercises and Tests in	Unit One	Unit Two	Unit Three	Unit Four	Unit Five
Sequence in time	L117, 118, 120, 129, 131, 133, 137	L144, 145, 147, 149, 151, 152, 154, 159, 161, 163, 164, 167, 168, 172, 173	L180, 187, 191, 194, 198, 205, 207, 208, 209	L219, 221, 223, 238, 240, 241	L250, 253, 262, 263, 265, 268
Imagination: Descriptive	L120, 124, 129, 135, 136	L143, 147, 150, 154, 159, 163, 167, 170	L180, 184, 190, 194, 205	L219, 222, 231, 238	L246, 253, 257, 268
Constructive	L117, 120, 129	L159, 163	L177, 184, 187	L214	L250
Comparison and contrast	L120, 129, 132, 133	L144, 148, 151, 154, 155, 160, 163, 166, 167, 170	L181, 187, 188, 191, 195, 198, 199, 201, 205	L212, 215, 219, 226, 227, 231, 234, 235	L247, 254, 259, 260, 263, 266, 268, 269
Cause and effect	L120, 121, 126, 127, 129, 133, 136	L144, 145, 146, 147, 148, 149, 151, 155, 159, 160, 161, 163, 167, 170	L181, 185, 188, 191, 192, 195, 196, 198, 199, 201, 202, 205, 206	L215, 219, 220, 223, 224, 227, 228, 231, 235, 236, 238, 239	L244, 246, 247, 250, 254, 257, 258, 260, 263, 264, 265, 266, 267
Evaluation	L117, 120, 129, 133, 136, 137	L144, 148, 149, 151, 160, 170, 171	L181, 182, 185, 188, 191, 198, 199, 201, 202, 206	L219, 220, 223, 224, 231, 235, 238	L246, 247, 254, 255, 257, 262, 265, 266
Drawing inferences	L117, 122, 126, 127, 132, 133, 136	L144, 146, 151, 152, 154, 155, 156, 163, 167, 170	L177, 180, 185, 186, 188, 189, 195, 196, 198, 206	L212, 216, 221, 223, 225, 227, 229, 231, 236, 238	L248, 250, 251, 254, 255, 258, 261, 268
Synthesis	L120, 121, 135	L144, 155, 156	L180, 184, 188, 189	L232	L244, 247, 254, 257, 259, 263, 268
Analysis	L117, 120, 130, 132, 134	L144, 148	L206, 219	L221, 223, 224, 238	L254, 260, 263
Generalization: Formulating	L126	L148, 155	L181, 206	L235	L250, 254, 269
Applying	L126	L160, 163, 165	L181, 188, 199, 201	L219, 227, 231, 235	L250, 257, 263
Organization: Listing	L118, 120, 131	L144, 155, 156, 161, 168	L184, 185, 188, 196	L232	L251

Exercises and Tests in	Unit One	Unit Two	Unit Three	Unit Four	Unit Five
II. Judgment (continued): Summarizing	B18, 28, 38, 50, 58, 71 L118, 121, 127, 131	B88, 99, 114, 125, 133, 145, 155, 163, 172, 182 L149, 156, 161	B201, 207, 226, 239, 252, 260, 275, 289, 308, 318, 326 L182, 188, 192, 196, 199, 202	B337, 345, 355, 368, 385, 391, 398, 406, 417, 429, 438, 445, 450 L224, 239	B466, 477, 498, 509, 518, 532, 539, 546 L251, 260, 263
Outlining	L133	L145, 152, 164	L192, 207	L215, 228, 236, 239	L248, 255, 258, 267
III. Skills: Map-reading	B32, 34, 35, 46, 47, 48, 62 L115, 117, 118, 120, 121, 122, 124, 126, 127, 128, 129, 130, 134, 135	B84, 87, 96, 108, 123, 132, 141, 170, 178 L142, 144, 145, 147, 149, 152, 154, 155, 159, 161, 166, 168, 169, 171	B189, 195, 228, 229, 234, 236, 240, 241, 243, 257, 269, 280, 284, 314, 316, 322, 323 L179, 182, 187, 188, 190, 192, 194, 196, 197, 199, 204, 207	B348, 349, 351, 352, 358, 362, 364, 366, 370, 374, 377, 378, 387, 389, 390, 400, 403, 405, 410, 411, 412, 414, 415, 432, 436, 439, 448 L217, 219, 220, 222, 224, 226, 228, 230, 232, 233, 234, 236, 237, 238, 239	B470, 473, 476, 482, 483, 486, 488, 490, 491, 492, 493, 502, 505, 520, 523, 526, 527, 528 L248, 251, 252, 253, 254, 255, 256, 258, 263
Map-making	L124, 126, 127, 135	L144, 147, 151, 152, 154, 159, 170	L180, 187, 191, 194, 198, 205, 207	L214, 219, 223, 227, 231, 235, 238	L250, 253, 257, 262
Locating	L118, 126, 130, 136	L145, 148, 151, 160, 167, 171	L181, 188, 191, 194, 198, 206	L215, 220, 223, 228, 231, 235, 237	L249, 251, 254, 257, 263
Interpreting pictures	B9, 15, 21, 31, 45, 48, 56, 67 L116, 120, 124, 128, 132, 135	B83, 94, 109, 121, 131, 139, 151, 159, 167, 177 L143, 147, 150, 153, 159, 162, 166, 169	B192, 195, 205, 211, 213, 225, 228, 233, 247, 249, 254, 257, 267, 278, 283, 291, 301, 313 L179, 184, 187, 190, 194, 204	B331, 339, 351, 361, 371, 379, 388, 397, 401, 413, 425, 428, 435, 443 L214, 217, 222, 226, 230, 234, 237	B461, 463, 469, 475, 479, 507, 515, 537 L245, 249, 253, 256, 258, 262, 264, 268
Using books [1] (Index, contents, etc.)	L121, 127	L145, 156, 161, 164, 168	L182, 185, 188, 196, 199, 202	L221, 228, 234	L251, 255, 258, 260

[1] See also the more specific suggestions in the Manual to accompany *The Beginnings of the American People and Nation.*

TABULATION OF EXERCISES AND TESTS IN UNDERSTANDING, JUDGMENT AND REASONING, AND SKILLS USED IN PART THREE ("LEARNING AND TEACHING LATER AMERICAN HISTORY")

G = Kelty's *The Growth of the American People and Nation* (a textbook which carries into effect the principles outlined here)
L = Kelty's *Learning and Teaching History in the Middle Grades*

Exercises and Tests in	Unit One	Unit Two	Unit Three	Unit Four	Unit Five	Unit Six	Unit Seven
I. Understanding:							
Of persons	G21, 35, 42, 59, 78 L296	G98, 110, 120, 136, 158, 171 L328	C222, 227, 232, 252, 256, 265 L354	G290, 328, 335, 342, 353, 358, 365, 374 L384	G395, 401, 407, 418 L404	G437, 443, 461, 466, 500, 508 L434-435	G520, 534, 555, 577, 586, 604, 607, 613 L474
Of places	G13, 28, 35, 49, 78 L294	G98, 110, 128, 171, 181, 190, 196 L327	G265	G285, 290, 295, 308, 322, 342, 353, 365, 374 L382	G407	G430, 437 L413	G534, 545, 555, 565, 577, 586, 593, 604, 613 L471
Of time	G28, 59 L278, 280, 283, 285, 289, 292, 294, 295	G98, 120, 128, 136, 171, 181, 190, 196 L301, 328	G222, 227, 252, 256 L354, 355	G280, 310, 316, 335, 342, 374 L361, 363, 366, 368, 371, 382-383	G388, 418 L390, 394, 402, 404, 405	G443 L412, 422, 423, 434, 435	G520, 534, 545, 555, 577, 586, 604 L441, 444, 446, 448, 453, 460, 471-474
Of vocabulary meanings	G13, 21, 28, 42, 49, 59, 78 L276, 277, 280, 282, 284, 286, 287, 288, 290, 293, 296-297	G87, 98, 110, 120, 128, 136, 150, 158, 164, 171, 181, 190, 196 L299, 300, 302, 304, 307, 309, 310, 312, 314, 317, 318, 319, 321, 323, 324, 326, 329-330	G211, 214, 218, 222, 227, 232, 243, 247, 252, 256, 260, 265, 270, 274 L333, 334, 336, 337, 338, 340, 342, 344, 346, 349, 350, 351, 353, 354-356	G280, 285, 290, 295, 302, 310, 316, 322, 328, 335, 342, 353, 358, 365, 374 L359, 360, 362, 364, 367, 369, 370, 372, 374, 375, 376, 378, 379, 381, 384-385	G383, 388, 395, 401, 407, 413 L388, 389, 391, 393, 395, 396, 398, 400, 403, 404-406	G430, 437, 443, 448, 454, 461, 466, 470, 476, 480, 487, 495, 500, 508, 613 L409, 410, 413, 415, 418, 420, 422, 424, 425, 427, 429, 430, 432, 433, 436-438	G520, 534, 545, 549, 555, 560, 565, 577, 586, 593, 604, 607, 613 L440, 442, 444, 445, 447, 448, 450, 452, 454, 456, 457, 459, 461, 463, 466, 468, 469, 470, 475-476

Exercises and Tests in	Unit One	Unit Two	Unit Three	Unit Four	Unit Five	Unit Six	Unit Seven
II. Judgment and reasoning: Sequence in thought (See also Organization)	G13, 21, 27–28, 35, 42, 49, 59, 78, L276, 277, 281, 282, 286, 287, 290, 291	G87, 98, 110, 120, 128, 136, 150, 158, 164, 171, 181, 190, 196, 202, L299, 300, 304, 305, 309, 314, 318, 319, 323, 324	G211, 214, 217, 222, 227, 232, 237, 243, 247, 252, 256, 260, 265, 270, 274, L333, 334, 337, 338, 342, 346, 347, 350, 351	G280, 285, 290, 295, 301, 308, 316, 322, 328, 335, 341–342, 353, 357, 364, 365, 373, L359, 360, 361, 364, 365, 369, 370, 374, 375, 378, 379	G383, 388, 394–395, 400–401, 407, 413, 418, L388, 391, 395, 396, 400, 401	G430, 437, 443, 447–448, 454, 461, 465, 470, 476, 480, 487, 495, 500, 508, L409, 410, 415, 420, 424, 425, 429, 430	G520, 533–534, 544–545, 549, 555, 560, 565, 577, 586, 593, 603, 607, 613, L440, 444, 447, 448, 450, 452, 456, 459, 463, 468, 469
Sequence in time	L278, 280, 283, 285, 289, 292, 294, 295, 296	L301, 302, 306, 308, 311, 312, 315, 320, 322, 327	L339, 341, 349, 366	L363, 368, 371, 373, 376, 380	L390, 394, 402, 404, 405	L412, 422, 423	L441, 444, 446, 448, 453, 458, 460, 465, 471–474
Imagination: Descriptive	L278, 287, 292	L300, 306		L351	L361, 366, 371, 401	L426	L441, 444, 469
Constructive	L278	L300, 306, 311, 315, 320	L335		L375, 392		
Comparison and contrast	L278, 279, 283, 284, 288, 293	L300, 306, 307, 311, 313, 315, 321	L335, 338, 339, 343, 344, 348, 352	L361, 364, 372, 376, 380	L389, 392, 393, 397, 403	L408, 412, 413, 416, 417, 421, 422, 426, 432–433	L440, 441, 449, 450, 453, 454, 461, 462, 465, 470
Cause and effect	L275, 279, 280, 284, 288, 289, 293, 294	L302, 303, 307, 308, 312, 314, 316, 317, 320–321, 326, 327	L335, 338, 339, 340, 341, 344, 346, 348, 349, 350, 352, 353	L361, 362, 363, 366, 367, 372, 373, 376, 380	L387, 389, 390, 392, 393, 394, 397, 398, 403	L408, 412, 417, 421, 426, 427, 428, 431, 432, 438	L441, 442, 445, 449, 450, 452, 453, 454, 458, 460, 461, 465, 466, 467, 470

Exercises and Tests in	Unit One	Unit Two	Unit Three	Unit Four	Unit Five	Unit Six	Unit Seven
Evaluation	L284, 288, 289, 293	L302, 307, 316, 321, 326, 327	L335, 340, 344, 345, 348, 349, 352, 353	L361, 362, 363, 366, 367, 372, 376, 380, 382	L389, 393, 397, 398	L412, 414, 417, 418, 420, 422, 426, 428, 432, 433	L440, 441, 443, 445, 446, 448, 449, 450, 454, 458, 461, 462, 465, 467, 470, 471
Drawing inferences	L277, 279, 286, 290, 293	L298, 299, 302, 307, 308, 309, 312, 317, 322, 326	L335, 338, 341, 346, 349, 350, 352	L361, 362, 364, 365, 368, 369, 372, 373, 374	L393, 394, 397, 399, 403	L412, 415, 417, 421, 423, 424, 425, 426, 428	L439, 440, 442, 443, 452, 453, 454, 455, 458, 461, 465, 467, 469, 470, 471
Synthesis	L284, 287	L301, 312, 315, 321	L334, 335, 342, 344, 353	L361, 362, 368, 373, 381	L399, 421	L426, 431	L446, 454, 455, 464
Analysis	L283, 284, 288, 289, 292	L302, 312, 316, 317, 320, 326	L335, 336, 340, 342, 344	L362, 371, 372, 377	L387, 389, 397, 398, 402	L413, 417, 422, 426, 428, 432	L441, 445, 454
Generalization: Formulating		L308, 313, 321	L336, 341	L373	L394, 399, 403	L418, 428	L454, 467, 471
Applying	L284, 293	L312, 316, 321, 326	L335, 345	L367, 372, 380	L398, 402	L422, 423, 429, 432	L445, 457, 460, 461, 465
Organization: Listing	L284, 287	L327	L335, 344, 349	L373	L390, 399	L433	L450
Summarizing	G13, 21, 28, 35, 42, 49, 59, 78; L285, 294	G87, 98, 110, 120, 128, 136, 150, 158, 164, 171, 181, 190, 196, 202; L308, 322	G211, 218, 222, 227, 232, 237, 243, 247, 252, 256, 260, 265, 270, 274; L349	G280, 285, 290, 295, 302, 310, 316, 322, 328, 335, 342, 353, 358, 365, 374; L363, 373	G383, 388, 395, 401, 407, 413, 418; L390, 399, 423	G430, 437, 443, 448, 454, 461, 466, 470, 476, 480, 487, 495, 500, 508; L414, 418, 428, 433	G520, 534, 545, 549, 555, 560, 564, 577, 586, 593, 604, 607, 613; L443, 462
Outlining	L289	L303, 313, 317, 322	L336, 345, 353	L368, 382	L394, 403	L428, 433	L446, 455, 467

Exercises and Tests in	Unit One	Unit Two	Unit Three	Unit Four	Unit Five	Unit Six	Unit Seven
III. Skills: Map-reading	G24, 60, 62, 63, 66, 68, 74, 75 L282, 285, 290, 291, 294	G83, 84, 92, 95, 104, 109, 154, 159, 160, 172, 174, 178, 181, 186, 191, 192 L300, 303, 305, 308, 310, 311, 315, 317, 318, 319, 322, 324, 327	L348	G288, 293, 303, 305, 306, 307, 313, 317, 320, 339, 341, 346, 347, 348, 352, 359, 362, 363, 367, 368, 370, 371 L365, 370, 373, 375, 376, 378, 379, 380, 381	G428 L396, 399, 401	L411	G514, 521, 528, 529, 532, 538, 540, 544, 551, 552, 570, 572, 573, 574, 576, 579, 584, 585 L440, 442, 443, 444, 448, 450, 452, 455, 456, 458, 459, 462, 464
Map-making	L283		L339, 352	L360, 371		L416	L444, 456
Locating	L278, 284, 288, 293	L302, 307, 312, 321, 326		L362, 367, 376, 381	L398	L413	L445, 449, 454, 457, 466, 470
Interpreting pictures	G9, 11, 25, 30, 39, 46, 55, 67, 69, 73 L277, 282, 287, 291	G83, 86, 89, 97, 101, 102, 103, 107, 113, 119, 124, 126, 131, 134, 139, 143, 145, 149, 161, 166, 169, 179, 183, 193, 201 L300, 305, 310, 315, 319, 324	G208, 209, 213, 217, 221, 225, 239, 242, 245, 255, 258, 263, 267, 273 L334, 338, 343, 347, 351	G279, 292, 297, 307, 315, 327, 331, 333, 340, 344, 345, 356, 360, 367, 372 L360, 365, 370, 375, 379	G379, 387, 391, 393, 397, 404, 405, 409, 411, 417 L388, 392, 396, 401	G423, 427, 433, 441, 445, 451, 453, 456, 459, 463, 469, 475, 478, 485, 489, 493, 499, 502, 507 L410, 416, 420, 425, 430	G513, 525, 529, 531, 537, 539, 547, 548, 551, 553, 571, 579, 582, 584, 588, 590, 595, 599, 609, 611 L440, 444, 448, 452, 456, 459, 464, 469
Using books [1] (Index, table of contents, etc.)	L280, 288, 294	L303, 308, 313, 327	L336, 345, 349, 350	L358, 368, 371, 373, 376	L390, 399	L414, 418, 428, 433	L443, 446, 450, 455, 458, 467

[1] See also the more specific suggestions in the Manual to accompany Kelty's *The Growth of the American People and Nation.*

TABULATION OF EXERCISES AND TESTS IN UNDERSTANDING, JUDGMENT AND REASONING, AND SKILLS USED IN PART FOUR: THE BEGINNINGS OF CIVILIZATION

C = Kelty's *How Our Civilization Began* (a textbook which carries into effect the principles outlined here)
L = Kelty's *Learning and Teaching History in the Middle Grades*

Exercises and Tests in	Unit One	Unit Two	Unit Three	Unit Four	Unit Five	Unit Six
I. Understanding:						
Of persons		C72–73, 93, 110 L527	C121, 140, 151, 160 L554–555	C169–170, 180, 190–191, 213, 220–221 L584–585	C245, 267, 274, 284, 294, 300 L623–624	
Of places		C72, 93, 103 L527	C121, 134, 140, 151, 160 L554	C169, 180, 190–191, 213, 221 L561, 570, 582, 583	C254, 259–260, 267, 274, 284, 300 L622–623	
Of time	C4, 17, 28, 47 L482, 483, 485, 487, 488, 490, 493, 497, 498, 499, 500, 501	L508, 515, 517, 520, 524, 527	C140, 160 L542, 543, 551, 554	C180, 191, 221 L564, 569, 583–584	C230, 236, 245, 267, 294, 300 L591, 597, 602, 607, 620, 623	
Of vocabulary meanings	C17, 28, 38–39 L480, 481, 484, 487, 489, 490, 492, 494, 495, 497, 499, 501, 502	C72–73, 93, 103, 110 L506, 507, 510, 512, 514, 516, 519, 521, 523, 526, 528	C121, 134, 140, 151, 160 L530, 534, 536, 538, 541, 543, 544, 545, 548, 551, 553, 555–556	C169–170, 180, 190–191, 213, 221 L559, 561, 563, 566, 568, 570–571, 574, 577, 580, 582, 585–586	C230, 236, 245, 254, 259–260, 267, 274, 284, 294, 300 L589, 590, 593, 595, 596, 598, 599, 600, 602, 604, 606, 608, 611, 612, 615, 617, 619, 621, 624, 625	C308, 317, 322, 327–328, 339, 344 L628, 630, 632, 635, 637, 638, 640, 642, 644, 646, 649, 651, 652–653

Exercises and Tests in	Unit One	Unit Two	Unit Three	Unit Four	Unit Five	Unit Six
II. Judgment and reasoning: Sequence in thought (See also Organization)	C17, 28, 38, 47 L480, 481, 487, 492, 497	C71–72, 92–93, 102–103, 110 L506, 507, 512, 514, 519, 523	C120, 134, 140, 151, 159 L530, 536, 541, 544, 545, 551	C169, 179–180, 190, 213, 220 L559, 563, 568, 573, 580	C230, 236, 245, 253, 259, 267, 274, 283–284, 293, 300 L589, 590, 595, 596, 600, 602, 606, 611, 615, 619	C308, 317, 322, 327, 339, 344 L628, 632, 637, 640, 644, 649
Sequence in time	L482, 483, 485, 488, 493, 498, 499, 500	L508, 515, 517, 520, 524, 527	L542, 551, 554	L564, 569, 583–584	L591, 597, 602, 607, 620, 623	
Imagination: Descriptive	L483, 488, 498	L508, 515	L532, 537, 542, 551	L559, 560, 564	L591, 592, 597, 602, 607	L633, 637, 645
Constructive	L483, 488	L508, 509, 515, 520, 524	L537, 547, 552	L575	L591, 597, 607, 611, 615	L633, 637, 641
Comparison and contrast	L479, 483, 484, 485, 489, 493, 494, 497, 498, 499	L509, 510, 514, 516, 517, 521, 522, 525, 526	L533, 534, 537, 538, 542, 547, 548, 552	L560, 564, 565, 567, 570, 575, 576, 577, 581	L592, 597, 598, 603, 607, 608, 612, 616, 620	L629, 630, 631, 634, 636, 637, 638, 641, 645, 646, 650
Cause and effect	L484, 485, 488, 489, 490, 493, 494, 495, 498, 499, 500, 502, 503	L509, 510, 511, 515, 516, 517, 518, 520, 521, 522, 525, 527, 528, 529	L533, 537, 538, 539, 542, 543, 544, 548, 549, 552, 553, 556, 557	L560, 562, 565, 569, 570, 571, 572, 576, 579, 581, 582, 583, 586, 587	L588, 592, 593, 597, 598, 603, 604, 605, 607, 608, 612, 613, 616, 620, 625, 626	L629, 630, 634, 636, 638, 642, 643, 645, 646, 648, 651, 653
Evaluation	L488, 490, 494	L517, 520, 529	L533, 538, 539, 542, 543, 547, 552	L560, 565, 570, 576, 577, 581, 582	L592, 598, 607, 611, 618, 620	L629, 630, 631, 635, 646, 653
Drawing inferences	L479, 484, 485, 486, 489, 490, 494, 495, 496, 499	L504, 509, 510, 512, 515, 516, 518, 521	L530, 535, 538, 540, 542, 548, 549, 552	L557, 560, 562, 567, 569, 572, 579, 581	L592, 594, 598, 605, 609, 612, 616	L627, 631, 634, 635, 636, 638, 639, 642, 646
Synthesis	L483, 484, 488, 493	L511	L532, 537, 538, 543, 547	L564, 569	L599, 612, 613	L629, 631, 639, 646
Analysis	L484, 485, 489, 493	L509, 510, 515, 517, 520, 521, 525	L552, 570	L572, 576, 577	L592, 594, 603	L629, 630

Exercises and Tests in	Unit One	Unit Two	Unit Three	Unit Four	Unit Five	Unit Six
Generalization: Formulating	L494		L533	L581	L599, 612	L638
Applying	L484, 489, 493, 494, 499, 500	L516, 525	L533, 534, 542, 548, 552	L560, 570, 576, 577	L621	L629, 630, 650
Organization: Listing	L483, 493	L511	L534, 553	L561, 578	L593, 599, 613	L629, 631, 639, 647
Summarizing	C17, 28, 39, 47 L485, 490, 500	C73, 93, 103, 110 L517, 521	C121, 134, 140, 151, 160 L549, 553	C170, 180, 191, 213, 221 L561, 566, 578	C230, 236, 245, 254, 260, 267, 274, 284, 294, 300 L604, 609, 622	C308, 317, 322, 328, 339, 344 L631, 639, 651
Outlining	L495	L511, 517, 526	L539, 544	L571, 583	L599, 613	L635, 643
III. Skills: Map-reading		C52, 54, 74, 76, 79, 86, 94, 99, 104 L504, 507, 509, 511, 512, 514, 517, 518, 519, 521, 526	C114, 118, 130, 135, 136, 138, 139, 154 L530, 532, 533, 534, 536, 539, 541, 544, 552	C163, 181, 188 L557, 559, 561, 567, 568, 570, 571, 581	C225, 230, 241, 248, 268, 279 L591, 593, 596, 599, 602, 603, 605, 611, 613	
Map-making	L488	L508, 515, 520	L542, 551	L559, 564, 569, 575	L591, 603, 607	
Locating		L510, 516, 521, 524, 526	L534, 538, 543, 553	L561, 570, 582	L598, 604, 608, 612	
Interpreting pictures	C7, 9, 10, 14, 15, 19, 20, 21, 22, 27, 31, 33, 37, 42, 46 L482, 487, 492, 497	C56, 60, 61, 62, 64, 65, 68, 77, 78, 82, 83, 84, 85, 88, 89, 90, 95, 97, 99, 108 L507, 514, 519, 524	C117, 119, 120, 124, 125, 126, 127, 131, 132, 133, 142, 145, 147, 149, 157, 158 L532, 536, 541, 546, 551	C166, 168, 174, 176, 177, 179, 182, 183, 185, 187, 194, 195, 196, 201, 203, 204, 205, 206, 207, 211, 217, 219 L559, 563, 568, 574, 580	C229, 235, 240, 247, 251, 257, 263, 265, 271, 277, 281, 287, 292, 299 L591, 596, 602, 606, 611, 615, 619	C306, 310, 313, 316, 319, 321, 325, 332, 335, 337, 341, 343 L628, 633, 637, 641, 644, 649
Using books	L485, 490, 495	L521, 526	L534, 549, 553	L561, 583	L593, 599, 609, 617	L639, 643

Examples of Exercises in Judgment and Reasoning

Sequence in Thought. EXAMPLE: One child tells the first part of the story; the teacher stops him and calls on another to continue, etc.

Sequence in Time. EXAMPLE: Put the figure 1 before the event which happened first, the figure 2 before the event which happened next, and so on:

> The Crusades tried to win back the Holy Land.
> Northmen discovered Greenland.
> Dias reached the Cape of Storms.

Imagination: Descriptive. EXAMPLE: Imagine that you are a sheep-herder on the Western plains. Tell how you spend your days.

> *Constructive.* EXAMPLE: Set a stage for the scene in which Commodore Perry was received by the officials of Japan.

Comparison and Contrast. EXAMPLE: From the encyclopedia and from the advertising literature of a modern steamship company compare Columbus's ships with the *Normandie* in length, speed per hour, number of passengers and crew, and length of time required to cross the Atlantic. Graph the results.

Cause and Effect. EXAMPLE: Why did the Jamestown colonists live on corn rather than wheat?

Evaluation. EXAMPLE: All these statements are true. Put a mark before the one which tells the most important reason why the United States entered the World War.

> The Central Powers might win the war.
> Great Britain would not let food supplies reach Germany.
> Many Germans lived in the United States.
> Some Americans wanted to help France.
> Unrestricted submarine warfare interfered with our commerce.

Synthesis. EXAMPLE: Make a list of the persons needed to dramatize a session of the Peace Conference in 1917–1918.

Analysis. EXAMPLE: Plan a series of acts and scenes necessary to dramatize a complete story of the Monroe Doctrine.

Generalization: Formulating. EXAMPLE: Make a map locating the first permanent settlements in each colony. From the locations, what rules can you draw up as to good locations for early settlements?

> *Applying.* EXAMPLE: We sometimes hear it said that great men differ from ordinary people because they have stronger wills. Apply this saying to the life of La Salle.

Organization: Listing. EXAMPLE: List the steps by which the North and the South tried to solve the question of slavery in the territories.

> *Summarizing.* EXAMPLE: One child tells the story of Part I of the outline, another of Part II, and so on. Sometimes a single sentence is required rather than the short oral résumé.

> *Outlining.* EXAMPLE: The children and the teacher make a co-operative outline of every story in the fourth-grade text until the children can make acceptable outlines independently. Then those who are able continue by themselves; the teacher helps the others.

The Place of Problem-Solving in the Learning of History

Years of experience with the problem-solving method in history have indicated pointedly its unsuitability for general use.[1] The materials are such that they do not lend themselves to the procedure of (1) sensing a problematical situation; (2) setting up various hypotheses; (3) testing each in turn; and (4) verifying the final result. Such a procedure implies a control of all the factors, which simply is not true to the conditions of history.

The attempt to use this method has resulted too often in a wild scramble of guessing, partly because the children have had little basis in fact upon which to proceed, and partly because history has not always followed what seem to be logical lines and hence has been unpredictable. Moreover, certain children have usually read ahead; they have found out what society determined in the case under consideration, or what fortuitous circumstances brought about; therefore no real problem-solving has been possible.

But to decide that the problem-solving method cannot be followed consistently throughout the course does not mean that there is no place in the learning of history for any problem-solving exercises. Nothing could be farther from the truth. Such exercises are particularly needed. Many children have been so repressed because of the faulty training they have received, and so habituated to merely reproducing what they have read, that they make no attempt to *think* or *reason* about it. They assume a passive attitude, and the teacher is compelled to force a reaction.

In many cases, however, she has made the mistake of introducing exercises in reasoning too early in the learning process, — before children were in possession of the basic facts needed as raw materials. Another instance of trying to make bricks without straw! It is quite obvious that one cannot reason without regard to the content of the reasoning.[2]

Consequently the general technique under discussion, as exemplified in Parts Two, Three, and Four of this book, delays reasoning exercises until after reading, study, discussion, picture and map study, and general activities have been completed. By that time children are presumably in possession of the raw materials; and they are ready to reason, so far as their mental development will allow. Exercises are therefore provided which will stretch the children's ability to its fullest capacity.

[1] W. H. Burton, "The Problem Solving Technique: Its Appearance and Development in American Texts on General Methods," *Educational Method*, XIV: 189–195, 248–253, 338–342 (January, February, March, 1935).

[2] See the psychological analysis on page 449 of the *Historical Outlook* article mentioned in footnote 1 on page 6.

The exercises and tests tabulated on pages 82–91 provide such exercise and practice in their simplest terms; but even on that level the performance of the group will be uneven. Teachers who understand the psychology of the situation will not be unduly distressed by the difference in rate of growth.

The Function of Drill [1]

Teachers whose philosophy of education recognizes no function for drill are invited to pass over this section and to turn immediately to the discussion of testing on page 98.

Opposition to drill, however, can no longer rest upon children's supposed abhorrence of it. On the contrary, years of experimentation with individualized materials in arithmetic and spelling have shown that they actually enjoy it, provided that it is intelligently administered. And the shortcomings of incidental learning have become evident.

However, the teacher should understand clearly the function of drill. It has only one purpose, and that is a narrow one. Its function is not to develop the understanding of large movements or to exercise the reasoning powers. It may indirectly assist in both processes by furnishing clear-cut and definite ideas with which to work, but its direct function is to strengthen the association of ideas.

Professor Freeman's test results have led him to conclude that the simple memory span, upon which association rests, is almost as strong in the middle-grade period as it will ever be, although the memory for meaningful materials continues to advance until well into maturity. This advance is partly because concentration of attention has been improved with the years and partly because the habit of classification has been formed. Teachers therefore need have no fear that drill is unsuited to the level of development of middle-grade children.

The question remaining is whether or not it is worth while for children to concentrate attention upon the simple types of association which can be made more permanent by drill. The fact that reasoning is so largely dependent on content (one of the explanations why it matures more slowly than sensory processes) would seem to support the thesis that the content which goes to make up simple concepts should be mastered as completely as possible.

The use of drill, then, depends for its validity on two assumptions: the value of certain fixed associations, and the value of providing for individual differences in the fixing of associations by supplying children with equipment for drill on their own difficulties. The second of these two points will be considered at length under the heading "Providing for Drill Exercises" (pp. 97–98).

[1] For a psychological analysis of the drill process see *The Social Studies*, XXV: 28–29 (January, 1934).

Clearly, not all content is of equal value. Some ideas are presented because they are crucial and necessary centers about which to organize other ideas, and some are only supporting details. An attempt must be made to determine by objective methods the relative values of certain historical materials on the simple level appropriate to the function of drill.

Numbers of scientific investigations have concerned themselves with this problem. Such studies of names of persons [1] has determined the emphasis given to different personalities in Parts Two, Three, and Four of this book. Studies of dates and of time comprehension have furnished the basis for the time expressions emphasized.[2] Studies of places [3] have helped to determine the place locations and the place relationships stressed. The special vocabulary exercises have been determined by vocabulary investigations.[4]

The Problem of Time Apprehension

The question of apprehension of time constitutes one of the teacher's most serious problems. Numbers of investigations have shown the inadequacy of children's understanding of time. Many teachers have therefore hastened to the conclusion that the time factor should be completely disregarded in the social-science program, — a conclusion with which the social scientists have registered their complete disagreement.[5] Other teachers have believed that the best way to develop this time sense is to begin with the present and work backward, — a dubious conclusion at best. Fortunately, in practice this counter-chronological method usually resolves itself into a method of *approach* only, not of the entire organization of materials.

The very coherence and continuity so stressed in the foregoing list of objectives [6] and in the principles of selection [7] and organization [8] of materials help to develop the idea of the time stream. So also does human thinking behavior, which "is unquestionably in continuous trains,"[9] and the feeling of sequence afforded by the routine of school life itself.[10]

[1] Reviewed in the bibliography, Nos. 3, 4, 5, 27, 28, 39, 47, 77, 78, on pages 447–455 of W. H. Burton's *The Supervision of Elementary Subjects*. See also R. M. Tryon's *The Teaching of History in Junior and Senior High Schools* (Ginn and Company, 1921).

[2] Ibid. Nos. 32 and 83 in the bibliography of W. H. Burton's *The Supervision of Elementary Subjects*. Reviewed in *The Social Studies*, XXV: 25 (January, 1934); also M. Lucille Harrison's "Nature and Development of Concepts of Time among Young Children," *Elementary School Journal*, XXXIV: 507–514 (March, 1934).

[3] No. 66 in the bibliography of W. H. Burton's *The Supervision of Elementary Subjects*.

[4] Ibid. Nos. 2, 23, 37, 41, 59, 61, 76. See also Kelley and Krey's *Tests and Measurements in the Social Sciences*, Chaps. I, III, VI and the studies listed on pages 227–229.

[5] See C. A. Beard's *The Nature of the Social Sciences*, pp. 189 ff.; Harold Rugg's *Teacher's Guide for an Introduction to Problems of American Culture*, pp. 53–54.

[6] See pages 7 and 8.   [7] See pages 14–19.   [8] See pages 19–25.

[9] J. F. Dashiell, *Fundamentals of Objective Psychology*, p. 526 (Houghton Mifflin Company, 1928).

[10] Charles H. Judd, *Psychology of Secondary Education*. Ginn and Company, 1927.

Investigations [1] indicate that by the age of eight or nine sufficiently definite and clear-cut time concepts have been developed to serve as a basis for training. Presenting to such children materials which are themselves arranged in a topical-chronological order would seem a logical means of developing the time concepts further.

The mastery of number also assists greatly in the ordering of events which can be marked off quantitatively. Dates, then, have relative meaning, just as numbers do; they help in the organization of time. Provided that the number of dates to be learned is kept reasonably small, there is no reason why a date may not mean to middle-grade children much the same thing that it means to adults who are not widely read, that is, relationship of the time of an event with reference to the time of other events which took place before or after it, the time depending on the *number*, or date.

Graphic devices such as a time line or time chart probably help.[2] Children grasp the idea better if they themselves make the chart, adding each event of importance as they study it. The average number of dates included will probably be less than one a week. The time chart may be made on the back of a roll of wallpaper and may extend around the room above the blackboard or under it.

Games may be played by the class. A certain date is selected from the chart. One child stands with his back to the time line, while others hurl at him the names of events studied. He must answer "Before" or "After" with reference to the original date selected.

Another valuable exercise is requiring children to number two events as 1 and 2 in the order in which they occurred.[3] It cannot be too strongly emphasized, however, that if exercises of this sort are to be included in the test, previous practice should have been provided *in this form* of time-testing during the drill periods, although not comprising exactly the same items. After children have demonstrated their ability to handle sets consisting of two items, the number may be increased to three, and in the upper middle grades even to four or five.

Some writers have suggested learning time by centuries rather than by definite dates, but results of experiments in that direction have not been encouraging.[4] Older children should be able to name the centuries correctly, but it is probable that a definite date will be the key to association which will be used.

To summarize, children's understanding of history is partly depend-

[1] Reviewed in *The Social Studies*, XXV: 25 (January, 1934). See also M. Lucille Harrison's "Nature and Development of Concepts of Time among Young Children," *Elementary School Journal*, XXXIV: 507–514 (March, 1934).

[2] See "Sequence in time" in the tabulation on pages 83, 86, 90; also examples of a time chart on pages 137, 295, 501, etc.

[3] See examples on pages 127, 280, 500.

[4] W. H. Winch, "Dates versus Centuries in Teaching Chronology to School Children," *Forum of Education*, VII–VIII: 32–41, 120–129 (February, June, 1930).

ent on their understanding of time. Sequence in stories, the numbering devices of dates and graphic aids, help to hold the train of historical ideas in order. Tests have shown that even untrained children increase rapidly in their mastery of time, and that children who are trained to do so give a satisfactory performance in a time test. Definiteness as to what is expected is of great value. If children know exactly what they are to remember, they can teach and drill themselves to a great extent, the record of their progress furnishing the needed incentive.

Providing for Drill Exercises

In order to provide for individual differences in rate of acquisition and in permanence of fixed associations, it is necessary to devise a plan by which the children can work sometimes individually and sometimes in small groups.

Drill on place locations can best be done at the map. Children may work by twos or in small groups, testing one another on their ability to locate the places selected for drill purposes. After developing skill by means of the type of map on which names are printed, it is helpful to turn to another type on which few names are given, for example, physical maps, to ascertain whether the relative locations are clearly in mind or whether the child is depending on the printed names. The use of maps of different sizes and colors is also helpful, to assist in divorcing mastery from any one medium. Outline maps are useful.

For drill on the names of persons and on dates, cards[1] may be prepared, bearing on one side the name of a person and on the other side his greatest achievement, about which learning is to be focused, or on one side a date and on the other side the event which occurred at that time. There is no difficulty in preparing the legend for the side bearing the name of the person or the date. What is printed on the other side should be stated so clearly that only one right answer is possible and the identification is unmistakable. Drill games may be played with both sides of the cards.

Repetition of the gradations of meaning to be associated with vocabulary terms is probably as necessary as is repetition of other types of association. Meaning has already been developed during the period of discussion,[2] but stating the correct meaning once does not ensure the children's remembering it. Repetition is needed, not to increase speed but to secure clearness. The use of a good children's dictionary is helpful in selecting a phraseology distinct from the *definition*, and not stated as a synonym but embodying the idea in phrases or clauses of child language. Many difficulties are encountered in making adequate statements, and improvements can be made from year to year as experience points out the unsatisfactory items.

[1] See examples on pages 118, 280, 484, etc. A standard size is desirable for ease in filing.
[2] See pages 57–64.

The usual principles of drill apply to history materials, except that speed is not a particularly important factor. The laws of repetition of correct models with attention, distributed practice periods, the detecting of mistakes early in the process, the avoidance of repetition in a fixed series (unless the series as a whole is to be fixed), and cumulative drill on materials as new items are added unit by unit, all are applicable to history. The number of items added at a given time should be small, since amount has a significant relationship to retention.[1]

A common error is the attempt to drill on material which has not yet been thoroughly understood. For this reason drill should not be introduced too early, — not until there has been ample time and opportunity afforded for the assimilation of ideas. In the plan projected here the periods of conversational approach, reading and study, discussion, picture and map study, and general activities all precede drill by the class as a whole. Any time after the general activities have been initiated seems appropriate for beginning short periods of drill, to be repeated for several days. Cumulative addition of new items without dropping the old helps to keep them all in mind.

As to *how* the drill cards are to be used, a wide range of choices is possible. It is desirable to have them accessible to the children any time after the later part of their period of reading and study, so that they may prepare themselves, individually or in small groups. Each child may develop the habit of carrying with him during the period of practice a paper on which he jots down the items about which he makes mistakes. He then knows which items are difficult for him, and concentrates his efforts on those. By the time the class is ready for the drill games each child has in this way had ample opportunity to prepare himself. During the drill games, also, each child keeps a record of his mistakes and does remedial work preparatory to the testing period. A graphic record of the test scores helps to motivate all such individual drill.

Testing

The essay type of examination was never widely used in the middle grades because of the mechanical difficulties in written expression. Tests of many kinds have long been used, however. The questions asked on the readings constitute one kind of test, and the products produced by projects furnish another; they exhibit the clearness of comprehension and range of detail mastered. The discussion[2] furnishes a splendid opportunity for testing. All these may properly be classified as teaching tests with the objective of diagnosis and remedy.

[1] William Pyle, *Psychology of Learning*, p. 129 (Warwick and York, 1921).
[2] See pages 57–64.

When the objective-test movement first reached the field of the social studies in the middle grades it found there a virgin territory. After the first few years of enthusiastic use, however, the movement slowed down considerably because of the difficulties that had presented themselves.[1]

The chief difficulty was the failure of the social scientists to agree on the desirable objectives to be achieved, the content or subject matter to be included, and the relative values. Accordingly the testing movement in the social sciences came to a halt for several years. The scientific investigations referred to above[2] made some progress toward determining relative values in certain limited aspects of American history, but the larger aspects remained untouched.

For this reason many progressive teachers have reacted against the whole testing theory. Instead of attempting to agree on objectives and content and then devising more effective instruments to measure values, they have dispensed with all attempt at measurement. Such a reaction is typical of American school practice.[3]

But to continue series of child experiences over a period of years without any attempt to appraise results is too great a social risk to be undertaken lightly. All but the extremists now realize that some form of testing is not only necessary but desirable [4] if education is to advance beyond the stage of blind wandering in a fog or wishful thinking. Educators may not know yet how to carry on such testing, but they know that it should be done. An obvious line of attack is the *improvement of the measuring instrument* or the devising of new instruments.

Tests of Facts

For the reasons stated above, the tests in the social sciences have not advanced far beyond the fact level. On this level, however, a considerable degree of improvement has been effected. Many statistical problems have been solved, and the greater degree of objectivity on the question of relative values has led to the exclusion of much of the unimportant detail. The best of the standard tests at present are criticized not so much on the basis of what they do as on the basis of what they do not do. There is rather general agreement that their exercises are better tests of important facts than would be any tests made hurriedly by the teacher whose grasp of subject matter is inadequate and whose technique of test construction is faulty in the extreme.

The best of the existing tests, then, may be conceded to do well

[1] See Harold Rugg's "After Three Decades of Scientific Method in Education," *Teachers College Record*, XXXVI: 111–122 (November, 1934).

[2] See first four footnotes, p. 95.

[3] As in the case of "methods" described on pages 32–34 above.

[4] J. L. Stenquist, "Recent Developments in the Uses of Tests," *Review of Educational Research*, III: 49–61 (February, 1933); also Chapter XIII in the Fourteenth Yearbook of the Department of Superintendence of the National Education Association (1936).

what they have attempted, but there are important aspects of the whole problem of measurement which have not been attempted successfully. These lie largely outside the field of facts.

The testing on persons, places, dates, and simple events may be rendered extremely effective by the great variety of cumulative exercises which have preceded it, — by the study-guide questions (pp. 43–44), the discussion (p. 57), the picture and map study (p. 64), the projects (p. 69), and the drill exercises (p. 94). Many years of experience show conclusively that lower middle-grade children *can* make satisfactory progress in the learning of facts, with no diminution of interest or enjoyment, and that they can be stimulated to use these facts in situations which call for reasoning.

The tests on persons, places, and dates [1] in Parts Two, Three, and Four of this book are designed to give help to teachers in the testing of basic facts.

In view of the necessity for providing mental *content* before reasoning can take place, administrators and supervisors need not feel apologetic in the least because their teachers test for facts.[2] If the teachers *teach only for facts*, however, they are derelict in their duty, and the supervisory force needs to turn its attention to the problem of training them to prepare for and give other types of tests.

A strong protest is again registered against a practice in which the statisticians have engaged in the making of even the fact tests. Without giving adequate consideration to the widely varying circumstances, they have assumed that a satisfactory picture of what children *can* do may be obtained by a picture of what they *are doing*. For example, a picture of adequate fourth-grade performance is supposed to be gained if the conditions of random sampling are met. In certain fields this assumption might be justified, — conceivably in arithmetic, where life experience tends constantly to reinforce school instruction, or in general reading, where children have at least been exposed to one type of reading material. But in the social sciences the assumption fails completely to meet the facts.

For example, some fourth grades still give no opportunity whatever for the reading of history stories, and the communities in which they are situated provide only the scantiest of such materials, if any at all. If a child has never even heard of Cortez or the spinning jenny or mass production, not only is he unable to reason about such subjects, but he cannot by any process known to man even teach himself the facts. To draw from such data conclusions about what fourth-grade

---

[1] See pages 138–139, 294–296, 527, and the tabulations on pages 82, 85, 89.

[2] In fact, a high correlation exists (.58) between knowledge of American history as measured by tests and liberal attitudes on civic problems. See the *School Review*, XLII: 54–55 (January, 1934).

children can or cannot or should or should not learn about the social sciences is vicious in the extreme. Examples from one "average" school system which has at least *tried* to expose its children to the materials on which they are to be tested are worth examples from hundreds of school systems in which the children have had no such opportunities, in formal training, in informal reading, or in incidental experience.

Tests of Understanding [1]

There is doubtless a difference between knowledge of facts and *understanding* of movements. That the one is necessary to the other, however, is obvious.

A valuable contribution to this question of understanding was made by the Commission on the Social Studies of the American Historical Association.[2] The study was limited to terms involving relationships, in which was found steady and consistent growth. Here again, however, the picture shows what *is* and not what *can be* or *should be.*

The exercises in vocabulary development (pp. 63–64), vocabulary drill (p. 64), and vocabulary testing (p. 64), as well as the suggestions for wide reading which follow in Parts Two, Three, and Four of this book, are aimed directly at the development of such understanding as the commission had in mind.

Tests at the end of each unit, as well as at the end of each story, are particularly helpful in diagnosing different kinds of understanding. If the elements of time, place, persons, and terms are provided with separate test exercises, the teacher may be able to discover the specific difficulties of individual children.

1. A particular child's chief difficulty may be with time relationships, and he therefore needs special help in drawing time lines, drilling on date-event cards, and arranging events in time order.
2. Another child does not visualize the locational setting and needs help through modeling sand-table maps, locating places on wall maps, and making maps. It may even be that poor eyesight is the cause of his weakness.
3. The difficulty of another child may be that he does not associate names of persons with events, and needs more repetition.
4. A very common error is the lack of understanding of historical terms (see the discussion of vocabulary on pages 60–64).

In fairness to the commission it should be recognized that a study going more deeply into the understanding of movements must await

[1] See A. C. Krey and E. B. Wesley's "Does the New Type Test Measure Results of Instruction in the Social Studies?" in *Historical Outlook*, XXIII: 7–21 (January, 1932), and E. B. Wesley's "Facts or Ideas in the Social Studies?" in *Historical Outlook*, XXIV: 28–30 (January, 1933).

[2] Kelley and Krey, *Tests and Measurements in the Social Sciences*, chaps. i–iii, vi; also Appendix I.

a larger degree of agreement as to the *content* of the social-science program. Grade placement is, by comparison, a simpler problem for the determination of which known techniques can be applied. But until the whole matter of subject content has been placed on a more secure foundation than divergent opinion or theory, little progress can be made in the study of understanding on a nation-wide scale.

It is gratifying to discover, however, that the many years of study and effort which the commission devoted to its arduous task resulted in a statement of objectives on which there is very substantial agreement on the part of the field, from extreme right wing to extreme left. Since so much has been accomplished in a field hitherto in chaos, perhaps greater unanimity in the even more baffling problem of content may be hoped for eventually.

Exercises in Reasoning [1]

Knowledge of facts is not the same as understanding of movements, and neither is comprehension the same as reasoning. Investigations have shown that knowledge of facts does not of necessity bring ability to use the facts in reasoning.[2] Objective exercises which test reasoning are, however, so difficult to devise that the experience of the commission with such tests seems to have discouraged them completely.

An examination of the conditions under which their tests were given suggests the causes of the unsatisfactory results. The children tested had obviously in many cases never been exposed to such reasoning materials, and they were completely at sea as to what was expected. Equally obviously, their teachers had not understood the ends aimed at and had not directed the teaching along those lines. The results simply show that the children tested did not possess the abilities aimed at. No conclusion can be drawn as to how children of the same age and at the same grade level might have responded *if they had been exposed to the materials and had been differently taught.*

The discussion of reasoning and its development (pages 79–94 above) points out clearly the dependence of children's reasoning upon their direct experience, and the way that experience is utilized by the teacher as a foundation for new content. If experience is totally lacking, or if the teacher fails to make the necessary tie-up from the old to the new, discouraging results are to be expected.

---

[1] See Chapter IV in Kelley and Krey's *Tests and Measurements in the Social Sciences* (in this instance somewhat ambiguously labeled "Skills") and also *Conclusions and Recommendations*, pp. 96–101. For dissenting views see Ernest Horn's "Another Chapter on Tests for the volume of 'Conclusions and Recommendations,'" *Social Studies*, XXVI: 13–22 (January, 1935); and M. E. Haggerty's "The Low Visibility of Educational Issues," *School and Society*, XLI: 273–282 (1935).

[2] Ralph W. Tyler, "Measuring the Ability to Infer," *Educational Research Bulletin*, IX: 475–480 (November, 1930); Joseph C. Dewey, "The Acquisition of Facts as a Measure of Reading Comprehension," *Elementary School Journal*, XXXV: 346–348 (January, 1935).

But to maintain that adequate exercises in reasoning can be, and have been, devised is not to maintain that they can be applied on a nation-wide scale. The difficulties in using a particular reasoning test on a nation-wide scale are manifold.

1. The social-science program varies so greatly in different parts of the country that exposure to given materials cannot be assumed.
2. The reading materials accessible to children vary equally widely. If they do not supply the factual background needed as content for reasoning, the techniques of reasoning cannot be applied.
3. Attempting to overcome the two former difficulties by printing given paragraphs in a test in order to supply content does not solve the difficulties. The materials are taken out of their context and the long cumulative background in understanding of what went before is missing. The conditions do not supply a fair set-up for testing reasoning.
4. On the other hand, the particular exercises chosen for testing reasoning may have been included by chance in the children's own preparation in some schools. Their texts may have printed the solution outright, as a statement. If so, the recall of such statements tests memory rather than reasoning power.
5. And, lastly, the great body of teachers who are themselves inadequately prepared can give little direction or guidance to children's native ability to reason. Children so taught will do poorly until they have had much opportunity to develop their reasoning powers through text or manual suggestions. The results of any reasoning test for such children will fail to show what they might be able to do under different conditions.

However discouraging the prospects may be for the perfecting of nation-wide tests in reasoning, there can be no doubt that tests have been devised which are applicable wherever conditions are roughly similar.[1] For example, wherever the course of study indicates exposure to roughly similar materials, wherever the reading opportunities are somewhat the same, and wherever there is not too great divergence in the quality of the school population or the teaching personnel, the same test of reasoning may be applied with expectations of fairly satisfactory results. Such conditions might apply within a given school system or within a group of systems where the opportunities which were offered approximated one another on the whole.

Preceding the *test* in reasoning should naturally occur many *exercises* demanding reasoning, for the child needs not only content but also some degree of mastery over the technique of the process itself. Numerous opportunities for such exercises appear during the integrated technique under consideration in this book, in the questions on the reading (pp. 43–44), in the discussion (pp. 57–64), in the projects of various kinds (pp. 69–77), and in the application to present-day conditions (pp. 77–79),

[1] See E. F. Lindquist and H. R. Anderson's "The Improvement of Objective Testing in History," Second Yearbook of the National Council for the Social Studies, pp. 97–117 (1932).

as well as in the exercises specifically labeled "exercises in reasoning" (pp. 79–94). It will be noticed that exercises in reasoning are provided for every subunit in Parts Two, Three, and Four, preceding tests in reasoning, which are also given for each story.

The text studied must give the factual material necessary to accomplish the tasks suggested, but it should not answer the questions directly. Otherwise the child is tested only as to his memory, not as to his reasoning powers. For example, "Compare colonial fireplaces with our methods of heating today" is *not* a reasoning exercise if the text which has been read makes the comparison itself. "Why were the white people able to defeat the Indians?" is not a reasoning exercise if the text supplies the answer and the children only repeat it as given.

Moreover, any test of reasoning must give children time to think. Quick jumping at conclusions and snap judgments cannot be prevented if children are under pressure of time. But as soon as they are in possession of the basic facts they should be led to advance to the *meanings behind the facts.*

It is to be noticed that the exercises in developing reasoning are termed "exercises" rather than "tests" (see pages 79–105 for examples). The purpose of this terminology is to impress upon the minds of teachers the fact that such exercises are designed to help ascertain the mental growth and development of children, and not to serve as means for determining marks or grades to be assigned.

The tabulation on pages 82–91 shows the specific instances in which provision has been made for both exercises and tests of the sort described.

Special mention should be made of the tests and exercises involving the organization of materials. The tabulations on pages 83–84, 87, 91 show that organization is accomplished, on the middle-grade level, chiefly by listing, by summarizing, and by outlining.

The values of organization are variously stated as follows: Koffka[1] says, "Learning consists essentially in an organization of the whole procedure." Pyle[2] says, "The most significant aspect of memory is organization." And John Dewey[3] agrees, "The growth is through logical organization of subject matter."

Newlun's[4] experiment in the use of summaries showed that

most children . . . can be taught to summarize in history by devoting a portion of their class period to this training for a period of twelve weeks or less. . . . Summarizing in history, if properly developed and used, can improve the achievement in history.

[1] Koffka, *The Growth of the Mind*, p. 176 (Harcourt, Brace and Company, Inc., 1924).
[2] William Pyle, *Psychological Principles Applied to Teaching*, p. 118 (Warwick and York, 1924). [3] *How We Think*, p. 39.
[4] Chester O. Newlun, *Teaching Children to Summarize in Fifth-Grade History*, Teachers College Contributions to Education, No. 404. Bureau of Publications, Columbia University, 1930.

The result of a year's work in teaching fourth-grade children to make outlines was reported to the writer by Miss Nelle Moore, then of the State Teachers' College at Oshkosh, Wisconsin. She reported that by the end of the year 25 per cent of the children were able to make acceptable outlines independently, while the rest of the group worked with the teacher in the making of a co-operative outline.

The view of the whole story which can be achieved through some form of organization helps children to keep in mind the important points and to subordinate details. It also helps them to follow varying thought patterns.

Tests of Skills

A useful analysis of skills in the social studies was made for the Commission.[1] The tests administered to determine possession of those skills, however, yielded negative results. But, again, it is not necessary to conclude because of those findings that children of the same ages and grade levels *cannot* master the skills enumerated. No one seems to question the desirability of such mastery, and the experience of favorably conditioned school systems shows that it can be achieved. More satisfactory results throughout the nation as a whole await the better preparation of teachers and the more widespread use of adequate materials of instruction.

The tabulations on pages 84, 87–88, 91 indicate where specific examples of exercises involving skills may be found. They comprise map-reading, map-making, location exercises, interpreting pictures, and using books (index, table of contents, unit half-title pages, running heads, summaries, etc.). The examples serve as suggestions. Naturally, however, much better exercises can be devised when reference is made to interpreting a particular picture or map[2] rather than to pictures and maps in general. Likewise, while exercises involving the use of the index and of reference books may be of general value, those referring to a specific table of contents and to specific chapter, page, and topic headings are much more helpful in the development of skills.[2]

Graphic Records of Test Scores

The experimental literature of education abounds in investigations[3] showing the value of keeping records of test scores, of children's noticing

---

[1] See "Skills," pp. 57–75, 234–339 in Kelley and Krey's *Tests and Measurements in the Social Sciences.* See also Howard R. Anderson's "Testing Basic Skills in the Social Studies," *Elementary School Journal,* XXXVI : 424–435 (February, 1936).

[2] See, for example, the teachers' manuals to accompany Kelty's *The Beginnings of the American People and Nation,* and Kelty's *The Growth of the American People and Nation.*

[3] See S. L. Pressey's *Psychology and the New Education,* pp. 94–96; the Twenty-ninth Yearbook of the National Society for the Study of Education, Part II, pp. 611–621 (1930); and Thomas S. Kirby's *Practice in the Case of School Children* (Teachers College Contributions to Education, Bureau of Publications, Columbia University, 1913).

their own progress on successive tests and graphing the results, and of assistance furnished thereby to teachers in the ascertaining of weaknesses in the test items or in their own teaching, or in both. Since the child's reward of effort should be the satisfaction derived from success, since it should be inherent in the situation and the teacher should not "hand out" satisfaction or annoyance, it follows that the child should see clearly whether he succeeded or failed, and to what extent. A graphic record makes the results appear objective and impersonal but unmistakable. He then enjoys having something definite to work for, working for it, and seeing definite results.

That the test scores need not be used to spur the competitive spirit is obvious. If desired, each child's graphic record may be kept by the child himself in a notebook at his own desk, and no invidious comparisons with others need be made.

The number of records kept can be reduced to a minimum. Records should not mechanize the learning process, nor make the teacher merely a timekeeper in the educational business world. A usable form for class results is shown in W. H. Burton's *Supervision of Elementary Subjects*, p. 434, Table No. 1. The form kept by each child to follow his own progress may be most easily understood by reducing the raw scores to per cents before graphing.

Remedial Work [1]

Probably the best advice that can be given with regard to remedial work is to adjust expectations according to ability and to utilize such a variety of meaningful experiences before the testing stage arrives that the need for remedial work is reduced to a minimum. Often testing has been introduced too early, and often it has been preceded by no other activities than reading and questioning. The technique under discussion in this book provides for a variety of activities. After those activities are completed or are well under way, specific drill is introduced, and formal testing is postponed to a late stage in the learning process.

A test is given at the end of every story; consequently ample opportunity is provided for discovering weaknesses and correcting misapprehensions as the work progresses. The test over the entire unit, given when the work has been completed, proves the efficacy of such remedial work as was done after the test on each story. (See the discussion of the diagnosis of unit tests on page 101.)

Some specific suggestions as to the conduct of such work have already been given: requiring children to keep a record of their own mistakes during drill (p. 98), encouraging them to ask the study-guide questions

[1] See L. J. Brueckner and E. O. Melby's *Diagnostic and Remedial Teaching* (Houghton Mifflin Company, 1931), and *Educational Diagnosis*, The Thirty-fourth Yearbook of the National Society for the Study of Education (Public School Publishing Company, Bloomington, Illinois, 1935).

of one another and allowing them to practice together on the drill materials (p. 97).

Moreover, when the test papers have been corrected and returned to the writers (as they *always* should be) each child should be required to correct his mistakes. The corrected test papers may well be filed in a notebook. Often children who made no mistakes may help those who made mistakes, hearing them give the right answer before any correcting is done on the test paper itself.

Not the least of the diagnostic values is the assistance given the teacher in diagnosing the particular respects in which her own presentations of meanings have been faulty, and in locating the places at which she has attempted to skim over materials too hastily. An examination of the particular test items on which most children failed may also show that the item itself was faulty in construction or in wording.

The test questions should be stated in a form of wording different from that used in the text. *Neither the test questions nor the answers should employ the same wording as does the text.* Care in this matter will help to prevent word memory or mere verbalism.

Lists of History Tests for Middle Grades

Standard tests in history are available as parts of batteries for middle-grade use, such as the following:

Metropolitan Achievement Tests: "History, Grades 4–8." World Book Company.

Modern School Achievement Tests: "History and Civics, Grades 3–9." Bureau of Publications, Teachers College, Columbia University.

New Stanford Achievement Tests: "History and Civics, Grades 4–9." World Book Company.

Public School Achievement Test: "History, Grades 5–8." Public School Publishing Company, Bloomington, Illinois.

Unit Scales of Attainment: "American History, Grades 4–8." Educational Test Bureau, Minneapolis, Minnesota.

Certain history tests have been standardized to measure achievement in entire fields of history, from the middle grades on, as follows:

Co-operative History Tests. Co-operative Test Service, New York City.

History Tests for Grades 4–7. Maryland State Department of Education.

PENNELL, *Boston Research Tests in United States History:* "Grades 6–8." Boston Public Schools, Boston, Massachusetts.

PRESSEY and RICHARDS, *Test on Understanding of American History:* "Grades 6–12." Public School Publishing Company, Bloomington, Illinois.

RAYNER, *American History Test:* "Elementary Grades." University of Illinois Bureau of Research, Urbana, Illinois.

VAN WAGENEN. *Revised American History Scales:* "Grade 5 to High School." Bureau of Publications, Teachers College, Columbia University.

Other tests cover certain phases of the learning of history at any level, such as the following:

PRESSEY, L. C. *Test of Special Vocabulary of History.* Public School Publishing Company, Bloomington, Illinois.

And still others cover the same phases but are directed especially toward the middle-grade and upper-grade level, such as the following:

KELTY-MOORE, *Test of Concepts in the Social Studies.* Charles Scribner's Sons.

From an examination of the lists given above, it becomes evident that the teacher has much assistance at her command in giving an inventory test at the beginning of the year and also in testing an entire field at the end of the year. As yet, however, no good standard instruments are available for unit testing. The tests which appear at the end of each unit in Parts Two, Three, and Four of this book have been widely used for a number of years but have not been standardized.

The tests of understanding given at the end of each story hereinafter have likewise been subjected to a decade of experimental use but are not standardized. The tests in reasoning and skills suggested in connection with each story are new.

If the teacher does not choose to use such helps, she will be obliged to devise tests of her own.[1]

A Suggested Time Distribution

Experienced teachers will have no difficulty in planning the activities of the basic technique, which have been described in the previous pages, in terms of the time units of their own school systems. In a program of integration the problem is simple, as the periods are usually flexible.

In the separate-studies program, with fixed hours for each subject, planning in terms of correlation of subjects is essential. In the more progressive schools teachers feel the advisability of devoting more time to the social studies than the scant fifteen minutes to twenty-five minutes each for geography and history in the middle grades which represent the maximum of the practice at present.[2] Correlation makes this possible.

---

[1] See Truman L. Kelley's "Objective Measurement of the Outcomes of the Social Studies," *Historical Outlook,* XXI: 66–72 (February, 1930); W. J. Osburn's "Selection of Test Items," *Review of Educational Research,* III: 21–32 (February, 1933); Howard R. Anderson and Everett F. Lindquist's "The Improvement of Objective Testing in History," Second Yearbook of the National Council for the Social Studies (1932); M. J. Stormzand's *Study-Guide Tests in American History: Part One, 1492–1860; Part Two, 1815 to the Present* (The Macmillan Company, 1925); W. J. Osburn's *Are We Making Good at Teaching History?* (Public School Publishing Company, 1926); and G. M. Ruch and others, *Objective or New-Type Examination* (Scott, Foresman and Company, 1929).

[2] See Mann's *How Schools Use their Time,* p. 97 (Teachers College Contributions to Education, No. 333 (1928), Bureau of Publications, Columbia University); Covert's *Time Allotments in Selected Consolidated Schools,* p. 2 (United States Department of the Interior, Office of Education, 1930); and the Fourteenth Yearbook of the Department of Superintendence of the National Education Association, pp. 67, 70–80 (1936). Harold Rugg, in *Culture and Education in America,* states that investigations have shown the necessity and the possibility of a social-studies program of two to two and a half hours daily.

A SUGGESTED TIME DISTRIBUTION FOR EARLY AMERICAN HISTORY (AS OUTLINED IN PART TWO) FOR SCHOOLS HAVING A YEAR OF THIRTY-SIX WEEKS

Unit One	Unit Two	Unit Three	Unit Four	Unit Five
Six Weeks	Eight Weeks	Seven Weeks	Seven Weeks	Eight Weeks
Story 1 . . . . . *One week*	A	A	A	A
Story 2 . . . . . *One week*	Story 1 . . . . . *One week*	Stories 1 and 2 . *One week*	Stories 1 and 2 . *One week*	Story 1 . . . . *One week*
Story 3 . . . . . *One week*	Story 2 . . . . . *One week*	Story 3 . . . . *One week*	Stories 3 and 4 . *One week*	B
Story 4 . . . . . *One week*	Story 3 . . . . . *One week*	Story 4 . . . . *One week*	B	Story 1 . . . . *One week*
Story 5 . . . . . *One week*	Story 4 . . . . . *One week*	Stories 5 and 6 . *One week*	Story 1 . . . *One week*	Story 2 . . . . *Seven days*
Story 6 (including the unit tests) . . . . . *One week*	B	B	C	Story 3 . . . . *Four days*
	Stories 1 and 2 . *One week*	Stories 1 and 2 . *Six days*	Stories 1 and 2 . *One week*	Story 4 . . . . *Four days*
	Story 3 . . . . . *One week*	Story 3 . . . *Four days*	Story 3 . . . } D . *One week*	Story 5 . . . . *One week*
	C	Stories 4 and 5 (including the unit tests) *One week*	Story 1 . . . *Four days*	C
	Stories 1 and 2 . *One week*		Stories 2 and 3 . *One week*	Story 1 . . . . *Four days*
	Story 3 (including the unit tests) . . . . *One week*		Stories 4 and 5 (including the unit tests) *One week*	Story 2 (including the unit tests) . . . . *Six days*

A SUGGESTED TIME DISTRIBUTION FOR LATER AMERICAN HISTORY (AS OUTLINED IN PART THREE) FOR SCHOOLS HAVING A YEAR OF THIRTY-SIX WEEKS

Unit One Four Weeks	Unit Two Six Weeks	Unit Three Five Weeks	Unit Four Five Weeks	Unit Five Four Weeks	Unit Six Five Weeks	Unit Seven Seven Weeks
Stories A, 1, 2 — One week	Stories A, 1, 2 — One week	Stories A, 1, 2, 3 — One week	Stories A, 1, 2, 3, 4, 5 — One week	Story A, 1 — One week	Stories A, 1, 2, 3 — One week	Story A, 1 and Story B, 1 — One week
Stories A, 3, 4 — One week	Stories A, 3, 4 — One week	Stories A, 4, 5, 6 — One week	Stories B, 1, 2, 3 — One week	Stories B, 1, 2 — One week	Stories A, 4, 5 — One week	Stories B, 2, 3 — One week
Story A, 5 and Story B, 1 — One week	Stories A, 5, 6 — One week	Story A, 7 and Stories B, 1, 2 — One week	Stories B, 4, 5, 6 — One week	Stories B, 3, 4 — One week	Stories B, 1, 2, 3 — One week	Stories 4, 5, 6 — One week
Stories B, 2, 3 (including the unit tests) — One week	Stories A, 7, 8, 9 — One week	Stories B, 3, 4 and Story C, 1 — One week	Stories C, 1, 2 — One week	Stories B, 5, 6 (including the unit tests) — One week	Stories C, 1, 2, 3 — One week	Story C, 1 — One week
	Stories B, 1, 2 — One week	Story C, 2 and Stories D, 1, 2 (including the unit tests) — One week	Stories C, 3, 4 (including the unit tests) — One week		Stories D, 1, 2 and Story E, 1 (including the unit tests) — One week	Story C, 2 — One week
	Stories B, 3, 4, 5 (including the unit tests) — One week					Story C, 3 and Story D, 1 — One week
						Stories D, 2, 3, 4 (including the unit tests) — One week

A SUGGESTED TIME DISTRIBUTION FOR "THE BEGINNINGS OF CIVILIZATION" (AS OUTLINED IN PART FOUR) FOR SCHOOLS HAVING A YEAR OF THIRTY-SIX WEEKS

Unit One	Unit Two	Unit Three	Unit Four	Unit Five	Unit Six
Five Weeks	Six Weeks	Six Weeks	Six Weeks	Seven Weeks	Six Weeks
Story 1 . . . Two weeks	Story 1 . Two weeks	Story 1 . . One week	Story 1 . . One week	Stories 1 and 2 One week	Story 1 . . One week
Story 2 . . . One week	Story 2 . Two weeks	Story 2 . . One week	Story 2 . . One week	Stories 3 and 4 One week	Story 2 . . One week
Story 3 . . One week	Story 3 . One week	Story 3 . . One week	Story 3 . . One week	Stories 5 and 6 One week	Story 3 . . One week
Story 4 (including the unit tests)	Story 4 (including the unit tests)	Story 4 . . Two weeks	Story 4 . . Two weeks	Story 7 . . . One week	Story 4 . . One week
One week	One week	Story 5 (including the unit tests)	Story 5 (including the unit tests)	Story 8 . . . One week	Story 5 . . One week
		One week	One week	Story 9 . . . One week	Story 6 (including the unit tests)
				Story 10 (including the unit tests)	One week
				One week	

The subunits which follow in Parts Two, Three, and Four are planned on the basis of a week's work each. A possible weekly time distribution follows:

First day	Conversational approach and reading
Second day	Reading
Third day	Reading
	Discussion (language period)
	Multisensory aids (art period)
Fourth day	Creative activities (art period) (planned during this period; may occupy several days)
	Application to present-day conditions and exercises in reasoning (language period)
	Drill and report on activities (other than art)
Fifth day	Testing and remedial work

The time distribution of the work of an entire year of thirty-six weeks for each of the three fields described in this book may be planned as shown in the tables on pages 109–111.

Equipment

Many studies of equipment [1] which have been made are very helpful to teachers, supervisors, and administrators in laying out programs toward fitting the schools for the tasks they have to perform. Administrators, on the whole, are becoming convinced of the necessity for adequate laboratory facilities for the social sciences on the high-school and junior-high-school levels. In exceptional cases they are also providing suitable equipment for the middle grades, but such cases are in the woeful minority. Some systems which provide a dozen sets of readers for the primary grades and room libraries for the upper grades still seem to feel that one textbook (often an antiquated one at that!) for each subject is sufficient for the middle grades. Quite possibly they might find in that same spot the weakness in the cumulative growth of children.

Few suggestions are available for building up adequate social-science equipment specifically for the middle grades. To assist in remedying such a deficiency, the following list is offered. It makes no attempt to list every piece of equipment that should be in the room, but focuses attention on materials needed for social science.

---

[1] Of special value is J. W. Baldwin's *The Social Studies Laboratory* (Teachers College Contributions to Education, No. 371. Bureau of Publications, Columbia University, 1929); a special section is devoted to Grades 4 to 6. See also Rose Knox's *School and Equipment* (Houghton Mifflin Company, 1927).

EQUIPMENT NEEDED FOR THE STUDY OF HISTORY
IN THE MIDDLE GRADES[1]

I. Books

Textbooks. See the lists on pages 45–46.
For extensive reading see the lists on pages 48–49.
For the lower group see the lists on pages 54–55.
For recreational reading, lists may be assembled from the specific books given
  for each story in Parts Two, Three, and Four.
Dramatic readers. See the books listed under "Creative Activities" for each story.
Reference books. See the books referred to or needed under "General Activities"
  for each story. Add

> A good children's encyclopedia
> An unabridged dictionary
> A children's dictionary
> An atlas
> A historical atlas

Books of illustrations, such as the Pageant of America series.

II. Pictured materials, including graphs, diagrams, etc.

Flat pictures
Wall pictures   } A list may be assembled from the suggestions under "Multi-
Slides   } sensory Aids" for each story in Parts Two, Three, and Four.
Motion pictures

III. Maps

One good set of wall maps for American history; one set for European history
One set of slated maps
Outline maps for seat use (preferably showing water bodies in color or land
  bodies in shading)
One globe

IV. Cards, of uniform size (for the drill cards)

V. Tests

Intelligence, achievement, and vocabulary tests
Mimeographed tests and exercises for each story and unit, if not supplied in
  printed form.

VI. Construction materials

Drawing and painting materials: paper, colored crayons, paints, equipment for
  hanging pictures, paste, etc.
Manual training equipment: saws, hammers, nails, stains, paints, knives, etc.

VII. General equipment of the room

Ample bookshelf space
Ample cupboard and storage space with plenty of shelf room
Filing cabinets for pictures, drill charts, tests, pupil records
Individual lockers for children
Portable lantern
Stereoscopes
Sand table (a good size is 8 ft. by $3\frac{1}{2}$ ft.), zinc-lined
Bulletin board

[1] See *Aids to Teaching in the Elementary School*, Thirteenth Yearbook of the Department
of Elementary School Principals of the National Education Association (1934). See also
Edgar C. Bye's *A Bibliography of the Teaching of the Social Studies*, Revised Edition (The
H. W. Wilson Company, 1933).

Card catalogues of equipment of various sorts
Worktables
Running water
Movable seats

VIII. School equipment

Rotary mimeograph
Typewriter
Block-printing set
Phonograph and phonograph records
Radio
Museum collections
Camera
Periodicals

PART TWO. LEARNING AND TEACHING EARLY AMERICAN HISTORY

UNIT ONE · *Why Men wanted to find a Short Route to the East* [*6 Weeks*

ADDITIONAL STORIES FOR MORE ADVANCED READERS

The Northmen in Europe and America

STORY 1. MARCO POLO [*1 Week*

Conversational Approach

"How many of you went on trips last summer? Did anyone go outside our state? Did any go outside the United States? How long did the trips take? Did any of you travel by any other way than by automobile or by railroad?

"Today we begin a story about a boy who lived long, long ago, and who took a trip longer than any of yours. It took him three years just to go to the country he visited. Do you suppose he went by automobile, railway, or steamship? Why not?"

At this point the teacher shows a map of Europe, northern Africa, and Asia modeled in the sand table, with the water bodies lined with blue paper. A flat map or even a relief map will not serve nearly so well in aiding these inexperienced children to distinguish between land and water bodies. The teacher tells the name of the boy traveler and writes the word on the board [*Marco Polo*]. She also points out on the sand table his outward route. Several children trace the same route.

"For some reason this boy did not even know how his father looked. What might the reason have been?" Children offer conjectures. "The story will tell you."

Reading and Study

The class is now divided into two groups: the Independent Readers and the Lower Group. They remain in the same classroom and carry on their activities at the same time. The Independent Readers proceed by themselves while the teacher helps the Lower Group.

The Reading Periods

Independent Readers

This group reads the entire story through silently, as given in their textbook. After the reading they test their comprehension by the study-guide questions furnished by the teacher or the textbook. If they cannot answer (to themselves) they must reread. They should not write the answers.

Texts

BARKER, DODD, WEBB, *Our Nation Begins*, 40–47.

BURNHAM and JACK, *Beginnings of Our Country*, 24–28.

CLARK-GORDY, *Westward toward America*, 325–331.

KELTY, *Beginnings of the American People and Nation*, 7–18.

KNOWLTON and WHEELER, *Our Past in Western Europe*, 168–177 (hard).

NIDA, *Following Columbus*, 18–22.

SMALLIDGE and PAXSON, *Finding America*, 1–5, 30–37.

Extensive Reading

FARIS, *Real Stories of the Geography Makers*, 48–54.

FIELD, *Finding the New World*, 30–49.

FOOTE and SKINNER, *Explorers and Founders of America*, 18–23.

HAAREN and POLAND, *Famous Men of the Middle Ages*, 213–218.

JONES, *Geography by Discovery*, 16–34.

MILLER, *My Bookhouse*, II : 204–205.

SHAW, *Discoverers and Explorers*, 16–22.

SOUTHWORTH, *Builders of Our Country*, I : 10–23.

TAPPAN, *European Hero Stories*, 152–156.

TERRY, *History Stories of Other Lands*, IV : 170–174.

VAN LOON, *Short History of Discovery*, 52–57.

Lower Group

If these children are very much below grade in reading ability, the teacher should first tell them the story orally, writing on the board the names of the principal persons and places as she mentions them. Children practice the pronunciations.

Then the teacher and this group read together the story as given in the text. The teacher guides the silent reading, section by section, by the same type of questions that she would use in a silent-reading period; for example, "Read to find out where Marco Polo's father and uncle had been."

After the entire story has been read in this manner the children test themselves by the study-guide questions.

Other Books

HANCOCK, Children of History : *Later Times*, 45–52.

Reading for Recreation (*Both Groups*)

The teacher puts on the bookshelf for recreational reading for both groups such books as

COLE, *The A B C Book of People*.

ELDRIDGE, *Yen-Foh*.

KENT, *He Went with Marco Polo* (harder).

The Discussion

The children give complete answers to the study-guide questions. This exercise gives the opportunity for clearing up half comprehensions and for correcting misapprehensions. The teacher insists on the children's using their own words rather than the words in the book.

She writes on the board the words *Far East, overland, route*. Children discuss the meanings.

Multisensory Aids

The teacher and the children talk over together the pictures in the text. Features of historical significance should be noted, such as the methods of transportation used and the costumes.

GABRIEL (Ed.). Pageant of America, I, 80–83.
National Geographic Magazine, XLIII : 745–780 (June, 1933).
MILLER. *Picturesque Tale of Progress*, VII : 11–24, 199–203.
Yale Pageant Educational Slides : 3.

Music. Play phonograph records of Rimsky-Korsakoff's *Scheherazade Suite*, Ketèlbey's "In a Chinese Temple Garden," and Tschaikowsky's "Danse Chinoise" from the *Nutcracker Suite*.

General Activities

Creative Activities: Group and Individual, Correlated with Other Subjects or Voluntary Projects

Committees of children mark Venice and China on the sand table. They construct ships and camels and load them with the articles mentioned in the text. With these ships and camels they illustrate the outward journey and the return journey.

Volunteers write a title-page for Marco Polo's book. (See Kelty's *How Our Civilization Began*, pp. 251, 325; Compton's Pictured Encyclopedia, B, pp. 175–181.)

Children may make designs for a headpiece for the story.

A traveler to China describes interesting activities which Marco Polo must have seen.

A committee begins to make the time chart. (See pages 95–97.)

Application to Present-Day Conditions

How far is it from Peking to Venice? (Turn to your geography and use the scale of miles for the overland route; for the return by sea.)

How long does it take a ship today to go from Peking to Venice? (Use the advertising folders of steamships. You can find many addresses in the advertising pages of magazines.)

Can you tell of any person who has recently made a voyage to unknown lands? What is the present-day name of Peking? [*Peiping.*] of the "Roof of the World"? Look at the map of Asia to find out. Do people today ever enter the service of other nations?

Exercises in Reasoning

Before their journey to China, what things did the Polos actually *know* about the Far East? What things had they only heard? Do you actually *know* anything about the Far East?

Do you blame the two teachers for refusing to go on with the Polos?

Would Marco Polo have been better off if he had stayed at home?

If you were the Great King, would you have taken a foreigner into your service?

Drill Games

Large drill cards may be made for the persons, places, dates, and terms. For example:

ONE SIDE		THE OTHER SIDE
Marco Polo	⟷	a man who wrote a book about China
Venice	⟷	the city in which Marco Polo was born
China	⟷	Marco Polo lived here seventeen years
1300	⟷	about the date the Polos returned
Far East	⟷	a term describing China and India
overland	⟷	a word meaning " not by sea "
route	⟷	a road or way used in travel

Children work individually, preparing themselves for the games played with both sides of these cards. When the games are played, each child has a blank sheet of paper and a pencil before him. He records on the paper all the items which he missed. Later he writes the correct identifications in his notebook.

Testing

Tests of Understanding of persons, places, dates, and vocabulary meanings are provided on page 18 of Kelty's *Beginnings of the American People and Nation* under the heading "Something to Do."

An *Additional Test on Reasoning* follows.[1] Check the right answer.

1. From the route shown on the sand-table map, did Marco Polo travel all the way by land, both in going to China and in coming home? Yes [ ] No [√]

Exercise in Organization

1. Following is a list of events in the story. Put the figure *1* before that which took place first, the figure *2* before that which happened next, and so on.

    [__1__] Marco Polo's father and uncle went to China.

    [__4__] Marco Polo made a book about his travels.

    [__2__] Marco went with his father and uncle on the second trip.

    [__3__] Nobody in Venice knew them when they came home.

2. Make one or two summary sentences telling about the story.

STORY 2.   THE EFFECT OF THE CRUSADES ON COMMERCE [1 Week

Conversational Approach

"Have you ever gone to see any church outside your own city, or any religious shrine? Why do you suppose that a church member might especially like to visit a church in the country where Jesus lived and died? Do you know what that land is called?" [The teacher writes *Holy Land* on the board.] On the

---

[1] Other reasoning exercises appear under the heading "General Activities." See the tabulation on pages 82–84 for the complete list of types of exercises and tests used.

sand-table map the teacher shows the Holy Land. Children decide how the name can be shown on the sand-table model. They mark it. They find out what the principal city is and decide how it can be marked on the model. "Why do many people think that Christians ought to own the Holy Land? Do you remember from your Bible stories what people lived there before the time of Christ? Our story today tells whether or not Christians do own the Holy Land."

Reading and Study

The Reading Periods

Independent Readers

This group reads the entire story through silently as given in their textbook. After the reading they test their comprehension by the study-guide questions furnished by the teacher or the textbook. If they cannot answer (to themselves) they must reread. They should not write the answers.

TEXTS

BARKER, DODD, WEBB, *Our Nation Begins*, 27–38.

CLARK-GORDY, *Westward toward America*, 311–322.

KELTY, *Beginnings of the American People and Nation*, 19–28.

KNOWLTON and WHEELER, *Our Past in Western Europe*, 157–163 (hard).

SMALLIDGE and PAXSON, *Finding America*, 10–15, 18–26, 62–67.

EXTENSIVE READING

BUTTERWORTH, *Zigzag Journeys in Classic Lands*, 177–182.

TAPPAN, *European Hero Stories*, 136–151, 161–165.

Lower Group

The teacher tells the story orally, writing on the board the names of the principal persons and places as she mentions them. The children practice the pronunciations.

Then the teacher and this group read together the story as given in the text. The teacher guides the silent reading, section by section, by the same type of questions that she would use in a silent-reading period; for example, "In the first section are named four places that Jesus knew. Find the sentence which tells about them."

After the entire story has been read in this manner the children test themselves by the study-guide questions.

OTHER BOOKS

PRATT, *Exploration and Discovery*, 11–16.

TERRY, *History Stories of Other Lands*, I: 49–57

READING FOR RECREATION (*Both Groups*)

The teacher puts on the bookshelf for recreational reading such books as

SCALES, *Boys of the Ages*, 65–88.

STEIN, *Our Little Crusader Cousin of Long Ago*.

The Discussion

The children give complete answers to the study-guide questions. This exercise enables the teacher to set up adequate standards as to what constitutes understanding. During the first units she will show the children repeatedly that they were not ready to answer the questions when perhaps they thought they were. By insisting that children's answers show a real grasp of the story the teacher is furnishing excellent training in "the ability to follow a coherent, cumulative train of thought" (see page 7).

The teacher writes on the board the words *pilgrim, siege, capture, conquer, crusade*. Children discuss the meanings.

Multisensory Aids

The teacher and the children talk over together the pictures in the text. Features of historical significance should be noted, such as the horses, weapons, and armor.

AUDIO-VISUAL MATERIALS OBTAINABLE

ARNOLD. Historical Pictures: A. H. P. 14.
EASTMAN. Educational Slides: The Crusades.
International Educational Pictures: Holy Land, Jerusalem.
LEHMANN. Historical Pictures: L. H. 206.
LONGMAN. Historical Wall Pictures: Richard Cœur de Lion's Sight of Jerusalem.
McKINLEY. Illustrated Topics: M. M. 5.
MILLER. *Picturesque Tale of Progress*, VI, 31–65, 104–108.
National Geographic Magazine, LIX, 369–390 (March, 1931); LXIV, 645–694 (December, 1933).

Music. Play records of the "Crusader's Hymn"; the "Pilgrims' Chorus."

General Activities

Creative Activities: Group and Individual, Correlated with Other Subjects or Voluntary Projects

Children trace the Crusaders' routes on the sand table by means of colored yarn. (Shepherd's Historical Atlas, pp. 66, 70.)

Boys may wish to construct some of the simpler siege engines and explain how they work.

Committees dramatize the meeting of the Crusaders with the Mohammedans.

The class makes a trip to the museum, if possible, to see weapons and armor of the time of the Crusades.

A volunteer makes a speech in which he urges his countrymen to join a Crusade which he is organizing.

The class continues the time chart.

Application to Present-Day Conditions

Who uses the red cross as an emblem today? Are pilgrimages ever made today? Make a list of articles used in warfare by the Crusaders (see the pictures in the books you read); of articles used in warfare today.

Do people today have to pay any kind of tax to visit foreign lands? [*Passport visa.*]

From your geography map find out what country owns the Holy Land.

How are armies raised today? (See *Conscription* in an encyclopedia for children.) Compare with the methods used in the time of the Crusades.

What is the city of Constantinople called today? To whom does it belong?

Exercises in Reasoning

Did the Crusades do Europe any good?
In what way did the Crusades and Marco Polo's book have the same effect?
Did the Crusaders enjoy themselves when on the Crusades?

Drill Games

Drill cards such as the following are made for the persons, places, and vocabulary terms needed.

Crusaders	⟷	men who fought in the "Holy Wars"
Mediterranean Sea	⟷	a large body of water between Europe and Africa
Constantinople	⟷	a large city near the Black Sea
pilgrims	⟷	persons who journey to holy places
siege	⟷	trying to capture a place by surrounding it and starving it out
to capture	⟷	to win by force
crusade	⟷	a war for a cause which men think is holy
to conquer	⟷	to overcome in war

Children drill themselves on their own difficulties, pointed out by their mistakes in the drill games.

Testing

Tests of Understanding of persons, places, and terms are supplied in parts II and III of "A Memory Test" on pages 27 and 28 of Kelty's *Beginnings of the American People and Nation*.

Additional Tests of Reasoning and Skills follow.[1]

1. Check: Tell from the sand-table map whether or not the Holy Land is near the Mediterranean Sea.   Yes [✓]   No [ ]

2. Check the best answer: Travel is good for people because   it helps them spend their money.   ✓ they learn many new ideas.   they have a good time when traveling.   they do not have to work when traveling.

3. In this list check all the articles which the men from the West learned to use while they were in the East.

✓ lemons	wheat	✓ sugar	wool	✓ pepper	✓ mattresses
iron	boats	stone	✓ glass	horses	✓ soap
honey	✓ silk	✓ rice	wagons	✓ watermelons	

4. Turn to the Index. On what pages in your book can you read about Constantinople? _ _ _ _ _ _

Exercise in Organization (Teacher and pupils work together)

1. Here is a list of section headings. Number them as the events happened in the story.

     [_ _5_ _] End of the Crusades
     [_ _1_ _] Journeys to the Holy Land
     [_ _3_ _] The Crusades
     [_ _2_ _] The Turks Conquer the Holy Land
     [_ _4_ _] Trade Grows Up

2. Make summary sentences of the main points in the story.

[1] Other exercises in reasoning are included under "General Activities."

STORY 3. MAIN TRADE ROUTES TO THE EAST   [1 Week

Conversational Approach

"By how many different ways could you come from your home to the school-house? Which is the best way? What is the best road to your nearest large city?

"Men from the West had the same problem about how to travel to the East. Which is the best way to make such a long journey? By land or by sea? Why?" The children gather around the sand-table model and select ways to travel from the West. Whenever they select one of the three routes actually used, it may be marked on the sand table by a long string of colored yarn. If some children suggest the routes around Africa or around northern Europe, they may be told that these routes were tried much later.

"Our story today tells about the three main trade routes."

Reading and Study

The Reading Periods

Independent Readers

This group reads the entire story through silently, as given in their textbook. After the reading they test their comprehension by the study-guide questions furnished by the teacher or the textbook.

TEXTS

KELTY, *Beginnings of the American People and Nation*, 29–38.
KNOWLTON and WHEELER, *Our Past in Western Europe*, 163–168 (hard).
SMALLIDGE and PAXSON, *Finding America*, 52–59.
WOODBURN and MORAN, *Finders and Founders of the New World*, 23–27.

EXTENSIVE READING

DAVIDSON, *Founders and Builders of Our Nation*, 7–9.
LAWLER, *Story of Columbus and Magellan*, 14–15.
SHAW, *Discoverers and Explorers*, 10–11.
SOUTHWORTH, *Builders of Our Country*, I, 24–25.

Lower Group

The teacher tells the story orally, illustrating the routes at the sand-table model as she mentions them. Children practice the pronunciation of the words stressed.

Then the teacher and this group read together the story as given in their text. The teacher guides the silent reading, section by section, by the type of questions that she would use in a silent-reading period; for example, "The first two paragraphs tell you what goods the ships carried. What were they?"

After the entire story has been read in this manner, the children test themselves by the study-guide questions.

OTHER BOOKS

ATWOOD and THOMAS, *Home Life in Far-Away Lands*, 65–70.
BARROWS and PARKER, *Geography: Journeys in Distant Lands*, 10–14.
CHAMBERLAIN, *How We Travel*.
FAIRGRIEVE and YOUNG, *Children of Many Lands*, 79–96.

READING FOR RECREATION (*Both Groups*)

The teacher puts on the bookshelf for recreational reading such books as

HARTMAN, *These United States* (hard).
RATZESBERGER, *Camel Bells*.
WELLS, *Ali, the Camel*.

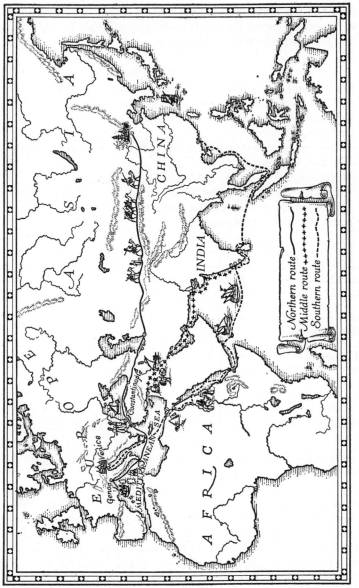

Early Trade Routes to the East

The Discussion

The children give complete answers to the study-guide questions. The teacher emphasizes the importance of children's answering in their own words, by commending those who do so.

She writes on the board the words *trade route, caravan, products, water route, East, West*. Children discuss the meanings.

Multisensory Aids

The teacher and the children talk over together the pictures in the text. Features of historical and geographical significance should be noted.

"In the map on page 123 how can you tell which is the northern route? the middle? the southern?

"Show the northern route on the sand table and then on the map." (Same with middle and southern routes.)

"Show Europe, Asia, Africa. Which looks the largest?

"At what city does the northern trade route begin? the southern trade route? Which one passes the city of Constantinople? How could men from Europe reach the middle trade route?

AUDIO-VISUAL MATERIALS OBTAINABLE

Compton's Pictured Teaching Materials: *Middle Ages*, II, Plate V, 3; Plate XI, 1, 2.
EASTMAN. Classroom Films: The Ship of the Desert.
GABRIEL (Ed.). Pageant of America, I, 84–86.
GRANT. *Story of the Ship.*
LEHMANN. Historical Pictures: L. H. 222.
McKINLEY. Illustrated Topics: M. M. 6.
MILLER. *Picturesque Tale of Progress*, VII, 204–205.
National Geographic Society Series: Sahara Life.
Yale Pageant Educational Slides: No. 4.

General Activities

Creative Activities: Group and Individual, Correlated with Other Subjects or Voluntary Projects

The class takes a trip to a museum, if possible, to see articles typical of Iran (Persia), India, China, and Japan.

Volunteers make a ship after models shown in the pictures, load it with goods mentioned in the text, and show why the unloading at Antioch and reloading on camels' backs was a process expensive in time, effort, and money.

To a volunteer: "Imagine that you are a citizen of Venice who has just read Marco Polo's book. Make the speech that you would make to a rich Venetian in trying to persuade him to build a ship for the Eastern trade."

The teacher reads to the children the beginning of Kipling's "Ballad of the King's Jest" (*Barrack Room Ballads*).

Volunteers draw a picture of a caravan to use as part of a backdrop for the dramatization. (See page 176.)

The class traces co-operatively on a slated outline map the three trade routes in different colors: northern, red; middle, blue; southern, yellow.

Sand-table Illustration of the Trade Routes, Showing Europe, Northern Africa, and Eastern Asia

Ships and camels are loaded with the goods of the country from which they came

Application to Present-Day Conditions

Why did the men from the West not use the Suez Canal?

Which of these three trade routes is most used today? (See a map of world trade routes in an advanced geography.)

The teacher shows the children the table of United States imports in the World Almanac. Do we today still carry on trade with the Far East?

In what way is the motor truck taking the place of the camel, just as it took the place of the horse?

Why are dishes called china? (See *Porcelain* in a children's encyclopedia.)

Is the indigo plant much used today as a dye? (See *Indigo* in a children's encyclopedia.)

Is there any trade route between your community and the nearest large city?

How did the war between Italy and Ethiopia show the importance of the southern trade route?

Exercises in Reasoning

The children state in one sentence a truth which they have learned about routes on which goods have frequently to be loaded and unloaded.

How were the lives of men in the West changed by the trade that grew up with the East?

We are likely to think of the people of Europe as more civilized than those of Asia. Were they more civilized at the time of our story? Prove your answer.

Why could the northern route not handle heavy goods?

Why were Eastern goods sold at so high a price in Europe?

Prove the truth of this statement: The main reason why the three trade routes were not satisfactory was that they were too expensive.

Drill Games

The place relationships are best drilled upon by maps. Outline maps are passed. Each child traces the northern route in red, the middle in blue, and the southern in yellow. (Outline maps which show water bodies in blue or shading are preferable for young children.)

Drill cards are made for the dates and terms needed.

India	↔	as far as the men from the West went themselves
Genoa	↔	the city which used the northern trade route
Europe	↔	the continent that was called the West
Asia	↔	the continent that was called the East
1453	↔	the year when Constantinople was captured by the Turks
trade route	↔	a road or way used to carry goods for buying and selling
caravan	↔	a company of camels and men
products	↔	goods raised, found, or made in a country
water route	↔	a way for travel used only by boats

Children drill individually on their own errors.

Testing

Tests of Understanding of places, dates, and terms are given in exercises II and III on pages 37 and 38 of Kelty's *Beginnings of the American People and Nation*.

Additional Tests of Reasoning and Skills follow.[1]

1. Turn to the map on page 123. Check the right answers.　　**Yes**　　**No**
a. Does the northern trade route pass Constantinople?　　[√]　　[ ]
b. Does the middle trade route begin in Africa?　　[ ]　　[√]
c. Can camels be used on the southern trade route most of the way?　　[ ]　　[√]

2. Check the best answer: None of the trade routes were as good as they ought to be because they all　　went to places very far away.　　needed too many men to carry on trade.　　brought home goods that were not needed. √ needed too much time and money for loading and unloading.

3. Turn to the index of your text. On what pages can you read about camels? _ _ _ _ _ _ Does this word come before or after the word *clearing*? _ _ _ _ _ _

4. Put the figure *1* in front of the thing which happened first and the figure *2* in front of the thing which happened later.

[_ _*1*_ _] Marco Polo came home from China.
[_ _*2*_ _] Men in Europe wanted to find an all-sea route.

Exercises in Organization

1. Children record from memory on outline maps the northern route in red, the middle in blue, and the southern in yellow.

2. One child tells orally about the northern route, another about the middle route, and another about the southern route.

STORY 4. PRINCE HENRY AND THE PORTUGUESE EXPLORATIONS

Conversational Approach　　　　　　　　[*1 Week*

"We found out in our last story that it was a bad thing to have to keep loading and unloading goods so many times before reaching the East. Can anyone see a way by which this might be avoided?" Children study the sand-table model and compare it with a globe if necessary. They themselves will suggest possible routes. (Some child may have suggested this route during the introductory conversation of the preceding story. If so, his solution is recalled now.) "Our story today tells how an all-sea route was first found."

Reading and Study

The Reading Periods

Independent Readers

This group reads the entire story through silently, as given in their textbook. After the reading they test their comprehension by the study-guide questions furnished by the teacher or by the text.

Lower Group

The teacher tells the story orally, writing on the board the most important names and using sketches to illustrate her points. Children practice the pronunciation of the names.

---

[1] Other exercises in reasoning are included under "General Activities."

TEXTS

BURNHAM and JACK, *Beginnings of Our Country*, 28–29.

CLARK-GORDY, *Westward toward America*, 344–345.

KELTY, *Beginnings of the American People and Nation*, 39–50.

KNOWLTON and WHEELER, *Our Past in Western Europe*, 212–223 (hard).

NIDA, *Following Columbus*, 24–27.

SMALLIDGE and PAXSON, *Finding America*, 5–6, 76–80, 83–90.

WOODBURN and MORAN, *Finders and Founders of the New World*, 27–28.

EXTENSIVE READING

FARIS, *Real Stories of the Geography Makers*, 55–59, 81–86.

LAWLER, *Story of Columbus and Magellan*, 1–13.

LUTHER, *Trading and Exploring*, 148–153, 174–191.

SHAW, *Discoverers and Explorers*, 40–43.

TAPPAN, *European Hero Stories*, 177–179.

VAN LOON, *Short History of Discovery*, 50–51, 58–59.

The teacher and the lower-ability group then read together the story as given in the text. The teacher guides the silent reading, section by section, by the same type of questions that she would use in a silent-reading period; for example, "In the first paragraph read to find what country first found an all-water route."

After the entire story has been read in this manner the children test themselves by the study-guide questions.

OTHER BOOKS

ATWOOD-THOMAS, *Home Life in Far-Away Lands*, 17–29.

BARROWS and PARKER, *Geography; Journeys in Distant Lands*, 55–61.

READING FOR RECREATION (*Both Groups*)

The teacher puts on the bookshelf for recreational reading for both groups such books as

BEST, *Steer for New Shores.*

HEWES, *Spice and the Devil's Cave.*

The Discussion

The children answer the study-guide questions as fully as possible. The teacher emphasizes the point that they should say these answers to themselves when they are studying. If they cannot say the answers, they need to reread the part of the story in which each answer is to be found.

She writes on the board the words *navigator, continent, all-sea route, Sea of Darkness*. Children discuss the meanings.

Multisensory Aids

Children and teacher talk over together the pictures in the text. Points of historical or geographical significance are noted. They turn to a map showing the world in Prince Henry's time compared with the world of today.

"From this map can you tell how much of the world was known shortly after Prince Henry's time? How are the unknown parts marked? How is the route of Dias shown? Show it on a large wall map. How is the route of Da Gama shown? Show it on a large wall map. Show Portugal on the large wall map; show India."

AUDIO-VISUAL MATERIALS OBTAINABLE

BRADLEY. Village Series of Cut-outs: African Village.

GABRIEL (Ed.). Pageant of America, I, 88–93.

International Educational Pictures: Pageantry of India.

McKINLEY. Illustrated Topics for American History: S. 3.

MILLER. *Picturesque Tale of Progress*, VII, 206–230.

National Geographic Magazine, LVI (October, 1929); LIX, LX (April, August, and October, 1931).
Society for Visual Education. Africa — The People of the Congo.
Yale Pageant Educational Slides: 5, 591.

Music. Play selections from Meyerbeer's *L'Africaine* (Vasco da Gama).

General Activities

Creative Activities: Group and Individual, Correlated with Other Subjects or Voluntary Projects

A committee constructs sand-table villages to represent the African Negroes. (See Miller's *Picturesque Tale of Progress*, VII : 211–223.)

Volunteers model in clay the imaginary dangers of the Sea of Darkness.

A volunteer writes a letter that Bartholomew Columbus, a member of Dias's crew, might have written to his older brother, Christopher, describing the voyage that was made to the Cape of Storms.

The teacher reads aloud to the children selected portions of Vachel Lindsay's "The Congo."

The class dramatizes the scene represented in some of the pictures in their text.

The class continues the time chart.

Applications to Present-Day Conditions

How far is it from Lisbon to the Cape of Good Hope? (Use the scale of miles in your geography book.) Compare with the distance traveled by Marco Polo. Make a graph of the two.

To whom does India belong at present? Does Portugal still own any land in the Far East? (See geography maps of Asia.)

Are any attempts being made today which seem to some people as silly as Prince Henry's seemed to his people? [*Stratosphere ascents.*]

Are any people today afraid to cross the ocean? What do they fear nowadays?

Are there slaves anywhere in the world today?

Have any places in the world been given names within the last few years? [*Antarctica.*]

Are any people today trying to build up new routes? [*Air routes; road to Mexico; proposed road to South America.*]

Exercises in Reasoning

Why did Prince Henry study the stars in order to become a better sailor?

Why did Portuguese sailors become the best in the world?

Does Henry deserve the title *Navigator*, since he himself did not go exploring?

Much of the world's gold and silver and jewels have always been collected by the people of India and kept there. Why?

Drill Games

The best drill for the place names (*Africa, Portugal, India, Cape of Good Hope*) is at the map. Drill cards are prepared for the persons, date, and vocabulary terms as follows:

Prince Henry	↔	the man who planned the route around Africa
Dias	↔	the first man to sail around the southern point of Africa
Vasco da Gama	↔	the first man to reach India by an all-sea route
1498	↔	the year when Vasco da Gama reached India
Cape of Storms	↔	the first name given to the Cape of Good Hope
navigator	↔	a man skilled in directing vessels at sea
continent	↔	one of the great bodies of land on the globe
all-sea route	↔	a route, or way, entirely by water
Sea of Darkness	↔	a name given because of the terrors of the Atlantic Ocean

Children are given access to these cards at any time during the week's work.

Testing

Tests of Understanding. Check the right answer.

1. The man who did most to open up an all-sea route to the Indies was   Dias.   √ Prince Henry.   Vasco da Gama.

2. The man who first reached the southern point of Africa was   Marco Polo.   Columbus.   √ Dias.

3. A man who knows a great deal about sailing and directing ships is a √ navigator.   captain.   prince.

4. Sailors used to call the Atlantic Ocean   √ Sea of Darkness.   Our Sea. The Middle Sea.

5. The year when Vasco da Gama reached India was   1300.   1453. √ 1498.

6. The king of Portugal did not like the name   √ Cape of Storms.   Cape of Good Hope.   Cape Bojador.

7. The man who fully carried out Prince Henry's plan was   Dias. √ Vasco da Gama.   a Turk.

8. The large bodies of land on the surface of the globe are called   nations. countries.   √ continents.

9. A road used for travel which does not cross any bodies of land is called √ an all-sea route.   an overland route.   a trade route.

Additional Tests of Reasoning and Skills follow.[1]

1. After Prince Henry's time most of the foreign trade of Europe was carried on   across the Mediterranean Sea.   √ on the Atlantic Ocean.   by long overland routes.

2. Turn to the map of the Portuguese explorations. Did the Portuguese sailors cross the Mediterranean Sea?   Yes [ ]   No [√]

[1] Other exercises in reasoning are included under "General Activities."

3. Put the figure *1* in front of the thing which happened first and the figure *2* in front of the thing which happened later.

[__2__] Vasco da Gama reached India by sea.

[__1__] Men from Europe went on the Crusades.

Exercise in Organization

1. Make a list of the section headings in the story in the order given.

2. Make summary sentences of the main points in the story.

STORY 5. NEW INVENTIONS AND DISCOVERIES [1 Week

Conversational Approach

The teacher brings to the class a magnet and a compass. The children experiment with the magnet, and the teacher explains that the compass is governed by the same principle. Children carry the compass about the room, to discover how it behaves. They name as many uses of the compass as they can. "Our story today tells how the compass came to be used.

"It also tells about another great invention." At this point the teacher has ready an ordinary schoolroom printing outfit. One child prints his name with it. The teacher then shows how much faster the work could be done if the block letters composing a word were tied together.

"How much faster yet the work could be done if a whole line could be fastened together and all the lines on a page could be printed at once! That idea was carried out by a man about whom we shall read today."

Reading and Study

The Reading Periods

Independent Readers

This group reads the entire story through silently, as given in their textbook. After the reading they test their comprehension by the study-guide questions furnished by the teacher or the text.

TEXTS

KELTY, *Beginnings of the American People and Nation*, 51–58.

KNOWLTON and WHEELER, *Our Past in Western Europe*, 198–201, 209–212 (hard).

NIDA, *Following Columbus*, 25–27.

SMALLIDGE and PAXSON, *Finding America*, 70–73.

EXTENSIVE READING

HAAREN and POLAND, *Famous Men of the Middle Ages*, 257–262.

PERRY and PRICE, *American History*, I: 46–47.

ROCHELEAU, *Story of Printing*.

TAPPAN, *European Hero Stories*, 165–169.

VAN LOON, *Short History of Discovery*, 46–49.

Lower Group

The teacher tells the story orally. Then teacher and lower-group children read together the story as given in the text. The teacher guides the silent reading, section by section, by the same type of question that she would use in a silent-reading period; for example, "The first paragraph tells us what a compass is used for."

After the entire story has been read in this manner the children test themselves by the study-guide questions.

OTHER BOOKS

BALDWIN, *Thirty More Famous Stories*, 40–49.

GRANT, *Story of the Ship*.

TERRY, *History Stories of Other Lands*, I: 80–88.

READING FOR RECREATION

STEIN, *Gabriel and the Hour Book*.

The Discussion

Children answer the study-guide questions. If a child's answer leaves out important phases of the subject, the teacher questions him. She calls the attention of the class to what she is doing and tells them that as soon as they learn how it is done, they may question one another for the same purpose.

She writes on the board the words *inventor, invention, compass, sailing charts, block printing, movable type.* Children discuss the meanings.

Multisensory Aids

The teacher and the children talk over together the pictures in the text.

AUDIO-VISUAL MATERIALS OBTAINABLE

ARNOLD. Historical Pictures: A. H. P. 23.
BRADLEY. Modern Trade Pictures: The Printer.
Compton's Pictured Teaching Materials: *Middle Ages*, II, 1, 3 4.
LEHMANN. Historical Pictures: L. H. 219, 220.
Yale Pageant Educational Slides: 6.

General Activities

Creative Activities: Group and Individual, Correlated with Other Subjects or Voluntary Projects

Boy scouts tell how they learned to use the compass.

Children draw a diagram of a ship and label the different parts. They compare it with drawings in the advertising literature of modern steamship companies.

A volunteer demonstrates how a magnetized needle floating on a cork in a basin of water can serve as a compass.

A volunteer makes a mold of sand or wood and fills it with melted lead to make a letter of type.

The class secures a copy of a sailing chart. (Write to the United States Coast and Geodetic Survey, Commerce Building, Washington, D.C.)

Several trips are possible: to a local newspaper plant to see how type is set up (or to a small job-printing plant); to a vessel near by which uses a compass (if there is any such); to a museum to see handwritten books.

A committee makes a collection of all the different kinds of maps that can be found.

Application to Present-Day Conditions

Children illustrate to visitors from other rooms how a compass works, and explain its purpose.

What inventions of the present day help to make ships more comfortable? [*Gyroscope.*]

In what ways would your own daily life be changed if there were no printing presses in the world?

Are there any copies of the Gutenberg Bible still? (See *Bible* in World Book Encyclopedia.)

Compare measurements of old-time ships with ships of today. Graph the figures. (See advertising literature of steamship companies and also *Ship* in a children's encyclopedia.)

Are there any laws today to make sailing safe? any steamboat inspection? (See *Department of Commerce* in encyclopedias for children.)

What is a "printer's devil"?

Has any improvement in printing been made since Gutenberg's day?

Exercises in Reasoning

Why does a globe represent the earth better than flat maps do?

Why did sailors dare to sail farther out at sea after they had a compass?

Is every book that is printed a blessing to the world?

From the map of Vasco da Gama's voyage do you think that he had a compass? Give your reasons.

How were children educated before the days of printing?

Drill Games

Drill cards are prepared as follows:

John Gutenberg	⟷	the man who began printing with movable type
inventor	⟷	a person who makes an article that has never been used before
compass	⟷	an instrument to tell direction
invention	⟷	the thing that is made by an inventor
movable type	⟷	letters that can be fastened together to print words

Children drill themselves especially on those which they find difficult. Games follow.

Testing

Tests of Understanding of persons and vocabulary meanings are provided on page 58 of Kelty's *Beginnings of the American People and Nation.*

Additional Tests of Reasoning and Skills.[1] Check the best answer.

1. At any time of the day or night sailors can guide their ships by the use of   the stars.   √ the compass.   the moon.   landmarks.

2. The compass was invented by   the Portuguese.   the Arabs.   the Chinese.   √ no one knows whom.

3. Complete this sentence: The invention of printing was a good thing because _ _ _ _ _ _.

4. Put the figure *1* in front of the way of sailing which was used first, and the figure *2* in front of the way that was used later.

[__2__] Sailors sailed by the use of the compass.

[__1__] Sailors sailed by looking at the stars.

Exercise in Organization. The teacher and the children together make a very simple outline of the story under a few main headings, the teacher supplying the main headings and the children supplying a few subheads under each.

[1] Other exercises in reasoning are included under "General Activities."

STORY 6. COLUMBUS'S PLAN

Conversational Approach

The teacher brings to class as large a globe as can be procured. (A map will not serve this purpose.) Children show on the globe all the routes that have been used in traveling to the Indies. [*Four.*]

"Can you see any other possible way to reach the Indies from the Mediterranean countries?" Children work on this problem until the solution presents itself, — sailing westward to reach the East.

"Our story today is about the man who first tried to prove that this could be done. Do you know who he was?"

Reading and Study

The Reading Periods

Independent Readers

This group reads the entire story through silently, as given in their text. After the reading they test their comprehension by the study-guide questions furnished by the teacher or the text.

TEXTS

BARKER, DODD, WEBB, *Our Nation Begins*, 53–59.

BEARD and BAGLEY, *First Book in American History*, 1–9.

BURNHAM and JACK, *Beginnings of Our Country*, 29–33.

CLARK-GORDY, *First Three Hundred Years*, 22–23 (hard).

CLARK-GORDY, *Westward toward America*, 346–348.

KELTY, *Beginnings of the American People and Nation*, 59–71.

KNOWLTON and WHEELER, *Our Past in Western Europe*, 226–234 (hard).

NIDA, *Following Columbus*, 29–35.

SMALLIDGE and PAXSON, *Finding America*, 6–8, 97–108.

WOODBURN and MORAN, *Finders and Founders of the New World*, 17–23, 28–34.

EXTENSIVE READING

CHANDLER and CHITWOOD, *Makers of American History*, 1–18.

COE, *Founders of Our Country*, 7–16.

DAVIDSON, *Founders and Builders of Our Nation*, 6, 10–12.

FIELD, *Finding the New World*, 50–58.

FOOTE and SKINNER, *Explorers and Founders of America*, 24–29.

LAWLER, *Story of Columbus and Magellan*, 17–41.

Lower Group

The teacher tells the story orally, writing on the board the names of the most important persons and places mentioned. Children practice the pronunciations.

Then the teacher and the children together read the story as given in the text. The teacher guides the silent reading, section by section, by the same type of questions that she would use in a silent-reading period; for example, "Our first paragraph tells us some of the things this boy liked. What were they?"

After the entire story has been read in this manner the children test themselves by the study-guide questions.

OTHER BOOKS

BLAISDELL and BALL, *American History for Little Folks*, 1–7.

BLAISDELL and BALL, *Child's Book of American History*, 1–3.

DAVIS, *Stories of the United States*, 27–37.

LUCIA, *Stories of American Discoverers for Little Americans*, 1–19.

PRATT, *Beginners' Book*, 23–29.

WAYLAND, *History Stories for Primary Grades*, 91–93.

WILSON, *A History Reader*, 33–42.

MONTGOMERY, *Beginners' American History*, 1–6.

PERRY and PRICE, *American History*, I : 1–4.

PRATT, *Exploration and Discovery*, 17–22.

SHAW, *Discoverers and Explorers*, 9–15, 24–30.

SOUTHWORTH, *Builders of Our Country* I: 26–31.

TAPPAN, *American Hero Stories*, 1–5.

TAPPAN, *European Hero Stories*, 170–173.

VAN LOON, *Short History of Discovery*, 60–77.

READING FOR RECREATION (*Both Groups*)

The teacher puts on the bookshelf for recreational reading such books as

HUTCHINSON, *The Men Who Found America.*

LENNES and PHILLIPS, *The Story of Columbus.*

LOWITZ, *The Cruise of Mr. Christopher Columbus.*

The Discussion

Children answer the study-guide questions as completely as possible. Again the teacher questions them as to phases omitted, in preparation for their questioning one another. She points out that only the most important matters need be included, not everything told in the text.

She writes on the board the words "Indies," "royal court." Children discuss the meanings.

Multisensory Aids

The children and the teacher talk over together the pictures in the text. Features of historical or geographical significance are noted.

The teacher shows a map on which North and South America are superimposed upon the map showing what Columbus thought he was going to do. What route did Columbus think he was going to follow? Is Japan really as close to Europe as the map shows? (Compare with a map in the geography.)

AUDIO-VISUAL MATERIALS OBTAINABLE

BROWN. Famous Pictures: 2248.

Chronicles of America Photoplays: Columbus.

Compton's Pictured Teaching Materials: *Holidays*, Plates I, II.

GABRIEL (Ed.). Pageant of America, I, 96–104.

GRANT. *Story of the Ship.*

Keystone View Slides: 11, 13.

McKINLEY. Illustrated Topics for Medieval and Modern History: M. M. 4.

National Geographic Magazine, LXVI, 370 (September, 1934), Columbus's flag.

MILLER. *Picturesque Tale of Progress*, VIII, 16–30.

Yale Pageant Educational Slides: 7, 592–594.

General Activities

Creative Activities: Group and Individual, Correlated with Other Subjects or Voluntary Projects

The class makes a list of the supplies needed for a long sea voyage.

Volunteers draw or paint Columbus's ships.

Children divide into committees and read the dramatizations given in Hubbard's *Little American History Plays* (3–12), Shoemaker's *Colonial Plays for the Schoolroom* (9–17), and Bird and Starling's *Historical Plays for Children* (1–17).

Volunteers write the letter that a member of Columbus's crew might have written to his mother the night before sailing.

The class make on the slated globe a map of what Columbus thought he was going to do, then outlines on it in red the world as it really is.

Application to Present-Day Conditions

Do many people today think that the stratosphere ascents and Byrd's expeditions to Antarctica are silly?

Name some tasks today that are too big for anyone except the government to undertake. [*For example, distributing the mail.*]

Do you know anyone who has kept on with a hard task after almost everyone else would have given it up?

If Columbus had received help from France instead of Spain, might it have made a difference to South and Central America? [*Language and customs.*]

Exercises in Reasoning

Do you think the fact that Columbus was born in Genoa had any effect on his life?

Would Marco Polo's book have had any influence on Columbus?

Was it a good thing that Columbus went to Portugal?

Imagine yourself in Columbus's place. Prove to your audience that the world is round.

What was the principal mistake that Columbus made in his reasoning? [*He knew nothing about North and South America.*] Was it a good thing that he made this mistake?

How do we know that these events took place, since they happened before all of us were born?

Why is Columbus so highly honored today, when wise men had known long before his time that the world is round?

Drill Games

Drill on the place names (*Atlantic, France, Spain*) is best done at the map.

Drill cards are prepared for the names of persons and for the vocabulary terms somewhat as follows:

Ferdinand	↔	king of Spain in Columbus's time
Isabella	↔	queen of Spain who decided to help Columbus
Columbus	↔	the first man who had courage enough to try to sail around the world
Indies	↔	a name given to the Far East
royal court	↔	where the king and queen live
sailing chart	↔	special kinds of maps for sailing

These cards are added to those of the preceding stories, and the drill games include all used during Unit One.

Testing

Tests of Understanding are supplied on page 71, exercise II, of Kelty's *Beginnings of the American People and Nation.*

Additional Tests of Reasoning and Skills.[1] Check the best answer.

[1] Other exercises in reasoning are included under "General Activities."

1. Columbus was the first man who believed that the world is round.

True [　]　　False [✓]

2. The events in this story took place　　in my father's lifetime　　in my grandfather's lifetime　　✓ long before grandfather's time.

3. Put the figure *1* in front of the thing which happened first and the figure *2* in front of the thing which happened later.

[_ _1_ _] Prince Henry studied the stars.

[_ _2_ _] Columbus had a new idea.

Exercises in Organization. Teacher and children working together select the main points in each section of the story and arrange them in outline form.

Tests on the Entire Unit

Test of Place Sense. Pass outline maps of the world which show water bodies in color or shading. Provide the children with colored crayons. Work is to be done in pencil except when color is specifically directed. Give the following directions:

1. Put a figure *1* where Venice should be.

2. Put a figure *2* where Genoa should be.

3. Write the word *China* in the right place.

4. Put a figure *3* where the Holy Land should be.

5. Put a figure *4* in the Mediterranean Sea.

6. Draw in red crayon the northern trade route.

7. Draw in blue crayon the middle trade route.

8. Draw in yellow crayon the southern trade route.

9. Write the word *India* in the right place.

10. Draw in green crayon Vasco da Gama's route.

11. Put a figure *5* where the Cape of Good Hope is.

12. Put the figure *6* where Portugal should be.

13. Write the word *Atlantic* in the right place.

Test of Time Sense. Pass mimeographed sheets of the following.

I. In each of the following exercises put the figure *1* before the name of the person who lived first and the figure *2* before the name of the person who lived later.

a. [_ _2_ _] Columbus
　　[_ _1_ _] Marco Polo

b. [_ _1_ _] Prince Henry
　　[_ _2_ _] Vasco da Gama

c. [_ _1_ _] Diaz
　　[_ _2_ _] Vasco da Gama

d. [_ _2_ _] Ferdinand
　　[_ _1_ _] John Gutenberg

e. [_ _2_ _] Isabella
　　[_ _1_ _] Prince Henry

II. Here is a list of things which happened in the stories. In each of the following exercises put the figure *1* before that which happened first and the figure *2* before that which happened later.

    a. [__1__] The Crusaders tried to win the Holy Land.

    [__2__] Diaz reached the Cape of Storms.

    b. [__2__] Vasco da Gama reached India.

    [__1__] Marco Polo went to China.

    c. [__2__] Columbus got help from Spain.

    [__1__] John Gutenberg printed from movable type.

III. Here is a list of dates:

              1300 1453 1498

Below is a list of things which happened. Take each date from this list and write it before the right event.

    [_____] Vasco da Gama reached India.

    [_____] Marco Polo returned home.

    [_____] Capture of Constantinople by the Turks.

Test on Persons. Pass mimeographed sheets of the following.

Here is a list of persons:

Turks	Vasco da Gama	Ferdinand	Columbus
Dias	John Gutenberg	Isabella	

Below are sentences which tell about these persons. Take one name at a time and put it in the right place.

    1. _____ wanted to reach the East by going West.

    2. _____ was king of Spain.

    3. _____ captured the Holy Land.

    4. _____ was queen of Spain.

    5. _____ went as far as the Cape of Storms.

    6. _____ invented our kind of printing.

    7. _____ was the first to reach India by sea.

Test on Historical Terms. The teacher prepares descriptions such as the following, which may have been used previously, as the subject of drill games, although using exactly the same wording should be avoided.

I. Here is a list of words:

overland	trade route	pilgrim
sea route	conquers	siege
route	capture	Far East
caravan		

Put each term in the right place in the sentences below.

    1. This word means that people always travel over the same way. The word is _____.

    2. This word means that in traveling you go always by land, not by water. The word is _____.

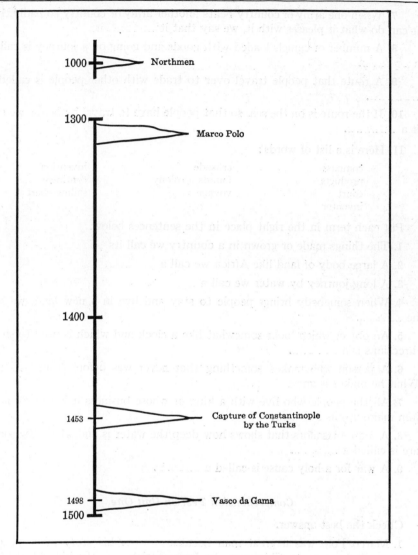

Time Chart — Unit I

3. People used to call both China and India the _ _ _ _ _ _.

4. This word means a person who makes a voyage to a place he thinks is holy. The word is _ _ _ _ _ _.

5. When an army stays outside a town, will not let anyone out or in, and tries to take the town, we say the army is making a _ _ _ _ _ _.

6. When armies take a person or place that belongs to an enemy, we say they _ _ _ _ _ _ the person or place.

7. When one army or country beats another army or country so badly that it can do what it pleases with it, we say that it _ _ _ _ _ _ _ it.

8. A number of camels loaded with goods and going on a journey is called a _ _ _ _ _ _ .

9. A route that people travel over to trade with other people is called a _ _ _ _ _ _ .

10. If the route is on the sea, so that people have to travel by boats, we call it a _ _ _ _ _ _ .

II. Here is a list of words:

compass	crusade	invention
products	founds a colony	continent
court	voyage	sailing chart
inventor		

Put each term in the right place in the sentences below.

1. The things made or grown in a country we call its _ _ _ _ _ _ .

2. A large body of land like Africa we call a _ _ _ _ _ _ .

3. A long journey by water we call a _ _ _ _ _ _ .

4. When somebody brings people to stay and live in a new land, we say he _ _ _ _ _ _ .

5. An object which looks somewhat like a clock and which is used to show directions is a _ _ _ _ _ _ .

6. A person who makes something that never was before is an _ _ _ _ _ _ . What he makes is an _ _ _ _ _ _ .

7. All the people who live with a king or whose business it is to stay near him make up his _ _ _ _ _ _ .

8. A map for sailors that shows how deep the water is and where the rocks are is called a _ _ _ _ _ _ _ .

9. A war for a holy cause is called a _ _ _ _ _ _ .

Comprehension Test on Unit One

Check the best answer.

1. Marco Polo was a great man because   √ his story made people eager to find a way to China.   he became rich.   the king liked him. he wrote a book.

2. The first people who knew that the earth is round were   Prince Henry and his men.   √ wise men who lived long before Columbus.   the three Polos.   the Turks.

3. The invention of printing was a good thing for the world because √ new ideas could be spread faster.   John Gutenberg was a great man. nobody knew how to read before that.   the printers grew rich.

4. People wanted to find an all-sea route to the Indies because   they did not like to ride camels.   ships can go very fast.   √ it cost a great deal of money to change from land routes to sea routes.   it is more fun to sail ships.

5. The first people who reached the Indies by sea were   √ men of Portugal.   Columbus and his men.   the Northmen.   the Crusaders.

6. The compass helped sailors because   they could see a long way with it.   it stopped the wind from blowing.   √ it showed in which direction they were going.   it told the time.

7. We honor Columbus because   √ he had the courage to try to sail west to reach China.   many kings knew him.   he was the first man who knew that the earth is round.   the king helped him.

8. The men who went on the Crusades learned   to fight bravely. √ to like the products of the East, so that they wanted to set up trade to get them.   that they were much better than the Turks.   to print with movable type.

9. After Vasco da Gama sailed around Africa, the country which traded most with the Indies was   Venice.   Genoa.   √ Portugal.   Spain.

10. What is the title of Unit One in the history which you have been studying?

Have any of the children in the lower group improved sufficiently by the end of Unit One to be shifted to the group of independent readers?

UNIT TWO · *How the Nations tried to get Wealth from the New World*

[8 Weeks

ADDITIONAL STORIES FOR MORE ADVANCED READERS

Balboa
Ponce de Leon
Conquest of Peru
Coronado
Spanish Life in the New World
John Hawkins and the English SlaveTrade
England and the Spanish Armada

Life in the French Colonies
Champlain and the Iroquois Indians
Americus Vespucius
Portugal in Brazil
Portugal in the Indies
The Age of Pirates

A. THE SPANISH EXPLORATIONS

STORY 1. THE SUCCESS AND FAILURE OF COLUMBUS   [1 Week

Conversational Approach

"From our last story we know what Columbus was trying to do. What was it? Does anyone happen to know whether or not he succeeded in doing that particular thing?" Turn to two maps, — one showing the world as Columbus thought it was, and one as it actually is. "What was in the way that Columbus knew nothing about?

"Our story today tells what Columbus found."

Reading and Study

The Reading Periods

Independent Readers

This group reads the entire story through silently, as given in their text. They then test their comprehension by the study-guide questions furnished by the teacher or the text.

TEXTS

BARKER, DODD, WEBB, *Our Nation Begins,* 59–70.

BEARD and BAGLEY, *First Book in American History,* 10–20.

BURNHAM and JACK, *Beginnings of Our Country,* 33–36.

CLARK-GORDY, *First Three Hundred Years,* 23–28 (hard).

CLARK-GORDY, *Westward toward America,* 348–354.

KELTY, *Beginnings of the American People and Nation,* 75–88.

KNOWLTON and WHEELER. *Our Past in Western Europe,* 234–244 (hard).

NIDA, *Following Columbus,* 36–42.

SMALLIDGE and PAXSON, *Finding America,* 109–118.

WOODBURN and MORAN, *Finders and Founders of the New World,* 1–9, 34–46.

EXTENSIVE READING

CHANDLER and CHITWOOD, *Makers of American History,* 18–23.

COE, *Founders of Our Country,* 16–35.

DAVIDSON, *Founders and Builders of Our Nation,* 12–21.

FARIS, *Real Stories of the Geography Makers,* 68–74.

FIELD, *Finding the New World,* 58–88.

FOOTE and SKINNER, *Explorers and Founders of America,* 29–36.

JONES, *Geography by Discovery,* 36–45.

Lower Group

The teacher tells the story orally to the children, writing on the board the names of the most important persons and places as she mentions them. Children practice the pronunciations.

Then the teacher and the lower-group children read together the story as given in the text. The teacher guides the silent reading, section by section, by the same type of questions she would use in a silent-reading period; for example, "What do the first two paragraphs tell about the trouble the ship had?"

After the entire story has been read in this manner, the children test themselves by the study-guide questions.

OTHER BOOKS

BALDWIN, *Thirty More Famous Stories,* 8–9.

BLAISDELL and BALL, *American History for Little Folks,* 7–11.

BLAISDELL and BALL, *Child's Book of American History,* 3–7.

DAVIS, *Stories of the United States,* 37–47.

LUCIA, *Stories of American Discoverers for Little Americans,* 19–32, 39–40.

PRATT, *Beginners' Book,* 29–36.

TERRY, *History Stories from Other Lands,* I: 89–96.

WAYLAND, *History Stories for Primary Grades,* 91–94.

WILSON, *History Reader,* 42–49.

LAWLER, *Story of Columbus and Magellan,* 41–65.
MONTGOMERY, *Beginners' American History,* 6–13.
PERRY and PRICE, *American History,* I: 4–7, 13–16, 37–46.
PRATT, *Exploration and Discovery,* 22–32.
SHAW, *Discoverers and Explorers,* 24–39.
SOUTHWORTH, *Builders of Our Country,* I: 31–36.
TAPPAN, *American Hero Stories,* 5–13.
TAPPAN, *European Hero Stories,* 173–176.
VAN LOON, *Short History of Discovery,* 78–89.

READING FOR RECREATION (*Both Groups*)

HUTCHINSON, *The Men Who Found America.*
LENNES and PHILLIPS, *The Story of Columbus.*
LOWITZ, *The Cruise of Mr. Christopher Columbus.*
STABLES, *Westward with Columbus.*

The Discussion

Children answer the study-guide questions as completely as possible. If important phases are omitted, they question one another in order to bring out the most important points. Those who have read from several books may have new material to contribute.

The teacher writes on the board the words *to discover, a discovery, a discoverer, mutiny.* Children discuss the meanings.

Multisensory Aids

The teacher and the children talk over together the pictures in the text, noting features of historical or geographical significance. They turn to a map of Columbus's voyages. Children tell how the different voyages are marked. They point out the arrows showing the direction of the ship. They tell whether or not Columbus ever reached the Indies (according to the map).

AUDIO-VISUAL MATERIALS OBTAINABLE

BRADLEY. Straight-Line Picture Cut-outs: Landing of Columbus.
BROWN. Famous Pictures: 1921, 704–M.
Chronicles of America Photoplays: Columbus.
Compton's Pictured Teaching Materials: *Middle Ages,* II, Plate XII, 4; *Holidays,* Plate III.
EASTMAN. Classroom Films: From Haiti to Trinidad.
GABRIEL (Ed.). Pageant of America, I, 105–110.
National Geographic Magazine, LIX, 80–112 (January, 1931); LXVI, 435–485 (October, 1934).
Perry Pictures: 1323–1326, 1269, 1328–1329, 658.
Yale Pageant Educational Slides: 8, 504, 505.

Music. Play selections from Franchetti's opera *Cristoforo Colombo.*

General Activities

Creative Activities: Group and Individual, Correlated with Other Subjects or Voluntary Projects

Committees of children read to the class such dramatizations as Hubbard's *Little American History Plays* (6–12) and Shoemaker's *Colonial Plays for the Schoolroom* (17–20).

Children give floor talks on the third and fourth voyages; on the Sargasso Sea.

The class makes a picture collection of Columbus's ships and of steamships of today.

Committees make a list of articles not native to the New World which Columbus introduced here. Can you find anything about the annual value of those articles now? (See World Almanac.)

Committees report on different articles which white people learned to use by watching the Indians. One reports on the history of the so-called Irish potato; another, on Indian corn and popcorn; another, on pumpkins, squash, and beans; another, on American cotton; another, on chocolate.

A volunteer recites Joaquin Miller's poem, "Columbus."

The class continues the time chart.

Each child makes a map showing all of Columbus's voyages, using different colors. (Save this and add later Spanish explorations.)

Application to Present-Day Conditions

Look in the index of an atlas and select places named for Columbus. Find these places on the map. Name all the other ways you can think of in which Columbus has been honored?

Do you think that Columbus Day should be celebrated every year? How do you think it should be done?

How many years have passed since the discovery of America?

How long does it take today to make the voyage that Columbus made? (See the advertising folders of steamship companies.) Graph the two figures of time needed.

What do we now call the group of islands on which Columbus first landed? Who owns them now? What is the present name of "The Spanish Island"? (See a large map.)

In what way is the name *Indians* the record of a mistake? the name *West Indies*?

Does the United States today own any land actually touched by Columbus?

Exercises in Reasoning

Why did the Indians not use rowboats instead of canoes?

Was Columbus ever able to deliver his letter to Marco Polo's Great King?

Are ships still troubled by the fact that the northeast trade winds always blow northeast?

Why did the sailors feel new hope when they saw articles floating on the waves?

Since Columbus did not bring back much gold, why did people become so excited about his first voyage?

Why was it a mistake to sell the Indians as slaves?

How do we know about what happened on the voyage? [*Columbus's Journal.*]

In what way was Columbus both a success and a failure?

Drill Games

Place names (*Spain, Canary Islands*) are best drilled upon at the map. Drill cards are made as follows for the names of persons and for dates and vocabulary terms.

Indians	⟷	a name given to the natives of America
1492	⟷	the year when Columbus discovered America
discovery	⟷	something which is discovered is called a _ _ _ _ _ _ _ _ _ _ _ _
to discover	⟷	to find something that was there before but that nobody knew about
discoverer	⟷	the person who makes a discovery
mutiny	⟷	an uprising against the leaders

Drill games, using both sides of the cards.

Testing

Tests of Understanding are provided on page 88 of Kelty's *Beginnings of the American People and Nation.*

Additional Tests of Reasoning and Skills.[1] Check the best answers.

1. People in Europe were excited about Columbus's supposed finding of the Indies because   they wanted to take trips to the Indies.   √ they could make money trading with the Indies.   Columbus brought back so much gold.   they wanted to go to the Indies to live.

2. Columbus's colony in the Spanish Island failed because   the climate was too hot.   the Indians were not friendly.   the colonists did not like Columbus.   √ the colonists were not working people.

3. Turn to the map of Columbus's voyages. Did Columbus touch North America?   Yes [ ]   No [√]

4. Turn to the index of your text. Material about the *Pinta* will be found on what pages? _ _ _ _ _ _

Does this word come before or after the word *printing.*

Before [√]   After [ ]

5. Put the figure *1* in front of the thing which happened first and the figure *2* in front of the thing which happened later.

[_ _2_ _] Vasco da Gama reached India.
[_ _1_ _] Columbus discovered America.

Exercises in Organization. Continue the outline begun on page 138 to include this story also.

One child tells the complete story of point one; another, of point two; and so on.

Children are shown how to keep their own test scores.

[1] Other exercises in reasoning are included under "General Activities."

STORY 2. MAGELLAN'S CIRCUMNAVIGATION OF THE GLOBE [1 Week

Conversational Approach

"What had been Columbus's purpose in making his voyages? Had he succeeded in this purpose? Do you think that the people of Europe would give up the idea then? Why not? [*Desire for trade by means of an all-sea route.*] Would Portugal be interested any longer? Why not? [*The route around Africa.*] Why were not all the nations satisfied after the route around Africa had been found?

"Our story today tells about the man who succeeded where Columbus failed. However, this success cost him his life."

Reading and Study

The Reading Periods

Independent Readers

TEXTS

BARKER, DODD, WEBB, *Our Nation Begins*, 78–83.

BEARD and BAGLEY, *First Book in American History*, 24–32.

BURNHAM and JACK, *Beginnings of Our Country*, 40–45.

CLARK-GORDY, *Westward toward America*, 360–364.

KELTY, *Beginnings of the American People and Nation*, 89–99.

KNOWLTON and WHEELER, *Our Past in Western Europe*, 257–263 (hard).

NIDA, *Following Columbus*, 49–57.

SMALLIDGE and PAXSON, *Finding America*, 154–166.

WOODBURN and MORAN, *Finders and Founders of the New World*, 59–64.

EXTENSIVE READING

COE, *Founders of Our Country*, 63–74.

FARIS, *Real Stories of the Geography Makers*, 87–92.

FIELD, *Finding the New World*, 136–150.

FOOTE and SKINNER, *Explorers and Founders of America*, 81–86.

JONES, *Geography by Discovery*, 47–61.

LAWLER, *Story of Columbus and Magellan*, 94–144.

PERRY and PRICE, *American History*, I: 48–56.

SHAW, *Discoverers and Explorers*, 62–67.

SOUTHWORTH, *Builders of Our Country*, I: 58–59.

TAPPAN, *American Hero Stories*, 14–24.

TAPPAN, *European Hero Stories*, 179–183.

VAN LOON, *Short History of Discovery*, 98–99.

Lower Group

The teacher tells the story orally to these children, writing on the board the names of the most important persons and places as she mentions them. Children practice the pronunciations.

Then the teacher and the lower group together read the story as given in the text. The teacher guides their silent reading, section by section, by the same type of questions that she would use in a silent-reading period; for example, "The first two paragraphs tell who had come to the king's court. Who was it?"

After the entire story has been read in this manner the children test themselves by the study-guide questions.

OTHER BOOKS

BRAINE, *Merchant Ships and What They Bring Us*.

BURKS, *Barbara's Philippine Journey*, 42–49.

LUCIA, *Stories of American Discoverers for Little Americans*, 79–87.

WADE, *Our Little Philippine Cousin*, 88–102.

READING FOR RECREATION (*Both Groups*)

The teacher puts on the bookshelf for recreational reading for both groups such books as

BURKS, *Barbara's Philippine Journey*.
HARTMAN, *These United States* (hard).
OBER, *Ferdinand Magellan*.
WADE, *Our Little Philippine Cousin*.

The Discussion

Children answer the study-guide questions as fully as possible. If important phases are omitted, they question one another in order to bring out the most important points. Those who have read from several books may have new material to contribute.

The teacher writes on the board the words *natives* and *circumnavigation*. Children discuss the meanings.

Multisensory Aids

The teacher and the children talk over together the pictures in the text, noting features of historical or geographical importance. They turn to a map of Magellan's voyage. Children show how Magellan's voyage is marked and in which direction his ships were going all along the line. They trace his route on a large wall map and on a globe.

AUDIO-VISUAL MATERIALS OBTAINABLE

Compton's Pictured Teaching Materials: *Middle Ages*, II, Plate XI, 3.
Gabriel (Ed.). Pageant of America, I, 117–119.
International Educational Pictures: In the Lee of the Horn.
Keystone View Slides: 14.
National Geographic Magazine, LXII, 699–740 (December, 1932).
Yale Pageant Educational Slides: 10, 11, 598.

General Activities

Creative Activities: Group and Individual, Correlated with Other Subjects or Voluntary Projects

A committee makes a collection of the trade goods carried by Magellan. (Are such goods used anywhere today in trading?)

Volunteers write a diary of the voyage, noting especially the search for an opening through South America, the winter in Patagonia and the mutiny, the passage through the straits, the long voyage across the Pacific, the fight in the Philippines, the trials of the homeward voyage, the return.

A committee reads to the class the dramatization given in Bird and Starling's *Historical Plays for Children* (97–115).

Some children may wish to write poems about Magellan.

A round-the-world traveler may tell the children of his experiences in the South Seas.

Each child adds the voyage of Magellan to the map of Spanish explorations begun in the last story.

The class continues the time chart.

Application to Present-Day Conditions

Why were the Philippines given their name? Why has the United States been particularly interested in them? What change in their government takes place in 1945? (See periodicals of 1935 under heading *Philippines*.)

In what way would Magellan's voyage have been much shorter if either the Panama or the Suez Canal had been built then?

What does the word *Patagonia* mean? (See Webster's New International Dictionary, unabridged.)

Is Magellan's route one that is much used nowadays? (Compare with geography maps of world trade routes.) Why not?

How long does it take to sail around the world today? (See advertising folders of steamship companies.) to fly around the world? (See *Aviation* in a children's encyclopedia.)

Can you find the Islands of Thieves [*Ladrones, or Marianne Islands*] on a map of the world today? Under whose control are they?

Exercises in Reasoning

How did Magellan know that South America was a separate continent and not just a group of islands off Asia? When did he come to this belief?

Would you believe everything in a journal written by a sailor who had not liked Magellan? Would he mean to tell an untruth?

From what you read in the story, can you make a sentence telling what a strait is?

Compare the way in which Magellan set up a mark to claim the new land with the way the Portuguese had marked their claims.

Did Magellan discover the Pacific Ocean?

Why is Magellan classed as a Spanish sailor when he was born in Portugal?

Drill Games

The place names (*Strait of Magellan, Philippines, South America, Pacific Ocean*) should be drilled upon at the map.

Drill cards are also made as follows:

1519–1522	↔	the years of Magellan's voyage
natives	↔	persons born in that country
Magellan	↔	the first man whose ship circumnavigated the globe
circumnavigation	↔	sailing around the world is called _ _ _ _ _ _ _ _ _ _ _

Children practice by themselves, recording their own errors.

Testing

Tests of Understanding are provided on page 99 of Kelty's *Beginnings of the American People and Nation.*

Additional Tests of Reasoning and Skills.[1] Check the right answer.

1. Magellan knew that South America could not be an island because   it had very high mountains.   it had so many bays.   √ it was so large. it was so far to the south.

2. Magellan discovered the Pacific Ocean.   True [ ]   False [√]

---

[1] Other exercises in reasoning are included under "General Activities."

3. Magellan named the Pacific Ocean.   True [√]   False [ ]

4. Turn to a map of Magellan's voyage. Did Magellan touch the shore of North America?   Yes [ ]   No [√]

5. Put the figure *1* in front of the thing which happened first and the figure *2* in front of the thing which happened later.

[_ _2_ _] Magellan sailed around the world.

[_ _1_ _] Columbus discovered America.

Exercise in Organization. Make summary sentences telling the main points of the story.

Children record their own test scores.

STORY 3. CORTEZ IN MEXICO

Conversational Approach

"How many Spanish sailors have we read about so far? Had Spain become rich from trade with the Indies? Do you suppose, then, that Spaniards would give up trying to trade with India by an all-sea route? Why did they not use the route of Magellan? Our story today tells us how Spaniards kept up the search for the riches of the East."

Reading and Study

The Reading Periods

Independent Readers

TEXTS

BARKER, DODD, WEBB, *Our Nation Begins,* 87–94.

BURNHAM and JACK, *Beginnings of Our Country,* 46–52.

CLARK-GORDY, *First Three Hundred Years,* 33–38 (hard).

KELTY, *Beginnings of the American People and Nation,* 100–114.

KNOWLTON and WHEELER, *Our Past in Western Europe,* 263–276 (hard).

NIDA, *Following Columbus,* 125–137.

SMALLIDGE and PAXSON, *Finding America,* 179–185.

EXTENSIVE READING

COE, *Founders of Our Country,* 41–51.

FIELD, *Finding the New World,* 151–175.

FOOTE and SKINNER, *Explorers and Founders of America,* 63–71.

LAWLER, *Story of Columbus and Magellan,* 73–81.

PERRY and PRICE, *American History,* I: 59–68.

PRATT, *Exploration and Discovery,* 51–67

SHAW, *Discoverers and Explorers,* 68–77.

Lower Group

The teacher tells the story orally to this group, writing on the board the names of the most important persons and places as she mentions them. Children practice the pronunciations.

Then these children and the teacher read the story together as given in the text. The teacher guides their silent reading, section by section, by the type of questions that she would use in a silent-reading period; for example, "Why did this boy dream of far-away lands?"

After the entire story has been read in this manner the children test themselves by the study-guide questions.

OTHER BOOKS

LUCIA, *Stories of American Discoverers for Little Americans,* 54–78.

PRATT, *Beginners' Book,* 37–52.

READING FOR RECREATION

The teacher puts on the bookshelf for recreational reading for both groups such books as the following:

SOUTHWORTH, *Builders of Our Country*, I: 43–46.

VAN LOON, *Short History of Discovery*, 104–105.

LANG (Ed.), *Conquest of Montezuma's Empire*.

HUTCHINSON, *The Men Who Found America*.

JANVIER, *Aztec Treasure House*.

PERKINS, *Mexican Twins*.

PLUMMER, *Roy and Ray in Mexico*.

WADE, *Ten Big Indians*, 11–44.

The Discussion

Children answer the study-guide questions as fully as possible. The teacher takes advantage of the occasion to check firmly those children who read rapidly but inaccurately and who have run through the stories in four or five books but who still cannot answer the study-guide questions.

The teacher writes on the board the words *capital city, conquest, interpreter*. Children discuss the meanings.

Multisensory Aids

The teacher and the children talk over together the pictures in the text, noting features of historical or geographical significance. They turn to a map of Cortez's route and show where he burned his ships.

The teacher shows prints of modern Mexican pictures by Diego Rivera and Orozco.

AUDIO-VISUAL MATERIALS OBTAINABLE

Compton's Pictured Teaching Materials: *Middle Ages*, II, Plate XII, 2.

EASTMAN. Classroom Films: Mexico.

GABRIEL (Ed.). Pageant of America: I, 128–136.

International Educational Pictures: Land of Montezuma.

Keystone View Slides: 1, 2.

National Geographic Magazine, LVIII, 45–84 (July, 1930).

MILLER. *Picturesque Tale of Progress*, VIII, 65–174.

Society for Visual Education. Picturols: Mexico City; A Trip through Old Mexico; Mexico and its People; Mexico, the Old and the New; The Conquest of Mexico and Peru.

Yale Pageant Educational Slides: 12, 16, 600.

Music. Play records of Mexican songs.

General Activities

Creative Activities: Group and Individual, Correlated with Other Subjects or Voluntary Projects

From the local automobile club the class secures maps of the highway to Mexico and advertising booklets with pictures.

A committee dramatizes the story in a succession of scenes, such as (1) Cortez in Spain; (2) Cortez in the Spanish Island and Cuba; (3) Landing at Veracruz; (4) The Advance on the City of Mexico and the First Conquest; (5) The Loss of the City of Mexico; (6) Reconquering the City.

Children make a collection of Indian designs. They themselves draw designs with which to decorate pottery for the program described on page 176.

The teacher reads to the children selected portions of Archibald MacLeish's poem "Conquistador."

A volunteer finds a picture of the great Aztec calendar stone and explains what it tells about Aztec science.

A volunteer draws Cortez's flag in color. (*National Geographic Magazine,* LXVI: 371 (September, 1934).

Volunteers make a picture collection of Egyptian and Mexican pyramids and compare the two.

Each child adds the route of Cortez to the map of Spanish explorations.

The class continues the time chart.

Application to Present-Day Conditions

Are there any Indians in Mexico today?

Does Spain own Mexico today?

What does *Veracruz* mean? [*True cross.*] Find Veracruz on the map.

Does Mexico today produce gold and silver? (See World Almanac.)

Do people traveling in foreign lands nowadays ever need an interpreter?

Ask a traveler to the city of Mexico to describe Xochimilco. What connection has it with our story?

What language is spoken in Mexico today?

In what part of our country are there many Mexicans today? What do they do?

Exercises in Reasoning

Compare the route of Cortez with the route of General Scott in the Mexican War. (See Kelty's *The Growth of the American People and Nation,* p. 173.) Why are they so much alike?

What right had Cortez to take Mexico away from the Indians?

Now that the Spaniards have found riches, will they give up trying to reach the Indies?

Why were a few Spaniards able to conquer so many Indians? [*Guns and gunpowder.*]

Should you believe that the Spaniards' side of the story about the conquest of Mexico was entirely true, or should you want to hear the Indians' side too?

Drill Games

Drill on the place names (*Gulf of Mexico, Mexico, city of Mexico*) can best be done at the map.

Drill cards are also made as follows:

Cortez	⟷	the man who conquered Mexico
Aztecs	⟷	Indians who lived in Mexico
capital city	⟷	city where the laws are made or where the ruler lives
conquest	⟷	the act of conquering is called _
interpreter	⟷	a person who tells the meaning of what is said in a foreign language

Drill with both sides of the cards.

Testing

Tests of Understanding follow.

1. Pass outline maps of North America and give the following directions:
a. Shade Mexico lightly.
b. Put a star where the city of Mexico should be.
c. Write the words *Gulf of Mexico* in the right place.
Check the best answer.

2. The Aztecs were the Indians who   helped Cortez's soldiers to fight.
√ lived in and around Mexico City.   lived on islands in the Gulf.

3. Cortez was the man who   discovered the Pacific Ocean.   acted as governor of Cuba.   √ conquered Mexico for Spain.

4. A capital city is   the largest city in a country.   √ the city where the laws are made.   the oldest city in the country.

5. The conquest of a place means   √ taking it by force.   discovering it for the first time.   a changing of rulers.

6. An interpreter is any person   who speaks a different language from yours.   who listens to what everyone says.   √ who explains what has been said in a foreign language.

Additional Tests on Reasoning and Skills.[1] Check the right answer.

1. The Spaniards knew there were gold and precious stones in Mexico √ from the reports of sailors.   from the voyages of Columbus.   from the stories of Indians.

2. The Spaniards did not need the Indies any more because   they had found the best route to the Indies.   √ they had found a land as rich as the Indies.   the Indies no longer produced any goods.

3. Turn to the map of Cortez's journey. Did Cortez reach the Pacific Coast?   Yes [ ]   No [√]

4. Put the figure *1* in front of the thing which happened first and the figure *2* in front of the thing which happened later.

[_ _2_ _] Cortez conquered Mexico.
[_ _1_ _] Vasco da Gama reached India.

Exercise in Organization. Teacher and children make co-operatively an outline of the story. Different children tell the story of each part of the outline.
Children record their own test scores.

STORY 4. DE SOTO DISCOVERS THE MISSISSIPPI   [*1 Week*

Conversational Approach

"When the people in Spain heard of the riches of Mexico, why would many of them want to go there? What would happen if too many went? Do you suppose that some of them would rather go somewhere else? Why? [*To*

---

[1] Other exercises in reasoning are included under "General Activities."

find new sources of riches for their own glory.] What places have not yet been explored? Our story today is about a man who struck out for himself. We shall see what he found."

Reading and Study

The Reading Periods

Independent Readers

TEXTS

BARKER, DODD, WEBB, *Our Nation Begins,* 111–116.

BURNHAM and JACK, *Beginnings of Our Country,* 56–58.

CLARK-GORDY, *First Three Hundred Years,* 30–32 (hard).

CLARK-GORDY, *Westward toward America,* 356–359.

KELTY, *The Beginning of the American People and Nation,* 115–125.

KNOWLTON and WHEELER, *Our Past in Western Europe,* 279–281 (hard).

NIDA, *Following Columbus,* 63–73.

SMALLIDGE and PAXSON, *Finding America,* 198–207.

WOODBURN and MORAN, *Finders and Founders of the New World,* 72–76.

EXTENSIVE READING

CHANDLER and CHITWOOD, *Makers of American History,* 39–43.

COE, *Founders of Our Country,* 52–62.

FIELD, *Finding the New World,* 212–232.

FOOTE and SKINNER, *Explorers and Founders of America,* 47–56.

MONTGOMERY, *Beginners' American History,* 20.

PERRY and PRICE, *American History,* I : 78–82.

PRATT, *Exploration and Discovery,* 77–83.

SHAW, *Discoverers and Explorers,* 84–91.

SOUTHWORTH, *Builders of Our Country,* I : 50–53.

VAN LOON, *Short History of Discovery,* 108–109.

Lower Group

The teacher tells the story orally to this group, writing on the board the names of the most important persons and places as she mentions them. Children practice the pronunciations.

This group and the teacher then read together the story as given in the text. The teacher guides the silent reading, section by section, by the same type of questions that she would use in a silent-reading period; for example, "The first section tells what kinds of things were brought in the ships to Florida. Read to find out what they were."

After the entire story has been read in this manner the children test themselves by the study-guide questions.

OTHER BOOKS

LUCIA, *Stories of American Discoverers for Little Americans,* 126–138.

READING FOR RECREATION

HUTCHINSON, *Men Who Found America.*

The Discussion

Children answer the study-guide questions as completely as possible. The teacher makes an effort to include children from the lower-ability group in the discussion.

She writes on the board the words *explore, explorer, exploration, score of years.* Children discuss the meanings.

Multisensory Aids

The teacher and the children talk over together the pictures in the text, noting features of geographical or historical importance. They turn to a map of De Soto's wanderings, and trace his route on a large wall map by the use of the data supplied.

AUDIO-VISUAL MATERIALS OBTAINABLE

BROWN. Famous Pictures: 97.
GABRIEL (Ed.). Pageant of America: I, 143–144.
McKINLEY. Illustrated Topics for American History: S. 1.
Perry Pictures: 1330.
Society for Visual Education (BRIGGS). Spanish Conquerors and Explorers.
Yale Pageant Educational Slides: 601.

Music. Play selections from Ferdie Grofé's *Mississippi Suite.*

General Activities

Creative Activities: Group and Individual, Correlated with Other Subjects or Voluntary Projects

The class plans an automobile trip, following De Soto's route.

Volunteers draw a series of three theme illustrations representing (1) the setting out of the expedition, (2) the burial of De Soto, (3) the return of the survivors to Mexico.

If possible secure a piece of copper ore and a piece of gold ore. Compare a finished article of copper with one of gold.

A volunteer gives a floor talk on the conquest of Peru (during which De Soto first became a rich man); another reports on Ponce de Leon's experiences in Florida.

Volunteers compare De Soto's death with the death of other explorers in far-away lands; for example, Scott, Livingstone, Amundsen, Magellan.

Each child adds De Soto's route to the map of Spanish explorations and shades lightly all the land now claimed by Spain in the New World.

The class continues the time chart.

Application to Present-Day Conditions

Name the present-day states of the United States which De Soto passed over. (Compare a geography map of the United States with the map given in the text.)

Does Spain own the territory which De Soto explored?

Do any states of the United States use the term *New* as part of their name, just as Mexico was formerly called *New* Spain?

How can you account for the fact that the Indians of the Western plains used horses after the arrival of the Spaniards when they never had had any horses before?

What does the word *Mississippi* mean? (See Webster's New International Dictionary, unabridged.) Is this river the largest river in the world? the longest?

Do you think you could make a ship if you had nothing more to work with than the Spaniards had on their return to Mexico?

Are there any unexplored regions in the world today? (See Bowman's *Geography in Relation to the Social Sciences*, p. 116.)

Exercises in Reasoning

When the people who wanted to join De Soto's party came to him, why did he send home the Spaniards who were dressed in silk?

Why did the Indians come to hate white men?

If tin cans had been known in De Soto's time, how would that fact have changed the equipment for his expedition?

Do you think that De Soto died happy?

Compare De Soto's burial with other cases of secret burial in early American history.

Why would other Spaniards not be eager to go to the lands which had been explored by De Soto?

Drill Games

Drill cards are made as follows:

De Soto	⟷	the Spaniard who discovered the Mississippi
Mississippi River	⟷	the river discovered by De Soto
to explore	⟷	to travel over new lands
explorer	⟷	a person who travels over new lands
exploration	⟷	traveling through new lands is called making an _ _ _ _ _
score of years	⟷	twenty years are called a _ _ _ _ _ _ _ _ _ _ _ _ _ _ _ _ _ _ _

These cards are accessible to the children all through their period of study.

Testing

Tests of Understanding are supplied on page 125 of Kelty's *Beginnings of the American People and Nation.*

Additional Tests of Reasoning and Skills [1]

Check the best answer: 1. Other Spaniards did not want to settle the Mississippi region because   the Indians would not help them.   it was very hard work.   De Soto had been buried in the river.   √ the country had no supply of gold.

2. Make a list of all the titles of stories in Unit Two up to date.

3. Turn to a map of De Soto's journey. Check: Does the map show the route by which De Soto's men at last made their way to Mexico?

Yes [ ]   No [√]

4. Make a sentence telling whether De Soto's journey would have been easier or harder if he had been kind to the Indians.

Exercise in Organization

1. Make a list of the headings in the story. Give a few summary sentences about each heading.

[1] Other exercises in reasoning are included under "General Activities."

2. Make a table headed "Spanish Exploration." Under it write the names of the explorers studied, and opposite each explorer's name write a statement of what he did and why it was important.

Name of Explorer	What he Did	Why Important

Children record their own test scores. The teacher shows them how to make a table, leaving space in the first column for the name or number of the story; in the second column, for the number of items that they themselves wrote correctly on each test; in the third, for the highest possible score on each test.

B. THE ENGLISH EXPLORATIONS

STORY 1. THE CABOTS DISCOVER NORTH AMERICA · STORY 2. FRANCIS DRAKE AND THE SPANIARDS   [1 Week

[Stories treated separately for reading and discussion; for other activities, both together]

Conversational Approach

"Name the explorers about whom we have been reading in this unit. They were all sent out by what country?

"How do you suppose other countries would feel when they heard of the wealth pouring into Spain? What should you expect them to do about it?

If the text used contains a table of contents, it will be helpful to turn to it and notice how the author shows that the explorations were made by different nations. Does the title of the unit indicate the purpose of all the explorations?"

Reading and Study

The Reading Periods (First Story)

Independent Readers

This group reads the entire story through silently, as given in their text. They then test their comprehension by the study-guide questions furnished by the teacher or by the text.

TEXTS

BARKER, DODD, WEBB, *Our Nation Begins*, 176–179.

BEARD and BAGLEY, *First Book in American History*, 26–29.

BURNHAM and JACK, *Beginnings of Our Country*, 36–38.

CLARK-GORDY, *First Three Hundred Years*, 151–155 (hard).

CLARK-GORDY, *Westward toward America*, 374–375.

Lower Group

The teacher tells the story orally to this group, writing on the board the names of the most important persons and places as she mentions them. Children practice the pronunciations.

This group and the teacher then read together the story as given in the text. The teacher guides the silent reading, section by section, by the same type of questions that she would use in a silent-reading period; for example, "Why was Spain growing poor while England was beginning to grow rich?"

After the entire story has been read in this manner the children test themselves by the study-guide questions.

A Model Representing the Spanish Treasure Fleet

The picture shows the town of Nombre de Dios, with the Spanish galleons in the harbor. Notice the train of llamas bringing down the gold and silver from the mines. The main church of the mission is in the right foreground, and the fort at the left in the background

KELTY, *Beginnings of the American People and Nation*, 126–133.
NIDA, *Following Columbus*, 44–47.
SMALLIDGE and PAXSON, *Finding America*, 129–135.
WOODBURN and MORAN, *Finders and Founders of the New World*, 48–54.

EXTENSIVE READING

CHANDLER and CHITWOOD, *Makers of American History*, 30–33.
COE, *Founders of Our Country*, 75–79.
FIELD, *Finding the New World*, 89–95.
FOOTE and SKINNER, *Explorers and Founders of America*, 87–90.
MONTGOMERY, *Beginners' American History*, 14–18.
SHAW, *Discoverers and Explorers*, 44–47.
SOUTHWORTH, *Builders of Our Country*, I: 37–40.
VAN LOON, *Short History of Discovery*, 90–91.

OTHER BOOKS

BLAISDELL and BALL, *Child's Book of American History*, 8–11.
DAVIS, *Stories of the United States*, 53–55.
LUCIA, *Stories of American Discoverers for Little Americans*, 33–38.
WILSON, *A History Reader*, 58–61.

READING FOR RECREATION

ROLT-WHEELER, *The Coming of the Peoples.*

The Discussion (First Story)

Children answer as fully as possible the study-guide questions. The teacher writes on the board the words *claims* (*of a country*) and *mainland*. Children discuss the meanings.

The Reading Periods (Second Story)

Independent Readers

This group reads the entire story through silently, as given in their text. They then test their comprehension by the study-guide questions furnished by the teacher or by the text.

TEXTS

BARKER, DODD, WEBB, *Our Nation Begins*, 179–183.
BEARD and BAGLEY, *First Book in American History*, 38–44, 47.
BURNHAM and JACK, *Beginnings of Our Country*, 70–74.
CLARK-GORDY, *First Three Hundred Years*, 155–156 (hard).
CLARK-GORDY, *Westward toward America*, 375–379.
KELTY, *Beginnings of the American People and Nation*, 134–145.
KNOWLTON and WHEELER, *Our Past in Western Europe*, 320–326 (hard).
NIDA, *Following Columbus*, 107–117.
SMALLIDGE and PAXSON, *Finding America*, 222–234.
WOODBURN and MORAN, *Finders and Founders of the New World*, 78–84.

Lower Group

The teacher tells the story orally to this group, writing on the board the names of the most important persons and places as she mentions them. Children practice the pronunciations.

This group and the teacher then read together the story as given in the text. The teacher guides the silent reading, section by section, by the same type of questions that she would use in a silent-reading period; for example, "The first paragraph tells us why Francis Drake hated the Spaniards. Why was it?"

After the entire story has been read in this manner the children test themselves by the study-guide questions.

OTHER BOOKS

BALDWIN, *Thirty More Famous Stories Retold*, 17–22.
DAVIS, *Stories of the United States*, 55–57.
LUCIA, *Stories of American Discoverers for Little Americans*, 139–150.

EXTENSIVE READING

COE, *Founders of Our Country*, 80–97.
FARIS, *Real Stories of the Geography Makers*,
93–98.
FIELD, *Finding the New World*, 310–338.
FOOTE and SKINNER, *Explorers and Found-
ers of America*, 91–102.
JONES, *Geography by Discovery*, 82–97.
PRATT, *Exploration and Discovery*, 127–136.
SHAW, *Discoverers and Explorers*, 108–113.
SOUTHWORTH, *Builders of Our Country*, I:
57–62.
TAPPAN, *American Hero Stories*, 24–37.

READING FOR RECREATION

HARTMAN, *These United States* (hard).

The Discussion (Second Story)

Children answer as fully as possible the study-guide questions. The teacher
writes on the board the words *Spanish Main, South Sea, to confer knighthood,
decade, pirate, sack of a city, attack*. Children discuss the meanings.

Multisensory Aids

The teacher and the children talk over the pictures for both stories in the
text, pointing out features of geographical or historical importance. They
turn to a map and show how the routes of the Cabots are marked as distinguished from that of Drake. They show these same routes on a large wall
map and point out the Spanish Main.

AUDIO-VISUAL MATERIALS OBTAINABLE

GABRIEL (Ed.). Pageant of America, I : 112–113, 162–164, 166.
Keystone View Slides : 19.
Yale Pageant Educational Slides : 19, 595, 605, 606.

General Activities

Creative Activities: Group and Individual, Correlated with Other Subjects or Voluntary Projects

Give a speech in which John Cabot describes the new lands he has found.
Draw and color the English flag which John Cabot planted on the shore of
Labrador. (See Webster's dictionary, unabridged.)
Make a stage set and on it show Drake's raid on the mule train in Panama.
Each child begins a map of "English Explorations in America" and marks
the routes of Cabot and Drake.
The class continues the time chart.

Application to Present-Day Conditions

Are any of Cabot's discoveries part of the British Empire today?
Is Labrador even colder than England? Why (since they are in nearly
the same latitude)? Do the waters round about still produce great numbers
of fish?

Do mothers ever frighten their children nowadays by telling them that someone will get them? What names are used today?

Are there any pirates in the world today?

Does the king of England ever confer knighthood on people nowadays?

The teacher tells the children about the "Drake fortune" fraud of recent times.

Exercises in Reasoning

Why could England not send her explorers to the same lands that Spain had found?

Could this story be called "England Enters the Game"? In what way was exploration a game?

Compare the aid given to John Cabot by the king of England on his first voyage with the aid given to Columbus by the queen and king of Spain.

Why was England disappointed in Cabot's new lands?

Sometimes you hear that certain sailors *sailed the Spanish Main.* Is that expression correct?

Do you think Drake's reasons for attacking Spanish towns were good ones?

Why did the English before Drake know so little about the Pacific Ocean?

Compare what Drake was trying to do with what Magellan had been trying to do.

Drill Games

Names of places are best drilled upon at the map: *North America, England, Pacific Coast of North America, Spanish Main, South Sea, California.*

Drill cards are made as follows:

1497	↔	the year John Cabot discovered North America
claims	↔	parts of a country that a nation calls its own are its _ _ _ _
mainland	↔	land on a continent and not on an island
John Cabot	↔	the man who discovered the mainland of North America
Francis Drake	↔	the first Englishman who circumnavigated the globe
to confer knighthood	↔	to give a man the title "Sir"
decade	↔	ten years are called a _ _ _ _ _ _ _ _ _ _ _ _ _ _ _ _ _ _
pirate	↔	one who robs at sea
sack of a city	↔	the robbing of a captured city
to attack	↔	to try to take by force

Children prepare themselves by drilling on their own difficulties.

Testing

Tests of Understanding are supplied on pages 133 and 144–145 of Kelty's *Beginnings of the American People and Nation.*

Additional Tests of Reasoning and Skills follow.[1] Check the best answer.

1. England laid claim to all the eastern coast of North America because of the voyages of   √ John Cabot.   Columbus.   Francis Drake.

[1] Other exercises are included under "General Activities."

2. The man who discovered the mainland of North America was   Columbus.   De Soto.   √ Cabot.

3. The first Englishman to circumnavigate the globe was   Magellan. √ Drake.   Cortez.

4. Drake sailed home around the world because   he wanted adventures in the Pacific.   that was the shortest way home.   it was too stormy around the Strait of Magellan.   √ he was afraid the Spaniards would catch him.

5. Drake helped to bring on war between England and Spain because √ he attacked Spanish towns in time of peace.   he sailed through Spanish waters.   he earned more money than the Spaniards.   the queen liked him so well.

6. A table of contents in a book is a list   √ at the beginning, telling the chief topics.   of words in the back of the book, telling the pages on which all the words listed can be found.

7. Turn to a map of the voyages of Cabot and Drake. Did John Cabot sail around the world?   Yes [ ]   No [√]   Did Drake go around the world?   Yes [√]   No [ ]

8. Put the figure *1* in front of the event which took place first and the figure *2* in front of the event which took place later.

[__1__] Columbus discovered America.

[__2__] John Cabot touched North America.

9. Do the same.

[__1__] Magellan sailed around the world.

[__2__] Drake sailed around the world.

Exercise in Organization. The lower group makes a list of the headings in the story of John Cabot. One child gives a summary of the first section; another, of the second section; and so on.

The upper group makes a list of the headings in the story of Francis Drake. One child gives a summary of the first section; another, of the second section; and so on.

Children record their own test scores.

STORY 3. WALTER RALEIGH'S COLONIES   [*1 Week*

Conversational Approach

"What was Columbus trying to do? Magellan? Cortez? De Soto? Cabot? Drake? Now we find a man who had a different idea. He wanted to find new homes for Englishmen. Why do you suppose Englishmen needed any new homes? Would some people in our country today be glad to go to a place where they might be given free land for a farm? Our story today is about the man who had this new idea. His name was Walter Raleigh."

Reading and Study

The Reading Periods

Independent Readers

TEXTS

BARKER, DODD, WEBB, *Our Nation Begins*, 186–190.

BEARD and BAGLEY, *First Book in American History*, 47–48.

BURNHAM and JACK, *Beginnings of Our Country*, 74–79.

CLARK-GORDY, *First Three Hundred Years*, 156–160 (hard).

CLARK-GORDY, *Westward toward America*, 379–382.

KELTY, *Beginnings of the American People and Nation*, 146–155.

KNOWLTON and WHEELER, *Our Past in Western Europe*, 328–333 (hard).

NIDA, *Following Columbus*, 146–156.

SMALLIDGE and PAXSON, *Finding America*, 238–251.

WOODBURN and MORAN, *Finders and Founders of the New World*, 84–92.

EXTENSIVE READING

BEEBY, *Community Life Today and in Colonial Times*, 222–225.

CHANDLER and CHITWOOD, *Makers of American History*, 44–50.

COE, *Founders of Our Country*, 98–110.

FIELD, *Finding the New World*, 280–309.

FOOTE and SKINNER, *Explorers and Founders of America*, 103–111.

INGRAHAM, *Story of Democracy*, 146–148.

JONES, *Geography by Discovery*, 99–111.

MONTGOMERY, *Beginners' American History*, 22–25.

SOUTHWORTH, *Builders of Our Country*, I: 64–72.

VAN LOON, *Short History of Discovery*, 116–117.

Lower Group

The teacher tells the story orally to this group, writing on the board the names of the most important persons and places as she mentions them. Children practice the pronunciations.

Then these children and the teacher read together the story as given in the text. The teacher guides the silent reading, section by section, by the same type of questions that she would use in a silent-reading period; for example, "Why did Walter Raleigh leave school?"

After the entire story has been read in this manner, children test themselves by the study-guide questions.

OTHER BOOKS

BALDWIN, *Fifty Famous Stories Retold*, 54–57.

DAVIS, *Stories of the United States*, 59–61.

WAYLAND, *History Stories for Primary Grades*, 13–14, 89–90.

WELSH, *Colonial Days*, 5–24.

WILSON, *A History Reader*, 90–92.

READING FOR RECREATION

ANDREWS, *Ten Boys Who Lived on the Road from Long Ago to Now*.

HUTCHINSON, *Men Who Found America*.

OBER, *Sir Walter Raleigh*.

The Discussion

Children answer as fully as possible the study-guide questions. One of the chief difficulties which will be revealed, doubtless, will be that some children read rapidly but inaccurately. In flagrant cases it may be necessary to transfer such children from the group of independent readers to the lower group until their study habits have improved.

The teacher writes on the board the words *courtier, failure, found a colony*. Children discuss the meanings.

Multisensory Aids

Children and teacher talk over together the pictures in the text, noting points of geographical or historical significance.

AUDIO-VISUAL MATERIALS OBTAINABLE

GABRIEL (Ed.). Pageant of America: I, 7–8, 159–161.
LONGMAN. Historical Illustrations: Pictures of English Court Life.
National Geographic Magazine, LXIV, 696, 698, 703 (December, 1933).
Yale Pageant Educational Slides: 17, 18, 42, 44, 604.

General Activities

Creative Activities: Group and Individual, Correlated with Other Subjects or Voluntary Projects

Some of the girls may dress dolls in the costumes of an English court gentleman, a court lady, a serving man, a serving woman.

Volunteers hold a conversation between Raleigh and Queen Elizabeth in which Raleigh argues the advantages of colonies in the New World and the Queen presents objections.

A committee reads to the class the dramatization given in Bird and Starling's *Historical Plays for Children* (79–95).

Volunteers present floor talks about Queen Elizabeth.

The class continues the time chart.

Applications to Present-Day Conditions

Look at a map of North Carolina. In what way is Raleigh's name honored there?

Is it ever dangerous to cross the North Atlantic today? Why?

Are potatoes produced today in any of the British Isles?

In what way does the name *Virginia* remind us of the history of these far-away times?

Is tobacco still sent to the British Isles? (See *Great Britain — Foreign Trade* in the New International Yearbook.)

Exercises in Reasoning

Is there any difference between *finding* a colony and *founding* a colony? Explain.

Compare Walter Raleigh with Prince Henry of Portugal.

Why did Raleigh send his colonies to the south?

Why were the Indians at first friendly and later unfriendly?

What do you think might have happened to the second colony?

What did Raleigh mean when he said of the ax which was to cut off his head, "'Tis a sharp medicine, but a cure for all diseases"?

How can Walter Raleigh be called "the Father of the English Colonies" when his colonies failed?

Did England prove grateful to Raleigh?

Should the story of Walter Raleigh's velvet cape and the mud puddle be put in history books whether it is true or not?

Drill Games

Prepare drill cards similar to the following:

Walter Raleigh	⟷	a man who tried to found English colonies in America
Virginia	⟷	land in America named for Queen Elizabeth
to found a colony	⟷	to begin a settlement in a new land
courtier	⟷	a follower at the court of a king
failure	⟷	something that is tried but does not succeed is a _ _ _ _ _ _

Some of the children will enjoy helping to make the cards.

Testing

Tests of Understanding are supplied in exercises II and III on pages 154–155 of Kelty's *Beginnings of the American People and Nation.*

Additional Tests of Reasoning and Skills.[1] Check the best answer.

1. The failure of Walter Raleigh's colonies showed that   colonies ought not to be made in the New World   English people did not know how to make colonies   √ not even a rich man could pay for a colony all by himself   the Spanish were the only nation that could make colonies.

2. We cannot say surely that the Indians destroyed the second colony, because _ _ _[*No sort of evidence was left.*]_ _ _

3. Turn to the back of the book. Write here the pages in the text on which you might read about Queen Elizabeth. _ _ _ _ _ _

4. Under which word did you look?   Queen [ ]   Elizabeth [√]

5. Put the figure *1* before the name of the man who lived first and the figure *2* before the name of the man who lived later. [_ _2_ _] Walter Raleigh [_ _ _1_ _ _] John Cabot

Exercises in Organization. The teacher and the children make a co-operative outline of the story.

The same sort of tabulation is made for "English Exploration" as appears on page 156.

C. THE FRENCH AND THE DUTCH EXPLORATIONS

STORY 1. CARTIER DISCOVERS THE GULF · STORY 2. CHAMPLAIN IN NEW FRANCE [1 Week

[Stories treated separately for reading and discussion; for other activities, both together]

Conversational Approach

"What two nations have now sent out their men to the New World? Where has Portugal sent her sailors? What great nation seems to have been left out of the race?

_____

[1] Other exercises in reasoning are included under "General Activities."

"The king of France once said, 'Show me the will of Father Adam which divides up the New World between other countries.' What did he mean? What, then, do you suppose he will do?'"

Reading and Study

The Reading Periods (First Story)

Independent Readers

This group reads the entire story through silently, as given in their text. They then test themselves by the study-guide questions furnished by the teacher or by the text.

TEXTS

BARKER, DODD, WEBB, *Our Nation Begins*, 129–135.

BEARD and BAGLEY, *First Book in American History*, 32–34.

BURNHAM and JACK, *Beginnings of Our Country*, 191–193.

CLARK-GORDY, *First Three Hundred Years*, 98–103 (hard).

CLARK-GORDY, *Westward toward America*, 367–369.

KELTY, *Beginnings of the American People and Nation*, 156–163.

KNOWLTON and WHEELER, *Our Past in Western Europe*, 290–293 (hard).

NIDA, *Following Columbus*, 75–81.

SMALLIDGE and PAXSON, *Finding America*, 210–218.

EXTENSIVE READING

BEEBY, *Community Life Today and in Colonial Times*, 316–317.

FIELD, *Finding the New World*, 255–279.

FOOTE and SKINNER, *Explorers and Founders of America*, 187–193.

JONES, *Geography by Discovery*, 63–70.

PRATT, *Exploration and Discovery*, 68–76.

SOUTHWORTH, *Builders of Our Country*, I: 144–148.

Lower Group

The teacher tells the story orally to the lower group, writing on the board the names of the principal persons and places as she mentions them. Children practice the pronunciation of the difficult names.

Then these children and the teacher read together the story as given in the text. The teacher guides the silent reading, section by section, by the same type of questions that she would use in a silent-reading period; for example, "Why had French sailors already been coming to our shores?"

After the entire story has been read in this manner the children test themselves by the study-guide questions.

OTHER BOOKS

LUCIA, *Stories of American Discoverers for Little Americans*, 113–125.

READING FOR RECREATION

McNEIL, *The Shores of Adventure; France in America.*

The Discussion (First Story)

The children give orally the answers to the study-guide questions. The teacher writes on the board the word *attempt*. Children discuss the meaning.

The Reading Periods (Second Story)

Independent Readers

This group reads the entire story through silently, as given in their text. They then test their comprehension by the study-guide questions furnished by the teacher or by the text.

Lower Group

The teacher tells the story orally to the lower group, writing on the board the names of the most important persons and places as she mentions them. Children practice the pronunciations.

TEXTS

BARKER, DODD, WEBB, *Our Nation Begins*, 135–142.

BURNHAM and JACK, *Beginnings of Our Country*, 193–198.

CLARK-GORDY, *First Three Hundred Years*, 103–109 (hard).

CLARK-GORDY, *Westward toward America*, 369.

KELTY, *Beginnings of the American People and Nation*, 164–172.

KNOWLTON and WHEELER. *Our Past in Western Europe*, 293–298 (hard).

NIDA, *Following Columbus*, 83–91, 94–95.

SMALLIDGE and PAXSON, *Builders of Our Nation*, 189–202 (hard).

EXTENSIVE READING

BEEBY, *Community Life Today and in Colonial Times*, 318–322.

COE, *Founders of Our Country*, 111–122.

FOOTE and SKINNER, *Explorers and Founders of America*, 195–206.

SOUTHWORTH, *Builders of Our Country*, I: 153–160.

TAPPAN, *American Hero Stories*, 49–59.

Then these children and the teacher read together the story as given in the text. The teacher guides the silent reading, section by section, by the same type of questions that she would use in a silent-reading period; for example, "How long did France wait before building cities?"

After the entire story has been read in this manner the children test themselves by the study-guide questions.

OTHER BOOKS

LUCIA, *Stories of American Discoverers for Little Americans*, 151–160.

PRATT, *Beginners' Book*, 53–66.

READING FOR RECREATION

HARTMAN, *These United States* (hard).

HUTCHINSON, *Men Who Found America*.

The Discussion (Second Story)

Children answer the study-guide questions as fully as possible. The teacher writes on the board the words *fur trade* and *New France*. Children discuss the meanings.

Multisensory Aids

Children and teacher talk over together the pictures in the text, pointing out features of historical or geographical significance. They compare maps of early New France with maps of today and notice how many of the Great Lakes were then known by name.

AUDIO-VISUAL MATERIALS OBTAINABLE

Compton's Pictured Teaching Materials: *American Indians*, Plate I.

GABRIEL (Ed.). Pageant of America: I, 292, 296, 298, 299.

Keystone View Slides: 7, 39.

McKINLEY. Illustrated Topics for American History: S. 5 A, S. 9.

Society for Visual Education (BURTON HOLMES–BRAY). Quaint Quebec.

Yale Pageant Education Slides: 22–24, 617–618.

General Activities

Creative Activities: Group and Individual, Correlated with Other Subjects or Voluntary Projects

A committee makes a sand-table model of North America east of the Mississippi. On it they mark Cartier's route; Champlain's routes. They show Quebec and Montreal, the Gulf of St. Lawrence, and the Lachine Rapids. They show where the French hoped that a Northwest Passage might be found. They mark the land of the Iroquois Indians.

A volunteer writes the diary that Champlain might have kept on his first exploring trip inland.

The class visits the local museum to observe relics of the French colonial days, if any are available.

Volunteers compose music on themes of rushing rivers, sunny forests, and Indians of New France.

The class continues the time chart.

Application to Present-Day Conditions

In what way is the name *Lachine* the record of a mistake? (Encyclopædia Britannica.)

Compare the Russian attempt today to open up a Northeast Passage with the old attempt to find a Northwest Passage.

Are there any place names in your vicinity that were given by the French? What does the word *Montreal* mean? (Encyclopædia Britannica.)

What is the land of New France called today? What people own it?

How is the disease called scurvy treated today? (See a children's encyclopedia.)

Do you know of any other man who has been given the title of "Father of his Country"?

Exercises in Reasoning

How could an explorer tell whether a body of water was a strait or a river?

Why was it easier to travel through the new lands belonging to France than through those of Spain or England?

Compare Champlain with Walter Raleigh. In what way were they alike and in what ways were they different?

Why did so many early colonies fail because of lack of food?

Why was fishing such an important industry in those days?

Why did the French wait so long before founding colonies in their new lands?

Why do the French and Spanish names of many places begin with the word *Saint,* while few English place names begin thus?

Drill Games

Drill on the following names is best done at the map: *France, Montreal, Gulf of St. Lawrence, St. Lawrence River, Quebec, Canada.*

Drill cards may be made for the following:

Cartier	⟷	the man who discovered the St. Lawrence River
attempt	⟷	trying to do a thing is called an _ _ _ _ _ _ _ _ _ _ _ _ _ _
fur trade	⟷	buying and selling the skins of animals
Quebec	⟷	a great city founded by Champlain
Champlain	⟷	" the Father of New France "
Canada	⟷	the country which now includes New France
New France	⟷	the name given to the lands settled by France in the New World

Testing

Exercises and Tests in Understanding are provided on pages 163 and 172 of Kelty's *Beginnings of the American People and Nation.*

Additional Tests of Reasoning and Skills follow.[1] Check the best answer.

1. Prisoners do not become good colonists because they ____ have to stay in the prison. ____ never know how to farm. ____ √ are not the right kind of people.

2. Champlain thought that the French colonists ought to spend most of their time in ____ catching fish. ____ hunting for furs. ____ exploring for gold. √ making farms.

3. Turn to a map of Champlain's explorations. The easiest way for⋅the early French colonists to reach Lake Huron was to go _ _ _ _ _ _.

4. What is the title of the entire unit that you are now reading? _ _ _ _ _ _ Where did you find it? _ _ _ _ _ _

5. Put the figure *1* before the thing that happened first and the figure *2* before the thing that happened later.

[_ _2_ _] Champlain made a settlement at Quebec.

[_ _1_ _] Walter Raleigh tried to make settlements for England.

Exercise in Organization. The lower group copies the topic headings of the story of Cartier and prepares to give a summary of each heading.

The independent readers copy the topic headings of the story of Champlain and prepare to give a summary of each heading.

A tabulation of "French Exploration" is prepared, similar to that shown on page 156.

STORY 3. HENRY HUDSON'S VOYAGE
[*1 Week. Save one day for the test on the entire unit*

Conversational Approach

"Still one other country wants to find a short route to the Indies. It is the Netherlands [writing *The Netherlands* on the board], sometimes called Holland. Can anyone point it out on the map?

"How do you suppose that such a small country could pay the expenses of colonizing?" [*It carried on much trade with the Indies by the route around Africa.*]

Reading and Study

The Reading Periods

Independent Readers

This group reads the entire story through silently, as given in their text. They then test their comprehension by the study-guide questions furnished by the teacher or by the text.

Lower Group

The teacher tells the story orally to the lower group, writing on the board the names of the principal persons as she names them. Children practice the pronunciation of any difficult names.

[1] Other exercises in reasoning are included under "General Activities."

TEXTS

BARKER, DODD, WEBB, *Our Nation Begins,* 163–168.

BEARD and BAGLEY, *First Book in American History,* 65–67.

KELTY, *Beginnings of the American People and Nation,* 173–182.

KNOWLTON and WHEELER, *When We Were Colonies,* 177–183 (hard).

McGUIRE and PHILLIPS, *Adventuring in Young America,* 33–35.

NIDA, *Following Columbus,* 100–106.

SMALLIDGE and PAXSON, *Finding America,* 254–266.

WOODBURN and MORAN, *Finders and Founders of the New World,* 162–164.

EXTENSIVE READING

BEEBY, *Community Life Today and in Colonial Times,* 247–250.

CHANDLER and CHITWOOD, *Makers of American History,* 75–77.

COE, *Founders of Our Country,* 123–128.

FIELD, *Finding the New World,* 367–393.

FOOTE and SKINNER, *Explorers and Founders of America,* 168–173.

MONTGOMERY, *Beginners' American History,* 36–40.

PERRY and PRICE, *American History,* I : 165–168.

PRATT, *Exploration and Discovery,* 137–143.

SHAW, *Discoverers and Explorers,* 114–120.

SOUTHWORTH, *Builders of Our Country,* I : 123–129.

VAN LOON, *Short History of Discovery,* 112–115.

Then these children and the teacher read together the story as given in the text. The teacher guides the silent reading, section by section, by the same type of questions that she would use in a silent-reading period; for example, "Where did the Dutch hope to find a short route to the Indies?"

After the entire story has been read in this manner the children test themselves by the study-guide questions.

OTHER BOOKS

BLAISDELL and BALL, *American History for Little Folks,* 38–42.

DAVIS, *Stories of the United States,* 115–119.

LUCIA, *Stories of American Discoverers for Little Americans,* 160–164.

WILSON, *A History Reader,* 110–112.

READING FOR RECREATION

LUTHER, *Trading and Exploring.*

McNAB, *Picture Book of Rivers.*

WADE, GRADY, KELTY, *Founding of Our City.*

The Discussion

Children answer as fully as possible the study-guide questions. The teacher takes advantage of the answers to clear up misapprehensions. She writes on the board the words *Northwest Passage.* Children discuss the meaning.

Multisensory Aids

The children and the teacher talk over together the pictures in the text, noting points of historical and geographical significance. They trace Hudson's voyages on the maps in their text and on the large wall map.

AUDIO-VISUAL MATERIALS OBTAINABLE

GABRIEL (Ed.). Pageant of America : I, 227–228.

Keystone View Slides : 35.

McKINLEY. Illustrated Topics for American History : S. 4.

Society for Visual Education (BRIGGS). Discovery of the Western World.

Yale Pageant Educational Slides : 530.

General Activities

Creative Activities: Group and Individual, Correlated with Other Subjects or Voluntary Projects

A volunteer reports on "The Rise of the Dutch Republic." (See Kelty's *The American Colonies*, pp. 111–118.)

A volunteer draws in colors the flag of the Netherlands and Hudson's flag. (See the *National Geographic Magazine*, LXVI, 370 (September, 1934).)

Volunteers try to act out a fur-trading scene in which neither party understands the language of the other.

Committees of children read the dramatizations found in Stevenson's *Children's Classics in Dramatic Form* (IV: 116–135), Hubbard's *Little American History Plays* (42–45: Act I), Tucker and Ryan's *Historical Plays of Colonial Days* (50–55, 75–82), and Bird and Starling's *Historical Plays for Children* (117–127). They read also "Henry Hudson" in *Dramatic Hours in History* (Teachers College, Columbia University).

A committee makes a collection of pictures comparing Manhattan Island in Hudson's time with Manhattan Island today.

Each child makes a map of "The Dutch in America."

The class continues the time chart.

Application to Present-Day Conditions

For what are windmills used today?

Where has Hudson left his name on the map of North America?

In what way was the building of the Panama Canal like the search for the Northwest Passage?

Find on a map of Europe the original York and Amsterdam from which New York and New Amsterdam were named.

Do any of our states today call their capitol buildings the state house? [*Massachusetts*.]

What are ice-breakers? Why are they necessary if a Northeast Passage is to be used by the Russians?

Is the fur trade carried on anywhere today?

Exercises in Reasoning

What must have happened to Portugal, since the Dutch sailors used the Portuguese route around Africa? [*It had sunk in importance; was not strong enough to keep strangers away from its possessions*.]

Who else that we have studied about had to have an interpreter?

Did Hudson have any right to take his ship to the New World?

Why did Hudson think that a river must flow into New York Bay?

Which do you think knew more about the Indians, Henry Hudson or Champlain?

What other explorer was Hudson near when he sailed up the river?

Have we any right to say that Henry Hudson was frozen to death? [*Lack of evidence*.]

Drill Games

The place names (*Holland* and *Hudson River*) are best drilled on at the map. Drill cards are made for the following:

| Henry Hudson | ⇔ | an Englishman who sailed for the Dutch |
| Northwest Passage | ⇔ | a hoped-for route cutting through northern North America |

Children also review the drill cards from all the stories in Unit Two.

Testing

Tests of Understanding are suggested on page 182 of Kelty's *Beginnings of the American People and Nation.*

Additional Tests of Reasoning and Skills follow.[1] Check the best answer.

1. Henry Hudson was an Englishman. Because of his exploration the land he explored was claimed by   England.   Spain.   √ Holland.   Portugal.

2. After he had sailed nearly as far as Lake Champlain, Hudson turned back because   √ he decided the body of water was a river.   the French would not let him go on.   the Indians were not friendly.   he decided that he wanted to go home.

3. All these sentence endings are true. Mark the one which gives the most important reason: The Dutch decided to make towns in the new land because   one of their sailors had found it.   they wanted a foothold in the New World.   their nation would win honor.   √ they wanted to carry on the fur trade.

4. Turn to a map of Hudson's voyages. Did Henry Hudson reach the Great Lakes?   Yes [ ]   No [√]

Did he sail along the eastern coast of the United States?
                                                    Yes [√]   No [ ]

Exercise in Organization. Make a tabulation for "Dutch Exploration" similar to that given on page 156.

Make a tabulation of explorers according to date, if the date is in the stories. It will differ from the preceding tabulation, because it will be arranged chronologically rather than by countries. For example:

> Columbus, 1492
> John Cabot, 1497
> Cartier, 1599–1521, etc.

Drill games may be played, using all the drill cards of the unit.

Tests on the Entire Unit

Tests of Place Sense. **I.** Pass outline maps of the world which show the water bodies in color or shading. Words to be written on the maps may be written on the board beforehand to give assistance in spelling. Give the following directions.

1. Put the figure *1* where England is.

2. Write the word *Canada* in the right place.

[1] Other exercises in reasoning are included under "General Activities."

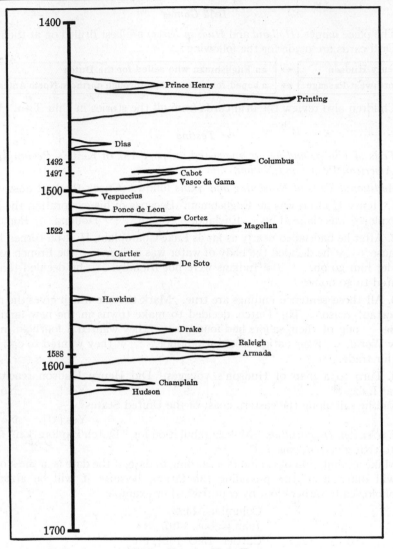

Time Chart — Unit Two

3. Write *eastern coast of North America* in the right place.
4. Write *Pacific coast of North America* in the right place.
5. Put the figure *4* where the Mississippi River is.
6. Put the figure *5* where the Gulf of Mexico is.
7. Write *South America* in the right place.
8. Write *North America* in the right place.
9. Put the figure *7* where the Philippine Islands are.
10. Put the figure *10* where Holland is.

II. Pass outline maps of North America which show the water bodies in blue or shading. Give the following directions.

1. Write the word *Pacific* in the right place.
2. Write the word *Mexico* in the right place.
3. Put the figure *5* where Virginia is.
4. Put the figure *6* where the St. Lawrence River is.
5. Put the figure *7* where Montreal is.
6. Put the figure *8* where Quebec is.
7. Put the figure *9* where Lake Champlain is.
8. Put the figure *10* where the Hudson River is.

Tests of Time Sense. Pass mimeographed sheets of the following.

I. Here are the names of persons. In each exercise put the figure *1* before the name of the person who lived first and the figure *2* before the name of the person who lived later.

1. [__*1*__] Columbus   3. [__*2*__] De Soto   5. [__*2*__] Champlain
   [__*2*__] Cortez   [__*1*__] Magellan   [__*1*__] Cartier

2. [__*1*__] Cabot   4. [__*1*__] Raleigh
   [__*2*__] Drake   [__*2*__] Hudson

II. Here is a list of things which happened. In each exercise put the figure *1* before the name of the event which happened first and the figure *2* before the name of the event which happened later.

1. [__*1*__] John Cabot discovered North America.
   [__*2*__] Magellan sailed around the globe.
2. [__*2*__] Henry Hudson explored the Hudson River.
   [__*1*__] Columbus discovered America.
3. [__*2*__] Champlain settled Quebec.
   [__*1*__] De Soto discovered the Mississippi.

III. Here is a list of dates:

1519–1522   1492   1497

Put each date in the right blank in the sentences below.

1. Columbus discovered America in _____.
2. Magellan's trip around the world was made in _____.
3. John Cabot discovered North America in _____.

Tests on Persons. Pass mimeographed sheets of the following.

I. Here is a list of names of persons:

Cortez	Henry Hudson	Champlain
Cartier	De Soto	Magellan
John Cabot	Aztecs	Francis Drake

Put each name in the right blank in the sentences below.

1. The first person whose ship sailed around the world was _____.
2. North America was discovered by _____.

3. The Dutch claimed land because of the voyage of _____.

4. Mexico was conquered by _____.

5. _____ discovered the St. Lawrence River.

6. The _____ lived in Mexico before Cortez came.

7. The Mississippi River was discovered by _____.

8. _____ built Quebec.

9. The first Englishman to sail around the world was _____.

Test on Historical Terms. **I.** Here is a list of words:

discover	mutiny	explore	governor
conquest	native	circumnavigation	interpreter
coast	capital city		

Put each word in the right blank in the sentences below.

1. This word means to travel over a country or sea in order to find out what kind of place it is. The word is _____.

2. This word means sailing all around the world. The word is _____.

3. A city which is the place where the ruler lives is called a _____.

4. Any person who was born in a place is called a _____ of that place.

5. To find any place and to tell the world about it is to _____ the place.

6. Any person who explains in one language what has been said in another is an _____.

7. Getting a country by force is called _____.

8. When men in an army or on a ship refuse to do what their leaders say, it is called _____.

9. The part of a country which is next to the sea is called the _____.

10. A man whose duty is to control or govern is called the _____.

II. Here is a list of words:

score of years	fort	Spanish Main	mainland
attacks	decade	Northwest Passage	claims
slaves	sack		

Put each word in the right blank in the sentences below.

1. A short way to India which France, England, and the Dutch hoped to find was called the _____.

2. Twenty years are a _____.

3. The lands which the countries said belonged to them were their _____.

4. When an army tries to take a place by force, it _____ the place.

5. A large body of land, not an island, is called the _____.

6. A strong building in which people can protect themselves is a _____.

7. People who are owned by others are called _____.

8. Ten years are a _____.

9. The northern coast of South America was called the _____.

10. Long ago, when an army captured a city, the soldiers used to take any-thing they saw which they wanted. When soldiers do this they _ _ _ _ _ _ the city.

III. Here is a list of words:

defeat	confers knighthood	New World
battle	courtier	attempt
fur trade	Old World	failure

Put each word in the right blank in the sentences below.

1. When two armies fight, they are having a _ _ _ _ _ _.

2. Buying and selling furs is called the _ _ _ _ _ _.

3. The part of the world which is not America is called the _ _ _ _ _ _.

4. America is called the _ _ _ _ _ _.

5. Whatever you try to do you _ _ _ _ _ _.

6. The army which loses a battle suffers a _ _ _ _ _ _.

7. What anybody tries to do and cannot is a _ _ _ _ _ _.

8. Anyone who spends much time in the king's court is called a _ _ _ _ _ _.

9. When a king gives a man the title *Sir*, we say the king _ _ _ _ _ _ on him.

Comprehension Test on Unit Two

Check the best answer.

1. Columbus thought that he had   discovered a new world.   √ found India.   sailed clear around the world back to Spain.   reached Africa.

2. England claimed the eastern coast of North America because   √ John Cabot discovered it.   Henry Hudson was English.   England was a strong country.   England had many ships.

3. The French could go to their part of America easily because   they had many ships.   the Indians liked them.   √ they found a great river lead-ing into the country.   New France was large.

4. The Dutch claimed some of the same land that England did because √ Henry Hudson discovered a river for them in North America.   they did not know about the English claim.   they hated England.   they were great traders.

5. When different countries claimed the same land, they usually   √ went to war about it.   gave up their claims.   gave the land to the church. sold it to the strongest.

6. Magellan's voyage around the world proved that   it is a long way around the world.   √ America is a continent, not part of Asia.   Magel-lan was a brave man.   sailing is easy work.

7. Champlain's great idea was   to go exploring.   to fight with the Iroquois.   √ to build towns and live in the new land.   to make friends with the English.

8. Francis Drake's voyage around South America   made England and Spain friends.   √ made Spain very angry at England.   made England very angry at Spain.   made his country rich.

9. Walter Raleigh was the first Englishman about whom we have read
√ who had the idea of building towns in the new land.   who sailed around
the world.   who wore beautiful clothes.   who had great courage.

10. After Cortez conquered Mexico   the Spaniards gave it to the Indians.
√ the Spanish people took the gold of Mexico.   the Spaniards killed all
the Indians.   the Spaniards went back home.

11. The Spanish people did not build towns along the great river that
De Soto found because   they liked to live on the sea.   they were afraid.
√ there was no gold there.   it was too far away.

12. Most of the people in South America today speak   Portuguese.
√ Spanish.   English.   French.

13. What is the title of the second unit of history about which you have
been studying?

**Are any children now ready to be transferred from the lower group to the
group of independent readers?**

An Integrating Center

Very early in the year the teacher and the children may begin to plan an
assembly program or a program for the Parent-Teacher Association, which will
include all of Units One and Two. This program will serve as an integrating
center about which all the activities of the two units that are outlined under
"General Activities" may revolve. Every group and individual project engaged in may be judged by the class as to its suitability for inclusion in the
program. Those chosen are kept or are recorded for use.

See page 274 for the next integrating agency. Both teacher and class may
keep this activity in mind during all of Units Three, Four, and Five.

UNIT THREE · *Why English People came to live in the New World*   [7 Weeks

ADDITIONAL STORIES FOR MORE ADVANCED READERS

Roger Williams and the Settlement of Rhode Island
The Founding of the Connecticut Colony
The Early Indian Wars
Sir William Johnson in New York
The Early History of New Hampshire and Vermont
Maine as a Possession of Massachusetts
The Settlement of New Jersey

Preparation for Unit Three

Before beginning Unit Three it is desirable to initiate some project which will give the children a life experience in terms of which they can interpret the meaning of the idea of representation.

For example, all the fourth and fifth grades in a city or all the rural schools of a section may arrange to co-operate in beginning a school museum. Each teacher may discuss with her class the desirability of keeping in a permanent place their own best projects and of collecting relics of colonial days, and so on, so that future classes may use them. Possible places are suggested for housing the exhibits.

Children then plan how it would be possible for many different grades or schools to work together. Some will suggest appointing committees from each room or school to meet and confer together. Such suggestions offer the opportunity to elect the members who are to take part. The name *representatives* should be introduced, and the committee members henceforth should be referred to only as representatives. They then meet and decide upon lines of action, which they report back to their individual rooms or schools.

This is obviously not the only exercise which could be used, but some such activity is absolutely necessary if children are to comprehend the abstract idea of representation, which is a key idea in all American history. If the idea is explained to them in words alone, the words cannot possibly develop a real concept of representation.

A. THE ECONOMIC MOTIVE FIRST   [4 Weeks

STORY 1. JAMESTOWN IS SETTLED · STORY 2. THE VIRGINIA
COLONY IS A SUCCESS   [1 Week

[Stories treated separately for reading and discussion; for other activities, both together]

Conversational Approach

"What had Walter Raleigh tried to do? Why had he failed? Can you think of any way in which enough money could be raised without one man's having to give it all?

"Even after enough money was raised, another problem remained. Would any people be willing to leave a country like England and come to live in a wild land like America? Who? What are some of the hard things they would have to do here? Our story today tells us about people who made an attempt to settle in the new country. Let us find out whether or not they succeeded."

Reading and Study

The Reading Periods (First Story)

Independent Readers

This group reads the entire story through silently, as given in the text. They then test their comprehension by the study-guide questions furnished by the teacher or by the text.

TEXTS

BARKER, DODD, WEBB, *Our Nation Begins,* 190–195.

BEARD and BAGLEY, *First Book in American History,* 51–54.

BURNHAM and JACK, *Beginnings of Our Country,* 85–89.

CLARK-GORDY, *First Three Hundred Years,* 177–192 (hard).

KELTY, *Beginnings of the American People and Nation,* 185–201.

KNOWLTON and GILL, *When We Were Colonies,* 23–36 (hard).

McGUIRE and PHILLIPS, *Adventuring in Young America,* 3–9.

NIDA, *Following Columbus,* 158–169.

SMALLIDGE and PAXSON, *Builders of Our Nation,* 4–36 (hard).

WOODBURN and MORAN, *Finders and Founders of the New World,* 93–114.

EXTENSIVE READING

BEEBY, *Community Life Today and in Colonial Times,* 225–238.

COE, *Founders of Our Country,* 132–152.

FIELD, *Finding the New World,* 343–366.

FOOTE and SKINNER, *Explorers and Founders of America,* 112–135.

INGRAHAM, *Story of Democracy,* 146–158.

MONTGOMERY, *Beginners' American History,* 25–33.

TAPPAN, *Letters from Colonial Children,* 1–40 (selections).

PERRY and PRICE, *American History,* I: 122–131.

SOUTHWORTH, *Builders of Our Country,* I: 73–81.

TAPPAN, *American Hero Stories,* 38–49.

Lower Group

The teacher tells the story orally, writing on the board the names of the most important persons and places as she mentions them. Children practice the pronunciations.

The teacher and the lower-ability group then read the story together as given in the text. The teacher guides the silent reading, section by section, by the same type of questions she would use in a silent-reading period; for example, "Why would Englishmen not try to make colonies?"

After the entire story has been read in this manner children test themselves by the study-guide questions.

OTHER BOOKS

BLAISDELL and BALL, *American History for Little Folks,* 12–17.

BLAISDELL and BALL, *Child's Book of American History,* 24–35.

DAVIS, *Stories of the United States,* 63–71.

DODGE, *Stories of American History,* 26–33.

WAYLAND, *History Stories for Primary Grades,* 151–154.

WELSH, *Colonial Days,* 25–70.

WILSON, *A History Reader,* 97–108.

READING FOR RECREATION

BALDWIN, *Fifty Famous Stories Retold.*

HUTCHINSON, *Men Who Found America.*

OTIS, *Richard of Jamestown.*

WADE, *Ten Big Indians.*

The Discussion

Children give answers to the study-guide questions as fully as possible. The teacher again watches for the rapid but inaccurate readers.

The teacher writes on the board the words *permanent colony* and *colonization.* Children discuss the meanings.

The Reading Periods (Second Story)

Independent Readers

This group reads the entire story through silently, as given in their text. They then test their comprehension by the study-guide questions furnished by the teacher or by the text.

TEXTS

BARKER, DODD, WEBB, *Our Nation Begins*, 195–197.
BEARD and BAGLEY, *First Book in American History*, 55.
BURNHAM and JACK, *Beginnings of Our Country*, 90–91.
KELTY, *Beginnings of the American People and Nation*, 202–209.
KNOWLTON and GILL, *When We Were Colonies*, 36–45 (hard).
McGUIRE and PHILLIPS, *Adventuring in Young America*, 9–11, 223–224.
NIDA, *Following Columbus*, 171–178.
SMALLIDGE and PAXSON, *Builders of Our Nation*, 36–43 (hard).

EXTENSIVE READING

BEEBY, *Community Life Today and in Colonial Times*, 238–245.
HAZARD and DUTTON, *Indians and Pioneers*, 149–157.
INGRAHAM, *Story of Democracy*, 159–160.
MONTGOMERY, *Beginners' American History*, 33–35.
PERRY and PRICE, *American History*, I: 131–135.
SOUTHWORTH, *Builders of Our Country*, I: 81–84, 201–207.

Lower Group

The teacher tells the story orally to this group, writing the most difficult words on the board as she mentions them. Children practice the pronunciations.

Then the teacher and the children read together the story as given in the text. The teacher guides the silent reading, section by section, by the same type of study-guide questions that she would use in a silent-reading period; for example, "The first section tells what good things the new governor did. What were they?"

After the entire story has been read in this manner the children test themselves by the study-guide questions.

OTHER BOOKS

WELSH, *Colonial Days*, 71–83.
WILSON, *A History Reader*, 108–109.

READING FOR RECREATION

DIX, *Blithe McBride.*
LUTHER, *Trading and Exploring.*
McNAB, *Picture Book of Rivers.*
WADE, GRADY, KELTY, *Founding of Our City.*

The Discussion

Children give as full answers to the study-guide questions as possible. The teacher explains that they need not try to remember every fact told in the story. The study-guide questions point out which facts to remember.

The teacher writes on the board the words *representatives, voting, plantation, making laws, colonists.* Children discuss the meanings.

Multisensory Aids

Children and teacher together talk over the pictures in the text, noting features of geographical or historical significance. They turn to the map and discuss not only *what* is shown but *how* it is shown.

AUDIO-VISUAL MATERIALS OBTAINABLE

BROWN. Famous Pictures: 115, 2251.
Chronicles of America Photoplays: Jamestown.
Compton's Pictured Teaching Materials: *American Colonies*, Plate III; *Land Transportation*, Plate VI, 2; Plate VII, 1.

GABRIEL (Ed.).   Pageant of America: I, 172–178, 183–192; V, 8; XI, 9–10, 33;
    XIII, 13–15.
International Educational Pictures: North America before the White Man Came.
Keystone View Slides: 21, 22.
McKINLEY. Illustrated Topics for American History: S. 6.
Perry Pictures: 1342–G, 1343–H.
Society for Visual Education. Picturol: Early Settlers.
Yale Pageant Educational Slides: 47, 48, 49, 51, 52, 53.

General Activities

Creative Activities: Group and Individual, Correlated with Other Subjects or Voluntary Projects

The class makes a complete list of all the things that colonists would need
to do in order to found a settlement, beginning with the moment that they
leave the ship.

A volunteer reports on the growing of tobacco and explains why it needs
many workers.

Committees of children read to the class the following dramatizations:
Tucker and Ryan's *Historical Plays of Colonial Days* (28–33, 44–49, 68–74,
131–136, 148–153); Stevenson's *Children's Classics in Dramatic Form* (II:
97–115); Bird and Starling's *Historical Plays for Children* (129–142).

The class holds a meeting of the representatives in Jamestown and discusses
some of the questions which they had to consider.

A volunteer makes a poster advertising for settlers to go to Virginia.

A volunteer investigates as to whether corn (maize) is a native of any other
continent than the Americas.

Each child begins a map of "English Settlements in the New World,"
marking Virginia, Jamestown, James River.

The class continues the time chart.

Application to Present-Day Conditions

Make a list of the business firms in your neighborhood which use the word
company as part of their name.

What is the name of your representative to Congress?

Have you ever heard of taking poor people from the large cities and putting
them out to work on farms? Should you expect such a plan to succeed
generally?

Are there any Indians left in the United States today?

Is there any place in the United States today where a settler is given free
land?

Does Virginia still produce tobacco? (Show children how to look up such
a question in the World Almanac under *Virginia*.) What is the price per pound
today? (Inquire at stores.)

Collect pictures of Jamestown today. A visitor tells the class what it looks
like today.

Exercises in Reasoning

Why were the English merchants willing to risk some of their money in a colony?

Which do you think had the best of the bargain, the settlers or the members of the company?

Can you make a sentence telling what kind of people ought to go to new lands for the purpose of making a colony?

Why was tobacco called the "dollar bush"?

Which do you think was the better plan, for all the settlers to work together or for each man to have his own farm? Why?

Do you think the story about Pocahontas's saving Captain John Smith's life ought to be told in a history book, whether it is true or not?

Why did John Smith not want the Indians to have any cannon?

Why is it best to have all the laws written down plainly?

Drill Games

Map drill is best for the place names: *James River, Jamestown, Virginia.* Drill cards similar to the following may be made:

John Smith	↔	the man who did most for the Jamestown colony
Pocahontas	↔	an Indian chief's daughter who helped the white people
Powhatan	↔	a chief of the Virginia Indians
1607	↔	the year when the first permanent English colony was settled in America
permanent colony	↔	a settlement which lasts
1619	↔	the year when the first Negro slaves were brought to an English colony
representatives	↔	persons elected to serve the interests of the people who elect them
voting	↔	telling your choice
plantation	↔	a large farm for growing one kind of crop
making laws	↔	making rules that all people must obey
colonists	↔	persons who leave their homes to live in a new settlement

Children are allowed to prepare themselves for the games by the use of these cards during the period of general activities.

Testing

Tests of Understanding are provided on pages 201 and 209 of Kelty's *Beginnings of the American People and Nation.*

Additional Tests of Reasoning and Skills.[1] Check the best answer.

1. A colony should not depend on the mother country for its food, because √ the colonists die if the ships do not come.   it costs so much money to carry food.   the mother country needs its own food.

[1] Other exercises in reasoning are included under "General Activities."

2. Colonists who are very far away from the mother country   should not have to obey any laws at all.   should bring all their laws from the homeland. √ should make their own local laws.

3. Turn to a map of the Virginia colony. Was Virginia an *inland* colony?

Yes [ ]   No [√]

Exercise in Organization. Teacher and children turn back to the first subtitle. Children are requested to give the gist of the entire section in one sentence. They do the same with all the following subtitles in the two stories read. Children record their own scores.

STORY 3. LIFE IN EARLY VIRGINIA   [1 Week

Conversational Approach

"Do you think you should have liked to live in Virginia in the early days? What things should you have liked about such a life? What things should you not have liked? Our story today tells you some more things that you would have liked, and probably some others that you would not have liked so well."

Reading and Study

The Reading Periods

Independent Readers

This group reads the entire story through silently as given in their text. They then test their comprehension by the study-guide questions furnished by the teacher or by the text.

TEXTS

BARKER, DODD, WEBB, *Our Nation Begins*, 241–250.

BURNHAM and JACK, *Beginnings of Our Country*, 151–168.

CLARK-GORDY, *First Three Hundred Years*, 286–328 (hard).

KELTY, *Beginnings of the American People and Nation*, 210–226.

KNOWLTON and GILL, *When We Were Colonies*, 52–55, 320–334 (hard).

McGUIRE and PHILLIPS, *Adventuring in Young America*, 78–79, 81–141 (selections).

NIDA, *Following Columbus*, 253–281.

EXTENSIVE READING

BEEBY, *Community Life Today and in Colonial Times*, 312–313.

HART and HAZARD, *Colonial Children*, 63–64, 149–152, 224–232.

PERRY and PRICE, *American History*, I : 225–229.

WAYLAND, *A History of Virginia for Boys and Girls*.

Lower Group

The teacher and the lower-ability group read together the story as given in the text. The teacher guides the silent reading, section by section, by the same type of questions that she would use in a silent-reading period; for example, "The first three paragraphs tell where most of the settlers in Virginia lived. Where was it?"

After the entire story has been read in this manner, the children test themselves by the study-guide questions.

OTHER BOOKS

BLAISDELL and BALL, *Short Stories from American History*, 104–110.

WILSON, *A History Reader*, 138–139.

READING FOR RECREATION

GOODWIN, *Southern Life before the Revolution*.

JENKS, *When America Was New*.

LACEY, *Light Then and Now*.

PERKINS, *Colonial Twins of Virginia*.

PYLE, *Story of Jack Ballister's Fortunes*.

Model of One of the Earliest Virginia Plantations

The Discussion

Children answer the study-guide questions as fully as possible. This exercise gives a good opportunity for others to add material after one child has given his contribution.

The teacher writes on the board the words *coach, slave quarters, Church of England, overseer, wharf.* Children discuss the meanings.

Multisensory Aids

Children and teacher talk over together the pictures in the text, pointing out features of geographical and historical significance.

AUDIO-VISUAL MATERIALS OBTAINABLE

Compton's Pictured Teaching Materials: *American Colonies,* Plates IV; X; XI, 5; XII, 2–5.

GABRIEL (Ed.). Pageant of America: III, 29–31, 50–54, 60–68; V, 8–9; XIII, 43–49.

Keystone View Slides: 87, 88, 90.

Yale Pageant Educational Slides: 538, 544, 701.

Music. Play records of spinning songs, music of the Cavaliers, the minuet.

General Activities

Creative Activities: Group and Individual, Correlated with Other Subjects or Voluntary Projects

Committees draw the plan of a plantation; the plan of a "great house."

A volunteer tries to make hominy, and reports on his success to the class. Another tries to dip candles or to tan leather.

A committee reads to the class the dramatization in Shoemaker's *Colonial Plays for the Schoolroom* (23–26).

Volunteers make replicas, for the school museum, of articles used in colonial days.

Girls dress dolls to represent a Southern gentleman and lady, and slaves.

The class writes the order for goods wanted which a Southern planter might have sent to his agent in England.

Application to Present-Day Conditions

Make a list of items about colonial life: houses, wharves, furniture, food, dishes, clothing, farm work, housework, manufacturing, churches, schools, travel, amusements, punishments. Compare each with our methods of living today, pointing out the differences.

Do some people today own both a town house and a country house? Why?

Are mosquito nets used over the beds in any lands today? [*In a great many tropical countries.*]

Are there any laws today about the kind of clothes people must wear?

Is the College of William and Mary still in existence? (See a children's encyclopedia.)

What is the origin of the expression "My latchstring is always out"?

Exercises in Reasoning

How do people today know anything about the way the colonists lived?

Why could little cotton be raised at this early date? [*There was not enough labor; power machinery was not yet invented.*]

Do you think the clothing of the men in colonial days more attractive than men's clothing today or less so?

Why were most of the plantations near rivers?

Why did each plantation need so many outhouses?

Why was it cheaper to burn wood than coal?

Why could the Virginians not have bathrooms?

Why was corn grown rather than wheat?

How could the people get along without clocks and watches?

Why did the planters not want poor tobacco sent to England?

Did the very severe punishments keep people from breaking the laws?

Drill Games

Drill cards are prepared similar to the following:

coach	⟷	a large closed carriage
slave quarters	⟷	a row of huts where the Negroes lived
Church of England	⟷	in America, the Episcopal Church
overseer	⟷	the man who directed the slaves' work
wharf	⟷	a landing place for ships

The children will enjoy being allowed to help in making these cards.

Testing

Tests of Understanding are suggested on page 226 of Kelty's *Beginnings of the American People and Nation.*

Additional Tests of Reasoning and Skills.[1] Check the best answer.

1. Each plantation had to be a little world in itself because   there were so many people on each one.   it cost too much to send goods by railroad. √ it took months to get needed articles from other places.   there were so many buildings on each one.

2. Did punishing people very severely keep them from breaking the laws?
Yes [ ]   No [√]

3. Schools could not be very good in these early days because   √ people lived so far apart.   people were not interested in education.   people would rather hunt and fish.   the grown people could not read and write.

4. Turn to the index in the back of your book. On what pages can you find the pillory mentioned? _ _ _ _ _ _

Exercise in Organization. Children make sets of questions of their own to test the most important points under each heading. They ask one another these questions.

---
[1] Other exercises in reasoning are included under "General Activities."

STORY 4. OTHER SOUTHERN COLONIES (CAROLINAS AND GEORGIA)
[1 Week

Conversational Approach

"When people in England learned that some of the settlers in Virginia were beginning to make money, what do you suppose they would do? Show on the map some of the places belonging to England where they might go.

"Our story today tells about the founding of three new colonies in the south."

Reading and Study

The Reading Periods

Independent Readers

This group reads the entire story through silently, as given in their text. They then test their comprehension by the study-guide questions furnished by the teacher or by the text.

TEXTS

BARKER, DODD, WEBB, *Our Nation Begins*, 226–227.

BEARD and BAGLEY, *First Book in American History*, 55–57, 77–78.

BURNHAM and JACK, *Beginnings of Our Country*, 108–112.

CLARK-GORDY, *First Three Hundred Years*, 249–256 (hard).

KELTY, *Beginnings of the American People and Nation*, 227–239.

KNOWLTON and GILL, *When We Were Colonies*, 78–105 (hard).

MCGUIRE and PHILLIPS, *Adventuring in Young America*, 43–47, 63–66.

NIDA, *Following Columbus*, 232–236.

SMALLIDGE and PAXSON, *Builders of Our Nation*, 150–166, 168–182 (hard).

WOODBURN and MORAN, *Finders and Founders of the New World*, 187–194.

EXTENSIVE READING

BEEBY, *Community Life Today and in Colonial Times*, 290–298.

COE, *Founders of Our Country*, 251–265.

FOOTE and SKINNER, *Explorers and Founders of America*, 235–242.

MONTGOMERY, *Beginners' American History*, 84–89.

PERRY and PRICE, *American History*, I: 193–199.

SOUTHWORTH, *Builders of Our Country*, I: 197–200.

STONE and FICKETT, *Everyday Life in the Colonies*, 103–144.

TAPPAN, *Letters from Colonial Children*, 296–319

Lower Group

The teacher tells the story orally to this group, writing on the board the names of the most important persons and places as she mentions them. Children practice the pronunciations.

Then the teacher and this group read together the story as given in the text. The teacher guides the silent reading, section by section, by the same type of study-guide questions that she would use in a silent-reading period; for example, "Why do we read next about some colonies which were not settled until many years later?"

After the entire story has been read in this manner, the children test themselves by the study-guide questions.

OTHER BOOKS

SHEPHERD, *Geography for Beginners*, 124–127.

WELSH, *Colonial Days*, 133–246.

WILSON, *A History Reader*, 325–326.

READING FOR RECREATION

ALLEN, *North Carolina History Stories*.

FARJEON, *Kings and Queens*.

HARRIS, *Stories of Georgia*.

MEANS, *Palmetto Stories*.

OERTEL, *Jack Sutherland*.

PAINE, *Blackbeard, Buccaneer*.

PENDLETON, *King Tom and the Runaways*.

The Discussion

Children answer as completely as possible the study-guide questions. The more able readers will enjoy adding material not given in the text. The teacher should encourage them to try to remember the name of the book in which they found it.

The teacher writes on the board the words *debtors, the South*. Children discuss the meanings.

Multisensory Aids

Children and teacher talk over together the pictures in the text, pointing out features of historical and geographical significance. They also turn to a colonial map and show the boundaries of each of the three colonies. How many of the cities were then large enough to be shown on the map?

AUDIO-VISUAL MATERIALS OBTAINABLE

GABRIEL (Ed.). Pageant of America: I, 264–275; III, 55–59.
Yale Pageant Educational Slides: 84, 90.

General Activities

Creative Activities: Group and Individual, Correlated with Other Subjects or Voluntary Projects

A committee draws a large picture map of North Carolina, decorating it in the right places with small drawings representing the industries of its colonial period.

A committee models on the sand table a South Carolina rice farm and explains how the irrigation ditches work.

A volunteer explains how turpentine is obtained; another tells how molasses is made; a third tells about the use of indigo.

A committee reads the dramatization given in Shoemaker's *Colonial Plays for the Schoolroom* (49–50).

Volunteers give floor talks on Blackbeard and other famous pirates; on James Oglethorpe.

Each child adds the Carolinas and Georgia to the map of'English settlements.

The class continues the time chart.

Application to Present-Day Conditions

Do people ever move away nowadays in search of adventure? Where do they go?

Does North Carolina still produce forest products? Does South Carolina still produce rice? (See *North Carolina* in the World Almanac; also *South Carolina*.) [*Rice is not listed as a principal product.*]

Is indigo widely used today as a dye? (See a children's encyclopedia.)

Compare the size of Charleston at the time of the Revolution with its size today. Graph the figures. Name a city today which is about the same size that Charleston was then.

Is South Carolina a manufacturing state today?

Does the government today try to help poor people? If so, how?

Can a man be sent to prison for debt today?

Why is Virginia often called "the Mother of Colonies"?

Is any house in your community built in the Georgian style of architecture? If so, study its features.

In which of our states was the first state university founded? When? [*North Carolina; 1795.*]

Exercises in Reasoning

In what ways are the Carolinas and Georgia more like Virginia than Maine and Massachusetts are like Virginia?

Was King Charles's purpose in giving Carolina to the eight lords merely to be generous to them?

Would it be a good thing to have one man serve as governor of Virginia as well as lord of Carolina?

Make a list of the things which marked the town life of South Carolina as different from the country life of Virginia.

Why does it seem foolish to put a man in prison for debt?

Drill Games

Drill on the place names (*North Carolina, South Carolina, Charleston, Georgia*) can best be done at the map.

Drill cards may be prepared for the following:

debtors	⟷	persons who owe money
the South	⟷	the colonies from Virginia and Maryland to Florida were called _ _ _

Testing

Tests of Understanding are suggested on page 239 of Kelty's *Beginnings of the American People and Nation.*

Additional Tests of Reasoning and Skills.[1] Check the best answer.

1. Georgia did not take a great part in the Revolution because   √ it had fewer people than any of the other colonies.   it was so far to the south. the climate was too warm for fighting.

2. South Carolina grew faster than North Carolina because   people liked to live in cities.   √ its port towns carried on trade by sea.   it was nearer to Georgia.

3. Turn to a map of the Southern colonies. Which colony is nearest to the Spanish settlements? _ _ _ _ _ _

Exercises in Organization

1. Children copy the topic headings of the story. With the teacher's help they tell in one sentence the principal thought of each topic.

---

[1] Other exercises in reasoning are included under "General Activities."

2. The class makes a tabulation of English colonies as follows:

Name	Settled by Whom	Principal Settlement	Why Settled	Time

This tabulation is for the purpose of synthesizing the materials and is not to be memorized.

STORY 5. LIFE IN NEW NETHERLAND · STORY 6. NEW NETHERLAND BECOMES NEW YORK   [1 Week

Conversational Approach

"Now we must go back a long time. What other nation did we find making a colony along the eastern coast of North America? What things do you know about life in Holland that you might also expect to find in the Dutch colonies in the New World? Do you think you should have liked to live in the Dutch colony?

"How would England like to have a neighbor so near her own colonies? What do you think she might do about it?"

Reading and Study

[The two stories are read consecutively before any discussion is held]

The Reading Periods

Independent Readers

This group reads the two stories through silently, as given in their text. They then test their comprehension by the study-guide questions furnished by the teacher or by the text.

TEXTS

BARKER, DODD, WEBB, *Our Nation Begins*, 168–174.
BEARD and BAGLEY, *First Book in American History*, 68–72.
BURNHAM and JACK, *Beginnings of Our Country*, 103–105, 112–114, 170–175.
CLARK-GORDY, *First Three Hundred Years*, 221–231 (hard).
KELTY, *Beginnings of the American People and Nation*, 240–252, 253–260.
KNOWLTON and GILL, *When We Were Colonies*, 183–194, 198–203 (hard).
McGUIRE and PHILLIPS, *Adventuring in Young America*, 35–41, 76–78.
NIDA, *Following Columbus*, 204–218.
SMALLIDGE and PAXSON, *Builders of Our Nation*, 130–147 (hard).
WOODBURN and MORAN, *Finders and Founders of the New World*, 164–175.

Lower Group

The teacher tells the stories orally to the lower group, writing on the board the names of the principal persons and places as she mentions them. Children practice the pronunciations.

This group and the teacher then read together the stories as given in the text. The teacher guides the silent reading, section by section, by the same type of questions that she would use in a silent-reading period; for example, "The first section tells why few Dutch colonists had made farms. Read to find the reason."

After both stories have been read in this manner, children test themselves by the study-guide questions.

OTHER BOOKS

BLAISDELL and BALL, *American History for Little Folks*, 42–44.
FAIRGRIEVE and YOUNG, *The World*, 9–10.
PRATT, *Beginners' Book*, 101–107.
WADE, GRADY, KELTY, *Founding of Our City*, 12–63, and 64–77.
WAYLAND, *History Stories for Primary Grades*, 161–162.
WILSON, *A History Reader*, 137–138.

EXTENSIVE READING

BEEBY, *Community Life Today and in Colonial Times*, 252–262.
FOOTE and SKINNER, *Explorers and Founders of America*, 175–185.
HAZARD and DUTTON, *Indians and Pioneers*, 233–239.
MONTGOMERY, *Beginners' American History*, 41–42.
PERRY and PRICE, *American History*, I: 170–179.
SOUTHWORTH, *Builders of Our Country*, I: 130–141.
TAPPAN, *American Hero Stories*, 73–83.
TAPPAN, *Letters from Colonial Children*, 188–232 (selections).

READING FOR RECREATION

BRADEN, *Little Brother of the Hudson.*
HOLLAND, *Blue Heron's Feather.*
KNIPE, *Maid of Old Manhattan.*
LEETCH, *Annetje and Her Family.*
OTIS, *Peter of New Amsterdam.*
PERKINS, *Dutch Twins.*
WILLIAMS, *Stories from Early New York History.*

The Discussion

The children answer as fully as possible the two sets of study-guide questions.

The teacher writes on the board the words *patroon, estates, surrender*. Children discuss the meanings.

Multisensory Aids

Children and teacher talk over together the pictures in the text, noting features of geographical and historical significance. They turn to a map of the period and show how the Dutch possessions are marked; they compare with a map of New York today. They show New Amsterdam and Fort Orange.

AUDIO-VISUAL MATERIALS OBTAINABLE

BRADLEY. Village Series of Cut-Outs: Dutch Village.
Chronicles of America Photoplays: Peter Stuyvesant.
Compton's Pictured Teaching Materials: *American Colonies*, Plates V; IX, 2; XII, 1. *Holland* (series).
GABRIEL (Ed.). Pageant of America: I, 230–238; XI, 16; XIII, 36–40.
International Educational Pictures: Rip Van Winkle.
Society for Visual Education (BRIGGS). English and Dutch Ambitions in the New World.
Yale Pageant Educational Slides: 85, 609–611.

General Activities

Creative Activities: Group and Individual, Correlated with Other Subjects or Voluntary Projects

Committees of children read before the class the dramatizations given in Tucker and Ryan's *Historical Plays of Colonial Days* (50–55, 75–82, 92–100), Hubbard's *Little American History Plays* (42–49), and Shoemaker's *Colonial Plays for the Schoolroom* (45–47).

A committee may wish to make a sand-table model of New Amsterdam.

Volunteers attempt to make cheese and butter and report to the class.

A volunteer makes the speech which Peter Stuyvesant might have given in attempting to stir his people to resist the English.

A committee makes a drawing to show the relative size of the three largest cities in colonial times; of the three largest cities of the United States today.

The class compares Rosa Bonheur's picture "The Horse Fair" with the picture of the cattle fair in the text.

A volunteer gives a floor talk on the tulip craze in Holland.

Each child adds New York and New Jersey to the map of English colonies. The class continues the time line.

Application to Present-Day Conditions

Make a picture collection of modern houses in the Dutch colonial style.

Make a collection of Dutch names prominent in American history, such as *Roosevelt, Vanderbilt*.

What is the title of the oldest brother of the king of England? Find a picture of him to show to the class.

Make a list of some of the languages spoken today in New York City.

Look in the dictionary to find out from what language our words *sled*, *sleigh*, and *skate* come.

Are knockers ever used on houses today?

Make a list of the present names of New York City streets which were given in Dutch times. (Wade, Grady, Kelty's *Founding of Our City*, 73–75.)

Are "Dutch ovens" used today? Are they the same as the ovens used by early Dutch colonists?

Are you glad or sorry that the English people took the Dutch colony?

Exercises in Reasoning

Why would many farms be bad for the fur trade?

Which do you think had the better of the bargain — the patroons or their settlers?

What other colony grew slowly until the people were allowed to own their own land?

Did England have a claim to the land along the Hudson River because Henry Hudson was an Englishman?

Why did the English care that the Dutch colony cut their colonies into two sections?

Do you think it is fair to begin war without warning the country you are going to fight?

Drill Games

The place names (*New Netherland*,[1] *New Amsterdam*, and *New York*) are best drilled on at the map.

Drill cards are made similar to the following:

patroon	↔	a wealthy Dutchman who paid the expenses of his settlers
estates	↔	large tracts of settled land
Peter Stuyvesant	↔	the last governor of New Netherland
surrender	↔	to give up to an enemy

Children drill on their own difficulties.

[1] Call the children's attention to the difference in spelling between *the Netherlands* and *New Netherland*.

Testing

Tests of Understanding are suggested on pages 251 and 252 ("Choices to Make") and on page 260 of Kelty's *Beginnings of the American People and Nation.*

Additional Tests of Reasoning and Skills.[1] Check the best answer.

1. The English wanted the colony of New Netherland because   it was more beautiful than their colonies.   √ it had the best harbor anywhere on the coast.   Peter Stuyvesant was a bad governor.   John Cabot had discovered the land.

2. When the English took the colony of New York, the Dutch colonists had to get out of the land immediately.   √ could stay and keep their own lands.   could move to land farther north.   had to go to live with the Indians.

3. Turn to a map of the Dutch colony. Did New Netherland extend very far from the east to the west?   Yes [ ]   No [√]

4. Should you believe all the bad things written about Peter Stuyvesant by a colonist whom he had punished? Why? _ _ _ _ _ _

Exercises in Organization

1. Teacher and children together make one outline which includes the two stories. One child recites on the first point as fully as he can; a second child, on the next point; and so on.

2. A tabulation for the Dutch colony (including both New York and New Jersey) is made, similar to that made for the English colonies (see page 189).

B. THE RELIGIOUS MOTIVE FIRST

STORY 1. THE PILGRIMS IN PLYMOUTH   [½ *Week*

Conversational Approach

"At last we come to a story about which you probably know a good deal already. It explains why we hold a day of Thanksgiving every year. Who knows the story?" Children contribute as much as they can. "Why were the Pilgrims living in Holland? Why did they decide to come to America instead of moving to some country much nearer home?"

Reading and Study

The Reading Periods

Independent Readers

TEXTS

BARKER, DODD, WEBB, *Our Nation Begins,* 200–204, 208–213.
BEARD and BAGLEY, *First Book in American History,* 57–59.

Lower Group

The teacher tells the story orally to this group, writing on the board the names of the most important persons and places as she mentions them. Children practice the pronunciations.

[1] Other exercises in reasoning are included under "General Activities."

BURNHAM and JACK, *Beginnings of Our Country*, 93–97.

CLARK-GORDY, *First Three Hundred Years*, 192–204 (hard).

KELTY, *Beginnings of the American People and Nation*, 261–275.

KNOWLTON and GILL, *When We Were Colonies*, 109–124 (hard).

MCGUIRE and PHILLIPS, *Adventuring in Young America*, 14–21.

NIDA, *Following Columbus*, 179–192.

SMALLIDGE and PAXSON, *Builders of Our Nation*, 46–78 (hard).

WOODBURN and MORAN, *Finders and Founders of the New World*, 116–135.

EXTENSIVE READING

BEEBY, *Community Life Today and in Colonial Times*, 173–206.

COE, *Founders of Our Country*, 153–166, 214–217.

FARIS, *Where Our History Was Made*, I : 37–40.

FIELD : *Finding the New World*, 394–418.

FOOTE and SKINNER, *Explorers and Founders of America*, 136–148.

HAZARD and DUTTON, *Indians and Pioneers*, 167–193.

INGRAHAM, *Story of Democracy*, 161–188.

MONTGOMERY, *Beginners' American History*, 44–53.

PERRY and PRICE, *American History*, I : 141–151.

SOUTHWORTH, *Builders of Our Country*, I : 89–98.

STONE and FICKETT, *Everyday Life in the Colonies*, 1–12.

TAPPAN, *American Hero Stories*, 59–72.

TAPPAN, *Letters from Colonial Children*, 85–127 (selections).

TOMLINSON, *Places Young Americans Want to Know*, 1–13.

USHER, *Story of the Pilgrims for Children* (selections).

Then the teacher and this group read the story together, as given in the text. The teacher guides the silent reading, section by section, by the same type of questions that she would use in a silent-reading period; for example, "The first three paragraphs tell us about the conditions in England. What were they like?"

After the entire story has been read in this manner, the children test themselves by the study-guide questions.

OTHER BOOKS

BALDWIN, *Stories of Old New England*, 3–23.

BLAISDELL and BALL, *American History for Little Folks*, 18–29.

BLAISDELL and BALL, *American History Story Book*, 1–18.

BLAISDELL and BALL, *Short Stories from American History*, 1–21.

CURTIS, *Why We Celebrate Our Holidays*, 124–129, 130–141.

DAVIS, *Stories of the United States*, 73–84.

DODGE, *Stories of American History*, 18–25.

PRATT, *Beginners' Book*, 89–100.

PRATT, *Stories of Colonial Children*, 7–12, 19–72 (selections).

PUMPHREY, *Pilgrim Stories*.

WAYLAND, *History Stories for Primary Grades*, 15–20, 96–102.

WILSON, *A History Reader*, 65–83.

READING FOR RECREATION

BARBOUR, *Giles of the Mayflower*.

BROOKS, *Lem, A New England Village Boy*.

BUTTERWORTH, *Pilot of the Mayflower*.

Colonial Stories Retold from St. Nicholas, 27–55.

DIX, *Soldier Rigdale*.

Indian Stories Retold from St. Nicholas, 136–154.

JENKS, *Captain Myles Standish*.

KNIPE, *A Mayflower Maid*.

LOWITZ, *The Pilgrims' Party*.

OTIS, *Mary of Plymouth*.

TAGGART, *A Pilgrim Maid*.

The Discussion   [*In a Language Period*

Children answer the study-guide questions as completely as possible. The teacher watches closely the performance of any pupils who may recently have been transferred from the lower group to the group of independent readers.

She writes on the board *Pilgrims, freedom of religion.* Children discuss the meanings.

Multisensory Aids

Children and teacher talk over together the pictures in the text, pointing out features of geographical and historical significance. They turn to a map of early New England and locate the village of Plymouth and the colony of Plymouth.

AUDIO-VISUAL MATERIALS OBTAINABLE

Chronicles of America Photoplays: The Pilgrims.
Compton's Pictured Teaching Materials: *Water and Air Transportation*, Plate II, 4; *Holidays*, Plates IV, V, VI.
EASTMAN. Educational Slides: The Pilgrims in America.
GABRIEL (Ed.). Pageant of America: I, 194–225.
International Educational Pictures: Pilgrims at Plymouth, Courtship of Miles Standish.
Keystone View Slides: 25, 27, 28, 30.
Perry Pictures: 1331, 1331–B, 1331–C, 1332, 1332–B, 1334, 1340.
Society for Visual Education. Schoolfilm: Beside the Zuider Zee.
Society for Visual Education (MUIR). Discovery and First Settlements through 1621.
Yale Pageant Educational Slides: 37, 59–61, 63, 508, 512, 816.

Music. Play records of long-meter hymns.

General Activities

Creative Activities: Group and Individual, Correlated with Other Subjects or Voluntary Projects

The children plan their own Thanksgiving program.
The children meet and draw up for themselves some rules "for the good of all," similar to the *Mayflower* Compact.
A volunteer draws a plan of the village of Plymouth.
The teacher reads to the children selections from Longfellow's *The Courtship of Miles Standish.*
Committees read to the class the dramatizations given in Tucker and Ryan's *Historical Plays of Colonial Days* (34–43, 56–59, 64–68, 143–147); Johnson and Barnum's *Book of Plays for Little Actors* (121–135); Shoemaker's *Colonial Plays for the Schoolroom* (19–26); and Hubbard's *Little American History Plays* (23–28).
A volunteer reads Felicia Hemans's poem "The Landing of the Pilgrims."
Each child adds Plymouth to the map of English settlements.
The class continues the time line.

Application to Present-Day Conditions   [A Language Exercise

Find a copy of your governor's last Thanksgiving proclamation; of the President's.
Is there any place in the world today where people do not have freedom of religion?
What is the Church of England called today?
Does your church believe in plain and simple buildings or in richly decorated buildings? Why?
Find on the map of England the city for which Plymouth was named.

Do people today ever make for themselves the laws by which they are to be ruled? [*In forming a club or similar organization.*]

Did the Pilgrims actually land *on* Plymouth Rock? A traveler who has seen the rock describes it to the children.

Exercises in Reasoning   [A Language Exercise

Compare the purpose of the founding of Plymouth with the purposes of the other colonies about which we have read.

Why did the gift of land from the London Company prove to be worth nothing to the Pilgrims?

Compare the pilgrims who went on the Crusades with the pilgrims who came to Plymouth.

There is a list of all the people who came over on the *Mayflower*. How could this list be used by anyone who wanted to find out whether or not his ancestors were among them?

Why did the Pilgrims have to take all their household goods with them? Why did they not know how to hunt?

Why was there so much sickness among most of the early colonists?

Drill Games

The location of *Plymouth colony* can best be drilled upon at the map. Drill cards may be made as follows:

William Bradford	⟷	governor of Plymouth
Miles Standish	⟷	the great captain of Plymouth
Massasoit	⟷	an Indian chief friendly to the Pilgrims
pilgrims	⟷	people who make a journey for a religious purpose
Plymouth	⟷	the settlement made by the Pilgrims
1620	⟷	the year Plymouth was settled
Mayflower	⟷	the Pilgrims' ship
freedom of religion	⟷	the right to worship God in one's own way

Children keep a record of their own errors, and drill on these.

Testing

Tests of Understanding are suggested on page 275 of Kelty's *Beginnings of the American People and Nation.*

Additional Tests of Reasoning and Skills [1]

1. Two of the colonies named below were settled for the same kinds of reasons. Draw lines under the names of the two.

Virginia   (Plymouth)   Carolina   Mexico

2. Draw a circle around the name of the colony that was settled to win freedom of religion.

[1] Other exercises in reasoning are included under "General Activities."

3. Check the best answer: The king would not give Plymouth a charter because   Plymouth was too far away from England.   Plymouth belonged to the London Company.   √ the Pilgrims had once left England without his consent.   the Pilgrims were the kind of people he did not like.

4. Turn to a map of the Plymouth colony. There was a village called Plymouth and also a whole colony named Plymouth.

True [√]   False [ ]

5. If you had to find out whether the Pilgrims were more religious than the people of Virginia, should you ask only the descendants of the Pilgrims? Tell why. ------

Exercise in Organization. Children copy the topic headings in a list. They give orally a summary sentence telling the main thought of each section.

STORY 2. THE PURITANS IN MASSACHUSETTS BAY COLONY [3 Days

Conversational Approach

"The Pilgrims have now solved their problem. Do you remember any other people in England who were not satisfied with the Church? When they heard of the success of the Pilgrims, what do you think that they would be likely to do?"

Reading and Study

The Reading Periods

Independent Readers

This group reads the entire story through silently, as given in their text. They then test their comprehension by the study-guide questions furnished by the teacher or by the text.

TEXTS

BARKER, DODD, WEBB, *Our Nation Begins,* 204–208, 213–215.

BEARD and BAGLEY, *First Book in American History,* 59–65.

BURNHAM and JACK, *Beginnings of Our Country,* 97–100.

CLARK-GORDY, *First Three Hundred Years,* 205–212 (hard).

KELTY, *Beginnings of the American People and Nation,* 276–289.

KNOWLTON and GILL, *When We Were Colonies,* 125–144, 339–342 (hard).

MCGUIRE and PHILLIPS, *Adventuring in Young America,* 24–28, 222–223.

NIDA, *Following Columbus,* 194–196.

SMALLIDGE and PAXSON, *Builders of Our Nation,* 80–82 (hard).

WOODBURN and MORAN, *Finders and Founders of New World,* 136–142.

Lower Group

The teacher tells the story orally to this group, writing on the board the names of the most important persons and places as she mentions them. Children practice the pronunciations.

The teacher and these children then read together the story as given in the text. The teacher guides the silent reading, section by section, by the same kind of questions that she would use in a silent-reading period; for example, "The first two paragraphs tell how the Puritans got their name. How did they get it?"

After the entire story has been read in this manner, the children test themselves by the study-guide questions.

OTHER BOOKS

DAVIS, *Stories of the United States,* 85–106.
PRATT, *Stories of Colonial Children,* 73–76.

READING FOR RECREATION

ANDREWS, *Ten Boys Who Lived on the Road from Long Ago to Now,* 193–209.
OTIS, *Ruth of Boston.*
PERKINS, *Puritan Twins.*

EXTENSIVE READING

BEEBY, *Community Life Today and in Colonial Times*, 264, 273.
FOOTE and SKINNER, *Explorers and Founders of America*, 150–159.
HAZARD and DUTTON, *Indians and Pioneers*, 194–202.
MONTGOMERY, *Beginners' American History*, 53–54.
MOORE, *Pilgrims and Puritans*, 115–152 (selections).
PERRY and PRICE, *American History*, I: 151–154.
SOUTHWORTH, *Builders of Our Country*, I: 101–106.

Continue using the books listed for the last story (p. 193).

The Discussion [*In a Language Period*

Children answer the study-guide questions as fully as possible. The teacher continues to follow up carefully the performance of children recently transferred from the lower group.

She writes on the board the words *town meeting, settled, assembly*, and discusses the meanings with the children.

Multisensory Aids

Children and teacher talk over together the pictures in the text, pointing out the features of geographical or historical significance. They turn to a map of early New England and notice the limits of the Massachusetts Bay Colony. They name the towns shown. They compare the Massachusetts Bay Colony with Plymouth.

AUDIO-VISUAL MATERIALS OBTAINABLE

Chronicles of America Photoplays: The Puritans.
GABRIEL (Ed.). Pageant of America: I, 210–216.
Yale Pageant Educational Slides: 65, 71, 72, 76, 78, 501.

Music. Play the record "Music of the Puritans."

General Activities

Creative Activities: Group and Individual, Correlated with Other Subjects or Voluntary Projects

Committees read to the class the dramatizations given in Hubbard's *Little American History Plays* (34–41) and Tucker and Ryan's *Historical Plays of Colonial Days* (1–6, 20–27, 101–105, 115–121, 154–157).

A committee makes an estimate of the present-day cost of a gentleman's equipment for colonizing.

The class holds a "town meeting" and decides in it some of the problems which children meet in their efforts to live together happily; for example, How can we see that everyone has a chance to learn to operate the slide lantern?

Children who own stamp collections may show commemorative stamps.

Children who live in the country report their attendance at town meetings.

Each child adds Massachusetts Bay to the map of English settlements, coloring both the Bay Colony and Plymouth red, to show that they were later united, and marking Boston and Salem.

The class continues the time chart.

Application to Present-Day Conditions   [A Language Exercise

Look at a present-day map of New England. Why is Boston called "the Hub"? (Are there any cultural implications?)

What do towns do today when their water supply is not good?

Can you find on a map the city of Boston in England?

Are women allowed to preach in your church today?

Do any people today believe in witches and spells and bad luck?

Why did the town meeting work better in early New England than it would in a large city today?

What arguments do people who have no children sometimes give against paying taxes for schools? What reasons can you think of in favor of supporting the schools by taxes?

What league today tries to help the nations to work together?

Exercises in Reasoning   [A Language Exercise

Do you think that *freedom of religion* is the right phrase to use in the case of people who mean by it freedom for themselves alone? Did the Puritans in New England act very differently from the way the king had acted in England?

Why did the Massachusetts Bay Colony have a better chance to live than Plymouth did? [*It had a charter; the people were more well-to-do.*]

Was Maine one of the thirteen original colonies?

Compare the Puritans with the Pilgrims.

Why is Massachusetts sometimes called "the Mother of Colonies"?

What is the difference between a town meeting and an assembly?

Drill Games

At the map, drill on the place names: *Massachusetts, Boston, Salem.*
Drill cards are made as follows:

1630	↔	the year when Boston was settled
Massachusetts Bay Colony	↔	the first colony settled by the Puritans
town meeting	↔	a gathering of all the citizens of the community to make their own laws
assembly	↔	a gathering of representatives from the towns
Puritans	↔	people who wanted to make the Church of England services more simple and plain
John Winthrop	↔	the first governor of Massachusetts Bay
Boston	↔	the largest town in Massachusetts

Children drill with both sides of the cards.

Testing

Tests of Understanding are suggested on page 289 of Kelty's *Beginnings of the American People and Nation.*

Additional Tests of Reasoning and Skills.[1] Check the best answer.

1. The Puritans liked their new colony of Massachusetts because   √ it was too far away for the king to control it well.   its soil was much better than that of England.   it was very near the colony of Plymouth.   it was the most thickly settled colony.

2. Draw a line under the right word: The men in the assembly came from a   larger   smaller   area than the men in the town meeting.

3. Here is a list of words: well-to-do, educated, large numbers of people. Which do these words describe, the Pilgrims or the Puritans? _ _ _[*Puritans.*]_ _ _

4. Turn to a map of the Massachusetts Bay Colony. Check: Massachusetts Bay Colony was smaller than Plymouth.   True [   ]   False [√]

5. On what pages in your book can you find facts about the town meeting? _ _ _ _ _ _

6. Where did you look to find out? _ _ _[*In the index.*]_ _ _

Exercise in Organization. Children explain the significance of the title of the story and give the main points of the discussion under each section heading.

STORY 3. LIFE AMONG THE PURITANS   *[4 Days*

Conversational Approach

"From what you have already read, do you think that you should have liked to live among the Puritans?" Different views are presented. Children tell features that they would have enjoyed and others that they would not. "Perhaps our story today will help you to decide more intelligently."

Reading and Study

The Reading Periods

Independent Readers

TEXTS

BARKER, DODD, WEBB, *Our Nation Begins,* 230–238.

BURNHAM and JACK, *Beginnings of Our Country,* 131–150.

KELTY, *Beginnings of the American People and Nation,* 290–308.

KNOWLTON and GILL, *When We Were Colonies,* 304–320, 342–355 (hard).

MCGUIRE and PHILLIPS, *Adventuring in Young America,* 71–76, 143–187 (selections).

Lower Group

The teacher and the lower group read together the story as given in the text. The teacher guides the silent reading, section by section, by the same type of questions that she would use in a silent-reading period; for example, "The first three paragraphs tell where the Puritans liked to live. Where was it?"

After the entire story has been read in this manner, the children test themselves by the study-guide questions.

[1] Other exercises in reasoning are included under "General Activities."

.40651

NIDA, *Following Columbus*, 237–251.
SMALLIDGE and PAXSON, *Builders of Our Nation*, 82–89 (hard).

EXTENSIVE READING

BAILEY, *Boys and Girls of Colonial Days*, 33–44, 101–109.
BEEBY, *Community Life Today and in Colonial Times*, 208–218, 300–312.
EARLE, *Child Life in Colonial Days*.
EARLE, *Home Life in Colonial Days*.
HART and HAZARD, *Colonial Children*, 55–57, 67–70, 152–155, 194–196, 220–221.
INGRAHAM, *Story of Democracy*, 205–209.
PRESCOTT, *A Day in a Colonial Home*, 1–13.
STONE and FICKETT, *Everyday Life in the Colonies*, 13–35, 36–41, 61–68, 94–102.
WARREN, *Little Pioneers*, 52–75, 86–99, 141–154, 172–182, 209–230.

OTHER BOOKS

BALDWIN, *Stories of Old New England*, 23–48.
PRATT, *Stories of Colonial Children*, 13–18, 77–104, 155–163.
WILSON, *A History Reader*.

READING FOR RECREATION

HOLLIDAY, *A Day in a Colonial Home*.
LAMPREY, *Days of the Colonists*.
MACELROY, *Work and Play in Colonial Days*.
SMITH, *Made in America*.
WILKINS, *Weavers' Children*.

The Discussion

Children answer as completely as possible the study-guide questions. This story offers an excellent opportunity for additions from other books. The children are encouraged to tell the name of the book from which they cite material.

The class reviews the meanings of the words *stocks* and *pillory*, and discusses also what an hourglass is.

Multisensory Aids

Teacher and children talk over together the pictures in the text, pointing out features of historical and geographical significance.

AUDIO-VISUAL MATERIALS OBTAINABLE

BRADLEY. Village Series of Cut-Outs : Pilgrim Village.
BROWN. Famous Pictures : 1444, 1497, 2069, 2070.
Compton's Pictured Teaching Materials : *American Colonies*, Plates I, II, VII, VIII, IX, XI, 1–4.
EASTMAN. Classroom Films : New England Fisheries, Parts I and II.
GABRIEL (Ed.). Pageant of America : III, 24–28, 32–40, 69–89, 298–306, 314–324 ; V, 9–13 ; XI, 12–15 ; XIII, 29–36.
International Educational Pictures : Thar She Blows, New England Fisheries.
Keystone View Slides : 31, 32.
Perry Pictures : 1333-E, 1337.
Yale Pageant Educational Slides : 66–70, 74, 77, 79–81, 538, 663, 809.

Music. Play records of Saint-Saëns's *Omphale's Spinning Wheel*.

General Activities

Creative Activities: Group and Individual, Correlated with Other Subjects or Voluntary Projects

Children take a trip to the museum to see articles used in colonial times. If possible, they take a trip to some home to observe spinning on a spinning wheel; to observe weaving on a hand loom.

Committees make soap, and make candles by the use of molds. If possible, they bring a sampler to show to the class.

A volunteer draws a plan of a New England village from the description in the text.

A volunteer shows how a quilt is pieced.

Girls dress dolls to represent Puritans.

Committees read to the class the dramatizations given in Hubbard's *Little American History Plays* (29–33), Parsons's *Red Letter Day Plays* (5–14), and Shoemaker's *Colonial Plays for the Schoolroom* (35–39).

Some children may wish to compose poems about Puritan life · other children may set these poems to music.

Application to Present-Day Conditions

Is fishing still an important industry of New England? Is farming? Is whaling? Is trade? (Consult a geography.)

What do we today call the church descended from the church of the Puritans? [*Congregational*.]

Why are clocks better than the hourglass?

What is the meaning of the expression *blue laws*?

Compare the Puritans' farms with the farms of today.

Is Massachusetts settled today entirely by people descended from the English?

Is furniture ever put together today with wooden pegs?

Compare the colonial methods of fire protection with those of today.

Why are people today so eager to secure antique furniture?

Is any house in your neighborhood furnished in Early American style?

Is any house built in the Colonial style of architecture?

Compare electric pads with warming pans.

Where is seed corn hung up to dry nowadays?

What is done with the rest of the crop not needed for seed?

Why did the Puritans use more maple sugar than cane sugar, while with us the contrary is true?

Exercises in Reasoning

Do you think boys and girls have more fun now or that they had more fun in colonial days?

Why did the Puritans live in towns instead of on scattered plantations?

Why was it easier for the Puritans to give each family what it needed than it is for us today to give each family what it needs?

Compare the number of different nationalities in Massachusetts with the number in New Amsterdam.

Why is cornmeal mush sometimes called Indian pudding? Why were tomatoes called love apples?

Why did the colonists eat much more salted and smoked fish and meat than we do?

Why were the fences around New England fields made of stone?

Why did New England build more ships than any other section of the country?

Drill Games

The only additional terms on which drill is needed are the following:

stocks	↔	a wooden frame into which a man's feet were fastened to punish him
pillory	↔	a wooden frame into which a man's head and hands were fastened to punish him
hourglass	↔	an article used to measure time by the running of sand

Testing

Tests of Understanding are suggested on page 308 of Kelty's *Beginnings of the American People and Nation.*

Additional Tests of Reasoning and Skills.[1] Check the best answer.

1. The Puritans had to live in towns because   the land was overgrown by forests.   √ the soil was not good enough for large plantations.   they liked to be near one another.

2. A Puritan's daily life was ruled most by   √ the church.   the school.   the town meeting.

3. The Puritans secured freedom of religion   for everybody.   √ for themselves alone.

4. The Puritans made laws to start schools because   they all had good educations themselves.   √ their children had to learn to read the Bible. they were more interested in education than the people of Virginia were.

5. Here is a list of early New England industries. Check the most important one: trade   fishing   shipbuilding   √ farming

Exercise in Organization. Children copy the section headings. They try to substitute a one-word heading for those which now use more than one.

Children give topical recitations on each heading.

STORY 4. THE CATHOLICS IN MARYLAND · STORY 5. THE QUAKERS IN PENNSYLVANIA   *[1 Week*

[Stories treated separately for reading and discussion; for other activities, both together]

Conversational Approach

"Why do you suppose we have not read of any Catholics in the new English settlements? Were they persecuted in England? Another religious group that needed a new home was the Quakers." The teacher writes *Quakers* on the board.

"Have any of you ever heard of Quakers? Do you happen to know which colony was settled for the Quakers? which for the Catholics?"

[1] Other exercises in reasoning are included under "General Activities."

Reading and Study

The Reading Periods (First Story)

Independent Readers

This group reads the entire story through silently, as given in their text. They then test their comprehension by study-guide questions furnished by the teacher or by the text.

TEXTS

BARKER, DODD, WEBB, *Our Nation Begins*, 218–222.

BURNHAM and JACK, *Beginnings of Our Country*, 91–93.

CLARK-GORDY, *First Three Hundred Years*, 236–240 (hard).

KELTY, *Beginnings of the American People and Nation*, 309–318.

KNOWLTON and GILL, *When We Were Colonies*, 67–76 (hard).

McGUIRE and PHILLIPS. *Adventuring in Young America*, 49–52.

NIDA, *Following Columbus*, 220–224.

SMALLIDGE and PAXSON, *Builders of Our Nation*, 98–108 (hard).

EXTENSIVE READING

BEEBY, *Community Life Today and in Colonial Times*, 286–291.

FOOTE and SKINNER, *Explorers and Founders of America*, 219–224.

HART and HAZARD, *Colonial Children*, 143–144.

MONTGOMERY, *Beginners' American History*, 55–60.

PERRY and PRICE, *American History*, I : 135–137, 193.

SOUTHWORTH, *Builders of Our Country*, I: 179–186.

Lower Group

The teacher tells the story orally to the lower group, writing on the board the names of the most important persons and places as she mentions them. Children practice the pronunciations.

The teacher and this group then read together the story as given in the text. The teacher guides the silent reading, section by section, by the same type of questions she would use in a silent-reading period; for example, "The first two paragraphs tell who was a friend of the Catholics."

After the entire story has been read in this manner, children test themselves by the study-guide questions.

OTHER BOOKS

DODGE, *Stories of American History*, 40–45.
WELSH, *Colonial Days*, 84–132.

READING FOR RECREATION

HILLYER, *Child's Geography of the World*, Tale 7.
OTIS, *Calvert of Maryland*.

The Discussion (First Story)

Children give as fully as possible the answers to the study-guide questions. Are they succeeding in separating the main thread of the story from the supporting details? The teacher writes on the board the words *proprietor* and *persecution*. Children discuss the meanings.

The Reading Periods (Second Story)

Independent Readers

TEXTS

BARKER, DODD, WEBB, *Our Nation Begins*, 222–226.

BEARD and BAGLEY, *First Book in American History*, 73–76.

Lower Group

The teacher tells the story orally to this group, writing on the board the names of the most important persons and places as she mentions them. Children practice the pronunciations.

BURNHAM and JACK, *Beginnings of Our Country*, 116–123, 175–182.

CLARK-GORDY, *First Three Hundred Years*, 240–248 (hard).

KELTY, *Beginnings of the American People and Nation*, 319–326.

KNOWLTON and GILL, *When We Were Colonies*, 231–248, 320, 334–337 (hard).

McGUIRE and PHILLIPS, *Adventuring in Young America*, 54–60, 189–217 (selections).

NIDA, *Following Columbus*, 225–230.

SMALLIDGE and PAXSON, *Builders of Our Nation*, 110–128 (hard).

WOODBURN and MORAN, *Finders and Founders of the New World*, 176–186.

EXTENSIVE READING

BEEBY, *Community Life Today and in Colonial Times*, 278–285.

COE, *Founders of Our Country*, 233–243.

HAZARD and DUTTON, *Indians and Pioneers*, 252–262.

MONTGOMERY, *Beginners' American History*, 76–83.

PERRY and PRICE, *American History*, I: 183–192.

SOUTHWORTH, *Builders of Our Country*, I: 187–196.

TAPPAN, *American Hero Stories*, 108–117.

TAPPAN, *Letters from Colonial Children*, 249–288.

The teacher and the lower group then read together the story as given in the text. The teacher guides the silent reading, section by section, by the same type of questions that she would use in a silent-reading period; for example, "The first two paragraphs tell you some of the things that the Quakers believed. What were they?"

After the entire story has been read in this manner, the children test themselves by the study-guide questions.

OTHER BOOKS

BLAISDELL and BALL, *American History for Little Folks*, 45–52.

DAVIS, *Stories of the United States*, 45–52.

DODGE, *Stories of American History*, 46–51.

WAYLAND, *History Stories for Primary Grades*, 169–171.

READING FOR RECREATION

ALBERT, *Little Pilgrims to Penn's Woods*.

OTIS, *Stephen of Philadelphia*.

WALTON and BRUMBAUGH, *Stories of Pennsylvania*.

The Discussion (Second Story)

Children answer the study-guide questions as fully as possible. The teacher writes on the board the words *half century* and *treaty*. Children discuss the meanings.

Multisensory Aids

Children and teacher talk over together the pictures in the texts, noting the features of geographical or historical significance. They turn to a map showing early Maryland and early Pennsylvania, and point out the disputed territory, Mason and Dixon's line, and the Lower Counties.

AUDIO-VISUAL MATERIALS OBTAINABLE

Compton's Pictured Teaching Materials: *American Colonies*, Plate VI.

GABRIEL (Ed.). Pageant of America: I, 247–255; XI, 36.

Keystone Views: 37.

McKINLEY. Illustrated Topics for American History: S. 10.

National Geographic Magazine, LXII, 643–698 (December, 1932).

Perry Pictures: 1395-A.

Society for Visual Education. Picture Story of Pennsylvania: The Coming of William Penn and the Quakers.

Yale Pageant Educational Slides: 86, 87, 531.

Music. Children sing "Maryland, My Maryland."

General Activities

Creative Activities: Group and Individual, Correlated with Other Subjects or Voluntary Projects

A volunteer writes the letter which a colonist on board the *Dove* might have written to his mother in England after the ship left the West Indies.

A committee turns to the graph mentioned on page 190 to find how the size of Philadelphia compared with that of other colonial cities.

Children who have stamp collections may show commemorative stamps.

The teacher may read to the class Whittier's "Quaker of the Olden Time."

Committees read to the group the dramatizations given in Bird and Starling's *Historical Plays for Children* (233–246) ; Tucker and Ryan's *Historical Plays of Colonial Days* (7–9) ; and Shoemaker's *Colonial Plays for the Schoolroom* (41–43).

Children take a trip to the museum to see designs in beads.

Two committees dramatize the meetings in which Calvert buys land from the Indians and in which Penn promises the Indians friendship.

Girls dress dolls in Quaker costume.

Each child adds Maryland and Pennsylvania to the map of English settlements, showing Philadelphia, St. Marys, the Lower Counties. Print the word *Delaware* in parentheses under the words *Lower Counties.*

Using the scale of miles, the class estimates the length of Pennsylvania's coast.

The class continues the time chart.

Application to Present-Day Conditions

Do Catholics and Protestants live peaceably in the same states today?

Compare the equipment needed for travel in those days with the equipment needed today.

Find a colored picture of the Baltimore oriole. Why was it given this name? (See a children's encyclopedia.)

Is the Society of Friends still in existence?

Do law courts today have a special wording of promises to tell the truth because some people will not "swear"?

Is the office of admiral in the navy a high office today? (See a children's encyclopedia.)

Do the streets in your city follow the "checkerboard plan" of the streets in Philadelphia? Find a plan of the city of Philadelphia. (International Encyclopedia.)

Is Delaware still connected with Pennsylvania?

Have you ever heard the expression *as quiet as a Quaker meeting?* What does it mean?

Exercises in Reasoning

State in a sentence what you think was the best way for the colonies to avoid trouble with the Indians.

Why would not the king be glad to have the Catholics set up a colony for themselves? Why did Baltimore allow all Christians to come to his colony?

Do you think, from the settlers' letters, that bananas or pineapples were grown in England?

Why did the Indians think that the white men's boats must have been made of one tree?

Why did Baltimore have a law made promising freedom of religion to all Christians?

Do you think the "inner light" does tell people what is right?

What changes would be made in the lives of working people after clocks came to be in common use?

Drill Games

Map drill is held for the place names: *Maryland, Philadelphia, Pennsylvania, Delaware.*

Drill cards are made similar to the following:

Catholics	↔	those people for whom the colony of Maryland was made
proprietor	↔	an owner
Lord Baltimore	↔	the founder of the colony of Maryland
persecution	↔	injury because of religious belief
William Penn	↔	the founder of the colony of Pennsylvania
Quakers	↔	a name given to the Society of Friends
half century	↔	fifty years are called a _ _ _ _ _ _
treaty	↔	an agreement between governments
Lower Counties	↔	an old name used for Delaware

Children drill themselves in their free time.

Testing

Tests of Understanding are suggested on pages 318 and 326 of Kelty's *Beginnings of the American People and Nation.*

Additional Tests of Reasoning and Skills [1]

1. Draw a line under the name of the colony which gave the most freedom of religion to its settlers: Plymouth   <u>Maryland</u>   Massachusetts Bay

2. Check the right answer: Lord Baltimore was called a proprietor because he   could tax his colonists.   could coin his own money.   √ owned all the land in the colony.   could try cases at law.

Draw a line under the right word.

3. The chief troubles of the colony of Maryland were about   education. the Indians.   representation.   <u>religion.</u>

4. The chief trouble of the Pennsylvania colony was about   <u>coastlands.</u> freedom of religion.   Indian wars.   payment of debts.

5. Turn to a map of Pennsylvania and Maryland. The Lower Counties were bought by   Maryland.   <u>Pennsylvania.</u>   New Jersey.

6. Put the figure *1* in front of the thing which happened first, and the figure *2* in front of the thing which happened later.

[1] Other exercises in reasoning are included under "General Activities."

a. [__*1*__] the Carolinas were settled.

[__*2*__] William Penn came to Pennsylvania.

b. [__*2*__] A settlement was made in Georgia.

[__*1*__] Lord Baltimore founded Maryland.

Exercise in Organization. Teacher and children working together make a very brief outline of each story.

The tabulation begun on page 189 is continued, all the rest of the thirteen colonies being added.

Tests on the Entire Unit

Test of Place Sense. **I.** Pass outline maps of North America which show water bodies in shading or color, and give the following directions.

1. Put the figure *1* where Philadelphia is.

2. Put the figure *2* where Boston is.

3. Put the figure *3* where Plymouth is.

4. Color New England red.

5. Put the figure *4* where Jamestown was.

6. Draw a wavy line ($\sim\!\sim\!\sim$) to represent the James River.

7. Color the South yellow.

II. Pass outline maps of the United States on which the boundaries of the states are shown. Give the following directions.

1. Put a capital *P* in Pennsylvania.

2. Put a capital *C* in North Carolina and another in South Carolina.

3. Put a capital *M* in Maryland.

4. Put a capital *G* in Georgia.

5. Write *Mass.* in Massachusetts.

Test of Time Sense. Pass mimeographed sheets of the following.

I. Here is a list of names of persons. In each exercise put the figure *1* before the name of the person who lived first, and the figure *2* before the name of the person who lived later.

1. [__*2*__] Governor Bradford
   [__*1*__] John Smith

2. [__*1*__] Pocahontas
   [__*2*__] Massasoit

3. [__*2*__] Lord Baltimore
   [__*1*__] John Winthrop

4. [__*2*__] William Penn
   [__*1*__] Peter Stuyvesant

5. [__*1*__] Powhatan
   [__*2*__] Miles Standish

II. Here is a list of things which happened in the stories. Put the figure *1* before the event which happened first, and the figure *2* before the event which happened later.

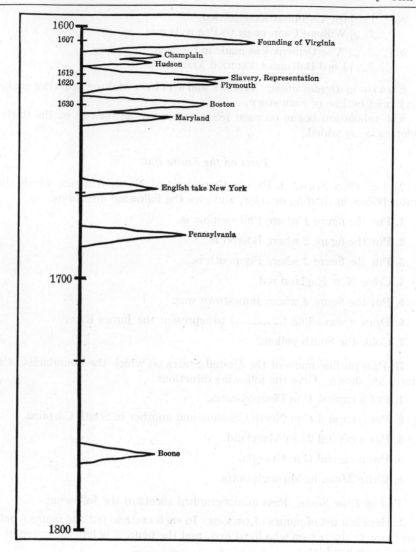

Time Chart — Unit Three

1. [_ _1_ _] Settlement of Jamestown.
   [_ _2_ _] Settlement of Plymouth.

2. [_ _2_ _] Quakers came to Pennsylvania.
   [_ _1_ _] Dutch came to New Netherland.

3. [_ _2_ _] Georgia settled.
   [_ _1_ _] Slavery begun in Virginia.

4. [_ _1_ _] Puritans came to Massachusetts.
   [_ _2_ _] The Carolinas settled.

III. Here is a list of dates:

1619   1607   1630   1620

Below is a list of things which happened. Take each date from this list and put it before the right event.

------ Founding of Jamestown.
------ Settlement of Boston.
------ Slavery begun in Virginia.
------ Settlement of Plymouth.

Tests on Persons. Pass mimeographed sheets of the following.

I. Here is a list of persons:

John Smith	John Winthrop	Puritans
Pocahontas	Peter Stuyvesant	Catholics
William Penn		

Take one name at a time and put it in the right place in the sentences below.

1. ------ founded Pennsylvania as a home for Quakers.

2. ------ wanted his people to fight against the English.

3. ------ came to live in Maryland.

4. ------ helped to found Virginia.

5. ------ was a governor of Massachusetts Bay Colony.

6. ------ helped the English in Jamestown.

7. ------ came to live in Boston.

II. Here is a list of names of persons:

Powhatan	Lord Baltimore	Pilgrims
Quakers	Massasoit	William Bradford
Miles Standish	Roger Williams	

Take one name at a time and put it in the right place in the sentences below.

1. ------ was the Indian chief who was a friend of the Pilgrims.

2. ------ founded Maryland as a home for the Catholics.

3. ------ was driven out of Massachusetts.

4. ------ was the brave soldier of Plymouth.

5. ------ was the Indian chief who was a friend to Virginia.

6. ------ went from England to Holland and then to America.

7. ------ came to live in Pennsylvania.

8. ------ was a governor of Plymouth.

Test on Historical Terms. **I.** Here is a list of words:

permanent colony	persecution	proprietor
treaty	plantations	colonists
representatives	colonial period	

Take one word or expression at a time and put it in the right place in the sentences below.

1. Persons who are chosen by vote of the people to make laws for them are _ _ _ _ _ _.

2. Settlers in a colony are called _ _ _ _ _ _.

3. The years during which many new colonies were being made are called the _ _ _ _ _ _.

4. Punishing people because they have a certain belief is _ _ _ _ _ _.

5. Large farms where a great deal of one crop is raised are called _ _ _ _ _ _.

6. A settlement in which the people stay is a _ _ _ _ _ _.

7. A man who owned all the land of a colony was called a _ _ _ _ _ _.

8. When two nations agree to do a certain thing, we call it making a _ _ _ _ _ _.

II. Here is another list of words:

making laws	hourglass	coach
colonization	Church of England	wharf
slave quarters	town meeting	

Take one word or expression at a time and put it in the right place in the sentences below.

1. The place where a ship ties up near the shore is called a _ _ _ _ _ _.

2. The church which the king wanted all people to attend was the _ _ _ _ _ _.

3. When the people or their representatives make a rule which all must obey, they are _ _ _ _ _ _.

4. The houses where the slaves lived were called _ _ _ _ _ _.

5. A large carriage drawn by many horses is a _ _ _ _ _ _.

6. Making colonies is called _ _ _ _ _ _.

7. An article used to tell time by means of sand running from one part to the other is an _ _ _ _ _ _.

8. When all the people of a town come together to make their laws, they form a _ _ _ _ _ _.

III. Here is another list of words:

pillory	settled	freedom of religion
debtors	patroon	surrender
stocks	estate	*Mayflower*

Take one word or expression at a time and put it in the right place in the sentences below.

1. When new people began to live in a town or colony, they _ _ _ _ _ _ there.

2. A large amount of land owned by anyone is an _ _ _ _ _ _.

3. The name of the ship in which the Pilgrims came to America was the _ _ _ _ _ _.

4. The block of wood in which one's head and hands were held in order to punish him was a _ _ _ _ _ _.

5. To give up to an enemy is to _ _ _ _ _ _.

6. People who owe money are _ _ _ _ _ _ .

7. A Dutchman who owned a large estate in New Netherland was a _ _ _ _ _ _ .

8. The block of wood in which one's legs were held in order to punish him was called the _ _ _ _ _ _ .

9. The right to go to the church one chooses is _ _ _ _ _ _ .

Comprehension Test on Unit Three

Check the best answer.

1. The first lasting English colony in the New World was   Plymouth. √ Virginia.   Maryland.   Boston.

2. The Pilgrims came to America   √ to win freedom of religion for themselves.   to trade with the Indians.   to find a new route to the Indies.   to have a good time.

3. Virginia did not grow well until   the Carolinas were settled.   √ each man had his own farm.   John Smith left the colony.   Catholics came to Maryland.

4. The first representatives in America met in   √ Virginia.   Massachusetts.   Rhode Island.   Maryland.

5. The Quakers got along well with the Indians because   they were quiet people.   they would not fight.   the Indians liked them.   √ they treated the Indians fairly.

6. After many years Boston and Plymouth   fought each other. √ joined as one colony.   both disappeared.   were the same size.

7. Georgia was founded as   a home for Catholics.   a neighbor to Florida.   a good place to trade with Mexico.   √ a home for debtors.

8. The Puritans lived   √ in small towns.   on large plantations. in large cities.   in the woods.

9. The Puritans got most of their goods in this way:

> They brought them from England.
> They sent back to England for them.
> They got them from the Spanish colonies.
> √ They made them for themselves.

10. The Dutch people would not fight for their town because   they wanted to be English.   √ only rich men had been able to own a farm there. their rulers were cruel.   they were lazy people.

11. What is the title of the third unit in history that you have been studying?

Are any other children ready to be transferred from the group of slow readers to the independent group?

UNIT FOUR · *How England came to own Most of North America*
[*7 Weeks*

ADDITIONAL STORIES FOR MORE ADVANCED READERS

Nicolet
Verendrye
John Sevier
James Robertson
Johnny Appleseed

The Settling of Marietta, Ohio
Benjamin Franklin and the Albany Plan
Sir William Johnson and the Iroquois
Pontiac's Conspiracy

A. THE FRENCH ADVANCE INTO THE INTERIOR

STORY 1. THE FRENCH FUR-TRADERS · STORY 2. THE FRENCH MISSIONARIES [*1 Week*

[Stories treated separately for reading and discussion; for other activities, both together]

Conversational Approach

A model is prepared in the sand table showing North America east of the Mississippi. The St. Lawrence, the Great Lakes, and the Mississippi and Ohio rivers are marked plainly, as well as Green Bay and the Fox and Wisconsin rivers, though not by name. The Appalachian ridges are built up.

The children and the teacher gather about the model and locate the French and English settlements. "Which of the two can travel into the interior of the country more easily?" The children study the model to find out which routes could be made entirely by water; which by passing overland for short distances. "Why should either the French or the English want to travel into the interior?" Children offer various suggestions. "Our story today will tell us."

Reading and Study

The Reading Periods (First Story)

Independent Readers

This group reads the entire story through silently, as given in their text. They then test their comprehension by the study-guide questions furnished by the teacher or by the text.

TEXTS

BARKER, DODD, WEBB, *Our Nation Begins*, 145–146.

CLARK-GORDY, *First Three Hundred Years*, 135–138 (hard).

KELTY, *Beginnings of the American People and Nation*, 329–337.

EXTENSIVE READING

BEEBY, *Community Life Today and in Colonial Times*, 324–325.

CARPENTER, *How the World is Clothed*, 176–192.

COE, *Founders of Our Country*, 288–295.

LAUT, *Story of the Trapper*, 50–64, 102–116, 181–205.

SOUTHWORTH, *Builders of Our Country*, I: 160–161.

VOLLINTINE, *Making of America*, 12–13.

Lower Group

The teacher tells the story orally to this group, writing on the board the most difficult words as she mentions them.

Then the teacher and the children read together the story as given in the text. The teacher guides the silent reading, section by section, by the same kind of questions that she would use in a silent-reading period; for example, "Why do you suppose white men were traveling with Indians?"

After the entire story has been read in this manner, children test themselves by the study-guide questions.

OTHER BOOKS

BASS, *Stories of Pioneer Life*, 29–32.

CHAMBERLAIN, *How We Are Clothed*, 129–153.

FAIRGRIEVE and YOUNG, *The World*, 90–99.

SHEPHERD, *Geography for Beginners*, 91–95.

READING FOR RECREATION

GRINNELL, *Jack the Young Trapper*.

OTIS, *Antoine of Oregon*.

SAXE, *Our Little Quebec Cousin*.

SKINNER, *Roselle of the North*.

WILSON and DRIGGS, *White Indian Boy*.

·The Discussion (First Story)

Children answer the study-guide questions as fully as possible. The teacher writes on the board *fur-traders, trading posts, woodrangers*. Children discuss the meanings.

The Reading Periods (Second Story)

Independent Readers

TEXTS

KELTY, *Beginnings of the American People and Nation*, 338–345.

NIDA, *Following Columbus*, 92–98.

EXTENSIVE READING

BEEBY, *Community Life Today and in Colonial Times*, 322–326.

COE, *Founders of Our Country*, 279–287.

VOLLINTINE, *Making of America*, 10–12.

Lower Group

The teacher tells the story orally to this group, writing on the board the most difficult names as she mentions them. Children practice the pronunciations.

Then teacher and children together read the story as given in the text. The teacher guides the silent reading, section by section, by the same type of questions that she would use in a silent-reading period; for example, "The first section tells us why the Jesuits were asked to come to New France. What was the reason?"

After the entire story has been read in this manner, the children test themselves by the study-guide questions.

The Discussion (Second Story)

The children answer the study-guide questions as fully as possible. The teacher writes on the board *mission stations*. Children discuss the meaning.

Multisensory Aids

Children and teacher talk over together the pictures in the text, noting features of geographical and historical significance.

AUDIO-VISUAL MATERIALS OBTAINABLE

Compton's Pictured Teaching Materials: *American Colonies*, Plate II, 4; *Clothing*, Plate VII, 1–3; *Trade*, Plate V, 1.
EASTMAN. Classroom Films: Beavers.
GABRIEL (Ed.). Pageant of America: I, 301.
International Educational Pictures: With the Trappers in the North.
SCHMEIL. Animal Pictures: S. Z. 17.
Society for Visual Education (BRAY). Where Our Furs Come From.
Yale Pageant Educational Slides: 21, 619–621, 626, 634, 635, 803–805.

Music. Play records of songs of French voyageurs and habitants.

General Activities

Creative Activities: Group and Individual, Correlated with Other Subjects or Voluntary Projects

Committees construct a fur-trading post similar to those which children have seen in the moving pictures.

A volunteer finds a picture of a French gentleman of the seventeenth century wearing a beaver hat, and explains how beaver hats were made.

The class makes a picture collection of animals whose skins are used as furs, and takes a trip to a local fur store to see the skins.

The teacher reads to the children short extracts from the *Jesuit Relations*, and from Parkman's *Jesuits in North America*.

A child who knows French may explain the French form of the word *wood-rangers*. [*Coureurs de bois*.]

Each child marks Mackinac Island on his map of French explorations.

Application to Present-Day Conditions

Are there any places near your home which were visited by early fur-traders or missionaries? If so, are they adequately marked?

Is the Jesuit order in existence today? (See a children's encyclopedia.)

Is trapping still carried on in North America? What city in the United States is the center of our fur trade? Why? (See *Fur trade* in a children's encyclopedia.)

Is it lawful nowadays to sell liquor to Indians?

Are there certain kinds of businesses nowadays that are kept for the government only? [*Sending the mail*.]

Why do many people not believe in trapping animals for their furs? [*A very painful death*.]

Have you ever heard of fur farms?

How do we know anything about what went on among the missionaries so many years ago? [*Jesuit Relations.*]

Exercises in Reasoning

Why did not the woodrangers wait until the Indians with furs to sell came to the French settlements? [*Might go to the English instead.*]

Why is trapping done during the later winter or early spring?

Compare the fur fair with the cattle fair of New Netherland.

Explain how an Indian war in America might raise the price of furs in France.

Why did the fur trade make the French unwilling to settle down on farms?

Drill Games

The location of *Mackinac Island* is best drilled on at the map.

Drill cards are made as follows:

fur-traders	↔	men who buy and sell the skins of animals
trading post	↔	a station for buying or selling
woodrangers	↔	white men who went into the forest for furs
Jesuits	↔	an order of missionaries
mission stations	↔	places where the missionaries taught

Children use these cards for help on their own errors.

Testing

Tests of Understanding are offered on pages 337 and 345 of Kelty's *Beginnings of the American People and Nation.*

Additional Tests of Reasoning and Skills.[1] Check the best answer.

1. The missionaries could not get at the Indians to teach them because √ the Indians were always moving about.   the Indians lived in the forests. the Indians were very far away.   the settlements were too small.

2. Few of the Indians became Christians because   they did not know how to read the Christian Bible.   √ they could not understand the ideas of the Christian religion.   they did not like white people.

3. Because Frenchmen were interested in the fur trade they did not want to   build ships.   spend time drying fish.   sell rum to the Indians. √ settle down on farms.

Exercise in Organization. Teacher and children working co-operatively make a brief outline of each of the two stories.

Children tell orally the main facts belonging under each heading.

---

[1] Other exercises in reasoning are included under "General Activities."

STORY 3.　MARQUETTE AND JOLIET · STORY 4.　LA SALLE [1 Week

[Stories treated separately for reading and discussion; for other activities, both together]

Conversational Approach

The class turns again to the sand-table model. "What is the longest possible journey by water through the interior? Can it be made entirely by water?" Children point out the places at which portages would have to be made. "What would travelers have to do when they came to such places? Then what kind of boats should they have? Where had they seen such boats in use? Of what were the canoes made?

"Our stories today tell about two voyages which tried to reach the mouth of the Mississippi. The first one failed; the second succeeded."

Reading and Study

The Reading Periods (First Story)

Independent Readers

TEXTS

BARKER, DODD, WEBB, *Our Nation Begins*, 146–151.

BURNHAM and JACK, *Beginnings of Our Country*, 200–202.

CLARK-GORDY, *Westward toward America*, 370–371.

KELTY, *Beginnings of the American People and Nation*, 346–355.

KNOWLTON and WHEELER, *Our Past in Western Europe*, 298–302 (hard).

SMALLIDGE and PAXSON, *Builders of Our Nation*, 205–216 (hard).

WOODBURN and MORAN, *Finders and Founders of the New World*, 197–207.

EXTENSIVE READING

BEEBY, *Community Life Today and in Colonial Times*, 326–331.

CHANDLER and CHITWOOD, *Makers of American History*, 103–105.

COE, *Founders of Our Country*, 266–268.

FARIS, *Real Stories of the Geography Makers*, 230–236.

PERRY and PRICE, *American History*, I : 99–103.

SOUTHWORTH, *Builders of Our Country*, I : 161–169.

TAPPAN, *American Hero Stories*, 96–103.

Lower Group

The teacher tells the story orally to this group, writing on the board the names of the most important persons and places as she mentions them. Children practice the pronunciations.

Teacher and lower group then read together the story as given in the text. The teacher guides the silent reading, section by section, by the same type of questions that she would use in a silent-reading period; for example, "The first two paragraphs tell what the leader was sent out to do. What was it?"

After the entire story has been read in this manner, children test themselves by the study-guide questions.

OTHER BOOKS

BASS, *Stories of Pioneer Life*, 21–28.

READING FOR RECREATION

HUTCHINSON, *Men Who Found America*.

The Discussion (First Story)

Children answer the study-guide questions as completely as possible, using care to avoid the words of the book. The teacher then writes on the board and discusses with the children the meanings of *portage, pipe of peace.*

The Reading Periods (Second Story)

Independent Readers

TEXTS

BARKER, DODD, WEBB, *Our Nation Begins,* 152–158.

BEARD and BAGLEY, *First Book in American History,* 83–91.

BURNHAM and JACK, *Beginnings of Our Country,* 202–208.

CLARK-GORDY, *First Three Hundred Years,* 111–115 (hard).

CLARK-GORDY, *Westward toward America,* 124–135, 371–373.

KELTY, *Beginnings of the American People and Nation,* 356–368.

KNOWLTON and WHEELER, *Our Past in Western Europe,* 303–310 (hard).

SMALLIDGE and PAXSON, *Builders of Our Nation,* 221–239 (hard).

WOODBURN and MORAN, *Finders and Founders of the New World,* 209–212, 217–224.

EXTENSIVE READING

BEEBY, *Community Life Today and in Colonial Times,* 331–335.

CHANDLER and CHITWOOD, *Makers of American History,* 105–110.

COE, *Founders of Our Country,* 268–278.

FOOTE and SKINNER, *Explorers and Founders of America,* 208–218.

PERRY and PRICE, *American History,* I : 103–109.

SOUTHWORTH, *Builders of Our Country,* I : 169–178.

TAPPAN, *American Hero Stories,* 103–107.

Lower Group

The teacher tells the story orally to this group, writing on the board the names of the most important persons and places as she mentions them. Children practice the pronunciations.

The teacher and the lower group then read the story together as given in the text. The teacher guides the silent reading, section by section, by the same type of questions that she would use in a silent-reading period; for example, "Why did La Salle not want to stay in France?"

After the entire story has been read in this manner, the children test themselves by the study-guide questions.

NOTE. The teacher by this time makes a conscious effort to lengthen the amount which children read at one stretch, — not paragraph by paragraph but several paragraphs for each question.

READING FOR RECREATION

CATHERWOOD, *Story of Tonty.*

HASBROUCK, *La Salle.*

The Discussion (Second Story)

Children answer the study-guide questions as fully as possible in their own language rather than in the words of the book. The teacher then writes on the board *seventeenth century.* Children discuss the meaning.

Multisensory Aids

Children and teacher talk over together the pictures in the texts, noting features of historical and geographical importance. They turn to a map showing the routes of Marquette and Joliet and La Salle. They notice how the routes are marked, and trace them on a large wall map. They point out Louisiana, the Illinois Country, Green Bay, the Fox River, the Mississippi, the Ohio and the Missouri River.

AUDIO-VISUAL MATERIALS OBTAINABLE

GABRIEL (Ed.). Pageant of America : I, 317–322.

McKINLEY. Illustrated Topics : M M 16.

Society for Visual Education. Schoolfilm : French Explorations in North America.

Yale Pageant Educational Slides : 25, 26, 527, 624, 806.

Children's Drawings of Frenchmen making a Portage. Initial Attempts are at the Left; Finished Drawings, at the Right

General Activities

Creative Activities: Group and Individual, Correlated with Other Subjects or Voluntary Projects

Children draw pictures of expeditions making a portage. (See opposite page.)

A volunteer explains how Indian guides shoot the rapids.

The class goes to the museum to see a pipe of peace, or calumet.

Some children may wish to write poems on phases of La Salle's work and suffering.

Committees read to the group the dramatizations in Hubbard's *Little American History Plays* (50–57) and Bird and Starling's *Historical Plays for Children* (33–52, 143–172).

Others dramatize the scene in which La Salle fails to find the mouth of the Mississippi on returning from France.

Each child adds the routes of Marquette and Joliet and La Salle to the map "French Exploration in America," starring the portages and naming Louisiana.

The class continues the time chart.

Application to Present-Day Conditions

Make a list of all the things you can find named for Marquette, Joliet, and La Salle.

Do wild ducks still feed on wild rice?

How long did it take Marquette and Joliet to travel from Mackinac to the Mississippi? [*One month.*] How long would it take to travel that distance today by automobile?

Are there any buffalo near the Wisconsin River today?

The mouth of which river is farther north, the Ohio or the Missouri?

Was La Salle's Louisiana country the same as today's state of Louisiana? Was the Illinois country the same as today's state of Illinois?

Does Louisiana still belong to France?

Exercises in Reasoning

Do you think it is correct to call Marquette the first white Chicagoan?

What was Marquette trying to find? Does that fact tell you whether or not the French yet had any idea of the width of the continent of North America?

Why did a missionary go with each exploring party?

Do you think that Joliet was given a good enough reward?

Who do you think has the best right to the title "Discoverer of the Mississippi"—De Soto or Marquette and Joliet?

About what other kings have we read who had colonies named for them? About what two queens?

Why was it necessary to build forts in order to carry on the fur trade?

We are often told that one difference between great men and ordinary people is that great men have stronger wills. Apply this saying in the case of La Salle.

Drill Games

Place names are drilled upon at the map: *Lake Michigan, Great Lakes, Louisiana country, mouth of Mississippi River.*

Drill cards are made for the following:

Marquette	↔	a missionary who journeyed with Joliet
Joliet	↔	a fur-trader who found the route from the Great Lakes to the Mississippi
portage	↔	a narrow neck of land between two waterways, across which goods are carried
pipe of peace	↔	an Indian sign of friendship
La Salle	↔	the man who gave France a claim to the Louisiana country
the *Griffin*	↔	the name of La Salle's sailing ship
seventeenth century	↔	all the years from 1600 up to 1700

Drill games are played with both sides of these cards.

Testing

Tests of Understanding are supplied on pages 354–355 and 368 of Kelty's *Beginnings of the American People and Nation.*

Additional Tests of Reasoning and Skills.[1] Check the best answer.

1. Marquette and Joliet turned back because   they thought that fierce Indians would attack them.   they believed that it would be very hot farther south.   √ they knew now that the Mississippi was not the way to China.   they were told that the Mississippi River was very dangerous.

2. The chief result of Marquette and Joliet's journey was that it   √ showed Frenchmen they could go by water from the Great Lakes to the Mississippi.   made the king believe that he could reach India by way of the Mississippi.   showed everybody how hard work it was to explore.   showed the missionaries where more Indians lived.

3. La Salle built a sailing ship because   sailing ships look better than canoes.   √ canoes could not hold enough goods.   sailing ships cost less money.   canoes could not travel fast enough.

4. All these statements are true. Put a check mark before the one which tells the most important result of La Salle's work: He built a fort called Heartbreak.   He had more trouble with his own people than with Indians. √ He claimed the Louisiana country for France.   He carried the fur trade to the Mississippi Valley.

5. Turn to a map showing the journeys of Marquette and Joliet and La Salle. Mark the following:

Marquette and Joliet passed the Ohio River.   True [√]   False [ ]
La Salle once reached the mouth of the Mississippi.   True [√]   False [ ]
La Salle discovered Lake Superior.   True [ ]   False [√]

[1] Other exercises in reasoning are included under "General Activities."

6. Which of the following sailed down the Mississippi first, La Salle or Marquette and Joliet? _ _ _[*Marquette and Joliet.*]_ _ _

Exercises in Organization. The lower group copies the topic headings of the first story. One child tells the principal points of the first section, another the principal points of the second section, and so on. The upper group does the same with the second story.

The table of French explorers begun in Unit Two (p. 168) is continued.

B. THE ENGLISH ADVANCE INTO THE INTERIOR

Conversational Approach

[*1 Week*

The class turns again to the sand-table model formerly used. "Now we have shown how the French could reach the heart of the country. Will the English be able to do as well?" Children try to study out the best ways for them to go beyond the mountains.

"Our story today tells how the English went beyond the mountains. Some of them had exciting adventures with Indians."

Reading and Study

The Reading Periods

Independent Readers

TEXTS

BARKER, DODD, WEBB, *Our Nation Begins,* 270–283.

BEARD and BAGLEY, *First Book in American History,* 83–91.

BURNHAM and JACK, *Beginnings of Our Country,* 270–281.

KELTY, *Beginnings of the American People and Nation,* 369–385.

McGUIRE and PHILLIPS, *Adventuring in Young America,* 239–265 (selections).

NIDA, *Following the Frontier,* 24–25, 48–52, 96–104.

EXTENSIVE READING

COE, *Makers of the Nation,* 131–150.

FARIS, *Where Our History Was Made,* 119–123, 141–145.

FOOTE and SKINNER, *Explorers and Founders of America,* 274–275.

MILLER, *My Book House,* II : 323.

MONTGOMERY, *Beginners' American History,* 132–139.

PERRY and PRICE, *American History,* I : 208–209.

SOUTHWORTH, *Builders of Our Country,* II : 116–121.

TAPPAN, *American Hero Stories,* 200–207.

VOLLINTINE, *Making of America,* 14–16, 54–72.

Lower Group

The teacher tells the story orally to this group, writing on the board the names of the most important persons and places as she mentions them. Children practice the pronunciations.

The teacher and the lower group then read together the story as given in the text. The teacher guides the silent reading, section by section, by the same type of questions that she would use in a silent-reading period; for example, "Was all the land east of the mountains now settled?"

After the entire story has been read in this manner, the children test themselves by the study-guide questions.

OTHER BOOKS

BASS, *Stories of Pioneer Life,* 29–45, 51–53, 103–136.

BLAISDELL and BALL, *American History for Little Folks,* 109–114.

BLAISDELL and BALL, *Short Stories from American History,* 92–98.

WAYLAND, *History Stories for Primary Grades,* 106–108.

READING FOR RECREATION

ATKINSON, *Johnny Appleseed.*
AVERILL and STANLEY (Ed.), *Daniel Boone*
   (illustrated by Rojankovsky).
DRAKE, *Pioneer Life in Kentucky.*
EVERSON and POWER, *Early Days in Ohio.*
GROVE, *Story of Daniel Boone.*

OTIS, *Benjamin of Ohio.*
OTIS, *Hannah of Kentucky.*
PERKINS, *Pioneer Twins.*
SCHAARE, *Life of Daniel Boone.*
SKINNER, *Silent Scot, Frontier Scout.*
TOMLINSON, *Scouting with Daniel Boone.*

The Discussion

Children answer the study-guide questions as completely as possible. The teacher checks carefully to see that the same children do not do all the talking while some never participate.

The teacher writes on the board *interior, pioneers, colonial period, eighteenth century.* Children discuss the meanings.

Multisensory Aids

Children and teacher talk over together the pictures given in the text, noting the features of geographical and historical importance. They turn to a map of early routes used by the English and show the only practicable road from North Carolina to Kentucky. They point out the Wilderness Road and the Cumberland Gap and discuss the importance of the gap.

AUDIO-VISUAL MATERIALS OBTAINABLE

Chronicles of America Photoplays: Daniel Boone.
EASTMAN. Classroom Films: The Boone Trail.
Keystone View Slides: 43.
Society for Visual Education. Picturol: First Westward Movement.
Society for Visual Education. Schoolfilm: Settling the Ohio Valley.
Yale Pageant Educational Slides: 134–136, 139–141, 551–552, 578–579, 629–630, 633, 819.

Music. Selections from Ryan's *Music for the Dances of Our Pioneers.*

General Activities

Creative Activities: Group and Individual, Correlated with Other Subjects or Voluntary Projects

On the sand-table model, committees show the parallel valleys of the Appalachians furnishing natural roads to the South.

A volunteer gives the speech which George Washington might have made to the assembly of Virginia, urging the importance of settling the West.

Girls dress dolls as the pioneers dressed.

Volunteers make soap carvings of pack horses.

Floor talks are given on how meat was dried or smoked for the winter.

Committees read to the group the dramatizations given in Stevenson's *Children's Classics in Dramatic Form* (IV: 142–154) and Hubbard's *Little American History Plays* (125–129).

The teacher reads to the class selections from Whitman's "O Pioneers"; from Vachel Lindsay's "Johnny Appleseed."

Each child begins to make a map called "The English and the French Have Trouble," showing the Appalachian Mountains, the Wilderness Road, and Kentucky.

The class continues the time chart.

Application to Present-Day Conditions

Is there still land in the United States that can be taken up by settlers? Is it good land?

Are the "Pennsylvania Dutch" really Dutch? (See a children's encyclopedia.)

Can you explain why some of the mountain people in Kentucky and Tennessee still live much as the pioneers did? [*They have been isolated ever since their ancestors settled there; no new ideas.*]

Do travelers today ever follow animal trails?

Have you ever seen a stump fence? a blazed tree?

Have you ever seen surveyors measuring land or laying out a road or sewer? How did they do it?

What are salt licks? (See *lick* in Webster's Dictionary, unabridged.)

Are tunnels used in warfare nowadays?

What is a deed to land? Is it necessary to have a deed?

Exercises in Reasoning

How could the products of the frontier farms be carried to the cities to be sold?

Why were so many different stories told about the interior? [*Different people had seen different parts of it.*]

Why were younger sons more eager to go West than the oldest son? [*Because of primogeniture.*]

We are told that most of the frontiersmen were usually in debt. Does the story of Boone tell you why?

Why did the Wilderness Road lead through the Cumberland Gap?

Why were the farms outside the stockade?

How did the pioneers help to keep alive the American spirit?

Do you think that the pioneers were as happy as we are today?

Drill Games

Drill on place names, such as *Kentucky, Appalachian Mountains, Wilderness Road, Cumberland Gap*, is best carried on at the map.

Drill cards are made for the following:

Daniel Boone	⟷	a famous pioneer in Kentucky
Kentucky	⟷	the first section settled by the English beyond the mountains
pioneers	⟷	persons who go into a new land very early
interior	⟷	the inland region of a country
colonial period	⟷	the time during which colonies were being settled
eighteenth century	⟷	the years from 1700 up to 1800

Children have access to these cards during the periods of reading and study.

Testing

Tests of Understanding are suggested on page 385 of Kelty's *Beginnings of the American People and Nation.*

Additional Tests of Reasoning and Skills.[1] Check the best answer.

1. Americans on the frontier did not work for wages, because   there was little money in the country.   everyone was rich.   there was not much work to be done.   √ everyone could have a farm of his own.

2. Mark the following as either true or false.

True   False

[ ]   [√] By 1750 the country was settled as far as the Mississippi.

[√]   [ ] Settlement beyond the mountains was very slow.

[√]   [ ] Settlements could not grow very fast until the Indians were driven out.

[ ]   [√] Daniel Boone lived about the time of the founding of Pennsylvania.

[ ]   [√] Most of the people living along the coast were foreigners.

[√]   [ ] Many foreigners lived in the back country.

[ ]   [√] It was very easy to cross the mountains.

[√]   [ ] People went beyond the mountains because they wanted cheap land.

[ ]   [√] The pioneers had many government officers to help them.

3. Turn to the map of early routes. Did the Wilderness Road cross the Ohio River?   Yes [ ]   No [√]

Is the Cumberland Gap north or south of the Ohio River?   North [ ] South [√]

Exercise in Organization. Children attempt to make two or three summary sentences.

C. THE FRENCH AND THE ENGLISH WANTED THE SAME LAND

STORY 1. TWO LINES OF FORTS · STORY 2. GEORGE WASHINGTON'S YOUTH   [1 Week

[Stories treated separately for reading and discussion; for other activities, both together]

Conversational Approach

The class gathers again about the sand-table model. They show the territory explored by the French; that explored by the English. "Do you remember how La Salle had planned to protect the French routes? Where would you build forts if you were the French governor?" The children select what seem to them to be good places. "Turn to a map showing the forts and see whether you have selected any of the right places. How are the French forts marked on this map?

[1] Other exercises on reasoning are included under "General Activities."

"Would the English have any interest in what the French were doing? Especially along what river? Why? What do you think they would probably do about it? Find the English forts on the map."

Reading and Study

The Reading Periods (First Story)

Independent Readers

TEXTS

BARKER, DODD, WEBB, *Our Nation Begins*, 255–256.

BEARD and BAGLEY, *First Book in American History*, 83, 91–92.

BURNHAM and JACK, *Beginnings of Our Country*, 215–216.

KELTY, *Beginnings of the American People and Nation*, 386–391.

NIDA, *Following the Frontier*, 19–22, 25–26.

EXTENSIVE READING

FOOTE and SKINNER, *Explorers and Founders of America*, 274–275.

TAPPAN, *American Hero Stories*, 117–118.

VOLLINTINE, *Making of America*, 16–19.

Lower Group

The teacher tells the story orally to this group, writing on the board the names of the most important places as she mentions them. Children practice the pronunciations.

Teacher and children then read together the story as given in the text. The teacher guides the silent reading, section by section, by the same type of questions that she would use in a silent-reading period; for example, "What did the French do when they became worried about the English?"

After the entire story has been read in this manner, children test themselves by the study-guide questions.

OTHER BOOKS

BASS, *Stories of Pioneer Life*, 51–53.

READING FOR RECREATION

ALTSHELER, *Rulers of the Lakes*.

The Discussion (First Story)

The children answer as fully as possible the study-guide questions. The teacher attempts to draw the members of the lower group into the discussion as well as those of the upper group. The following words are written on the board: *lead plates, blockhouses, forks of the Ohio.* Children discuss the meanings.

The Reading Periods (Second Story)

Independent Readers

TEXTS

BARKER, DODD, WEBB, *Our Nation Begins*, 256–258.

BEARD and BAGLEY, *First Book in American History*, 92–94.

BURNHAM and JACK, *Beginnings of Our Country*, 216–217.

KELTY, *Beginnings of the American People and Nation*, 392–398.

KNOWLTON and GILL, *When We Were Colonies*, 55–64 (hard).

Lower Group

The teacher and the lower group read together the story as given in the text. The teacher guides the silent reading, section by section, by the same type of questions that she would use in a silent-reading period; for example, "Why do we begin to read about George Washington at this particular time?"

After the entire story has been read in this manner, the children test themselves by the study-guide questions.

SMALLIDGE and PAXSON, *Builders of Our Nation*, 266–278 (hard).

WOODBURN and MORAN, *Finders and Founders of the New World*, 226–234.

EXTENSIVE READING

CHANDLER and CHITWOOD, *Makers of American History*, 144–146.

COE, *Founders of Our Country*, 296–302.

DAVIDSON, *Founders and Builders of Our Nation*, 56–59.

MONTGOMERY, *Beginners' American History*, 103–108.

SOUTHWORTH, *Builders of Our Country*, II: 24–31.

OTHER BOOKS

BALDWIN, *Fifty Famous People*, 60–62.

BALDWIN, *Fifty Famous Stories Retold*, 59–61.

BLAISDELL and BALL, *Child's Book of American History*, 77–85.

CURTIS, *Why We Celebrate Our Holidays*, 24–30.

DAVIS, *Stories of the United States*, 139–151.

WAYLAND, *History Stories for Primary Grades*, 21–23, 109–115, 155–157.

WILSON, *A History Reader*, 199–207.

READING FOR RECREATION

LOWITZ, *General George the Great*.

MIRRIAM, *Washington's Boyhood*.

The Discussion (Second Story)

Children answer the study-guide questions as completely as possible. This exercise offers a good opportunity to clear up misapprehensions or half-understandings. The teacher writes on the board the word *surveyor*. Children discuss the meaning.

Multisensory Aids

Children and teacher talk over together the pictures in the text, pointing out features of geographical and historical significance.

They turn to a map of the French and the English in America and locate the French forts and the English forts.

AUDIO-VISUAL AIDS OBTAINABLE

BRADLEY. Straight-Line Cut-Outs: George Washington, his Mount Vernon Home.

Compton's Pictured Teaching Materials: *American Colonies*, Plate IV, 1; *Holidays*, Plate XI.

EASTMAN. Classroom Films: George Washington, his Life and Times.

International Educational Pictures: George Washington (3 sets).

Keystone Views: 44–46, 49.

Society for Visual Education (MUIR). 1626–1759: Early Settlements and French and Indian Wars.

Society for Visual Education. Picturol: George Washington.

Yale Pageant Educational Slides: 28–30, 550, 817.

Music. Children sing "Mount Vernon Bells."

General Activities

Creative Activities: Group and Individual, Correlated with Other Subjects or Voluntary Projects

A committee sets up French and English forts on the sand-table model.

Children make a graph to show the comparative numbers of French and English in America.[1]

[1] See A. B. Hart's *Formation of the Union* (Longmans, Green & Co.), p. 27.

The teacher puts on the board a list of the names of French forts and a list of the names of English forts. Children attempt to determine which is which from the form of the name.

Fort St. Louis	Fort Cumberland	Fort Le Bœuf
Fort William Henry	Fort Duquesne	Fort Venango
Fort Crevecœur	Fort Vincennes	
Fort Frontenac	Fort Edward	

A volunteer models and paints plates like the lead plates buried by the French.

A traveler describes Mount Vernon to the class.

A volunteer explains by a blackboard drawing why the Forks of the Ohio are called forks.

Each child adds the two lines of forts to the map begun last week.

Application to Present-Day Conditions

By how many different methods might a message be sent from Virginia to the Ohio? Are there any iron mines in Virginia today? (See *Virginia* in the World Almanac.)

Do you know of any people today who are spreading out into lands held by another people? [*Japanese into China; Italians into Africa.*]

How long would it take today to travel from Canada to the Ohio River? How long did it take the French? [*Forty-four days.*] Graph the two sets of figures.

How large is a good-sized farm today? Compare with the size of George Washington's father's lands. Do you suppose his land was all planted?

Exercises in Reasoning

What is meant by the following statement? "The English were hemmed in by the French forts."

Why would the Indians need blacksmiths?

Why should you expect the Forks of the Ohio to become a railway center many years later?

Why was George Washington called "a promising young Englishman"?

Which was older, George Washington or Benjamin Franklin? (See the encyclopedia for the date of birth of each.) Compare their boyhood days.

Children and teacher together discuss why legends grow up about great men (cherry tree, "never told a lie," etc.). Should such stories be included in history books?

Was it of any importance to George Washington that his brother was manager of the Ohio Company? [*Brought home to him very early the importance of possession of the Ohio.*]

Was Martha Washington's name "Martha Washington" when she was a little girl?

Drill Games

Place names are best drilled upon at the map: *Mohawk River, Forks of the Ohio.*

Drill cards are made as follows:

lead plates	↔	articles buried by the French to prove their claims
blockhouse	↔	a fort made of logs
George Washington	↔	a young Virginia surveyor
Martha Washington	↔	wife of " the Father of his Country "
Mount Vernon	↔	home of George Washington
surveyor	↔	a person who measures land

Children prepare for the drill games by practicing on the items which they find most difficult.

Testing

Tests of Understanding are supplied on pages 391 and 398 of Kelty's *Beginnings of the American People and Nation.*

Additional Tests of Reasoning and Skills.[1] Check the best answer.

1. Both the French and the English wanted the Forks of the Ohio because √ a fort there could keep boats from going up or down the river.   the soil there was good for farming.   boats could sail easily up and down the river.   there were many coal mines near the river.

2. Quarrels between nations have usually been settled by   talking the matter over.   prayer.   buying each other's claims.   √ force.

3. The English people did not need to build as many forts as the French because   √ the mountains protected them.   the French were much better fighters.   the English had better guns.   forts cannot be built along rivers.

4. Washington's work as a surveyor was useful for his country many years later because   he made a great deal of money from it.   he surveyed so much land.   √ it taught him to live in the wilderness.   it made him hate the French.

5. Turn to a map of the French forts. Did the French build forts to connect their settlements on the Mississippi with the settlements near the Great Lakes and the St. Lawrence?   Yes [√]   No [ ]

6. On what pages in the book can you find Mount Vernon mentioned?

- - - - - -

Where did you find out? _ _ _[*Index.*]_ _ _
Under which word did you look?   Mount [√]   Vernon [ ]

Exercise in Organization. The teacher supplies the skeleton outline for the two stories, and the children fill the blank spaces.

---

[1] Other exercises in reasoning are included under "General Activities."

STORY 3. WASHINGTON'S JOURNEY

D. WARS BETWEEN THE FRENCH AND THE ENGLISH

STORY 1. THE THREE EARLY WARS BETWEEN THE FRENCH AND THE ENGLISH   [1 Week

[Stories treated separately for reading and discussion; for other activities, both together]

Conversational Approach

"When your mother intends to punish you, does she ever warn you first? Do nations ever warn one another? How do you suppose that they can send such warnings? From what particular spot do you think the French and the English would warn one another away? Our first story tells how that was done and who did it.

"Then we must go back and find out what had happened in the first three wars between the English and the French. Which do you think had the best chance to win? Why? List all the points in favor of the French and those in favor of the English."

Reading and Study

The Reading Periods (First Story)

Independent Readers

TEXTS

BARKER, DODD, WEBB, *Our Nation Begins*, 258–259.

BEARD and BAGLEY, *First Book in American History*, 94–96.

BURNHAM and JACK, *Beginnings of Our Country*, 218–219.

KELTY, *Beginnings of the American People and Nation*, 399–406.

NIDA, *Following the Frontier*, 27–30.

SMALLIDGE and PAXSON, *Builders of Our Nation*, 280–289 (hard).

WOODBURN and MORAN, *Finders and Founders of the New World*, 235–238.

EXTENSIVE READING

CHANDLER and CHITWOOD, *Makers of American History*, 146.

COE, *Founders of Our Country*, 302–306.

DAVIDSON, *Founders and Builders of Our Country*, 59–62.

FOOTE and SKINNER, *Explorers and Founders of America*, 275–276.

MONTGOMERY, *Beginners' American History*, 108–110.

PERRY and PRICE, *American History*, I: 209–210.

SOUTHWORTH, *Builders of Our Country*, II: 31–39.

TAPPAN, *American Hero Stories*, 118–123.

VOLLINTINE, *Making of America*, 19–23.

Lower Group

The teacher tells the story orally to this group, writing on the board the names of the most important persons and places as she mentions them. Children practice the pronunciations.

The teacher and these children then read together the story as given in the text. The teacher guides the silent reading, section by section, by the same type of questions that she would use in a silent-reading period; for example, "Why did the governor of Virginia send a trader to the Indians?"

After the entire story has been read in this manner, the children test themselves by the study-guide questions.

OTHER BOOKS

BLAISDELL and BALL, *Child's Book of American History*, 86–90.

WILSON, *A History Reader*, 207–212.

READING FOR RECREATION

ALTSHELER, *Rulers of the Lakes.*

The Discussion (First Story)

Children answer as completely as possible the study-guide questions. They question one another to bring out points of importance which were omitted in the discussion.

The Reading Periods (Second Story)

Independent Readers

TEXTS

BURNHAM and JACK, *Beginnings of Our Country*, 210–215.
CLARK-GORDY, *First Three Hundred Years*, 353–358 (hard).
KELTY, *Beginnings of the American People and Nation*, 407–417.
KNOWLTON and GILL, *When We Were Colonies*, 267–274 (hard).
NIDA, *Following the Frontier*, 10.

EXTENSIVE READING

FOOTE and SKINNER, *Explorers and Founders of America*, 296–306.
PERRY and PRICE, *American History*, I : 203–208.
VOLLINTINE, *Making of America*, 8–9.

READING FOR RECREATION

GRINNELL, *Beyond the Old Frontier*.
MCNEIL, *Shadow of the Iroquois*.
SMITH, *Boys of the Border*.
SMITH, *Boy Captive of Old Deerfield*.

Lower Group

The teacher tells the story orally to this group, writing on the board the names of the most important persons and places as she mentions them. Children practice the pronunciations. Teacher and children then read together the story as given in the text. The teacher guides the silent reading, section by section, by the same type of questions that she would use in a silent-reading period; for example, "What did both France and England want?"

When the entire story has been read in this manner the children test themselves by the study-guide questions.

OTHER BOOKS

BLAISDELL and BALL, *American History for Little Folks*, 53–58.
BLAISDELL and BALL, *American History Story Book*, 19–27.
BLAISDELL and BALL, *Child's Book of American History*, 64–76.
BLAISDELL and BALL, *Short Stories from American History*, 22–29.
PRATT, *Stories of Colonial Children*, 121–129, 136–154.

The Discussion (Second Story)

Children answer the study-guide questions with their books open before them. Several sets of answers may be given by different children.

The teacher writes on the board the words *outlying settlements*, *war whoop*, *stockade*. Children discuss the meanings. Are there any outlying settlements in your city?

Multisensory Aids

Children and teacher talk over together the pictures in the text, noting features of geographical and historical significance. They turn to the map and point out territory which changed owners during the first three wars.

AUDIO-VISUAL MATERIALS OBTAINABLE

MCKINLEY. Illustrated Topics for American History : S 11.
Society for Visual Education (BRIGGS). The Struggle between the French and the English.
Yale Pageant Educational Slides : 31.

General Activities

Creative Activities: Group and Individual, Correlated with Other Subjects or Voluntary Projects

A visit is made to the museum to see letters and seals used before the days of envelopes, and to see firearms of the colonial period.

A volunteer writes the message which George Washington carried.

A committee reads to the class the dramatizations given in Shoemaker's *Colonial Plays for the Schoolroom* (53–57).

A volunteer writes the letter which George Washington might have written, describing his journey to the Ohio.

The teacher reads to the class selections from Cooper's *Last of the Mohicans* illustrating the methods of Indian warfare.

On the map "The English and the French Have Trouble" each child shades the territory won by the English in the first three wars.

Application to Present-Day Conditions

How long does it take to travel from your home to the Ohio River? Compare this with the time George Washington's journey took.

How do armies today carry their big guns from one place to another?

Is Newfoundland a part of the Dominion of Canada today? (See a children's encyclopedia.)

Show on a map the railroad leading to Hudson's Bay. Compare with the condition of the country at the time of our story.

Exercises in Reasoning

Why did armies in past times almost never fight in the winter?

How was news carried from the frontier settlements?

Do you blame the Indians for taking the side of those they thought would win? Should they have helped the English? the French?

From this story give examples of the fact that the colonies were not willing to work together.

Why had New France spread out to the north and west more than to the south?

Do you suppose that only the French and the Indians were cruel, or were the English cruel too? Do you think that the trouble between the French and the English is going to be settled peaceably? Why?

Drill Games

Drill cards are made for the following:

Fort Duquesne	⟷	the fort built by the French at the Forks of the Ohio
Sir William Johnson	⟷	the great friend of the Iroquois
stockade	⟷	a fence of stout posts
war whoop	⟷	a loud shout given by Indians during an attack
outlying settlements	⟷	villages far out on the frontier

Testing

Tests of Understanding are suggested in Kelty's *Beginnings of the American People and Nation*, pp. 406, 417.

Additional Tests of Reasoning and Skills.[1] Check the best answer.

1. The real purpose of Washington's journey to the Ohio was ____ to show the other English colonies that Virginia meant business. ____ √ to show the French that the English claimed the Forks. ____ to drive away the French already there.

2. During the three early wars the French and the English were fighting for the land along the ____ √ St. Lawrence River. ____ Great Lakes. ____ Atlantic coast. ____ Mississippi River.

3. Turn to a map of the early wars. Show in this square how the map marks the land northeast of Maine which was won by the English. □

4. Why would the story of the war as told by a man who fought in it be likely to be a true story? ___[*Eyewitness.*]___

5. In what ways might it not be a completely true story? ___[*Saw only small part of action. Likely to be prejudiced.*]___

Exercises in Organization. Make a list of the causes of the wars.
Make a list of the advantages of the French.
Make a list of the advantages of the English.
Make a list of the changes in land ownership caused by the three wars.

STORY 2. BENJAMIN FRANKLIN'S SERVICES · STORY 3. THE
FRENCH AND INDIAN WAR BEGINS   [*1 Week*]

[Stories treated separately for reading and discussion; for other activities, both together]

Conversational Approach (First Story)

"Is any building or company or any article in your town called the Franklin? Why was this name given to it? Have you ever heard anything about Benjamin Franklin?"

Reading and Study

The Reading Periods (First Story)

Independent Readers

BARKER, DODD, WEBB, *Our Nation Begins*, 324–328.

BEARD and BAGLEY, *First Book in American History*, 136–140.

BURNHAM and JACK, *Beginnings of Our Country*, 182–185.

KELTY, *Beginnings of the American People and Nation*, 418–429.

KNOWLTON and GILL, *When We Were Colonies*, 250–257 (hard).

SMALLIDGE and PAXSON, *Builders of Our Nation*, 246–263 (hard).

WOODBURN and MORAN, *Finders and Founders of the New World*, 244–259.

Lower Group

The teacher and the lower group read together the story as given in the text. The teacher guides the silent reading, section by section, by the same type of questions that she would use in a silent-reading period; for example, "The first page tells us about Franklin's very early boyhood with his family."

When the entire story has been read in this manner, the children test themselves by the study-guide questions.

[1] Other exercises in reasoning are included under "General Activities."

EXTENSIVE READING

COE, *Founders of Our Country*, 310–320.
DAVIDSON, *Founders and Builders of Our Nation*, 35–45.
FARIS, *Real Stories of the Geography Makers*, 213–216.
FOOTE and SKINNER, *Explorers and Founders of America*, 261–267.
MONTGOMERY, *Beginners' American History*, 89–101.
PERRY and PRICE, *American History*, I : 214.
SOUTHWORTH, *Builders of Our Country*, I : 208–222.

OTHER BOOKS

BALDWIN, *Fifty Famous People*, 21–24.
McFEE, *Story of Benjamin Franklin*.
WILSON, *A History Reader*, 141–152.

The Discussion (First Story)

Children answer the study-guide questions as fully as possible.

Conversational Approach (Second Story)

"Now we must go back and find out what has been happening between the French and the English while Franklin was growing up.

"Turn to a map of the French and Indian War. Why may we feel quite sure that some of the fighting will take place at the Forks of the Ohio? Has there been fighting there already? Where must supplies come from to reach the French fort here?

"Find the French forts on Lakes Erie and Ontario. If the English could take these, would it make any difference about the supplies' reaching Fort Duquesne?

"Our story today tells about fighting in these two places: at the Forks of the Ohio; and at the French forts on Lakes Erie and Ontario."

Reading and Study

The Reading Periods (Second Story)

Independent Readers

TEXTS

BARKER, DODD, WEBB, *Our Nation Begins*, 259–262.
BEARD and BAGLEY, *First Book in American History*, 96–97.
BURNHAM and JACK, *Beginnings of Our Country*, 219–223.
KELTY, *Beginnings of the American People and Nation*, 430–438.
KNOWLTON and GILL, *When We Were Colonies*, 274–289 (hard).
NIDA, *Following the Frontier*, 31–33.
SMALLIDGE and PAXSON, *Builders of Our Country*, 289–291.
WOODBURN and MORAN, *Finders and Founders of the New World*, 238–242.

Lower Group

The teacher tells the story orally to this group, writing on the board the names of the most important persons and places as she mentions them. Children practice the pronunciations.

The teacher and the children then read together the story as told in the text. The teacher guides the silent reading, section by section, by the same type of questions that she would use in a silent-reading period; for example, "The first two paragraphs tell how France and England made ready. What did they do?"

After the entire story has been read in this manner the children test themselves by the study-guide questions.

EXTENSIVE READING

CHANDLER and CHITWOOD, *Makers of American History*, 109–114.
COE, *Founders of Our Country*, 306–309.
FOOTE and SKINNER, *Explorers and Founders of America*, 276–280.
MONTGOMERY, *Beginners' American History*, 110–112.
PERRY and PRICE, *American History*, I : 210–216.
SOUTHWORTH, *Builders of Our Country*, II : 36–43.
TAPPAN, *American Hero Stories*, 123–125.
VOLLINTINE, *Making of America*, 22–29.

OTHER BOOKS

BLAISDELL and BALL, *Child's Book of American History*, 97–103.
DAVIS, *Stories of the United States*, 131–134.
DODGE, *Stories of American History*, 52–59.
WILSON, *A History Reader*, 212–215.

READING FOR RECREATION

FIELD, *Calico Bush*.
GREGOR, *Jim Mason, Scout*.

The Discussion (Second Story)

Children answer the study-guide questions as fully as possible. The teacher writes on the board *aide, retreat, regiment*. Children discuss the meanings.

Multisensory Aids

Children and teacher talk over together the pictures in the text, noting points of historical or geographical significance. They turn to a map of the French and Indian War and show Braddock's route and the French forts taken by the English.

AUDIO-VISUAL MATERIALS OBTAINABLE

BROWN. Famous Pictures: 2133.
Compton's Pictured Teaching Materials: *American Indians*, Plate II, 1.
GABRIEL (Ed.). Pageant of America: XI, 61–66.
International Educational Pictures: Benjamin Franklin.
Society for Visual Education (SPENCER). Benjamin Franklin.
Yale Pageant Educational Slides: 119, 301, 716, 772.

General Activities

Creative Activities: Group and Individual, Correlated with Other Subjects or Voluntary Projects

The class consults the index of a large atlas to find out how many places have been named for Franklin, and adds to the list the names of buildings or other articles named for him.

A volunteer writes an article for the school newspaper.

Groups form a reading club like Franklin's.

Committees compare an almanac of today with *Poor Richard's Almanac*.

The class takes a trip to the museum to see a Franklin stove.

The class makes as long a list as possible of Franklin's public services.

The teacher reads to the class selections from Franklin's *Autobiography*.

Volunteers choose adages from *Poor Richard's Almanac* and draw illuminated mottoes.

A volunteer draws a plan of Braddock's expedition.

Girls dress dolls in the uniform of a British soldier, a British officer, and an American soldier of the period.

A committee reads to the class the dramatization given in Bird and Starling's *Historical Plays for Children* (199–220).

On the map "The French and the English Have Trouble" each child traces Braddock's route and draws a red circle around all the French forts taken by the English.

Application to Present-Day Conditions

Find on a map of today the city which occupies the site of Fort Duquesne.

Can you name any present-day scientists?

Do we have child labor nowadays?

Are any people today vegetarians?

Are newspapers ever punished nowadays by having their printing places closed down? Why?

Compare the length of time it took Franklin to go from Boston to New York with the length of time such a journey takes today.

Why are advertisements a very important part of the newspaper of today? [*They pay a large part of the costs.*]

What takes the place of Franklin's night watch today?

Does France still have a great army and England a great fleet?

Do Canada and the United States have to have forts along the Great Lakes today?

Exercises in Reasoning

From Franklin's life can we learn a lesson about the possibility of each American's educating himself, no matter how poor he may be? Write a sentence containing the statement of such a lesson.

Does a man have to go through college in order to become well educated?

Can you think of a case where you can apply to yourself the rule "Don't pay too much for your whistle"?

How is a public library supported?

Why has Franklin been called "the Schoolmaster of a Nation"?

Why is a lightning rod supposed to protect a house?

Why should Braddock have listened to the colonial officers?

Does a brave soldier ever retreat? [*Case of Braddock.*]

Does the second story tell why Washington could take no part later in the capture of Quebec?

Drill Games

Place names can best be drilled upon at the map: *Fort Duquesne, Pittsburgh.*

Drill cards are made for the following:

Benjamin Franklin	⟷	America's first great scientist
Poor Richard's Almanac	⟷	a book printed every year by Benjamin Franklin
General Braddock	⟷	a British officer killed while going to Fort Duquesne
Fort Pitt	⟷	the British fort built where Fort Duquesne had stood
aide	⟷	an officer who helps the general
regiment	⟷	a large group of soldiers
to retreat	⟷	to withdraw, or go back

Testing

Tests of Understanding are suggested on pages 429 and 438 of Kelty's *Beginnings of the American People and Nation.*

Additional Test of Reasoning and Skills.[1] Check the best answer.

1. In the French and Indian War   the Indians were fighting both the French and the English.   √ the English were fighting both the French and the Indians.   the French were fighting on the same side as the Indians and the English.   the French were fighting the Indians.

2. The river about which most fighting was done at this time was the √ Ohio.   St. Lawrence.   Mississippi.   Hudson.

3. The English wanted to take the French forts on the Great Lakes because   those were the most heavily fortified of all forts.   √ the supplies from Quebec to Fort Duquesne passed there.   those forts were very easy to get at.   the Indians liked to come to those forts.

4. Turn to a map of the French and Indian War. In order to reach Fort Duquesne, Braddock had to march   east   √ west.

Exercise in Organization. The teacher supplies the main headings for the outline of the French and Indian War. The children co-operatively decide what the subheadings should be.

STORY 4. THE BATTLE OF QUEBEC · STORY 5. THE END OF FRANCE IN NORTH AMERICA   [1 Week

[Stories treated separately for reading and discussion; for other activities, both together]

Conversational Approach

The class gathers once more around the sand-table model of North America east of the Mississippi. "What important places does France now have left in North America? What is the best way for the English to get at them? Why will England's large fleet be a help to her in this attempt? Why will the task be a hard one?"

Reading and Study

The Reading Periods (First Story)

Independent Readers

TEXTS

BARKER, DODD, WEBB, *Our Nation Begins,* 262–267.

BEARD and BAGLEY, *First Book in American History,* 97–101.

BURNHAM and JACK, *Beginnings of Our Country,* 223–226.

CLARK-GORDY, *First Three Hundred Years,* 358–368 (hard).

KELTY, *Beginnings of the American People and Nation,* 439–445.

Lower Group

The teacher tells the story orally to this group, writing on the board the names of the most important persons and places as she mentions them. Children practice the pronunciations.

The teacher and these children then read together the story as given in the text. The teacher guides the silent reading, section by section, by the same kind of questions that she would use in a silent-reading

[1] Other exercises in reasoning are included under "General Activities."

KNOWLTON and GILL, *When We Were Colonies,* 289–292 (hard).
NIDA, *Following the Frontier,* 33–36.

EXTENSIVE READING

CHANDLER and CHITWOOD, *Makers of American History,* 112–120.
FOOTE and SKINNER, *Explorers and Founders of America,* 281–295.
PERRY and PRICE, *American History,* I : 216–220.
SOUTHWORTH, *Builders of Our Country,* I : 226–243.
TAPPAN, *American Hero Stories,* 126–134.
VOLLINTINE, *Making of America,* 25–34.

period; for example, "Why was the St. Lawrence River so important?"

After the entire story has been read in this manner the children test themselves by the study-guide questions.

OTHER BOOKS

DAVIS, *Stories of the United States,* 136–137.
WAYLAND, *History Stories for the Primary Grades,* 158–160.

READING FOR RECREATION

BRANDEIS, *Little Anne of Canada.*
CROWNFIELD, *Joscelyn of the Forts.*
PLUMMER, *Roy and Ray in Canada.*
TAPPAN, *American History for Very Young Readers.*

The Discussion (First Story)

Children answer the study-guide questions as completely as possible, questioning one another to bring out important matters that were omitted.

The Reading Periods (Second Story)

Independent Readers

TEXTS

KELTY, *Beginnings of the American People and Nation,* 446–450.
KNOWLTON and GILL, *When We Were Colonies,* 296–298 (hard).
PERRY and PRICE, *American History,* I : 221.
VOLLINTINE, *The Making of America,* 35, 37–53.

Lower Group

The teacher and these children read together the story given in the text. The teacher guides the silent reading, section by section, by the same type of questions that she would use in a silent-reading period; for example, "What happened to the French colonists when the war was over?"

After the entire story has been read in this manner children test themselves by the study-guide questions.

The Discussion (Second Story)

Children answer the study-guide questions as completely as possible. They recite at the map all those topics which require the pointing out of locations.

Multisensory Aids

Children and teacher talk over together the pictures in the text, noting the features of geographical and historical significance. They turn to a map of North America in 1763 and notice how the Spanish lands are marked; the English; the French.

AUDIO–VISUAL MATERIALS OBTAINABLE

ARNOLD. Historical Pictures: A. H. P. 71.
BROWN. Famous Pictures: 1421.
Chronicles of America Photoplays: Wolfe and Montcalm.
Keystone View Slides: 47, 48.

LONGMANS. Historical Wall Pictures: Wolfe on the Plains of Abraham.
National Geographic Magazine, LXVII, 167–200 (February, 1935).
Society for Visual Education. Schoolfilm: Struggle of the French and the English for North America.
Yale Pageant Educational Slides: 33–35, 717.

General Activities

Creative Activities: Group and Individual, Correlated with Other Subjects or Voluntary Projects

On the sand-table model, committees place ships to represent the British fleet. They mark out the path by which the British climbed to the heights. They place the Montcalm-Wolfe monument on the Plains of Abraham.

A committee reads to the class the dramatization given in Bird and Starling's *Historical Plays for Children* (221–231).

The teacher reads to the children selections from Gray's "Elegy in a Country Churchyard."

A group of children representing the French and a group representing the English meet to make and sign the treaty.

Each child shows the terms of the treaty by coloring the map "The French and the English Have Trouble."

The class continues the time chart.

Application to Present-Day Conditions

If two armies are fighting today in Far Northern lands, which one does the bitter northern winter help the more? [*The defense.*]

Are Canada and the United States at peace today? How long has there been peace between them? [*Since 1815.*]

Does it make any difference to you personally that the British won instead of the French?

A traveler who has been to Quebec and Montreal tells the children what signs of French life and customs can still be seen in eastern Canada.

Does France still own Haiti? Does she still own the two small islands in the Gulf of St. Lawrence?

Does Great Britain still have control over the sea?

Exercises in Reasoning

Which of the two generals do you think you should like better?

Do you think that the French themselves were largely to blame for their defeat? Why?

Why was it a bad thing to have all the French farmers fighting in the army?

In what language must the English who were coming down the river have replied to the French guards?

Why would the French nobles in Canada be more likely to go back to France after the war than the French common people?

Why were the English colonies glad that France was defeated?

Is a battle called "great" because many men were killed in it? Why has the battle of Quebec been called one of the greatest battles ever fought?

Drill Games

Drill on place names and on the terms of the treaty is best done at the map. Children should be able to point out what was given to England and Spain, and what was left for France.

Drill cards are made for the following:

General Wolfe	↔	the British general at the battle of Quebec
General Montcalm	↔	the French general at the battle of Quebec
Plains of Abraham	↔	where the battle of Quebec was fought
1763	↔	year of the treaty ending the French and Indian War
treaty of peace	↔	a solemn agreement to stop fighting

Testing

Tests of Understanding are supplied on pages 445 and 450 of Kelty's *Beginnings of the American People and Nation.*

Tests of Reasoning and Skills.[1] Check the best answer.

1. After the French and Indian War was over, the strongest nation in North America was France. Spain. √ England. Russia.

2. The fact that Great Britain won the war was important because it meant that French life and speech would completely disappear. England could keep control of the sea. √ English life and speech would spread over the continent. France could never again be as strong as England.

3. Turn to a map of North America in 1763. The first French fort that a ship coming from England could attack was _ _[*Quebec*]_ _.

4. Show in these squares how the map marks the land belonging to the English □ Spanish □ French □ after 1763.

5. Put the figure *1* in front of the thing which happened first, and the figure *2* in front of the thing which happened later:

[_ _*2*_ _] The treaty of peace was signed.
[_ _*1*_ _] Quebec was taken by the English.

Exercise in Organization. The teacher and the children together make one co-operative outline of the two stories. Children then give a topical recitation on each point in the outline.

Test on the Entire Unit

Test of Place Sense. Pass outline maps of North America, double size, which show water bodies in blue or shading. Give the following directions.

1. Put the initials *GL* in each one of the Great Lakes.

2. Put the letter *M* in Lake Michigan.

3. Put the letter *D* where Detroit is.

---

[1] Other exercises in reasoning are included under "General Activities."

4. Write *Miss.* at the mouth of the Mississippi River.

5. Write *La.* where Louisiana is.

6. Put the figure *1* where Mackinac is.

7. Put the figure *2* where Fort Duquesne was.

8. Write *Ohio* where the Ohio River is.

Test of Time Sense. Pass mimeographed sheets of the following.

I. Here is a list of people. In each exercise put the figure *1* before the name of the person who lived first and the figure *2* before the name of the person who lived later.

1. [__*1*__] Marquette
   [__*2*__] La Salle

2. [__*1*__] Joliet
   [__*2*__] Franklin

3. [__*2*__] Braddock
   [__*1*__] La Salle

4. [__*2*__] Montcalm
   [__*1*__] Marquette

5. [__*1*__] Joliet
   [__*2*__] George Washington

II. Here is a list of things which happened in the stories. In each exercise put the figure *1* before the event which happened first and the figure *2* before that which happened later.

1. [__*1*__] La Salle sailed to the mouth of the Mississippi.
   [__*2*__] The French drove Braddock back.

2. [__*2*__] The French lost almost all their land in North America.
   [__*1*__] George Washington was sent to warn the French away.

3. [__*2*__] The French built a fort at the Forks of the Ohio.
   [__*1*__] Marquette and Joliet sailed past the mouth of the Ohio.

4. [__*1*__] Benjamin Franklin became a printer.
   [__*2*__] General Wolfe took Quebec.,

III. Here is a list of dates:

1607   1620   1763   1754   1492

Choose the right one and place it in the following blank.

_____ End of the French and Indian War.

Test on Persons. Pass mimeographed sheets of the following.

I. Here is a list of names:

Jesuits   Marquette   General Braddock
General Montcalm   Sir William Johnson

Take one name at a time and put it in the right place in the sentences below.

1. _____ was the Frenchman who fought at Quebec.

2. _____ were missionaries to the Indians.

3. _____ sailed down the Mississippi with Joliet.

4. _____ was killed near Fort Duquesne.

5. _____ made the Iroquois help the English.

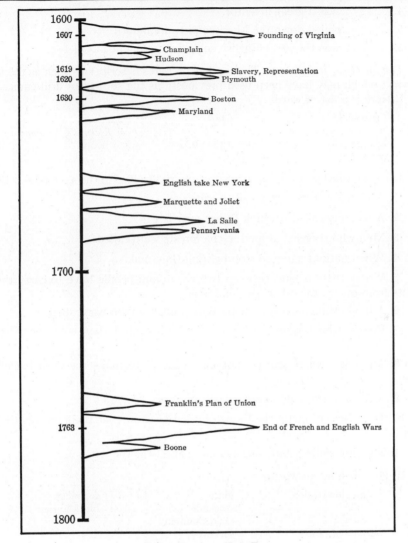

Time Chart — Unit Four

II. Here is a list of names:

Joliet	La Salle	Benjamin Franklin
General Wolfe	Martha Washington	George Washington

Take one name at a time and put it in the right place in the sentences below.

1. _ _ _ _ _ _ sailed on the upper Mississippi.

2. _ _ _ _ _ _ was with General Braddock.

3. _ _ _ _ _ _ was the wife of George Washington.

4. _ _ _ _ _ _ was a great inventor.

5. _ _ _ _ _ _ sailed down the Mississippi to its mouth.

6. _ _ _ _ _ _ was the great English soldier who fought at Quebec.

Test on Historical Terms. The teacher prepares descriptions such as the following, which may have been used previously as the subject of drill games.

I. Here is a list of words:

fur-traders	woodrangers	*Griffin*
treaty of peace	council	*Poor Richard's Almanac*
trading post	Forks of the Ohio	war whoop
portage	lead plates	

Take one word at a time and put it in the right place in the sentences below.

1. A loud shout used as a call to war is a _ _ _ _ _ _.

2. A meeting called to think things over is a _ _ _ _ _ _.

3. Men who traveled around in the forests were called _ _ _ _ _ _.

4. When nations agree to stop fighting they make a _ _ _ _ _ _.

5. Where there is land between two rivers and people have to carry their boats from one to the other, the land is a _ _ _ _ _ _.

6. A book printed every year by Benjamin Franklin was called _ _ _ _ _ _.

7. People who bought furs from the Indians and then sold them were _ _ _ _ _ _.

8. The place where two rivers come together to make the Ohio is called the _ _ _ _ _ _.

9. A settlement made in order to trade is a _ _ _ _ _ _.

10. The pieces of metal the French buried to show that the land was theirs were _ _ _ _ _ _.

11. The first sailing ship on the Great Lakes was the _ _ _ _ _ _.

II. Here is a list of words:

mission station	unite	regiment
aide	stockade	blockhouse
retreat	Ohio Company	
pipe of peace	surveyor	

Put each word in the right place in the sentences below.

1. To go back, away from an enemy, is to _ _ _ _ _ _.

2. A high fence around a place to protect it is a _ _ _ _ _ _.

3. A heavy fort made of logs with little holes to shoot from is a_ _ _ _ _ _.

4. An Indian sign of peace was to smoke a _ _ _ _ _ _.

5. A man who helps a general to give his orders is an _ _ _ _ _ _.

6. A man who measures land is a _ _ _ _ _ _.

7. Part of an army is a _ _ _ _ _ _.

8. To join together is to _ _ _ _ _ _ .

9. A place where missionaries stay is a _ _ _ _ _ _ .

10. The people who owned land near the Ohio made up the _ _ _ _ _ _ .

Comprehension Test on Unit Four

Check the best answer.

1. The wars between the French and the English   left the French half the land.   √ drove the French out of North America.   drove the English out of North America.   left all of the land to the Spanish.

2. When Washington made his journey to the Ohio River the French told him that they   would leave the Ohio River.   would share the land with the English.   √ would not leave the Ohio River.   had never been near the river.

3. The English people wanted to settle along the Ohio River because they   did not like to live by the sea.   did not want the French to hold the land.   could have boat rides.   √ could control the land along the river.

4. La Salle's great idea was   √ to build forts along the rivers in the French claims.   to discover the Mississippi.   to go back to France.   to build mission stations in Louisiana.

5. Both the French and the English built a line of forts   because they had no ships.   √ in order to protect the land they claimed.   because they were afraid of the Indians.   in order to show how strong they were.

6. Marquette and Joliet showed the French people that   if they sailed to the mouth of the Mississippi they would become rich.   all Indians were friendly.   the Mississippi was a route to India.   √ they could travel most of the way by water through the Great Lakes and down the Mississippi.

7. The English wanted to take Quebec because   Champlain had founded it.   it was a beautiful city.   √ it was the strongest city along the St. Lawrence.   it was on a great river.

8. The first three wars between the French and the English   √ did not show which was going to win.   showed that the English would win.   showed that the French would win.   showed that they would both lose.

9. The missionaries and fur-traders helped France   to fight the Indians.   √ to explore the land.   to fight the English.   to rule the sea.

10. What is the title of the fourth unit in history which you have just finished studying?

Are any members of the lower group now ready to be transferred to the group of independent readers for the last unit?

UNIT FIVE · *How the English Colonies came to separate themselves from the Mother Country*   [*8 Weeks*

ADDITIONAL STORIES FOR MORE ADVANCED READERS

Samuel Adams	Marion, Sumter, and Pickens
James Otis	Lafayette
Patrick Henry	Steuben
Benedict Arnold	Pulaski

A

CAUSES OF THE REVOLUTION   [*1 Week*

Conversational Approach

"While a war may settle one problem, it also makes many new problems. For example, a war always costs enormous sums of money. Why? The wars between the French and the English had cost Great Britain enormous sums." (The class makes a list of articles for which the money had been spent.) "Now the time had come to pay.

"Who got most of the immediate benefit from driving France out of the New World? [*The colonies could now take up land, trade in furs, and fish without hindrance.*] Then do you think that the colonists should help to pay the bills?" (One group of children may tell why the colonists should pay; another group may tell why some colonists thought they ought not to pay.)

"But who was to decide how much the colonists should pay and how much Great Britain should pay? Would either one be willing to let the other decide? Which one do you think should have been allowed to decide? Why? And then how should the money be raised? How is money usually raised to pay government expenses? Do you know anyone who pays taxes today? Who would decide what kind of taxes the colonists ought to pay? Why did Great Britain think that she ought to decide? Why did the colonists think that they should decide?" (The series of key questions should be written on the board and left as a statement of the problem.)

"We can see that a great deal of trouble must arise over these questions."

Reading and Study

The Reading Periods

Independent Readers

This group reads the entire story through silently, as given in their text. They then test their comprehension by the study-guide questions furnished by the teacher or by the text.

TEXTS

BARKER, DODD, WEBB, *Our Nation Begins,* 289–296.

BEARD and BAGLEY, *First Book in American History,* 103–118.

BURNHAM and JACK, *Beginnings of Our Country,* 231–245.

CLARK-GORDY, *First Three Hundred Years,* 343–345, 377–390 (hard).

KELTY, *Beginnings of the American People and Nation,* 453–466.

SMALLIDGE and PAXSON, *Builders of Our Nation,* 298–307 (hard).

WOODBURN and MORAN, *Makers of America,* 8–32.

EXTENSIVE READING

CHANDLER and CHITWOOD, *Makers of American History,* 130–143.

COE, *Makers of the Nation,* 9–29.

FOOTE and SKINNER, *Makers and Defenders of America,* 9–30.

MONTGOMERY, *Beginners' American History,* 113–115.

SOUTHWORTH, *Builders of Our Country,* II: 1–18.

Lower Group

The teacher tells the story orally to this group, writing the key words and phrases on the board as she mentions them. The teacher and the lower group then read together the story as given in the text. The teacher guides the silent reading, section by section, by the same type of questions that she would use in a silent-reading period; for example, "What happened because the colonies and the mother country were so far apart?"

After the entire story has been read in this manner the children test themselves by the study-guide questions.

OTHER BOOKS

BLAISDELL and BALL, *American History for Little Folks,* 59–79.

BLAISDELL and BALL, *Child's Book of American History,* 104–119.

BLAISDELL and BALL, *Short Stories from American History,* 38–44, 51–57.

DAVIS, *Stories of the United States,* 153–159.

DODGE, *Stories of American History,* 60–78.

PRATT, *Stories of Colonial Children,* 165–188.

WILSON, *A History Reader,* 223–225.

READING FOR RECREATION

PERKINS, *American Twins of the Revolution.*

The Discussion

Children answer the study-guide questions as fully as possible. Since the causes of the war are basic to an understanding of it, several sets of answers may well be given.

The teacher writes on the board the words *tax, port cities.* Children discuss the meanings.

Multisensory Aids

Children and teacher talk over together the pictures in the text, noting features of historical or geographical significance.

AUDIO-VISUAL MATERIALS OBTAINABLE

Chronicles of America Photoplays: Eve of the Revolution.
GABRIEL (Ed.). Pageant of America: XI, 51–53.
Keystone View Slides: 58–60, 62–63, 66, 307, 309.
Perry Pictures: 1383-F, 1384-C.

Society for Visual Education (MUIR). 1765–1776, Beginning of the Revolution.
Yale Pageant Educational Slides: 92, 94–98, 386, 668, 769, 771, 776.

Music. Use the following phonograph records: "Patrick Henry's Speech,"
"The Rising of '76," "Yankee Doodle."

General Activities

Creative Activities: Group and Individual, Correlated with Other Subjects or Voluntary Projects

Committees draw scenes from this section. They paste them on a long roll
of wallpaper and fasten each end securely to a wooden roller. The scenes may
then be shown as a continuous motion picture, different children giving the
necessary descriptions and explanations as the pictures are unrolled.

Two committees present the views of Great Britain and the colonists in
regard to taxation; two others present the varying views in regard to representation.

Committees read to the class the dramatizations given in Hubbard's *Little
American History Plays* (61–65); Stevenson's *Dramatized Scenes from American
History* (145–215); and Hand's *Historical Studies in Dramatic Form*, "George
Washington," "Boston Tea Party."

Volunteers give floor talks on Samuel Adams and Patrick Henry.

The class illustrates by the use of a puzzle map of the United States that
each state can be separate and yet that all together make up the United States.

Application to Present-Day Conditions

Does the United States compel the use of stamps today? (Show the children internal revenue stamps and explain their use.)

Does the United States today lay taxes on its colonies at their port cities?
[*For example, in Puerto Rico.*] Who decides upon the kind and amount of
those taxes?

Show tax receipts.

Are goods ever smuggled into the country today? Do we think that smug-
gling is right now?

What does *tightening up the laws* mean?

Are there any laws nowadays that are not well enforced?

Can officers today search houses and barns for stolen goods? (Ask the local
police or the sheriff.)

Does the United States today lay both "direct taxes" and "taxes at the
ports"?

Do people today ever agree not to buy goods from countries that they do
not like? [*Boycott of Jews against Hitler.*]

Is there any tax nowadays on tea? (Write to the Treasury Department,
Washington, D.C., for tariff schedules.)

Does your state govern itself and yet remain part of the United States?
Why was not the same plan followed at the time of the Revolution?

Exercises in Reasoning

Why could not England continue her older practice of letting the colonies alone?

In what way was it a good thing for the colonies that they were so far away from England?

Make a list showing what the people at that time believed that colonies ought to produce; what England ought to send back to them.

Why did England want the colonies to sell certain goods only to her? [*She needed them because she could not produce her own.*]

Did England treat her colonies worse than other countries in Europe treated theirs at the time?

Why did England not want the colonies to manufacture certain kinds of goods? [*If they did, English merchants couldn't sell their goods to the colonists.*]

What is the difference between a direct tax and taxes at the ports?

Why was the meeting which was held called the First *Continental* Congress? Do you think that that was the right name?

Drill Games

Drill cards are made as follows:

Samuel Adams	↔	a man who helped to bring on the Revolution in the North
Patrick Henry	↔	a great Southern speaker
George III	↔	king of England at the time of the Revolution
1765	↔	the year the Stamp Act was passed
tax	↔	money which must be paid for the support of the government
smuggling	↔	bringing goods into a country secretly without paying the tax
the Revolution	↔	the war which made a great change in American ways of living
Continental Congress	↔	a meeting of representatives from all the colonies

These cards are made accessible to the children during the periods of reading and study.

Testing

Tests of Understanding are suggested on page 466 of Kelty's *Beginnings of the American People and Nation.*

Additional Tests of Reasoning and Skills. Check the best answer.

1. In the seventeenth and eighteenth centuries the purpose in sending out colonies was to   make life better for the colonists.   get rid of some citizens of the mother country.   claim land for the colonists.   √ earn money for the mother country.

2. In the quarrel between the colonies and the mother country   the right was all on the side of the colonies.   the right was all on the side of England.   √ there was right on both sides.

3. The chief subject on which they could not agree was   √ how to lay the taxes.   how to get out of paying taxes.   where taxes ought to be paid.   how to tax the pioneers.

4. A tax at the port cities   is   √is not   a direct tax on the citizens.

Exercise in Organization. The teacher writes the following outline on the board. Children recite on each subheading.

QUARREL BETWEEN ENGLAND AND AMERICA

> Trouble about taxes and trade
> > shipping laws
> > trade laws
> > > buying goods
> > > selling goods
> > > smuggling
> > laws about manufacture
> > tightening up the laws at the ports
> > a direct tax
> > > hated by colonists
> > back to taxes at the ports
> > > on many goods
> > > on tea : Boston Tea Party
> Trouble about representation

B

STORY 1. THE REVOLUTION IN NEW ENGLAND   *[1 Week*

Conversational Approach

"We have found that trouble has already broken out. Where? Then in what section will war probably begin?

"You may possibly have heard something about the Revolution in New England. Has anyone ever heard of Paul Revere? Our story today tells us about the war in New England."

Reading and Study

The Reading Periods

Independent Readers

TEXTS

BARKER, DODD, WEBB, *Our Nation Begins,* 296–299, 306–307.

BEARD and BAGLEY, *First Book in American History,* 121–123.

BURNHAM and JACK, *Beginnings of Our Country,* 247–250.

CLARK-GORDY, *First Three Hundred Years,* 290–298 (hard).

KELTY, *Beginnings of the American People and Nation,* 467–477.

SMALLIDGE and PAXSON, *Builders of Our Nation,* 307–312 (hard).

Lower Group

The teacher tells the story orally to this group, writing on the board the names of the most important persons and places as she mentions them. Children practice the pronunciations.

Then the teacher and the children read together the story as given in the text. The teacher guides the silent reading, section by section, by the same type of questions that she would use in a silent-reading period; for example, "How did people make ready for war?"

EXTENSIVE READING

COE, *Makers of the Nation*, 37–61.
FOOTE and SKINNER, *Makers and Defenders of America*, 31–37, 51–56.
INGRAHAM, *Story of Democracy*, 190–209.
MONTGOMERY, *Beginners' American History*, 115–120.
SOUTHWORTH, *Builders of Our Country*, II: 19–23, 44–58.
TAPPAN, *American Hero Stories*, 143–157.

After the entire story has been read in this manner the children test themselves by the study-guide questions.

OTHER BOOKS

BALDWIN, *Fifty Famous People*, 37–42.
BALDWIN, *Fifty Famous Rides and Riders*, 104–107.
BLAISDELL and BALL, *Child's Book of American History*, 120–129.
DAVIS, *Stories of the United States*, 161–170.
DODGE, *Stories of American History*, 79–117.
PRATT, *Stories of Colonial Children*, 195–207.
WAYLAND, *History Stories for Primary Grades*, 175–178.

READING FOR RECREATION

BARTON, *When Boston Braved the King*.
CARTER, *Patriot Lad of Old Boston*.
CARTER, *Patriot Lad of Old Connecticut*.
CARTER, *Patriot Lad of Old New Hampshire*.
SAGE, *A Little Daughter of the Revolution*.
THOMPSON, *The Green Mountain Boys*.
Revolutionary Stories Retold from St. Nicholas.

The Discussion

Children answer the study-guide questions as completely as possible, questioning one another about important points omitted. Those who have read additional material will enjoy making contributions of items not mentioned in the text.

The teacher writes on the board the words *New England, Tory, Yankee, British*. Children discuss the meanings.

Multisensory Aids

The children and the teacher talk over together the pictures given in the text, noting features of geographical and historical significance. They turn to a map of the Revolution in New England and point out the location of the battles and the plan of the siege of Boston. They show Boston, Lexington, and Concord on the test map and then on a large wall map. They trace the route to Lake Champlain and estimate the distance from the scale of miles in the geography maps. They estimate how far the British had to go to sail away to Halifax.

AUDIO-VISUAL MATERIALS OBTAINABLE

GABRIEL (Ed.). Pageant of America: XI, 55–60.
International Educational Pictures: New England Shrines, Historic Boston, Historic New England.
Keystone View Slides: 60–63, 311–314.
McKINLEY. Illustrated Topics for American History: S. 14.
Society for Visual Education. Picturol: Campaigns of the Revolution.
Yale Pageant Educational Slides: 103–108, 305, 338, 718.

Music. Play records of "Paul Revere's Ride." Sing "Yankee Doodle."

General Activities

*Creative Activities: Group and Individual, Correlated with Other Subjects or
Voluntary Projects*

A volunteer committee models in the sand table the northern theater of war.

Committees read to the class the dramatizations given in Hubbard's *Little
American History Plays* (66–76); Hand's *Historical Stories in Dramatic Form:*
"Battle of Lexington," "Israel Putnam."

A volunteer draws the Bunker Hill flag in colors (*National Geographic Magazine*, XXXII, 338).

Floor talks are given on Ethan Allen and his "Green Mountain Boys."

Children who own stamp collections may show commemorative stamps.

The teacher reads to the children Emerson's "Concord Hymn"; Oliver
Wendell Holmes's poems "Lexington" and "Grandmother's Story of Bunker-
Hill Battle."

Volunteers make soap carvings of Paul Revere and his horse.

The class continues the making of the motion-picture film. (See page 246.)

Each child makes a map of the Revolution in New England, marking Lexington, Concord, Bunker Hill, Ticonderoga, and the plan of the siege of Boston.

The class continues the time chart.

Application to Present-Day Conditions

Have you ever heard the expression *Go to Halifax?* Can you trace its beginnings to Revolutionary times? [*British went to Halifax from Boston.*]

Is the term *Tory* ever used today? [*Of persons opposed to change.*]

What was the condition of Maine during Revolutionary times?

How was that different from today?

Do the men in armies today supply their own guns and clothing? Why do
we think uniforms necessary nowadays?

Who is commander-in-chief of our armies today? [*The President.*]

Does the Revolutionary War have anything to do with the fact that many
people nowadays like to spend their vacations in traveling through New
England? [*To see historic spots and relics.*]

Exercises in Reasoning

How could signals be sent by bonfires in Revolutionary times?

Why did the British want to seize Samuel Adams?

From the story, can you draw up a statement about the difficulty of conquering thinly settled areas when the people are determined not to be conquered?

What difference would it make if the British did come down from Canada
and "cut the colonies in two"?

Why did the colonists think that Canada might join in the Revolution?

Why did both sides want Bunker Hill?

Can an army ever learn lessons from a battle which was lost? [*Bunker Hill.*]

Review the meaning of the word *siege.* Does it properly apply to the siege
of Boston?

Drill Games

Place names are best drilled upon at the map: *Lexington, Concord, Bunker Hill, New England.*

Drill cards are made for the following:

British	⟷	the people of Great Britain
1775	⟷	the date of the battles of Lexington and Concord
Tories	⟷	persons who took the British side in the war
Yankees	⟷	New Englanders who fought the mother country
"Yankee Doodle"	⟷	a song making fun of the New Englanders

Children may drill one another by using these cards.

Testing

Tests of Understanding are supplied on page 477 of Kelty's *Beginnings of the American People and Nation.*

Additional Tests of Reasoning and Skills.[1] Check the right answer.

1. During the first year of the war the British   √ still hoped that war might be prevented.   wanted to begin fighting with large armies.   wanted to wait until they had larger armies.   still believed that Washington would not fight.

2. Of the people living in the English colonies   all joined in the fight against the king.   √ some joined the king's troops and some did not.   all joined the troops of the British.

3. Which troops were better supplied and managed?   the Americans. √ the British.

4. Turn to a map of the Revolution in New England. Did the Americans draw up their troops in a circle around Boston?   Yes [√]   No [ ]

Exercise in Organization. Children copy the topic headings of the story and give a brief summary of each topic.

STORY 2. THE REVOLUTION IN THE MIDDLE COLONIES [7 Days

Conversational Approach

"When the British left Boston do you suppose that they intended to give up punishing the colonies? Then they will come back. Where would be a good place for them to land?

"Sometimes we can almost read an entire story from the map. Turn to a map of the Revolution in the middle colonies. Find New York, where Washington went from Boston. How is his route marked from now on? Where did he go on leaving New York City? That particular route ends where? [*Near Valley Forge.*] The British were following him most of this time; so they went to most of the same places that the Americans did.

[1] Other exercises in reasoning are included under "General Activities."

"Find Philadelphia. How did the British go there? Why do you suppose they would go such a long roundabout way?

"Now we will look for a third line of action." (Summarize the first two.) "Look in the north. See if you can find the route of a British army coming down from Lake Champlain. See if you can find another coming from farther west.

"Our story today is about these three general lines of action." (Summarize the three.)

Reading and Study

The Reading Periods

Independent Readers

TEXTS

BARKER, DODD, WEBB. *Our Nation Begins*, 307–310.
BEARD and BAGLEY, *First Book in American History*, 124–127, 136–142.
BURNHAM and JACK, *Beginnings of Our Country*, 254–260.
CLARK-GORDY, *First Three Hundred Years*, 407–413 (hard).
KELTY, *Beginnings of the American People and Nation*, 478–498.
SMALLIDGE and PAXSON, *Builders of Our Nation*, 314–318 (hard).
WOODBURN and MORAN, *Makers of America*, 108–111.

EXTENSIVE READING

COE, *Makers of the Nation*, 71–77, 88–94, 120–130.
DAVIDSON, *Founders and Builders of Our Nation*, 74–82.
FARIS, *Where Our History Was Made*, Book II, 259–261.
FOOTE and SKINNER, *Makers and Defenders of America*, 56–68, 74–87, 98–102.
MONTGOMERY, *Beginners' American History*, 121–122.
SOUTHWORTH, *Builders of Our Country*, II: 51–60, 63–74, 93–96.
TAPPAN, *American Hero Stories*, 158–178.

Lower Group

A large-scale map should be drawn on a slated map or on the blackboard, similar to the map discussed above. The three general lines of action mentioned should be shown in different colors.

The teacher tells the story orally, pointing to the places on the map as she mentions them, and writing on the board the names of the most important persons and places.

Then teacher and children read together the story as given in the text. The teacher guides the silent reading, section by section, by the same type of questions that she would use in a silent-reading period; for example, "Why did Washington think that the British would come next to New York?"

After the entire story has been read in this manner the children test themselves by the study-guide questions.

OTHER BOOKS

BALDWIN, *Fifty Famous People*, 43–47.
BALDWIN, *Fifty Famous Rides and Riders*, 111–119.
BLAISDELL and BALL, *American History for Little Folks*, 86–92, 98–102.
BLAISDELL and BALL, *American History Story Book*, 37–58.
BLAISDELL and BALL, *Short Stories from American History*, 58–63, 72–79, 80–85, 122–129.
DODGE, *Stories of American History*, 125–147.
WAYLAND, *History Stories for Primary Grades*, 28–30, 184–187.

READING FOR RECREATION

COOKE, *The Fortunes of John Hawk*.
CURTIS, *A Little Maid of Old Philadelphia*.
KNIPE, *The Lucky Sixpence*.
MASON, *Tom Strong, Washington's Scout*.

SHERMAN, *Mistress Madcap*.
SMITH, *Boys and Girls of '77*.
Revolutionary Stories Retold from St. Nicholas.

The Discussion

Several different sets of children answer the study-guide questions as fully as possible, using the map when necessary.

The teacher writes on the board the words *retreat, surrender, traitor*. Children discuss the meanings.

Multisensory Aids

Children and teacher talk over together the pictures in the text, noting features of historical or geographical significance. They turn to the map and point out the three general routes mentioned in the conversational approach. They locate Long Island, New York City, the Hudson River, New Jersey, the Delaware River, Trenton, Philadelphia, Lake Champlain, Albany, the St. Lawrence River, Lake Ontario, Saratoga, and Valley Forge.

AUDIO-VISUAL MATERIALS OBTAINABLE

International Educational Pictures: Historic Hudson, Philadelphia and Valley Forge, Philadelphia Yesterday and Today, Benedict Arnold, Heart of a Hero (Nathan Hale).
Perry Pictures: 1386, 1387, 1414, 1415, 1416-F.
Society for Visual Education (MUIR). Origin of the United States Flag.
Yale Pageant Educational Slides: 113, 115–117, 120, 533, 623, 719–725.

General Activities

Creative Activities: Group and Individual, Correlated with Other Subjects or Voluntary Projects

Volunteers model in the sand table the theater of war in the middle colonies.

The class takes a trip to the museum to see articles connected with the Revolution.

A volunteer draws a picture of the first flag. (Compare it with the present flag. See the *National Geographic Magazine*, XXXII, 338.)

Committees read the following dramatizations to the class:

HAND, *Historical Stories in Dramatic Form:* "Nathan Hale," "Robert Morris."
HUBBARD, *Little American History Plays*, 81–98.
SHOEMAKER, *Colonial Plays for the Schoolroom*, 59–64.
STEVENSON, *Children's Classics in Dramatic Form:* V, 1–23.
TUCKER and RYAN, *Historical Plays of Colonial Days*, 121–125.
WALKER, *Little Plays from American History for Young Folks*, 57–120.

Floor talks are given on Lafayette, Steuben, Pulaski, Robert Morris, Benedict Arnold.

A volunteer impersonates Benjamin Franklin and gives his speech trying to persuade the king of France to help the American colonies.

The class continues the making of the motion-picture film. (See page 246.)

Each child makes a map of the Revolution in the middle colonies, showing the three general lines of action, marking the places mentioned above, and circling New York and Philadelphia in red, to show that the British still held them in 1777.

The class continues the time chart.

Application to Present-Day Conditions

Is it possible that more stars yet may be added to our flag? To represent what places?

In what other war have France and the United States fought side by side?

What does the expression *not worth a Continental* mean?

List the states which were included in the term *middle colonies*.

Are foreigners hired to fight in armies nowadays?

Compare the length of time men are enlisted in the army nowadays with the length of Revolutionary enlistments. Which is better? Why?

Turn to a population map of the United States today. Which are the more thickly populated, the New England states or the middle states?

Exercises in Reasoning

Why did both the Americans and the British want to hold New York? Why did they consider Philadelphia important?

Should spies be shot?

Was it because they were afraid of the colonists that the British continued to offer peace?

Why was the retreat across New Jersey called the darkest hour of the Revolution?

Compare Washington's disadvantages with the British disadvantages.

Can you make up a sentence telling what advantage it is to an army to fight on its own ground?

Why did some colonists sell their products to the British when they would not sell to the Americans? Are such people patriotic?

What kind of man does General Burgoyne seem to have been?

What do you think of France's reasons for helping the colonies?

Drill Games

Place names are best drilled upon at the map: *Saratoga, Valley Forge, Albany.*

Drill cards are made as follows:

Lafayette	↔	a French nobleman who fought for the colonies
Burgoyne	↔	the British general who came south from Lake Champlain
Robert Morris	↔	an American who helped to raise money to carry on the war
Nathan Hale	↔	an American spy in the British camp
1777	↔	date of the battle of Saratoga
traitor	↔	a person who betrays his country

Children may help one another to drill on these items.

Testing

Tests of Understanding are suggested on pages 497–498 of Kelty's *Beginnings of the American People and Nation.*

Additional Tests of Reasoning and Skills. Check the best answer.

1. A city which was held by the British throughout the war was   Philadelphia.   Boston.   √ New York.   Charleston.

2. The following statements are all true. Check the one which gives the most important reason : France helped the American colonies because   the French people liked the Americans.   Lafayette worked for the American cause.   √ France wanted to injure Great Britain.   Benjamin Franklin asked the French to help.   France thought the colonies would win.

3. When it came to furnishing money for the Continental army,   √ Congress was slow and careless.   the states paid most of the bill.   Congress voted plenty of money and supplies.   the men served entirely without pay.

4. These statements are all true. Mark the most important one : Burgoyne wanted to   come down as far as Albany.   get help from the city of New York.   send his scouts out for food.   √ cut Massachusetts and Virginia apart.

5. Turn to a map of the Revolution in the middle colonies.

a. From New York the British went to Philadelphia   √ by sea.   by land.

b. Burgoyne succeeded in reaching Albany.   True [   ]   False [√]

6. In looking up *Robert Morris* in the index, under which word should you look?   *Robert* [   ]   *Morris* [√]

7. If you read one account of the battle of Saratoga written by a British soldier and another account written by an American soldier, should you find them much alike or would they be different? Why? Would either one intend to tell a lie?

Exercise in Organization. The teacher puts on the board three headings corresponding to the routes discussed in the "Conversational Approach." With their books open, children select subheadings to place under each of the three main headings. They then tell the story of each subhead.

STORY 3. THE REVOLUTION IN THE NORTHWEST   [*4 Days*

Conversational Approach

"What have been the titles of our last two stories? Now we turn to the Northwest." Children show on the wall map which part was called the Northwest.

"Let us see how much we can learn about the story from a map of the Revolution in the Northwest before doing any reading. Where do the British come from and how far do they go? The American forces are led by Clark. Where do they start? Trace their route. How do you suppose they will travel when they leave the river? To how many forts do they go?

"Our story today tells us why the Americans wanted to take the Northwest."

Reading and Study

The Reading Periods

Independent Readers

TEXTS

BARKER, DODD, WEBB, *Our Nation Begins,* 311–315.

BURNHAM and JACK, *Beginnings of Our Nation,* 281–291.

KELTY, *Beginnings of the American People and Nation,* 499–509.

NIDA, *Following the Frontier,* 78–84.

SMALLIDGE and PAXSON, *Builders of Our Nation,* 318–319 (hard).

WOODBURN and MORAN, *Makers of America,* 150–168.

EXTENSIVE READING

CHANDLER and CHITWOOD, *Makers of American History,* 158–164.

COE, *Makers of the Nation,* 158–178.

DAVIDSON, *Founders and Builders of Our Nation,* 101–108.

MONTGOMERY, *Beginners' American History,* 143–150.

TAPPAN, *American Hero Stories,* 185–192.

Lower Group

The teacher tells the story orally to this group, writing on the board the names of the most important persons and places as she mentions them.

The teacher and this group then read together the story as given in the text. The teacher guides the silent reading, section by section, by the same type of question that she would use in a silent-reading period; for example, "What kind of forts did the British have in the Northwest?"

After the entire story has been read in this manner, the children test themselves by the study-guide questions.

OTHER BOOKS

BLAISDELL and BALL, *Short Stories from American History,* 64–71, 99–103.

PRATT, *Stories of Colonial Children,* 189–194.

READING FOR RECREATION

EGGLESTON, *Long Knives.*

OTIS, *Hannah of Kentucky.*

SKINNER, *Becky Landers.*

The Discussion

Children give as full answers as possible to the study-guide questions. The teacher attempts to draw the lower group into the discussion. She writes on the board the word *expedition.* Children discuss the meaning.

Multisensory Aids

Children and teacher together talk over the pictures in the text, noting features of historical and geographical significance. They turn to a map of the Revolution in the Northwest and point out both American and British routes.

AUDIO-VISUAL MATERIALS OBTAINABLE

Chronicles of America Photoplays: Vincennes.

Yale Pageant Educational Slides: 118, 557, 631.

General Activities

Creative Activities: Group and Individual, Correlated with Other Subjects or Voluntary Projects

Volunteers model in the sand table the scene of the war in the Northwest.

Committees read to the class the dramatizations given in Hubbard's *Little American History Plays* (111–124) and Bird and Starling's *Historical Plays for Children* (54–78).

A volunteer imagines himself an old grandfather telling to his grandchildren his exploits as a member of Clark's band.

The class continues the making of the motion-picture film. (See page 246.)

Each child makes a map of the Revolution in the Northwest. He shows the routes of Clark and the British and marks the three forts.

Application to Present-Day Conditions

The class makes a list of the states later cut out of the Northwest.

Have you ever heard the expression "They are after his scalp"? Explain.

What city today is located at the falls of the Ohio River?

Are conquered people of much help to their conquerors when war comes? [An example is the case of the French, who were indifferent to both British and American occupation of the Western forts.]

Why is it hard for men with rifles to fight against men with cannon?

Do you think Congress ought to build a memorial to George Rogers Clark?

How do people try to prevent rivers from overflowing their banks now?

Exercises in Reasoning

How did it happen that there were French farmers around the British forts?

Why would the Indians rather help the British than the colonists?

Why could the governor of Virginia not give Clark much help in money?

In what way did the French treaty help Clark's work?

Extra: Some child may be able to explain in what way Clark's plan illustrates the truth of the saying "The best defense is an offense."

Drill Games

Drill on the term Northwest can best be done at the map.

Drill cards are made as follows:

George Rogers Clark	⟷	the American leader who conquered the Northwest
expedition	⟷	many persons making a journey together

Games are played with the accumulated drill cards of the entire unit.

Testing

Tests of Understanding are supplied on page 509 of Kelty's Beginnings of the American People and Nation.

Additional Tests of Reasoning and Skills.[1] Check the best answer.

1. The United States had a claim to the land north of the Ohio River because ___ Americans first explored it. ___ √ George Rogers Clark conquered forts there. ___ George Rogers Clark bought it. ___ the French people gave it up.

2. The people who were most eager to have an expedition sent to the Northwest were ___ the governor and assembly of Virginia. ___ the Indian friends of the British. ___ the French people living around the forts. ___ √ the pioneers living in Kentucky.

[1] Other exercises in reasoning are included under "General Activities."

3. Turn to a map of the Revolution in the Northwest. Did George Rogers Clark march to Detroit?   Yes [ ]   No [✓]

4. On what pages does the text tell about George Rogers Clark? _ _ _ _ _ _
Where did you find out? _ _ _[*In the index*]_ _ _
Under which word did you look?   George [ ]   Rogers [ ]   Clark [✓]

Exercise in Organization. Those children who believe that they can make their own outlines of the story work independently. The teacher and the rest of the group make a co-operative outline of the main points.

STORY 4. THE REVOLUTION AT SEA   [*4 Days*

Conversational Approach

"Where do you suppose all the British soldiers came from whom we have seen fighting in New England, the middle colonies, and the Northwest? How were they carried across the ocean? And where could their officers get clothing for them to wear, guns and powder for them to fight with, and food enough for them to eat? How could all these be carried across the ocean?

"Then, if the colonists could keep the British ships from sailing the seas freely, they might be able to cut off the supplies of soldiers and fighting material. Do you think that they could do this? Our story will tell us."

Reading and Study

The Reading Periods

Independent Readers

TEXTS

BARKER, DODD, WEBB, *Our Nation Begins*, 315–318.

BEARD and BAGLEY, *First Book in American History*, 128–131.

BURNHAM and JACK, *Beginnings of Our Country*, 260–262.

KELTY, *Beginnings of the American People and Nation*, 510–518.

WOODBURN and MORAN, *Makers of America*, 113–117.

EXTENSIVE READING

COE, *Makers of the Nation*, 110–119.

DAVIDSON, *Founders and Builders of Our Nation*, 83–90.

FOOTE and SKINNER, *Makers and Defenders of America*, 103–110.

SOUTHWORTH, *Builders of Our Country*, II: 84–92.

TAPPAN, *American Hero Stories*, 193–200.

Lower Group

The teacher tells the story orally to this group, writing the most difficult words on the board as she mentions them. Children practice the pronunciations.

The teacher and the children then read together the story as given in the text. The teacher guides the silent reading, section by section, by the same type of questions that she would use in a silent-reading period; for example, "What kinds of ships were there in the colonies before the war?"

After the entire story has been read in this manner, the children test themselves by the study-guide questions.

OTHER BOOKS

DODGE, *Stories of American History*, 148–153.

GROVE, *American Naval Heroes*, 3–12.

PRATT, *Stories of Colonial Children*, 195–207.

WILSON, *A History Reader*, 308–309.

READING FOR RECREATION

PAINE, *Privateers of '76.*
SEAWELL, *Paul Jones.*

The Discussion

Children answer the study-guide questions as completely as possible, the teacher still exercising vigilance that the words of the book be not followed. She writes on the board and discusses with the children the meaning of *privateer* and *high seas*.

Multisensory Aids

Children and teacher talk over together the pictures given in the text, noting features of geographical and historical significance.

AUDIO-VISUAL MATERIALS OBTAINABLE

Keystone View Slides: 320.
National Geographic Magazine, LXVI, 370 (September, 1934).
Yale Pageant Educational Slides: 731–732.

General Activities

Creative Activities: Group and Individual, Correlated with Other Subjects or Voluntary Projects

Committees make a collection of pictures of warships of the Revolutionary period; of warships of today.

Volunteers bring ship models to show to the class.

The teacher may read to the children Arthur Hale's poem "The Yankee Privateer." (Stevenson, *Poems of American History*, 221.)

Volunteers draw a picture of the first navy jack with the legend "Don't Tread on Me"; of flags of Washington's cruisers. (See the *National Geographic Magazine*, XXXII, 338, 339.)

The class makes a graph to show the losses of the United States navy in the Revolution.

A committee draws a plan of the arrangement of the troops and the fleets at Yorktown.

Children read to the class the dramatization given in Hand's *Historical Stories in Dramatic Form*, "John Paul Jones."

A committee makes a collection of pictures, comparing the navy uniforms with the army uniforms.

A floor talk is given on John Barry, "the Father of the American Navy."

A visitor to Annapolis describes John Paul Jones's grave and the great naval academy at Annapolis.

The class continues the making of the motion-picture film. (See page 246.)

Application to Present-Day Conditions

Is it lawful for a person to have his name changed nowadays? How? (Ask a lawyer.)

Compare merchant ships of today with warships. Can merchant ships be easily changed to warships?

Make a list of the titles of officers in the navy; in the army. (See *Rank in army and navy* in a children's encyclopedia.)

Are privateers used by nations nowadays? (See a children's encyclopedia.)

What is the difference between the law of the "high seas" and the law within the "three-mile limit"? (See *High seas* in a children's encyclopedia.)

How does the French fleet today compare with the British? (See *Navies* in the World Almanac.)

Exercise in Reasoning

At the beginning of the war, why did the colonies have no navy?

Why would a privateer not want to fight a man-of-war?

Why were rich men eager to send out their ships as privateers?

What is the difference between privateers and a regular navy?

What did Americans expect from the French fleet?

Why were the colonies not able to build a large navy of their own?

If John Paul Jones had written an account of the great sea battle, and the British captain had written one, would the two accounts probably be alike? Does that mean that one would be right and the other wrong?

Are the waters of Lake Michigan "high seas"?

Drill Games

Drill cards are made as follows:

John Paul Jones	⟷	a great naval leader of the Revolution
Annapolis	⟷	a school for training naval officers
high seas	⟷	water more than three miles away from land
privateer	⟷	a fighting ship sent out by a private person

Children help one another to find out which items are most difficult for them.

Testing

Tests of Understanding are suggested on page 518 of Kelty's *Beginnings of the American People and Nation.*

Additional Tests of Reasoning and Skills.[1] Check the right answer.

1. During the Revolutionary War the use of privateers was carried on by the British.   √ both British and Americans.   the Americans.   neither Americans nor British.

2. People who sent out privateers sent them in order to   get even with the British.   show that they were patriotic.   build up trade with the British.   √ make money for themselves.

3. During most of the war the side which had control of the sea was   √ the British.   the Americans.   the French.

4. Did the use of the French fleet help to decide the success or failure of the Revolution?   Yes [√]   No [ ]

Exercise in Organization. Children copy the topic headings of the story and prepare one summary sentence for each. The summary sentence tells the main thought brought out in the section.

[1] Other exercises in reasoning are included under "General Activities."

STORY 5. THE REVOLUTION IN THE SOUTH [1 Week

Conversational Approach

"We have studied the course of the Revolution now through what different sections of the country? About which part have we not yet heard? Do you suppose that fighting was going on in the South? About which cities might we expect it to center?

"Do you know which side finally won the war? How can you tell?"

Reading and Study

The Reading Periods

Independent Readers

TEXTS

BARKER, DODD, WEBB, *Our Nation Begins*, 318–324.

BEARD and BAGLEY, *First Book in American History*, 127–128, 145.

BURNHAM and JACK, *Beginnings of Our Country*, 264–268.

CLARK-GORDY, *First Three Hundred Years*, 413–416 (hard).

KELTY, *Beginnings of the American People and Nation*, 519–532.

SMALLIDGE and PAXSON, *Builders of Our Nation*, 320–323 (hard).

WOODBURN and MORAN, *Makers of America*, 88–108.

EXTENSIVE READING

COE, *Makers of the Nation*, 78–87, 95–109.

FOOTE and SKINNER, *Makers and Defenders of America*, 68–71, 89–97.

INGRAHAM, *Story of Democracy*, 209–214.

MONTGOMERY, *Beginners' American History*, 122–129.

SOUTHWORTH, *Builders of Our Country*, II : 60–62, 75–83.

TAPPAN, *American Hero Stories*, 179–184.

Lower Group

The teacher tells the story orally to this group, writing on the board the names of the most important persons and places as she mentions them. Children practice the pronunciations.

Then the teacher and the group read together the story as told in the text. The teacher guides the silent reading, section by section, by the same type of questions that she would use in a silent-reading period; for example, "Why did the British decide to turn to the South?"

After the entire story has been read in this manner, the children test themselves by the study-guide questions.

OTHER BOOKS

BALDWIN, *Fifty Famous Rides and Riders*, 120–129.

BLAISDELL and BALL, *American History for Little Folks*, 80–85, 103–108.

BLAISDELL and BALL, *American History Story Book*, 59–72, 86–91.

BLAISDELL and BALL, *Short Stories from American History*, 45–50.

DODGE, *Stories of American History*, 154–170.

WAYLAND, *History Stories for Primary Grades*, 26–27, 179–181, 188, 191.

READING FOR RECREATION

Revolutionary Stories Retold from St. Nicholas.
VARBLE, *A Girl from London.*

The Discussion

Several different sets of children give the answers to the study-guide questions, helping one another to bring out important points that may have been omitted. The teacher writes on the board *swamp foxes*. Children discuss the meaning.

Multisensory Aids

Children and teacher talk over together the pictures in the text, noting features of historical and geographical importance. They turn to a map of the Revolution in the South, and trace the course of the British armies, state by state; the same for the American armies. The route of the French fleet is shown.

AUDIO-VISUAL MATERIALS OBTAINABLE

Chronicles of America Photoplays: Yorktown.

Keystone View Slides: 73, 83.

Perry Pictures: 1388.

Society for Visual Education (MUIR). 1776–1789: End of the Revolution and Inauguration of Washington.

Society for Visual Education. Picturols: Campaigns of the Revolution, George Washington.

Society for Visual Education. Schoolfilm: War of the American Revolution.

Yale Pageant Educational Slides: 122–123, 126–127, 532, 727.

General Activities

Creative Activities: Group and Individual, Correlated with Other Subjects or Voluntary Projects

Volunteers model in the sand table the Southern theater of war.

Floor talks are given about prison ships.

The class continues the making of the motion-picture film. (See page 246.)

The teacher may read to the class Bryant's poem "The Song of Marion's Men" and W. G. Simms's poem "The Swamp Fox."

A volunteer shows to the class from the Standard Dictionary (under "Revolution") the uniforms used during the Revolution.

A visitor to Yorktown and Williamsburg, Virginia, describes his experiences to the children.

Each child makes a map of the Southern campaigns showing the British and American routes and the route of the French fleet and marking Yorktown.

The class continues the time chart.

Application to Present-Day Conditions

Does it make any difference to you personally that the colonists won, rather than the British? How?

Can the pay of a private soldier in the army today support a family?

Are ships very important in winning wars today? Why?

Have you ever heard of the societies called the Daughters of the American Revolution and the Sons of the American Revolution? What is the purpose of these societies? (See a children's encyclopedia.)

Exercises in Reasoning

Why was Georgia the weakest of the states? How old was it?

In what way were the slaves in South Carolina a disadvantage to the colonists?

A great commander once said, "An army travels on its stomach." What did he mean? Was this true of the war in the South?

Compare the discouraging times which the American armies had in the South with the hardships at Valley Forge.

In what way did Spain and the Netherlands help the colonies whether they meant to or not?

Why did the band at Yorktown play "The World's Upside Down"?

Make a list of the most important battles in New England, in the middle colonies, in the Northwest, at sea, and in the South.

Drill Games

Drill on the place names (*Yorktown* and *Paris*) can best be done at the map. Drill cards are made as follows:

General Cornwallis	↔	the British officer who surrendered at Yorktown
Nathanael Greene	↔	the greatest American general of the Revolution in the South
Yorktown	↔	the place where the great battle was fought which ended the Revolutionary War
1783	↔	date of the treaty of peace ending the Revolution
" swamp foxes "	↔	men who carried on irregular fighting against the British in the South

Testing

Tests of Understanding are supplied on pages 531–532 of Kelty's *Beginnings of the American People and Nation.*

Additional Tests of Reasoning and Skills.[1] Check the best answer.

1. During the greater part of the Revolution the fighting in the South was done by   large armies around Charleston.   large armies sent from the North.   George Washington himself.   √ small groups of colonists.

2. The war ended because   √ other nations in Europe also fought England.   the colonists completely defeated England.   England grew tired of fighting.   the colonists were ready to stop.

3. The Revolution took place   in my father's time.   in my grandfather's time.   √ before my grandfather's time.

4. How do you suppose we know anything about the Revolution, which happened so long ago? _ _ _ _ _ _

5. Turn to a map of the United States in 1783. Show in a square how the map marks the land belonging to the United States.

Exercise in Organization. The teacher supplies the main headings concerning the British advance through the South, Washington's advance southward, the French fleet, the battle of Yorktown, and the treaty of peace. Children give oral summaries for each heading.

[1] Other exercises in reasoning are included under "General Activities."

C. GOVERNMENTAL CHANGES

STORY 1. THE DECLARATION OF INDEPENDENCE   [4 Days

Conversational Approach

"When the war began, what were the colonies fighting for? And yet we found in our last story that they were recognized in the treaty of peace as an independent nation. Why do you suppose they changed their minds about what they wanted? What is meant by an 'independent' country?

"Why do we celebrate the Fourth of July every year?"

Reading and Study

The Reading Periods

Independent Readers

TEXTS

BARKER, DODD, WEBB, *Our Nation Begins*, 299–302.

BEARD and BAGLEY, *First Book in American History*, 131–136.

BURNHAM and JACK, *Beginnings of Our Country*, 250–254.

KELTY, *Beginnings of the American People and Nation*, 533–539.

SMALLIDGE and PAXSON, *Builders of Our Nation*, 313–314 (hard).

EXTENSIVE READING

COE, *Makers of the Nation*, 62–69.

MONTGOMERY, *Beginners' American History*, 120–121.

Lower Group

The teacher tells the story orally to this group, writing the difficult words on the board as she mentions them.

Teacher and lower group then read together the story as given in the text. The teacher guides the silent reading, section by section, by the same kind of questions that she would use in a silent-reading period; for example, "In 1775 what did the Second Continental Congress think about independence?"

After the entire story has been read in this manner, the children test themselves by the study-guide questions.

OTHER BOOKS

BALDWIN, *Fifty Famous Rides and Riders*, 108–110.

BLAISDELL and BALL, *American History Story Book*, 28–36.

CURTIS, *Why We Celebrate Our Holiday*, 93–99.

DODGE, *Stories of American History*, 118–124.

WAYLAND, *History Stories for Primary Grades*, 24–25, 182–183.

The Discussion

Several different sets of children answer the study-guide questions as completely as possible. The teacher makes a particular attempt to ascertain whether they are only repeating words or whether the words represent in their own minds definite and clear-cut ideas. The teacher writes on the board and discusses with the children the meanings of *independent, state, Declaration of Independence.*

Multisensory Aids

Teacher and children talk over together the pictures in the texts, noting features of historical significance.

AUDIO-VISUAL MATERIALS OBTAINABLE

Chronicles of America Photoplays: The Declaration of Independence.
EASTMAN. Educational Slides: The Declaration of Independence.
Keystone View Slides: 68–70, 72, 308.
McKINLEY. Illustrated Topics for American History: S 15.
Society for Visual Education (SPENCER). Independence Day; Picture Story of Pennsylvania; Story of Independence Hall.
Yale Pageant Educational Slides: 101, 109, 110, 112, 775.

General Activities

Creative Activities: Group and Individual, Correlated with Other Subjects or Voluntary Projects

The teacher reads to the children the parts of the Declaration of Independence which they can understand, including the sentence which actually declares independence. Children then draw up a "Declaration of Independence" in their own words.

Children examine a photostatic copy of the Declaration itself.

The class plans a program for the Fourth of July which each child can carry out in his own home. Copies are sent to the parents.

The class continues the making of the motion-picture film. (See page 246.)

The teacher may read to the class the poem "Independence Bell" (author unknown) in Persons's *Our Country in Poem and Prose* (88–90).

Committees read to the class the dramatizations given in Hubbard's *Little American History Plays* (77–80); Johnston and Barnum's *Book of Plays for Little Actors* (165–171); Stevenson's *Dramatized Scenes from American History* (217–262).

The class continues the time chart.

Application to Present-Day Conditions

What does this expression mean: "I'll put my John Hancock on that"?

Where is the original copy of the Declaration of Independence kept? (See a children's encyclopedia.)

Is Independence Hall still in existence? (See encyclopedia.)

Do large bodies of men still carry on much of their business by committees?

Do you think it would be a good thing for every small country and island to be independent? For example, Puerto Rico? the Philippines? Give reasons.

Exercise in Reasoning

Is *setting off* firecrackers the best way to celebrate the Fourth of July?

Why did the colonists ask the king for their rights before they commenced fighting?

Why did it require great courage for the representatives to sign the Declaration of Independence? What would probably have happened to them if the war had failed?

What is the difference between a colony and a state?

How do you suppose we know what went on in the meetings of the Second Continental Congress?

Do you think that *declaring* themselves independent really *made* the colonies independent?

What duties did independence bring to the colonies that they had not had before?

Drill Games

Drill cards are made as follows:

John Hancock	⟷	a president of the Continental Congress
Independence Hall	⟷	the building in which the Declaration of Independence was signed
July 4, 1776	⟷	the date of the signing of the Declaration of Independence
Declaration of Independence	⟷	the paper which said that the states were free and independent
state	⟷	one of the parts of which the United States is made up
independent	⟷	separate and free

These cards are accessible for the children's use during their periods of reading and study.

Testing

Tests of Understanding are suggested on page 539 of Kelty's *Beginnings of the American People and Nation.*

Additional Tests of Reasoning and Skills.[1] Check the best answer.

1. When the colonists asked their "rights as Englishmen" they meant the right to   √ decide how much tax they would pay.   declare war whenever they wanted to.   coin money for themselves freely.   keep up an army for their own defense.

2. The Americans became a separate nation when   they fought their first battle against the king.   England took the last of her soldiers away. √ the Declaration of Independence was signed.   the treaty of peace was signed.

3. The new state governments were made by   the king's officers.   the Continental Congress.   the Declaration of Independence.   √ each state for itself.

4. We know what was written down in the Declaration of Independence because _ _ _ _ _ _. (Finish the sentence.)

[1] Other exercises in reasoning are included under "General Activities."

Exercise in Organization. Children who believe themselves able to do so attempt to make a brief outline of the story independently. The teacher and the rest of the group make a co-operative outline. Children tell the principal events which belong under each heading.

STORY 2. THE CONSTITUTION   [6 *Days*

Conversational Approach

"After the Declaration of Independence, could the colonists get along with the same government that they had had before? Why not? Who had been their chief officers before?

"Each state could decide upon its own government for itself, but who could decide upon a government for the whole of the United States? Do you suppose it is an easy matter to make a good government? Do all nations have the same kind of government?"

Reading and Study

The Reading Periods

Independent Readers

TEXTS

BARKER, DODD, WEBB, *Our Nation Grows Up,* 4–17 (hard).

BEARD and BAGLEY, *First Book in American History,* 149–157.

BURNHAM and JACK, *Beginnings of Our Country,* 293–305.

CLARK, *Westward to the Pacific,* 21–44, 47–51 (hard).

KELTY, *Beginnings of the American People and Nation,* 540–548.

SMALLIDGE and PAXSON, *Builders of Our Nation,* 330–333 (hard).

WOODBURN and MORAN, *Makers of America,* 169–174.

EXTENSIVE READING

COE, *Makers of the Nation,* 179–185.

FOOTE and SKINNER, *Makers and Defenders of America,* 111–116.

INGRAHAM, *Story of Democracy,* 221–225.

MONTGOMERY, *Beginners' American History,* 129–130.

STONE and FICKETT, *Days and Deeds a Hundred Years Ago,* 36–52.

Lower Group

The teacher tells the story orally to this group, writing on the board the most difficult words as she mentions them. Children practice the pronunciations.

The teacher and the group then read together the story as given in the text. The teacher guides the silent reading, section by section, by the same type of questions that she would use in a silent-reading period; for example, "Why was it hard to make a change in the old government?"

After the entire story has been read in this manner, the children test themselves by the study-guide questions.

OTHER BOOKS

PRATT, *Stories of Colonial Children,* 217–221.

WAYLAND, *History Stories for Primary Grades,* 116–118.

The Discussion

Several different sets of children answer the study-guide questions as fully as possible. Since this material is rather abstract in nature, the teacher uses especial care to ascertain whether children are expressing real ideas or are merely repeating words. She writes on the board *constitution.* Children discuss the meaning.

Multisensory Aids

Children and teacher talk over together the pictures in the text, pointing out features of historical importance.

AUDIO-VISUAL MATERIALS OBTAINABLE

Keystone View Slides: 85, 322.
Society for Visual Education (SPENCER). The Constitution of the United States.
Yale Pageant Educational Slides: 128, 780, 781.

General Activities

Creative Activities: Group and Individual, Correlated with Other Subjects or Voluntary Projects

Photostatic copies of parts of the Constitution are shown to the group. Children select the names of the signers about whom they have heard. (Children's encyclopedias give extracts.) Children make a list of the powers given to Congress. How was each group to be enforced?

The group divides into sections representing the large states and the small states. Each expresses its ideas about representation. At last a plan is suggested to which both can agree.

A committee reads for the class the dramatization given in Shoemaker's *Colonial Plays for the Schoolroom* (65–72).

The class continues the making of the motion-picture film. (See page 246.)

Volunteers prepare speeches telling why they would have signed the Constitution if they had been there.

The class continues the time chart.

Application to Present-Day Conditions

Under what government do we live today?

Is the original copy of the Constitution in existence today? Where is it kept? How old is it? Would ordinary paper have lasted so long? (See a children's encyclopedia.)

How many states are there in the United States today?

Can you tell of anything which has been named for James Madison? Did he ever become president? Can you tell of anything named for Hamilton?

Do people today ever think that certain changes should be made in the Constitution? Can you name any changes that have been made? What are the changes called?

Give examples of compromises which you yourself have made.

Is Washington, D.C., the only capital city the United States has had?

A club shows the class its written constitution.

Exercises in Reasoning

Do you suppose any improvement can ever be made in our kind of government?

Compare the great meeting for drawing up the Constitution with the Continental Congresses held during the Revolution.

Why did George Washington make a good chairman for the meeting?

[Make a list of the different men who have been called "the Father of" various things throughout history.

How do we know about what took place in the meeting, since its work was done in secret?

Compare the problem facing the meeting with the problem facing the colonies just before the Revolution.

From your knowledge of history, write a sentence telling whether or not conditions usually remain the same in a country for century after century.

Drill Games

Drill cards are made for the following:

Constitution	↔	the general plan of government and law
1789	↔	the date when the Constitution went into effect

Drill games are played in which all the drill cards of Unit Five are included.

A series of drill games may be played with cards chosen at random from all the units studied thus far.

Testing

Tests of Understanding are suggested on page 546 of Kelty's *Beginnings of The American People and Nation.*

Additional Tests of Reasoning and Skills.[1] Check the best answer.

1. It was hard to make a government for the United States because   √ different people wanted different plans.   the country was so large.   so many people lived in the country.   nobody could think of a good plan.

2. In the years that are to come it is reasonable to expect that   the Constitution will be thrown away.   no change will ever be made in the Constitution.   the Constitution will be out of fashion.   √ further changes will be made in the Constitution.

Exercise in Organization. Children prepare their own sets of questions covering the main points of the story and ask these questions of one another.

Tests on the Entire Unit

Test of Place Sense

Trace an outline of the United States east of the Mississippi. Make it on as large a scale as possible. Supply each child with a copy. Give the following directions.

1. Put the figure *1* where Lexington is.

2. Put the figure *2* where Bunker Hill is.

3. Put the figure *3* where Saratoga is.

4. Put the figure *4* where Valley Forge is.

5. Put the figure *5* where Yorktown is.

[1] Other exercises in reasoning are included under "General Activities."

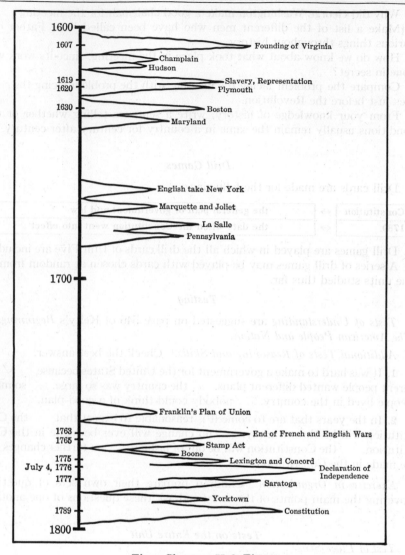

Time Chart — Unit Five

6. Write the word *Northwest* in the proper place.

7. In what city is Independence Hall? _ _ _ _ _ _

Test of Time Sense

I. Here is a list of things which happened. In each exercise place the figure *1* before the event which happened first, and the figure *2* before the event which happened later.

1. [_ _*1*_ _] George III decided to tax the colonies.
    [_ _*2*_ _] The Declaration of Independence was signed.

2. [__2__] General Burgoyne surrendered at Saratoga.
   [__1__] Samuel Adams made speeches against the taxes.

3. [__2__] The British had to leave Boston.
   [__1__] Boston Tea Party.

4. [__1__] Robert Morris collected money to pay for the war.
   [__2__] Cornwallis surrendered at Yorktown.

5. [__2__] A strong government was made.
   [__1__] The Declaration of Independence was signed.

II. Here is a list of dates:

   1789   1765   July 4, 1776   1783   1775   **1777**

Put each date in the right blank in the sentences below.

1. The Stamp Act was passed in _____.

2. The battle of Saratoga was fought in _____.

3. The treaty which ended the war was signed in _____.

4. The Constitution went into effect in _____.

5. The Declaration of Independence was made in _____.

6. The first battle of the Revolution was fought in _____.

Test on Persons. Pass mimeographed sheets of the following:

I. Here is a list of the names of persons.

   Robert Morris   John Hancock   Patrick Henry
   John Paul Jones   George III   Nathan Hale

Put each name in the right blank in the sentences below.

1. A great hero of the American navy was _____.

2. _____ said, "I only regret that I have but one life to give for my country."

3. The king of England at the time of the Revolution was _____.

4. The man who helped to collect money for the army was _____.

5. The first man to sign the Declaration of Independence was _____.

6. The man who said "Give me liberty or give me death" was _____.

II. Here is another list of the names of persons. Do the same.

   Samuel Adams   Lafayette   General Burgoyne
   Nathanael Greene   George Rogers Clark   Cornwallis

1. The man who surrendered at Yorktown was _____.

2. The man who told Boston not to take the tea was _____.

3. A great American general in the South was _____.

4. A noble Frenchman who helped the Americans was _____.

5. The man who surrendered at Saratoga was _____.

6. The Northwest was won by _____.

Test on Historical Terms. The teacher prepares descriptions such as the following, which may have been used previously as the subject of drill games.

I. Here is a list of words:

Yankee	tax	Continental Congress
Constitution	surrender	Fourth of July
Tory		

Put each word in the right place in the sentences below.

1. A citizen of the United States was called a _____.

2. When men of one army give themselves up to another army, we say they _____.

3. The day on which the Declaration of Independence was signed was the _____.

4. Money which must be paid to support the government is a _____.

5. An American who sided with England during the Revolution was called a _____.

6. The most important law of the United States is its _____.

7. Representatives from all the colonies met and made up the _____. It carried on the war.

II. Here is a list of words

retreat	the North	traitor
revolution	expedition	high seas
Declaration of Independence	"swamp fox"	

Do the same as above.

1. The paper in which the representatives said that they were no longer part of England is the _____.

2. Marion was called the _____ because he would hide in the forests and swamps when the British came after him.

3. A great change in the kind of government a country has is called a _____.

4. A man who helps the enemies of his country is a _____.

5. The waters of the oceans are called the _____.

6. The part of the United States east of New York was called _____.

7. To go back from before an enemy is to _____.

8. When many persons make a journey together for a certain purpose, they make an _____.

Comprehension Test on Unit Five

Check the best answer.

1. The government which we have in the United States today is based on the   Continental Congress.   Articles of Confederation.   √ Constitution.   Stamp Act.

2. The colonies and the mother country quarreled because   √ the colonies wanted to trade as they pleased.   the colonies wanted to make a new country. England made them pay too much money.   England was cruel to them.

3. The war in the North resulted in a victory for   England.   √ the United States.   neither.   both.

4. When the war began the colonies were fighting because   √ they wanted the rights of Englishmen.   they wanted to make a new country. England started the fighting.   England liked to fight.

5. After the British had failed at Saratoga   Russia decided to help the United States.   America decided she was going to win.   England decided to give up the war.   √ France decided to help the United States.

6. The United States began when   the Revolution began.   France agreed to help us.   the war was over.   √ the Declaration of Independence was signed.

7. The United States claimed the Northwest because   √ George Rogers Clark had won it.   the colonists had settled it.   the king had given it to them.   many French people lived there.

8. The British navy did not finally decide the war in favor of England because   John Paul Jones won many victories.   √ the French fleet was helping the Americans.   England did not have many ships.   the United States had many ships.

9. What is the title of the fifth unit in history which you have just finished studying?

A progress test on the year's work should now be given. Form B of the "Unit Scales of Attainment" (History Section)[1] should be used, so that comparisons may be made with the preliminary scores on Form A given at the beginning of the year (see page 39). The results should be graphed for easy study. Other tests which may be used for the same purpose are these:

Co-operative History Tests. Co-operative Test Service, New York City.
History Tests for Grades 4–7. Maryland State Department of Education.
Metropolitan Achievement Tests: "History. Grades 4–8." World Book Company.
Modern School Achievement Tests: "History and Civics, Grades 3–9." Bureau of Publications, Teachers College, Columbia University.
New Stanford Achievement Tests: "History and Civics, Grades 4–9." World Book Company.
Public School Achievement Test: "History, Grades 5–8." Public School Publishing Company, Bloomington, Illinois.

[1] Educational Test Bureau, Minneapolis, Minnesota.

The teacher may wish also to use the "Analytical Scales of Attainment in American History"[1] to assist her in the diagnosis of individual difficulties, although this particular test was designed for upper grades.

An Integrating Agency

While interest still runs high in the program described on page 176, the project of a pageant for the end of the year may be broached. From that time on, children select from the variety of general activities suggested under each story those which can be incorporated directly into the pageant. Thus, by the time actual rehearsals begin, the composition of the pageant will have been completed through this cumulative process.

[1] Educational Test Bureau, Minneapolis, Minn.

PART THREE. LEARNING AND TEACHING LATER AMERICAN HISTORY

UNIT ONE · *How the United States won the Respect of the Nations* [4 Weeks

ADDITIONAL STORIES FOR MORE ADVANCED READERS

Life of John Adams
Benjamin West and Early American Painters
American Authors: Bryant, Cooper, Irving
Tecumseh's Conspiracy

A

STORY 1. THE BEGINNINGS OF THE NEW GOVERNMENT
STORY 2. FINANCIAL PROBLEMS [1 Week

[Stories treated separately for conversational approach, the reading periods, and the discussion; for other activities, both together]

Conversational Approach (First Story)

"Why do you suppose that the great nations of the world paid little attention to the small nation that had just been born in far-away America? Would they consider it their equal? Can you name some small country in the world today which we consider of little importance? Should we pay much attention if it changed its form of government?

"The United States in 1789 was in somewhat the same position as a small boy who enters a new school in a strange city. What things is he likely to have to do before he wins the respect of the other boys?

"Our new unit tells how the United States won the respect of the other nations many years ago."

275

Reading and Study

The class is now divided into two groups: the independent readers and the lower group. They remain in the same classroom and carry on their activities at the same time.

The Reading Periods (*First Story*)

Independent Readers

This group reads the entire story through silently, as given in their text. They then test their comprehension by the study-guide questions furnished by the teacher or by the text. Reading from several other texts may follow.

TEXTS

BARKER, DODD, WEBB, *Our Nation Grows Up*, 18–22, 24–27.
BEARD and BAGLEY, *First Book in American History*, 154–155, 158.
BURNHAM and JACK, *Growth of Our Country*, 3–5, 8–11.
CLARK, *Westward to the Pacific*, 51–54.
HALLECK and FRANTZ, *Makers of Our Nation*, 60–63.
KELTY, *Growth of the American People and Nation*, 7–13.
SMALLIDGE and PAXSON, *Builders of Our Nation*, 326–336, 339–340.
WOODBURN and MORAN, *Makers of America*, 169–174.

EXTENSIVE READING

COE, *Makers of the Nation*, 181–185.
GORDY, *Leaders in Making America*, 240–246.
LEFFERTS, *American Leaders*, I : 87–88, 90–92.

Lower Group

If these children are very much below grade in reading ability, the teacher first tells them the story orally, writing on the board the most important of the new words used. Children practice the pronunciations.

Then the teacher and this group read together the story as given in the text. The teacher directs the silent reading, section by section, by such questions as "Why did Washington find everything in such bad condition?"

The children read silently and answer orally. Those who cannot find the answer are shown where it is, by those who can.

This process is continued throughout the entire story. Then the children test themselves by the study-guide questions at the end of the story.

OTHER BOOKS

BLAISDELL and BALL, *American History Story Book*, 86–91.
BLAISDELL and BALL, *Short Stories from American History*, 104–110.
DAVIS, *Stories of the United States*, 173–175.

READING FOR RECREATION (*Both Groups*)

GERWIG, *Washington, the Young Leader.*
LOWITZ, *General George the Great.*

The Discussion (*First Story*)

The children give complete answers to the study-guide questions. This exercise gives opportunity for clearing up half-comprehensions and for correcting misapprehensions. The teacher insists on the children's using their own words rather than the words in the book.

The teacher writes on the board the words *president, inauguration, administration.* The children discuss the meaning of each.

Conversational Approach (*Second Story*)

"Now we come to a very hard question. What is a debt? Why was the new nation very heavily in debt? Should it try to pay its debts? How could it do so? What do you think would be the difference between state debts and the debt of the entire nation? Do you think both ought to be paid? Our story today will tell us."

The Reading Periods (Second Story)

Independent Readers

This group reads the entire story through silently, as given in their text. They then test their comprehension by the study-guide questions furnished by the teacher or by the text. Reading from several other texts may follow.

TEXTS

BARKER, DODD, WEBB, *Our Nation Grows Up*, 22–24.
BEARD and BAGLEY, *First Book in American History*, 155–158.
BURNHAM and JACK, *Growth of Our Country*, 5–8.
HALLECK and FRANTZ, *Makers of Our Nation*, 91–94.
KELTY, *Growth of the American People and Nation*, 14–21.
SMALLIDGE and PAXSON, *Builders of Our Nation*, 336.

EXTENSIVE READING

BURNHAM, *Hero Tales from History*, 301–309.
COE, *Makers of the Nation*, 187.
LEFFERTS, *American Leaders*, I: 193–216.
SOUTHWORTH, *Builders of Our Country*, II: 97–107.
UHRBROCK and OWENS, *Famous Americans*, 134–149.

Lower Group

If the children are very much below grade in reading ability, the teacher tells them the story orally, writing on the board the most important names as she mentions them. Children practice the pronunciations.

Then the teacher and this group read together the story as given in the text. The teacher directs the silent reading, section by section, by such questions as "What was Hamilton's job in the new government?"

The children read silently and answer orally. Those who cannot find the answer are shown where to look for it, by those who can.

This process is continued throughout the entire story. Then the children test themselves by the study-guide questions at the end of the story.

READING FOR RECREATION (*Both Groups*)

FRYER, *Book of Boyhoods*.
"Story of Money," in *Junior Red Cross News* (March, April, 1933).

The Discussion (Second Story)

The children give complete answers to the study-guide questions. This exercise enables the teacher to set up adequate standards as to what constitutes understanding. During the first units she will show the children repeatedly that they were not ready to answer the questions when perhaps they thought that they were. By insisting that children's answers show a real grasp of the story, the teacher is furnishing excellent training in the "ability to follow a coherent, cumulative train of thought."[1]

The teacher writes on the board the words *debts, treasurer, Secretary of the Treasury*. Children discuss the meanings.

Multisensory Aids

The teacher and the children talk over together the pictures in the text, noting features of historical significance.

[1] See page 7.

Chronicles of America Photoplays: Alexander Hamilton.
Compton's Pictured Teaching Materials: *Holidays*, Plate XII.
International Educational Pictures: Alexander Hamilton.
Keystone Views: 85, 86, 87, 89, 90, 91, 92, 94, 322.
Yale Pageant Educational Slides: 129, 130, 782, 783.

Music. Children sing "Mount Vernon Bells."
The teacher plays a recording of the "President's March," which was played at Washington's inauguration.

General Activities

Creative Activities: Group and Individual, Correlated with Other Subjects or Voluntary Projects

A committee makes graphs to show the following facts:

In 1789 the United States had about the same population as the Netherlands, Portugal, and Sweden. Compare their populations today. (See World Almanac for figures.)

A committee makes up a tabulation of imports, and estimates the amount that could be raised by a tax on imports. (See the text as to rates and articles taxed.)

The class carries on some project which will necessitate the election of a treasurer.

A volunteer writes a diary of one of Washington's days at Mount Vernon.

A volunteer describes a fox hunt.

A committee sets a stage to represent a city welcoming President Washington on his way to New York to the inauguration.

Another committee may wish to enact the scene by means of a puppet show.

The class makes a picture collection of the inauguration of a new president in our own times. (Cut out the inaugural address from a newspaper.)

A volunteer dresses a doll in the costume in which President Washington was inaugurated.

A volunteer gives a floor talk on "John Adams, the First Vice-President."

The teacher uses the phonographic record of Washington's Farewell Address.

A visitor to Mount Vernon describes the place to the class.

The class finds the island of Nevis, in the West Indies, where Alexander Hamilton was born.

A visitor to the West Indies describes the small islands to the class.

The class begins to make a new time line.

Application to Present-Day Conditions

Who is president of the United States now? How many presidents have we had?

What can a farmer do today for worn-out soil?

Compare the wooden plow of Washington's time with plows in use today. (See a children's encyclopedia.)

Are the best men in your community today always willing to serve their country as officials? Would many of them rather spend their time in making money for themselves?

How long does it take nowadays to go from Mount Vernon (just outside Washington) to New York? (See railway schedules.) Compare with the length of time needed in Washington's day.

How many guns (shots) are the official greeting to the president today? (See Chicago Daily News Almanac, " Official salutes.")

Can you find a picture showing how New York welcomes famous visitors today?

When is a new president inaugurated nowadays? [*In January; by the Twentieth Amendment to the Constitution.*]

What salary is paid the president of the United States today?

What four cabinet offices were created by President Washington? What men hold these offices today? Can you find pictures of them?

Why does the government always need a great deal of money? What is done with it?

Hamilton believed that the country should be run by the upper classes — the rich, the well-born, and the most able. He had little faith in the common people. Do you know anyone who holds such views today?

Does a captain in the army today have to furnish the supplies for his company?

How much money does the United States spend in a year today? Compare this with the two and a half millions in Hamilton's time.

The teacher shows the class a government bond (one form in which the public debt is represented today).

Does the United States owe any public debt today?

Exercises in Reasoning

Why did General Washington's farms run down during the eight years that he had been away?

Why did Washington seem an old man at fifty-seven years of age?

Why was New York not made the permanent capital of the United States? Can you think of any reasons why it might have been wise to choose New York?

Why did it take so long for the new members of Congress to arrive in New York?

Why did Washington think he needed some cabinet officers?

What things could a secretary do for a great general? Why would a knowledge of the French language be a help to Washington's secretary during the war?

How do we know anything about what the president wore at his inauguration so many years ago? [*Newspaper accounts, letters, diaries.*]

Why would Washington not allow himself to be made president for a third time?

Drill Games

Cards for drill games may be made as follows:

ONE SIDE		THE OTHER SIDE
president	⟺	the highest officer of our country
inauguration	⟺	the ceremony by which the president takes his office
administration	⟺	the years during which one president manages the affairs of the nation
Alexander Hamilton	⟺	the first Secretary of the Treasury
debt	⟺	money owed
treasurer	⟺	the officer who has charge of the money for a group
Secretary of the Treasury	⟺	chief officer of the department which takes charge of United States money

Children have access to these cards at any time and drill themselves on their own difficulties. Later on, drill games are played.

Testing

Tests of Understanding of persons and terms are provided on pages 13 and 21 of Kelty's *The Growth of the American People and Nation.*

Tests of Reasoning and Skills. All the following statements are true. Check the one which gives the best answer.

1. George Washington was elected as the first president because   he had been a great soldier.   he was a rich man.   √ he was trusted by all parts of the country.   Virginia was one of the most important states.

2. Washington chose four men to be cabinet officers so that   √ they might give him their advice.   they would not have so much to do.   they might win votes for him.   he might have a guard.

3. On what pages in your book can you find Alexander Hamilton mentioned?

------

4. Where did you look to find out? ___[*In the index.*]___

5. Check the word under which you looked.
                                              [ ] *Alexander*   [√] *Hamilton*
Did it come before or after the word *Havana?*   Before [√]   After [ ]

6. Put the figure 1 before the thing which happened first and the figure 2 before the thing which happened later.

[__2__] George Washington was inaugurated as president.
[__1__] The Constitution went into effect.

Exercise in Organization. Children in the lower group copy the section headings of the first story.

A

STORY 3. THE NEW CAPITAL · STORY 4. BUILDING UP TRADE WITH CHINA   [1 Week

[Stories treated separately for reading and discussion; for other activities, both together]

Conversational Approach

"In our history stories of last week we found that the first capital of the United States was what city? Then where was it moved? Can you think of any reasons why Philadelphia was chosen? Is Philadelphia still our national capital? What city is? In what state is the city of Washington?" (To find out whether or not children already have some vague idea about the District of Columbia.) "Our story today tells how Washington came to be built."

Reading and Study

The Reading Periods (First Story)

Independent Readers

This group reads the entire story through silently as given in their text. They then test their comprehension by the study-guide questions furnished by the teacher or by the text. Reading from several other texts may follow.

TEXTS

KELTY, *The Growth of the American People and Nation*, 22–28.
WOODBURN and MORAN, *Makers of America*, 174–180.

EXTENSIVE READING

COE, *Makers of the Nation*, 186–189.
FARIS, *Where Our History Was Made*, II: 325–333.
INGRAHAM, *Story of Democracy*, 243–257.
LEFFERTS, *American Leaders*, I: 88–90.
LEFFERTS, *Our Own United States*, 84–90.

Lower Group

If these children are very much below grade in reading ability, the teacher first tells them the story orally, writing on the board the most important new names used. Children practice the pronunciations.

Then the teacher and this group read together the story as given in the text. The teacher directs the silent reading, section by section, by such questions as "What three places hoped to be chosen as the capital?"

The children read silently and answer orally; those who cannot find the answer are shown where to look for it, by those who can.

Children then test their comprehension of the story by the study-guide questions at the end of the story.

OTHER BOOKS

CARROLL and CARROLL, *Around the World*, III: 47–53.

READING FOR RECREATION (*Both Groups*)

HILLYER, *Child's Geography of the World*, Tale 6.
ROOSEVELT, *A Trip to Washington with Bob and Betty.*
TAYLOR, *Our U.S.A.*

The Discussion (First Story)

Children answer the study-guide questions. The teacher emphasizes the importance of the children's answering in their own words, by commending those who do so.

She writes on the board the words *Capitol, capital city, White House, nineteenth century, Pennsylvania Avenue.* Children discuss the meaning or significance of the terms; they notice the difference in spelling and meaning between *capital* and *capitol.*

Reading Periods (Second Story)

Independent Readers

This group reads the entire story through silently, as given in their text. They then test their comprehension by the study-guide questions furnished by the teacher or by the text.

TEXTS

CLARK, *Westward toward America,* 316–317.
KELTY, *Growth of the American People and Nation,* 29–35.

EXTENSIVE READING

DAKIN, *Great Rivers of the World,* 105–108.
JUDSON, *Early Days in Old Oregon,* 25–30.
MONTGOMERY, *Beginners' American History,* 209–212.

Lower Group

The teacher tells the story orally, writing on the board the names of the most important persons and places mentioned.

Then the teacher and this group read together the story as given in the text. The teacher directs the silent reading, section by section, by such questions as "Why did the Americans now have to make a move for themselves?"

The children read silently and answer orally; those who cannot find the answer are shown where to look for it, by those who can.

They then test their understanding of the story by the study-guide questions at the end of the story.

READING FOR RECREATION (*Both Groups*)

BAILEY, *Children of the Handicrafts.*
COLE, *A B C Book of People.*
ELDRIDGE, *Yen-Foh.*
FRENCH, *Stories of Hawaii.*
SWAN, *Deep-Water Days.*
WADE, GRADY, KELTY, *Tales of Adventures in History,* 87–100 (Cook).

The Discussion (Second Story)

The children answer the study-guide questions as fully as possible. The teacher stresses the importance of their saying the answers to themselves while they are studying, and going back to the story when they are unable to answer a given question.

Multisensory Aids

The teacher and the children talk over the pictures in the text, pointing out features of historical and geographical significance.

They turn to a map of the District of Columbia and notice by what states it is surrounded and on what body of water it is. On a large wall map they trace the routes used at the time in sailing to China.

AUDIO-VISUAL MATERIALS OBTAINABLE

BROWN. Famous Pictures: 43, 44.
EASTMAN. Classroom Films: Washington, the Capital City.
GABRIEL (Ed.). Pageant of America: XIII, 116–122.
International Educational Pictures: China (series).
Keystone Views: 261, 529.

National Geographic Magazine, LVII, 372–392 (March, 1930); LX, 517–619 (November, 1931); LXVII, 457–488 (April, 1935).
Society for Visual Education. Picturols: Washington, D.C., Parts I and II.
Yale Pageant Educational Slides: 167.

General Activities

Creative Activities: Group and Individual, Correlated with Other Subjects or Voluntary Projects

A committee models in the sand table the locale of the District of Columbia and the city of Washington, marking the location of some of the principal buildings mentioned.

Volunteers draw scenes illustrating life in the new capital.

The class makes a trip to a local department store or museum to examine articles imported from China.

A committee dramatizes the story of Captain Robert Gray.

The teacher reads to the class Abigail Adams's letter describing the new capital.[1]

A volunteer models in clay the medal struck for the voyage of the *Columbia*.[2]

Volunteers report on other countries building new capitals: Peter the Great and St. Petersburg in Russia, Canberra in Australia, Delhi in India.

A volunteer reports on the revival in America of "classical" architecture and shows pictures to illustrate the influence of classical buildings on public buildings in America.

Another volunteer reports on furniture designed by Duncan Phyfe.

The class makes a picture collection of the present-day city of Washington, displaying it on the bulletin board.

A visitor to Washington describes the city to the children.

Each child begins to make a map of the United States in the early nineteenth century. As base, a double-sized map of the United States east of the Mississippi is used. Washington, Boston, and Salem are marked.

The class continues the time line.

Application to Present-Day Conditions

Is the District of Columbia one of the forty-eight states? How is it governed? (See a children's encyclopedia.)

Is Washington, D.C., in about the central part of the country today? Do you think that the capital ought therefore to be changed again? Why not?

Does the United States still carry on trade with China? In what articles? (See the World Almanac.)

Where do the Chinese people get their furs today?

What does the expression *rounding the Horn* mean?

How long does it take to sail around the world today? Compare with the three years which Captain Robert Gray's voyage took.

[1] A. B. Hart, *American History Told by Contemporaries,* Vol. III, pp. 331–333. The Macmillan Company, 1902.

[2] E. E. Sparks, *Expansion of the American People,* p. 211. Scott, Foresman and Company, 1900.

Exercises in Reasoning

Last year you learned the meaning of the word *compromise*. Was the agreement about debts and the location of the capital city a compromise?

Why did so many cities wish to be the capital?

Is there any advantage in locating the capital in a large city?

What effect should you expect the moving of the capital to have on the city of Philadelphia?

Did the naming of the new district *Columbia* right the injustice which had been done Columbus when the continent he discovered was called *America*?

Why did the United States have to build up a new trade with China?

Why did the Chinese people need furs?

What class of people in New England grew rich from the trade with China and India? Who had been the rich people there before this time?

What part of the story proves that the world had not even yet given up its dream of a Northwest Passage to the Indies?

Compare the way in which Captain Gray laid claim to the land along the Columbia with the way in which earlier explorers had marked their claims.

Who was the first man to sail around the world? the first Englishman? the first American?

Drill Games

Drill on place names can best be carried on at the map: *District of Columbia, Washington, Potomac, Boston, Salem, Oregon, Columbia River*.

Cards may be made for the drill games as follows:

Pennsylvania Avenue	↔	street leading from Capitol to White House
nineteenth century	↔	all the years from 1800 up through 1899
White House	↔	official home of the president
the Capitol	↔	building in which Congress meets
capital city	↔	city from which government of a country is carried on
Captain Robert Gray	↔	man who discovered the Columbia River

Children test themselves by using both sides of these cards.

Testing

Tests of Understanding are supplied in Kelty's *The Growth of the American People and Nation*, pp. 28, 35.

Tests of Reasoning and Skills

1. Make a list of the reasons why the capital city was located in the District of Columbia. Use your book if you want to.

2. Check the best answer: The United States had to build up a new trade with China because   it had lost so many ships during the Revolution. China had always kept American ships out of its ports.   ✓ it could no longer depend on Great Britain's trade with China.   China had taken the side of Great Britain during the Revolution.

3. Turn to a map of the District of Columbia. Check the following:

a. The District of Columbia is a perfect square.   Yes [ ]   No [√]

b. The District of Columbia is between Maryland and Virginia.   Yes [√]
No [ ]

4. Put the figure *1* before the thing which happened first, and the figure *2* before the thing which happened later.

[_ _2_ _] the United States built up trade with China.

[_ _1_ _] the United States declared its independence.

Exercises in Organization. Teacher and children together make summary sentences of the two stories.

A

STORY 5. THOMAS JEFFERSON

B

STORY 1. THE BARBARY PIRATES   [1 *Week*

[Stories treated separately for conversational approach, the reading periods, and the discussion; for other activities, both together]

Conversational Approach (*First Story*)

"Who remembers Alexander Hamilton's beliefs about who should run the government? Today we begin a story about a man who had entirely different ideas about government. Let us see if we can find out what those ideas were."

Reading and Study

The Reading Periods (*First Story*)

Independent Readers

This group reads the entire story through silently, as given in their text. They then test their comprehension by the study-guide questions furnished by the teacher or the text. Reading from other texts may follow.

TEXTS

BURNHAM and JACK, *Growth of Our Country*, 11–17.

HALLECK and FRANTZ, *Makers of Our Nation*, 132–141, 151–152.

KELTY, *Growth of the American People and Nation*, 36–42.

WOODBURN and MORAN. *Makers of America*, 189–195.

EXTENSIVE READING

BURNHAM, *Hero Tales from History*, 309–314.

CHANDLER and CHITWOOD, *Makers of American History*, 176–182.

Lower Group

If these children are very much below grade in reading ability, the teacher tells the story orally, writing on the board the most important of the new words used. Children practice the pronunciations.

Then the teacher and this group read together the story as given in the text. The teacher directs the silent reading, section by section, by such questions as "What had Jefferson already done in France and in the United States?"

The children read silently and answer orally. Those who cannot find the answer are shown where to look for it, by those who have found it.

This process is continued throughout the entire story. Children then test their comprehension by the study-guide questions at the end of the story.

COE, *Makers of the Nation*, 213–216.

DAVIDSON, *Founders and Builders of Our Nation*, 109–114.

EVANS, *America First*, 236–240.

FARIS, *Where Our History Was Made*, II: 292–296.

FOOTE and SKINNER, *Makers and Defenders of America*, 117–125.

GORDY, *American Leaders and Heroes*, 241–243.

LEFFERTS, *American Leaders*, I: 94–109.

MONTGOMERY, *Beginners' American History*, 162–168, 170.

SOUTHWORTH, *Builders of our Country*, II: 108–113.

UHRBROCK and OWENS, *Famous Americans*, 72–80.

OTHER BOOKS

BALDWIN, *Fifty Famous People*, 54–57.

EGGLESTON, *Stories of Great Americans*, 87–96.

WAYLAND, *History Stories for Primary Grades*, 119–121.

The Discussion (First Story)

Children answer the study-guide questions. If a child's answer leaves out important phases of the subject, the teacher questions him. She calls the attention of the class to what she is doing, and tells them that as soon as they learn how it is done they may question one another for the same purpose.

The teacher writes on the board the words *Democratic party, political party*. Children discuss the meanings.

Conversational Approach (Second Story)

".The United States had made a good beginning at home. Now it had to turn to the problem of getting along with other countries.

"On the map of Africa, show the countries bordering the Mediterranean. These were then called the Barbary States." (The teacher writes *Barbary States* on the board.) "Some of their people were pirates. What does that mean? What would happen, then, to United States ships sailing in the Mediterranean? Our next story tells what the United States decided to do about this matter."

Reading and Study

The Reading Periods (Second Story)

Independent Readers

This group reads the entire story through silently. They then test their comprehension by the study-guide questions furnished by the teacher or the text.

TEXTS

KELTY, *Growth of the American People and Nation*, 43–49.

EXTENSIVE READING

CHANDLER and CHITWOOD, *Makers of American History*, 192–195.

EVANS, *America First*, 240–244.

Lower Group

The teacher tells the story orally to this group, writing on the board the names of the most important persons and places as she mentions them. Children practice the pronunciations.

Then the teacher and this group read together the story as given in the text. The teacher directs the silent reading, section by section, by such questions as "What things were the Barbary pirates in the habit of doing?"

The children read silently and answer orally. Those who cannot find the answer

LEFFERTS, *American Leaders*, I : 217–222.
SOUTHWORTH, *Builders of Our Country*, II : 146–148.
UHRBROCK and OWENS, *Famous Americans*, 167–171.

READING FOR RECREATION

AUSTIN, *Uncle Sam's Secrets*, 235–236.
KAUFFMAN, *Barbary Bo*.
SEAWELL, *Decatur and Somers*.

are shown where to look for it, by those who have found it.

This process is continued throughout the entire story. Children then test their comprehension by the study-guide questions at the end of the story.

OTHER BOOKS

EGGLESTON, *Stories of Great Americans*, 83–87.

The Discussion (Second Story)

Children answer the study-guide questions. Again the teacher questions them as to phases omitted, in preparation for their questioning one another. She points out that only the most important matters need be included, not everything told in the text.

She writes on the board the words *Barbary States, ransom, paying tribute.* Children discuss the meanings.

Multisensory Aids

Children and teacher talk over together the pictures in the text, pointing out features of historical and geographical importance. They point out the Barbary States on a large wall map.

AUDIO-VISUAL MATERIALS OBTAINABLE

BROWN. Famous Pictures : 1786.
Compton's Pictured Teaching Materials : *American Colonies*, Plate IV, 2.
International Educational Pictures : Thomas Jefferson.
Keystone Views : 93.
Perry Pictures : 116, 116B.
Yale Pageant Educational Slides : 58, 387.

General Activities

Creative Activities: Group and Individual, Correlated with Other Subjects or Voluntary Projects

A volunteer writes a letter Jefferson might have written to a friend, urging him to join the new party.

A volunteer finds the name of Thomas Jefferson among the signers of the Declaration of Independence.

A volunteer reports on the United States Military Academy at West Point, established during Jefferson's presidency.

The class makes a picture collection of Monticello. A visitor to Monticello describes the place to the class.

Volunteers make a list of Jefferson's services to his country.

A committee shows the flags of the Barbary States (*National Geographic Magazine*, XXXII : 358 (October, 1917)).

Application to Present-Day Conditions

To what political parties do your father and mother belong? Why does each one belong to this party instead of some other?

Do you know any people today whose beliefs are like Jefferson's?

Which political party today claims to be carrying out Jefferson's ideas?

Did the present president of the United States read his own message to Congress, like Washington, or did he send it to be read, like Jefferson?

Does our government today have the same views about the army and navy that Jefferson had?

What are the names of the countries which today are situated along the southern Mediterranean coast? Are there still pirates there?

Are people ever held for ransom today?

From the index of an atlas find out how many places have been named in honor of Jefferson. Do you know any other things named in his honor?

Exercises in Reasoning

Jefferson believed in common working people, like farmers. He wanted them all to have a chance for a good life. Compare his beliefs with those of Alexander Hamilton. Why were these two men bound to be enemies?

Why do you suppose Jefferson did not want people to work in factories and live in cities?

What does this mean: "The voice of the people is the voice of God"? Do you believe it?

Before this time the oldest son got all the father's property when the father died. Why do you suppose the law was changed at this time?

Why was it harder to start a political party in 1800 than it is today?

What does the word *Monticello* mean? (See New International Encyclopedia.)

Why did American sailors burn their own ship, the *Philadelphia*?

Did the troubles with the Barbary pirates have any good results?

Drill Games

Place names are best drilled on at the map: *Tripoli, Barbary States.*
Drill cards may be made as follows:

Thomas Jefferson	↔	a leader who had great faith in common people
political party	↔	a group of people who try to elect their own members to offices
Democratic party	↔	political party founded by Thomas Jefferson
ransom	↔	money paid to set free someone who has been captured
to pay tribute	↔	to give money in order to avoid being attacked

Children practice in small groups, each child making a record of the items on which he makes mistakes.

Testing

Tests of Understanding are given in Kelty's *The Growth of the American People and Nation*, pp. 42, 49.

Tests of Reasoning and Skills

1. Put one of these names in each of the spaces below : *Jefferson, Hamilton.* We should expect that farmers would vote for the party of _ _ _ _ _ _ . We should expect that business men would vote for the party of _ _ _ _ _ _ .

2. Finish the following sentence: It is almost useless to try to buy peace from pirates, because _ _ _ _ _ _ .

3. Put the figure *1* before the thing which happened first, and the figure *2* before the thing which happened later.

[_ _*1*_ _] The Revolutionary War was fought.
[_ _*2*_ _] There was trouble with the Barbary pirates.

Exercises in Organization. Children who believe themselves able to do so make an independent outline of the first story, while the teacher and the other children make a co-operative outline of the second story. The outlines of the first story are then presented to the group for appraisal.

B

STORY 2. CAUSES OF THE WAR OF 1812 · STORY 3. THE WAR OF 1812
[*1 Week*
[Stories treated separately for conversational approach, the reading periods, and the discussion ; for other activities, both together]

Conversational Approach (First Story)

"Now the United States had to face a problem which has never yet been satisfactorily solved. It is about trading with countries which are at war with one another. Suppose that France and England are fighting each other. Why will France not want us to send any goods to England? Why will England not want us to send any goods to France? How could either one prevent us?

"Undoubtedly the United States has a right to trade where she pleases. So has a man a right to cross the street in front of a team of runaway horses. Is he wise to insist on his right?

"We have insisted on the right to trade with countries which were at war with one another twice in our history, and twice we have been drawn into the war. Which do you think is better, to give up our right to trade until the war is over or to send men to be killed in fighting for that right?

"Our story today tells how we were once drawn into war over this question."

Reading and Study

The Reading Periods (First Story)

Since this story deals with rather abstract topics, it probably will be wise for the teacher to tell the story orally to both groups, writing on the board the most important new words as she mentions them. Children practice the pronunciations.

The teacher and the entire class then read together the story as given in the text. The teacher directs the silent reading, section by section, by such questions as "Why had Napoleon not been able to conquer Great Britain also?"
ꜰ Children read silently and answer orally. Those who cannot find the answer are shown where to look for it, by those who have found it. They then test their comprehension by the study-guide questions at the end of the story.

Independent Readers

This group reads the entire story through silently, as given in their text. They then test their comprehension by the study-guide questions furnished by the teacher or by the text. Reading from other texts may follow.

TEXTS

BARKER, DODD, WEBB, *Our Nation Grows Up*, 47–50.
BURNHAM and JACK, *Growth of Our Country*, 35–40.
CLARK, *Westward to the Pacific*, 146–147, 161–163.
KELTY, *Growth of the American People and Nation*, 50–59.

EXTENSIVE READING

DAVIDSON, *Founders and Builders of Our Nation*, 121–124.
EVANS, *America First*, 265–269.
FARIS, *Where Our History Was Made*, II: 32–38.
FOOTE and SKINNER, *Makers and Defenders of America*, 149–151.
MONTGOMERY, *Beginners' American History*, 193–194.

Lower Group

The lower group may find it necessary to reread the story in order to answer the study-guide questions.

OTHER BOOKS

BLAISDELL and BALL, *American History Story Book*, 121–125.
EGGLESTON, *Stories of Great Americans*, 107–111.

READING FOR RECREATION (*Both Groups*)

ALTSHELER, *A Herald of the West*.
KNIPE, *Lost— A Brother*.
PERKINS, *American Twins of 1812*.

The Discussion (*First Story*)   [*In a Language Period*

The children answer the study-guide questions with their books open before them. The teacher makes a special attempt to find out whether children understand what they are saying. Answering in their own words will help.

The teacher writes on the board the words *neutral, impressment, freedom of the seas*. Children discuss the meanings.

Conversational Approach (*Second Story*)

"We have found that the United States could not keep out of the war in Europe because our people insisted on trading with the countries at war. Let us see how much of the action of the war we can read from the map.

"Turn to a map of the War of 1812. What does the key tell us? Where did General Hull start from and how far did he go? What seems to have stopped him there? Where did General Harrison start from and how far did he go?

"In the north the British made two advances. Where? They made one in the Chesapeake Bay region. What do you suppose they were trying to do there? What action took place in the extreme south?

"There were also a good many battles at sea which the map does not show.

"Turn constantly to this map as you read the story, and it will help you to understand what happened."

Reading and Study

The Reading Periods (Second Story)

Independent Readers

This group reads the entire story through silently, as given in their text. They then test their comprehension by the study-guide questions furnished by the teacher or by the text. Reading from other texts may follow.

TEXTS

BARKER, DODD, WEBB, *Our Nation Grows Up*, 50–55.

BEARD and BAGLEY, *First Book in American History*, 181–186.

BURNHAM and JACK, *Growth of Our Country*, 40–49.

KELTY, *Growth of the American People and Nation*, 60–78.

EXTENSIVE READING

CHANDLER and CHITWOOD, *Makers of American History*, 195–199.

EVANS, *America First*, 274–278.

FARIS, *Where Our History Was Made*, II: 24–32.

FOOTE and SKINNER, *Makers and Defenders of America*, 152–160.

HORTON, *A Group of Famous Women*, 13–24.

LEFFERTS, *American Leaders*, I: 222–236.

SOUTHWORTH, *Builders of Our Country*, II: 140–146.

TAPPAN, *American Hero Stories*, 218–223, 224–236.

TOMLINSON, *Fighters Young Americans Want to Know*, 148–181.

UHRBROCK and OWENS, *Famous Americans*, 178–184.

Lower Group

The teacher tells the story orally to this group, writing on the board the names of the most important persons and places as she mentions them. Children practice the pronunciations.

Then the teacher and this group read together the story as given in the text. The teacher directs the silent reading, section by section, by such questions as "Why did the backwoodsmen want to march immediately to Detroit?"

Children read silently and answer orally. This procedure is continued throughout the story. Children then test their understanding by the study-guide questions at the end of the story.

OTHER BOOKS

BLAISDELL and BALL, *Short Stories from American History*, 111–121.

GROVE, *American Naval Heroes*, 14–19.

TAPPAN, *American History Stories for Very Young Readers*, 110–117.

WAYLAND, *History Stories for Primary Grades*, 195–199.

READING FOR RECREATION

BARNES, *The Hero of Erie*.

BARNES, *Yankee Ships and Yankee Sailors*.

MARSHALL, *Old Hickory's Prisoner*.

PALMER, *Men and Ships of Steel*.

SEAWELL, *Little Jarvis*.

SWAN, *Anchors Aweigh*.

TOMLINSON, *The Boys with Old Hickory*.

The Discussion (Second Story)   [In a Language Period

Children answer the study-guide questions with their books open. They point out on a large wall map all the places mentioned. The teacher calls special attention to the circumstances attending the writing of "The Star-Spangled Banner."

Multisensory Aids

Children and teacher talk over together the pictures in the text, pointing out features of historical or geographical significance.

Turning to the map, the children trace each of the lines of the campaigns mentioned in the text.

GRANT. *Story of the Ship*: the *Constitution*, the *Victory*, the *Niagara*.
Keystone Views: 99, 102, 326–333.
McKINLEY. Illustrated Topics for American History: S. 20.
National Geographic Magazine: LXVI, 371 (September, 1934).
Society for Visual Education (MUIR). 1789–1815: First Presidents and War of 1812.
Yale Pageant Educational Slides: 133, 536, 575, 640, 733, 734, 736, 737, 738, 739, 740,
790.

Music. Sing "The Star-Spangled Banner" and "Hail Columbia."
Play a record of "Anchors A-Weigh."

General Activities

*Creative Activities: Group and Individual, Correlated with Other Subjects or
Voluntary Projects*

A volunteer gives the speech which a representative of Great Britain might
have given, trying to persuade the United States not to sell to France. Another
volunteer gives the speech which a representative of France might have given,
trying to persuade the United States not to sell to Great Britain.

Three children impersonate the three plans tried to solve the problem of
neutral trade. Each explains his purpose.

A committee may draw a picture map of Europe under the domination of
Napoleon, showing French soldiers holding the land areas and British ships
guarding the seas. (Shepherd's Historical Atlas, 153.)

A volunteer draws a scroll bearing Perry's message of victory.

Committees read to the class the dramatizations given in Hubbard's *Little
American History Plays* (101–108), Bird and Starling's *Historical Plays for
Children* (247–270), and Hague and Chalmers's *Dramatic Moments in American
History* (129–151).

The teacher reads to the class Oliver Wendell Holmes's poem "Old Iron-
sides."

A committee dramatizes the impressment of a seaman.

Volunteers draw posters to recruit men for the army and navy in 1812.

Each child draws a map showing the lines of British and American advance,
similar to that mentioned in the conversational approach to the second
story.

The class continues the time line.

Application to Present-Day Conditions

Did the United States insist on its right to trade with both nations during
the war between Italy and Ethiopia? (See periodicals of 1935 and 1936.)

Is it still true that when Europe suffers the United States must suffer also?

Have you ever heard the word *neutral* used in any other connection than
in wars? [*For example, in labor disputes or other quarrels.*]

Is it possible for a man to change his citizenship nowadays? How? (See
Naturalization in a children's encyclopedia.) Do you know anyone who is a
naturalized citizen?

How did the League of Nations try to stop the war between Italy and Ethiopia? [*By refusing to trade with Italy or to lend her money.*]

Does Canada today have any desire to join the United States as one country?

Have the United States and Canada ever been at war since 1814?

Do you know of anything named for Dolly Madison? [*Silver patterns, cakes.*]

Exercises in Reasoning

Which is worth more — the money which might be made from trade during a war between other nations, or the lives of the soldiers who would be killed defending our right to such trade?

Is there any difference between fighting for trade rights and fighting for some high principle, such as independence?

Can you starve your enemy if other countries continue to trade with him?

Why did so many people object to serving in the British navy?

Is it patriotic to run the risk of drawing the United States into war by trading with countries at war?

Do you think that the War of 1812 was necessary? Might it have been prevented if there had been an Atlantic cable at that time? Why?

Why did we go to war with England instead of with France?

Why were the American army and the American navy so unprepared to carry on the war?

How could the battle of New Orleans also have been prevented if there had been an Atlantic cable at that time?

How do the relations between Canada and the United States since 1814 help to explain this statement: "The relations between the two countries are 'the greatest object lesson which the world has ever seen of how nations might learn to live together in peace and trust'"?

Many people believe that neither side ever really wins in a war. How does the War of 1812 support this view?

Drill Games

Place names are best drilled upon at the map: *New Orleans, Lake Erie.*
Association cards are made as follows:

neutral	↔	not taking either side in a war
freedom of the seas	↔	freedom of neutral countries to trade in ordinary goods with countries at war
impressment	↔	forcing sailors into service
James Madison	↔	president during the War of 1812
War of 1812	↔	our second war with England
"Star-Spangled Banner"	↔	the national anthem of the United States
Andrew Jackson	↔	the victor at New Orleans
Oliver Hazard Perry	↔	American sailor who won a victory on Lake Erie

These cards are added to those already used in the unit, and the drill games include them all.

Testing

Tests of Understanding are supplied in Kelty's *The Growth of the American People and Nation,* pp. 59 and 78.

Tests of Reasoning and Skills

1. Check the best answer: The events about which we are reading took place   a thousand years ago.   in my father's lifetime.   in my grandfather's time.   √ before my grandfather's time.

2. Which of the causes of the War of 1812 is still a problem for the nations of the World? _ _ _[*Neutral trade.*]_ _ _

3. Check the best answer: Why did the backwoodsmen and the War Hawks want to enter the War of 1812?   They were eager to fight in a war. √ They wanted Canada.   They believed England would not fight.   They wanted to free American sailors.

4. Make a list of the topic headings of the first story as given in the text. Use your book to do so.

5. Turn to a map of the War of 1812. Check the following: **Yes**   **No**

a. General Hull went on from Detroit into Canada.   [ ]   [√]

b. General Harrison remained at Detroit.   [ ]   [√]

c. The British went to Washington, D.C.   [√]   [ ]

d. The British went north from Baltimore to Pennsylvania.   [ ]   [√]

e. Andrew Jackson marched his soldiers to New Orleans.   [√]   [ ]

f. The British came to New Orleans by boat.   [√]   [ ]

g. The Americans went from Lake Champlain to Montreal.   [ ]   [√]

6. Put the figure *1* before the thing which happened first, and the figure *2* before the thing which happened later.

[_ _*1*_ _] The Barbary Wars   [_ _*2*_ _] The War of 1812

Exercises in Organization. The children give brief topical recitations on the topic headings that they copied. (See 4 above.)

The teacher makes a brief outline of the second story, and the children point out on the map the action under each subhead in her outline.

Tests on the Entire Unit

Test of Place Sense. Pass double-sized outline maps of the United States. Give the following directions:

1. Draw a square where the District of Columbia is.

2. Put the figure *1* where Washington, D. C., is.

3. Draw a wavy line (〰〰〰) to represent the Potomac River.

4. Put the letter *O* where Oregon is.

5. Draw another wavy line (〰〰〰) to represent the Columbia River.

6. Put the initials *N O* where New Orleans is.

7. Write the word *Erie* in Lake Erie.

8. Pass to the wall map of the world and show where Tripoli is.

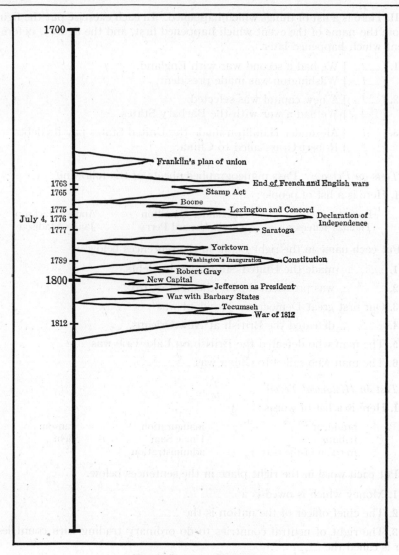

Time Chart — Unit One

Tests of Time Sense. Pass mimeographed sheets of the following:

I. Here are some names of persons. In each exercise put the figure *1* before the name of the person who did his great work first, and the figure *2* before the name of the person who did his great work later.

1. [__*1*__] Alexander Hamilton   3. [__*2*__] James Madison
   [__*2*__] Oliver Hazard Perry   [__*1*__] Captain Robert Gray

2. [__*2*__] Andrew Jackson
   [__*1*__] Thomas Jefferson

II. Here is a list of things which happened. In each exercise put the figure *1* before the name of the event which happened first, and the figure *2* before the event which happened later.

1. [__2__] We had a second war with England.
   [__1__] Washington was made president.

2. [__1__] A new capital was selected.
   [__2__] We had a war with the Barbary States.

3. [__1__] Alexander Hamilton made the United States pay its debts.
   [__2__] Robert Gray sailed to China.

Tests on Persons. Pass mimeographed sheets of the following:

I. Here is a list of people:

Robert Gray	Alexander Hamilton	Andrew Jackson
Thomas Jefferson	Oliver Hazard Perry	James Madison

Put each name in the right blank in the sentences below:

1. _____ made the United States pay its debts.
2. _____ was president during the War of 1812.
3. Our first great Democratic president was _____.
4. _____ defeated the British at New Orleans.
5. The man who defeated the British on Lake Erie was _____.
6. The man who sailed to China was _____.

Test on Historical Terms

I. Here is a list of words:

president	inauguration	ransom
tribute	Uncle Sam	debt
freedom of the seas	administration	

Put each word in the right place in the sentences below.

1. Money which is owed is a _____.
2. The chief officer of the nation is the _____.
3. The right of neutral countries to do ordinary trading with countries at war is called the _____.
4. The years during which a man is president are his _____.
5. Money paid to set someone free is _____.
6. Money paid to keep people from attacking us is _____.
7. The _____ is the occasion when a man begins to act as president.
8. The United States government is sometimes called _____.

II. Here is another list of words:

neutral	White House	capitol
treasurer	impressment	political party
Democratic party	capital city	

Do the same.

1. The city from which the government of a country is carried on is the
_ _ _ _ _ _.

2. A man who takes care of the money for a society or a nation is the
_ _ _ _ _ _.

3. People who do not take either one side or the other in a quarrel are
_ _ _ _ _ _.

4. The house in which the president lives is the _ _ _ _ _ _.

5. The party of Thomas Jefferson was the _ _ _ _ _ _.

6. The building in which the lawmakers of the United States have their
meetings is called the _ _ _ _ _ _.

7. Forcing a man into military or naval service contrary to law is _ _ _ _ _ _.

8. Men who unite to elect some of their members to government offices
make up a _ _ _ _ _ _.

Comprehension Test on Unit One

Check the right answer.

1. The first president of the United States was   Thomas Jefferson.
Benjamin Franklin.   √ George Washington.

2. We fought England instead of France in 1812 because   √ we could
not get at France.   we had nothing against France.   we wanted to
fight England.

3. The greatest thing that Alexander Hamilton did was   to fight with
Aaron Burr.   to act as treasurer.   √ to make the new nation pay its
debts.

4. The War of 1812 was really   a war to gain more land.   a war
to gain sea power.   √ a second war for independence.

5. The lasting capital of the United States was placed in   √ Washington, D.C.   New York.   Philadelphia.

6. The claim of the United States to the Oregon country was based on
the work of   √ Captain Robert Gray.   Francis Drake.   George
Rogers Clark.

7. The war with the Barbary pirates was fought because   √ they
robbed our ships.   they took our lands.   they impressed our sailors.

8. The first president to belong to the Democratic party was   George
Washington.   John Adams.   √ Thomas Jefferson.

9. We did not want a war with France because   we liked the French
people.   √ France had helped us in the Revolution.   France had a
larger navy than we had.

10. What is the title of Unit One? _ _ _ _ _ _

**Are there any children now ready to be transferred from the lower group
to the group of independent readers?**

Unit Two · *How the United States moved Westward to the Pacific*   [6 Weeks

A

STORY 1. THE FIRST SETTLERS BEYOND THE MOUNTAINS · STORY 2. THE LOUISIANA PURCHASE   [1 Week

[Stories treated separately for conversational approach, the reading periods, and the discussion; for other activities, both together]

Conversational Approach (First Story)

Volunteers have modeled in the sand table continental United States, showing mountain chains and principal rivers. They mark the Wilderness Road and Braddock's Road, Pittsburgh, Cincinnati, Louisville, and the Cumberland Gap.

The class gathers about the sand-table model and shows the routes that would naturally be chosen by persons wishing to go beyond the mountains. After returning to their seats they discuss possible methods or means of travel in the wilderness.

Reading and Study

The Reading Periods (First Story)

Independent Readers

This group reads the entire story through silently, as given in their text. Then they test their comprehension by study-guide questions furnished by the teacher or by the text. Reading from other texts may follow.

Lower Group

The teacher tells the story orally to this group, writing on the board the most important names as she mentions them. Children practice the pronunciations.

Then the teacher and these children read together the story as given in the

TEXTS

BEARD and BAGLEY, *First Book in American History*, 163–164.

BURNHAM and JACK, *Growth of Our Country*, 18–20, 76–80.

CLARK, *Westward to the Pacific*, 61–71, 81–100.

KELTY, *Growth of the American People and Nation*, 81–87.

NIDA, *Following the Frontier*, 39–43, 45–48, 96–104.

EXTENSIVE READING

BEEBY, *How the World Grows Smaller*, 20–32, 98–107.

BRIGHAM, *From Trail to Railway*, 67–70.

HART, *How Our Grandfathers Lived*, 97–98, 109–113.

INGRAHAM, *Story of Democracy*, 215–221.

SOUTHWORTH, *Builders of Our Country*, II : 135–136.

STONE and FICKETT, *Days and Deeds a Hundred Years Ago*, 16–35, 68–77.

VOLLINTINE, *Making of America*, 14–16, 75–91, 106–115, 120–130.

text. The teacher directs the silent reading, section by section, by such questions as "Why did the frontier keep moving westward?"

This process is continued throughout the entire story. Children then test themselves by the study-guide questions at the end of the story.

OTHER BOOKS

FAIRGRIEVE and YOUNG, *The World*, 16–20.

READING FOR RECREATION (*Both Groups*)

CATHERWOOD, *Rocky Fork.*

GROSVENOR, *Strange Stories of the Great Valley.*

HARTMAN, *These United States.*

OTIS, *Benjamin of Ohio.*

PETERSHAM, *Story Book of Transportation.*

The Discussion (*First Story*)

Children answer the study-guide questions as fully as possible. If important phases are omitted, they question one another in order to bring out the most important points.

The teacher writes on the board the words *frontier, pioneers, flatboat, pack horse.* Children discuss the meanings.

Conversational Approach (*Second Story*)

Children gather once more around the sand-table model. "When these people at last do succeed in making little farms, what will they do with their hogs and tobacco and wheat?" Children try to determine possible routes and means of transportation. The route by river is the only feasible one.

"But who owns the land west of the Mississippi and at its mouth? Suppose that Spain refused to allow any American flatboats to come down the river. What could the Americans do?" Children speculate as to what might be done.

"Our story today is about this very problem."

Reading and Study

The Reading Periods (*Second Story*)

Independent Readers

TEXTS

BARKER, DODD, WEBB, *Our Nation Grows Up*, 29–41.

BEARD and BAGLEY, *First Book in American History*, 164–179.

Lower Group

The teacher first tells the story orally to this group, writing on the board the most important new words as she mentions them. Children practice the pronunciations.

Then the teacher and this group read

4 0 6 5 1

BURNHAM and JACK, *Growth of Our Country,* 20–32.
CLARK, *Westward to the Pacific,* 146–160.
HALLECK and FRANTZ, *Makers of Our Nation,* 142–151.
KELTY, *Growth of the American People and Nation,* 88–98.
MCGUIRE and PHILLIPS, *Building Our Country,* 5–7.
NIDA, *Following the Frontier,* 217–230.
SMALLIDGE and PAXSON, *Builders of Our Nation,* 367–383.
WOODBURN and MORAN, *Makers of America,* 195–207.

EXTENSIVE READING

BURNHAM, *Hero Tales from History,* 247–258.
COE, *Makers of the Nation,* 198–212.
DAKIN, *Great Rivers of the World,* 78–79, 108–110.
DAVIDSON, *Founders and Builders of Our Nation,* 114–115.
EVANS, *America First,* 244–259.
FAIRBANKS, *Western United States,* 151–161.
FARIS, *Real Stories from Our History,* 100–109.
GORDY, *Leaders in Making America,* 255–263.
LEFFERTS, *American Leaders,* I : 276–288.
MONTGOMERY, *Beginners' American History,* 168–170.
SOUTHWORTH, *Builders of Our Country,* II : 113–114.
UHRBROCK and OWENS, *Famous Americans,* 158–166.
VOLLINTINE, *Making of America,* 130–144.

together the story as given in the text. The teacher directs the silent reading, section by section, by such questions as "What products did the Westerners raise?"

This procedure is continued throughout the story. Children then test themselves by the study-guide questions at the end of the story.

OTHER BOOKS

EGGLESTON, *Stories of Great Americans,* 90–96.
TAPPAN, *American History Stories for Very Young Readers,* 102–109.

READING FOR RECREATION

MEADER, *Down the Big River.*
MEIGS, *As the Crow Flies.*
RADFORD, *Marie of Old New Orleans.*
SABIN, *Opening the West with Lewis and Clark.*

The Discussion (Second Story)

Children answer the study-guide questions as completely as possible. Those who have read from several books may have new material to contribute.

The teacher writes on the board the words *purchase* and *territory.* Children discuss the meanings.

Multisensory Aids

Children and teacher talk over together the pictures in the text, pointing out features of historical and geographical significance.

They turn to a map of the Louisiana Purchase. They compare it in size with the rest of the United States. "To whom does the land west of the Louisiana Purchase belong? Can you see the island of Santo Domingo? Why is it named on this map?"

AUDIO-VISUAL MATERIALS OBTAINABLE

Chronicles of America Photoplays: The Frontier Woman.
Compton's Pictured Teaching Materials: *Land Transportation*, Plate V, 1, 2.
EASTMAN. Classroom Films: New Orleans.
National Geographic Magazine, LVII, 398, 402, 473, 476; Plates X, XI (April, 1930).
Society for Visual Education. Picturols: The First Westward Movement, The Louisiana Purchase.
Society for Visual Education. Schoolfilms: Breaking through the Appalachians, Settling the Ohio Valley, Louisiana Purchase and the Lewis and Clark Expedition.
Yale Pageant Educational Slides: 164–166, 636–639, 643–648.

Music. Play selections from Ferdie Grofé's *Mississippi Suite.*

General Activities

Creative Activities: Group and Individual, Correlated with Other Subjects or Voluntary Projects

A volunteer constructs a Conestoga wagon and explains how it is made.

A volunteer carves from soap a loaded pack horse.

A committee writes a series of letters which a pioneer settler might have written to his family in the East, telling of the progress he has made; and from his family to him telling of their preparations to join him.

A committee begins to make a list of new states added to the Union, with the date of each, beginning with Vermont, Kentucky, Tennessee, Ohio.

Volunteers report on the Society of the Cincinnati and on the life of Toussaint L'Ouverture. (See a children's encyclopedia.)

Some children may wish to draw decorative designs for iron railings or doors, like those in New Orleans.

The teacher may read to the children the poem "Sacajawea" from Stevenson's *Poems of American History* (340).

A traveler who has used a pack horse tells his experiences to the children. A traveler to New Orleans describes the city.

A committee reads to the class the dramatization given in Bird and Starling's *Historical Plays for Children* (173–198).

Each child begins to make a map of the Westward movement. On it he shows the Louisiana Purchase.

The teacher reads to the children selections from Parkman's *Oregon Trail.* The class continues the time line.

Applications to Present-Day Conditions

Are there any regions in the world today in which the only people are explorers? any regions in which the only white people are traders? any in which the settlers are pioneers?

Find the present population of Pittsburgh, Cincinnati, and Louisville. (See the World Almanac.)

Do any farmers still have trouble in getting their products to markets? Why? [*Because of bad roads.*]

Is the United States today allowed to trade in any foreign port which it chooses?

Under what governments are Santo Domingo and Haiti today?

Count the number of states or parts of states that have been made from the Louisiana Purchase.

Exercises in Reasoning

After the War of 1812 how did the United States turn its back on Europe? Why were so many people eager to leave the East?

Do you think you would have liked to move West during the early days? What things should you have liked? What things should you not have liked?

Can you explain this statement: "The first great change caused by the Revolutionary War was independence; the second was the opening up of the West"? Why was this considered so important?

Why did not the pioneers try to send their goods to New York and Boston instead of to New Orleans?

Could the owner get his flatboat back home again?

Why was the United States afraid to have Napoleon as a neighbor?

Why did many of the Eastern states not like the idea of adding a huge territory like Louisiana out of which many new states might later be made?

Drill Games

Place names are best drilled upon at the map: *Rocky Mountains, Missouri River, Wilderness Road.*

Drill cards for the games may be made as follows:

frontier	↔	where settlement ends and wilderness begins
flatboat	↔	a boat with a flat bottom
pack horse	↔	horse used to carry bags and boxes of goods
pioneers	↔	the first people to come into a region
purchase	↔	that which is bought
territory	↔	a large tract of land not yet a state
Lewis and Clark	↔	explorers of the upper Missouri country
1803	↔	date of the Louisiana Purchase

Children drill one another in small groups in preparation for the drill games.

Testing

Tests of Understanding are given in Kelty's *The Growth of the American People and Nation,* pp. 87, 98.

Tests of Reasoning and Skills

1. In each of the following put the figure *1* before the name of the people who reached the West first, and the figure *2* before the name of those who came later:

a. [_ _2_ _] traders   b. [_ _1_ _] pioneer settlers
  [_ _1_ _] explorers   [_ _2_ _] farmers

2. In the following list, check all the means of travel used at this time in the West:

stagecoach	camels	railways
√ flatboat	√ wagons	√ on foot
√ pack horses	automobiles	

3. Check the best answer: The chief reason for buying the Louisiana territory was   to make the United States twice as large as before.   √ to give the Westerners a chance to send out their products.   to push France away from the Mississippi River.   to get land enough to make many new states.

4. Turn to a map of the Louisiana Purchase. Did the Louisiana Purchase reach as far as the Pacific Ocean?   Yes [ ]   No [√]

5. Turn to the table of contents.   Under what subheading do you find these two stories? _____

Exercises in Organization. The entire class attempts to make independent outlines of the first story, using the topic headings as guides. The teacher prepares the outline of the second story. Children give one summary sentence about each subheading in the two stories.

A

STORY 3. ROADS AND CANALS · STORY 4. STEAMBOATS [1 *Week*

[Stories treated separately for reading and discussion; for other activities, both together]

Conversational Approach

"When you have been driving around the country, have you ever struck bad roads? What kind of roads were they? You can perhaps imagine, then, what kind of roads there were in the West in the early days. Who do you suppose paid for building the Western roads?

"Which is cheaper, to move goods by water or overland? Why? Can you see any possible way to move goods from the Great Lakes to New York most of the way by water?" Children study the sand-table model in order to decide. "Our story tells how an all-water route was made."

Reading and Study

The Reading Periods (First Story)

Independent Readers

TEXTS

BARKER, DODD, WEBB, *Our Nation Grows Up*, 74–76, 78–81.
BEARD and BAGLEY, *First Book in American History*, 212–213, 224–227.
BURNHAM and JACK, *Growth of Our Country*, 63–67.
CLARK, *Westward to the Pacific*, 100–106.
HALLECK and FRANTZ, *Makers of Our Nation*, 159–167, 173–176.

Lower Group

The teacher tells the story orally to this group, writing on the board the most important names as she mentions them. Children practice the pronunciations.

Then the teacher and these children read together the story as given in the text. The teacher directs the silent reading, section by section, by such questions as "Why had no roads been built to the West?"

KELTY, *Growth of the American People and Nation*, 99–110.

McGUIRE and PHILLIPS, *Adventuring in Young America*, 303–309, 316–324, 328–332.

McGUIRE and PHILLIPS, *Building Our Country*, 118–119.

NIDA, *Following the Frontier*, 55–62, 164–178, 191–195, 201–203.

SMALLIDGE and PAXSON, *Builders of Our Nation*, 512–520, 525–530.

WOOBDURN and MORAN, *Makers of America*, 211–212, 215–220.

EXTENSIVE READING

BEEBY, *How the World Grows Smaller*, 74–80.

BRIGHAM, *From Trail to Railway*, 40–52, 87–97.

COE, *Makers of the Nation*, 241–245.

EVANS, *America First*, 278–282.

FARIS, *Real Stories from Our History*, 110–115, 134–168.

FOOTE and SKINNER, *Makers and Defenders of America*, 219–223.

GORDY, *American Leaders and Heroes*, 246–252.

HART, *How Our Grandfathers Lived*, 102–104.

LEFFERTS, *American Leaders*, II : 38–51.

MOWRY, *American Inventions and Inventors*, 215–222.

SOUTHWORTH, *Builders of Our Country*, II : 176–179.

TAPPAN, *Travelers and Traveling*, 89–93.

UHRBROCK and OWENS, *Famous Americans*, 223–229.

VOLLINTINE, *Making of America*, 115–162.

Children read silently and answer orally. When the entire story has been read in this manner, they test themselves by the study-guide questions at the end of the story.

OTHER BOOKS

FAIRGRIEVE and YOUNG, *The World*, 20–27.

READING FOR RECREATION

ABBOTT, *Low Bridge.*

EGGLESTON, *The Last of the Flatboats.*

MULLER, *How They Carried the Goods.*

ORTON, *Treasure in the Little Trunk.*

The Discussion (*First Story*)

Children answer the study-guide questions as fully as possible. The teacher checks firmly those children who read rapidly but inaccurately, and who have run through four or five books but who still cannot answer the study-guide questions.

The teacher writes on the board the words *canal, turnpike, Erie Canal, National Road.* Children discuss their significance.

The Reading Periods (*Second Story*)

Independent Readers

TEXTS

BARKER, DODD, WEBB, *Our Nation Grows Up*, 76–78.

BEARD and BAGLEY, *First Book in American History*, 220–224.

BURNHAM and JACK, *Growth of Our Country*, 59–63.

CLARK, *Westward to the Pacific*, 106–112.

Lower Group

The teacher tells the story orally to this group, writing on the board the most important words as she mentions them. Children practice the pronunciations.

Then the teacher and these children read together the story as given in the text. The teacher directs the silent reading, section by section, by such questions

HALLECK and FRANTZ, *Makers of Our Nation*, 167–173.

KELTY, *Growth of the American People and Nation*, 111–120.

McGUIRE and PHILLIPS, *Adventuring in Young America*, 324–326.

McGUIRE and PHILLIPS, *Building Our Country*, 115–118.

NIDA, *Following the Frontier*, 155–162, 179–190.

SMALLIDGE and PAXSON, *Builders of Our Nation*, 520–525.

WOODBURN and MORAN, *Makers of America*, 212–215.

EXTENSIVE READING

BEEBY, *How the World Grows Smaller*, 91–97.

BURNHAM, *Hero Tales from History*, 270–273.

CHANDLER and CHITWOOD, *Makers of American History*, 187–191.

COE, *Makers of the Nation*, 225–232.

DAVIDSON, *Founders and Builders of Our Nation*, 130–136.

FARIS, *Real Stories from Our History*, 220–249.

FOOTE and SKINNER, *Makers and Defenders of America*, 213–218.

GORDY, *Leaders in Making America*, 269–275.

HART, *How Our Grandfathers Lived*, 99–102.

LEFFERTS, *American Leaders*, II : 16–37.

McFEE, *Stories of American Inventions*, 14–28.

MONTGOMERY, *Beginners' American History*, 171–178.

PARKMAN, *Conquests of Invention*, 222–241.

SOUTHWORTH, *Builders of Our Country*, II : 127–134.

UHRBROCK and OWENS, *Famous Americans*, 215–220.

VOLLINTINE, *Making of America*, 145–150.

as "What were some of the early plans for moving boats?"

Children read silently and answer orally. When the entire story has been read in this manner, they test themselves by the study-guide questions at the end of the story.

OTHER BOOKS

BALDWIN, *Fifty Famous People*, 146–149.

CHAMBERLAIN, *How We Travel*, 161–170.

EGGLESTON, *Stories of Great Americans*, 96–101.

READING FOR RECREATION

BLACKIE, *A Book of Engines*.

BUSH AND WADDELL, *How We Have Conquered Distance*.

CARTWRIGHT, *Boys' Book of Ships*.

DUKELOW and WEBSTER, *The Ship Book*.

GRANT, *Story of the Ship*.

McFEE, *Story of Robert Fulton*.

Picture Book of Ships (Macmillan).

PRYOR, *The Steamship Book*.

RUSSELL, *Snowy for Luck*.

TOUSEY, *Steamboat Billy*.

The Discussion (Second Story)

Children answer the study-guide questions. The teacher makes an effort to draw children of the lower-ability group into the discussion.

Multisensory Aids

Children and teacher talk over the pictures in the text, pointing out features of historical or geographical significance.

They turn to a map of railroads and canals in 1850, name the states in which there are as yet no railroads or canals, and point out the Erie Canal and the National Road.

AUDIO-VISUAL MATERIALS OBTAINABLE

Building America : Transportation.

Compton's Pictured Teaching Materials : *Water and Air Transportation*, Plates IV, VII, 1 ; *Land Transportation:* Plate V, 2, 3 ; Plate VI, 1, 3 ; Plate VIII.

EASTMAN. Classroom Films : The Mohawk Valley.

GABRIEL (Ed.). Pageant of America : V, 85.

McKINLEY. Illustrated Topics for American History: S 26, 30.
Keystone Views: 108, 109, 110.
Society for Visual Education. Picturol: Canals.
Society for Visual Eucation (SPENCER). Beginnings, Waterways, Primitive methods; Rivers, Canals; Steamboats.
Society for Visual Education. Schoolfilms: Canals in United States History, The Steamboat in United States History.
Yale Pageant Educational Slides: 142–147, 149, 154, 226, 227, 229, 546, 553, 571, 682, 683, 1833.

Music. Children sing "Wagon Wheels."
The teacher sings to the children songs of the Erie Canal from Lomax's *American Ballads and Folk Songs.*

General Activities

Creative Activities: Group and Individual, Correlated with Other Subjects or Voluntary Projects

A committee constructs a corduroy road on the sand table.

The teacher may read to the children some of Dickens's descriptions of coach travel; for example, from *Pickwick Papers.*

Volunteers draw scenes of an inn of the period.

A committee makes a graph comparing the four-mile-an-hour travel over bad roads and the ten-mile-an-hour travel over the National Road with rates of travel today.

A committee constructs in the sand table a model of a lock canal.

A volunteer prepares a physical map which explains why the Erie Canal was built just where it was.

A volunteer explains what makes a steamboat move through the water. He may use a model or pictures in his explanation.

A news commentator prepares a radio speech broadcasting the news of the *Clermont's* trial trip.

Children who have forded streams describe their experiences.

A volunteer draws a poster advertising the first trip of the *Clermont.*

A volunteer explains to the class the tabulation on canals given in the World Book Encyclopedia ("Canals").

A committee reads to the class the dramatization given in Hubbard's *Little American History Plays* (161–165).

The class makes a picture collection of canal boats, locks, early roads and vehicles, and early steamboats. These are displayed on the bulletin board.

The teacher reads to the children selections from Mark Twain's *Life on the Mississippi.*

Children add the Erie Canal and the National Road to the map begun on page 301.

The class continues the time line.

Application to Present-Day Conditions

Could automobiles do much better over such roads than the wagons did?

Are corduroy roads anywhere in existence today? Are fords in use anywhere?

Does the national government pay any part of the expense of building roads today?

Have you ever driven over a toll road or a toll bridge?

What are the most famous canals in the world today? [*Panama and Suez.*]

Is the Erie Canal in use today?

How much does it cost today to move a ton of goods from Buffalo to New York? (Ask the local railway agent.) Compare with the $100 rate before the Erie Canal, and the $18 rate by way of the canal in early days.

Are all roads highways? (See a children's encyclopedia.)

Are wood-burning steamers in use anywhere today? [*In Alaska; on the rivers of Africa.*]

Have you ever heard the expression *low bridge*? How did it originate?

Exercises in Reasoning

Why were few corduroy roads built west of the Mississippi? [*Because of lack of timber.*]

Why was each state not willing to pay for building a good road to the West across its territory? [*People from other states also would benefit.*]

Why did most people think the national government had no right to build roads? [*It would be done by tax money, some of which would come from states not directly benefited.*]

Why do better roads help people from different parts of the country to understand one another better?

In what way was the Erie Canal an offset to the National Road?

The Erie Canal was only four feet deep. Do you think it deserved its title "the Big Ditch"?

Why might one expect that many cities would grow up along the Erie Canal?

Why was the Erie Canal built to Lake Erie instead of to Lake Ontario?

Should you expect the New England farmers to be glad that the Erie Canal was built?

Which do you think was the greater invention, the building of a steam engine or putting that steam engine to work in running a ship?

How did the invention of the steamboat help to throw sailors out of work?

Drill Games

Place names are best drilled upon at the map: *Erie Canal, National Road.*

Drill cards are made as follows:

De Witt Clinton	⇔	the governor of New York who had the Erie Canal dug
turnpike	⇔	a road on which there are toll gates
canal	⇔	a channel dug between two natural waterways
Robert Fulton	⇔	inventor of the steamboat
Clermont	⇔	the first commercially successful steamboat
1807	⇔	the year when the steamboat was invented

Testing

Tests of Understanding are suggested in Kelty's *The Growth of the American People and Nation*, pp. 110, 120.

Tests of Reasoning and Skills

1. Can you make up a sentence telling what effect ease of travel has upon the settling of a new country? _____

2. Finish this sentence: Moving goods by water is easier than moving goods by land because _____.

3. In the following list put the figure *1* before the method of travel that men used earliest in the world, the figure *2* before the method used next, and so on.

[__2__] horses   [__1__] on foot   [__4__] canals
       [__3__] wagons   [__5__] steamboat

4. From the story, do you think that Fulton himself invented all the machinery used in the steamboat?   Yes [ ]   No [✓]

5. Turn to a map of roads, railroads, and canals in 1850.
Does the map show any road? If so, show here how it is marked. _____
Does the map show any railroads? If so, tell here how they are marked. _____
Does the map show any canals? If so, show here how they are marked. _____

Exercises in Organization. Children copy the topic headings in the first story and tell a few facts about each.

They make summary sentences for the second story, similar to the summary sentences made previously.

A

STORY 5. RAILROADS · STORY 6. FARMING MACHINERY [1 Week

[Stories treated separately for conversational approach, the reading periods, and the discussion; for other activities, both together]

Conversational Approach (First Story)

Children point out on the map which parts of the Western lands could not be reached by steamboats. "Would it pay the United States in the early 1800's to build roads there? Then it seems as if settlement there would have to be very slow. Can you think of any invention which would speed up settlement in this area? Our story today will tell us."

Reading and Study

The Reading Periods (First Story)

Independent Readers

TEXTS

BARKER, DODD, WEBB, *Our Nation Grows Up*, 81–84.
BEARD and BAGLEY, *First Book in American History*, 227–228.

Lower Group

The teacher tells the story orally to this group, writing on the board the names of the most important persons and places as she mentions them. Children practice the pronunciations.

BURNHAM and JACK, *Growth of Our Country,* 67–70.

HALLECK and FRANTZ, *Makers of Our Nation,* 176–180.

KELTY, *Growth of the American People and Nation,* 121–128.

MCGUIRE and PHILLIPS, *Building Our Country,* 107–115.

NIDA, *Following the Frontier,* 205–214.

SMALLIDGE and PAXSON, *Builders of Our Nation,* 532–536.

WOODBURN and MORAN, *Makers of America,* 220–224.

EXTENSIVE READING

BEEBY, *How the World Grows Smaller,* 145–153.

BRIGHAM, *From Trail to Railway,* 53–56, 98–106.

COE, *Makers of the Nation,* 233–240.

FARIS, *Real Stories from Our History,* 250–282.

FARIS, *Where Our History Was Made,* II : 268–275.

FOOTE and SKINNER, *Makers and Defenders of America,* 223–229.

GORDY, *Leaders in Making America,* 278–281.

LEFFERTS, *American Leaders,* II : 52–67.

SOUTHWORTH, *Builders of Our Country,* II : 136–139.

STONE and FICKETT, *Days and Deeds a Hundred Years Ago,* 112–121.

TAPPAN, *Travelers and Traveling,* 1–14.

UHRBROCK and OWENS, *Famous Americans,* 230–237.

Then the teacher and this group read together the story as given in the text. The teacher guides the silent reading, section by section, by such questions as "What were the earliest kinds of railroads ever used?"

Children read silently and answer orally. When the entire story has been read in this manner, they test themselves by the study-guide questions at the end of the story.

OTHER BOOKS

SMITH, *Railroad Book.*

READING FOR RECREATION

BLACKIE, *A Book of Engines.*

BUSH and WADDELL, *How We Have Conquered Distance.*

COOLIDGE and DI BONA, *Story of Steam.*

DALGLIESH, *America Travels.*

GABRIEL, *Book of Trains.*

HENDERSON, *Trains — Stories and Pictures.*

HOSKINS, *The Iron Horse.*

MEIGS, *The Wonderful Locomotive.*

PETERSHAM, *Story Book of Transportation.*

Picture Book of Travel (Macmillan).

PRYOR, *The Train Book.*

SWIFT, *Little Black Nose.*

The Discussion *(First Story)*

Children answer the study-guide questions as completely as possible. The teacher notices particularly the progress toward accuracy made by the children who read rapidly but inaccurately.

The teacher writes on the board the words *locomotive, transportation, era.* Children discuss the meanings.

Conversational Approach *(Second Story)*

"How would most of the settlers in the Mississippi Valley earn their living? What kind of farming implements did the early colonists have in our country? Are such implements in use anywhere today? [*For trimming the edges of lawns, or for cutting grass in small fields or on a railway right of way.*] Would it do a settler much good now to have a hundred acres of good Western land if he had to till it with such instruments? Why not? What, then, is needed before Western farms can be profitable? Our story today tells us how the problem was solved.

"Have you ever seen great machines working on a farm? Describe them."

Reading and Study

The Reading Periods (Second Story)

Independent Readers

TEXTS

BARKER, DODD, WEBB, *Our Nation Grows Up*, 88–92.

BEARD and BAGLEY, *First Book in American History*, 217–218.

BURNHAM and JACK, *Growth of Our Country*, 72–74.

HALLECK and FRANTZ, *Makers of Our Nation*, 181–183.

KELTY, *Growth of the American People and Nation*, 129–136.

MCGUIRE and PHILLIPS, *Building Our Country*, 45–49.

SMALLIDGE and PAXSON, *Builders of Our Nation*, 505–510.

WOODBURN and MORAN, *Makers of America*, 322–324.

EXTENSIVE READING

BURNHAM, *Hero Tales from History*, 279–282.

CHANDLER and CHITWOOD, *Makers of American History*, 251–254.

COE, *Makers of the Nation*, 356–360.

DAVIDSON, *Founders and Builders of Our Nation*, 145–151.

FOOTE and SKINNER, *Makers and Defenders of America*, 305–308.

LEFFERTS, *American Leaders*, II : 68–80.

MCFEE, *Stories of American Inventions*, 29–49.

PARKMAN, *Conquests of Invention*, 8–26.

SOUTHWORTH, *Builders of Our Country*, II : 249–251.

TAPPAN, *Heroes of Progress*, 20–29.

UHRBROCK and OWENS, *Famous Americans*, 239–247.

Lower Group

The teacher tells the story orally to these children, writing on the board the most important words as she mentions them. Children practice the pronunciations.

Then the teacher and this group read together the story as given in the text. The teacher guides the silent reading, section by section, by such questions as "Why could large farms not be worked?"

Children read silently and answer orally. When the entire story has been read in this manner, they test themselves by the study-guide questions at the end of the story.

READING FOR RECREATION

BEATY, *How We Farm.*

WATSON, *Story of Bread.*

WILDER, *Farmer Boy.*

The Discussion (Second Story)

Children answer the study-guide questions as fully as possible.

The teacher tries especially to clear up misapprehensions as to farm life and machinery on the part of city children.

Multisensory Aids

Children and teacher talk over together the pictures in the text, pointing out features of geographic and historical significance. They turn again to the railway map of 1850 and note advances made.

AUDIO-VISUAL MATERIALS OBTAINABLE

Building America : Food, Transportation.

Compton's Pictured Teaching Materials : *Land Transportation*, Plate IX ; *Food*, Plate IV, 3, 4 ; *Trade*, Plate II, 4 ; *American Colonies*, Plate III, 4.

GABRIEL (Ed.). Pageant of America: III, 114–141, 207–210, 216–220.
Keystone Views: 104–106, 112, 295–297.
LEHMANN. Historical Pictures: L. H. 225.
MCKINLEY. Illustrated Topics for American History: S. 26, 28.
MCKINLEY. Illustrated Topics for Mediæval and Modern History: M M 26.
Society for Visual Education. Picturols: Railroads, Bridges.
Society for Visual Education. Schoolfilm: Railroads in United States History.
Yale Pageant Educational Slides: 148, 149, 235–238, 506, 555, 658–660, 686, 687.

General Activities

Creative Activities: Group and Individual, Correlated with Other Subjects or Voluntary Projects

The class makes a picture collection of early railways and early farming implements. The pictures are mounted on the bulletin board.

A committee constructs on the sand table a "railroad" like those used from the mines to the port towns in England.

A volunteer reports on the life of James Watt.

A volunteer brings to class a model of a steam engine and explains how it works. Another shows the class his toy locomotive.

The teacher reads to the children John G. Saxe's "Rhyme of the Rail."

An aged person in the community tells his memories of early railway travel.

A committee makes a graph showing the number of people engaged in farming at the time of the Revolution; the number today. (For today, see World Almanac. Compare with total population.)

The class visits the local museum to observe early farming implements, and a local hardware store to observe modern farming implements. Where possible, a visit is made to a farm to see a reaper and binder.

A volunteer explains the poster of the evolution of travel as given in the World Book Encyclopedia, under "Railroad."

The class continues the time line.

Application to Present-Day Conditions

Compare the number of miles of railroads in the United States with the mileage of other countries. (World Almanac.)

Is the Baltimore and Ohio Railroad still in existence?

How do railways carry baggage nowadays? freight? Compare with the first railroads.

What is a narrow-gauge railroad? a standard-gauge railroad? (See *Railroad* in a children's encyclopedia.)

Can you secure a railway map of your own state? What sections have not been reached by railways? Is it likely that railways ever will be built to them? Why not?

Are sickles ever used nowadays? Where?

Does the International Harvesting Company sell any of its machines in your community?

Is there an agricultural society in your community?

Exercises in Reasoning

Why does steam raise the lid of a teakettle?

How did it happen that Baltimore was more interested in building railroads than most other cities were at that time?

Why do you suppose the engine built in New York was called the *De Witt Clinton?*

Notice that the early railroad coaches looked like wagons or stagecoaches, and the earliest automobiles looked like carriages. Can you explain why?

Why could large factories never have been built if there were no railways?

In what way do the cities depend on the farms and the farms depend on the cities?

Can reapers and binders be used on all kinds of fields?

Why did McCormick choose Chicago as the place for his factory?

In what way have all the inventions about which you have been reading helped men to control nature?

Why did the invention of the reaper give the railroads more to carry?

Drill Games

The location of Baltimore is best drilled upon at the map.

Drill cards are made as follows:

1830	⟷	date of the beginning of railroad-building
locomotive	⟷	the engine that pulls railway cars
transportation	⟷	carrying things from one place to another
era	⟷	a period of time
Baltimore and Ohio	⟷	the first American road to use a locomotive
Cyrus McCormick	⟷	the man who invented the reaping machine
reaper	⟷	a machine to cut grain
1831	⟷	date of the invention of the reaper

Children devise riddles from the drill cards and ask the riddles of one another.

Testing

Tests of Understanding are given in Kelty's *The Growth of the American People and Nation*, pp. 128, 136.

Tests of Reasoning and Skills

1. Make here a list of all the improvements and inventions mentioned in the last four stories which helped the rapid settlement of the Western lands. Use your book if you need to do so. ___[*Roads, steamship, railways, canals, reapers.*]___

2. In the following list, check the two events which took place at almost the same time:

invention of steamboat	digging the Erie Canal	√ building of railways
√ invention of reaper	making the National Road	Purchase of Louisiana

3. Tell in a sentence what effect the reaper had on the size of farms. _ _ _ _ _ _

4. On what page in the text can you find material about plows? _ _ _ _ _ _
Where did you look to find out? _ _ _[*In the index.*]_ _ _

Exercise in Organization. Children choose which of the two stories they wish to outline. The teacher helps those who cannot work alone.

A

STORY 7. LIFE ON THE FRONTIER · STORY 8. ANDREW JACKSON
STORY 9. PURCHASE OF FLORIDA   [*1 Week*

[For conversational approach, reading periods, and discussion, the first story is treated separately; then the second and third stories together; for other activities all three stories together]

Conversational Approach (*First Story*)

"Our story today tells us how these pioneers lived. In what ways was their life like camping out today? In what ways was it very different?"

Reading and Study

The Reading Periods (*First Story*)

Since much must be done this week, and since the first story is comparatively easy, all children begin independent reading immediately. The teacher goes about the room helping members of the lower group who encounter difficulties. Upon finishing the text all children test their comprehension by the study-guide questions furnished by the teacher or by the text.

Independent Readers

TEXTS

BEARD and BAGLEY, *First Book in American History*, 197.

BURNHAM and JACK, *Growth of Our Country*, 80–92.

CLARK, *Westward to the Pacific*, 112–129, 194–197.

KELTY, *Growth of the American People and Nation*, 137–150.

McGUIRE and PHILLIPS, *Adventuring in Young America*, 267–300.

McGUIRE and PHILLIPS, *Building Our Country*, 7, 86–94, 97–104.

NIDA, *Following the Frontier*, 63–76, 106–153 (selections).

EXTENSIVE READING

EVANS, *America First*, 260–264.

FARIS, *Real Stories from Our History*, 116–120.

FARIS, *Where Our History Was Made*, II: 178–182, 276–279.

GORDY, *Leaders in Making America*, 221–225.

VOLLINTINE, *Making of America*, 115–118, 163–169.

Lower Group

OTHER BOOKS

BLAISDELL and BALL, *American History for Little Folks*, 109–114.

BLAISDELL and BALL, *Child's Book of American History*, 138–143.

BLAISDELL and BALL, *Log Cabin Days*, 19–23.

BLAISDELL and BALL, *Pioneers of America*.

READING FOR RECREATION

ALTSHELER, *Young Trailers*.

BASS, *Stories of Early Times in the Great West*.

EVERSON and POWER, *Early Days in Ohio*.

FLETCHER, *Old Settler Stories*.

GREGOR, *Jim Mason, Backwoodsman*.

SWAN, *Frontier Days*.

WILDER, *Farmer Boy*.

The Discussion (First Story)   [In a Language Period

Children answer the study-guide questions. The teacher writes on the board the words *clearing* and *house-raising*. Children discuss the meanings.

Conversational Approach (Second and Third Stories)

"Why would some of the people in the East not want the people in the West to be allowed to vote? But the people in the West were given the vote for president when their states were admitted to the Union. What kind of man would they want for president? Do you know of any such man? Our story will tell us."

Reading and Study

The Reading Periods (Second and Third Stories)

[These two stories are read consecutively before any discussion is held]

Independent Readers

TEXTS

BARKER, DODD, WEBB, *Our Nation Grows Up*, 41–42, 65–71.

BEARD and BAGLEY, *First Book in American History*, 199–205.

BURNHAM and JACK, *Growth of Our Country*, 33–34, 94–106.

HALLECK and FRANTZ, *Makers of Our Nation*, 152–155, 155–157.

KELTY, *Growth of the American People and Nation*, 151–158, 159–164.

WOODBURN and MORAN, *Makers of America*, 207–210.

EXTENSIVE READING

BURNHAM, *Hero Tales from History*, 315–320.

CHANDLER and CHITWOOD, *Makers of American History*, 201–207.

COE, *Makers of the Nation*, 217–224.

DAVIDSON, *Founders and Builders of Our Nation*, 117–127.

EVANS, *America First*, 294–298.

FARIS, *Where Our History Was Made*, II: 314–317.

FOOTE and SKINNER, *Makers and Defenders of America*, 168–177.

GORDY, *American Leaders and Heroes*, 253–262.

MONTGOMERY, *Beginners' American History*, 184–194.

SOUTHWORTH, *Builders of Our Country*, II: 149–157.

Lower Group

The teacher tells both stories orally to the lower group, writing on the board the words most important for them to remember.

Then the teacher and these children read together the two stories, as given in the text. The teacher guides the silent reading, section by section, by such questions as "Why did men from the West want Andrew Jackson as president?"

Children read silently and answer orally. When both stories have been read in this manner, children test their comprehension by the study-guide questions at the end of the stories.

OTHER BOOKS

BALDWIN, *Fifty Famous People*, 75–78.

The Discussion (Second and Third Stories)   [In a Language Period

Children answer both sets of study-guide questions as fully as possible. The teacher writes on the board the words *invasion, boundary line, frontier settlements*. Children discuss the meanings.

Multisensory Aids

Children and teacher together talk over the pictures in the text, pointing out features of geographic and historical importance.

They turn to a map of the period and show East Florida, West Florida, and the Southwest Territory. They show that rivers from the Southwest Territory reach the Gulf through West Florida.

AUDIO-VISUAL MATERIALS OBTAINABLE

Compton's Pictured Teaching Materials: *Food*, Plate III, 1; *Trade*, Plate VI, 1, 2; Plate VIII, 4.

GABRIEL (Ed.). Pageant of America: III, 91–97, 106–111; XIII, 141–144.

Keystone Views: 103, 334, 337.

McKINLEY. Illustrated Topics for American History: S. 19.

Yale Pageant Educational Slides: 144, 541, 663–665, 702, 703, 741, 818.

Music. The teacher plays selections from Ryan's *Music for the Dances of the Pioneers.*

General Activities

Creative Activities: Group and Individual, Correlated with Other Subjects or Voluntary Projects

Pioneers tell the children stories of their experiences. Children interview their grandparents or other aged persons in order to get first-hand stories.

A committee constructs a "clearing" on the sand table.

Committees estimate the cost of farms of 40, 60, 80, 100, and 120 acres under the varying plans of purchase.

Volunteers draw a series of illustrations showing the successive waves of immigration into the West.

A committee makes a list of all the kinds of work done by the pioneers, and compares the list with the work that a family does today.

The class visits the local museum to see relics of pioneer life.

The teacher reads to the children a comparison of American and British farmers just before the War of 1812 as given in Counts's *Social Foundations of Education* (15–17). She also reads selections from such books as Hamlin Garland's *A Son of the Middle Border, A Daughter of the Middle Border, Trail Makers of the Middle Border.*

The class holds a spelling match, using the old-time rules.

Volunteers may wish to compose music or poems on phases of pioneer life.

Children collect pictures of Andrew Jackson's home, "The Hermitage." A traveler who has seen it describes it to the class.

Volunteers graph the figures showing the comparative costs of the Louisiana Territory and of Florida.

Children show East Florida and West Florida and the Southwest Territory on the map begun on page 283. They add Florida to the map begun on page 301.

The class continues the time line.

Application to Present-Day Conditions   [In a Language Period

What is a squatter? (See children's encyclopedia.) Are there any squatters nowadays?

What is a deed to land? Why is a deed necessary?

Do people today ever make smudges as protection against mosquitoes?

What disease do people who live near swamps suffer from today? [*Malaria.*] How do they treat it? [*With quinine.*] Where does quinine come from? Who discovered its use?

Is furniture ever put together today with wooden pegs?

What has happened to the wild passenger pigeon in America?

Is the West as a section still poorer than the East?

Sometimes today you hear people say that they are going to the shops and stores to do their trading. How did this expression originate?

Are our presidents in modern times men of the common people in the same sense that Jackson was?

Who are the Scotch-Irish? [*Scots living in northern Ireland, and their descendants.*]

Are men today given appointments to office because they are members of a certain political party? Is this system good for the country? What could be done to change it?

Ask a Democrat why the Democratic party holds a Jackson Day dinner each year.

Why has Florida never become a great cotton-growing state?

Why do many people go to Florida for the winter? [*See mean temperature.*]

Exercises in Reasoning   [In a Language Period

Was it wise to cut down all the trees in the Western lands?

Does a man pay more or less tax after he makes improvements on his land? (What are improvements?) Do you think he ought to pay more or less?

Why does draining swampy land help to kill off the mosquitoes?

Why was pioneer life particularly hard for the women?

Why would few of the pioneers work for wages?

Should you expect such pioneers to have much respect for "book learning"?

You often hear that the American spirit of today owes its hopefulness to the influence of the pioneers. Can you explain this?

Why was it harder to make people obey the laws on the frontier than in the older sections of the country?

Why do you suppose that Jackson chose to belong to Jefferson's Democratic party?

Why are not the men who can do the work best always given offices?

Do you think the United States had a right to take Florida?

Do you think the pioneers were happier than we are today?

What did Jackson mean by his slogan "Let the people rule"?

Drill Games

Game cards are made as follows:

clearing	⟷	a tract of land on which the trees have been cut down
house-raising	⟷	putting logs together to make a house
Andrew Jackson	⟷	the first president chosen from among the common people
"Old Hickory"	⟷	a nickname given to Andrew Jackson
boundary line	⟷	a line showing the limits of a tract of land
invasion	⟷	entering another land with an armed force
frontier settlements	⟷	homes on the edge of the wilderness

Testing

Tests of Understanding are suggested in Kelty's *The Growth of the American People and Nation*, pp. 150, 158, 164.

Tests of Reasoning and Skills. Check the best answers.

1. People in pioneer settlements   √ do not obey the law as well as people in older places.   obey the law better than people in older communities.

2. When a new president is elected, he should   √ put only the best men into office.   put into office those who voted for him.

3. The United States wanted Florida. For this reason   it had a right to take the land by force.   √ it had no right to take the land by force.

4. The people of Jackson's time would be expected to favor   private schools.   √ free public schools.

5. Do you think that a Democratic newspaper of the time would give a completely fair account of Jackson's giving office to those who voted for him? Explain your answer. ___[*It would be prejudiced in Jackson's favor.*]___

6. Turn to a map showing the purchase of Florida. Which part of Florida was nearest to Louisiana? ___[*West Florida.*]___

The rivers from the Southwest Territory flow into the Gulf through   East Florida.   √ West Florida.

Exercise in Organization. The teacher makes one outline including the last two stories. Children give topical recitations on each subhead.

B

STORY 1. THE ANNEXATION OF TEXAS · STORY 2. THE MEXICAN WAR
[*1 Week*

[Stories treated separately for conversational approach, the reading periods, and the discussion; for other activities, both together]

Conversational Approach (First Story)

"What is the next foreign territory that Americans would meet if they kept on moving west? Why do you suppose many of them would want to go to Texas? What country had owned Texas? Would Spain want Americans to enter her lands? Our story will tell us."

Reading and Study

The Reading Periods (First Story)

Independent Readers

TEXTS

BARKER, DODD, WEBB, *Our Nation Grows Up*, 112–119.

BEARD and BAGLEY, *First Book in American History*, 235–242.

BURNHAM and JACK, *Growth of Our Country*, 111–125.

CLARK, *Westward to the Pacific*, 163–166, 170–172, 197–207.

HALLECK and FRANTZ, *Makers of Our Nation*, 185–196.

KELTY, *Growth of the American People and Nation*, 165–171.

NIDA, *Following the Frontier*, 249–251.

SMALLIDGE and PAXSON, *Builders of Our Nation*, 400–416.

WOODBURN and MORAN, *Makers of America*, 230–235.

EXTENSIVE READING

CHANDLER and CHITWOOD, *Makers of American History*, 208–215.

COE, *Makers of the Nation*, 253–263.

EVANS, *America First*, 317–324.

FARIS, *Real Stories from Our History*, 127–133.

FARIS, *Where Our History Was Made*, II: 38–43.

GORDY, *Leaders in Making America*, 287–292.

LEFFERTS, *American Leaders*, I: 289–303.

MONTGOMERY, *Beginners' American History*, 205–208.

UHRBROCK and OWENS, *Famous Americans*, 187–196.

VOLLINTINE, *Making of America*, 212–220.

Lower Group

The teacher tells the story orally to this group, writing on the board the names of the most important persons and places as she mentions them. Children practice the pronunciations.

Then the teacher and these children read together the story as given in the text. The teacher guides the silent reading, section by section, by such questions as "What kinds of homes did the poorer settlers make in the Southwest?"

Children read silently and answer orally. When the entire story has been read in this manner, they test themselves by the study-guide questions at the end of the story.

OTHER BOOKS

BLAISDELL and BALL, *American History for Little Folks*, 115–121.

WAYLAND, *History Stories for Primary Grades*, 56–58.

READING FOR RECREATION

ALTSHELER, *Texan Scouts*.

BRITT, *Boys' Own Book of Frontiersmen*.

CORBY, *Story of David Crockett*.

JAMES and JAMES, *Six Feet Six*.

OTIS, *Philip of Texas*.

SCHAARE, *Life of Davy Crockett*.

The Discussion (First Story)

Children answer the study-guide questions. Have they shown satisfactory progress in giving the main thread of a story and eliminating unnecessary details?

The teacher writes the word *annexation* on the board. Children discuss the meaning.

Conversational Approach (Second Story)

"Our last story showed us that trouble would probably come between Mexico and the United States because of the question of Texas. Turn to a map showing the Mexican War. Perhaps we can learn from it how the war was fought. What does the key tell us about the main lines of attack?" Children point out each.

"How does the map show the land claimed by both Texas and Mexico? We shall expect that trouble will begin about this section."

Reading and Study

The Reading Periods (Second Story)

Independent Readers

TEXTS

BARKER, DODD, WEBB, *Our Nation Grows Up*, 121–123.

BEARD and BAGLEY, *First Book in American History*, 242–247.

BURNHAM and JACK, *Growth of Our Country*, 142–153.

CLARK, *Westward to the Pacific*, 209–221.

HALLECK and FRANTZ, *Makers of Our Country*, 197–199, 200.

KELTY, *Growth of the American People and Nation*, 172–181.

McGUIRE and PHILLIPS, *Building Our Country*, 9–11.

NIDA, *Following the Frontier*, 243–247.

SMALLIDGE and PAXSON, *Builders of Our Nation*, 418–431.

WOODBURN and MORAN, *Makers of America*, 235–241.

EXTENSIVE READING

BURNHAM, *Hero Tales from History*, 258–265.

COE, *Makers of the Nation*, 264–271.

EGGLESTON, *Stories of American Life and Adventure*, 166–171.

FAIRBANKS, *Western United States*, 106–114.

FARIS, *Where Our History Was Made*, II : 149–153, 160–165.

GORDY, *Leaders in Making America*, 292–297.

LEFFERTS, *American Leaders*, II : 304–318.

MONTGOMERY, *Beginners' American History*, 217–218.

TAPPAN, *American Hero Stories*, 237–253.

UHRBROCK and OWENS, *Famous Americans,* 197–206.

Lower Group

The teacher tells the story orally to this group, writing on the board the names of the most important persons and places as she mentions them.

Teacher and children then read together the story as given in the text. The teacher guides the silent reading, section by section, by such questions as "What land did both Texas and Mexico claim?"

Children read silently and answer orally. When the entire story has been read in this manner they test themselves by the study-guide questions at the end of the story.

READING FOR RECREATION

ARMER, *Waterless Mountain.*

DARBY, *Skip-Come-a-Lou.*

SABIN, *Into Mexico with General Scott.*

The Discussion (Second Story)

Children answer the study-guide questions as fully as possible. Those who have read additional material of special interest are given an opportunity to contribute.

The teacher writes on the board the word *cession*. Children discuss the meaning.

Multisensory Aids

Children and teacher talk over together the pictures in the text, pointing out features of geographic and historical importance. They turn to a map of the Mexican War. Children show all the lines of campaigns. They point these out also on a large wall map. They show the Rio Grande and the Mexican cession.

AUDIO-VISUAL MATERIALS OBTAINABLE

Keystone Views: 116, 119, 121.
MCKINLEY. Illustrated Topics for American History: S. 29.
National Geographic Magazine, LVII, 419, 439 (April, 1930).
Society for Visual Education. Picturol: The Pacific Coast.
Society for Visual Education. Schoolfilm: Trans-Mississippi Trails.
Society for Visual Education (MUIR). 1817–1850: Modes of Travel, Discovery of Gold,
    Mexican War.
Yale Pageant Educational Slides: 160, 162, 163, 177–179, 649, 742–744.

Music. The teacher plays selections from Ferdie Grofé's *Grand Canyon Suite*. She tells the children the story of Victor Herbert's opera *Natoma* and plays some of the selections.

General Activities

Creative Activities: Group and Individual, Correlated with Other Subjects or Voluntary Projects

A committee constructs in the sand table a model of the double houses, with a space between, used in the Southwest.

A volunteer shows a picture of the Alamo today.

Two volunteers hold a conversation between Santa Anna and Sam Houston, each upholding his country's claim to Texas.

Volunteers make a sand model showing the American lines of attack.

A volunteer explains the graph of Texas products shown in Compton's Pictured Encyclopedia, under "Texas."

A volunteer makes a list of the names of some of the Mexican states.

Children make a picture collection of old California missions.

A committee reads to the class the dramatization given in Hague and Chalmers's *Dramatic Moments in American History* (152–173).

The teacher shows the flag of the Alamo, the flag of Texas, the Bear Flag of California (*National Geographic Magazine*, XXXII : 330, 342 (October,1917)).

The teacher reads to the class selections from Joaquin Miller's poem "Defense of the Alamo" and from Lowell's *Biglow Papers*.

A visitor to Mexico describes the country to the children.

The children add Texas and the Mexican cession to the map begun on page 301.

The class continues the time line.

Application to Present-Day Conditions

Why is Texas called the "Lone-Star State"?

Does Texas still produce much cotton? (See World Almanac.)

Does Mexico today still bear marks of the years that it was under Spanish rule? [*Language, buildings, many of the customs.*]

What kind of government does Mexico have today?

What does *Rio Grande* mean? [*The Big River.*]

Would Americans today, if called to war, know as much about fighting as the backwoodsmen who made up the American army in the Mexican War?

What do the initials *D. F.* mean which one often sees after the name of the city of Mexico? [*Federal District.*] Compare it with the District of Columbia.

What states and parts of states have been made from the Mexican cession? How many of them have Spanish names?

Exercises in Reasoning

Why did Texas have only one star on its flag?

Why do you think that Mexico wanted to be free from Spain?

Should the Americans have obeyed the Mexican laws as long as they lived in Mexican territory?

How does the Mexican War prove that after fighting once begins, people will claim more land than they did in the beginning?

Did the fact that the Mexicans lost the war prove that they are afraid to fight?

Why were Americans in the North not so eager for the Mexican War as the people in the South?

On what other occasion had the United States gained as much land as the Mexican cession?

Now that you have read about the Mexican War and the annexation of Texas, do you understand why many South Americans and Mexicans are still suspicious of the United States?

Drill Games

Place names are best drilled upon at the map: *Texas, Rio Grande, city of Mexico.*

Drill cards are made as follows:

Sam Houston	⟷	a leader of the Texans in their struggle for independence
1845	⟷	date when Texas was annexed to the United States
annexation	⟷	joining one country to another
Alamo	⟷	a famous old mission in Texas
1848	⟷	date of the end of the Mexican War
cession	⟷	territory given up by one country to another

Children play the game " Who am I?" with their cards. Each shows the identification side of his card and calls on someone to name it.

Testing

Tests of Understanding are suggested in Kelty's *The Growth of the American People and Nation*, pp. 171, 181.

Tests of Reasoning and Skills

1. Make a list of the famous men who took part in the Mexican War. Use your book.

2. From what you read about Texas, can you make up a sentence telling what is likely to happen when many settlers from one country settle in an unoccupied territory that belongs to another country?

3. From what two directions did American settlers move into Texas? √ north   south   √ east   west

4. Check the best answer: General Taylor's expedition showed that   the Americans had more courage than the Mexicans.   the Mexicans would not fight for their country.   √ it is almost impossible to march an army far across sandy deserts.   it is easy to conquer a people as scattered as the Mexicans.

5. Turn to a map of the Mexican War.

How does the map show the land that was claimed by both Texas and Mexico? _____

How does the map mark the troops that marched to California? _____ the troops that conquered the states of northeastern Mexico? _____ the troops that took the city of Mexico ? _____

How does the map mark the land given up by Mexico at the close of the war? _____

6. Put the figure *1* before the thing which happened first, and the figure *2* before the thing which happened later.

a. [__1__] Louisiana Purchase   *b.* [__1__] Mexican cession
    [__2__] Purchase of Florida   [__2__] Annexation of Texas

Exercise in Organization. The class makes a co-operative outline of the first story.

Each child makes a brief oral summary of the action along the three lines of campaign described in the second story.

B

STORY 3. DISCOVERY OF GOLD IN CALIFORNIA · STORY 4. THE OREGON QUESTION · STORY 5. THE PURCHASE OF ALASKA
[*1 Week*

[Stories treated separately for conversational approach, the reading periods, and the discussion; for other activities, both together]

Conversational Approach (First Story)

The class turns to a map showing the Mexican cession. "Which part of these new lands would it be reasonable to expect to find settled first? [*That nearest the older settlements.*] Why? But it was not. California was settled first. Does anyone know the reason?"

The children turn to a map of the Western Hemisphere and speculate on possible ways to reach California.

Reading and Study

The Reading Periods (First Story)

Independent Readers

TEXTS

BARKER, DODD, WEBB, *Our Nation Grows Up*, 123–134.
BEARD and BAGLEY, *First Book in American History*, 248–250.
BURNHAM and JACK, *Growth of Our Country*, 153–157.

Lower Group

The teacher tells the story orally to this group, writing on the board the names of the most important persons and places as she mentions them. Children practice the pronunciations.

Then the teacher and these children read together the story as given in the

CLARK, *Westward to the Pacific*, 221–232.

HALLECK and FRANTZ, *Makers of Our Nation*, 201–203, 204–206.

KELTY, *Growth of the American People and Nation*, 182–190.

MCGUIRE and PHILLIPS, *Adventuring in Young America*, 332–338.

MCGUIRE and PHILLIPS, *Building Our Country*, 139–140.

NIDA, *Following the Frontier*, 253–272.

SMALLIDGE and PAXSON, *Builders of Our Nation*, 432–435.

WOODBURN and MORAN, *Makers of America*, 242–248.

EXTENSIVE READING

COE, *Makers of the Nation*, 272–277.

EGGLESTON, *Stories of American Life and Adventure*, 171–177.

EVANS, *America First*, 330–339.

FARIS, *Real Stories from Our History*, 191–195.

GORDY, *Leaders in Making America*, 302–305.

MONTGOMERY, *Beginners' American History*, 213–216.

SAMUEL, *Story of Gold and Silver*, 21–27.

VOLLINTINE, *The Making of America*, 221–232.

text. The teacher guides the silent reading, section by section, by such questions as "How did it happen that gold came to be discovered in California?"

Children read silently and answer orally. After the entire story has been read in this manner, they test their understanding by the study-guide questions at the end of the story.

OTHER BOOKS

BLAISDELL and BALL, *Child's Book of American History*, 144–151.

CARROLL and CARROLL, *Around the World*, III: 133–139.

TAPPAN, *American History Stories for Very Young Readers*, 118–123.

READING FOR RECREATION

BASS, *Stories of Early Times in the Great West.*

MCNEIL, *Boy Forty-niners.*

MCNEIL, *Early Days in California.*

MCNEIL, *Fighting with Frémont.*

MUNROE, *Golden Days of '49.*

OTIS, *Martha of California.*

PETERSHAM, *Story of Gold.*

SABIN, *Gold Seekers of '49.*

SKINNER, *Ranch of the Golden Flowers.*

The Discussion (First Story)

Children answer the study-guide questions as fully as possible. Those who add new material are encouraged to give the name of the book in which they found it. The children discuss the meaning of the term *forty-niners*.

Conversational Approach (Second and Third Stories)

"Have you ever been to a two-ring or three-ring circus? Could you watch what was going on everywhere at once? The United States was much like a three-ring circus. While the trouble with Mexico was going on in the Southwest, things were happening in the Northwest.

"Who owned this country?" The teacher points out the Oregon country at the map. "Did the United States have any claim to it? Who owns it now? Our story today tells how these matters were settled."

Reading and Study

The Reading Periods (Second and Third Stories)

[These two stories are read consecutively before any discussion is held]

Independent Readers

TEXTS

BARKER, DODD, WEBB, *Our Nation Grows Up*, 97–109.

BEARD and BAGLEY, *First Book in American History*, 252–263.

Lower Group

The teacher tells both stories orally to this group, writing on the board the most important words as she mentions them. Children practice the pronunciations.

The teacher and this group then read

BURNHAM and JACK, *Growth of Our Country*, 126–141.

CLARK, *Westward to the Pacific*, 245–274, 393–399.

HALLECK and FRANTZ, *Makers of Our Country*, 199–200, 203–204.

KELTY, *Growth of the American People and Nation*, 191–196, 197–202.

McGUIRE and PHILLIPS, *Building Our Country*, 8–9.

NIDA, *Following the Frontier*, 274–286.

SMALLIDGE and PAXSON, *Builders of Our Nation*, 385–398.

EXTENSIVE READING

EGGLESTON, *Stories of American Life and Adventure*, 207–214.

FARIS, *Where Our History Was Made*, II: 203–207.

GEORGE, *Little Journeys to Alaska and Canada*, 9–11.

GORDY, *Leaders in Making America*, 297–301.

JUDSON, *Early Days in Old Oregon*.

VOLLINTINE, *Making of America*, 198–211.

together the stories as given in the text. The teacher guides the silent reading, section by section, by such questions as "How many nations claimed the Oregon country?"

Children read silently and answer orally. After both stories have been read in this manner, they test themselves by the study-guide questions at the end of the stories.

READING FOR RECREATION

BUTLER, *Singing Paddles*.

CARR, *Children of the Covered Wagon*.

CHAFFEE, *Sitka*.

DARLING, *Baldy of Nome*.

GRINNELL, *Jack, the Young Trapper*.

HUDSPETH, *Oregon Chief*.

Kah-Da (Macmillan).

LANGE, *The Shawnee's Warning*.

MEEKER, *Ox Team Days on the Oregon Trail*.

MILLER, *Overland in a Covered Wagon*.

MONROE, *Fur Seal's Tooth*.

OTIS, *Antoine of Oregon*.

PACKARD, *Young Ice Whalers*.

PLOWHARD, *Lucretia Ann on the Oregon Trail*.

SCHULTZ, *The Danger Trail*.

SPRAGUE, *The Boy Pathfinder*.

SWAN, *Covered-Wagon Days*.

The Discussion (Second and Third Stories)

The children answer the study-guide questions as fully as possible. Has it become evident that children who have been transferred from the lower group to the group of independent readers are holding their own under the new conditions?

The teacher writes on the board the words *prairie schooner, " Seward's ice box."* Children discuss the meanings.

Multisensory Aids

Children and teacher talk over together the pictures in the text, pointing out features of geographic or historical significance. They turn to the map and point out the Oregon country, the part taken by Great Britain, the part taken by the United States, the Oregon Trail, the Santa Fe Trail, the South Pass.

AUDIO-VISUAL MATERIALS OBTAINABLE

Compton's Pictured Teaching Materials: *Food*, Plate XII.

EASTMAN. Classroom Films: Overland to California, The Oregon Country, Alaska.

GABRIEL (Ed.). Pageant of America: III, 170–171.

International Educational Pictures: California in '49, The Covered Wagon, Growth of the United States.

Keystone Views: 187–192, 340.

National Geographic Magazine, LIX, 191–224 (February, 1931).

Society for Visual Education. Picturols: The Pacific Coast, Alaska as a Whole.

Society for Visual Education. Schoolfilm: Across the Rockies to the Pacific. Society
for Visual Education (BRIGGS). Emigration to the West.
Yale Pageant Educational Slides: 169, 180–183, 502.

Music. Children sing "Oh, Susannah." The teacher plays records of
"Arkansas Traveler" and "Old Dan Tucker."

General Activities

Creative Activities: Group and Individual, Correlated with Other Subjects or Voluntary Projects

Committees draw a series of scenes on the back of a long roll of wallpaper,
which they show as reels of a motion picture. Reel One, "Route around Cape
Horn"; Reel Two, "Route across Panama"; Reel Three, "The Oregon Trail
Route"; Reel Four, "The Santa Fe Trail Route"[1]; Reel Five, "Life at the
Mines."

A volunteer explains how gold is assayed.

Another volunteer describes the dangers of a voyage around the Horn.

A committee reads to the class the dramatization given in Hubbard's *Little
American History Plays* (131–136).

The teacher reads to the class selections from Bret Harte's *Luck of Roaring
Camp*.

A committee models the South Pass in the sand table to show its importance
in reaching the west coast.

A volunteer shows the amount of gold produced annually in California
compared with its other products (graph in Compton's Pictured Encyclopedia,
under "California"); the gold of Alaska compared with its other products (ibid.
"Alaska"). (See also World Book Encyclopedia, under "California.")

The class makes a trip to the museum to see articles carved by the natives
of Alaska.

A volunteer makes a cut-up map showing the successive additions of territory to the United States.

The class discuss scenes from the motion pictures showing the Hudson's Bay
Company; showing travel on the Oregon Trail.

A visitor to a gold mine describes it to the class. A visitor to Alaska describes
the country.

Each child adds the Oregon country to the map begun on page 301.

Application to Present-Day Conditions

Have there been any gold rushes lately? [*To the Hudson Bay region in
Canada.*]

Does California produce most of our gold today? (See World Almanac.)
What is the annual value of the gold output of the United States?

What is the shortest way to reach California today from the eastern coast?
How long does it take? How much does it cost?

Name the states or parts of states of the United States which have been

[1] See *The Spanish Trail*, Teacher's Lesson Unit Series, Teachers College, Columbia
University.

made out of our part of the Oregon country. Name the Canadian provinces made out of the British part.

Is St. Louis still the center of the American fur trade?

Are any of John Jacob Astor's descendants living today?

Is Alaska a state? Is it likely to become a state?

Is Russia a near neighbor of the United States today?

How may Alaska become of great value to us in the future as a center of air travel?

Are Eskimos Indians?

What was the value of all Alaska's products last year? (See the World Almanac.) Do you think this shows that the land was worth the two cents an acre paid for it?

Exercises in Reasoning

Should a gold mine belong to the person who finds the vein, or should it belong to the nation that owns the land? Give arguments on both sides.

What kind of food could a miner prepare with only a coffeepot and a frying pan?

Did the gold rush have any effect on persuading Americans that there ought to be a quick method of transportation across the Isthmus of Panama?

Why did the value of land in California cities rise greatly during the gold rush?

Why would it not be satisfactory for two different nations to own the same land together?

Which nation do you think got the better of the Oregon bargain?

Jefferson had thought that it would take America a thousand years to reach the Pacific coast. Why was the task accomplished so much sooner than he had thought possible?

What does this sentence mean: "The flag follows the farmer"?

How did it happen that Russia owned Alaska?

Why had the United States made little advance in the arts during this busy era?

How may Alaska some day become of great value to us in our dealings with Japan?

Drill Games

Place names are best drilled upon at the map: *California, Columbia River, Oregon, Alaska.*

Drill cards are made as follows:

Forty-niners	⟷	those who went to California in the rush for gold in 1849
1848	⟷	date of the discovery of gold in California
"prairie schooners"	⟷	covered wagons on the plains
Santa Fe Trail	⟷	chief route to the Pacific coast through the Southwest
Oregon Trail	⟷	chief route to the Pacific coast through the Northwest
"Seward's ice box"	⟷	a nickname given to Alaska

Children spend their drill time on the items which they find difficult.

Testing

Tests of Understanding are supplied in Kelty's *The Growth of the American People and Nation*, pp. 190, 196, 202.

Test of Reasoning and Skills. Check the best answer.

1. The western coast was settled before the western part of the Great Plains largely because of   the building of railways.   √ the discovery of gold in California.   the use of steamboats on western rivers.   the annexation of Texas.

2. What do you think was the truth in regard to the Oregon country? The United States had the best claim.   Great Britain had the best claim. √ Both sides had good claims.

3. Has any part of America ever been settled from the West?   Yes [√] No [ ]   If so, what part? _ _ _[*The Rocky Mountain region.*]_ _ _

4. Turn to a map of the Oregon country. How does this map mark the Oregon Trail? _ _ _ _ _ _ How does it show that the United States and Great Britain settled their quarrel about the Oregon country? _ _ _ _ _ _

5. On what pages in your book is the Santa Fe Trail mentioned? _ _ _ _ _ _ Where did you find out? _ _ _[*In the index.*]_ _ _ Under which word did you look?   Santa [√]   Fe [ ]   Trail [ ]

6. Put the figure *1* before the thing which happened first, and the figure *2* before the thing which happened later.

   a. [_ _2_ _] discovery of gold in   *b.* [_ _1_ _] settlement of the Oregon
             California   boundary
   [_ _1_ _] Mexican War   [_ _2_ _] purchase of Alaska

Exercise in Organization. Each child copies the topic headings of one of the stories and prepares to give a brief topical recitation on each heading.

Tests on the Entire Unit

Test of Place Sense. Pass double-sized outline maps of North America. Lists of the words to be spelled may be placed on the board to assist the children in writing. Give the following directions:

1. Put the letter *C* where the Columbia River is.

2. Write the word *Alaska* in the proper place.

3. Write the word *California* in the proper place.

4. Draw two parallel lines where the Erie Canal is.

5. Put the letter *M* where the city of Mexico is.

6. Write the words *Missouri River* in the proper place.

7. Draw with green crayon a line to represent the Wilderness Road.

8. Write the word *Texas* in the proper place.

9. Write the words *Rio Grande* in the proper place.

10. Write the word *Oregon* in the proper place.

11. Pass to the map and show the Rocky Mountains.

Tests of Time Sense. Pass mimeographed sheets of the following:

I. Here are some names of persons. In each exercise put the figure *1* before the name of the person who did his great work first, and the figure *2* before the name of the person who did his great work later.

1. [__*2*__] Cyrus McCormick
   [__*1*__] William Clark

2. [__*1*__] Meriwether Lewis
   [__*2*__] Sam Houston

3. [__*2*__] De Witt Clinton
   [__*1*__] Alexander Hamilton

4. [__*1*__] Captain Robert Gray
   [__*2*__] Robert Fulton

5. [__*1*__] Thomas Jefferson
   [__*2*__] Andrew Jackson

II. Here is a list of things which happened. In each exercise put the figure *1* before the event which happened first, and the figure *2* before the event which happened later.

1. [__*1*__] McCormick's reaper was
       invented.
   [__*2*__] End of the Mexican War.

2. [__*2*__] Annexation of Texas.
   [__*1*__] Fulton's steamboat was
       invented.

3. [__*2*__] Beginning of railroads.
   [__*1*__] Purchase of Louisiana.

4. [__*1*__] Settlement of the Oregon
       trouble.
   [__*2*__] Purchase of Alaska.

III. Here is a list of dates:

    1803   1848   1830   1831   1845   1807

Put each date in the right blank in the sentences below.

1. The end of the Mexican War came in _____.

2. McCormick's reaper was invented in _____.

3. In _____ Louisiana was purchased.

4. In _____ Fulton's steamboat was successful.

5. Railroads were begun in _____.

6. In _____ Texas was annexed.

Test on Persons. Pass mimeographed sheets of the following:

Here is a list of people:

Jefferson	Cyrus McCormick	Robert Fulton
De Witt Clinton	Andrew Jackson	Sam Houston
Lewis	Clark	

Put each name in the right blank space in the sentences below.

1. _____ and _____ explored the Louisiana territory.

2. _____ was the first president from the West.

3. The reaper was invented by _____.

4. The steamboat was built by _____.

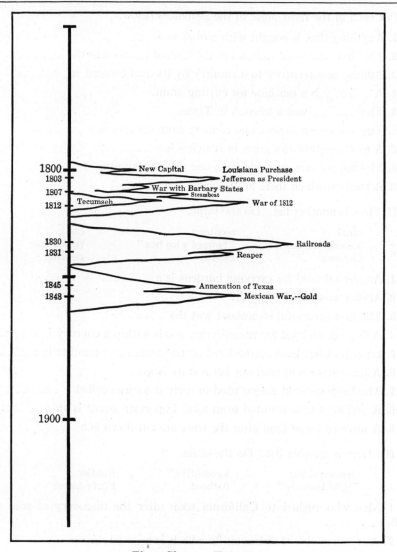

Time Chart — Unit Two

5. _ _ _ _ _ _ built the Erie Canal.

6. _ _ _ _ _ _ was a hero in the early history of Texas.

7. _ _ _ _ _ _ was president when Louisiana was purchased.

Test on Historical Terms

I. Here is a list of words:

Alamo	transportation	reaper
turnpike	Baltimore and Ohio	boundary line
annexation	binder	purchase

Put each in the right place in the sentences below.

1. Anything that is bought with money is a _____.

2. The first successful railroad in the United States was the _____.

3. Adding new territory to a country by its own consent is _____.

4. A _____ is a machine for cutting grain.

5. The _____ was a mission in Texas.

6. The line which divides one country from another is a _____.

7. A machine that ties grain in bunches is a _____.

8. Moving persons or goods from one place to another is _____.

9. A road on which there are tollgates is a _____.

II. Here is another list. Do the same.

canal	territory	era
"prairie schooner"	"Seward's ice box"	pack horse
Clermont	cession	clearing

1. An animal used for carrying burdens is a _____.

2. Alaska was called _____.

3. The first successful steamboat was the _____.

4. A large ditch used for transporting goods within a country is a _____.

5. Land that has been surrendered by one country to another is a _____.

6. A large stretch of land not yet a state is a _____.

7. The large covered wagon used in early days was called a _____.

8. A period of time counted from some important event is an _____.

9. A piece of forest land after the trees are cut down is a _____.

III. Here is another list. Do the same.

house-raising	locomotive	frontier
"Old Hickory"	flatboat	Forty-niners

1. Men who rushed to California soon after the discovery of gold were called _____.

2. A steam engine that travels on wheels is a _____.

3. The part of a country that is near the border is called the _____.

4. Andrew Jackson was called _____.

5. A boat with a flat bottom was called a _____.

6. Putting up the frame of a house was called a _____.

Comprehension Test on Unit Two

Check the two best answers: Early settlers in the West went there √ by way of the Ohio River.   by sailing around South America.   by the Panama Canal.   √ by gaps through the mountains.

Check the best answer.

1. People thought Alaska was not worth much because   we bought it from Russia.   √ it was so cold.   we had so much land already.

2. We bought Florida from   England.   France.   √ Spain.

3. The Louisiana Purchase was important because   √ it made it possible for Americans to move westward.   the land no longer belonged to Spain.   it made the map of the United States larger.

4. The settling of the Oregon question kept the peace with   Spain.   France.   √ England.

5. Andrew Jackson's election as president showed the power of the East.   √ West.   South.

6. Good roads and canals were needed   to save the wagons from wearing out.   to make riding comfortable.   √ to make it cheaper to send goods to the West.

7. California was settled before the other Pacific-coast states were settled because   people liked California better.   √ gold was discovered in California.   it was nearer.

8. Farming machinery was invented because   √ Western farms were too large for a few men to work.   men preferred to work by machinery.   inventors had to have work.

9. Steamboats and railroads helped to settle the West because   they were easy to build.   people liked to go fast.   √ they made it quicker and cheaper to transport men and goods.

10. When the Mexican War was over, the United States had   learned how to fight.   √ won a great deal of land.   made Mexico give us our rights.

11. The United States thought it had a right to annex Texas because of the fact that   the United States is larger than Mexico.   Texas no longer belonged to Mexico.   √ Americans in Texas asked for annexation.

12. What is the title of the unit which you have just completed? ＿＿＿＿＿＿

Are any children now ready to be transferred from the lower group to the group of independent readers?

UNIT THREE · *How One Machine called for Another
until All our Methods of Living were Changed*
[*5 Weeks*

EXTRA STORY FOR MORE ADVANCED READERS
The Growth of the Newspaper

A

**STORY 1. SPINNING · STORY 2. WEAVING · STORY 3. THE USE
OF POWER ·**   [*1 Week*

[For conversational approach, reading periods, and discussion the first two stories are taken
up together and then the third story; for other activities, all three together]

Conversational Approach (*First and Second Stories*)

The teacher brings to class a piece of coarse linen and asks the class if anyone can tell how it was made. Children experiment in drawing out threads from both warp and woof. The teacher calls their attention to the fact that these threads are made by twisting fibers. They untwist these threads, as well as twine, darning cotton, and sewing thread, in order to ascertain whether or not they are all made alike.

"Can such twisting be done in any other way than by hand?" Children tell what they know about the spinning wheel and about modern machinery. "What is the twisting process called? [*Spinning.*] What is the process called by which the threads are put together to make cloth? [*Weaving.*] Have you yourselves ever done any weaving?" Probably most of the children have woven paper, rushes, reeds, or raffia.

"Our stories today tell us how these two processes were first done by machinery."

Reading and Study

The Reading Periods (First and Second Stories)

[These two stories are read consecutively before any discussion is held]

Independent Readers

This group reads both stories through silently, as given in the text. They then test their comprehension by the study-guide questions furnished by the teacher or by the text.

TEXTS

KELTY, Growth of the American People and Nation, 205–211, 212–214.

EXTENSIVE READING

BROOKS, Story of Cotton, 84–89.
CARPENTER, How the World is Clothed, 40–43.
FORMAN, Stories of Useful Inventions, 116–119.
TURPIN, Cotton, 53–61.

Lower Group

The teacher tells both stories orally to this group, writing on the board the most important words as she mentions them.

Then the teacher and this group read the two stories together, as given in the text. The teacher guides the silent reading, section by section, by such questions as "Of what materials were the first threads made?"

Children read silently and answer orally. After the entire story has been read in this manner, they test themselves by the study-guide questions at the end of the stories.

OTHER BOOKS

CHAMBERLAIN, How We Are Clothed, 154–156.
KELTY, How Our Civilization Began, 30–31.
SHILLIG, Four Wonders, 51–52.

The Discussion (First and Second Stories)

The children answer the study-guide questions as fully as possible, the teacher watching closely the performance of children recently transferred from the lower group.

The teacher writes on the board the words *spinning, spindle, spinning wheel, weaving, shuttle, textile, loom.* Children discuss the meanings.

Conversational Approach (Third Story)

"These large machines are heavy, and men find it very difficult to run them. They look about for help.

"When men first had farm work too hard for a man to do, how had they secured help? [*From tamed animals.*] When they had found rowing boats too slow a process, how had they secured help? [*From the wind by means of sails.*]

"Can you mention any other means besides animals and wind that men have used to do their work for them? These are all called forms of power." (The teacher writes *power* on the board.) "Our story today tells us how power first came to be used with textile machinery."

The Reading Periods (Third Story)

Independent Readers

TEXTS

KELTY, *Growth of the American People and Nation*, 215–218.

EXTENSIVE READING

CARPENTER, *How the World is Clothed*, 43–44.
FORMAN, *Stories of Useful Inventions*, 119–120.
TURPIN, *Cotton*, 61.

Lower Group

The teacher and the lower group read together the story as given in the text. The teacher guides the silent reading, section by section, by such questions as "What kinds of power are described in the first section?"

Children read silently and answer orally. When the entire story has been read in this manner, they test themselves by the study-guide questions at the end of the story.

OTHER BOOKS

KELTY, *How Our Civilization Began*, 19–23.

The Discussion (Third Story)

Children answer the study-guide questions as fully as possible. The teacher writes on the board the words *the use of power, power loom*. Children discuss the meanings.

Multisensory Aids

Children and teacher talk over together the pictures in the text, pointing out features of geographic and historical importance.

AUDIO-VISUAL MATERIALS OBTAINABLE

Building America: Men and Machines, Power.
Compton's Pictured Teaching Materials: *American Colonies*, Plates II, 5; VII, 2; VIII, 5.
GABRIEL (Ed.). Pageant of America: V, 15–16, 29–32, 44, 153, 155–158.
International Educational Pictures: Story of Power.
Keystone Views: 293, 294.
McKINLEY. Illustrated Topics for Mediæval and Modern History: MM 21.
Yale Pageant Educational Slides: 215–222, 509.

Music. Play records of Saint-Saëns's *Omphale's Spinning Wheel*.

General Activities

Creative Activities: Group and Individual, Correlated with Other Subjects or Voluntary Projects

The class makes a poster to illustrate all the kinds of power. Under each heading they paste pictures illustrative of the application of that kind of power to man's work. For example, under the heading "Animal Power" they may show as many kinds of animals as possible doing as many kinds of work as possible.

If possible, the class observes spinning by means of a spinning wheel and weaving on a hand loom. (The household-economics department may be able to help.) They also, if possible, observe spinning and weaving by machinery.

The class makes a trip to observe machinery run by power.

Volunteers furnish lists of articles run by power in their own homes. These may be posted.

Volunteers illustrate spinning by twisting raw wool with the fingers.

The art class weaves rugs or mats and introduces simple designs into them.

The teacher may tell the children a brief outline of Hauptmann's drama *The Weavers.*

The class observes the shuttle of a sewing machine.

Application to Present-Day Conditions

How many articles in your home are made by the combined processes of spinning and weaving?

Has the invention of machinery today thrown any people out of work? Give specific examples.

What is homespun? Do you think that the so-called homespun which we buy in stores today was really spun by hand at home?

Do workers today own the tools and machines with which they work, as they used to do?

What is meant by *broadloom?*

People in olden days often made cloth to use for themselves. What do the people who make cloth today intend to do with it? Which would probably make cloth that would last longer?

In what way has the use of power made man's brain more important than his physical strength?

Does England still make more cloth than any other country? (See World Almanac.)

What is meant by *horsepower?* by *man power?*

Exercises in Reasoning

In what ways is clothing made of cloth better than clothing made of the skins of animals?

Why would the invention of spinning machinery and weaving machinery throw many people out of work? Do you think it would be better, then, not to have any machinery? What can be done for the people who are thrown out of work?

What does the word *manufacture* mean? [*To make by hand.*] Do you think that is a good name for most of our modern methods?

What change in women's work in the home was made by the invention of spinning and weaving machinery?

Do you think the earliest people who discovered how to weave could have been greatly below us in intelligence?

Why was the finest old Japanese and Chinese silk made in very narrow widths?

What does this sentence mean: "The machine multiplies men's hands and feet"?

Drill Games

Association cards are made as follows:

spinning	↔	drawing out and twisting into thread
spindle	↔	the rod on which thread may be wound
spinning wheel	↔	a tool for spinning, worked by a wheel
weaving	↔	interlacing threads in a loom
shuttle	↔	a case to carry the thread from one side to the other in weaving
textile	↔	cloth made by weaving
loom	↔	a frame set up for weaving
use of power	↔	a means of getting work done by other ways than man's strength
power loom	↔	a loom run by some other means than man's strength

Testing

Tests of Understanding are supplied in Kelty's *The Growth of the American People and Nation*, pp. 211, 214, 218.

Tests of Reasoning and Skills

1. Can you make up a sentence telling why the invention of machines has been a good thing? _____

2. Can you make up a sentence telling in what way the invention of machines has been bad for some people? _____

3. What is the title of the entire unit you are now studying? _____

4. Under what subheading are all three of the stories that you read this week? _____

Exercise in Organization. The teacher and the class make co-operatively one outline including all three stories.

A

STORY 4. THE COTTON GIN · STORY 5. THE SEWING MACHINE
STORY 6. THE BEGINNING OF THE FACTORY SYSTEM   [1 Week

[For conversational approach, reading periods, and discussion the first two stories are taken up together and then the third story; for other activities, all three together]

Conversational Approach (First and Second Stories)

"Now that so many textile machines have been invented, they will use great quantities of raw materials. Of what raw materials are textiles made? How could the supply of wool be increased? the supply of cotton? Can the sheep and the cotton be raised in England?

"When people tried to increase the supply of cotton, they ran into a stumblingblock. Here it is." At this point the teacher shows bolls of cotton, and the children try to pick out the seeds. They find out what a difficult task it is, and recognize that a fast method must be found.

Reading and Study

The Reading Periods (First and Second Stories)

[These two stories are read consecutively before any discussion is held]

Independent Readers

TEXTS

BARKER, DODD, WEBB, *Our Nation Grows Up*, 59–61, 86–88.

BEARD and BAGLEY, *First Book in American History*, 213–217, 218–220.

BURNHAM and JACK, *Growth of Our Country*, 55–59.

HALLECK and FRANTZ, *Makers of Our Nation*, 119–131.

KELTY, *Growth of the American People and Nation*, 219–222, 223–227.

McGUIRE and PHILLIPS, *Building Our Country*, 52–54, 54–58, 60–62.

SMALLIDGE and PAXSON, *Builders of Our Nation*, 495–501, 501–505.

WOODBURN and MORAN, *Makers of America*, 181–187.

EXTENSIVE READING

BROOKS, *Story of Cotton*, 89–99.

BURNHAM, *Hero Tales from History*, 266–269, 282–285.

CARPENTER, *How the World Is Clothed*, 29–33, 327–328.

COE, *Makers of the Nation*, 190–197.

DAVIDSON, *Founders and Builders of Our Nation*, 137–144.

EVANS, *America First*, 232–235.

FOOTE and SKINNER, *Makers and Defenders of America*, 205–209, 209–212.

GORDY, *Leaders in Making America*, 246–247.

LEFFERTS, *American Leaders*, II: 1–14.

McFEE, *Stories of American Inventions*, 1–13, 74–83.

MONTGOMERY, *Beginners' American History*, 156–162.

PARKMAN, *Conquests of Invention*, 63–79, 87–103.

SOUTHWORTH, *Builders of Our Country*, II: 123–126.

TURPIN, *Cotton*, 76–86.

UHRBROCK and OWENS, *Famous Americans*, 208–214.

Lower Group

The teacher tells both stories orally to this group, writing on the board the most important names as she mentions them.

Then the teacher and this group read together the two stories as given in the text. The teacher guides the silent reading, section by section, by such questions as "Why had the United States not yet raised much cotton for sale?"

Children read silently and answer orally. When both stories have been completed in this manner, they test themselves by the study-guide questions at the end of the stories.

OTHER BOOKS

CHAMBERLAIN, *How We Are Clothed*, 46–49, 163–166.

CHASE and CLOW, *Stories of Industry*, II: 13–15.

SHILLIG, *Four Wonders*, 10–11, 15–20.

READING FOR RECREATION

PETERSHAM, *Story Book of Clothes*.

The Discussion (First and Second Stories)

Children answer the study-guide questions as fully as possible. Are they by this time answering habitually in their own words rather than in the words of the book?

The teacher writes on the board the words *cotton gin, clothing industry.* Children discuss the meanings.

Conversational Approach (Third Story)

"Now we come to another difficulty. These huge new machines were very expensive. Could a workman buy his own? Who would have to do the buying of the machines? [*Rich men.*]

"Where had the spinning wheels and hand looms been kept in the old days? Do you think that the rich men will be willing to keep these machines in their own homes? Then where will they be kept?

"But why will a rich man be willing to let some poor man come in and work his machines? [*The product will belong to him.*] Why will the poor man be willing to work machines that belong to someone else? [*He will be paid money.*]

"In the old days to whom did a piece of cloth belong when it was finished? [*To the man who made it.*] Under the new system to whom will it belong? [*To the capitalist.*]

"This is a new idea in the world. We now find that most laborers are going to be paid in wages, and that most goods are going to be made in factories instead of in homes."

The Reading Periods (Third Story)

Independent Readers

TEXTS

BARKER, DODD, WEBB, *Our Nation Grows Up*, 36–59, 61.

KELTY, *Growth of the American People and Nation*, 228–232.

MCGUIRE and PHILLIPS, *Building Our Country*, 14–15, 58–60, 64–73, 199–205.

EXTENSIVE READING

BROOKS, *Story of Cotton*, 109–125, 253–254.

CARPENTER, *How the World Is Clothed*, 329–333.

TURPIN, *Cotton*, 61–65, 71–74.

READING FOR RECREATION

COOKE, *A Visit to a Cotton Mill.*

Lower Group

The teacher tells this story orally to the lower group, writing on the board the most important words as she mentions them.

The teacher and these children then read together the story as given in the text.

The teacher guides the silent reading, section by section, by such questions as "How did each family carry on work at home in the olden days?"

Children read silently and answer orally. When the entire story has been read in this manner, they test themselves by the study-guide questions at the end of the story.

OTHER BOOKS

SHILLIG, *Four Wonders*, 13–15.

WAYLAND, *History Stories for Primary Grades*, 41–43.

The Discussion (Third Story)

Children answer the study-guide questions as fully as possible. The teacher checks to see that the same children do not do all the talking while others never participate. She writes on the board the words *factory system, division of labor, quantity production.* Children discuss the meanings.

Multisensory Aids

Children and teacher talk over together the pictures in the text, pointing out the significant or interesting features.

AUDIO-VISUAL MATERIALS OBTAINABLE

Compton's Pictured Teaching Materials: *Clothing*, Plates III, IV, VIII, IX.
GABRIEL (Ed.). Pageant of America: III, 143–144; V, 35–41, 149–150.
Keystone Views: 96, 97.
Society for Visual Education (BRIGGS). Industrial and Social Development.
Yale Pageant Educational Slides: 223–225, 239.

General Activities

Creative Activities: Group and Individual, Correlated with Other Subjects or Voluntary Projects

Volunteers may wish to design friezes or headpieces for the beginning of each story.

A committee shows on a slated map the cotton-growing areas of the United States today.

A volunteer makes a graph showing the percentage of the world's cotton produced by the United States.

One of the girls demonstrates the many steps necessary to make a dress by hand.

Two girls may demonstrate to the class how much faster a long seam may be sewed on a machine than by hand.

The class takes a trip to a furrier and to a cobbler's shop to observe different kinds of sewing machines.

The class makes a trip to a factory to observe quantity production.

A committee reads to the class the dramatization "Eli Whitney" from *The Historical Outlook* (XVI: 130–131).

A volunteer explains the cartoon in Knowlton's *Making History Graphic* (31).

A volunteer draws a blueprint of a simple cotton gin.

Children make a picture collection to show how people dressed just before the Civil War.

The class continues the time line.

Application to Present-Day Conditions

Does the United States today produce more cotton than we can use ourselves? To whom do we sell it? (See World Almanac.) Why is it hard to find countries which will buy it?

What is the boll weevil? What efforts are made to combat it?

What kind of sewing is still done in the home?

Are there sewing machines today to sew other kinds of material than cloth?

Compare a sewing-machine needle with an ordinary needle. How do they differ?

Why are factory workers sometimes called "hands"? [*They have not much opportunity to use their brains.*]

Exercises in Reasoning

Does the supply of cotton furnish one reason why Japan is eager to spread her power over China?

What effect did the cotton gin have on slavery in the United States?

Why did tailors oppose the use of sewing machines? In the long run did the sewing machine make fewer jobs or more jobs?

How have women used the time saved for them by the sewing machine?

How did the building of factories change the ways that farmers spent their time in the evening? [*Tacks, nails, shoes, etc., were formerly made at home.*]

At first the rich people in New England had been the landowners; later they were those engaged in shipping. What change will take place now?

Why was the kind of factory work first introduced into America looked upon as women's work? [*Women had made the textiles in the home.*]

Why was it a bad thing for the factories to grow so large that the owners did not know their workmen?

How did the growth of factories affect the class of skilled mechanics?

Why was the War of 1812 a help to American factories? [*America couldn't get goods from England.*]

Why did factory work have a bad effect on family life?

Drill Games

Drill cards are made as follows:

Eli Whitney	⟷	inventor of the cotton gin
1793	⟷	date of invention of cotton gin
cotton gin	⟷	a machine for taking the seeds out of cotton
Elias Howe	⟷	inventor of the sewing machine
clothing industry	⟷	business of manufacturing and selling ready-made clothes
Samuel Slater	⟷	builder of the first American factory
factory system	⟷	production of goods in factories rather than in the home
quantity production	⟷	making a very large number of the article which a factory manufactures
division of labor	⟷	plan by which each worker performs only one small part of the entire task

These cards are added to those previously used, and the games are played with the entire number.

Testing

Tests of Understanding are suggested in Kelty's *The Growth of the American People and Nation*, pp. 222, 227, 232.

Tests of Reasoning and Skills. Check the best answer.

1. A great supply of raw cotton was needed because ✓ machines worked faster than hand workers.　people began to wear many more clothes.　the United States wished to sell much cotton.

2. The effects of the cotton gin were　all good.　all bad.　✓ partly good and partly bad.

3. From what you have read in this unit, should you expect that, from now on, the world will stay much the same or that there will probably be many other changes? _____

4. The clothing industry depends most upon the invention of the steamship. √ the sewing machine. the printing press. the reaper.

5. Here is a time ladder. Put the figure *1* in the space where the invention of the cotton gin belongs. Put the figure *2* in the space where the invention of the sewing machine belongs.

Exercise in Organization. Each child prepares orally a short summary paragraph of one of the three stories.

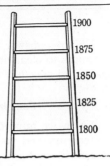

A

STORY 7. THE GROWTH OF CITIES

B

STORY 1. SENDING MESSAGES IN EARLY DAYS · STORY 2. SENDING MAIL BY RAILWAY [*1 Week*

[For conversational approach, reading periods, and discussion the first story is taken up separately, and then the second and third stories together; for other activities all three stories are taken up together]

Conversational Approach (First Story)

The teacher reviews with the children what they already know about the size of the cities in our early history.

"Now that factories are growing up at the waterfalls in the New England streams, where do you suppose they can get enough workers? [*They can draw from farms of countryside.*] Where can these workers live while working in the factories? What kinds of goods will they need? What kinds of services? How can the railroad help them?

"This is the way the cities grew. And the larger a city grew, the more factories wanted to come to it. Why? Our story today is about the growth of cities."

Reading and Study

The Reading Periods (First Story)

Independent Readers

TEXTS

KELTY, *Growth of the American People and Nation*, 233–237.
SMALLIDGE and PAXSON, *Builders of Our Nation*, 556–557.

EXTENSIVE READING

BROOKS, *Story of Cotton*, 125–131.
FARIS, *When America Was Young*, chap. viii.

Lower Group

The teacher and this group read together the story as given in the text. The teacher guides the silent reading, section by section, by such questions as "Where had the older cities grown up?"

Children read silently and answer orally. When the entire story has been read in this manner, the children test themselves by the study-guide questions at the end of the story.

READING FOR RECREATION

BEATY, *What We See in the City*.

The Discussion (First Story)

Children answer the study-guide questions as fully as possible. The teacher attempts to clear up misapprehensions or half-understandings. She writes on the board *growth of cities*. Children discuss the significance.

Conversational Approach (Second and Third Stories)

"Now we must consider another problem. Suppose that you were out in the country and your friend was on a hill far away. Is there some way that you could send him a message?" Children enumerate all the ways of sending messages about which they have heard or read.

"Our two stories today tell about some ways of sending messages."

Reading and Study

The Reading Periods (Second and Third Stories)

[These two stories are read consecutively before any discussion is held]

Independent Readers

TEXTS

HALLECK and FRANTZ, *Makers of Our Nation*, 253–254.
KELTY, *Growth of the American People and Nation*, 238–243, 244–247.
McGUIRE and PHILLIPS, *Building Our Country*, 272–279.

EXTENSIVE READING

AUSTIN, *Uncle Sam's Secrets*, 21–23.
BEEBY, *How the World Grows Smaller*, 191–216, 247–254.
EGGLESTON, *Stories of American Life and Adventure*, 137–147.
FORMAN, *Stories of Useful Inventions*, 226–228.
LARGE, *Everyday Wonders*, 106–108.
MONTGOMERY *Beginners' American History*, 197.
TAPPAN, *Travelers and Traveling*, 15–19.

Lower Group

The teacher and this group read together the stories as given in the text. The teacher guides the silent reading, section by section, by such questions as "How were messages sent in colonial times?"

Children read silently and answer orally. When both stories have been read through in this manner, the children test themselves by the study-guide questions at the end of the stories.

OTHER BOOKS

BAILEY, *What to Do for Uncle Sam*, 123–124.
CHAMBERLAIN, *How We Travel*, 18–23, 193–199.
KELTY, *How Our Civilization Began*, 43–47, 67–69.

READING FOR RECREATION

BUSH and WADDELL, *How We Have Conquered Distance*.
HUGHES, *Carrying the Mail*.
McSPADDEN, *How They Carried the Mail*.
ROLT-WHEELER, *The Boy with the United States Mail*.
SIEGEL, *Around the World in a Mailbag*.
WEBSTER, *The World's Messengers*.

The Discussion (Second and Third Stories)

Children answer the study-guide questions as completely as possible. They question one another in order to bring out phases omitted. The teacher writes on the board the words *communication, postrider, railway mail car, railway mail clerk, Post Office Department*. Children discuss the meanings.

Multisensory Aids

Children and teacher talk over together the pictures in the text, pointing out features of historical or geographical significance.

AUDIO-VISUAL MATERIALS OBTAINABLE

Building America: Communication.
Compton's Pictured Teaching Materials: *Communication,* Plates IV, V, VI; *American Colonies,* Plate X, 3.
Keystone Views: 336, 340.
McKINLEY. Illustrated Topics for American History: S. 21.
Society for Visual Education. Schoolfilm: Growth of Cities.
Society for Visual Education (BRAY-EYEGATE). Communication by Mail.
Yale Pageant Educational Slides: 524, 671.

General Activities

Creative Activities: Group and Individual, Correlated with Other Subjects or Voluntary Projects

The class divides itself into committees for a community survey. Each selects a certain number of blocks as its territory. Each committee records the number of grocery stores, meat markets, bakeries, drug stores, hardware stores, department or clothing stores, doctors, dentists, lawyers, shoemakers or cobblers, garages, restaurants, churches, libraries, banks, branch postal stations, etc.

A volunteer graphs the numbers out of every hundred in the United States who were city dwellers in 1790; in 1860; in 1930.

Volunteers report where great numbers of Irish settled; Germans; Scandinavians. Are their descendants there still?

The class makes a picture collection of great cities in the United States before the Civil War.

A volunteer shows how the Indians wrote. (See Hart's *How Our Grandfathers Lived,* 196–198.)

The class makes a trip to the local museum to see letters which were written before the days of envelopes.

A trip is arranged to the local post office to see how the mail is sorted and sent. If possible, the class is given a glimpse inside a railway mail car.

Volunteers explain how money orders are sent; how money may be deposited in the postal savings bank; how packages may be sent by the parcel post.

A language period is devoted to the proper addressing of letters.

A floor talk is given about the Dead Letter Office; about the rural free-delivery system.

The teacher reads to the class Browning's poems "How They Brought the Good News from Ghent to Aix" and "Pheidippides."

Boy Scouts illustrate wigwagging.

Volunteers attempt to write messages by picture-writing. The class attempts to read such messages.

Application to Present-Day Conditions

Find out the population of your own city in 1930, 1920, 1910, 1900 (the public library will help you). Graph the figures. Can you explain why your city is growing or is not growing?

Make a list of the ten largest cities in the United States in order of size.

The class makes a list of some of the problems caused by living in cities and tells how society is attempting to solve each one.

What is the latest improvement in carrying the mail?

Do we have to pay today according to the distance that a letter is going?

Make a list of foreign countries in which you are interested. Find out the postage rate to each. A stamp-collector shows his books.

Which is the only department of the United States government that the ordinary citizen comes in contact with daily? [*The Post Office Department.*]

Have you ever seen a train pick up or deliver mail at a station where it did not stop?

Why do many people prefer to keep their money in postal savings banks rather than in the ordinary banks?

Who is our present Postmaster-General? How did he get this office?

Is whispering in school communication?

Exercises in Reasoning

Do you think that the people in cities are happier than those who live on farms?

Why are cities almost certain to grow up wherever iron and coal are found close together?

Why is your city located just where it is?

Why did many cities grow up in the East and West, but few in the South?

Are the people who live in cities as independent as those who live on farms? Explain.

Why did the colonists write letters less frequently than we do?

Why is it better for the United States government to have charge of the mails than for each state to take charge of its own?

Why does the United States government pay certain ships to carry the mails to foreign countries instead of sending ships of its own?

Why are many people now moving back to the farms?

In what way does Paul Revere's ride illustrate our theme?

Drill Games

The following cards are added for the drill games:

communication	⟷	the sending of messages
postrider	⟷	a horseman who carried messages
railway mail car	⟷	a special coach in which mail is carried on the railroad
railway mail clerk	⟷	a man who sorts the mail in a railway mail car
Post Office Department	⟷	the division of the United States government in charge of the mail

Testing

Tests of Understanding are suggested in Kelty's *The Growth of the American People and Nation*, pp. 237, 243, 247.

Tests of Reasoning and Skills. Check the best answer.

1. The growth of cities has been   entirely good for the United States. √ partly good and partly bad.   entirely bad for the United States.

2. All these statements are true. Check that which gives the best reason why our cities grew so fast :   √ Factories were built in the cities.   Foreigners came to live there.   Many railroads were built.   Steamship lines were established.

3. Texts say that better communication made the people of the United States more alike. Why is this true? _ _ _ _ _ _

4. On what pages in your text can you find material about the Post Office Department? _ _ _ _ _ _ Where did you look to find out? _ _ _[*In the index.*]_ _ _ Under which word did you look?   *Post* [√]   *Office* [ ]   *Department* [ ]

Exercise in Organization. Children prepare sentence summaries for one of the stories.

B

STORY 3. THE TELEGRAPH · STORY 4. THE CABLE

C

STORY 1. CLIPPER SHIPS   [*1 Week*

[For conversational approach, reading periods, and discussion, the first two stories are taken up together and then the third story; for other activities, all three together]

Conversational Approach (First Two Stories)

"As more railroads were built a serious danger came to be seen. The railway trains were very likely to bump into one another. How is that prevented today? [*By signals and telegraphed instructions.*] It became clear, then, that some faster way of sending messages to trains was needed. Do you know what way was found? [*The telegraph.*] How does the telegraph help other people besides those working or traveling on the railroads?"

Reading and Study

The Reading Periods (First Two Stories)

[These two stories are read consecutively before any discussion is held]

Independent Readers

TEXTS

BARKER, DODD, WEBB, *Our Nation Grows Up*, 84–86.

BEARD and BAGLEY, *First Book in American History*, 228–231.

BURNHAM and JACK, *Growth of Our Country*, 70–72.

Lower Group

The teacher tells both stories orally to this group, writing on the board the most important names as she mentions them.

Then the teacher and these children read together both stories as given in the text. The teacher guides the silent reading, section by section, by such questions

CLARK, *Westward to the Pacific*, 386–390.

HALLECK and FRANTZ, *Makers of Our Nation*, 254–263.

KELTY, *Growth of the American People and Nation*, 248–252, 253–256.

McGUIRE and PHILLIPS, *Building Our Country*, 124–130, 130–134.

NIDA, *Following the Frontier*, 295–301.

SMALLIDGE and PAXSON, *Builders of Our Nation*, 560–562, 562–564.

WOODBURN and MORAN, *Makers of America*, 224–228.

EXTENSIVE READING

BEEBY, *How the World Grows Smaller*, 228–246, 254–259.

BURNHAM, *Hero Tales from History*, 274–278.

CHANDLER and CHITWOOD, *Makers of American History*, 247–251.

COE, *Makers of the Nation*, 246–252.

EVANS, *America First*, 325–330.

FARIS, *Real Stories from Our History*, 290–294.

FOOTE and SKINNER, *Makers and Defenders of America*, 309–314, 314–316.

FORMAN, *Stories of Useful Inventions*, 235–239.

GORDY, *American Leaders and Heroes*, 273–281.

LEFFERTS, *American Leaders*, II: 82–97.

McFEE, *Stories of American Inventions*, 50–73.

PARKMAN, *Conquests of Invention*, 350–378.

SOUTHWORTH, *Builders of Our Country*, II: 180–183, 184–185.

STONE and FICKETT, *Days and Deeds a Hundred Years Ago*, 121–130.

UHRBROCK and OWENS, *Famous Americans*, 249–256.

as "What new way of sending messages may now be used?"

Children read silently and answer orally. When both stories have been completed in this manner, they test themselves by the study-guide questions at the end of the stories.

OTHER BOOKS

CHAMBERLAIN, *How We Travel*, 204–211, 219–227.

READING FOR RECREATION

WEBSTER, *The World's Messengers*.

The Discussion (*First Two Stories*)

Children answer the study-guide questions. What progress toward accuracy is being made by the rapid but inaccurate readers?

The teacher writes on the board the words *telegraph*, *Morse code*, *transatlantic cable*. Children discuss the meanings.

Conversational Approach (*Third Story*)

"Not only did we need to send messages rapidly across the ocean but we also needed to be able to travel faster. Why are the steamships, at the time about which we are reading, not being much used for ocean travel? Our story today tells us about some of the most beautiful products ever built in America — sailing ships called clippers. Why do you suppose they were given that name?"

Reading and Study

The Reading Periods (Third Story)

Independent Readers

TEXTS

KELTY, *Growth of the American People and Nation*, 257–260.

EXTENSIVE READING

FARIS, *Where Our History Was Made*, II : 250–255.

ROCHELEAU, *Story of Ships and Shipping*, 14–17.

Lower Group

The teacher and this group read together the story as given in the text. The teacher guides the silent reading by such questions as "What are tramp ships?"

Children read silently and answer orally. When the entire story has been read in this manner, they test themselves by the study-guide questions at the end of the story.

READING FOR RECREATION

FARJEON, *Old Sailor's Yarn Box.*
GRANT, *Story of the Ship.*
SPERRY, *All Sails Set.*

The Discussion (Third Story)

Children answer the study-guide questions. Those who have read additional material are given the opportunity to contribute.

Multisensory Aids

Children and teacher talk over together the pictures in the text, pointing out features of historical and geographical significance.

AUDIO-VISUAL MATERIALS OBTAINABLE

Building America : Communication.
Compton's Pictured Teaching Materials : *Communication*, Plates VII, VIII ; *Water and Air Transportation*, Plate III.
GRANT. *Story of the Ship:* Clipper Ship and Plan of a Full-Rigged Ship.
International Educational Pictures : Laying the World's Fastest Ocean Cable.
Keystone Views : 335.
McKINLEY. Illustrated Topics for American History : S 28.
Society for Visual Education (BRAY). Repairing a Sub-sea Cable.
Yale Pageant Educational Slides : 228, 230–231, 513, 690.

Music. The teacher plays records of sea chanteys.

The teacher reads or sings to the children songs of sailors and sea fights from Lomax's *American Ballads and Folk Songs.*

General Activities

Creative Activities: Group and Individual, Correlated with Other Subjects or Voluntary Projects

The class makes a trip to the local railway station to observe a telegraph at work ; to the local newspaper office to observe how news comes in.

A committee looks up the Morse alphabet in the dictionary or encyclopedia (*telegraph*). Each member writes a word in it to show the class.

A committee shows telegram forms and explains how a message can be cut to a few words. The members explain day-letter and night-letter rates.

A committee explains how news is gathered by telegraph. The class examines newspapers to find items marked AP (Associated Press) or UP (United Press).

If possible, the class secures from the local telephone company an old piece of cable to see how it is made. If not, use a picture such as that in Compton's Pictured Encyclopedia or the World Book Encyclopedia.

If possible, an old sailor is invited to describe the life on a sailing ship.

Volunteers may wish to draw or paint pictures of clipper ships. Others may wish to compose poems about their voyages.

A picture collection of clipper ships is made.

A volunteer shows a ship model and names the different ropes, sails, and spars.

A volunteer finds out the distance in miles traveled by the fastest of the clipper ships, which could make 21 knots an hour. (See the dictionary.)

A committee reads to the class the dramatization given in Hubbard's *Little American History Plays* (166–169).

Volunteers find out the cost of sending cables to various foreign ports. (Consult local telegraph offices.)

The class studies a map showing cable lines of communication, to see where such lines are most numerous and where they are least numerous. (Goode, *School Atlas*, 13.)

Application to Present-Day Conditions

In what way has the use of radio somewhat lessened the importance of the telegraph?

What are the names of the most important telegraph companies in the United States? [*Western Union and Postal Telegraph.*]

Can you think of any project which would seem as silly today as the laying of the cable did then?

Are there any three-masters in the world today? four-masters? five-masters?

Are there any tramp ships today?

How many knots an hour can the fastest steamship make today? (World Almanac: *Merchant Marine.*)

How much of our own commerce do American ships carry today? (World Almanac: *Tonnage of Vessels.*) Compare American with foreign tonnage.

Compare the speed records of clipper ships with those of steamers. (World Almanac: *Ship Speed Records.*)

Exercises in Reasoning

Why do you suppose that both Fulton and Morse turned from art to invention? [*America not much interested in art at that time.*]

Why did it cost so much money for Morse to try out his invention?

Is it a good thing for citizens of one part of the country to learn instantly what is going on in another part? Why?

Why do you suppose that the use of rubber was discovered so late in the world's history? [*The South American Indians had known about it.*]

Why was Newfoundland chosen as the place to land the cable? (See the map.)

In what way did the clipper ships help in the California gold rush?

Is it a good thing to let ships of other countries carry almost all our goods?

Drill Games

Drill cards are made as follows:

Samuel F. B. Morse	↔	inventor of the telegraph
1844	↔	date of the invention of the telegraph
telegraph	↔	a means of sending written messages by electricity
Morse code	↔	the alphabet used in telegraphy
Cyrus W. Field	↔	the man who laid the Atlantic cable
transatlantic	↔	anything which crosses the Atlantic
clipper ships	↔	very fast sailing vessels

Testing

Tests of Understanding are suggested in Kelty's *The Growth of the American People and Nation*, pp. 252, 256, 260.

Tests of Reasoning and Skills

1. In the following list check the two which helped directly to make the people of the United States think alike:

canals	√ telegraph	cotton gin
reaper and binder	sewing machine	√ railroads

2. How might the War of 1812 have been prevented if there had been a cable then? Use your book to find the answer.

3. Should you expect that the owners of clipper ships would welcome the coming of steamboats?   Yes [ ]   No [√]   Tell your reason.

4. On what page is the table of contents for the unit you are now studying? _ _ _ _ _ _

5. Put the figure *1* before the thing which was used first and the figure *2* before the thing which was used later.

    a. [_ _1_ _] telegraph   *b.* [_ _2_ _] cable
        [_ _2_ _] telephone   [_ _1_ _] clipper ships

Exercise in Organization. Each child copies the topic headings of one of the stories and prepares to give a brief summary of each heading.

C

STORY 2. TRADE WITH JAPAN

D

STORY 1. CHEAP IRON AND STEEL · STORY 2. COAL   [1 Week

[For conversational approach, reading periods, and discussion, the first story is taken up first and then the last two together; for other activities, all three together]

Conversational Approach (First Story)

"American trade with China was begun at about what time? Would it seem reasonable, then, to expect that trade with Japan might have followed soon? Why? Why should you think that Americans would want to trade with Japan?

"And yet trade with Japan had not followed the opening up of trade with China. No country in the world was able to trade freely with Japan. Can you imagine why? Our story will tell us."

Reading and Study

The Reading Periods (First Story)

Independent Readers

TEXTS

KELTY, *Growth of the American People and Nation*, 261–265.

EXTENSIVE READING

BRAIN, *All about Japan*, 131–148.
GRIFFIS, *Japan in History*, 209–215.
VAN BERGEN, *Story of Japan*, 191–206.

READING FOR RECREATION

WHEELER and HOLMES, Burton Holmes Travel Stories: *Japan*, 7–10.

Lower Group

The teacher tells the story orally to this group, writing on the board the names of the most important persons and places as she mentions them.

Then the teacher and this group read together the story as given in the text. The teacher guides the silent reading, section by section, by such questions as "Why had the Japanese refused to trade?"

Children read silently and answer orally. When the entire story has been read in this manner they test themselves by the study-guide questions at the end of the story.

The Discussion (First Story)

Children answer the study-guide questions. The teacher may invite a visitor to hear these explanations. The teacher writes on the board the words *commodore, opening the ports*. Children discuss the meanings.

Conversational Approach (Last Two Stories)

"Turn to the table of contents for this unit. Under what heading are the last two stories? Glance at the other titles of stories in this unit and see if they tell you why a new metal industry was needed. And if a new metal industry was needed, how would the fuel supply be affected?"

Reading and Study

The Reading Periods (Last Two Stories)

[These two stories are read consecutively before any discussion is held]

Independent Readers

TEXT

KELTY, *Growth of the American People and Nation*, 266–270, 271–274.

EXTENSIVE READING

CHASE and CLOW, *Stories of Industry*, I : 3–5, 63–65, 74–80.
HUSBAND, *America at Work*, 20–31.
PARKMAN, *Conquests of Invention*, 298–309.
ROCHELEAU, Great American Industries: *Minerals*, 8–13, 96–101.
TAPPAN, *Diggers in the Earth*, 59–64.

READING FOR RECREATION

HOUGH, *The Story of Fire*.
PETERSHAM, *Story of Coal*.
PETERSHAM, *Story Book of Iron and Steel*.
PRYOR, *The Steel Book*.

Lower Group

The teacher and this group read together the stories as given in the text. The teacher guides the silent reading, section by section, by such questions as "What is the difference between iron and steel?"

Children read silently and answer orally. When both stories have been read in this manner they test themselves by the study-guide questions at the end of the stories.

OTHER BOOKS

SHEPHERD, *Geography for Beginners*, 45–50.
WAYLAND, *History Stories for Primary Grades*, 44–46, 47–49.

The Discussion (Last Two Stories)

The children answer the study-guide questions as completely as possible. The teacher listens closely for phrases that indicate a lack of comprehension of the ideas. She writes on the board the words *steel, smelting, fuel, Industrial Revolution, Coal Age, Iron Age, Steel Age*. Children discuss the meanings.

Multisensory Aids

Children and teacher talk over together the pictures in the text, pointing out features of special significance.

AUDIO-VISUAL MATERIALS OBTAINABLE

Compton's Pictured Teaching Materials: *Coal and Iron*, Plates II, III, IX–XII; *American Colonies*, Plate VIII, 2, 3.
EASTMAN. Classroom Films: Iron Ore to Pig Iron.
GABRIEL (Ed.). Pageant of America: V, 58, 60, 63, 65, 176–185.
Keystone Views: 282, 283.
McKINLEY. Illustrated Topics for Mediæval and Modern History: M M 32.
Society for Visual Education. Picturol: Mining Bituminous Coal.
Yale Pageant Educational Slides: 157, 232, 568, 704–707, 711–713.

Music. Play records of Japanese music.

General Activities

Creative Activities: Group and Individual, Correlated with Other Subjects or Voluntary Projects

The class makes a trip to the local museum or to a department store to see articles made by the Japanese.

Volunteers dramatize the scene of Perry's landing in Japan.

A volunteer brings to class a piece of cast iron, a piece of steel, and some carbon from a carburetor.

If possible, the class makes a trip to a local foundry or forge or repair shop. If not, visit a blacksmith shop to observe the working of iron. No attempt should be made to follow the various processes in detail.

Volunteers make lists of articles made of cast iron and articles made of steel.

A committee records on a slated map the iron-producing areas of the United States.

Volunteers demonstrate the difference between hard (anthracite) coal and soft (bituminous) coal.

Volunteers show the class a diagram of a coal mine and explain it. (Compton's Pictured Encyclopedia: *Mines and mining.*)

A volunteer explains the two-page diagram of the smelting of iron as shown in Compton's Pictured Encyclopedia (*Iron*).

Application to Present-Day Conditions

Does the United States carry on trade with Japan today? (See the World Almanac.)

Which has more trade in China today, the Japanese or the United States?

Compare the Japanese Empire (including Manchukuo) with the United States in area and population.

Is Japan a near neighbor of the United States today? (Find the most westerly point of the Aleutian Islands and measure the distance to Japan.)

What do these words mean, *Occidental* and *Oriental*? Which nations are Occidental and which are Oriental?

Does Japan belong to the League of Nations? Does the United States?

Compare the yearly value of the iron and steel output of the United States with the value of the gold output.

What is pig iron?

What fuel is now partly taking the place of both wood and coal?

Exercises in Reasoning

About what other famous brothers have we read besides Oliver Hazard Perry and Commodore Matthew Perry? [*George Rogers Clark and William Clark.*]

Do you think the Japanese had a right to keep from trading with other countries if they wanted to?

If you had wanted to introduce Japan to the civilization of the Western world, should you have taken the same gifts that Commodore Perry did?

Why did Japan grant Perry's request?

May the United States regret some day that she forced Japan to become modern? Why?

Why was the use of iron discovered later than many other metals?

Why was Valley Forge given its name?

In what way did the invention of the steam engine help work in the mines? Where do you suppose the water in the mines came from?

Why is more soft coal used today than hard coal?

Could the same period of time be called the Coal Age, the Age of Iron, and the Age of Steel? Why?

Drill Games

Cards are made as follows:

Commodore Matthew Perry	⬌	the man who opened up Japan to trade
commodore	⬌	the old name of the naval officer next higher than captain
opening the ports	⬌	beginning foreign trade in coast cities
steel	⬌	iron with most of the carbon taken out
smelting	⬌	melting in order to get metal
Industrial Revolution	⬌	the changes in the ways of doing work caused by the use of machinery
Coal Age	⬌	the period in history when coal is the chief fuel used
Age of Iron	⬌	the period in history when iron is one of the most important products used
Age of Steel	⬌	the period in history when steel is one of the most important products used
fuel	⬌	material used to feed a fire

Children may work by twos, hearing each other give the identifications.

Testing

Tests of Understanding are given in Kelty's *The Growth of the American People and Nation,* pp. 265, 270, 274.

Tests of Reasoning and Skills

1. Make a list of reasons why the United States wanted to trade with Japan. Use your book if it will help you.

2. Why had the United States not been much interested in Japan until 1846 and 1848? ___[*Had not faced the Pacific before.*]___

3. Underline the right words: Steel has   more   less   carbon than iron.

4. Check the best answer: The Industrial Revolution increased the need for iron and steel very much because   so many more people came to America.   cities grew so rapidly.   people now want to buy iron and steel.   √ most machines are made of iron or steel.

5. Is this statement true or false? Coal is a better fuel than wood because it takes trees a long time to grow, while coal can be dug out of the earth everywhere.   True [ ]   False [√]

Exercise in Organization. Each child chooses which of the first two stories he will outline, and works by himself.

Tests on the Entire Unit

Tests of Time Sense. Pass mimeographed sheets of the following.

I. Here are the names of persons. In each exercise put the figure *1* before the name of the person who did his great work first and the figure *2* before the name of the person who did his great work later.

1. [_ _2_ _] Cyrus W. Field   2. [_ _2_ _] Elias Howe
   [_ _1_ _] Eli Whitney   [_ _1_ _] Samuel Slater

3. [_ _2_ _] Commodore Perry
   [_ _1_ _] Samuel F. B. Morse

II. Here is a list of events. In each exercise put the figure *1* before the event which happened first and the figure *2* before the event which happened later.

1. [_ _1_ _] Spinning by machinery was begun.
   [_ _2_ _] The telegraph was invented.
2. [_ _2_ _] The United States made cheap iron.
   [_ _1_ _] Machines were run by power.
3. [_ _1_ _] Weaving by machinery was begun.
   [_ _2_ _] Trade was opened up with Japan.
4. [_ _1_ _] The factory system was begun.
   [_ _2_ _] Clipper ships were built.
5. [_ _2_ _] The Atlantic cable was laid.
   [_ _1_ _] The cotton gin was invented.

Test on Persons. Pass mimeographed sheets of the following:

Here is a list of names of noted men:

Cyrus W. Field	Elias Howe	Samuel Slater
Eli Whitney	Samuel F. B. Morse	

Put each one in the right blank in the sentences below.

1. The man who laid the Atlantic cable was _ _ _ _ _ _.

2. The English inventions in textile machinery were brought to America by _ _ _ _ _ _.

3. _ _ _ _ _ _ invented the cotton gin.

4. _ _ _ _ _ _ invented the telegraph.

5. The sewing machine was invented by _ _ _ _ _ _.

Test on Historical Terms

I. Below is a list of terms:

spin	Coal Age	power
fuel	spindle	factory system
growth of cities	Industrial Revolution	smelting
quantity production		

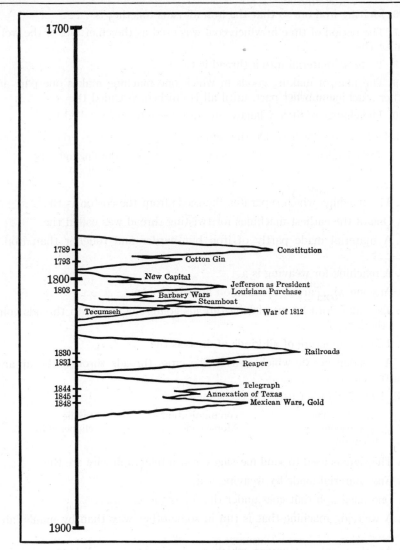

Time Chart — Unit Three

Put each one in the right blank in the sentences below.

1. Matter which will burn or produce heat is _ _ _ _ _ _.

2. Turning out huge lots of goods to sell is _ _ _ _ _ _.

3. Any kind of force that can be used to do any kind of work is _ _ _ _ _ _.

4. A rod which turns round and round and twists the thread is called a _ _ _ _ _ _.

5. The great changes in methods of work and living caused by the changes in machinery are called the _ _ _ _ _ _.

6. Melting iron ore so that the iron all runs together is _ _ _ _ _ _.

7. The period of time in which coal was used as the chief fuel of the world is called the _ _ _ _ _ _.

8. To twist material into a thread is to _ _ _ _ _ _.

9. The plan of making goods in which one machine makes one part and another machine another part, until all is finished, is called the _ _ _ _ _ _.

10. The change of little villages into very large towns is called the _ _ _ _ _ _.

II. Here is another list. Do the same.

spinning jenny	loom	clothing industry
steel	weave	cotton gin
shuttle	postrider	

1. The machine which separates the seeds from the cotton is the _ _ _ _ _ _.

2. One of the earliest machines for twisting thread was called the _ _ _ _ _ _.

3. A material made partly of iron but harder and tougher than iron is _ _ _ _ _ _.

4. A machine for weaving is a _ _ _ _ _ _

5. Anyone who carries the mail on horseback is a _ _ _ _ _ _.

6. To make cloth by interlacing threads going one way with threads going across them is to _ _ _ _ _ _.

7. The manufacture of all kinds of dress is the _ _ _ _ _ _.

8. A wooden needle which weaves the cross threads through the up-and-down threads is a _ _ _ _ _ _.

III. Here is another list. Do the same.

Atlantic cable	communication	textile
power loom	Morse code	clipper ship
telegraph		

1. The signals used to send messages over a telegraph wire are the _ _ _ _ _ _.

2. Any material made by weaving is a _ _ _ _ _ _.

3. One telegraph that goes under the sea is the _ _ _ _ _ _.

4. A weaving machine that is run in some other way than by man's labor is a _ _ _ _ _ _.

5. An electrical instrument which sends signals to a distant point is a _ _ _ _ _ _.

6. Exchanging ideas from one person to another in any way is _ _ _ _ _ _.

7. A sailing vessel built for speed is a _ _ _ _ _ _.

Comprehension Test on Unit Three

Check the best answer.

1. Everywhere coal was used as a fuel because   √ wood was not a good fuel to melt so much iron.   the supply of coal was increased greatly.   it takes little work to get coal out of the ground.

2. Cities began to grow to a great size because ___ life on the farms was too hard work. ___ ✓ the factories brought together so many people in one place. ___ people would rather live in towns than in the open country.

3. If we had not found new ways of working iron ___ our inventors would have been angry. ___ the iron workers would have been out of work most of the time. ___ ✓ there would not have been enough iron to make all the machines we needed.

4. The Atlantic cable was important because ___ it taught us much about the bottom of the sea and the fish. ___ ✓ it helped nations to know what others were doing and thinking. ___ it was laid by an American after many attempts and failures.

5. It was better to make goods in a factory than at home because ___ ✓ great quantities could be produced in the factories. ___ machines cost too much money for workers to own them. ___ factories are big buildings.

6. Telegraphing was better than sending messages in the old way because ___ it caused much less work than sending postriders on horses. ___ ✓ it could help all the people in the country to learn about news at the same time. ___ it does not cost so much to telegraph as it does to send a special messenger.

7. The chief effect of the invention of the sewing machine was ___ the improved appearance of clothes. ___ a change of style in clothing. ___ ✓ the growth of the clothing industry.

8. Railroads helped to send messages because ___ they carried letters free. ___ ✓ letters sent by rail traveled fast. ___ people went in trains to deliver their own messages.

9. The only way to supply enough raw cotton to keep all the spinning machines and weaving machines busy was ___ ✓ to find a quick way of taking out the seeds. ___ to send to other lands for more cotton. ___ to make every farmer grow some cotton.

10. The invention of spinning machinery was important because ___ no one had ever spun thread before. ___ ✓ it could spin many threads at once. ___ men did not have to work.

11. So much thread would not have been of much use ___ ✓ if someone had not learned to weave by machine also. ___ if someone had not bought the thread after it was made. ___ if it had not been good thread which would last long.

12. The power loom did the work of many men; and so these men could then ___ stay at home all day without working. ___ ✓ do work that had not been done before. ___ break the machines and get their old jobs back.

13. What is the title of the unit you have just completed? _____

Are any other children now ready to be transferred from the lower group to the group of independent readers?

UNIT FOUR · *How the Slavery Question almost split the Nation into Two Parts*   [5 *Weeks*

EXTRA STORIES FOR MORE ADVANCED READERS

Daniel Webster, Henry Clay, John C. Calhoun
The American Red Cross
Poets: Longfellow, Whittier, Holmes, Lowell
Writers: Poe, Hawthorne
Educators and Scientists: Horace Mann, Audubon
Advances in Science: Ether, Photography
The Temperance Movement

A

STORY 1. SLAVERY IN ALL THE COLONIES · STORY 2. THE SLAVE TRADE · STORY 3. END OF SLAVERY IN THE NORTH · STORY 4. COTTON AND SLAVERY · STORY 5. LIFE ON A SOUTHERN PLANTATION
[1 *Week*
[Stories treated separately for the reading periods and the discussion; for other activities, all together]

Conversational Approach

"Now we are ready to read about the greatest danger the United States had ever faced since the time of the Articles of Confederation. What does the title of the unit tell us about what almost happened? What were the two parts that could not agree? What was one of the questions that they quarreled about?

"Before beginning to read, can you say whether you think it is likely that one side was entirely in the right and the other side entirely in the wrong? Perhaps our stories will tell us."

Reading and Study

The Reading Periods (First Four Stories)

[These four stories are read consecutively before any discussion is held]

Independent Readers

This group reads the stories silently, as given in the test. As they finish each one, they test their comprehension by the study-guide questions furnished by the teacher or by the text.

TEXTS

BARKER, DODD, WEBB, *Our Nation Grows Up*, 139–142.

BEARD and BAGLEY, *First Book in American History*, 265, 265–266, 266–267.

BURNHAM and JACK, *Growth of Our Country*, 163–176 (four stories).

CLARK, *Westward to the Pacific*, 325–330 (two stories).

KELTY, *Growth of the American People and Nation*, 277–280, 281–285, 286–290, 291–295.

SMALLIDGE and PAXSON, *Builders of Our Nation*, 442–444.

EXTENSIVE READING

BROOKS, *Story of Cotton*, 74–75, 126–127, 129–131, 137.

COE, *Makers of the Nation*, 196–197.

GORDY, *Leaders in Making America*, 247, 314.

TURPIN, *Cotton*.

Lower Group

The teacher tells the main outline of all four stories as one story to this group, writing on the board the most important words as she mentions them.

Then the teacher and this group read all four stories together as given in the text. The teacher guides the silent reading, section by section, by such questions as "In the beginning, why were there slaves in all the colonies?"

Children read silently and answer orally. When all the stories have been read in this manner they test themselves by the study-guide questions at the end of the stories.

OTHER BOOKS

FAIRGRIEVE and YOUNG, *The World*, 60–62, 157–161.

SCHWARTZ, *Five Little Strangers*, 72–102.

READING FOR RECREATION

HARTMAN, *These United States*.

PETERSHAM, *Story Book of Clothes*.

ROLT-WHEELER, *Boy with the United States Census*, 165–209.

The Discussion (First Four Stories)   [In a Language Period

Children answer the study-guide questions as fully as possible, with their books open before them. The teacher writes on the board the following words: *slavery, Negro, slave trade, middle passage, abolition, freedmen, cotton states, plantation system, border states*. Children discuss the meanings.

The Reading Periods (Last Story)

Independent Readers

TEXTS

KELTY, *Growth of the American People and Nation*, 296–302.

McGUIRE and PHILLIPS, *Building Our Country*, 16–17, 20–23, 27–38, 41–45.

EXTENSIVE READING

BROOKS, *Story of Cotton*, 157–165, 167–171, 171–181.

EVANS, *America First*, 308–313.

GORDY, *Leaders in Making America*, 247–250.

Lower Group

The teacher and this group read together the story as given in the text. The teacher directs the silent reading, section by section, by such questions as "What picture of the 'great house' do you get from the story?"

Children read silently and answer orally. When the entire story has been read in this manner they test themselves by the study-guide questions at the end of the story.

HART, *Romance of the Civil War*, 1–8, 9–13, 13–39, 41–44.
TURPIN, *Cotton*, 96–98.

READING FOR RECREATION

CREDLE, *Across the Cotton Patch.*
KNOX, *The Boys and Sally Down on a Plantation.*
KNOX, *Miss Jimmy Dean.*
PERKINS, *Pickaninny Twins.*
STOWE, *Uncle Tom's Cabin.*

The Discussion (Last Story)   [In a Language Period

Children answer the study-guide questions. The teacher writes on the board the words *overseer, poor whites, field servants, house servants*. Children discuss the meanings.

Multisensory Aids

Children and teacher talk over the pictures in the text, pointing out features of geographic or historical interest.

AUDIO-VISUAL MATERIALS OBTAINABLE

Chronicles of America Photoplays: Dixie.
Compton's Pictured Teaching Materials: *American Colonies*, Plate IV, 1, 2; IX, 1; *Clothing*, Plates III; IV, 1.
EASTMAN. Educational Films: Cotton Growing, The Old South.
GABRIEL (Ed.). Pageant of America, III: 145–164; XIII: 81–91, 110–116.
Keystone Views: 123–125.
LEHMANN. Geographical Pictures: L. G. 604.
McKINLEY. Illustrated Topics for American History: S. 23, 27, 31.
Society for Visual Education (SPENCER). Cotton Production.
Yale Pageant Educational Slides: 55–57, 159, 240–242, 657.

Music. Children sing the Stephen Foster songs and "Old Man River."

The teacher plays records of Negro spirituals and selections from Dvořák's *New World Symphony.*

The teacher reads or sings to the children some of the songs of Southern chain gangs, Negro bad men, songs from the mountains, songs of childhood, breakdowns and play parties and spirituals, on pages 58–84, 89–118, 147–163, 267–299, 303–327, 577–613 of Lomax's *American Ballads and Folk Songs.*

General Activities

Creative Activities: Group and Individual, Correlated with Other Subjects or Voluntary Projects

A volunteer graphs the numbers of colored and of white in the colonies.

A volunteer reads sections from the Bible which the Southerners used to prove that slavery was proper. (Use a concordance under *bondmen, servant.*)

Children report scenes which they have observed in motion pictures showing the slave trade in Africa.

A committee draws on a slated map the triangle of trade from New England to Africa to the West Indies and back to New England. The middle passage is marked. On each leg of the journey is written the name of the product carried.

The teacher reads to the children selections describing the slave trade from Stephen V. Benét's *John Brown's Body*.

A volunteer finds phrases used in the Declaration of Independence which some Northerners used to show that slavery should not be permitted. [*Free and equal; right to liberty.*]

A volunteer explains why any one-crop system is bad.

Some of the children may wish to design headpieces for the stories read.

A committee graphs the increase in the cotton crop from 1800 to 1850; the increase in the colored population. (United States census.)

A committee reads to the class the dramatization given in Walker's *Little Plays from American History* (145–155).

A volunteer writes the letter which a Northern boy might have written to his parents about his Christmas holiday with a friend in the South.

The class makes a picture collection of beautiful Southern homes.

A volunteer explains the poster of the uses of cotton given in Compton's Pictured Encyclopedia (*Cotton*) or World Book Encyclopedia (*Cotton*).

Volunteers prepare advertisements announcing the sale of slaves.

The class continues the time line.

Application to Present-Day Conditions [*In a Language Period*

In what way is the population of the United States different today from what it would have been if slavery had never existed here?

How many colored people are there in the United States today?

Are there slaves anywhere in the world today?

Can you find in a copy of the Constitution of the United States the section which says that the foreign slave trade may be stopped in 1808?

A committee makes a list of all the different uses of cotton that it can find.

What problem does the South have on its hands today in regard to its cotton crop?

What does this expression mean, *wearing out the soil*? this expression, *cotton is king*?

Are overseers used in work today? Compare the overseer with the foreman of a job.

Are there still poor whites living in the mountains?

What gifts has the Negro brought to American life? [*For example, in music his spirituals and syncopation, his humor, his ability to find happiness.*]

Exercises in Reasoning [*In a Language Period*

Why were not free white men used to do all the work in colonial times instead of bringing in slaves?

Why do you suppose that black people were used as slaves instead of yellow people?

Does the fact that there were fewer slaves in the Northern colonies than in the South prove that the people of the North were better than the people in the South? What does it prove?

Were black tribes in Africa partly to blame for the constant supply of Negroes coming to this country?

Why are there more colored people in the North now than there were in the period about which you are reading?

Can you see any connection between the movement for democracy that we studied at the time of Jefferson and Jackson and the movement for abolition of slavery?

In what ways were the slaves worse off than the factory hands in the North? In what ways were they better off?

Would the Northern cotton manufacturers be likely to become abolitionists?

Do you think that the Southern planters should have used fertilizer on their fields, or was it a good thing to leave the worn-out fields and take up new ones?

In what way had the main businesses of the North and the South grown to be very different? Do they differ as much today?

Were the Southerners right in their belief that the Negro would not work unless he was a slave?

What effect would the great number of slaves in the South have upon poor white men who needed work? What could they do?

Name the border states. Were they all free? all slave? some free and some slave? State which was which.

Do the large wheat farms of the Northwest today use the plantation system?

Drill Games　　　　　　　　　　　　　　[*In a Study Period*

Place names are best drilled upon at the map: *Guinea Coast, border states.* Drill cards are made as follows:

1619	⇔	date when the first Negro slaves were brought to the United States
Negroes	⇔	blacks from Africa or their descendants
slavery	⇔	condition in which service is forced
slave trade	⇔	the buying or selling of Negroes
middle passage	⇔	voyage between Africa and the West Indies
William Lloyd Garrison	⇔	the most violent leader of abolition
Mason and Dixon's Line	⇔	the eastern part of the boundary between free and slave states
abolition	⇔	destroying, or putting an end to, slavery
freedmen	⇔	slaves who had been set free
The Liberator	⇔	a newspaper of the abolition movement
cotton states	⇔	states where cotton is grown as a principal product
border states	⇔	states on the line between North and South
plantation system	⇔	growing large amounts of a single crop on a farm with cheap labor
overseer	⇔	the man who superintended the work of slaves
poor whites	⇔	Southern whites who had few or no slaves
field servants	⇔	slaves who tended the crops
house servants	⇔	slaves who worked in the house or carriage house

Testing

Tests of Understanding are given in Kelty's *The Growth of the American People and Nation*, pp. 280, 285, 290, 295, 302.

Tests of Reasoning and Skills. Check the best answer.

1. Slavery grew in the South and died out in the North because √ it paid in the South and not in the North.   the people in the North were better than those in the South.   slaves liked the South better than the North.   the people in the North did not like black men.

2. Most of the people who sailed their ships to Africa to get slaves were from   the South.   √ New England.   the border states.

3. The blame for the selling of slaves in Africa belongs to   the white traders.   the black tribes of Africa.   √ both black tribes and white traders.

4. The invention of the cotton gin proved to be   a good thing for the Negro.   √ a bad thing for the Negro.

5. Most of the white people in the South owned   √ less than five slaves. more than a hundred slaves.   more than a thousand slaves.   no slaves at all.

6. Would you believe all the things written about slave-owners by leaders of the abolition movement? Explain your answer. ___[*Greatly prejudiced against slave-owners.*]___

7. Put the figure *1* before the thing which happened first, and the figure *2* before the thing which happened later.

a. [__*1*__] The slaves in the North were freed.
[__*2*__] The slaves in the South were freed.

b. [__*2*__] The slave trade inside the country was ended.
[__*1*__] The foreign slave trade was ended.

c. [__*1*__] The cotton gin was invented.
[__*2*__] The slavery system spread to the West.

Exercise in Organization. The class divides into five committees. The members of each committee prepare a brief oral summary of one of the stories.

B

STORY 1. THE MISSOURI COMPROMISE · STORY 2. THE COMPROMISE OF 1850 · STORY 3. THE KANSAS–NEBRASKA ACT   [*1 Week*

[For conversational approach, reading periods, and discussion, the first two stories are taken up together and then the third story; for other activities, all three together]

Conversational Approach (First Two Stories)

"So far, we might say: 'Why not let the North go its way without slaves, and the South go its way with slaves? Why need they quarrel about the matter?'" These two questions have been previously written on the board, and the teacher now points them out.

"Turn to a map showing the Louisiana Purchase. Here is the answer. To whom does the new land belong, to the North or the South? Then is it to be free territory or slave territory? Can you yourself think of any way in which the problem might be solved? Our first story today tells what was decided upon.

"Now turn to a map showing the Mexican Cession. Here is some more new land. To whom does the Mexican Cession belong? Then is it to be slave territory or free territory? Our second story today tells us what different plan was decided upon in this case."

Reading and Study

The Reading Periods (First Two Stories)

[These two stories are read consecutively before any discussion is held]

Independent Readers

TEXTS

BARKER, DODD, WEBB, *Our Nation Grows Up*, 142–151.
BEARD and BAGLEY, *First Book in American History*, 267–271, 274–283, 284–288.
BURNHAM and JACK, *Growth of Our Country*, 178–180, 180–184.
CLARK, *Westward to the Pacific*, 173–175.
HALLECK and FRANTZ, *Makers of Our Nation*, 209–211.
KELTY, *Growth of the American People and Nation*, 303–310, 311–316.
WOODBURN and MORAN, *Makers of America*, 249–261.

EXTENSIVE READING

BURNHAM, *Hero Tales from History*, 320–327.
CHANDLER and CHITWOOD, *Makers of American History*, 225–232, 233–246.
COE, *Makers of the Nation*, 283–295, 296–302.
EVANS, *America First*, 303–308.
FOOTE and SKINNER, *Makers and Defenders of America*, 178–190.
GORDY, *Leaders in Making America*, 308–311, 318–322.
SOUTHWORTH, *Builders of Our Country*, II: 158–165, 166–175.

Lower Group

The teacher tells both stories orally to this group, writing the most important words on the board as she mentions them.

Then the teacher and these children read together the stories as given in the text. The teacher directs the silent reading, section by section, by such questions as "What were the dividing lines between the two sections?"

The children read silently and answer orally. After both the stories have been read in this manner the children test themselves by the study-guide questions at the end of the stories.

READING FOR RECREATION

OGDEN, *Cherokee Trails*.

The Discussion (First Two Stories)   [In a Language Period

Children answer the study-guide questions with their books open before them if necessary. The teacher writes on the board the words *compromise, free states, slave states*. Children discuss the meanings.

Conversational Approach (Third Story)

"How was the decision about slavery in the Mexican Cession different from the earlier decision about the lands of the Louisiana Purchase? Some of the leaders believed that the decision in the Mexican Cession was the more fair of the two. What do you suppose they would want to have done then?" Children speculate as to possibilities.

"If the people who are to live in a territory are to decide, then it makes a good deal of difference who moves in. What do you suppose the Northern leaders will try to do? the Southern leaders?" Children speculate as to possibilities. "Our story tells us."

Reading and Study

The Reading Periods (*Third Story*)

Independent Readers

TEXTS

BARKER, DODD, WEBB, *Our Nation Grows Up*, 153–154.

BURNHAM and JACK, *Growth of Our Country*, 186–187.

CLARK, *Westward to the Pacific*, 332–335.

KELTY, *Growth of the American People and Nation*, 317–322.

EXTENSIVE READING

DAVIDSON, *Founders and Builders of Our Nation*, 181–187.

EGGLESTON, *Stories of Great Americans*, 124–128.

EVANS, *America First*, 299–303, 313–317.

GORDY, *Leaders in Making America*, 314–315.

Lower Group

The teacher tells the story orally to this group, writing on the board the most important words as she mentions them.

Then the teacher and these children read together the story as given in the text. The teacher directs the silent reading, section by section, by such questions as "Why did people in 1850 think that peace had come at last?"

Children read silently and answer orally. When the entire story has been read in this manner they test themselves by the questions at the end of the story.

READING FOR RECREATION

BROOKS, *Boy Settlers*.
SABIN, *The Boy Settlers*.

The Discussion (*Third Story*)   [*In a Language Period*

Children answer the study-guide questions. They question one another to bring out points which have been omitted.

Multisensory Aids

Children and teacher talk over together the pictures in the text, pointing out features of geographic and historical importance. They turn to maps showing the Missouri Compromise, the Compromise of 1850, and the Kansas-Nebraska Act. They read the keys and point out each factor shown. At each map they try to decide whether the North or the South seemed to have the better of the bargain. They notice changes from one map to the next.

AUDIO-VISUAL MATERIALS OBTAINABLE

GABRIEL (Ed.). *Pageant of America*, XI: 222–224.
Keystone Views: 338–339.
Perry Pictures: 144, 144-B, 144-D.
Society for Visual Education. Schoolfilm: *Trans-Mississippi Trails*.
Society for Visual Education (BRIGGS). *Territorial Expansion and the Slavery Question*.
Yale Pageant Educational Slides: 243.

General Activities

Creative Activities: Group and Individual, Correlated with Other Subjects or Voluntary Projects

A volunteer explains how Great Britain solved her problem of slavery in her colonies in 1833. [*Bought slaves from the owners.*]

Two volunteers take the parts of the North and the South. Each explains his views at the time of the Missouri Compromise. Another group explains the two points of view in 1850; and another, in 1854.

Volunteers give floor talks on the lives of John C. Calhoun, Daniel Webster, and Henry Clay.

Volunteers make diagrams for the Compromise of 1850, the Kansas-Nebraska Act, the Missouri Compromise, as follows:

The Questions	What the North Wanted	The Compromise	What the South Wanted

A committee reads to the class the dramatization given in Hague and Chalmers's *Dramatic Moments in American History* (199–210).

A committee makes a list of all the names of the states admitted to the Union, marking each *S* for slave state or *F* for free state. The list is posted.

A volunteer explains that it was Noah Webster, not Daniel Webster, who made a dictionary.

The class continues the time line.

Application to Present-Day Conditions

Children give examples of compromises which they themselves have seen in daily life or in which they have taken part.

Is life in Missouri today most like life in the North or life in the South?

Does every state still have the right to elect two senators whether it is large or small? Then how do the states with a larger population have any advantage?

Is it possible today for the majority constantly to pass laws that are unfair to the minority?

Are there many Negroes today in Kansas and Nebraska? (World Almanac: *Negro Population by States.*)

Exercises in Reasoning

Do you think that the ending of slavery in the colonies of Great Britain in 1833 might have an influence on the United States? Might it have been a good thing for the United States to follow the same plan? Would it have cost any more in the end?

In what way did the possession of new lands in the western territories bring on trouble between the North and the South?

Sometimes you hear the quarrel between the North and the South spoken of as "the quarrel between the slave and the machine." Can you tell why?

When did the question of slavery first come to be a topic which attracted the attention of the entire country? [*At the time of the Missouri Compromise.*]

What did Jefferson mean when he said the Missouri question was like a "fire bell in the night"?

Why was there no question but that Maine would enter the Union as a free state?

Why do you suppose that Mexico had not allowed slavery within its borders after it became independent? [*It was the Indians themselves who had been the slaves.*]

Why was Oregon declared free territory with little trouble? [*Partly to offset Texas, a slave state; largely because of its climate.*]

Do you blame the South for complaining that it could always be outvoted by the North?

Drill Games

Place names are best drilled upon at the map: *Missouri, Kansas, Nebraska.* Drill cards may be made as follows:

Missouri Compromise	↔	a plan for dividing the Louisiana Purchase lands between free and slave interests
1820	↔	date of the Missouri Compromise
Great Compromise	↔	a plan for settling the slavery question in the Mexican Cession
Henry Clay	↔	a great leader who always tried to make peace between the sections
1850	↔	date of the Great Compromise
free states	↔	states in which no slavery was allowed
slave states	↔	states which allowed slavery
Kansas-Nebraska Act	↔	the law which put an end to the Missouri Compromise

Children drill individually, keeping a record on a piece of paper of the items on which they make mistakes. Then drill games are played by the entire class.

Testing

Tests of Understanding are given in Kelty's *The Growth of the American People and Nation*, pp. 308–310, 316, 322.

Tests of Reasoning and Skills

1. What was the first plan tried to settle the question of freedom or slavery in the territories?   To enforce freedom everywhere.   To allow slavery everywhere in both states and territories.   √ To divide the territory between free and slave interests.   To let the people decide for themselves.

2. Complete the sentence: "Home rule" about slavery in the Mexican Cession means _ _ _ _ _ _ .

3. When people from the East settled the West they usually went west in horizontal lines. Since this is so, you would expect that Kansas would be settled by people from   slave states [√]   free states [ ]

4. Make a list of the plans tried to settle the quarrel over slavery in the territories.

5. If you wanted to know the truth about what happened in "bleeding Kansas" what newspapers and speeches should you read?   Those written by Northern men.   √ Those written by both sides.   Those written by Southern men.

6. Turn to the table of contents. Under what general heading are all three of these stories? _ _ _ _ _ _

7. Put the figure *1* before the thing which happened first and the figure *2* before the thing which happened later.

    a. [_ _2_ _] A plan was made for settling the slavery question in the Mexican Cession.

    [_ _1_ _] A plan was made for settling the slavery question in the Louisiana Purchase.

    b. [_ _1_ _] The Missouri Compromise.

    [_ _2_ _] The Compromise of 1850.

    c. [_ _1_ _] The admission of Maine as a state.

    [_ _2_ _] The Compromise of 1850.

    d. [_ _2_ _] The Kansas-Nebraska Act.

    [_ _1_ _] The Compromise of 1850.

    e. [_ _2_ _] The Kansas-Nebraska Act.

    [_ _1_ _] The Missouri Compromise.

Exercise in Organization. The teacher makes one outline including all three stories. Children decide what points should be included under each of the subheads.

B

STORY 4. FUGITIVE SLAVES AND THE DRED SCOTT DECISION · STORY 5. LIFE OF ABRAHAM LINCOLN · STORY 6. THE REPUBLICAN PARTY AND SECESSION [*1 Week*

[For conversational approach, reading periods, and discussion, the first two stories are taken up together and then the third story; for other activities, all three stories together]

Conversational Approach (First Two Stories)

"If slaves were unhappy on their plantations why didn't they run away and go to live in the free states? If they did, do you suppose their masters could make them go back?" Children speculate as to what might happen. "Our story today will tell us."

Reading and Study

The Reading Periods (First Two Stories)

[These two stories are read consecutively before any discussion is held]

Independent Readers

TEXTS

BARKER, DODD, WEBB, *Our Nation Grows Up*, 156–159.

BEARD and BAGLEY, *First Book in American History*, 291–292, 292–299.

BURNHAM and JACK, *Growth of Our Country*, 184–186, 193–197.

CLARK, *Westward to the Pacific*, 330–332, 335–336.

HALLECK and FRANTZ, *Makers of Our Nation*, 211–217.

KELTY, *Growth of the American People and Nation*, 323–328, 329–335.

SMALLIDGE and PAXSON, *Builders of Our Nation*, 446–460.

WOODBURN and MORAN, *Makers of America*, 262–268.

EXTENSIVE READING

EVANS, *America First*, 349–354.

HART, *Romance of the Civil War*, 51–56, 59–69.

Lower Group

The teacher tells the first story orally to this group, writing on the board the most important words as she mentions them.

Then teacher and children read together both stories as given in the text. The teacher directs the silent reading, section by section, by such questions as "What could a man do whose slave ran away?"

Children read silently and answer orally. After both stories have been completed in this manner they test themselves by the questions at the end of both stories.

READING FOR RECREATION

ALLEE, *Susanna and Tristram*.
TROWBRIDGE, *Cudjo's Cave*.

The Discussion (First Two Stories)

Children answer the study-guide questions as completely as possible. Visitors from the upper grades question them to test their understanding. The teacher writes on the board the words *fugitive slave, underground railroad*. Children discuss the meanings.

Conversational Approach (Third Story)

"Which section seems to be getting far ahead of the other? What different plans have been tried to try to satisfy both parties? Does either one seem to be really satisfied?

"What do you think the South will do when it makes up its mind that it can never equal the North in population and wealth? Our story will tell us."

Reading and Study

The Reading Periods (Third Story)

Independent Readers

TEXTS

BARKER, DODD, WEBB, *Our Nation Grows Up*, 154–156, 159–162.

BEARD and BAGLEY, *First Book in American History*, 299–320.

BURNHAM and JACK, *Growth of Our Country*, 187–191.

Lower Group

The teacher tells the story orally to this group, writing on the board the most important words as she mentions them. Children practice the pronunciations.

Then the teacher and this group read together the story as given in the text. The teacher directs the silent reading, section

CLARK, *Westward to the Pacific*, 337–343.
HALLECK and FRANTZ, *Makers of Our Nation*, 217–220.
KELTY, *Growth of the American People and Nation*, 336–342.
MCGUIRE and PHILLIPS, *Building Our Country*, 81–84.
SMALLIDGE and PAXSON, *Builders of Our Nation*, 461–482.
WOODBURN and MORAN, *Makers of America*, 268–273.

EXTENSIVE READING

BURNHAM, *Hero Tales from History*, 327–332.
CHANDLER and CHITWOOD, *Makers of American History*, 255–263, 265–269.
COE, *Makers of the Nation*, 303–313, 313–319.
DAVIDSON, *Founders and Builders of Our Nation*, 204–213.
EVANS, *America First*, 354–359.
FOOTE and SKINNER, *Makers and Defenders of America*, 230–244.
GORDY, *Leaders in Making America*, 323–329, 330–335.
LEFFERTS, *American Leaders*, II : 179–212, 216.
MONTGOMERY, *Beginners' American History*, 222–234, 235–237.
SOUTHWORTH, *Builders of Our Country*, II : 186–204, 206–209.
TAPPAN, *American Hero Stories*, 254–264.

by section, by such questions as "Had Lincoln ever appeared to be a great man before 1860?"

Children read silently and answer orally. When the entire story has been read in this manner they test themselves by the questions at the end of the story.

OTHER BOOKS

BALDWIN, *Fifty Famous People*, 7–11.
CURTIS, *Why We Celebrate Our Holidays*, 12–17.
DAVIS, *Stories of the United States*, 183–202, 203–209.
TAPPAN, *American History Stories for Very Young Readers*, 124–130.
WAYLAND, *History Stories for Primary Grades*, 125–128, 202–204.
WILSON, *History Reader*, 190–191.

READING FOR RECREATION

BALDWIN, *Abraham Lincoln*.
BUTTERWORTH, *In the Boyhood of Lincoln*.
GORDY, *Abraham Lincoln*.
MOORES, *Life of Abraham Lincoln for Boys and Girls*.
TARBELL, *Boy Scouts' Life of Lincoln*.

The Discussion (Third Story)

Children answer the study-guide questions. The teacher writes on the board the words *secession, Republican party*. Children discuss the meanings.

Multisensory Aids

Children and teacher talk over together the pictures in the text, pointing out features of geographic and historical importance.

They turn to a map and show all the territories theoretically opened to slavery by the Dred Scott decision. They turn to a map showing secession, and list the states which seceded. They count the number which seceded and the number which remained in the Union.

AUDIO-VISUAL MATERIALS OBTAINABLE

Compton's Pictured Teaching Materials : *Holidays*, Plate X.
EASTMAN. Classroom Films : Abraham Lincoln.
International Educational Pictures : Heart of Lincoln ; Abraham Lincoln (series).
Keystone Views : 128, 130, 131, 144–145, 345–346.
National Geographic Magazine, LXVI, 371 (September, 1934).
Perry Pictures : 2536.
Society for Visual Education. Picturol : Abraham Lincoln.
Yale Pageant Educational Slides : 54, 257–249, 503, 795–796, 798.

Music. Play records of "Chloe." Children sing "Dixie."

General Activities

Creative Activities: Group and Individual, Correlated with Other Subjects or Voluntary Projects

Volunteers draw up newspaper advertisements for runaway slaves.

Volunteers think up plans that might have been used to carry fugitives secretly from one station to the next of the underground railway.

Volunteers report on how the slavery question divided some of the churches. (For example, see *Methodists* and *Baptists* in a children's encyclopedia.)

A committee shows routes of the underground railroad. (D. R. Fox's *Harper's Atlas of American History*, 41.)

The class makes a trip to a local court to see how cases are tried. (No attempt is made to follow the details of a particular case.)

Volunteers draw theme illustrations for stories of fugitive slaves.

A committee makes a list of places named for Lincoln (from the index of an atlas); of things named for him.

The physical-education teacher may teach the boys a dance based on the rhythm of the woodcutter's ax.

The class makes a picture collection of Lincoln monuments.

Children make a map showing the states which seceded and those which remained in the Union.

Committees read to the class the dramatizations given in

> Johnston and Barnum, *Book of Plays for Little Actors*, 61–65.
> Wade, *Little Folks' Plays of American Heroes*, "Abraham Lincoln."
> Hubbard, *Little American History Plays*, 139–151.
> Walker, *Little Plays from American History*, 131–133.

A committee represents the Southern states. The members give arguments as to whether or not they will secede.

The class makes a trip to the museum to see hand-split rails.

A volunteer explains the cartoon in Knowlton's *Making History Graphic* (106–107).

The class plans an assembly program for Lincoln's birthday.

The class continues the time line.

Application to Present-Day Conditions

If a man's horse or cow strays away and someone else finds it, how can the owner secure his property?

If a man commits a crime in one state and hides in another, can the officers of the first state take him home with them when they find him? (See the heading *Extradition* in a children's encyclopedia.)

Are laws ever declared "against the Constitution" nowadays? Have you heard of any? Who declares them unconstitutional?

What chances in life do you have that Abraham Lincoln did not have?

Could we live as a nation today if each state could leave the Union when a law was passed that it did not like?

Is our president still inaugurated on March fourth? (See the Twentieth Amendment to the Constitution.)

Are armies nowadays made up of volunteers?

Is the Republican party today still against slavery in the territories?

Why is West Virginia a separate state from Virginia?

Exercises in Reasoning

Why did many fugitive slaves try to reach Canada?

Is it easy to make people obey a law that they think is wrong?

Why does Congress make a law that is against the Constitution?

How does Lincoln's life prove that a man may succeed in spite of all hardship?

Was Lincoln an uneducated man?

How did the fact that Lincoln had lived in border states help him to understand both sides of the slavery question?

Compare the secession of the Southern states from the Union with the revolt of the thirteen colonies from Great Britain.

Drill Games

Cards for drill games are made as follows:

Dred Scott	↔	a certain slave who had been taken by his master to live in a free state
underground railroad	↔	a method of helping fugitive slaves to escape
fugitive slaves	↔	slaves who ran away
Dred Scott decision	↔	the Supreme Court's statement that Congress could not keep slaves out of territories
"Honest Abe"	↔	a nickname given to Abraham Lincoln
Jefferson Davis	↔	president of the Confederacy
South Carolina	↔	the first state to secede
1860	↔	date of the secession of South Carolina
secession	↔	the act of leaving the Union
the Confederacy	↔	the government set up by the states that seceded
Republican party	↔	the political party that was against the spreading of slavery to any territories

Children practice by twos.

Testing

Tests of Understanding are given in Kelty's The Growth of the American People and Nation, pp. 328, 335, 342.

Tests of Reasoning and Skills. Check the best answer.

1. Slaves were not free by law when they reached free states because √ they were considered property, not persons.   the citizens there made them slaves again.   their masters always found them.

2. The Dred Scott decision said that Congress could   make any law it liked about slavery.   free the slaves in slave states.   √ not make a law to keep slaves out of any territories.   not let abolitionists enter slave states.

3. After reading of Lincoln's life, can you make up a sentence telling about opportunities in life for poor boys? _ _ _ _ _ _

4. The Southern states seceded when Lincoln was elected by the Republicans because   they hated Abraham Lincoln for his ideas about slavery.   they wanted Jefferson Davis as president.   the Republicans were going to put an end to slavery in the slave states.   √ the Republicans would try to prevent slavery from spreading to any territories.

5. In the quarrel between North and South   the right was all on the side of the South.   √ there was right on both sides.   the right was all on the side of the North.

6. Put the figure *1* before the thing which happened first, and the figure *2* before the thing which happened later.

  a. [_ _*1*_ _] The Compromise of 1850.
     [_ _*2*_ _] The Dred Scott decision.

  b. [_ _*2*_ _] The secession of South Carolina.
     [_ _*1*_ _] The election of Lincoln.

Exercise in Organization. Half the class copies the topic headings of the first story; the other half copies the headings of the second story. Each child prepares to give a brief summary of his headings.

C

STORY 1. THE FIRST TWO YEARS · STORY 2. THE BLOCKADE
[1 Week
[Stories treated separately for conversational approach, the reading periods, and the discussion; for other activities, both together]

Conversational Approach (First Story)

"Now that war has really begun, which side do you think will win? What advantage does the North have? What advantage does the South have?

"When nations are at war, why do you suppose that each one wants to capture the capital city of the other?

"Let us see how much we can learn about what happened from a map of the war." Children trace the lines of action shown and name the principal battles.

"Now we shall read about these attacks — four by one side and one by the other. Trace them on the map as you read about them and they will be much easier to understand."

Reading and Study

The Reading Periods (First Story)

Independent Readers

TEXTS

BARKER, DODD, WEBB, *Our Nation Grows Up*, 163–166.
BEARD and BAGLEY, *First Book in American History*, 320–324, 326–327, 336–340.

Lower Group

The teacher tells the story orally to this group, writing on the board the most important words as she mentions them.

Then the teacher and these children read together the story as given in the text.

BURNHAM and JACK, *Growth of Our Country*, 197–203.

CLARK, *Westward to the Pacific*, 343–349.

HALLECK and FRANTZ, *Makers of Our Nation*, 223–225.

KELTY, *Growth of the American People and Nation*, 343–353.

SMALLIDGE and PAXSON, *Builders of Our Nation*, 483–487.

WOODBURN and MORAN, *Makers of America*, 273–275, 282–285, 290–293.

EXTENSIVE READING

BURNHAM, *Hero Tales from History*, 341–346.

COE, *Makers of the Nation*, 325–337, 342–345.

EVANS, *America First*, 359–369, 374–383.

FOOTE and SKINNER, *Makers and Defenders of America*, 274–287.

GORDY, *Leaders in Making America*, 335–341.

HART, *Romance of the Civil War*, 117–124, 139–144, 192–196, 220–234.

LEFFERTS, *American Leaders*, II : 266–283.

SOUTHWORTH, *Builders of Our Country*, II : 209–210, 229–235.

The teacher directs the silent reading, section by section, by such questions as "Why did Robert E. Lee join the Confederate forces?"

Children read silently and answer orally. After the entire story has been read in this manner they test themselves by the questions at the end of the story.

OTHER BOOKS

BALDWIN, *Fifty Famous People*, 11–13.

WAYLAND, *History Stories for Primary Grades*, 122–124.

READING FOR RECREATION

ALTSHELER, *The Scouts of Stonewall*.

BARNES, *Son of Lighthorse Harry*.

CURTIS, *A Yankee Girl at Antietam*.

CURTIS, *A Yankee Girl at Fort Sumter*.

HILL, *On the Trail of Grant and Lee*.

The Discussion (First Story)

Children answer the study-guide questions with their maps open before them. The teacher writes on the board the words *Confederate, Union, Federal, The Blue and the Gray*. Children discuss the meanings.

Conversational Approach (Second Story)

"In which section of the country have we found that most of the factories were located? What will the South do now for manufactured goods? Name some of the kinds of goods it will need. Can it build factories of its own? Why not? Then where will it have to secure manufactured goods? [*Largely from Great Britain*.]

"Can you think of any way that the North might prevent this trade? Our story will tell us."

Reading and Study

The Reading Periods (Second Story)

Independent Readers

TEXTS

BARKER, DODD, WEBB, *Our Nation Grows Up*, 167–168.

BEARD and BAGLEY, *First Book in American History*, 324–326.

KELTY, *Growth of the American People and Nation*, 354–358.

EXTENSIVE READING

EVANS, *America First*, 383–387.

FOOTE and SKINNER, *Makers and Defenders of America*, 294–297.

Lower Group

The teacher tells the story orally to this group, writing on the board the most important words as she mentions them.

Then the teacher and these children read together the story as given in the text. The teacher directs the silent reading, section by section, by such questions as "Why did the Confederacy not win the war in the first two years?"

Children read silently and answer orally. When the entire story has been

HART, *Romance of the Civil War*, 347–366.
SOUTHWORTH, *Builders of Our Country*, II:
    210–211, 238–248.
TURPIN, *Cotton*, 109–110, 113–114.

read in this manner they test themselves
by the questions at the end of the story.

READING FOR RECREATION

AUSTIN, *Uncle Sam's Secrets*, 219–224, 237.
WORDEN, *The Monitor and the Merrimac*.

The Discussion (Second Story)

Children answer the study-guide questions as fully as possible, questioning
one another about important points omitted or misapprehended. The teacher
writes on the board the words *seaboard, blockade, ironclad*. Children discuss
the meanings.

Multisensory Aids

Children and teacher talk over together the pictures in the text, pointing
out the features of geographic or historical significance.

They turn to the map and children trace the four lines of Northern advance
and the line of Southern advance, describing each as they point it out.

AUDIO-VISUAL MATERIALS OBTAINABLE

EASTMAN. Educational Slides: Lincoln and the Civil War.
GRANT. *Story of the Ship:* The *Monitor*.
Keystone Views: 131, 134, 135, 342.
Society for Visual Education. Picturols: Battle Hymn of the Republic, Dixie.
Society for Visual Education (MUIR). 1850–1862: Beginning of the Civil War.
Yale Pageant Educational Slides: 250, 252, 746, 747, 799.

Music. Children sing Civil War songs: "Battle Hymn of the Republic,"
"Tenting on the Old Camp Ground," "Marching through Georgia," "Lorena,"
"Maryland, My Maryland," "When Johnny Comes Marching Home."

General Activities

Creative Activities: Group and Individual, Correlated with Other Subjects or Voluntary Projects

A committee models in the sand table the Southern states east of the
Mississippi. Other committees place strings of different colored yarns to represent the first four Northern advances and the first Southern advance.

Another committee places a circle of tiny ships outside each Southern port
to form a blockade.

The class makes a picture collection showing Arlington.

A volunteer explains how a vessel covered with iron plates can float.

A committee reads to the class the dramatization given in Hubbard's *Little
American History Plays* (152–157).

The teacher reads to the children selections from Stephen Vincent Benét's
John Brown's Body; Whittier's "Barbara Frietchie"; and from Persons's
Our Country in Poem and Prose the following: "The Black Regiment,"
"Keenan's Charge," "Roll Call," "Cavalry Song," "Cruise of the *Monitor*."

A man who has served in the navy describes a modern steel battleship to
the children.

Application to Present-Day Conditions

In what way has Lee's home, Arlington, been honored recently?

Are soldiers today sent into battle without any training at all?

Do people today still turn against their leaders when a task takes longer than they had thought that it would? Can you give examples?

Why does a war often make it appear that business is good? Is it good business in the long run?

What are profiteers? Can you give any examples from recent wars? (See unabridged dictionary under "New Words.")

Have you ever heard of any countries' being blockaded in recent years?

Are our battleships today ironclad?

Exercises in Reasoning

Why do you suppose that the men in the Southern armies were, on the whole, more interested in fighting than the men in the Northern armies?

What did each side hope to get from foreign countries?

Do you think that the people in the North understood what a task it would be to bring the South back into the Union? Explain your answer.

What advantage did Lee hope to get by invading the North?

In what way did the War between the States spread the use of McCormick's reaper?

Why was the paper money of the South worth very little?

Sometimes you hear people argue as to which is the more important, the army or the navy. Does this seem a sensible question? [*Both are needed.*]

How did the South plan to get money to buy guns and ammunition?

Compare a blockade with "opening the ports."

Drill Games

Place names are best drilled upon at the map: *Richmond, seaboard.*

Game cards are made as follows:

Robert E. Lee	⟷	the commander of the Confederate armies
"Stonewall" Jackson	⟷	one of the best of the Confederate generals
Civil War	⟷	the War between the States
the Union	⟷	the states that had not seceded
Federal	⟷	of the national government of the United States
the *Monitor*	⟷	the name of the Union ironclad
John Ericsson	⟷	a great engineer who built an ironclad
blockade	⟷	the closing of a seaport by an enemy
ironclad	⟷	a warship covered with armor
the *Merrimac*	⟷	the name of the Confederate ironclad

Children drill themselves, to make ready for the games played by the class.

Testing

Tests of Understanding are supplied in Kelty's *The Growth of the American People and Nation,* pp. 353, 358.

Tests of Reasoning and Skills

1. Turn to a map of the Civil War. Mark the following as true or false.

True False

[✓] [ ] The first advance of the North ended at Bull Run.

[✓] [ ] The second advance of the North was by water to Yorktown and by land from there to Richmond.

[ ] [✓] The third advance of the North was to Richmond.

[✓] [ ] The fourth advance of the North began at the Potomac River.

[ ] [✓] The first advance of the South into the North went beyond Antietam Creek.

2. Turn to a map of the Confederacy.

How many states did the North have to blockade? ___[9]___

How many Confederate states had no seacoast? ___[2]___

3. Mark the one statement among the following which is true.

[ ] Some unpatriotic people in the North made money from the war, but none in the South.

[ ] Some unpatriotic people in the South made money from the war, but none in the North.

[ ] No unpatriotic people made money from the war, in either the North or the South.

[✓] Unpatriotic people made money from the war in both the North and the South.

4. Number these events in the order in which they took place.

[__2__] The South advanced into the North.

[__1__] The North advanced into the South.

5. Under what heading do these stories stand in the table of contents?
_____

Exercise in Organization. The map-study exercise mentioned under "Multi-sensory Aids" serves as the exercise in organization.

C

STORY 3. CUTTING THE CONFEDERACY IN TWO · STORY 4.
THE END COMES   [1 Week

[Stories treated separately for conversational approach, the reading periods, and the discussion; for other activities, both together]

Conversational Approach (First Story)

"We have found out how the Northern blockade had kept the South from receiving manufactured goods from abroad. Now if the North could only keep the meat and food supplies of Texas and Louisiana from reaching the Southern armies, that too would help bring the war to an end."

The class turns to the map and tries to decide how the supplies from the West could be cut off. "Our story today tells how this was done."

Reading and Study

The Reading Periods (First Story)

Independent Readers

TEXTS

BARKER, DODD, WEBB, *Our Nation Grows Up*, 162–163, 168–169.
CLARK, *Westward to the Pacific*, 350–352.
HALLECK and FRANTZ, *Makers of Our Nation*, 225–227.
KELTY, *Growth of the American People and Nation*, 359–365.

EXTENSIVE READING

BURNHAM, *Hero Tales from History*, 346–352.
FOOTE and SKINNER, *Makers and Defenders of America*, 288–294.
HART, *Romance of the Civil War*, 177–179.

READING FOR RECREATION

LANIER, *Book of Bravery*, 349–360.
MILLER, *My Book House*, IV: 354–362.
PAGE, *Two Little Confederates*.

Lower Group

The teacher tells the story orally to this group, using the map for illustration as she talks.

Then the teacher and these children read together the story as given in the text. The teacher directs the silent reading, section by section, by such questions as "How could the North cut the Confederacy in two?"

The children read silently and answer orally. When the entire story has been read in this manner they test themselves by the questions at the end of the story.

OTHER BOOKS

GROVE, *American Naval Heroes*, 19–27.

The Discussion (First Story)

Children answer the study-guide questions. Those who have read additional material are given an opportunity to contribute. The teacher writes the word *admiral* on the board; children discuss the meaning.

Conversational Approach (Second Story)

"Turn to a map showing the last stages of the war. Do you see any way in which this part could be cut in two also? Trace two routes that the Northern armies followed in trying to do this very thing.

"Trace the route of a Southern army advancing into the North.

"Our story today tells us about all these actions. Together they brought the war to an end."

Reading and Study

The Reading Periods (Second Story)

Independent Readers

TEXTS

BARKER, DODD, WEBB, *Our Nation Grows Up*, 169–173.
BEARD and BAGLEY, *First Book in American History*, 326–335, 340–341.
BURNHAM and JACK, *Growth of Our Country*, 203–212.
CLARK, *Westward to the Pacific*, 352–358.
HALLECK and FRANTZ, *Makers of Our Nation*, 220–223, 228–230.
KELTY, *Growth of the American People and Nation*, 366–374.

Lower Group

The teacher tells the story orally to this group, using the map to illustrate her points.

Then the teacher and these children read together the story as given in the text. The teacher directs the silent reading, section by section, by such questions as "Why did President Lincoln change his mind about freeing the slaves?"

Children read silently and answer orally. When the entire story has been

SMALLIDGE and PAXSON, *Builders of Our Nation*, 487–488.
WOODBURN and MORAN, *Makers of America*, 275–282, 285–290, 293–295.

EXTENSIVE READING

BROOKS, *Story of Cotton*, 194–197.
BURNHAM, *Hero Tales from History*, 332–340.
CHANDLER and CHITWOOD, *Makers of American History*, 269–286.
COE, *Makers of the Nation*, 319–324, 338–342, 345–348.
EVANS, *America First*, 391–396.
FOOTE and SKINNER, *Makers and Defenders of America*, 258–273.
GORDY, *Leaders in Making America*, 341–356.
HART, *Romance of the Civil War*, 179–183, 189–191, 277–282.
LEFFERTS, *American Leaders*, II : 220–256.
MONTGOMERY, *Beginners' American History*, 237–239.
SOUTHWORTH, *Builders of Our Country*, II : 212–228.

read in this manner they test themselves by the questions at the end of the story.

OTHER BOOKS

BALDWIN, *Fifty Famous Rides and Riders*, 160–162.
BLAISDELL and BALL, *American History for Little Folks*, 122–127.

READING FOR RECREATION

LINDSAY, *Silverfoot*.
SINGMASTER, *A Boy at Gettysburg*.
SINGMASTER, *Sewing Susie*.
TAPPAN, *Ella, A Little Girl of the Sixties*.

The Discussion (Second Story)

Children answer the study-guide questions as completely as possible. The teacher writes on the board the words *emancipation, proclamation, draft, assassination.* Children discuss the meanings.

Multisensory Aids

Children and teacher talk over together the pictures in the text, pointing out features of geographic and historical significance. They turn to a map showing the late stages of the War between the States. They point out New Orleans, Island Number 10, the forts in Tennessee, Vicksburg, Port Hudson, and the "strip in the center." They show Atlanta and Savannah, and trace the routes of the last campaigns described.

AUDIO-VISUAL MATERIALS OBTAINABLE

Keystone Views: 136–138, 141, 149, 151, 341, 343, 344.
McKINLEY. Illustrated Topics for American History : S 32, 33.
National Geographic Magazine, LX, 66–75 (July, 1931).
Perry Pictures: 1422.
Society for Visual Education (MUIR). Finishing the Civil War — Assassination of Lincoln.
Yale Pageant Educational Slides: 255–260, 262–263, 516, 518, 748–750.

General Activities

Creative Activities: Group and Individual, Correlated with Other Subjects or Voluntary Projects

A committee models in the sand table the southern Mississippi Valley theater of war. They mark New Orleans, Vicksburg, Port Hudson, Island Number 10, and two forts in Tennessee. They mark with colored yarn the "strip in the center."

When the second story is read, another committee models the theater of war east of the Mississippi. It marks in colored yarn the different lines of advance in this section. Atlanta, Savannah, and Richmond are marked.

If any Confederate or Union veterans are living in the vicinity they may be invited to tell the children about their experiences.

A committee writes out the wording of an emancipation proclamation.

The teacher reads to the class Lincoln's "Gettysburg Address"; some of the most beautiful sentences from the "Second Inaugural Address"; Whitman's "O Captain, My Captain"; Harte's "John Burns of Gettysburg"; and parts of Mary Shipman Andrews's "The Perfect Tribute."

A committee reads to the class the dramatization given in Hague and Chalmers's *Dramatic Moments in American History* (246–294).

The class continues the time line.

Application to Present-Day Conditions

Is New Orleans fortified today? Why?

What is the name of the highest rank in the American navy today?

Is the city of New Orleans right on the Gulf of Mexico?

What are pensions? Who pays the pensions to the Union veterans? How much have the Civil War pensions cost the government? (See World Almanac, *Pensions*.) Does the Federal government pay pensions to Confederate veterans? How long since the Civil War ended?

In view of the amount of money which must be paid in pensions long after a war is over, do you think the United States should enter war needlessly?

Are soldiers drafted nowadays? How? (See *Conscription* in a children's encyclopedia.)

Do armies often fight "hand to hand" today? Why not?

How long do the hatreds bred by war last?

Can any signs of the War between the States still be seen in the South today? Why is it to be expected that signs of the conflict would remain longer in the South than in the North?

Exercises in Reasoning

Why did the North think it was wise to cut the Confederacy in two?

Why does an army not like to leave forts filled with enemy soldiers back of it?

Why is it hard to capture a hill held by the enemy?

Compare the plan of the North with Burgoyne's expedition in New York during the Revolution.

Why did not the Emancipation Proclamation free the slaves in the border states that had remained in the Union?

Do you think that General Sherman enjoyed destroying every building and all the crops in his path? Why did he do it? What did he mean when he said "War is hell"?

In what way did the end of the war mark the victory of coal, iron, and steam over farmers and planters? Does this situation still remain today?

Drill Games

Place names are best drilled upon at the map: *Atlanta, New Orleans, Gettysburg.*

Drill cards are made as follows:

Ulysses S. Grant	⟷	commander of all the Union armies in the last years of the War between the States
Admiral Farragut	⟷	the naval officer who took New Orleans
admiral	⟷	the highest-ranking officer of the navy
General Sherman	⟷	the Union general who cut the South in two for the last time
1861–1865	⟷	dates of the beginning and end of the War between the States
draft	⟷	system by which men are made to serve in the army and navy
Ford's Theater	⟷	the building in which Abraham Lincoln was shot
1863	⟷	the date of the Emancipation Proclamation
Emancipation Proclamation	⟷	the declaration that slaves in the seceding states were free

Children drill one another in preparation for the games.

Testing

Tests of Understanding are given in Kelty's *The Growth of the American People and Nation*, pp. 365, 374.

Tests of Reasoning and Skills

1. Make a list of all the reasons you can think of why the North won the war.

2. Turn to a map of the Civil War. Mark each of the following as true or false.

True False

[✓] [ ] New Orleans was a good place to begin cutting the Confederacy in two.

[ ] [✓] The "strip in the center" about which so much fighting took place was between Vicksburg and Island No. 10.

[✓] [ ] For years supplies for the Confederate troops had been coming from Texas and Louisiana.

3. Continue, using the map.

True False

[ ] [✓] The fifth advance from the North into the South went as far as North Carolina.

[ ] [✓] Sherman marched from Savannah into Virginia.

[✓] [ ] The second advance from the South into the North ended at Gettysburg.

[ ] [✓] The Union troops marched from Lookout Mountain to Vicksburg.

4. Do you think that it was a good thing or a bad thing that the North won? _____ Why? _____

Exercise in Organization. The teacher makes one outline including both stories. Children tell the most important points which belong under each.

Tests on the Entire Unit

Test of Place Sense. Pass outline maps of the United States showing the state boundaries by dotted lines. Give the following directions:

1. Put the letter *K* in the state of Kansas.
2. Put the letter *M* in the state of Missouri.
3. Put the letter *N* in the state of Nebraska.
4. Put the letter *S* in the state of South Carolina.
5. Draw Mason and Dixon's line in red.
6. Color the Mexican cession yellow.
7. Place a star (*) where Richmond, Virginia, is.
8. Place an *O* where New Orleans is.
9. Place a √ where Atlanta is.
10. Place a square (□) where Gettysburg is.

Test of Time Sense. Pass mimeographed sheets of the following.

I. 1. Here is a list of names. Put the figure *1* before the name of the person who lived first or whose great work was done first, the figure *2* before the name of the person who lived next, and so on.

[__1__] Andrew Jackson   [__3__] Abraham Lincoln
                      [__2__] Henry Clay

2. Here is another list. Do the same.

[__2__] Dred Scott   [__3__] Robert E. Lee   [__1__] Elias Howe

3. Here is another list. Do the same.

[__3__] General U. S. Grant   [__2__] Commodore Perry
                      [__1__] Samuel F. B. Morse

4. Here is another list. Do the same.

[__3__] Jefferson Davis   [__1__] Samuel Slater
                      [__2__] Sam Houston

5. Here is another list. Do the same.

[__2__] William Lloyd Garrison   [__3__] "Stonewall" Jackson
                      [__1__] Eli Whitney

6. Here is another list. Do the same.

[__1__] Alexander Hamilton   [__3__] John Ericsson
                      [__2__] Cyrus McCormick

II. Here is a list of dates:

1850	1865	1820
1619	1861	1863

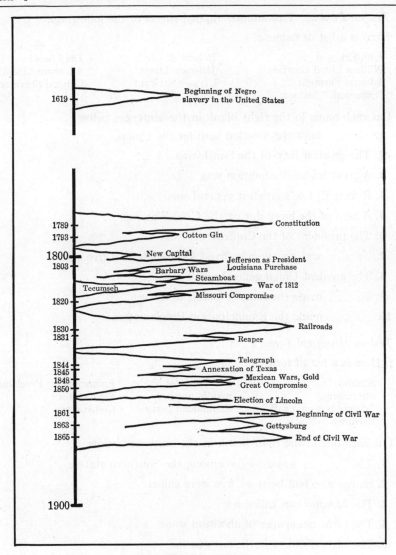

1619 — Beginning of Negro slavery in the United States

1789 — Constitution
1793 — Cotton Gin
1800 — New Capital
1803 — Jefferson as President / Louisiana Purchase
Barbary Wars
Steamboat
Tecumseh — War of 1812
1820 — Missouri Compromise

1830 — Railroads
1831 — Reaper

1844 — Telegraph
1845 — Annexation of Texas
1848 — Mexican Wars, Gold
1850 — Great Compromise
Election of Lincoln
1861 — Beginning of Civil War
1863 — Gettysburg
1865 — End of Civil War

1900

Time Chart — Unit Four

Put each in its right place in the sentences below.

1. The Missouri Compromise was made in _____.
2. Slaves were first brought into Virginia in _____.
3. The Civil War ended in _____.
4. The Civil War began in _____.
5. The Great Compromise was made in _____.
6. The Emancipation Proclamation was made in _____.

Test on Persons. Pass mimeographed sheets of the following.

Here is a list of names:

John Ericsson	Robert E. Lee	Dred Scott
William Lloyd Garrison	Jefferson Davis	Abraham Lincoln
Admiral Farragut	Ulysses S. Grant	General Sherman
"Stonewall" Jackson		

Put each name in the right blank in the sentences below.

1. _____ built the ironclad ship for the Union.

2. The greatest hero of the South was _____.

3. A great leader of abolition was _____.

4. Robert E. Lee's greatest general was _____.

5. A hero of the navy during the Civil War was _____.

6. The president of the Confederacy was _____.

7. _____ was a slave who lived for a while in a free state.

8. The greatest Union general was _____.

9. _____ made the famous march to the sea.

10. _____ made the Emancipation Proclamation.

Test on Historical Terms

I. Here is a list of terms:

admiral	*The Liberator*	Emancipation Proclamation
compromise	middle passage	slave states
"cheese box on a raft"	Republican party	Confederacy
freedmen		

Put each one in the right blank in the sentences below.

1. The _____ was a league among the Southern states.

2. Slaves who had been set free were called _____.

3. The *Monitor* was called a _____.

4. The great newspaper of abolition was _____.

5. The highest officer in the navy is the _____.

6. States in which there was slavery were the _____.

7. The party that believed there should be no slavery in the territories was the _____.

8. A settlement of a question by which each side gains something but has to give up something is a _____.

9. The part of the Atlantic between Africa and the West Indies which was used by the slave ships was called the _____.

10. The statement by President Lincoln that the slaves in the seceding states were free was the _____.

II. Here is another list. Do the same.

slavery	ironclad	plantation system
fugitive slave	Missouri Compromise	overseer
field servants	*Monitor*	underground railroad
"Honest Abe"		

1. A vessel covered with iron or steel is an _ _ _ _ _ _ .

2. The raising of one crop on a very large farm, usually by Negro labor, is the _ _ _ _ _ _ .

3. A slave who ran away was a _ _ _ _ _ _ .

4. A man who had charge of slaves at work was an _ _ _ _ _ _ .

5. The settlement of the question about slavery in the Louisiana Purchase was the _ _ _ _ _ _ .

6. Slaves who worked in agriculture were _ _ _ _ _ _ .

7. Lincoln was called _ _ _ _ _ _ .

8. The ironclad vessel belonging to the North was the _ _ _ _ _ _ .

9. The system of helping slaves to escape to Canada was the _ _ _ _ _ _ .

10. The condition of a human being who is the property of another is _ _ _ _ _ _ .

III. Here is another list. Do the same.

assassination	house servants	border states
cotton states	Civil War	poor whites
free states	Great Compromise	

1. The War between the States was the _ _ _ _ _ _ .

2. States between the North and the South were the _ _ _ _ _ _ .

3. Killing a person by sudden attack is _ _ _ _ _ _ .

4. Slaves who did work around the house were _ _ _ _ _ _ .

5. States in which the growing of cotton was a chief industry were called _ _ _ _ _ _ .

6. The Act of Congress which allowed the people in the Mexican Cession (except California) to choose for themselves whether they should have slavery or not was the _ _ _ _ _ _ .

7. States in which no slavery was allowed were _ _ _ _ _ _ .

8. Southerners who did not have slaves or large plantations were _ _ _ _ _ _ .

Comprehension Test on Unit Four

Check the best answer.

1. Slavery in America was begun _____ during the American Revolution.
√ in the colonial period.   after the Constitution was adopted.

2. The slave trade was the name given especially to the _____ selling of slaves inside the state.   selling of Negroes from the border states to the far South.
√ securing of Negroes in Africa and selling them in America.

3. In the Civil War each side wanted   to wait at home until the other attacked it.   √ to take the capital and the government of the other.   to starve the other out.

4. By 1800 slavery had almost disappeared in   √ the North.   the South.   the territories.

5. The reason why the Union fleet blockaded the Southern ports was √ to cut off trade with Europe.   to prevent armies' being sent from port to port.   to burn the Southern ports.

6. The main reason why the South wanted to have more slaves was because   the Southerners did not like to work.   √ they wanted to grow more cotton.   the Negroes made their population greater.

7. The reason why the Federal forces wanted to have all the cities along the Mississippi was   √ to cut the Confederacy in two.   to travel by water instead of by land.   to own the largest cities.

8. Should slavery be spread into the new territories? In the first settlement of the question in the Louisiana Purchase lands it was decided   √ to draw a line north of which was to be free soil and south of which was to be slave soil.   to let the people decide for themselves.   to allow no slavery at all anywhere in the territories.

9. Later in the same lands it was decided   to draw a line north of which was to be free soil and south of which was to be slave soil.   √ to let the people decide for themselves.   to allow no slavery at all anywhere in the territories.

10. The reason why the North won in the Civil War was that   its soldiers were braver.   its side was right.   √ it had more men and more money.

11. In the lands we got from Mexico, all but California were   √ to decide for themselves whether they would be slave or free.   to draw the Missouri Compromise line farther west.   not to try to settle the slavery question in any manner.

12. The Dred Scott decision said that   a slave was free if he went into free territory.   √ Congress could not prevent a master from taking his slaves into United States territory.   slaves must stay in the slave states and not attempt to run away from their masters.

13. The South seceded after the election of Lincoln because   they did not like Lincoln.   √ Lincoln's party stood for "no more slavery in the territories."   they believed Lincoln would free their slaves to please his party.

14. What is the title of the unit which you have just completed? _ _ _ _ _ _

Are any children now ready to be transferred from the lower group to the group of independent readers?

UNIT FIVE · *How the United States became really United in Spirit*

EXTRA STORIES FOR MORE ADVANCED READERS

Writers: Walt Whitman, Mark Twain
Musicians and Artists: Sargent, Homer, St. Gaudens, French, MacDowell
Our National Parks
Great World's Fairs
Child Labor
Improvements in Prisons and Asylums

A

RECONSTRUCTION IN THE SOUTH   [*1 Week*

Conversational Approach

"The end of the war left an enormous amount of work to be done. For example, what would the Southern soldiers have to do when they returned to their plantations?

"Under what government had the Southern states been living during the war? Could these governments continue? Why not? Had the Southern states been sending their Senators and Representatives to Washington during the war? Then these must be elected too.

"Some of the people in the North were afraid that the Southerners might not be fair to the Negroes. Can you think of any laws which might be passed to try to protect them?

"Our story today tells how the country tried to solve these many problems."

Reading and Study

The Reading Periods

Independent Readers

This group reads the story through silently, as given in their text. They then test their comprehension by the study-guide questions furnished by the teacher or the text.

Lower Group

The teacher tells the story orally to this group, writing on the board the most important new words as she mentions them. Children practice the pronunciations.

Then the teacher and these children

TEXTS

BARKER, DODD, WEBB, *Our Nation Grows Up*, 174–175.

BEARD and BAGLEY, *First Book in American History*, 360.

BURNHAM and JACK, *Growth of Our Country*, 212–215.

CLARK, *Westward to the Pacific*, 358–363.

KELTY, *Growth of the American People and Nation*, 377–383.

WOODBURN and MORAN, *Makers of Our Nation*, 297–303.

EXTENSIVE READING

BROOKS, *Story of Cotton*, 197, 199–202.

TURPIN, *Cotton*, 115–122.

read together the story as given in the text. The teacher guides the silent reading, section by section, by such questions as "How would the ending of slavery make a change in Southern life?"

Children read silently and answer orally. When the entire story has been read in this manner they test themselves by the questions at the end of the story.

OTHER BOOKS

CURTIS, *Why We Celebrate Our Holidays*, 81–85.

READING FOR RECREATION

BOOKER T. WASHINGTON, *Up from Slavery*.

The Discussion

Several different sets of children give the answers to the study-guide questions. The teacher writes on the board the words *amendment, voter, carpetbaggers, citizen, reconstruction, decade*. Children discuss the meanings.

Multisensory Aids

Children and teacher talk over together the pictures in the text, pointing out features of geographic and historical significance.

AUDIO-VISUAL MATERIALS OBTAINABLE

EASTMAN. Classroom Films: The New South.

McKINLEY. Illustrated Topics for American History: S 34.

Yale Pageant Educational Slides: 261, 264.

General Activities

Creative Activities: Group and Individual, Correlated with Other Subjects or Voluntary Projects

A volunteer makes a list of the tasks confronting the returned Southerners.

One pupil impersonates Lincoln and tells why his plan of reconstruction should be followed. Another acts as a member of Congress and tells why he thinks the Congressional plan should be followed.

A committee makes cards, like the drill cards used in games, with the words *Thirteenth Amendment, Fourteenth Amendment*, and *Fifteenth Amendment* on them. They decide what explanations should be printed on the other side.

A volunteer brings an old-fashioned carpetbag to show to the class.

Floor talks are given about Booker T. Washington and Tuskegee Institute; about the Peabody Fund for bringing better understanding between North and South; about Julius Rosenwald's work for Negro education.

The teacher reads to the children some of the poems of Paul Lawrence Dunbar and Countee Cullen, or others from Odum and Johnson's *The Negro and His Songs*.

The class studies Memorial Day as a factor in healing the wounds left by the war. The teacher reads Mayo's poem "The Blue and the Gray."

Committees read the dramatization given in Hubbard's *Little American History Plays* (173–177).

If there is a Confederate soldier in the community, he may tell the children about the tasks of the early years of reconstruction.

Application to Present-Day Conditions

Why is it always hard for men coming home from a war to find jobs?

Are pardons ever given nowadays? By whom?

Who becomes president if the president dies in the middle of his term?

Have any amendments been made to the Constitution recently? On what subjects?

Are you a citizen of the United States? Is your baby brother a citizen? (See the Fourteenth Amendment.) Is a citizen the same as a voter?

Why is a legislature made up of citizens who do not pay direct taxes likely to waste a great deal of money?

Compare the Ku Klux Klan of post-Civil-War days with the Ku Klux Klan of post-World-War days.

Is the "Solid South" still "solid" today? (See the latest election returns.)

Is the South still left to decide for itself whether or not the Negro should be given the right to vote? Are there any problems today in the relations of white people and colored people? [*For example, lynching, "Jim Crow" cars.*]

Exercises in Reasoning

What had the Civil War settled about slavery? about secession?

Why do you think that Lincoln's plan of reconstruction was wiser than the plan of Congress?

Do you think that it was wise to give the Negroes the right to vote immediately? Should ignorant people be allowed to vote now?

Why did the Negro legislatures in the South pass many laws that were not wise?

Why can the people who live in a country decide what ought to be done better than those who live outside?

Drill Cards

Cards are made as follows:

reconstruction	⟷	building up Southern life again
amendment	⟷	a change in the Constitution
carpetbaggers	⟷	cheap political leaders who went to the South after the war
citizen	⟷	a person who owes loyalty to a particular government
voter	⟷	one who has the right to tell his choice at an election or meeting
Ku Klux Klan	⟷	a society organized to regain control by white men in the South
decade	⟷	a period of ten years

Children choose whether to practice alone or in groups.

Testing

Tests of Understanding are suggested in Kelty's *The Growth of the American People and Nation*, p. 383.

Tests of Reasoning and Skills. Check the best answer.

1. New officers had to be elected all through the South because   the old officers had all died in the war.   √ the old officers had fought against the Union.   new officers would be younger men.   new officers would understand new problems.

2. The new legislatures in the South passed many bad laws because   the members were Negroes.   √ the members were not educated men.

3. Find two reasons why the plan of Congress for bringing the Southern states into the Union was more severe than Lincoln's plan.

4. Match the two columns below. Draw lines to connect the parts which belong together.

Fifteenth Amendment   about freedom
Thirteenth Amendment   about citizenship
Fourteenth Amendment   about voting

5. Put the figure *1* before the thing which happened first, the figure *2* before the thing which happened next, and the figure *3* before the thing which happened last.

[__3__] Thirteenth Amendment passed   [__2__] End of Civil War
[__1__] Emancipation Proclamation

Exercise in Organization. Children copy the topic headings of the story and prepare to give a brief topical recitation on each.

B

STORY 1. FREE LAND · STORY 2. THE OVERLAND STAGE AND THE PONY EXPRESS   [*1 Week*

[Stories treated separately for reading and discussion; for other activities, both together]

Conversational Approach

The teacher writes on the board the name of the unit. Children tell the bearing which the last story had on the unit. "Turn to the table of contents. What is the second subheading? What bearing does it have on the unit? Show how the titles of our two stories today relate to the unit theme."

Reading and Study

The Reading Periods (*First Story*)

Independent Readers

TEXTS

BARKER, DODD, WEBB, *Our Nation Grows Up*, 215–218.
BURNHAM and JACK, *Growth of Our Country*, 221–222, 235–236.

Lower Group

The teacher tells the story orally to this group, writing on the board the most important words as she mentions them. Children practice the pronunciations.

Then the teacher and this group read

CLARK, *Westward to the Pacific,* 166–169, 176–181.

KELTY, *Growth of the American People and Nation,* 384–388.

NIDA, *Following the Frontier,* 196–200, 238–242.

EXTENSIVE READING

GORDY, *Leaders in Making America,* 382–383.

VOLLINTINE, *Making of America,* 237–238.

READING FOR RECREATION

BUSH, *A Prairie Rose.*

CARRUTH, *Track's End.*

CATHERWOOD, *Rocky Fork.*

CHOWEN, *Living Wild.*

together the story as given in the text. The teacher directs the silent reading, section by section, by such questions as "What was the first price asked for Western lands?"

Children read silently and answer orally. When the entire story has been read in this manner they test themselves by the questions at the end of the story.

OTIS, *Seth of Colorado.*

TABER and BOETCHER, *Breaking Sod on the Prairie.*

WILDER, *Little House on the Prairie.*

The Discussion (First Story)

Children answer the study-guide questions as fully as possible. The teacher attempts to draw the lower group into the discussion. She writes on the board the words *free land, homesteaders, Land Office.* Children discuss the meanings.

The Reading Periods (Second Story)

Independent Readers

TEXTS

BARKER, DODD, WEBB, *Our Nation Grows Up,* 181–195.

BURNHAM and JACK, *Growth of Our Country,* 225–227.

McGUIRE and PHILLIPS, *Adventuring in Young America,* 309–311, 338–342.

KELTY, *Growth of the American People and Nation,* 389–395.

NIDA, *Following the Frontier,* 288–294.

SMALLIDGE and PAXSON, *Builders of Our Nation,* 557–560.

WOODBURN and MORAN, *Makers of America,* 328–330.

EXTENSIVE READING

EVANS, *America First,* 339–344.

FAIRBANKS, *Western United States,* 198–204.

FARIS, *Real Stories from Our History,* 169–190, 196–212.

FARIS, *Where Our History Was Made,* II: 165–174, 190–194.

GORDY, *Leaders in Making America,* 364–372.

HART, *How Our Grandfathers Lived,* 85–87.

VOLLINTINE, *Making of America,* 238–240.

Lower Group

The teacher and this group read together the story as given in the text. The teacher directs the silent reading, section by section, by such questions as "Why did so many people want to go West or send letters there?"

Children read silently and answer orally. When the entire story has been read in this manner they test themselves by the questions at the end of the story.

OTHER BOOKS

BLAISDELL and BALL, *Pioneers of America.*

MILLER, *My Book House,* I: 343–352.

READING FOR RECREATION

CODY, *Adventures of Buffalo Bill.*

DRIGGS, *The Pony Express Goes Through.*

GRINNELL, *Jack in the Rockies.*

HAUCK, *The Youngest Rider.*

HOOKER, *The Bullwhacker.*

NIDA, *Letters of Polly, the Pioneer.*

SABIN, *On the Overland Stage.*

WILSON and DRIGGS, *The White Indian Boy.*

The Discussion (Second Story)

Children answer the study-guide questions as fully as possible, the teacher watching with care the performance of children recently transferred from the lower group to the group of independent readers. She writes on the board the words *overland stage, pony express, scout.* Children discuss the meanings.

Multisensory Aids

Children and teacher talk over together the pictures in the text, pointing out features of geographic and historical significance.

AUDIO-VISUAL MATERIALS OBTAINABLE

Compton's Pictured Teaching Materials: *Communication*, Plate IV, 5.
GABRIEL (Ed.). Pageant of America: III, 113, 190–191.
International Educational Pictures: Pony Express.
McKINLEY. Illustrated Topics for American History: S 35.
Yale Pageant Educational Slides: 155–156, 175–176, 187–188, 491, 581, 677, 688–689.

Music. Children sing "Little Brown Church" (illustrating life in Iowa).

General Activities

Creative Activities: Group and Individual, Correlated with Other Subjects or Voluntary Projects

A volunteer draws up the wording of the Homestead Act. Another may try to make a miniature sod house.

Children draw scenes of life on a homestead, based on their reading.

A volunteer reports on the plague of grasshoppers; another on tornadoes and blizzards.

The class makes a picture collection of the phases of Western life represented in the two stories.

A floor talk is given on the life of "Buffalo Bill" Cody.

A relay game is played, so that all children may understand the principle of relaying as applied to the pony express.

A volunteer writes a diary of Buffalo Bill in the days when he was a pony expressman.

A volunteer graphs the comparative figures of speed per hour for the stage coach and the pony express.

Children who have seen the motion picture *Cimarron* describe the great land rush.

A volunteer graphs the changing figures for homestead size in the dry West; from 160 acres to 320 to 640. Why were larger homesteads allowed in the dry areas?

An old settler tells the children how he took up land from the government.

The teacher reads to the children selections from Hamlin Garland's *Boy Life on the Prairie* and from Bradley's *Story of the Pony Express*. She reads or sings "Songs of the Overlanders" from Lomax's *American Ballads and Folk Songs*.

A volunteer shows the table of public lands in the World Book Encyclopedia.

Application to Present-Day Conditions

A committee finds out how much 640 acres of land is in terms of a part of the city or neighboring farms; the same for 160 acres; for 80 acres; for 40 acres; for 1 acre.

Can any farming land be had from the government free nowadays?

Who owns the wild lands in your state, the state itself or the Federal
government?

Do you think you would rather live on scattered farms as in the United
States, or in farming villages as do the people of Europe?

Have you ever seen strips of sod used nowadays? [*In making lawns.*]

How are modern through busses somewhat like the old overland stage?

What are "gumbo" roads? Are they still holding back settlement? (See
unabridged dictionary.)

Are any parts of the West still supplied by freighting? Is this done by
wagons or trucks?

How did the word *bullwhacker* originate? (See unabridged dictionary.)

Compare the postage cost of $10 an ounce by pony express with the present
cost of air-mail postage.

Explain the expression *a land-office business*, meaning "a rushing business."

Exercises in Reasoning

Do you think it is fair for rich land companies or persons to buy up the
best land along riverbanks with no intention of working it, but only to sell at
a high price to some man who really needs it in order to reach the river?

How do you suppose that homesteaders proved that they had lived five
years on their claims?

What could homesteaders on the plains use for firewood?

Why could settlement in the tough-sod areas not have been made before
plows were improved?

Figure the daily cost of the overland stage journey.

Why were there so many holdups of the stage coaches? [*Some carried gold
from the mines.*]

Why did the telegraph make the pony express unnecessary?

We are told that different questions are asked of people in different parts
of the country: "What family do you come from?" "How much money have
you?" "What can you do?" Of these three questions, which do you think
was most important in the young West?

Drill Games

Cards are made as follows:

homesteaders	↔	persons who took up free land for homes
Homestead Act	↔	the law allowing settlers to take up free land for homes
free land	↔	land given by the government to settlers
Land Office	↔	the department of the government which managed the giving or sale of land
overland stage	↔	passenger coaches crossing the country
"Buffalo Bill" Cody	↔	the man who made Wild West shows famous
scout	↔	a man sent ahead of an army to find out about the country
pony express	↔	rapid transportation by horseback riders

Testing

Tests of Understanding are given in Kelty's *The Growth of the American People and Nation*, pp. 388, 395.

Tests of Reasoning and Skills

1. Can you make up a sentence telling how the means of communication make a difference in the speed of settlement of a country? Write it here.

------

2. Check the right answer: People who would be most interested in free land in the West would be   sailors.   manufacturers.   fur-traders. √ farmers.

3. What things should you expect to learn about stagecoaches by reading the advertisements of a stagecoach company? ------

4. Put the figure *1* before the one which reached the Pacific coast first, and the figure *2* before that which reached it later.

[--*1*--] the pony express   [--*2*--] the telegraph

Exercise in Organization. Children choose which of the two stories they will outline, working individually.

B

STORY 3. TRANSCONTINENTAL RAILROADS · STORY 4. THE END OF THE INDIAN QUESTION   [*1 Week*]

[Stories treated separately for reading and discussion; for other activities, both together]

Conversational Approach

"Read the title of the new story. How might the railroads help to bind the West to the East? Use the scale of miles to estimate about how far it is from the Mississippi River to the West coast. Why would it cost enormous sums of money to build railroads so far?

"After they were built, what effect should you expect them to have on the settlement of the West?

"Aside from the hard work, what do you suppose people feared most about going to settle in the West? If the Indians become peaceful, what difference do you suppose that will make? Our stories this week tell about these problems."

Reading and Study

The Reading Periods (First Story)

Independent Readers

TEXTS

BARKER, DODD, WEBB, *Our Nation Grows Up*, 195–202.

BURNHAM and JACK, *Growth of Our Country*, 266–270.

CLARK, *Westward to the Pacific*, 373–378.

Lower Group

The teacher tells the story orally to this group, writing on the board the most important words as she mentions them.

Then the teacher and this group read together the story as given in the text. The teacher guides the silent reading, section

KELTY, *Growth of the American People and Nation*, 396–401.

McGUIRE and PHILLIPS, *Adventuring in Young America*, 311–314.

McGUIRE and PHILLIPS, *Building Our Country*, 308–312.

NIDA, *Following the Frontier*, 304–310.

SMALLIDGE and PAXSON, *Builders of Our Nation*, 536–539.

WOODBURN and MORAN, *Makers of America*, 324–328.

EXTENSIVE READING

BEEBY, *How the World Grows Smaller*, 120–129.

BROOKS, *Story of Cotton*, 236–238.

FARIS, *Real Stories from Our History*, 283–289.

GORDY, *Leaders in Making America*, 373–378.

LARGE, *Everyday Wonders*, 134–144.

TAPPAN, *Heroes of Progress*, 168–178.

VOLLINTINE, *Making of America*, 240–242, 246–249.

by section, by such questions as "Which reached the Pacific coast first, the telegraph or the railroad?"

Children read silently and answer orally. When the entire story has been read in this manner they test themselves by the questions at the end of the story.

READING FOR RECREATION

BLACKIE, *A Book of Engines*.

CRUMP, *Boys' Book of Railroads*.

DUVOISIN, *All Aboard*.

HENDERSON, *Trains*.

HOLLAND, *Historic Trains*.

HOSKINS, *The Iron Horse*.

LENT, *Clear Track Ahead*.

LINCOLN SCHOOL, *Trains*.

MEIGS, *The Wonderful Locomotive*.

PRYOR, *The Train Book*.

REED, *Railway Engines of the World*.

REYNOLDS, *Famous American Trains and their Stories*.

SABIN, *Opening the Iron Trail*.

VAN METRE, *Trains, Tracks, and Travel*.

The Discussion (First Story)

Children answer the study-guide questions as fully as possible. Have they by this time quite broken themselves of the habit of using the words of the book? The teacher writes on the board the words *trunk line, transcontinental*. Children discuss the meanings.

The Reading Periods (Second Story)

Independent Readers

TEXTS

BARKER, DODD, WEBB, *Our Nation Grows Up*, 218–226.

BURNHAM and JACK, *Growth of Our Country*, 230–235.

CLARK, *Westward to the Pacific*, 175–176.

KELTY, *Growth of the American People and Nation*, 402–407.

WOODBURN and MORAN, *Makers of America*, 330–331.

EXTENSIVE READING

EGGLESTON, *Stories of American Life and Adventure*, 191–201.

EVANS, *America First*, 344–349.

FARIS, *Where Our History Was Made*, II: 66–70.

GORDY, *Leaders in Making America*, 388–391.

LAUT, *Story of the Trapper*.

Lower Group

The teacher tells the story orally to this group, writing on the board the most important words as she mentions them.

Then the teacher and these children read together the story as given in the text. The teacher directs the silent reading, section by section, by such questions as "What land had been promised to the Indians?"

Children read silently and answer orally. When the entire story has been read in this manner they test themselves by the questions at the end of the story.

OTHER BOOKS

DAVIS, *Stories of the United States*, 223–225.

WILLIAMS, *Boys' Book of Indians and the Wild West*.

READING FOR RECREATION

ALTSHELER, *Last of the Chiefs.*
CORMACK and ALEXANDER, *The Horns of Gur.*
DEMING, *Indians in Winter Camp.*
DOUBLEDAY, *From Cattle Ranch to College.*
FOX, *Uncle Sam's Animals*, 45–51.
GRINNELL, *Jack among the Indians.*
LANGE, *On the Trail of the Sioux.*
LANIER, *Book of Bravery.*
LINDERMAN, *Blackfeet Indians.*

NIDA, *Letters of Polly the Pioneer*, 51–56.
OTIS, *Antoine of Oregon.*
ROBERTSON, *On the Trail of Chief Joseph.*
SABIN, *Boys' Book of Indian Warriors.*
STODDARD, *Little Smoke.*
WADE, *Ten Big Indians*, 179–256.
WALKER, *Shining Star, the Indian Boy.*
WILSON and DRIGGS, *The White Indian Boy.*

The Discussion (Second Story)

Children answer the study-guide questions as completely as possible, questioning one another to bring out important points omitted. The teacher writes on the board the words *government Indian schools, reservation.* Children discuss the meanings.

Multisensory Aids

Children and teacher talk over together the pictures in the text, pointing out features of historical and geographical significance.

AUDIO-VISUAL MATERIALS OBTAINABLE

Building America: Transportation.
Compton's Pictured Teaching Materials: *Land Transportation,* Plate X; *American Indians,* Plate VI, 5; Plate XII.
GABRIEL (Ed.). Pageant of America: I, 37–39; III, 172–174.
International Educational Pictures: Transportation (series), Railway (series).
Keystone Views: 152, 153.
McKINLEY. Illustrated Topics for American History: S 36.
Society for Visual Education. Picturols: Railroads, West of the Mississippi, Life of the Plains Indians.
Society for Visual Education (BRAY-EYEGATE). Transportation by Railroads in the United States — Passenger Service, Freight Service.
Yale Pageant Educational Slides: 168, 186, 189, 192–209, 340, 583, 698.

Music. Play records of Honegger's *Pacific 231.*
Play records of native Indian music; Dvořák's "Indian Lament."

General Activities

Creative Activities: Group and Individual, Correlated with Other Subjects or Voluntary Projects

The class divides into committees which learn the names of the principal trunk railway lines east of the Mississippi, and the principal trunk lines west of it. Each committee writes for a map and an advertising folder of its line. It then reports to the group, tracing the route on the large wall map and describing its advantages.

Pictures are shown describing sleeping cars, dining cars, observation cars, club cars, maid and valet service, shower baths, etc.

The class examines a physical map of the United States and tries to account for the location of the principal railway lines.

A volunteer explains the difference between a Diesel engine and the engine of an old locomotive.

A traveler in Europe describes European trains.

Visitors to national parks describe the herds of buffalo to the children.

One child represents the Americans and explains why we kept moving westward. Another child represents the Indians and shows in what ways the white men did wrong.

A committee reads to the class the dramatization given in Hague and Chalmers's *Dramatic Moments in American History* (175–198).

The teacher reads to the class selections from Vachel Lindsay's "Ghosts of the Buffaloes" in *Johnny Appleseed and Other Poems*. She reads or sings some of the railroad songs from Lomax's *American Ballads and Folk Songs* (3–45).

A committee secures pictures of the nearest government Indian school.

A volunteer finds out from what source the plains Indians got their horses. [*After arrival of Spaniards in Mexico.*]

Application to Present-Day Conditions

What are streamlined trains? (Show pictures.)

Is it likely that the automobile and the bus and the truck will put the railroads out of business?

Why do we have no single trunk line running from the Atlantic to the Pacific?

Why is Chicago a great railway center?

Why do distances in our country now not seem so great as they once did? Shall we be likely ever to feel that we must change our capital to some city more nearly in the center of the country?

Do Americans have much reason to feel proud of their treatment of the Indians?

Are any place names in your state Indian names?

Do you think the Indian was any more dangerous to the people of those times than the automobile is to us today?

Are there Indians today near your home? If so, do they live on reservations or like any other citizens?

Do you think people who have Indian blood in their veins should be ashamed of it?

Exercises in Reasoning

Why is one trunk line better than many short lines?

In what ways might it be a good thing to have all the railroads in the country under one management? In what ways would it probably not be a good thing?

Why have the automobile and the autobus made the railroads lose much money?

Why were so many foreigners brought to this country to work on the railroads?

In what way did the building of the railroad to the Pacific help Columbus's old dream of a route to the Indies come true?

Why could the railroads not earn much money until the West was settled?

Explain this statement: "The Indian was considered for the most part a dangerous animal, like the panthers, wolves and wild cats, or a nuisance like the stones and tree stumps, to be cleared away."

How did the school for Indians take the place of the sword?

Explain this sentence: "The shining steel rails gripped firmly all the land they crossed and bound it together as one nation."

How do you suppose that we know anything about the battle of the Little Big Horn if every man of Custer's troops was killed?

Do you think that we should try to make the Indians give up all their ancient customs and become just like white people?

Drill Games

Place names are best drilled upon at the map: *Oklahoma, Little Big Horn.* Drill cards are made as follows:

Cornelius Vanderbilt	⟷	the first man to make a trunk line
Union Pacific Railroad	⟷	the first railroad through to the west coast
James J. Hill	⟷	a man who helped greatly in the settling of the great Northwest
the New York Central	⟷	the Vanderbilt railroad
the Pennsylvania Railroad	⟷	a trunk line which united many short lines in Pennsylvania
trunk line	⟷	a main line, not a side line
J. P. Morgan	⟷	a great banker who helped to develop the railroads
transcontinental	⟷	crossing the country from ocean to ocean
Sitting Bull	⟷	a great leader of the Sioux Indians
government Indian schools	⟷	schools run by the United States government to teach the Indians
General Custer	⟷	an American who made a rash attack on Indians in Montana
reservation	⟷	a tract of land set aside for a certain purpose

Children drill alone until they think that they know the items; then they practice by twos.

Testing

Tests of Understanding are given in Kelty's *The Growth of the American People and Nation*, pp. 401, 407.

Tests of Reasoning and Skills. Check the best answer.

1. Uniting many small railroads into one trunk line was a good thing because   the bigger a thing is, the better it is.   cars could hold more freight that way.   √ cars did not have to be unloaded so many times.   small railroads are un-American.

2. The United States government did not keep its promise to the Indians because   Americans do not usually keep their promises.   √ Amer-

icans wanted land and mines in the Indians' territory.   the government
wanted to get rid of the Indians.   the government was not strong
enough to keep its citizens back.

3. Make a list of the things you have studied that helped to bind different
sections of the country together. _ _ _[*Railroads, canals, telegraph, roads,
steamboats.*]_ _ _

4. What might have happened if the West had not been bound to the
East by good means of transportation and communication? Tell in one
sentence. _ _ _ _ _ _

5. On what pages in your text can you find material about Sitting Bull?
_ _ _ _ _ _

Where did you look to find out? _ _ _[*Index.*]_ _ _
Under which word did you look?   Sitting [✓]   Bull [ ]

Exercise in Organization. Children choose one story, and make summary
sentences for it.

B

STORY 5. THE COW COUNTRY · STORY 6. THE TELEPHONE
[1 Week
[Stories treated separately for conversational approach, the reading periods, and the
discussion; for other activities, both together]

Conversational Approach (First Story)

Review from geography lessons the number of inches of rainfall needed for
ordinary farming; the number needed for dry farming. Consult a rainfall
map of the United States to determine the areas in which ordinary farming
cannot be carried on without irrigation.

"And yet we know that people had long been moving into those areas.
How could they earn their living? What name is given to the men who watch
the cattle? Our story today is about cowboys."

Reading and Study

The Reading Periods (First Story)

Independent Readers

TEXTS

BARKER, DODD, WEBB, *Our Nation Grows
Up,* 209–215.
BURNHAM and JACK, *Growth of Our Country,*
227–230.
CLARK, *Westward to the Pacific,* 232–236.
KELTY, *Growth of the American People and
Nation,* 408–413.
McGUIRE and PHILLIPS, *Adventuring in
Young America,* 229–238, 345–350.

EXTENSIVE READING

ALLEN, *United States,* 209–251.
BARROWS and PARKER, *United States and
Canada,* 75–83.

Lower Group

The teacher and this group read together the story as given in the text. The
teacher directs the silent reading, section
by section, by such questions as "Where
did most of the cattle come from?"

Children read silently and answer
orally. After the entire story has been
read in this manner they test themselves
by the questions at the end of the story.

OTHER BOOKS

ALLEN, *How and Where We Live,* 26–30, 36–
37.
CARPENTER, *The Foods We Eat,* 35–45.

CARPENTER, *How the World Is Fed*, 73–98.
CHAMBERLAIN, *North America*, 119–122.
GORDY, *Leaders in Making America*, 379–381.
HUSBAND, *America at Work*, 96–102.
LANE (Ed.), *Industries of Today*, 12–18.
LEFFERTS, *Our Own United States*, 218–222, 253–257.
PITKIN and HUGHES, *Seeing America: Farm and Field*, 213–224.
SMITH, *Human Geography*, I : 83.
TAPPAN, *Farmer and his Friends*, 83–85.
VOLLINTINE, *Making of America*, 235–237, 243.

CARROLL, *Around the World*, III : 81–85, 139–141.
CHAMBERLAIN, *How We Are Clothed*, 59–71.
CHAMBERLAIN, *How We Are Fed*, 18–31.
FAIRBANKS, *Home Geography for Primary Grades*, 194–197.
FAIRGRIEVE and YOUNG, *The World*, 132–142.
KNOWLTON, *First Lessons in Geography*, 112–117.
SHEPHERD, *Geography for Beginners*, 69–75, 138–141.
WINSLOW, *The Earth and Its People*, 77–78.

READING FOR RECREATION

CANFIELD, *Boys of the Rincón Ranch.*
CARTER, *Shaggy, the Horse from Wyoming.*
CHAFFEE, *Wandy, the Wild Pony.*
DOUBLEDAY, *From Cattle Ranch to College.*
GAUSS, *Bang of the Diamond Tail.*
GILLETT and DRIGGS, *The Texas Ranger.*
GRINNELL, *Jack the Young Ranchman.*
HINKLE, *Tawney, a Dog of the Old West.*
JAMES, *Cow Country.*
JAMES, *In the Saddle with Uncle Bill.*

JAMES, *Smoky.*
JAMES, *Young Cow Boy.*
McCONNELL and DRIGGS, *Frontier Law.*
OTIS, *Philip of Texas.*
ROLLINS, *Cow Boy Life in Montana.*
SWAN, *Frontier Days.*
TOUSEY, *Cow Boy Tommy's Round-up; Cow Boy Tommy.*
Cowboys (Ward, Lock & Co.).

The Discussion (First Story)

Children answer the study-guide questions as fully as possible. They recommend to one another the books they have found especially interesting. The teacher writes on the board the words *cow country, brand, cowboys, round-up, stockyards, sheep-herders.* Children discuss the meanings.

Conversational Approach (Second Story)

"Of all the ways that you might send a message to someone far distant, which two have we not yet studied? [*Telephone and radio.*] Which one was invented first? Do you understand the process by which a voice can travel miles over a wire? Few people do. It was a very difficult problem to solve. Our story today tells who solved it and how hard he worked."

Reading and Study

The Reading Periods (Second Story)

Independent Readers

TEXTS

BURNHAM and JACK, *Growth of Our Country*, 241–243.
CLARK, *Westward to the Pacific*, 390–392.
HALLECK and FRANTZ, *Makers of Our Nation*, 263–268.
KELTY, *Growth of the American People and Nation*, 414–418.
McGUIRE and PHILLIPS, *Building Our Country*, 289–293.
NIDA, *Following the Frontier*, 301–302.

Lower Group

The teacher tells the story orally to this group, writing on the board the most important words as she mentions them. Children practice the pronunciations.

Then the teacher and this group read together the story as given in the text. The teacher directs the silent reading, section by section, by such questions as "Why was a great fair held in Philadelphia?"

Children read silently and answer

SMALLIDGE and PAXSON, *Builders of Our Nation*, 565–567.
WOODBURN and MORAN, *Makers of America*, 332–335.

EXTENSIVE READING

BEEBY, *How the World Grows Smaller*, 157–190.
CHANDLER and CHITWOOD, *Makers of American History*, 294–296.
EVANS, *America First*, 401–404.
FARIS, *Real Stories from Our History*, 295–301.
GORDY, *Leaders in Making America*, 409–412.
LARGE, *Everyday Wonders*, 56–70.
LEFFERTS, *American Leaders*, II: 99–115.
McFEE, *Stories of American Inventions*, 84–104.
PARKMAN, *Conquests of Invention*, 379–395.
SANFORD and OWEN, *Modern Americans*, 29–35.
TAPPAN, *Heroes of Progress*, 115–121.
UHRBROCK and OWENS, *Famous Americans*, 259–267.

orally. After the entire story has been read in this manner they test themselves by the questions at the end of the story.

OTHER BOOKS

CHAMBERLAIN, *How We Travel*, 212–218.
EVERETT and REED, *When They Were Boys*, 15–23.

READING FOR RECREATION

LAMBERT, *Talking Wires*.

The Discussion (Second Story)

Children answer the study-guide questions as fully as possible. The teacher tries particularly to guard against the mere use of words without any ideas back of them.

Multisensory Aids

Children and teacher talk over together the pictures in the text, pointing out features of historical and geographic importance. They show on the map the states which constituted the "last frontier."

AUDIO-VISUAL MATERIALS OBTAINABLE

Compton's Pictured Teaching Materials: *Clothing*, Plate II; *Food*, Plate X; *Communication*, Plate IX.
EASTMAN. Classroom Films: Cattle, Meat-Packing, Sheep Range.
GABRIEL (Ed.). Pageant of America: III, 166–167, 175–190, 202–205; V, Chap. XII.
International Educational Pictures: Cattle Ranch.
Keystone Views: 107.
Society for Visual Education. Schoolfilm: Great Plains.
Society for Visual Education (SPENCER). Wool Production.
Yale Pageant Educational Slides: 171–173, 424–431, 482, 507.

Music. Play records of cowboy songs: "Oh, Bury Me Not on the Lone Prairie," "The Last Round-Up," "Good-by, Old Paint."
Sing songs from Larkin's *Singing Cowboy*.

General Activities

Creative Activities: Group and Individual, Correlated with Other Subjects or Voluntary Projects

A volunteer investigates to discover whether cattle are native to the Americas.
Volunteers carve longhorns from soap.

A committee models the cattle country in the sand table, marks the railroads mentioned, and the long drive.

Volunteers draw scenes of a round-up.

Children design their own brand.

The teacher reads to the children Carl Sandburg's poem "Chicago."

A visitor to the stockyards describes them to the children.

The class makes a trip to the local freight yard to observe cattle cars and refrigerator cars.

Volunteers find out from the local telegraph and telephone companies the comparative cost of telegrams and long-distance calls to the nearest large city.

Children who have attended any world's fair explain the purpose of such exhibitions.

The class makes a visit to a local telephone exchange to observe how calls are handled. Perhaps a demonstration can be arranged by telephone employees, illustrating telephone courtesy. (Suggestions may be obtained from *The Story of Communication*, Teacher's Lesson Unit Series, Teachers College, Columbia University.)

A volunteer explains the graph in Marshall's *Story of Human Progress* (341).

Someone who has lived in the West tells the children how the modern cowboy differs from the old-time cowboy.

Volunteers demonstrate how to use a dial telephone.

The teacher sings or reads to the children cowboy songs from Lomax's *American Ballads and Folk Songs* (375–421).

The class continues the time line.

Application to Present-Day Conditions

Which states today are the great cattle-producing states? (See World Almanac.) How do the cattle obtain their food in the winter? What are "feeders"? (See unabridged dictionary.)

Is a round-up the same as a rodeo?

What is a dude ranch?

Explain the graph showing a cattle census of the world in the World Book Encyclopedia under *Cattle*.

Are cattle still fed on the open range?

Explain how the main frontiers left open today are for "the pioneers of ideas."

Do sheep still graze in national forests?

Children inquire at their local meat markets as to the sources of supply.

Has the closing of the frontier had any effect on the opportunities open to poor people today?

Can deaf persons be taught to speak today? (Read about the life of Helen Keller.)

Does Brazil still have an emperor today? (See *Government* under *Brazil* in a children's encyclopedia.)

How is Bell's name still honored in the telephone world?

Explain the telephone census of the world, shown graphically in the World Book Encyclopedia under *Telephone*.

Exercises in Reasoning

Why was there no market for the cattle of the Great Plains before the railroad reached the West? Why could they not be sent out by steamboats?

How do the farmers of the Middle West today profit from the herds of cattle raised on the Great Plains? (See *feeders.*)

Can you draw up a general rule, telling the kind of work that people will do in a given locality before factories are built?

Why could the cattle men and the sheep men not get along peaceably?

How did the invention of the tin can build many American fortunes?

Why did the closing of the frontier give the Americans more time to enjoy art?

What is the difference between the telegraph and the telephone?

Do you think that the establishment of free public high schools during this period helped to make the United States united in spirit?

Drill Games

Cards are made as follows:

brand	⟷	a mark burned with a hot iron
cowboys	⟷	men who manage herds of cattle
round–up	⟷	gathering all the cattle together
stockyards	⟷	a large collection of pens in which cattle are kept for market
sheep–herders	⟷	men who guard large flocks of sheep
rodeo	⟷	an exhibition of skillful riding
Alexander Graham Bell	⟷	the inventor of the telephone
1876	⟷	date of the invention of the telephone

Games are played with all the cards used during the unit.

Testing

Tests of Understanding are given in Kelty's *The Growth of the American People and Nation*, pp. 413, 418.

Tests of Reasoning and Skills

1. In the second column put the letter *a* before the words that match the telephone and the letter *b* before the words that match the telegraph.

a. the telephone   [__*b*__] sends written messages

b. the telegraph   [__*a*__] sends spoken messages

2. How did the invention of barbed wire help to break up the open range? Answer in one sentence. _ _ _ _ _ _

3. Can you make a sentence telling about the value of the frontier to poor people? _ _ _ _ _ _

4. Is the kind of telephone that we use today the invention of one man?

                                        Yes [ ]   No [✓]

Exercise in Organization. Teacher and class working together make a co-operative outline of the last story.

Tests on the Entire Unit

Test of Time Sense. Pass mimeographed sheets of the following:

I. Here is a list of names. In each exercise put the figure *1* before the name of the person who did his great work first, the figure *2* before the name of the person who came next, and so on.

1. [__*3*__] Alexander Graham Bell   **4.** [__*3*__] James J. Hill
   [__*1*__] Samuel Slater   [__*1*__] Robert Fulton
   [__*2*__] Samuel F. B. Morse   [__*2*__] Cyrus McCormick

2. [__*1*__] Paul Revere   **5.** [__*1*__] Alexander Hamilton
   [__*3*__] "Buffalo Bill" Cody   [__*2*__] John Jacob Astor
   [__*2*__] General Taylor   [__*3*__] J. P. Morgan

3. [__*1*__] Lewis and Clark
   [__*3*__] General Custer
   [__*2*__] "Stonewall" Jackson

II. Here is a list of events which took place. Put the figure *1* before the event which took place first, the figure *2* before the event which took place next, and so on.

[__*3*__] Invention of the telephone
[__*1*__] Homestead Act
[__*2*__] Reconstruction

Test on Persons. Pass mimeographed sheets of the following:

I. Here is a list of names:

homesteaders	J. P. Morgan	General Custer
Alexander Graham Bell	Cornelius Vanderbilt	"Buffalo Bill" Cody
Sitting Bull	James J. Hill	

Put each name in the right blank in the sentences below.

1. The Indian in charge of the forces that defeated General Custer was
_____.

2. A great banker who helped in railroad building was _____.

3. The man who made the first trunk railroad was _____.

4. People who went to take up free government land were called _____.

5. The man who invented the telephone was _____.

6. _____ built the Great Northern Railroad.

7. _____ was a rider for the pony express.

8. At the battle of the Little Big Horn _____ was defeated.

Test on Historical Terms

I. Here is a list of terms:

citizen	amendment	Ku Klux Klan
pony express	voter	overland stage
round-up	Land Office	Great Northern Railroad
carpetbagger		

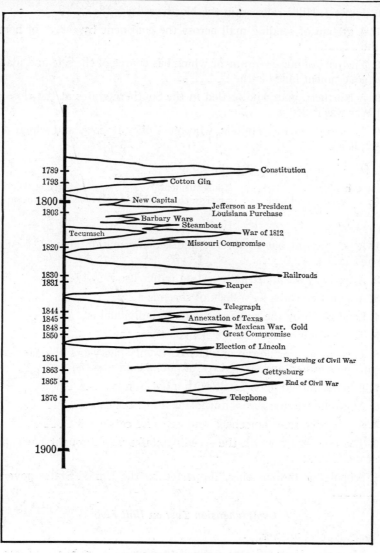

Time Chart — Unit Five

Put each one in the right blank in the sentences below.

1. A change made in our Constitution is an _ _ _ _ _ _.

2. A secret society in the South after the Civil War was the _ _ _ _ _ _.

3. Anyone who has by law the right to record his choice in an election is a _ _ _ _ _ _.

4. Driving cattle together to be branded is a _ _ _ _ _ _.

5. A carriage which made regular trips across country was the _ _ _ _ _ _.

6. James J. Hill's railroad in the Northwest was the _ _ _ _ _ _.

7. A system of sending mail across the continent by relays of horsemen was the _ _ _ _ _ _.

8. The part of our government which has charge of the sale and managing of the government lands is the _ _ _ _ _ _.

9. A Northern man who settled in the Southern states at the close of the Civil War was called a _ _ _ _ _ _.

10. A member of the republic, who must obey its laws and whom it must protect, is a _ _ _ _ _ _.

II. Here is another list. Do the same.

sheep-herder	transcontinental	reconstruction
Union Pacific Railroad	government Indian schools	reservation
cowboy	brand	free land
scout	Homestead Act	

1. A person sent out to observe and get information about the enemy in time of war is a _ _ _ _ _ _.

2. A territory set apart for a certain public use is a _ _ _ _ _ _.

3. A man who cares for a flock of sheep is a _ _ _ _ _ _.

4. Land given by the government to an individual is _ _ _ _ _ _.

5. The first railroad to the Pacific coast was the _ _ _ _ _ _.

6. The law which allowed any citizen twenty-one years of age or more to take up one hundred and sixty acres of public land was the _ _ _ _ _ _.

7. A mark burned upon cattle with a hot iron is a _ _ _ _ _ _.

8. Anything passing across a whole continent is called _ _ _ _ _ _.

9. A man who rides horseback and cares for cattle is a _ _ _ _ _ _.

10. The process by which the seceding states were brought back into the Union was _ _ _ _ _ _.

11. Schools for Indians only, supported by the United States government are _ _ _ _ _ _.

Comprehension Test on Unit Five

Check the best answer.

1. What the United States decided to do with its public land was   to sell it at a high price.   √ to give it to settlers.   to keep it all.

2. At the close of the war, which was left in worse condition?   The North.   √ The South.

3. Mails were carried in the West just after the Civil War by   √ the pony express.   railroads.   steamboats.

4. At this time in our history, passengers were carried by   railroads.   √ the overland stage.   automobiles.

5. After the Civil War the North   was very good to the South.   paid no attention to the South.   √ treated the South harshly.

6. The way in which affairs in the South were improved at last was that   the South let the Negroes run the states.   the North sent soldiers to the South.   √ the South took matters into its own hands.

7. One thing that bound the West to the East was the   √ transcontinental railroads.   discovery of gold.   defeat of the Indians.

8. A great business for which much of the land of the West could be used was the   growing of rice.   manufacturing of cotton.   √ cattle-raising business.

9. One of the greatest effects of the disappearance of the frontier was that   √ there was little free land left.   the people became lazy.   no one could live a life of adventure any more.

10. A great effect of the invention of the telephone was that   people could talk more.   people did not have to wait for letters from their families. √ business could be carried on more quickly.

11. Check two answers: Two great results of the defeat of the Indians were that   it showed how strong the United States was.   √ settlement of the West could go on faster.   √ the Indians had to give up their lands.

12. What is the title of the unit which you have just completed? _ _ _ _ _ _

Are any children now ready to be transferred from the lower group to the group of independent readers?

Unit Six · *How the United States became a Great Industrial Nation*

[5 Weeks

A

STORY 1. MINING · STORY 2. MAKING IRON AND STEEL · STORY 3. THE ELECTRICAL INDUSTRY   [1 Week

[For conversational approach, reading periods, and discussion, the first two stories are taken up together and then the third story; for other activities, all three together]

Conversational Approach (First and Second Stories)

"Read the title of our new unit. What is an industrial nation? If a nation is not industrial, what would you call it? Name some other countries besides the United States that are mainly industrial. Name some countries that are mainly agricultural.

"What was the title of Unit Three? Didn't the United States become an industrial nation then? [*It had only made a beginning.*] There were factories, to be sure, but they were small and employed few men. But by this time such factories were scattered everywhere. They could no longer spread over new territory; so they began to grow to a giant size instead.

"Why must an industrial country use enormous quantities of metal? Which of all our metals do you suppose is worth the most money each year?" Children speculate.

"Our stories today will tell us."

Reading and Study

The Reading Periods (First and Second Stories)

[These two stories are read consecutively before any discussion is held]

Independent Readers

This group reads both stories through silently, as given in the text. They then test their comprehension by the study-guide questions furnished by the teacher or by the text.

TEXTS

BARKER, DODD, WEBB, *Our Nation Grows Up*, 205–208.

BURNHAM and JACK, *Growth of Our Country*, 222–224, 250–252, 262–266.

CLARK, *Westward to the Pacific*, 459–462.

HALLECK and FRANTZ, *Makers of Our Nation*, 237–241.

KELTY, *Growth of the American People and Nation*, 421–430, 431–437.

McGUIRE and PHILLIPS, *Building Our Country*, 149–160, 164–167, 172–175, 195–199.

EXTENSIVE READING

ALLEN, *United States*, 138–208,

ATWOOD, *United States among the Nations*, 141–159, 166–170, 178–186.

BARROWS and PARKER, *United States and Canada*, 38–41, 117–119, 138, 141–142.

Lower Group

The teacher and this group read together the two stories as given in the text. The teacher directs the silent reading, section by section, by such questions as "What was one reason why the United States could become great industrially?"

Children read silently and answer orally. After both stories have been read in this manner, they test themselves by the questions at the end of the stories.

OTHER BOOKS

ALLEN, *How and Where We Live*, 97–102.

CARROLL, *Around the World*, III : 53–62, 75, 122–131.

CHAMBERLAIN, *How We Are Clothed*, 72–79, 222–225.

KNOWLTON, *First Lessons in Geography*, 172–177, 194–197.

SHEPHERD, *Geography for Beginners*, 51–55.

WINSLOW, *Earth and Its People*, 91–97.

BROOKS, *Story of Cotton*, 230–236, 242–248, 254–264.

CARPENTER, *How the World is Clothed*, 34–44, 44–50, 329–335.

CHASE and CLOW, *Stories of Industry*, I: 13–30, 39–80 ;] II : 17–76.

EGGLESTON, *Stories of American Life and Adventure*, 207–214.

FAIRBANKS, *Western United States*, 215–248.

GEORGE, *Little Journeys to Alaska and Canada*, 49–50.

GORDY, *Leaders in Making America*, 358–364.

HUSBAND, *America at Work*, 20–31.

LEFFERTS, *Our Own United States*, 12–15, 49–52, 55–56, 59–64, 98–100, 103–104, 174–177.

SAMUEL, *Story of Gold and Silver*.

SAMUEL, *Story of Iron*.

SANFORD and OWEN, *Modern Americans*, 169–175.

SMITH, *Human Geography*, I : 86–90, 136–139, 140–141.

SOUTHWORTH, *Builders of Our Country*, II : 266–269.

TAPPAN, *Diggers in the Earth*, 43–56, 65–75, 84–94.

TAPPAN, *Heroes of Progress*, 228–236.

VOLLINTINE, *Making of America*, 233–235.

WINSLOW, *United States*, 61–70, 148–155, 176–180.

READING FOR RECREATION

BORMANN, *Bridges*.

CARNEGIE, *Andrew Carnegie's Own Story for Boys and Girls*.

COOKE, *A Visit to a Cotton Mill*.

GARLAND, *The Long Trail*.

HODGINS and MAGOWN, *Sky High*.

JACKSON, *Nelly's Silver Mine*.

LAMPREY, *All the Ways of Building*.

LENT, *Diggers and Builders*.

MEANS, *Penny for Luck*.

NAUMBURG, LAMBERT, and MITCHELL, *Skyscraper*.

OTIS, *Seth of Colorado*.

PETERSHAM, *Story Book of Earth's Treasures*.

PETERSHAM, *Story Book of Houses*.

PETERSHAM, *Story Book of Oil*.

PRYOR, *The Steel Book*.

STANLEY-BROWN, *Young Architects*.

THOMPSON, *Gold-Seeking on the Dalton Trail*.

WADSWORTH, *Modern Story Book*.

WALDEN, *Dog Puncher on the Yukon*.

WIDDEMER, *In the Shadow of the Skyscrapers*.

The Discussion (First and Second Stories)
↓ [*In a Language Period*

Children answer the study-guide questions. Other children challenge them to present proof for their statements, and they must find the part of the text on which the statements were based.

The teacher writes on the board the words *claim, prospector, import, export, United States Steel Corporation, the New South*. Children discuss the meanings.

Conversational Approach (Third Story)

"This great industrial advance would have been much slower if all the factory machines had had to be run by steam. What other form of power is commonly used in factories? For what else is electricity used in factories besides for power? Do you know any other uses of electricity besides for power and light?"

Reading and Study

The Reading Periods (Third Story)

Independent Readers

TEXTS

BEARD and BAGLEY, *First Book in American History*, 344, 348–350.

BURNHAM and JACK, *Growth of Our Country*, 244–249.

HALLECK and FRANTZ, *Makers of Our Nation*, 241–247, 283–295.

Lower Group

The teacher and this group read together the story as given in the text. The teacher directs the silent reading, section by section, by such questions as "Did Americans make most of the discoveries about electricity?"

Children read silently and answer

KELTY, *Growth of the American People and Nation*, 438–443.

McGUIRE and PHILLIPS, *Building Our Country*, 167–172.

SMALLIDGE and PAXSON, *Builders of Our Nation*, 576–585.

WOODBURN and MORAN, *Makers of America*, 335–340.

EXTENSIVE READING

CHANDLER and CHITWOOD, *Makers of American History*, 289–294.

DAVIDSON, *Founders and Builders of Our Nation*, 160–167.

EVANS, *America First*, 405–408.

FORMAN, *Stories of Useful Inventions*, 36–37.

GORDY, *Leaders in Making America*, 404–408.

LEFFERTS, *American Leaders*, II : 116–129, 134–137, 139–142.

McFEE, *Stories of American Inventions*, 105–117, 117–142.

PARKMAN, *Conquests of Invention*, 158–168, 168–182.

SANFORD and OWEN, *Modern Americans*, 17–27.

SOUTHWORTH, *Builders of Our Country*, II : 260–265.

TAPPAN, *Heroes of Progress*, 199–207.

UHRBROCK and OWENS, *Famous Americans*, 269–279.

orally. When they have read the entire story in this manner, they test themselves by the questions at the end of the story.

OTHER BOOKS

EVERETT and REED, *When They Were Boys*, 15–22.

SHEPHERD, *Geography for Beginners*, 56–59.

READING FOR RECREATION

McFEE, *Story of Thomas A. Edison.*

MEADOWCROFT, *Boys' Life of Edison.*

ROLT-WHEELER *Thomas Alva Edison.*

The Discussion (Third Story)   [*In a Language Period*

Children answer the study-guide questions as completely as possible, with a high-school science student as guest.

The teacher writes on the board the words *electricity, phonograph, central power station.* Children discuss the meanings.

Multisensory Aids

Children and teacher together talk over the pictures in the text, pointing out features of geographic or historical significance.

AUDIO-VISUAL MATERIALS OBTAINABLE

Building America : Housing, Power.

Compton's Pictured Teaching Materials. *Water and Air Transportation*, Plate VIII, 2 ; *Clothing*, Plates II–IV ; *Coal and Iron*, Plates IV–IX.

EASTMAN. Classroom Films : The Mining and Smelting of Copper, Anthracite Coal, Bituminous Coal, Gold, Oil, Cotton Goods.

GABRIEL (Ed.). Pageant of America : V, 64–81, 95–96, 103–105, 109, 139–140, 143–145, 186–212, Chapter VIII.

International Educational Pictures : Golden Yukon, Oil (series), Mining (series), The Benefactor.

Keystone Views : 122, 187, 190, 211, 282, 283, 285, 286, 293, 294.

McKINLEY. Illustrated Topics for American History : S 35.

National Geographic Magazine, LXIII, 481–518 (April, 1933).

Perry Pictures: 2513.

Society for Visual Education. Picturols: Mining Bituminous Coal, Petroleum Refining.

Society for Visual Education (BRAY-EYEGATE). Story of Copper, Petroleum and Gas, Iron and Steel.

Yale Pageant Educational Slides: 233, 267, 396, 397, 405, 407, 411–412, 414–423, 457–458, 708.

The teacher shows the children a collection of Joseph Pennell's etchings.

Music. The teacher sings to the children songs of the miner from Lomax's *American Ballads and Folk Songs.*

General Activities

Creative Activities: Group and Individual, Correlated with Other Subjects or Voluntary Projects

A volunteer shows a mineral map of the world (as in Bowman's *Geography in Relation to the Social Sciences,* p. 207) and explains that "Great Powers" are those which use the most energy-giving minerals.

Other volunteers show maps or graphs of other natural resources to explain why the United States became great. (World Encyclopedia Book: graph, *Iron.*)

If possible, children show samples of ore of different kinds: iron, copper, silver, gold.

A volunteer reports on "ghost towns" like Central City, Colorado (see encyclopedia); another on the famous Comstock lode.

The teacher shows the children the daily report from the New York stock exchange of the value of such stocks as "The Homestake Mine" in the Black Hills; of the United States Steel Corporation.

A volunteer reports on such Wild West characters as "Wild Bill" Hickok and "Calamity Jane."

The teacher reads to the children some of Robert W. Service's poems of Alaska from *Songs of a Sour Dough.*

Visitors to different kinds of mines describe them to the class.

Volunteers search in the World Almanac to learn which nation of the world made the most cotton cloth last year; which nation was second; which nation was third.

A volunteer reports on the skyscraper as an American contribution to architecture.

A floor talk is given about the great steel plants in modern Russia.

The class makes a visit to a hardware store to find out how many different kinds of articles are made of steel; to a central power station to observe how power is sent to factories and homes.

A volunteer explains how Michael Faraday, a poor scientist, made many modern fortunes possible.

The teacher shows a map comparing the use of power in different parts of the world (as in Bowman's *Geography in Relation to the Social Sciences,* p. 208).

Children examine an electric-light bulb to see how it is made.

If there is an X-ray machine in any shoe shop in the city, the children make a visit to it. If not, they examine X-ray pictures.

A volunteer explains why such cities as Gary, Indiana, were built.

The class makes a visit to the local museum to observe mining exhibits.

The class continues the time line.

Application to Present-Day Conditions   [In a Language Period

Children compare the annual production of the United States with that of other countries in iron, coal, silver, gold, copper, oil. (World Almanac.)

Has the United States enough coal in the ground to last it for all the future? (See a children's encyclopedia.)

Does the great supply of natural resources in the United States help to explain the mad rush of all classes of people to get rich?

Which produced more gold, Alaska or the Yukon Territory of Canada?

Why do countries at war today want huge supplies of oil and copper? Why did the League of Nations want to stop the supply of oil to Italy during the war in Ethiopia?

What minerals did Italy hope to find in Ethiopia? Why did she need minerals so badly?

What is a "gusher"? How are oil wells dug? How is the oil stored? How is it moved to market? How is gasoline made?

Are there any Carnegie libraries in your vicinity? Why are they so called?

If Japan can sell cheaper cotton cloth than the United States can, what will happen to our customers?

How has electricity been used in air conditioning?

Point out the difference between poles used by power lines and telephone poles.

Exercises in Reasoning   [In a Language Period

Why have mineral supplies been the cause of many modern wars?

Why cannot nations buy mineral supplies from other nations instead of going to war over the matter?

Why were the earliest settlers little interested in minerals, except gold and silver?

Does every country have as good an opportunity as the United States to give each of its citizens a good living? (Compare maps of natural resources.)

Why do miners not make permanent settlements in a new country?

Explain the graph in the World Book Encyclopedia, p. 3820.

Compare Andrew Carnegie with many other millionaires as to his use of his money.

Why do you suppose that Japan can sell her cotton goods at a lower price than we can?

How did the phonograph help to improve American taste in music?

Is it possible that a scientist may make more money for his nation (if not for himself) than a businessman?

Children compare candles, oil lamps, gas lights, and electric lights.

Explain this sentence: "People used to spend their lives in the struggle with the frontier; now they spend their lives in the struggles to earn more money in order to buy more."

Drill Games

Place names are drilled upon at the map: *Yukon, Klondike.*
Drill cards are made as follows:

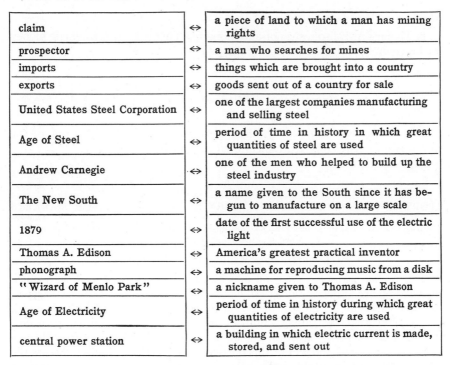

claim	⟷	a piece of land to which a man has mining rights
prospector	⟷	a man who searches for mines
imports	⟷	things which are brought into a country
exports	⟷	goods sent out of a country for sale
United States Steel Corporation	⟷	one of the largest companies manufacturing and selling steel
Age of Steel	⟷	period of time in history in which great quantities of steel are used
Andrew Carnegie	⟷	one of the men who helped to build up the steel industry
The New South	⟷	a name given to the South since it has begun to manufacture on a large scale
1879	⟷	date of the first successful use of the electric light
Thomas A. Edison	⟷	America's greatest practical inventor
phonograph	⟷	a machine for reproducing music from a disk
"Wizard of Menlo Park"	⟷	a nickname given to Thomas A. Edison
Age of Electricity	⟷	period of time in history during which great quantities of electricity are used
central power station	⟷	a building in which electric current is made, stored, and sent out

Children keep a record of their own difficulties while practicing.

Testing

Tests of Understanding are given in Kelty's *The Growth of the American People and Nation*, 430, 437, 443.

Tests of Reasoning and Skills

1. No country can become a great manufacturing country without (*a*) raw materials, (*b*) power, (*c*) labor, and (*d*) markets. Tell what the South has in each respect.

a. _ _ _ _ _ _   c. _ _ _ _ _ _
b. _ _ _ _ _ _   d. _ _ _ _ _ _

2. Check the right answer: The most valuable of the minerals mined in the United States every year is   gold.   silver.   ✓ iron.   copper.   coal.

3. Check: It is cheaper   ✓ to bring iron ore to a place near the coal mines.   to bring coal to a place near the iron mines.

4. The chief reason why the United States is so rich is   ✓ its supply of minerals.   its people work harder than others.

Mark the following as true or false:

5. *a.* Japan and the United States both want to sell cotton cloth to the world. This makes them feel friendly toward each other.   True [ ]   False [✓]

b. They both need to sell their cloth in order to have jobs for their working people.   True [✓]   False [ ]

6. Thomas A. Edison was not a millionaire. Therefore he made little money for his country.   True [ ]   False [✓]

7. Electricity is used to do much of our work nowadays.

True [✓]   False [ ]

8. Do you think Japan has a right to sell cotton cloth cheaper than we do? Explain. _ _ _ _ _ _

Exercise in Organization. Children copy the topic headings of one of the stories and prepare to give a topical recitation of the whole story.

A

STORY 4. MASS PRODUCTION · STORY 5. THE SEARCH FOR MARKETS
[1 Week
[Stories treated separately for conversational approach, reading periods, and discussion; for other activities, both together]

Conversational Approach (First Story)

The teacher brings to class some articles made of assembled parts with which the children are familiar; for example, a small clock, skates, a carpet-sweeper, etc. She selects for her illustration one of the parts which can be easily removed.

"Suppose that the rubber bumpers on this sweeper should be worn out. Would it be necessary to throw the sweeper away? Why not? How do you know that the new band will fit this particular sweeper?" Children discuss the principle of interchangeable parts.

"This idea of making articles in small pieces and bringing the pieces together was one of the greatest ideas ever developed in manufacture. Our story today tells us what effect it had."

Reading and Study

The Reading Periods (First Story)

Independent Readers

TEXTS

BARKER, DODD, WEBB, *Our Nation Grows Up*, 291–299.

HALLECK and FRANTZ, *Makers of Our Nation*, 128–130.

KELTY, *Growth of the American People and Nation*, 444–448.

READING FOR RECREATION

BOND, *On the Battle Front of Engineering*.

SMITH, *Made in America*.

Lower Group

The teacher tells the story orally to the lower group, writing on the board the most important words as she mentions them.

Then the teacher and this group read together the story as given in the text. The teacher guides the silent reading, section by section, by such questions as "How did the factories of the past differ from the factories of today?"

Children read silently and answer orally. When they have read the entire story in this manner they test themselves by the questions at the end of the story.

The Discussion (First Story)

The children answer the study-guide questions as fully as possible. The teacher attempts particularly to ascertain whether or not their sentences represent clear-cut and vivid concepts, as opposed to word-memory.

The teacher writes on the board the words *mass production, quantity production, assembling, standard parts, interchangeable parts, division of labor.* Children discuss the meanings.

Conversational Approach (Second Story)

"Now we must begin to look for the results of mass production. Soon our factories were making more sewing machines and reapers than our own people could buy. What do you suppose the owners could do with the rest of the machines?

"There are some countries to which we certainly cannot sell. Which are they? [*Those which manufacture similar articles.*] Can you think of countries which might buy?" Children speculate as to which they may be. "Our story is about this problem of selling the goods we cannot use ourselves."

Reading and Study

The Reading Periods (Second Story)

Independent Readers

TEXTS

KELTY, *Growth of the American People and Nation,* 449–454.

EXTENSIVE READING

AITCHISON and UTTLEY, *Across Seven Seas to Seven Continents,* 287–296.
ATWOOD, *United States among the Nations,* 216, 219–220, 224–225.
BEEBY, *How the World Grows Smaller,* 62–97.
BLAICH, *Three Industrial Nations,* 332–333, 341.
LARGE, *Everyday Wonders,* 23–24.
TAPPAN, *Travelers and Traveling,* 95–107.
WERTHNER, *How Man Makes Markets,* 9–14.

Lower Group

The teacher explains the story orally to this group, writing the most important words on the board as she mentions them.

Then the teacher and these children read together the story as given in the text. The teacher directs the silent reading, section by section, by such questions as "How fast did our steel production increase in twenty years?"

Children read silently and answer orally. When they have read the entire story in this manner they test themselves by the questions at the end of the story.

OTHER BOOKS

CHAMBERLAIN, *How We Travel,* 165–170.

READING FOR RECREATION

ADAMS, *Cork Ships and How to Make Them.*
BAXTER and YOUNG, *Ships and Navigation.*
BEATY, *What We See in the City.*
LENT, *Full Steam Ahead.*

LINCOLN SCHOOL, *Boats.*
PRYOR, *The Steamship Book.*
WASHBURNE, *Letters to Channy.*

The Discussion (Second Story)

Children answer the study-guide questions as fully as possible *in their own words.* The teacher writes on the board the words *home market, surplus, merchant marine, colonial market.* Children discuss the meanings.

Multisensory Aids

Children and teacher talk over together the pictures in the text, pointing out features of geographic or historical significance.

AUDIO-VISUAL MATERIALS OBTAINABLE

Building America: Men and Machines.
Compton's Pictured Teaching Materials: *Farm and City*, Plate X; *Water and Air Transportation*, Plates VI, IX.
EASTMAN. Classroom Films: Transportation on the Great Lakes, Ocean Liners.
GRANT. *Story of the Ship:* Unloading Machinery, Navigation, Whalebacks.
Society for Visual Education (SPENCER). United States Merchant Marine.
Yale Pageant Educational Slides: 580.

General Activities

Creative Activities: Group and Individual, Correlated with Other Subjects or Voluntary Projects

A committee reports on the apprentice system formerly used in training craftsmen. (See encyclopedia.) It explains why the system is not used in modern factory work.

The class makes a visit to any kind of factory in which division of labor and mass production may be observed.

If assembling cannot be observed at a local factory, perhaps one of the local hardware or jewelry stores can demonstrate it.

The art teacher may help a committee to show how the designs of machines have influenced modern art.

A visitor to an automobile factory tells the children how the parts are assembled.

A committee marks on a slated map of the world the figure *1* for our best foreign customer, the figure *2* for the next best customer, and so on. (World Almanac, *Imports and Exports: United States.*)

A volunteer explains why a screw-propeller is better than a side-wheeler or an end-wheeler.

A committee graphs the figures showing how the time needed to cross the Atlantic has been cut down since the time of Columbus. (See Counts's *Social Foundations of Education*, pp. 457 ff.)

The class collects from the advertising columns of magazines and newspapers the names of the world's principal steamship lines. It divides into committees. Each committee writes to one steamship line for maps and advertising folders. The results are presented before the Parent-Teachers' Association as a "Travel Night."

From the same advertising material a committee selects the diagrams showing the deck plans of the largest and finest ships. They show where the cabins are, where the dining-room is, how to go from one part of the ship to other parts, where the deck sports are carried on, the kitchens, laundry, space for dogs, etc.

A committee finds the number of ships in the American Merchant Marine as compared with that of other great countries. (World Almanac, *World's Merchant Shipping*.)

Travelers on Atlantic and Pacific liners describe the ships and the life on shipboard.

A volunteer shows the comparative size of ships as given in Compton's Pictured Encyclopedia (*Ships; Ships compared with buildings*) or in the World Book Encyclopedia (*Ships*); another shows and explains the diagram of a modern steamship as given in the World Book Encyclopedia (*Ship*).

Application to Present-Day Conditions

Is there any division of labor in your home? in the school? in the community?

What do boys do nowadays during the years they used to spend as apprentices? Why?

Are there any industries in your community which depend on quantity production?

How do articles "made to order" differ from other articles?

Can parts of one automobile be interchanged with parts of another make? Why not?

Compare the size of the home market of the United States with that of Great Britain; France; Russia. Use the census figures.

Is the foreign market for United States goods growing larger or smaller? (Consult export figures in the World Almanac for the last twenty years.)

Does the need for colonial markets explain why Italy wanted Ethiopia?

What happens to mass production when many workmen lose their jobs? [*They cannot buy; the home market shrinks.*]

Why did the United States give up the Philippines if all countries want colonial markets? [*Feeling of Filipinos, difficulty of defense, opposition of domestic interests.*]

Exercises in Reasoning

Is it a good thing for a laborer not to own the tools and machines he works with?

Which do you think would be more interesting work, making an entire gun or watching a machine which makes one part? Which is easier?

What effect does mass production have on expert workmanship?

Why did mass production bring about the end of the small factory?

Is there any difference between mass production and quantity production? between interchangeable parts and standard parts?

From the map which the committee made of our foreign markets, do you think it would be wise for us to try to increase the amount we sell to Canada, Mexico, and South America and not to depend too much on Europe and Asia?

Why does Japan have a good chance to take away much of our foreign market in Asia?

What do you think must happen to a manufacturing country which wants to sell its goods to neighboring countries but which refuses to buy any of its neighbors' goods?

Drill Games

Drill cards are made as follows:

mass production, or quantity production	↔	manufacture on a large scale of parts that can be assembled
assembling	↔	joining together of parts to make a whole
standard parts, or interchangeable parts	↔	parts made exactly alike, to be joined later
division of labor	↔	separating a complete job into many separate tasks
home market	↔	opportunity for sale within the boundaries of a country
surplus	↔	an amount more than is required
merchant marine	↔	the trading vessels of a country
colonial market	↔	opportunities for sale in places under the control of a certain nation

Testing

Tests of Understanding are given in Kelty's *The Growth of the American People and Nation*, pp. 448, 454.

Tests of Reasoning and Skills

1. Check those statements which truly describe mass production.

a. √ Factory-owner supplies the materials.
Each worker supplies his own materials.

b. Workers own their own tools and machines.
√ Factory-owners supply the tools and machines.

c. One man makes an entire article.
√ One man performs only one small task.

d. Men need long and careful training for work.
√ Workmen need little training.

e. √ The machine does more of the work than the man.
The man does more of the work than the machine.

f. √ Each part is made by itself.
Each part is made for only one completed article.

2. Mark the following as true or false: Each industrial country wishes to sell its surplus to other countries. Therefore it must be willing to buy from the neighbors also.   True [√]   False [ ]

3. Can you make up a sentence telling whether the desire of all industrial countries for colonial markets leads to peace or war between countries?

- - - - - -

4. Under what general heading do the two stories which you read this week belong? _ _ _ _ _ _ Where did you look to find out? _ _ _[*Table of contents.*]_ _ _

Exercise in Organization. Each child prepares a brief oral summary of one of the two stories. The principal of the building is invited to hear the reports.

B

STORY 1. SOME NEW INVENTIONS · STORY 2. THE USE OF RUBBER · STORY 3. PATENTS AND COPYRIGHTS   [1 Week

[For conversational approach, reading periods, and discussion the first two stories are taken up together, and then the third story; for other activities, all three together]

Conversational Approach (First and Second Stories)

"The time about which we are now reading is sometimes called 'The Age of Invention.' Why do you suppose it has been given that name? Glance through the next two stories and find the names of some of the inventions. Which do you expect to find most interesting?

"And these are only some of the most important inventions. One book is not large enough to name them all."

Reading and Study

The Reading Periods (First and Second Stories)

[These two stories are read consecutively before any discussion is held]

Independent Readers

TEXTS

BEARD and BAGLEY, *First Book in American History*, 348, 350–352.
BURNHAM and JACK, *Growth of Our Country*, 240–241, 249–250, 355–356.
CLARK, *Westward to the Pacific*, 281–289, 392–393.
HALLECK and FRANTZ, *Makers of Our Nation*, 232–236, 295–299.
KELTY, *Growth of the American People and Nation*, 455–461, 462–466.
McGUIRE and PHILLIPS, *Building Our Country*, 119–120, 266–269, 293–302.
NIDA, *Following the Frontier*, 323–325.
SMALLIDGE and PAXSON, *Builders of Our Nation*, 567–570.

EXTENSIVE READINGS

BEEBY, *How the World Grows Smaller*, 109–119.
BROWNE, *Peeps at Industries: Rubber*.
CHASE and CLOW, *Stories of Industry*, II: 89–113.
DAVIDSON, *Founders and Builders of Our Nation*, 164.
LARGE, *Everyday Wonders*, 84–96, 97–106, 112–123.
McFEE, *Stories of American Inventions*, 206–225.
PARKMAN, *Conquests of Invention*, 110–131, 182–185, 396–408.
TAPPAN, *Heroes of Progress*, 30–38.
TAPPAN, *Makers of Many Things*, 6–15.
TAPPAN, *Travelers and Traveling*, 54–62.
WADE, *Light Bringers*, 172–195.

Lower Group

The teacher and this group read together the stories as given in the text. The teacher directs the silent reading, section by section, by such questions as "What two kinds of inventions were being made?" Children read silently and answer orally. When both stories have been read in this manner they test themselves by the questions at the end of the stories.

OTHER BOOKS

ALLEN, *How and Where We Live*, 103–106.
CHAMBERLAIN, *How We Are Clothed*, 107–128.
EGGLESTON, *Stories of Great Americans*, 128–131.
FAIRGRIEVE and YOUNG, *The World*, 110–114.
KNOWLTON, *First Lessons in Geography*, 210–211.

READING FOR RECREATION

FLOHERTY, *Moviemakers*.
HAMMOND, *Charles Proteus Steinmetz*.
NIXON-ROULET, *Our Little Brazilian Cousin*.

The Discussion (First and Second Stories) [In a Language Period

Children answer the study-guide questions as fully as possible. The teacher writes on the board the words *wireless telegraph, wireless telephone, radio, trolley car.* Children discuss the meanings.

Conversational Approach (Third Story)

"Now let us suppose that a man has spent the best years of his life in inventing a typewriter. Do you think it would be fair for some other man to examine it carefully and then make some just like it to sell? Could such a thing happen?" Some children will undoubtedly know about patent laws.

"Does a person who writes a book have any such protection? See if your own book has a copyright mark."

Reading and Study

The Reading Periods (Third Story)

Independent Readers

TEXTS

KELTY, *Growth of the American People and Nation,* 467–470.

READING FOR RECREATION

ROLT-WHEELER, *The Boy with the United States Inventors.*

Lower Group

The teacher and this group read together the story as given in the text. The teacher directs the silent reading, section by section, by such questions as "What classes of people does the United States protect in their ideas?"

Children read silently and answer orally. When the entire story has been read in this manner they test themselves by the study-guide questions at the end of the story.

The Discussion (Third Story) [In a Language Period

Children answer the study-guide questions as fully as possible. The teacher writes on the board the words *patent, copyright, trade-mark, Patent Office.* Children discuss the meanings.

Multisensory Aids

Children and teacher talk over together the pictures in the text, noting the significant features.

AUDIO-VISUAL MATERIALS OBTAINABLE

Building America: Communication.
Compton's Pictured Teaching Materials: *Communication,* Plate X; *Clothing,* Plate VII, 4.
EASTMAN. Classroom Films: Rubber.
International Educational Pictures: Rubber (series).
Keystone Views: 212.
The Mentor, XIII, 3–12.
Perry Pictures: 123-B.
Yale Pageant Educational Slides: 484, 486.

General Activities

Creative Activities: Group and Individual, Correlated with Other Subjects or Voluntary Projects

A committee makes a collection of pictures showing trolley cars in various foreign countries.

Other committees show and explain pictures of subways and elevated lines.

A volunteer investigates what a franchise is, and why a streetcar franchise is granted to only one company instead of to as many companies as possible.

Children who have never used a typewriter are allowed to write a few lines on the school typewriter, under the supervision of an office worker.

A volunteer explains what television is and how we shall probably be using it soon.

If possible, the class, or at least a committee, visits a broadcasting station.

The teacher shows the class a roll of motion-picture film.

A volunteer reports on the Firestone rubber plantations in Liberia. (Ask your local Firestone dealer how to secure the material for it.)

A volunteer tells the class the story of Vulcan.

Children make a list of all the articles they can find which have a patent mark on them.

They look through all their books to find the copyright marks.

The class makes a large poster on which are pasted all the trade-marks the children can find.

Application to Present-Day Conditions

Why are busses taking the place of streetcars in many cities?

Have you ever heard the expression *off his trolley*? What does it mean?

Have you ever heard anyone call streetcars cable cars? How did this expression originate? Why are street cars called trolley cars?

How does the motion picture affect the clothes, manners, and speech of people in all parts of the country?

What effect has the radio had on keeping members of families at home? In what way may we say that the radio and the movies are working in exactly opposite directions?

How does the radio help us, even better than the newspaper, to know what is going on in the rest of the world and what the rest of the world is thinking and feeling?

What does the signal S O S mean?

What is the difference between the wireless telegraph and the wireless telephone?

How did rubber receive its name? (See the encyclopedia.)

How is Goodyear's name honored today in the rubber business?

For which of our essential imports is the United States most dependent on foreign countries? (See American Yearbook or World Almanac.)

Exercises in Reasoning

In what way is the growth of a large city dependent on trolley cars?

How has the typewriter been a great help to women who want to earn their own living?

Has the motion picture had any bad effects on American life?

Why are most of our motion pictures made in Hollywood?

The old Greeks believed that no state should ever be so large that the citizens could not come together in one place and listen to one man speaking. In what way might the radio have made them willing to see their state grow to a larger size?

Do you think that radio musicians should be allowed to sing or play music over the air without paying the man who wrote it?

In what way is the wireless an improvement over the cable?

In what way does the Patent Office prove that all opportunity has not disappeared from modern life?

Do you think that a patent or a copyright should last forever?

Drill Games

Drill cards are made as follows:

Marconi	⟺	the first man who made a workable wireless telegraph
wireless telegraph	⟺	instrument for sending and receiving written messages without wires
trolley car	⟺	a car run by electric current in a wire overhead
wireless telephone	⟺	instrument for sending the sound of the voice without wires
Charles Goodyear	⟺	the man who discovered how to vulcanize rubber
vulcanization	⟺	treating rubber with sulphur and heat
patent	⟺	a government protection given to an inventor for the making and sale of his invention
copyright	⟺	a government protection given to an author for the sale of his works
trade-mark	⟺	a name or sign on goods that can be used only by a certain company
Patent Office	⟺	the department of government which gives and keeps records of patents

These cards are added to those used previously in this unit; and the game includes them all.

Testing

Tests of Understanding are given in Kelty's *The Growth of the American People and Nation*, pp. 461, 466, 470.

Tests of Reasoning and Skills

1. Check the right answer: Most of the inventions about which we have been reading took place ____ during my own lifetime. √ during my grandfather's lifetime. ____ long before my grandfather lived.

2. Make a list of the inventions named in the first story which do not depend on electricity. _ _ _[*The typewriter.*]_ _ _

3. If the United States ever has to go to war about its supplies of raw material, the trouble will probably be caused by which material? _ _ _[*Rubber.*]_ _ _

4. Is this sentence true? "All inventions have been good for the world." Explain your answer. _ _ _ _ _ _

5. Put the figure *1* before the thing which was used first, the figure *2* before the thing which was used next, and the figure *3* before the thing which was used last.   [_ _*3*_ _] radio   [_ _*1*_ _] telegraph   [_ _*2*_ _] telephone

Exercise in Organization. The class makes summary sentences for the three stories.

C

STORY 1. IMMIGRATION · STORY 2. BEGINNING OF THE LABOR PROB- LEM · STORY 3. COMBINATIONS OF CAPITAL AND LABOR

[*1 Week*

[For conversational approach, reading periods, and discussion, the first story is treated separately and the second and third together; for other activities, all three together]

Conversational Approach (First Story)

"Sometimes one hears thoughtless persons making fun of newcomers to this country and calling them all sorts of names, such as 'Dagoes' and 'Chinks.' As a matter of fact, we all came from other countries in the first place, as our history stories have clearly showed. Who are the only persons who can claim to be real Americans for centuries back?" [*The Indians.*]

In order to insure the right attitude toward immigrants, the teacher undertakes the following exercise. She asks the children the following questions, recording the results in the table: "Are there any children here who were not born in the United States? If so, in what country were you born? Were your fathers and mothers born outside the United States? If so, where? Where were your two grandfathers and two grandmothers born?" The figures should be arranged in order, to show what countries are represented the greatest number of times in the ancestry of the class.

FOREIGN ANCESTRY OF OUR CLASS [1]

	Country of Birth													
	Germany	Norway	Sweden	Denmark	Scotland	Ireland	Canada	Austria	Hungary	Wales	France	Holland	Switzerland	England
Children	..	..	..	..	..	..	..	..	2	..	..	..	..	..
Fathers and mothers	12	4	..	2	..	5	1	..	2	3	3	..	..	..
Grandfathers and grandmothers .	22	9	3	6	11	16	2	2	5	6	7	1	3	1
Total	34	13	3	8	11	21	3	2	9	9	10	1	3	1

[1] Figures from one Wisconsin class of sixteen members. Some children did not know where their grandparents were born.

"What do we call people who come from some foreign country to the United States to live?" The teacher writes the word *immigrant* on the board.

"Our diagram shows that most of our forefathers were immigrants here only one or two generations ago."

Reading and Study

The Reading Periods (First Story)

Independent Readers

TEXTS

CLARK, *Westward to the Pacific*, 309–314, 443–450.

KELTY, *Growth of the American People and Nation*, 471–476.

MCGUIRE and PHILLIPS, *Building Our Country*, 18–20.

EXTENSIVE READING

INGRAHAM, *Story of Democracy*, 231–233.

VOLLINTINE, *Making of America*, 170–186.

WADE, *Pilgrims of Today*.

Lower Group

The teacher and these children read together the story as given in the text. The teacher guides the silent reading, section by section, by such questions as "What three kinds of work needed to be done all at once?"

Children read silently and answer orally. When the entire story has been read in this manner they test themselves by the questions at the end of the story.

OTHER BOOKS

MIRICK and HOLMES, *Home Life around the World*, 156–159.

SCHWARTZ, *Five Little Strangers*, 103–136.

READING FOR RECREATION

ANTIN, *Promised Land*.

HUSBAND, *Americans by Adoption*.

ROLT-WHEELER, *Boy with the United States Census*.

The Discussion (First Story)   [In a Language Period

Children answer the study-guide questions as fully as possible. The teacher writes on the board the words *immigrant, immigration*. Children discuss the meanings.

Conversational Approach (Second and Third Stories)

"Where would most of the immigrants have to earn their living? From what you already know of the early factories do you think they were very pleasant places in which to work? What could the laborer do if he thought he had to work too many hours or received too little money?

"Suppose that Smith Brothers' factory employed five hundred men and paid them all very low wages. If John Jones did not think the wages were fair he could quit work and Mr. Smith could easily find another man.

"But if John Jones could persuade all five hundred men to quit at once Mr. Smith would have a hard time to find so many more and therefore might be willing to raise their wages.

"Many workers saw this truth, and years ago they began to form societies of their own, called labor unions" (pointing to the words written on the board). "Each labor union tried to help its own members in every way.

There came into being a barbers' union, a steamfitters' union, a musicians' union, a brotherhood of railway trainmen, etc.

"Do you suppose the factory-owners would be likely to unite also? Can you tell what any of their societies are called? Our stories today will tell us."

Reading and Study

The Reading Periods (Second and Third Stories)

[These two stories are read consecutively before any discussion is held]

Independent Readers

TEXTS

BARKER, DODD, WEBB, *Our Nation Grows Up*, 262–266.

BEARD and BAGLEY, *First Book in American History*, 422–424.

BURNHAM and JACK, *Growth of Our Country*, 257–261, 290–293.

KELTY, *Growth of the American People and Nation*, 477–480, 481–487.

WOODBURN and MORAN, *Makers of America*, 367–374.

EXTENSIVE READING

VOLLINTINE, *Making of America*, 249–253.

Lower Group

The teacher and this group read together the two stories as given in the text. The teacher guides the silent reading, section by section, by such questions as "Why could not the immigrants work on farms?"

Children read silently and answer orally. When both stories have been read in this manner they test themselves by the questions at the end of the stories.

READING FOR RECREATION

HARTMAN, *These United States*, Chap. XX.
HILL, *Fighting a Fire*.
MYGATT (Ed.), *Julia Newberry's Diary*.
PHILLIPS, *Marty Comes to Town*.

The Discussion (Second and Third Stories) [In a Language Period

Children answer the study-guide questions as fully as possible. The teacher writes on the board the words *machine workers, employers, wages, employees, corporation, trade union, capital, strike, collective bargaining*. Children discuss the meanings.

Multisensory Aids

Children and teacher talk over together the pictures in the text, pointing out features of historical or geographic significance.

AUDIO-VISUAL MATERIALS OBTAINABLE

Compton's Pictured Teaching Materials: *Farm and City*, Plate XII.
GABRIEL (Ed.). Pageant of America: V, 150–159, 279, 290, 294, 299–301.
Keystone Views: 158–159, 276–279.
Perry Pictures: 7691, 7692.
Society for Visual Education. Schoolfilms: Immigration to the United States, Growth of Cities.
Society for Visual Education. Picturols of the great cities may be ordered by name.
Yale Pageant Educational Slides: 459.

Music. National music is played, according to the prevailing nationalities in the community: Irish, Scotch, Welsh, Canadian, English, French, Dutch, Polish, Czechoslovakian, Jugoslavian, Italian, German, Russian, Belgian, Swiss, etc. See the index of phonograph records produced by Victor, Columbia, Brunswick.

General Activities

Creative Activities: Group and Individual, Correlated with Other Subjects or Voluntary Projects

A volunteer impersonates a steamship agent visiting European cities. He gives the speech he might make in persuading immigrants to come to America.

Committees are formed to study the contributions to American life made by immigrants or the sons of immigrants. For example: in music, Theodore Thomas, Victor Herbert, John Philip Sousa; in modern music, George Gershwin, Irving Berlin; in art, Augustus Saint-Gaudens, etc.

Visitors to cities describe the little Italys or Russias or Hungarys that they have seen there.

Older immigrants are invited to tell the children about their trip across the ocean, the examination at Ellis Island, and other experiences.

Volunteers compare the life of early factory workers in the North with the slaves in the South, as to both comfort and security.

The teacher reads to the children Whitman's poem "Song of the Broad Axe."

A committee finds out from the local chamber of commerce the number of wageworkers; the total population. They make a graph showing the proportions.

A volunteer tells the story of the old man, his sons, and the bundle of sticks (Aesop's Fables, Stickney edition, p. 140). He applies the principle to both capital and labor.

If possible, the entire class or committees visit a labor-union meeting and a meeting of the chamber of commerce.

A volunteer shows the class a union card.

Children ask their local meat markets, grocery stores, drug stores, milkmen, etc., whether the business is conducted by a corporation, a partnership, or individual ownership.

Application to Present-Day Conditions   [In a Language Period

Children make a "black list" of all the bad names that they have heard immigrants called: dagoes, hunjacks or hunkies, chinks, japs, spicks, frog-eaters, micks, etc. They explain how such names show lack of understanding.

Are Chinese and Japanese allowed to come to this country to live today?

Are all the hardest jobs left to immigrants today?

Which of the great political parties particularly welcomed the immigrants into their own ranks?

Are many wage-earners today likely to become rich? Why not?

Why are there such tall buildings in our cities today? [*High land values, much business to be done.*]

What effect does city life have on the spirit of neighborliness?

Children make a list of the local business firms which are corporations. Are there any which are partnerships?

What do laborers do with the free time they have won by union action?

Do unions carry on collective bargaining today?

Exercises in Reasoning [*In a Language Period*

Did the United States allow the immigrants to come here because of charity or because we needed cheap labor?

Why are few immigrants allowed to enter the United States each year at present?

In what way did the closing of the frontier affect opportunities for immigrants?

Which is more sure of his living, a farmer or a wage-earner?

Did giving the laborer the right to vote solve for him his problem of earning a decent living?

Is it possible for one man to be both an employer and an employee? Give an example.

Why do so many people in New England live in cities? Why do so few people on the western plateaus live in cities?

Why have cities grown upward straight into the air as well as spreading out on the ground?

Why does the government find it hard to control the great corporations?

Why should you expect that the labor unions would be great friends of the public schools?

Why does the United States government need a Department of Labor?

Why is collective bargaining better than each man's trying to bargain with his employer by himself?

Why do most men prefer to do business today as a corporation rather than as a partnership?

Do you think capital could get along without labor? Could labor get along without capital? Then is it sensible for them to come to an agreement peaceably?

Drill Games

Drill cards are made as follows:

immigrant	⟷	a person who comes into a country
machine workers	⟷	people who earn their living by tending machines in factories
employers	⟷	persons who have other people in their service
immigration	⟷	the coming of foreigners into a country
wages	⟷	regular payment to laborers for their work
employees	⟷	persons who earn their living by working for others
corporation	⟷	a group of people joined by law to carry on business
trade union	⟷	an association of workers in the same trade
capital	⟷	wealth used for the making of goods
strike	⟷	stopping work in order to secure what is demanded
collective bargaining	⟷	coming to an agreement between employers and representatives of employees

Children practice individually, keeping a record of their own difficulties.

Testing

Tests of Understanding are given in Kelty's *The Growth of the American People and Nation*, pp. 476, 480, 487.

Tests of Reasoning and Skills

1. Should you expect a member of a labor union and an owner of a corporation to be on the same side in a labor quarrel? Explain your answer. _ _ _ _ _ _ _

2. Check the best answer: The United States allows few immigrants to enter the country nowadays because ⎯ other countries do not let Americans enter. √ there are not enough jobs to go around. ⎯ immigrants nowadays will not work hard. ⎯ there are no more farms to give away.

3. Can you make up a sentence telling whether or not immigrants have done any good in America? _ _ _ _ _ _

4. In the following list, check the subjects which the *employer* might think good for his business:

√ long hours of labor   high wages
  short hours of labor   √ no labor unions
√ low wages   strong labor unions

5. Check the sentence which seems true to you:
  The world does not need capital.
  The world does not need labor.
  The world could get along without either labor or capital.
√ The world needs both labor and capital.

Exercise in Organization. Teacher and children working co-operatively make a single outline comprising the last two stories. Children prepare a topical recitation on each subheading.

D

STORY 1. NEW TYPES OF FARMS · STORY 2. LUTHER BURBANK

E

STORY 1. CONSERVATION   [*1 Week*

[For conversational approach, reading periods, and discussion, the first two stories are taken up together and then the third story; for other activities, all three together]

Conversational Approach (First and Second Stories)

"Turn to the table of contents. What is the title of the unit? Read the sub-heads which make up the units. Explain the connection between the first subheading and the unit title; the second; the third; the fourth. What the fifth means is described by the title of the story. What is it? What does such a subject as that have to do with the unit title?

"Today we are going to begin the first two stories. In what ways shall you expect the farm of the new day to differ from farms before the Civil War? What is a wizard? Can you imagine, then, what a "plant wizard" might be?

Reading and Study

The Reading Periods (First and Second Stories)

[These two stories are read consecutively before any discussion is held]

Independent Readers

TEXTS

BARKER, DODD, WEBB, *Our Nation Grows Up*, 268–275.

BURNHAM and JACK, *Growth of Our Country*, 237–240.

KELTY, *Growth of the American People and Nation*, 488–495, 496–500.

McGUIRE and PHILLIPS, *Building of Our Country*, 178–190.

SMALLIDGE and PAXSON, *Builders of Our Nation*, 571–576

EXTENSIVE READING

ATWOOD, *United States among the Nations*, 80–83, 91.

BARROWS and PARKER, *United States and Canada*, 94–95.

BROOKS, *Story of Cotton*, 224–230, 280–290, 302–313, 317–328.

FORMAN, *Stories of Useful Inventions*, 84, 93–96.

GORDY, *Leaders in Making America*, 424–429.

SANFORD and OWEN, *Modern Americans*, 57–64.

TAPPAN, *Heroes of Progress*, 106–115.

WADE, *Wonder Workers*, 1–33.

Lower Group

The teacher and this group read together the stories as given in the text. The teacher guides the silent reading, section by section, by such questions as "How did the Civil War increase the use of the reaper?"

Children read silently and answer orally. When both stories have been read in this manner they test themselves by the questions at the end of the stories.

OTHER BOOKS

EVERETT and REED, *When They Were Boys*, 128–134.

MIRICK and HOLMES, *Home Life around the World*, 128–133.

READING FOR RECREATION

BEATY, *How We Farm*.

BEATY and ALLEN, *The Farm in Pictures*.

BEATY and ALLEN, *Vacation Days on the Farm*.

DE KRUIF, *Hunger Fighters*.

HADER, *The Farmer in the Dell*.

LENT, *Grindstone Farm*.

PERKINS, *Farm Twins*.

SLUSSER, WILLIAMS, BEESON, *Stories of Luther Burbank and his Plant School*.

WATSON, *Story of Bread*.

WILDER, *Farmer Boy*.

The Discussion (First and Second Stories) [In a Language Period

Children answer the study-guide questions as fully as possible. The teacher writes on the board the following words: *harvester, tractor, twine binder, threshing machine, codling moth, gang plow, rotation of crops, fertilizer, reaper and binder, Department of Agriculture, grafting*. Children discuss the meanings.

Conversational Approach (Third Story)

"Have you ever known the kind of boy or girl who is very saving of his or her own paper but who wastes school paper? the kind of man or woman who saves his or her money carefully, but who scatters papers about the streets and parks which someone must be paid by the city to pick up?

"The American nation as a whole has been very wasteful. How is it possible to be wasteful of forests? of bird and animal life? Can you think of other natural resources that have been wasted?

"What does this old saying mean, 'Waste not; want not'? How does it apply to our future as a nation?"

Reading and Study

The Reading Periods (Third Story)

Independent Readers

TEXTS

BEARD and BAGLEY, *First Book in American History*, 421–422.

CLARK, *Westward to the Pacific*, 480–484.

KELTY, *Growth of the American People and Nation*, 501–508.

EXTENSIVE READING

ALLEN, *United States*, 282–283, 313–317.

ATWOOD and THOMAS, *The Americas*, 159–160.

CHAMBERLAIN, *North America*, 282–287, 290–295.

FAIRBANKS, *Western United States*, 290–294.

FARIS, *Where Our History Was Made*, II: 207–222.

GORDY, *Leaders in Making America*, 385–388 (Powell).

LEFFERTS, *Our Own United States*, 223–227.

SMITH, *Human Geography*, I: 93–94.

Lower Group

The teacher and this group read together the story as given in the text. The teacher directs the silent reading, section by section, by such questions as "Why did not early Americans think about saving natural resources?"

Children read silently and answer orally. When the entire story has been read in this manner, they test themselves by the questions at the end of the story.

OTHER BOOKS

ALLEN, *How and Where We Live*, 71–72.

BAILEY, *What to Do for Uncle Sam*, 56–62, 160–169.

MIRICK and HOLMES, *Home Life around the World*, 134–146.

WINSLOW, *The Earth and Its People*, 75–76.

READING FOR RECREATION

CRUMP, *Boys' Book of Forest Rangers*.
DORRANCE, *Story of the Forest*.
FAIRBANKS, *Conservation Reader*.
ROLT-WHEELER, *Boy with the United States Foresters*.
ROLT-WHEELER, *Boy with the United States Fisheries*.

The Discussion (Third Story)　　　［*In a Language Period*

Children answer the study-guide questions as fully as possible. The teacher writes on the board the words *fish hatchery, conservation, forest rangers, closed season, game laws, natural resources*. Children discuss the meanings.

Multisensory Aids

Children and teacher talk over together the pictures in the text, pointing out features of geographic or historical significance.

AUDIO-VISUAL MATERIALS OBTAINABLE

Building America: Food.

Compton's Pictured Teaching Materials: *Farm and City*, Plates I–V, VII; *Food*, Plates III, V, IX.

EASTMAN. Classroom Films: Wheat, Wheat to Bread, Luther Burbank, Irrigation, Reforestation.

GABRIEL (Ed.). Pageant of America: III, 211–215, 220–228, 229–234, 234–238, 311–314.

International Educational Pictures: Irrigation in the Southwest.

Keystone Views: 209, 210–254, 295–299.

McKINLEY. Illustrated Topics in American History: S 39.

Perry Pictures: 7510.

Society for Visual Education. Schoolfilms: Central Plains, Reclaiming Arid Land by Irrigation, Making the Desert Blossom.
Society for Visual Education. Picturol: Reclamation.
Society for Visual Education (SPENCER). Wheat Raising, Irrigation, Forest Conservation.
Society for Visual Education (BRAY-EYEGATE). Fruit-Farming.
Yale Pageant Educational Slides: 235, 236, 349–355, 358–361, 378–384, 449–451.

General Activities

Creative Activities: Group and Individual, Correlated with Other Subjects or Voluntary Projects

If possible, the entire class makes a visit to a modern farm.

Children list all the improved farm machinery that they have seen. They divide into committees; each committee chooses one piece of machinery, makes a picture collection of this machine, and explains its working.

A volunteer investigates the materials used for the *twine* of the twine binder. (See *Hemp* and *Sisal* in an encyclopedia.)

A child who has observed the activities of threshing time on a farm describes them to the class.

Children interested in farming plan a good rotation of crops for a certain field and draw a diagram illustrating it.

The science teacher in the high school is invited to demonstrate grafting.

The teacher reads to the children some of the beautiful Bible passages about reaping and threshing. (See Concordance.)

A volunteer looks through seed catalogues and lists Burbank products.

Floor talks are given on the work of forest rangers.

A volunteer explains what a smoke-consumer is.

A committee reports on the game laws of the state and shows hunting and fishing licenses. They explain the "closed seasons" and the Izaak Walton League.

If possible, the class observes some work in tree surgery. A visitor to a fish hatchery describes it to the children.

The children explain the tabulation of the work of birds in Bailey's *What to do for Uncle Sam* (161–162).

A committee sets up in the sand table an irrigation system that will work.

Application to Present-Day Conditions   [*In a Language Period*

Does the United States still produce more food than our own people eat? (World Almanac, *Exports: United States.*)

What happened to all the men thrown out of work by the new machines? Where did they go?

Have you ever heard the expression *eats like a thresher*? What does it mean?

Can you estimate the amount of money needed to buy a farm, stock it, and supply it with machinery? Is there much reason, then, for a "city man" to feel that he is better off than a farmer?

What are tenant farmers? Why is it bad to have too many farms in the United States run by tenants?

When you have been driving through the country have you ever seen an experimental field?

Is there a county agricultural agent in your county?

Why was grapefruit not used until recent years? (See encyclopedia.)

What is the Boy Scout rule about putting out camp fires? Why was it made?

In what way is the safety movement an attempt to save our natural resources?

Why does Japan buy much of our scrap iron?

Exercises in Reasoning   [In a Language Period

Do you think it would be a good thing for our farmers to raise only as much food as our own people can buy?

Is a tractor better than a horse for all farms?

Explain this statement: "The harvester pushed the frontier westward at the rate of thirty miles a year."

In what two ways do the people of the city depend on the farmer? [*To raise their food and to buy their manufactures.*] In what two ways do the farmers depend on the city people? [*To buy their products and to supply them with manufactured articles.*] Could either get along without the others?

Has science always been used for the good of man? [*Poison gas, etc.*]

Why have many people returned to the farms in the last few years?

Which will be easier to replace, our forests or our mines?

Do you think it would be a good plan to keep any new mine discovered for the people as a whole, instead of allowing one man to own it?

Water power is used to generate electricity. Does that explain why every one of us ought to be interested in the control of water power? What effect does it have on the cost of our electricity?

What effect had irrigation and dry farming on the Westward movement?

Do you think it is fair to the people who will live in this country a hundred years from now for us to waste the natural resources? Explain.

Drill Games

Drill cards are made as follows:

harvester	↔	a machine that gathers grain
tractor	↔	a motor vehicle that pulls another implement
twine binder	↔	machine that ties up sheaves of grain with rope
threshing machine	↔	a machine which separates the grain from the stalk and chaff
codling moth	↔	an insect that attacks orchards
gang plow	↔	many plows fastened together and working at once
rotation of crops	↔	changing crops raised on a field for a period of years
fertilizer	↔	material added to the soil to make it richer

grafting	⟷	to unite a shoot of one tree with the stock of another
Department of Agriculture	⟷	the part of the United States government which tries to help farmers solve their problems
reaper and binder	⟷	a machine which cuts grain and also ties it into sheaves
Luther Burbank	⟷	" the Plant Wizard "
Gifford Pinchot	⟷	a leader in the movement for conservation of natural resources
conservation	⟷	saving natural resources and using them wisely

Testing

Tests of Understanding are given in Kelty's *The Growth of the American People and Nation,* pp. 495, 500, 508.

Tests of Reasoning and Skills

1. Does it take more brains or less brains to run a farm than it does to work in a factory?   More [✓]   Less [ ]

2. Under what heading do the titles of the first two stories this week belong? Use your book to find out. _ _ _ _ _ _ Where did you look to find out? _ _ _ [*Table of contents.*]_ _ _

3. In the following list, check those practices which are good for the soil:

Mining the soil	One-crop system
✓ Using fertilizer	✓ Rotation of crops

4. Check the best answer in each of the following.

a.   All the trees in a country should be cut down.
    ✓ Old trees may be cut, but young trees should be left.
    No trees in a country should ever be cut down.

b. ✓ Less wasteful methods of mining should be used.
    No minerals should be sent to foreign countries.
    Minerals should be mined only part of the year.

c.   All water power should be owned by the government.
    Water power should be owned by companies for profit.
    ✓ The government should control water power.

d.   No hunting or fishing should be allowed at any time.
    ✓ Hunting and fishing should have closed seasons.
    Hunting and fishing should be free and open at all times.

e. ✓ Irrigation is used where the soil is dry.
    Irrigation is used where the soil is rocky.
    Irrigation is used to drain the soil.

Exercise in Organization. Lower-group children copy the topic headings of the first or third story. They prepare brief oral summaries of their headings. Children who believe themselves able to do so make an outline of one of the stories independently.

Tests on the Entire Unit

Test of Time Sense. Pass mimeographed sheets of the following.

I. Here is a list of persons. Put the figure *1* before the name of the man who did his great work first, the figure *2* before the name of the one who was next, and so on.

1.

[__*3*__] Marconi
[__*2*__] Charles Goodyear
[__*1*__] Eli Whitney

2. Here is another list. Do the same.

[__*3*__] Luther Burbank
[__*2*__] Elias Howe
[__*1*__] Cyrus McCormick

3. Here is another list. Do the same.

[__*3*__] Andrew Carnegie
[__*1*__] Alexander Hamilton
[__*2*__] Oliver Hazard Perry

4. Here is another list. Do the same.

[__*2*__] Sam Houston
[__*1*__] Robert Fulton
[__*3*__] James J. Hill

5. Here is another list. Do the same.

[__*2*__] Andrew Jackson
[__*3*__] Gifford Pinchot
[__*1*__] Robert Gray

6. Here is another list. Do the same.

[__*1*__] Thomas Jefferson
[__*2*__] Cyrus W. Field
[__*3*__] Thomas A. Edison

7. Here is another list. Do the same.

[__*1*__] Robert Fulton
[__*3*__] Thomas A. Edison
[__*2*__] William Lloyd Garrison

II. Here is a list of events. Put the figure *1* before that which came first, the figure *2* before that which came next, and so on.

[__*1*__] Invention of the telegraph
[__*2*__] Invention of the telephone
[__*3*__] Invention of the phonograph

Tests on Persons. Pass mimeographed sheets of the following. Here is a list of names:

| Marconi | Andrew Carnegie | Charles Goodyear |
| Gifford Pinchot | Luther Burbank | Thomas A. Edison |

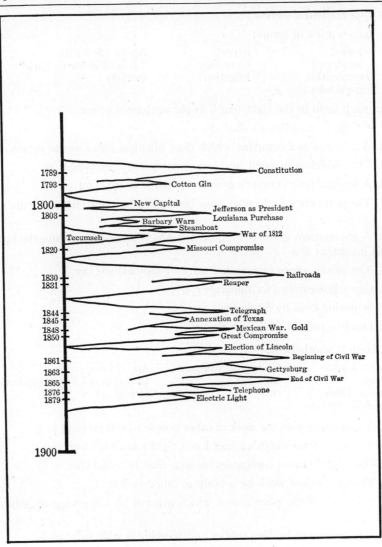

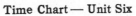

Time Chart — Unit Six

Put each name in the right blank in the sentences below.

1. _ _ _ _ _ _ made the electric light usable.
2. _ _ _ _ _ _ was a leader for conservation.
3. The man who vulcanized rubber was _ _ _ _ _ _.
4. The "Plant Wizard" was _ _ _ _ _ _.
5. _ _ _ _ _ _ discovered the use of the wireless.
6. _ _ _ _ _ _ gave much of his money to libraries.

Test on Historical Terms

I. Here is a list of terms :

patent	import	Age of Electricity
immigrant	prospector	"Wizard of Menlo Park"
corporation	irrigation	markets
game laws		

Put each term in the right blank in the sentences below.

1. Edison is sometimes called the _ _ _ _ _ _.

2. A _ _ _ _ _ _ is a company which does business like a single person.

3. That which is brought into one country from another is an _ _ _ _ _ _.

4. A foreigner who enters a country to settle there is an _ _ _ _ _ _.

5. The years during which we have been using so much electricity are called the _ _ _ _ _ _.

6. A government grant to an inventor which gives only to him the right to sell his invention is a _ _ _ _ _ _.

7. The places where our products are in demand are our _ _ _ _ _ _.

8. One who searches for minerals is a _ _ _ _ _ _.

9. Watering land by ditches is _ _ _ _ _ _.

10. Laws to protect wild animals are _ _ _ _ _ _.

II. Here is another list. Do the same.

vulcanization	interchangeable parts	Age of Steel
strike	employer	United States Steel Corporation
Patent Office	claim	surplus
machine workers		

1. Anyone who uses the work of other people whom he pays is an _ _ _ _ _ _.

2. A tract of land which a miner has a right to call his own is a _ _ _ _ _ _.

3. One of the largest companies making steel is called the _ _ _ _ _ _.

4. The quitting of work by a body of laborers is a _ _ _ _ _ _.

5. The part of the government which attends to the giving of patents is the _ _ _ _ _ _.

6. The process of heating rubber and treating it with sulphur is _ _ _ _ _ _.

7. Anything more than what is used or needed is a _ _ _ _ _ _.

8. Parts of one machine which can be changed for similar parts of a similar machine are called _ _ _ _ _ _.

9. Laborers who work at machines are called _ _ _ _ _ _.

10. The time during which much steel is used is called the _ _ _ _ _ _.

III. Here is another list. Do the same.

assembling	twine binder	standard parts
grafting	merchant marine	tractor
exports	United States Department of Agriculture	wireless telephone
harvester		

1. A machine which reaps crops is the _____.

2. An engine which pulls farm machinery is a _____.

3. Any goods sent out of one country to another are _____.

4. An instrument which sends sounds through the air without wires is the _____.

5. Joining together the parts of a machine is called _____.

6. A machine which ties up grain with heavy cord is a _____.

7. Ships used for commerce and trade on the high seas are the _____.

8. To fasten a shoot from one tree into another is _____.

9. Similar parts which are of exactly the same size and material are _____.

10. The part of the government which attends particularly to the business of farming is the _____.

IV. Here is another list. Do the same.

wages	New South	copyright
rotation of crops	fish hatchery	closed season
trade-mark	Department of Labor	fertilizer

1. Material put on land to make it produce more is _____.

2. A place where fish eggs are hatched is a _____.

3. The right given by the government to an author so that only he may sell his works is a _____.

4. The particular mark used by a manufacturer to show that certain goods were made by him is a _____.

5. Since the South has started many industries, it is often called the _____.

6. The time when it is against the law to shoot certain game is the _____.

7. The certain fixed sum of money paid to laborers is called _____.

8. The part of the government which attends particularly to the interests of laboring people is the _____.

9. Changing crops about by turns is called _____.

V. Here is another list. Do the same.

American Federation of Labor	employee	"Plant Wizard"
conservation	forest ranger	trolley car
codling moth	natural resources	

1. Burbank was often called the _____.

2. One who works for wages or a salary in the service of another is an _____.

3. Keeping or protecting natural resources from injury is _____.

4. The trade unions in the United States and Canada together make up the _____.

5. A streetcar is a _____.

6. The advantages that nature has supplied a country are its _ _ _ _ _ _.

7. A man who guards tracts of woods for the state is a _ _ _ _ _ _.

8. A great pest of apple orchards is the _ _ _ _ _ _.

Comprehension Test on Unit Six

Check the best answer.

1. Much land in the West was made useful for agriculture by   buying it from Canada.   √ irrigation.   inventing new machinery.

2. As the factory system spread, cities   grew worse.   grew smaller. √ grew larger.

3. A record of all inventions is kept   √ in the Patent Office.   in the United States Department of Labor.   in the United States Department of Agriculture.

4. Steamships had to be greatly improved because   it was so far to go to the other continents.   other countries improved their ships.   √ they had to carry so many more goods for export.

5. The man who did most to improve plants was   Thomas A. Edison. √ Luther Burbank.   Marconi.

6. Just as the laborers formed unions, the employers   destroyed the labor unions.   joined the labor unions.   √ formed associations of their own.

7. One of the greatest improvements in making machines was   √ to make them with interchangeable parts.   to make them of better materials.   to make more of them.

8. We had to find new markets because   the old ones were worn out.   we did not want any other country to have them.   √ we produced such great quantities of goods.

9. One of the greatest improvements in agriculture was   √ to plan the crops more wisely.   to build larger barns.   to buy more land.

10. Workers formed labor unions because   the employers formed associations of their own.   they could elect officers and have a club of their own.   √ all together they could accomplish more than each man working alone.

11. A new kind of power that we began to use was   steam.   √ electricity.   hand power.

12. Most workers were paid at this time   √ by wages.   by selling their own product.   by working land.

13. A new material that we learned to use was   cotton.   √ rubber.   wool.

14. Our population increased faster than it ever had before because   more children were born.   fewer people died.   √ many immigrants came.

15. Check three answers: The following industries grew to a huge size during this period:

embroidering	✓ textile manufactures	making pottery
✓mining	painting	lumbering
sewing by hand	✓ iron and steel manufactures	

16. What is the title of the unit which you have just completed? _ _ _ _ _ _

A Stunt Day may be held, when original plays, dramatizations, and other projects worked out during the unit are presented. The teacher has nothing to do with the planning of the program, which is the class's surprise for its guests.

Are any children now ready to be transferred from the lower group to the group of independent readers?

UNIT SEVEN · *How the United States became a World Power*

A

THE MONROE DOCTRINE   [½ *Week*

Conversational Approach

"Have you ever heard of any child's having a guardian? What does that mean? What things does a guardian have to decide?

"Do you suppose that it would be possible for one country to be guardian of another? What duties might the guardian country have to perform?"

At this point the class turns to a map of the Western Hemisphere and counts the number of small countries shown. "These are the countries which the United States used to try to guard.

"Can you see any reason why these little countries might not like to have a guardian? Do you think the United States ought to act as a guardian whether or not the other countries like it?" Children speculate as to the implications. "Our story today will tell us about this question."

Reading and Study

The Reading Periods

Independent Readers

This group reads the entire story through silently, as given in their text. They then test their comprehension by the study-guide questions furnished by the teacher or by the text.

TEXTS

BARKER, DODD, WEBB, *Our Nation Grows Up*, 61–63.

BEARD and BAGLEY, *First Book in American History*, 193–194.

CLARK, *Westward to the Pacific*, 191–194, 315–316, 423–424.

KELTY, *Growth of the American People and Nation*, 511–520.

McGUIRE and PHILLIPS, *Building Our Country*, 145–147.

Lower Group

The teacher tells the story orally to this group, writing on the board the names of the most important persons and places as she mentions them. Children practice the pronunciations.

Then the teacher and this group read together the story as given in the text. The teacher guides the silent reading, section by section, by such questions as "What questions are we to study during this unit?"

Children read silently and answer orally. When the entire story has been read in this manner, they test themselves by the questions at the end of the story.

The Discussion   [In a Language Period

Since this topic is somewhat difficult, several different sets of children give the answers to the study-guide questions. The teacher writes on the board the words *Monroe message* and *Monroe Doctrine*. Children tell the difference between them.

Multisensory Aids

Children and teacher talk over together the pictures in the text, pointing out the features of historical or geographical significance. They turn to a map of South America just before 1800, and name the South and Central American countries of today which were then Spanish possessions. They name the countries of today which were then Portuguese possessions. They compare with a map of South America today, and notice how few of the countries are now possessions of any foreign power.

If the children have studied Africa, they contrast this situation with that of Africa, where there is only one fully independent country left.

AUDIO-VISUAL MATERIALS OBTAINABLE

National Geographic Magazine, LXVI, 371 (September, 1934).
Perry Pictures: 2020.
Yale Pageant Educational Slides: 792.

General Activities

Creative Activities: Group and Individual, Correlated with Other Subjects or Voluntary Projects

A committee models South and Central America, Mexico, and the West Indies in the sand table. The letter *P* is put on all the countries of today which were once Portuguese possessions, and the letter *S* on all the countries of today which were once Spanish possessions.

The class plans a dramatization as follows:

ACT I. Scene in Spanish America when news comes that Napoleon's brother has been placed on the throne of Spain.

ACT II. A group of South American merchants discusses the satisfactory trade situation.

ACT III. Decision of South America to revolt.

ACT IV. *Scene 1.* A scene during the crossing of the Andes. *Scene 2.* Meeting of Bolívar and San Martín.

ACT V. *Scene 1.* The Spanish king surveys his American empire, at the end of the nineteenth century. *Scene 2.* The king gets help toward winning back his colonies.

ACT VI. President Monroe's message to Congress.

ACT VII. The Venezuela case as an illustration of Point 1 of the Monroe Doctrine.

ACT VIII. Money affairs of Haiti as an example of Point 2 of the Monroe Doctrine.

A volunteer shows Bolívar's flag, San Martín's flag, and the flag of the Army of the Andes (*National Geographic Magazine*, September, 1934, p. 371).

The class inserts the new date in the time line.

Application to Present-Day Conditions [*In a Language Period*

Is there any sign left today that Brazil was once a Portuguese possession, and that almost all the rest of South America was Spanish? [*What language is spoken in each?*]

Is there any means of getting across the Andes Mountains today? [*Airplanes and railways.*]

What are the A B C countries of South America today? [*Argentina, Brazil, Chile.*]

Do countries today ever "recognize" a new nation? [*Manchukuo.*]

Did the United States interfere with the governments of European countries when it sent an army to fight in the World War?

Does the United States today continue to interfere in the affairs of Haiti, Nicaragua, and other smaller American nations? (Look in a high-school history textbook.)

Exercises in Reasoning

What must a man have done to be called "the George Washington of South America"?

When the Spanish king came back to the throne, why did the South Americans change their minds about wanting to be under him again?

If Bolívar had succeeded in uniting all South America into one country, would it have been larger or smaller than the United States? (Compare the areas.)

Why would it be natural that the United States should sympathize with the South American countries that wanted to be independent?

Why did the United States not want the Spanish king and the Czar of Russia as neighbors in America? [*They might endanger our form of government.*]

Did the other American nations have any reason for their fears that the United States might swallow them up? [*Texas and the Mexican War.*]

Since South America has been known to white people even longer than North America, why is it so much less densely populated?

Do you think that the Monroe Doctrine may have still more changes in its meaning? Why?

If it had not been for the Monroe Doctrine, do you suppose that the same thing might have happened to South America which has happened to Africa?

Drill Games

Drill cards are made as follows:

1823	↔	the date of Monroe's message
Monroe message	↔	President Monroe's statement about colonization and interfering with governments
San Martín	↔	the hero of South American independence in the south
Bolívar	↔	the hero of South American independence in the north
Monroe Doctrine	↔	stretching Monroe message to cover (1) protection of liberty and (2) commercial interest

Children drill themselves in preparation for class games.

Testing

Tests of Understanding are given in Kelty's *The Growth of the American People and Nation*, p. 520.

Tests of Reasoning and Skills

1. Write here the three things which President Monroe's message talked about: _ _ _ _ _ _, _ _ _ _ _ _, _ _ _ _ _ _.

2. Write here the two things which the Monroe Doctrine added to the Monroe message. _ _ _ _ _ _, _ _ _ _ _ _.

3. The people in Spanish America would have nothing to do with Napoleon's brother as their king because   he was a cruel man.   they had not elected him.   √ he was not Spanish.

4. Turn to a map of South America before 1800. Check the following as true or false:

True False
[ ]   [√]   All South America could properly be called Spanish America.
[√]   [ ]   In 1795 Spain owned land in North America.
[√]   [ ]   Portugal had vast possessions in South America.

5. Show by means of squares how the map shows
                    Portuguese territory   Spanish Territory

6. From what you have read, do you think it is likely that the Monroe Doctrine will ever have any more changes made in its meaning?

Yes [√]   No [ ]

Exercise in Organization. Children copy the topic headings of the story and prepare a brief oral summary of each heading.

B

STORY 1.   THE SPANISH–AMERICAN WAR   [$\frac{1}{2}$ Week
Conversational Approach

The teacher places a map of the world before the class. Children point out on it all the possessions of the United States. The teacher will probably have to explain that the Phillippines are now a separate country and that they will be independent in 1945.

"What was the last annexation of territory about which we read in our book? [*Alaska.*] Do you think it is better for a country to be all in one piece or scattered about the globe?" Children present different views.

"Our story today will tell us how the United States got Puerto Rico and the Philippines. Does anyone know already?"

Reading and Study

The Reading Periods

Independent Readers

TEXTS

BEARD and BAGLEY, *First Book in American History*, 367–375.

BURNHAM and JACK, *Growth of Our Country*, 283–288.

CLARK, *Westward to the Pacific*, 408–411.

KELTY, *Growth of the American People and Nation*, 521–534.

WOODBURN and MORAN, *Makers of America*, 307–310.

EXTENSIVE READING

CHANDLER and CHITWOOD, *Makers of American History*, 299–307.

EVANS, *America First*, 414–422.

FOOTE and SKINNER, *Makers and Defenders of America*, 323–327.

GORDY, *American Leaders and Heroes*, 314–326.

LEFFERTS, *American Leaders*, II : 297–310.

MONTGOMERY, *Beginners' American History*, 241–255.

SOUTHWORTH, *Builders of Our Country*, II : 256–259.

TOMLINSON, *Fighters Young Americans Want to Know*, 217–224.

UHRBROCK and OWENS, *Famous Americans*, 337–346.

Lower Group

The teacher tells the story orally to this group, writing on the board the names of the most important persons and places as she mentions them.

Then the teacher and this group read together the story as given in the text. The teacher directs the silent reading, section by section, by such questions as "Find out two reasons why Spain did not feel very friendly toward the United States."

Children read silently and answer orally. When the entire story has been read in this manner, they test themselves by the questions at the end of the story.

OTHER BOOKS

DAVIS, *Stories of the United States*, 236–241.

GROVE, *American Naval Heroes*, 27–31.

READING FOR RECREATION

ALLEN, *Cleared for Action.*

GEROULD, *Filibuster*

The Discussion   *[In a Language Period*

Children answer the study-guide questions as fully as possible, each one pointing out on the large wall map all the places he mentions. The teacher writes on the board the words *the white man's burden*. Children discuss the meaning.

Multisensory Aids

Children and teacher talk over together the pictures in the text, pointing out features of geographic and historical significance. They turn to a map of the Caribbean area and locate Cuba, Havana, Santiago, Puerto Rico. They turn to a map of the Far East and locate the Philippines, Manila, Guam.

Audio-visual Materials Obtainable

BROWN. Famous Pictures: 3, 66, 2136, 2146.

Society for Visual Education (MUIR). 1865–1898: Presidents' Administrations and Beginning of Spanish-American War; 1898–1901: End of Spanish-American War and Assassination of McKinley.

Society for Visual Education (BRIGGS). The New Union — Spanish-American War.

Yale Pageant Educational Slides: 269, 751–753.

Music. "Hot Time in the Old Town Tonight" and "Just As the Sun Went Down" are played as representative of the war spirit.

Play Sousa's "Stars and Stripes Forever."

General Activities

Creative Activities: Group and Individual, Correlated with Other Subjects or Voluntary Projects

One committee models in half of the sand table the Caribbean arena of war, marking the scenes of important engagements; another does the same for the war in the Far East.

Volunteers may wish to design a headpiece for the story.

Volunteers draw scenes of life in the Cuban concentration camps.

A veteran of the Spanish-American War describes his experiences.

A volunteer reports on the history of the American Red Cross.

The children write two editorials: one for a European newspaper, declaring that the United States should not have gone to war with Spain; and one for an American newspaper, explaining why we went to war with Spain.

Children write cablegrams for the home newspapers announcing the principal battles.

The teacher reads to the class Elbert Hubbard's "A Message to García."

Each child makes two maps: one of the Caribbean war area, and the other of the Far Eastern war area.

The class continues the time line.

Application to Present-Day Conditions   *[In a Language Period*

Has Cuba had a peaceful and orderly government of late years?

How do newspapers learn about what is going on during a war? (See encyclopedia under "Newspapers.")

Why do Americans spend some of their money for property in foreign countries? [*High returns.*] What do they do when their property is in danger because of war? [*Ask the United States to protect it.*] This is likely to draw the United States into war. Is it a good thing?

Does any country have a right to send its warships into the territory of a foreign country?

Why is the United States interested in keeping so small an island as Guam? [*Coaling station; station for airships.*] From a map, find the names of other small islands owned by the United States in the Pacific.

How much of the territory won by the United States during the Spanish-American War does it still hold?

Why is Cuba called "the Pearl of the Antilles"?

Exercises in Reasoning

How many years of peace had the United States had between the Civil War and the Spanish-American War?

In what way did the Spanish-American War broaden the interests of the United States?

Why does the United States not want any other country to possess Cuba?

Are more newspapers sold during war times? Then why are some newspaper-owners always for war?

Do you think we should take much pride in fighting a war that might have been prevented?

Why is the health department of an army as important as the department which supplies the ammunition?

The United States has always believed that government ought to rest on the consent of the people. Do you think, then, that we should take lands inhabited by people who do not want to be American?

Explain why the results of the Spanish-American War made the United States a world power.

Why do comparatively few Americans live in our islands?

Do you suppose that yellow men and black men and brown men believe in "the white man's burden"? Do they like the idea?

Drill Games

Place names are best drilled upon at the map: *Cuba, Manila, Havana, Santiago, Guam.*

Drill cards are made as follows:

William McKinley	⟷	the president during the war with Spain
Admiral George Dewey	⟷	the sailor who took Manila
1898	⟷	date of the Spanish-American War
Spanish-American War	⟷	the hundred days' war with Spain
"Rough Riders"	⟷	Roosevelt's company of horsemen
"white man's burden"	⟷	the idea that white men should take backward lands and civilize them

Testing

Tests of Understanding are given in Kelty's *The Growth of the American People and Nation*, p. 534.

Tests of Reasoning and Skills

1. Here is a list of reasons why the United States went to war. They are all true. Check the most important reason.

    Cuba is very near the coastline of the United States.

√ American citizens had much money invested in Cuba.

    The Cubans were very cruelly treated.

    Newspapers were eager for war.

    Many young men were eager for adventure.

2. Make a list of all the places mentioned in your book where fighting took place. _ _ _[*Manila, Guam, Santiago, Puerto Rico.*]_ _ _

3. Make a list of what the United States gained as a result of the Spanish-American War. _ _ _[*Puerto Rico, Guam, Philippines, Cuba (to occupy).*]_ _ _

4. Put the figure *1* before that which happened first, the figure *2* before that which happened next, and so on.

    [_ _*1*_ _] Monroe message

    [_ _*3*_ _] Spanish American War

    [_ _*2*_ _] Invention of electric light

5. Where in your book can you find material about the *Maine*? _ _ _ _ _ _ Where did you look to find out? _ _ _[*Index.*]_ _ _

Exercise in Organization. Each child makes an independent outline.

B

STORY 2. ISLAND PROBLEMS · STORY 3. CUBA   [*1 Week*

[Stories treated separately for reading and discussion; for other activities, both together]

Conversational Approach

Children list the islands which belong to or are a part of the United States now. "How many of them came to us as a result of the Spanish-American War? There is one group in the Pacific which did not come to us as a result of the war. Which group is it? We must find how we came to include the Hawaiian Islands. Why is Cuba not in this list?"

Reading and Study

The Reading Periods (First Story)

Independent Readers	Lower Group
TEXTS	The teacher and this group read together the story as given in the text. The teacher guides the silent reading, section by section, by such questions as "What problem did the United States have to solve about its new possessions?"
BARKER, DODD, WEBB, *Our Nation Grows Up*, 326–333.	
BEARD and BAGLEY, *First Book in American History*, 378–380.	

CLARK, *Westward toward America*, 399–408, 411–415.

KELTY, *Growth of the American People and Nation*, 535–545.

McGUIRE and PHILLIPS, *Building Our Country*, 140–143, 145.

EXTENSIVE READING

ATWOOD and THOMAS, *The Americas*, 207–212, 214–216.

BARROWS and PARKER, *United States and Canada*, 249–257.

GEORGE, *Little Journeys to Cuba and Porto Rico*, 5–7.

GEORGE, *Little Journeys to Hawaii and the Philippines*, 10–15.

SMITH, *Human Geography*, I : 172–179, 181–182.

TOMLINSON, *Fighters Young Americans Want to Know*, 225–238.

WINSLOW, *Our American Neighbors*, 73–79, 80–85, 92–98.

Children read silently and answer orally. When the story has been completed in this manner they test themselves by the questions at the end of the story.

OTHER BOOKS

ALLEN, *How and Where We Live*, 193–197.

CARPENTER, *Around the World with the Children*, 74–81.

CARROLL, *Around the World*, II : 188–197; III : 215–222, 223–227, 228–266.

CHANCE, *Little Folks of Many Lands*, 83–93.

DAVIS, *Stories of the United States*, 235–236, 240–241, 270–271.

FAIRGRIEVE and YOUNG, *Homes Far Away*, 133–142.

FAIRGRIEVE and YOUNG, *The World*, 197–204.

SCHWARTZ, *Five Little Strangers*, 137–176.

READING FOR RECREATION

BURKS, *Barbara's Philippine Journey.*

FRENCH, *Stories of Hawaii.*

HADER, *Jamaica Johnny.*

KROUT, *Alice's Visit to the Hawaiian Islands.*

PERKINS, *Filipino Twins.*

SOWERS, *Carlos and Lola.*

SPERRY, *One Day with Manu.*

STUART, *Adventures of Piang, the Moro Jungle Boy.*

THOMPSON, *Our Atlantic Possessions.*

TIETJENS, *Boy of the South Seas.*

VAN DEUSEN, *Picturesque Porto Rico.*

WADE, *Our Little Cuban Cousin.*

WADE, *Our Little Hawaiian Cousin.*

WADE *Our Little Philippine Cousin.*

WADE, *Our Little Porto Rican Cousin.*

WADE, GRADY, KELTY, *Tales of Adventures in History*, 87–100 (Cook).

The Discussion (*First Story*)

Children answer the study-guide questions as fully as possible. Those who have read additional material will enjoy the opportunity to make their contributions. The teacher writes on the board the expression *Crossroads of the Pacific*. Children explain the significance.

The Reading Periods (*Second Story*)

Independent Readers

TEXTS

KELTY, *Growth of the American People and Nation*, 546–549.

Lower Group

The teacher and this group read together the story as given in the text. The teacher guides the silent reading, section by section, by such questions as "What did many people expect to happen after the war?"

Children read silently and answer orally. When the entire story has been read in this manner, they test themselves by the questions at the end of the story.

The Discussion (Second Story)

Children answer the study-guide questions as fully as possible. The teacher writes on the board the word *protectorate*. Children discuss the meaning.

Multisensory Aids

Children and teacher talk over the pictures in the text, pointing out features of geographic or historical importance.

AUDIO-VISUAL MATERIALS OBTAINABLE

EASTMAN. Classroom Films: Philippine Islands, Hawaiian Islands, Puerto Rico.
International Educational Pictures: Hawaii (series); Porto Rico (series); Cuba, the Island of Sugar; Under Cuban Skies; Our New Islands in the West Indies; St. Thomas, Uncle Sam's Ward.
Keystone Views: 172–179, 180–183.
National Geographic Magazine, LVII, 523–544 (May, 1930); LXIV, 345–380 (September, 1933).
National Geographic Society Series: The Philippines.
Perry Pictures: 7641–7644, 7655.
Society for Visual Education. Picturols: The Hawaiian Islands as a Whole; Philippine Islands, Parts I and II.
Society for Visual Education (BRAY-EYEGATE). Story of Pineapple.
Society for Visual Education (SPENCER). Porto Rico, Cuba.
United States Department of the Interior. National Parks Portfolio: Hawaii National Park.

Music. Sing West Indian folk songs from the music series used in your school. Records of Hawaiian music may be contrasted with records of Cuban and Puerto Rican music.

Play selections from Gruenberg's *Emperor Jones.*

General Activities

Creative Activities: Group and Individual, Correlated with Other Subjects or Voluntary Projects

The class divides into committees. Each committee selects one island or group of islands to investigate. It collects pictures and gathers interesting information to present to the class. It collects figures as to the amount of annual trade with the United States. (See World Almanac.)

Visitors to the islands are invited to describe them to the children.

A volunteer reports on the Virgin Islands as the old home of pirates. (See the encyclopedia.)

A volunteer reports on the voyages of Captain Cook.

A volunteer finds out how much sugar Cuba produces each year and explains why its prosperity depends on whether the United States will buy its crop.

A map is consulted to find out why Hawaii is called "the Crossroads of the Pacific" (Atwood and Thomas, *The Americas*, p. 203).

The class may wish to correspond with schools in one or more of the cities in the various islands.

The class continues the time line.

Application to Present-Day Conditions

Volunteers report on the new Philippine government. (See periodicals of November, 1935, and also current issues for later developments.)

The class investigates which steamship lines and air lines reach each of the islands. (The advertising columns of travel magazines will help. Also address the Chamber of Commerce of the chief city of each island group.)

What advantages does each group of islands offer to travelers?

Are all our islands heavily fortified? (See encyclopedia.) Which do you think need the strongest fortifications? Why?

Do you think that it is an easy task for any people to learn to govern themselves? Why?

Do you think that the United States ought to have protectorates over many other countries? Give reasons for your answer.

Why do many people fear that Japan will take the Philippines? (Study the map.)

Do you think Puerto Rico will ever be given independence? Give reasons. What other change might possibly satisfy its people?

What bill was introduced into Congress recently about Puerto Rican independence? (See periodicals of May, 1936.)

Exercises in Reasoning

What is the principal export of the Philippines? (See your geography.) To whom do they sell it? Why, then, did the beet-sugar growers of the United States want the Philippines to become an independent country? [*Their sugar could not compete with beet sugar in our markets.*]

Do you blame the Puerto Ricans for wanting the United States to tell them whether or not they are ever to become a state? Give reasons for their being made a state; reasons against.

Why did the United States want to buy the Virgin Islands? Do you think they are worth the money paid for them?

Why do you suppose there are so many Chinese and Japanese in Hawaii? How do they, the native Hawaiians, and the white people get along? (See the encyclopedia.)

Compare the revolution against the queen in Hawaii with the revolution of Texas against Mexico.

In what way was Hawaii useful during the Spanish-American War?

Why did the world not believe that we would give up Cuba?

In what way was the giving of independence to the Philippines an entirely new practice for the United States? [*First time we ever gave up any territory.*]

Contrast the way in which Hawaii was added with the way in which Puerto Rico was added.

Drill Games

Place names are best drilled upon at the map: *Philippines, Puerto Rico, Virgin Islands, Hawaii, Honolulu.*

Drill cards are made as follows:

Danish West Indies	↔	the former name of the Virgin Islands
1917	↔	date of the purchase of the Virgin Islands
" Gibraltar of America "	↔	a nickname given to the Virgin Islands
Filipinos	↔	the people who live in the Philippine Islands
" Crossroads of the Pacific "	↔	a nickname given to Hawaii
1898	↔	date of the annexation of Hawaii
protectorate	↔	part control over a weak nation by a stronger nation

Testing

Tests of Understanding are given in Kelty's *The Growth of the American People and Nation*, pp. 545, 549.

Tests of Reasoning and Skills

1. Finish this sentence, naming *three* answers: Our islands are useful to the United States because they ___[*supply raw materials*]___, ___[*supply markets*]___, ___[*some of them help in defense*]___.

2. Finish this sentence: The first time that the United States ever gave up any of its territory was ___[*when granting independence to the Philippines*]___.

3. The islands which will help most in keeping up our power in the Pacific are ___[*Hawaiian Islands*]___.

4. The two groups of islands that will help most in protecting the Panama Canal are ___[*Virgin Islands*]___, ___[*Puerto Rico*]___.

5. Check the right answer: Since we gave up the right to interfere in Cuba, the feeling of the Cubans toward us has been   [✓] more friendly.   [ ] less friendly.

Exercise in Organization. Children copy the topic headings of both stories. They choose one heading from each, about which to give a topical recitation.

B

STORY 4. THE PANAMA CANAL · STORY 5. THEODORE ROOSEVELT · STORY 6. RELATIONS WITH MEXICO   [*1 Week*

[For conversational approach, reading periods, and discussion, the first two stories are taken up together, and then the third story; for other activities, all three together]

Conversational Approach (First and Second Stories)

"When the United States wanted to send its ships from New York to the Hawaiian Islands, by what routes would the ships have to go?" Children show possibilities on the map.

"Use the scale of miles and estimate the distance. Why would such a great distance be very bad in time of war? Do you happen to know what was done to solve this problem? Our stories today tell what was done, and what man was most responsible for doing it."

Reading and Study

The Reading Periods (First and Second Stories)

[These two stories are read consecutively before any discussion is held]

Independent Readers

TEXTS

BARKER, DODD, WEBB, *Our Nation Grows Up*, 236–239, 239–243.

BEARD and BAGLEY, *First Book in American History*, 416–420, 424–427, 432–433.

BURNHAM and JACK, *Growth of Our Country*, 293–297, 311–325.

CLARK, *Westward to the Pacific*, 425–432.

HALLECK and FRANTZ, *Makers of Our Nation*, 301–313.

KELTY, *Growth of the American People and Nation*, 550–555, 556–560.

MCGUIRE and PHILLIPS, *Building Our Country*, 143–145.

NIDA, *Following the Frontier*, 312–315.

SMALLIDGE and PAXSON, *Builders of Our Nation*, 530–531.

WOODBURN and MORAN, *Makers of America*, 310–317.

EXTENSIVE READING

ATWOOD and THOMAS, *The Americas*, 213–214.

BARROWS and PARKER, *United States and Canada*, 254.

BURNHAM, *Hero Tales from History*, 352–358.

CHANDLER and CHITWOOD, *Makers of American History*, 308.

FARIS, *Real Stories of the Geography Makers*, 185–189.

GORDY, *Leaders in Making America*, 430–441.

INGRAHAM, *Story of Democracy*, 233–241.

LEFFERTS, *American Leaders*, II : 330–345.

NIDA, *Panama and Its Bridge of Water*.

SANFORD and OWEN, *Modern Americans*, 37–42, 73–80.

TAPPAN, *American Hero Stories*, 265–278.

TAPPAN, *Heroes of Progress*, 237–244, 254–263.

UHRBROCK and OWENS, *Famous Americans*, 348–366.

WINSLOW, *Our American Neighbors*, 66–71.

Lower Group

The teacher tells both stories orally to this group, writing on the board the most important words as she mentions them.

Then the teacher and this group read together the stories as given in the text. The teacher directs the silent reading, section by section, by such questions as "How long had people had the idea of digging a canal?"

Children read silently and answer orally. When both stories have been read in this manner, they test themselves by the questions at the end of the stories.

OTHER BOOKS

DAVIS, *Stories of the United States*, 247–248.

EVERETT and REED, *When They Were Boys*, 53–59, 77–90.

SMITH, *Human Geography*, I : 110.

READING FOR RECREATION

BOND, *Pick, Shovel, and Pluck*.

PIKE, *Basco, Our Little Panama Cousin*.

ROOSEVELT, *Theodore Roosevelt's Letters to His Children*.

SOWERS and VAN NEUMAN, *Let's Go Round the World with Bob and Betty*.

VERRILL, *Panama of Today*.

WADE, *The Master Builders*.

The Discussion (First and Second Stories) [In a Language Period

Children answer both sets of study-guide questions as fully as possible.

Conversational Approach (Third Story)

"During much of this time the United States has had another problem on its hands. This was what to do about Mexico. Mexico had had a good many revolutions, and governments came and went. What do you suppose the

Americans who owned property in Mexico wanted the government to do? And why would the world watch very suspiciously to see what the United States would do? [*Because we had taken land from Mexico before.*]

"On the whole, does it seem to you a good idea for the United States to interfere with the affairs of its neighbors? Our story will tell us what the government decided to do."

Reading and Study

The Reading Periods (Third Story)

Independent Readers

TEXTS

KELTY, *Growth of the American People and Nation*, 561–565.

EXTENSIVE READING

CHANDLER and CHITWOOD, *Makers of American History*, 311–312.

READING FOR RECREATION

BAYLOR, *Juan and Juanita.*
BRANDEIS, *Little Mexican Donkey Boy.*
LEE, *Pablo and Petra.*
MORROW, *Painted Pig.*
SMITH, *Made in Mexico.*

Lower Group

The teacher tells the story orally to this group, writing on the board the most important words as she mentions them.

Then the teacher and this group read together the story as given in the text. The teacher directs the silent reading, section by section, by such questions as "How long had Mexico been independent?"

Children read silently and answer orally. When the entire story has been read in this manner, they test themselves by the questions at the end of the story.

OTHER BOOKS

DAVIS, *Stories of the United States*, 256–259.

The Discussion (Third Story)   [In a Language Period

Children answer the study-guide questions as fully as possible. The teacher writes on the board the words *watchful waiting, Mexican border*. Children discuss the significance.

Multisensory Aids

Children and teacher talk over together the pictures in the text, pointing out features of historic or geographical significance. They turn to a map of the Panama Canal and show Colombia, Panama, Nicaragua, the Canal Zone. Which end of the canal is farther west, the Pacific end or the Atlantic end?

AUDIO-VISUAL MATERIALS OBTAINABLE

EASTMAN. Classroom Films: The Panama Canal.
International Educational Pictures: Panama Canal and Its Historical Significance; The Real Roosevelt; Theodore Roosevelt; Mexico, II; Mexico Rejuvenated.
MCKINLEY. Illustrated Topics for American History: S 40.
National Geographic Magazine, LXV, 329–356 (March, 1934); LXVI, 738–788 (December, 1934).
Society for Visual Education. Picturols: Panama Canal Zone as a Whole, Theodore Roosevelt.
Society for Visual Education. Schoolfilm: The Panama Canal and Its Historical Significance.
Yale Pageant Educational Slides: 270, 271, 473.

Music. Play records of Mexican music.

General Activities

Creative Activities: Group and Individual, Correlated with Other Subjects or Voluntary Projects

A committee models the area of the canal in the sand table, showing part of Colombia, Panama, the Canal Zone, the Panama Railroad, the canal, and the cities of Colón, Ancon, and Panama.

A volunteer reports on how the Suez Canal was built.

A visitor to Panama describes the voyage from the Atlantic to the Pacific through the canal.

A volunteer committee reports on the dramatic story of Walter Reed and the experiments with yellow fever.

The teacher reads to the class Percy Mackaye's poem "Goethals: Poet Engineer," in Edwin Markham's *The Book of Poetry*, II.

The class plans a trip to Panama — routes, fares, scenes to be enjoyed.

A committee reads to the class the dramatization given in Hague and Chalmers's *Dramatic Moments in American History* (212–245).

The teacher reads to the children selections from *Theodore Roosevelt's Letters to His Children* and shows some of the drawings.

The class plans an automobile trip to the city of Mexico. (See the local automobile club or gasoline dealers.)

A soldier who served on the Mexican border tells the children about his experiences.

A visitor to the city of Mexico tells of the interesting railway journey from Veracruz to the city of Mexico.

The class continues the time line.

Application to Present-Day Conditions   [In a Language Period

Compare the Panama Canal and the Suez Canal as to length and as to annual tonnage carried.

Why may the United States yet build a canal without locks across Nicaragua? Does this explain why the United States is always interested in Nicaragua?

Do other nations besides the United States use the Panama Canal? (See the encyclopedia or World Almanac.)

Graph the number of ships of each nation that passed through the canal last year. (World Almanac.)

Do you know any other of our recent presidents (besides Theodore Roosevelt) who were leaders rather than followers of their political party?

Which other of our recent presidents was vice-president when the president died, and therefore came into office in this way? [*Coolidge, on the death of Harding.*]

Why would the Panama Canal be particularly useful in case of war with Japan?

Exercises in Reasoning   [*In a Language Period*

How had our navy been divided at the beginning of the Spanish-American War? (Review the story.)

Compare the advantages of a sea-level canal without locks and a lock canal, such as that at Panama.

Do you think the United States was entirely fair to Colombia when Panama revolted? (See Kelty's *The Growth of the American People and Nation*, p. 552.)

Why was yellow fever worse in the tropics than in temperate regions?

Why did the Panama Canal lead to a great increase in the trade between the east coast and the west coast? Do you think it would do the railroads any good?

In what ways has the study of tropical medicine increased the possibilities of colonizing in the tropics?

In what ways did Thomas Jefferson, Andrew Jackson, and Theodore Roosevelt all try to give a "square deal" to the common man?

Why is the city of Mexico a fine summer resort though it is so very far south of us? (Find out the altitude.)

In what way did President Wilson show courage by *not* sending soldiers into Mexico?

Drill Games

Place names are best drilled upon at the map: *Panama, Canal Zone, Mexican border.*

Drill cards are made as follows:

Colonel Goethals	↔	the army officer in charge of digging the Panama Canal
Colonel Gorgas	↔	the officer in charge of the health work in the Canal Zone
1914	↔	date when the Panama Canal was completed
Theodore Roosevelt	↔	the president who had the Panama Canal dug
" watchful waiting "	↔	our policy of waiting to allow Mexico to solve her own problems

Children drill one another by twos.

Testing

Tests of Understanding are given in Kelty's *The Growth of the American People and Nation*, pp. 555, 560, 565.

Tests of Reasoning and Skills

1. Can you make up a sentence telling whether or not the Panama Canal was worth the money it cost, and why? _ _ _ _ _ _

2. Make a list of the political offices which Theodore Roosevelt held during his lifetime. Use your book. _ _ _[*State representative, head of New York police, public service at Washington, D.C., Navy Department, governor of New York, vice-president, president.*]_ _ _

3. Check the best answer: The United States did not interfere with the Mexican government because   many countries were already suspicious of the United States.   the president was afraid he might be defeated.   √ we

believe in allowing each country to solve its own problems.   England did
not want us to interfere.

Check the right answer:

4. Should you expect an American who owned property in Mexico to want
President Wilson to send the army into the country?   Yes [√]   No [ ]
Why? _ _ _ _ _ _

5. Should you expect an American who did not own property in Mexico to
want President Wilson to send the army into the country?   Yes [ ]
No [√]   Why? _ _ _ _ _ _

6. Turn to a map of the Panama Canal. Does the Panama Canal touch the
country of Colombia?   Yes [ ]   No [√]

7. Under what subheading do all three stories for this week belong?
_ _ _ _ _ _ Where did you look to find out? _ _ _[*Table of contents.*]_ _ _

Exercise in Organization. Each child makes an independent outline of the
first story. The class judges the results.

C

STORY 1. THE COMING OF THE WORLD WAR   [*1 Week*

Conversational Approach

"You have learned about all the wars we have studied so far mainly from
books. Now we come to one about which you probably have heard from your
fathers or grandfathers. How many had relations who fought in the last war?
Where did the fighting take place? Do you know any other countries which
fought on the same side as the United States?" The teacher lists as many
as children are sure of. "Do you know any countries fighting on the other
side?" The teacher lists as many as are given correctly. "Do you know what
the trouble was all about? Our story today will tell us."

Reading and Study

The Reading Periods

Independent Readers

TEXTS

KELTY, *Growth of the American People and
Nation*, 566–577.
SMALLIDGE and PAXSON, *Builders of Our
Nation*, 603–606.

EXTENSIVE READING

EVANS, *America First*, 428–433.
SANFORD and OWEN, *Modern Europeans*, 9–
20, 21–31, 32–41, 51–58, 59–71, 89–98,
99–109, 121–131, 149–157, 165–176, 177–
185.

READING FOR RECREATION

ALTSHELER, *Hosts of the Air*.
BARBOUR, *Fortunes of War*.
CARTER, *Shaggy*.

Lower Group

The teacher tells the story orally to this
group, illustrating places mentioned on the
slated map which she has already prepared. She writes the most important
words on the board as she mentions them.
Children practice the pronunciations.

Then the teacher and this group read
together the story as given in the text. The
teacher directs the silent reading, section
by section, by such questions as "Did any
one country cause the World War?"

Children read silently and answer
orally. When the entire story has been
read in this manner, they test themselves
by the questions at the end of the story.

· DYER, *Ben, the Battle Horse.*
MUKERJI, *Gay Neck.*
ROLT-WHEELER, *Boys' Book of the Great War.*
ROLT-WHEELER, *Wonder of War in the Air.*

OTHER BOOKS

CURTIS, *Why We Celebrate Our Holidays,* 117–119.
DAVIS, *Stories of the United States,* 259–262.

The Discussion

Several different sets of children answer the study-guide questions. The teacher writes on the board the words *Allies, Western Front, tanks, Eastern Front, alliance, trenches.* Children discuss the meanings.

Multisensory Aids

Children and teacher talk over together the pictures in the text, pointing out features of geographic or historical significance. They turn to a map of the World War and show the Western Front, the Eastern Front, the Italian Front, the Marne, Verdun, Tannenberg Forest, and the battle of Jutland.

AUDIO-VISUAL MATERIALS OBTAINABLE

EASTMAN. Educational Slides: World War and Peace.
McKINLEY. Illustrated Topics for Mediæval and Modern History; M M 35–38.
Yale Pageant Educational Slides: 295, 296.

General Activities

Creative Activities: Group and Individual, Correlated with Other Subjects or Voluntary Projects

A committee models the theater of war in the sand table, marking Germany, Russia, France, Belgium, Austria-Hungary, Italy. Name the Marne, Verdun, Tannenberg, Jutland. Show the Western Front, the Eastern Front, the Italian Front.

Another committee shows the Allies and the Central Powers on a slated map of the world, coloring the Allies and all their dependencies one color and the Central Powers with all their dependencies another. They show why the war was called the World War. (See Shepherd's *Historical Atlas* (179–182) or Bartholomew's *School Economic Atlas* (14–15, 16–17). The list is in the World Book Encyclopedia (" World War ").)

A volunteer draws a map showing the famous German plan for a Berlin-to-Bagdad railway.

A committee writes an article for a German newspaper telling the causes of the war as the Germans saw it; another committee writes a similar article for an Allied newspaper.

Volunteers draw pictures to illustrate the friendly countries making up the Central Powers; the Allies.

The teacher reads to the children some of the most famous war poems, such as McCrae's "In Flanders Fields."

Children report the part played by animals in the war (Dyer's *Ben, the Battle Horse;* Red Cross dogs, carrier pigeons).

The class makes a picture collection of war machines.

A volunteer reports on the use of poison gas.

The class continues the time line.

Application to Present-Day Conditions

Review the theme "Struggle for Markets and Raw Materials." Does this heading explain why Japan is taking land in northern China, and Italy is taking land in Africa? Explain.

Suppose that other nations got all the raw materials and markets that they needed. Would this have any effect on the United States?

What is a "standing," or "regular," army? Compare the size of the standing armies of different countries. (See encyclopedia or World Almanac.)

Why is the airplane of such value in modern war?

Under what government is Russia today? (See encyclopedia.)

What is the name of Constantinople today? (Consult a modern atlas.)

Exercises in Reasoning

From what you know of quarrels between boys and girls, do you think it likely that one side was entirely right and the other side entirely wrong?

Why did the German people feel that they did not have a fair chance in regard to colonies?

How does the assassination of the Austrian prince show that a very small thing may start a war if nations are ready for it?

Why was so much of the fighting done from the trenches?

Why was the withdrawal of Russia from the war a great blow to the Allies?

In what way did science make the World War more terrible than any war had ever been before?

Drill Games

Place names are best drilled upon at the map: *Marne, Western Front, Belgium, Verdun, Eastern Front, Serbia.*

Drill cards are made as follows:

General Foch	⟷	the French general who became commander in chief of the Allies
the Allies	⟷	all the countries fighting on the same side as Great Britain and France (except the United States)
1914	⟷	date of the beginning of the World War
World War	⟷	the war between the Allies and the Central Powers from 1914 to 1917
tanks	⟷	armored motor cars moving on treads
General Hindenburg	⟷	the great German general of the battle of the Tannenberg Forest
Central Powers	⟷	all the countries fighting on the same side as Germany and Austria-Hungary
Kaiser	⟷	the title of the emperor of Germany
alliance	⟷	an agreement between nations to help one another
trenches	⟷	long, narrow ditches to protect troops, from which they carry on war

Children drill individually, to get ready for class games.

Testing

Tests of Understanding are suggested in Kelty's *The Growth of the American People and Nation,* p. 577.

Tests of Reasoning and Skills

1. Check the best answer: In the World War ___ the Allies were entirely in the right. ___ the Central Powers were entirely in the right. ✓ right lay on both sides. ___ neither side had any reason to fight.

2. All the following are causes of the World War. Check the most important:

✓ Both sides wanted as many raw materials and markets as possible.
___ Both sides wanted large navies.
___ Germany wanted to build a Berlin-to-Bagdad railway.
___ Great Britain wanted to keep Germany away from India.
___ Both sides were heavily armed.

3. Was the assassination of the Austrian prince the real cause of the war?
Yes [ ]   No [✓]

4. Most of the fighting took place on ___ the Italian Front. ✓ the Western Front. ___ the Eastern Front.

5. Turn to a map of the World War. Check each of the following as true or false:

True False

[ ]   [✓] The submarine war zone touched Sweden and Italy.
[✓]   [ ] The Western Front touched Belgium and France.
[✓]   [ ] On the Eastern Front the Russians advanced into Austria-Hungary.
[ ]   [✓] The Italian Front was west of Italy.

Exercise in Organization. The children copy the topic headings and prepare to give a topical recitation on each.

STORY 2. AMERICA'S PART IN THE WAR   *[1 Week*

Conversational Approach

"Up to this point we have found no reason at all why the United States should fight. But you know that we did fight. Let us see why.

"Do you remember why we had been drawn into the war between Napoleon and Great Britain in 1812?" Children give the reasons. "Now we find the same thing happening again. If our ships try now to trade with Germany, what will the Allies do? [*Form a blockade to keep them out, or capture them.*]

"If our ships try to trade with the Allies, what do you suppose the Germans will do? [*Blow them up by submarines.*] Which do you think is worse, to capture our ships or to blow them up and kill our sailors? Then which side will the United States probably take? Our story today tells about our part in the war."

Reading and Study

The Reading Periods

Independent Readers

TEXTS

BARKER, DODD, WEBB, *Our Nation Grows Up*, 243–252.

BEARD and BAGLEY, *First Book in American History*, 435–449.

BURNHAM and JACK, *Growth of Our Country*, 327–339.

CLARK, *Westward to the Pacific*, 433–440.

HALLECK and FRANTZ, *Makers of Our Nation*, 315–328.

KELTY, *Growth of the American People and Nation*, 578–586.

SMALLIDGE and PAXSON, *Builders of Our Nation*, 606–611.

WOODBURN and MORAN, *Makers of America*, 317–320.

EXTENSIVE READING

EVANS, *America First*, 433–447.

GORDY, *Leaders in Making America*, 454–466.

SANFORD and OWEN, *Other Soldiers*.

TOMLINSON, *Fighters Young Americans Want to Know*, 239–256, 257–265, 266–275.

UHRBROCK and OWENS, *Famous Americans*, 368–376.

Lower Group

The teacher tells the story orally to this group, writing on the board the most important words as she mentions them, and pointing out places on the map.

Then the teacher and this group read together the story as given in the text. The teacher directs the silent reading, section by section, by such questions as "Why did the United States not take part on either side at first?"

Children read silently and answer orally. When the entire story has been read in this manner, they test themselves by the questions at the end of the story.

OTHER BOOKS

CURTIS, *Why We Celebrate Our Holidays*, 119–120.

DAVIS, *Stories of the United States*, 263–269.

EVERETT and REED, *When They Were Boys*, 65–70, 116–122, 123–127.

TAPPAN, *American History for Very Young Readers*, 131–137.

READING FOR RECREATION

ABBOTT, *Blue Jackets of 1918*.
COLLINS, *Naval Heroes of Today*.
CONNOR, *Sandy, the Tin Soldier of the A.E.F.*
DRIGGS, *Adventures of Arnold Adair, American Ace*.
DUPUY, *Uncle Sam, Fighter*.
TOMLINSON, *Scouting with General Pershing*.

The Discussion

Several different sets of children answer the study-guide questions, questioning one another to bring out important points omitted. The teacher writes on the board the words *draft, Liberty Loans, submarine war zone, armistice*. Children discuss the meanings.

Multisensory Aids

Children and teacher talk over together the pictures in the text, pointing out features of geographical and historical significance. They turn to a map of the World War and show the submarine war zone, the lane left for American ships, the Hindenburg Line, Château-Thierry, and the Argonne Forest.

AUDIO-VISUAL MATERIALS OBTAINABLE

Keystone Views: 229, 231–232, 235–236, 238–239, 241–244, 246, 350.
McKINLEY. Illustrated Topics for American History: S 45, 46.
Perry Pictures: 130–D, 132–F.
Society for Visual Education (BRIGGS). The World War and Its Results.
Yale Pageant Educational Slides: 275, 279, 280, 281, 283, 285–287, 289–291, 294, 295, 297, 300, 756–761.

Music. Play records of World War music or sing "Over There," "Long Way to Tipperary," "Where Do We Go from Here?" "Keep the Home Fires Burning," "Madelon," "Pack Up Your Troubles," "There's a Long, Long Trail," "I Hate to Get Up in the Morning," "Katy."

General Activities

Creative Activities: Group and Individual, Correlated with Other Subjects or Voluntary Projects

A committee marks on the sand-table model all the additional places mentioned above under "Multisensory Aids."

The class makes a visit to the local museum to see World War relics.

Veterans are invited to describe their experiences to the children.

A volunteer describes how ships and automobiles were camouflaged during the war to conceal them from the enemy. (See encyclopedia.)

A volunteer explains the use of depth bombs and mines.

A committee explains how the "draft" operates. (See *Conscription* in the encyclopedia.) It uses the class as subjects.

The teacher shows the children the graphic representation of the cost of war from the *Literary Digest*, CXX : 17 (September 1, 1935).

The teacher explains what a government bond is, and explains that the money will have to be paid back, much of it by the children themselves.

A volunteer reports on the later services of General von Hindenburg to his country. (See encyclopedia.)

A volunteer reports on the exploits of Sergeant York.

A volunteer committee makes a picture map of America's part in the war.

The class continues the time chart.

Application to Present-Day Conditions

America lent money to almost all the Allies during the War. Does this explain the term *America, a creditor nation*? Did we get the money back?

Why is a blockade as hard on the women and children of a country at war as it is on the soldiers?

What did our experience in the World War teach us as to the possibility of getting ready to fight a war quickly?

How do women and children and old men help in the winning of a war nowadays?

Why is it necessary to have one commander in chief, even if several nations are fighting?

Exercises in Reasoning

The hundred years from 1814 to 1914 are the only time in our history when we have had comparatively little to do with Europe. Prove that we have been greatly influenced by Europe before and since.

Compare the British blockade of Germany with the American blockade of the Southern ports during the Civil War.

Which do you think was more effective, Britain's blockade of Germany by her ships or Germany's blockade of the British Isles by her submarines?

Sometimes you hear people say that war is good for business. Is this true in the long run?

Why do you suppose the Allies had fought for several years without a commander in chief?

How do you suppose a ship would know when it entered the submarine war zone?

Drill Games

Drill cards are made as follows:

November 11, 1918	⟷	date of the armistice ending the World War
the draft	⟷	choosing men for forced service in the army or navy
Liberty Loans	⟷	United States government bonds to pay the costs of the war
Woodrow Wilson	⟷	the president of the United States during the World War
submarine war zone	⟷	the part of the ocean marked off, within which ships were likely to be blown up
General Pershing	⟷	the commander of the American troops in the World War
the *Lusitania*	⟷	a large passenger ship torpedoed by the Germans
1917	⟷	the date when the United States entered the World War
armistice	⟷	an agreement to stop fighting for a time

Children keep records of their mistakes while drilling individually.

Testing

Tests of Understanding are given in Kelty's *The Growth of the American People and Nation*, p. 586.

Tests of Reasoning and Skills

1. Between 1914 and 1917 the United States had cause for complaint against   Germany only.   Great Britain only.   ✓ both Germany and Great Britain.   neither Germany nor Great Britain.

2. What did we learn both in 1812 and in 1914–1917 as to the chances of a neutral trading country's staying out of a war? _ _ _[*It will be drawn in if the war lasts long.*]_ _ _

3. If we have another war we shall get our soldiers   ✓ by the draft. from volunteers.

4. Considering what the World War cost us and what we got out of it, do you think that we made a profit by going into it?   Yes [ ]   No [✓]

5. Turn to a map of the World War. Mark the following:

True False
[✓] [ ] The Argonne Forest was once in the hands of the Germans.
[ ] [✓] The Germans took Château-Thierry.
[ ] [✓] The Hindenburg Line was in Russia.
[✓] [ ] The Americans fought on the Western Front.

Exercise in Organization. Children prepare one or two summary sentences for each heading in the story.

C

STORY 3. THE PROBLEMS OF PEACE

D

STORY 1. TRANSPORTATION BY LAND, AIR, AND SEA   [*1 Week*

[Stories treated separately for reading and discussion; for other activities, both together]

Conversational Approach

Large wall maps are displayed showing Europe in 1914 and Europe today. Children study the differences. "Most of those differences were made by the treaty which ended the World War."

Children point out Geneva. "That is the home of another change brought about by the treaty, the League of Nations." Children tell what they already know about it.

"Since every nation is spending so much on war that not enough is left for better purposes, why do not the nations all agree to cut down the size of their armies and navies? Does this seem a good idea?"

Reading and Study

The Reading Periods (First Story)

Independent Readers

TEXTS

BEARD and BAGLEY, *First Book in American History*, 444–445.
BURNHAM and JACK, *Growth of Our Country*, 339–340, 356–357.
CLARK, *Westward to the Pacific*, 440–443.
KELTY, *Growth of the American People and Nation*, 587–593.
SMALLIDGE and PAXSON, *Builders of Our Nation*, 611–612.
WOODBURN and MORAN, *Makers of America*, 348–352, 355–366.

EXTENSIVE READING

SANFORD and OWEN, *Modern Americans*, 9–15.

Lower Group

The teacher explains these topics orally to the lower group, writing on the board the most important words as she mentions them. Children practice the pronunciations.

Then the teacher and these children read together the story as given in the text. The teacher directs the silent reading, section by section, by such questions as "Who would make the peace?"

Children read silently and answer orally. When the entire story has been read in this manner, they test themselves by the questions at the end of the story.

The Discussion (First Story)

Several different sets of children give the answers to the study-guide questions. The teacher attempts particularly to detect wrong impressions and half-comprehensions, from the answers. She writes on the board the following words: *peace conference, disarmament, limitation of armaments, reduction of armaments.* Children discuss the meanings.

The Reading Periods (Second Story)

Independent Readers

TEXTS

BARKER, DODD, WEBB, *Our Nation Grows Up*, 301–307.

BURNHAM and JACK, *Growth of Our Country*, 270–274, 347–355.

CLARK, *Westward to the Pacific*, 379–386.

HALLECK and FRANTZ, *Makers of Our Nation*, 247–251, 268–281.

KELTY, *Growth of the American People and Nation*, 594–604.

McGUIRE and PHILLIPS, *Building Our Country*, 280–283, 313–318, 322–339.

NIDA, *Following the Frontier*, 315–323.

SMALLIDGE and PAXSON, *Builders of Our Nation*, 539–554.

EXTENSIVE READING

BOND, *With the Men Who Do Things*, 197–213.

FORMAN, *Stories of Useful Inventions*, 161–165.

GORDY, *Leaders in Making America*, 414–421.

LARGE, *Everyday Wonders*, 17–22, 71–83.

McFEE, *Stories of American Inventions*, 166–205, 226–251.

PARKMAN, *Conquests of Invention*, 310–343.

SANFORD and OWEN, *Modern Americans*, 99–107, 125–130.

TAPPAN, *Heroes of Progress*, 217–227.

TAPPAN, *Travelers and Traveling*, 74–81.

WADE, *The Light Bringers*, 112–141.

Lower Group

The teacher and this group read together the story as given in the text. The teacher guides the silent reading, section by section, by such questions as "What was the first kind of horseless carriage?"

Children read silently and answer orally. When the entire story has been read in this manner, they test themselves by the questions at the end of the story.

OTHER BOOKS

CHAMBERLAIN, *How We Travel*, 131–136, 182–187.

EVERETT and REED, *When They Were Boys*, 38–44.

READING FOR RECREATION

D'AULAIRE, *Conquest of the Atlantic.*

BISHOP, *Story of the Submarine.*

BUSH and WADDELL, *How We Have Conquered Distance.*

CHARNLEY, *Boys' Life of the Wright Brothers.*

COLLINS, *Boys' Book of Submarines.*

DOBIAS, *Picture Book of Flying.*

FLOHERTY, *'Board the Airliner.*

GABRIEL, *Book of Airplanes.*

GABRIEL, *Book of Automobiles.*

HOLLAND, *Historic Airships.*

LARGE, *Air Travelers.*

LENT, *Wide Road Ahead.*

LINDBERGH, *We.*

PRYOR, *Airplane Book.*

SALT, *Automobiles.*

SIMONDS, *Henry Ford, Motor Genius.*

WEBSTER, *Travel by Air, Land, and Sea.*

The Discussion (Second Story)

Children answer the study-guide questions as fully as possible, questioning one another to bring out important points omitted. The teacher writes the following words on the board: *seaplanes, airships, airplanes, aviator, submarines, good roads.* Children discuss the meanings.

Multisensory Aids

Children and teacher talk over together the pictures in the text, pointing out features of geographic and historical significance.

AUDIO-VISUAL MATERIALS OBTAINABLE

Building America: Transportation.
Compton's Pictured Teaching Materials: *Land Transportation*, Plate VII, 5; Plates XI, XII; *Water and Air Transportation*, Plates X–XII.
International Educational Pictures: Aviation.
Keystone Views: 226, 227, 249, 299.
MCKINLEY. Illustrated Topics for Mediæval and Modern History: M M 36.
National Geographic Magazine, LVII, 653–688 (June, 1930); LXIII, 585–630 (May, 1933); LXIV, 728 (December, 1933).
Society for Visual Education (SPENCER). Aircraft.
Yale Pageant Educational Slides: 234, 476, 477, 479, 481, 691–699, 754–755.

Music. Play selections from Ferdie Grofé's suite *Wheels*.

General Activities

Creative Activities: Group and Individual, Correlated with Other Subjects or Voluntary Projects

A committee examines a map of the world and reports what nations were given the German colonies to manage.

A committee lists the countries which belong to the League of Nations and the countries which do not belong. (See the World Almanac.)

A committee reads to the class the dramatization given in Hague and Chalmers's *Dramatic Moments in American History* (296–314).

The class holds a conference on limitation of armaments and presents reasons why armaments of all countries should be cut down.

Volunteers draw diagrams to illustrate the 5: 5: 3 naval ratio.

The class makes a picture collection of the evolution of the automobile and the airplane; a map of air-mail routes.

A volunteer reports on Ford's early-American village at Dearborn. (Perhaps the local Ford dealer can suggest material.)

A committee makes a picture collection of highway markings. (See World Book Encyclopedia: "Automobiles.")

A volunteer graphs the automobile census of the principal countries of the world. (World Almanac.)

A stamp-collector shows his collection of air-mail stamps.

Persons who have made airplane flights describe their experiences.

Children stage an exhibit of model airplanes.

A sailor who has done submarine service describes his experiences to the children.

A volunteer explains the graphic representation of comparative loads on good and bad roads given in the World Book Encyclopedia: "Roads and Streets."

A volunteer explains Cruikshank's cartoon in the World Book Encyclopedia under "Aircraft."

The teacher reads to the class the poem "Darius Green and His Flying Machine."

A volunteer tells the story of Icarus.

The class continues the time line.

Application to Present-Day Conditions

The World War was often called "a war to end wars." Did it succeed in doing that?

In what ways do you think that the League of Nations is a good thing? Why does the United States not belong? Why is the League not stronger than it is?

Is Germany a republic today?

What is a baseball league? a basketball league? In what way are they similar to the League of Nations?

Is there any law which the nations of the world are bound to accept? (See *International law* in the encyclopedia.) How can they be forced to live up to these laws?

Are countries today cutting down their armies and navies? (World Almanac.)

In what way has the automobile made the township unnecessary as a government unit? Could counties today be much larger than they were in our earlier history? Why? Could school districts be larger and better?

Does the United States government today take any part in the building of roads? (See encyclopedia under *Roads*.) When had the United States taken any interest in road-building before? (See *National Road* in the text.)

A volunteer reports on the career of Lindbergh; another tells the services of the Wright brothers.

Has the United States progressed as fast in the welfare of its people as it has in its machine development?

Exercises in Reasoning

In the treaty of peace Germany was disarmed. The other nations promised that they would cut down their arms too. They did not do it. Do you blame Germany for feeling that she has not been treated fairly?

Why did many people think that President Wilson himself ought not to attend the Peace Conference?

Do you think Germany alone was to blame for the war, as the treaty said?

Why is co-operation among the nations better than war?

How do the automobile licenses of cars traveling along your main highways give you some idea of the extent of travel nowadays? [*From many different states.*]

How has the automobile helped criminals and made the enforcement of law more difficult?

Why should every automobile driver have to pass a test? What kind of test?

How has the automobile taken the place of the horse? Is it even taking the place of the camel?

Why did the automobile lead to the demand for good roads?

In what way have the automobile, the submarine, and the airplane made conservation of our national resources even more necessary?

Why are the poorer countries not willing to give up the use of submarines?
What does the following sentence mean? "In effect, the whole world is now smaller than the United States was in Jackson's time."

Drill Games

Place names are best drilled upon at the map: *Versailles, Geneva, Kitty Hawk, Detroit.*

Drill cards are made as follows:

Treaty of Versailles	↔	the treaty, signed in 1919, which ended the World War
League of Nations	↔	an organization of most of the nations of the world to help them solve world problems
disarmament	↔	laying aside arms completely
limitation of armaments	↔	naming a size beyond which no country's armaments may go
reduction of armaments	↔	cutting down the size of the armaments that a country now has
Briand-Kellogg Peace Pact	↔	a paper signed by almost every country, promising not to use war as a means of solving problems
Wright brothers	↔	the famous brothers who made the first successful airplane flight
seaplanes	↔	flying machines built for landing on the water
airships	↔	lighter-than-air flying machines
Henry Ford	↔	the man who began mass production in the manufacture of automobiles
1894	↔	date of the first successful automobile
airplanes	↔	heavier-than-air flying machines
aviator	↔	a man who operates a flying machine
Charles A. Lindbergh	↔	the first American to fly across the Atlantic alone
Zeppelins	↔	huge airships built by a German
1903	↔	date of the first successful airplane flight
submarines	↔	boats which can operate beneath the surface of the water
airport	↔	a landing field for aircraft

Children drill on these terms by twos.

Testing

Tests of Understanding are given in Kelty's *The Growth of the American People and Nation,* pp. 593, 604.

Tests of Reasoning and Skills

1. In order to secure a League of Nations through the Treaty of Versailles, President Wilson   had to give up some American territory to other nations.

√ had to accept many parts of the treaty that were not fair.   had to take the side of Germany against the Allies.

2. The League of Nations   has solved every problem of the nations since the war.   √ has solved some problems and been unable to solve others.   has never solved any problem of importance.

3. Which will it be easier to persuade the nations to accept?
√ Reduction of armaments.   Disarmament.

4. Which has done the most good to the American people so far?
The airplane.   The submarine.   √ The automobile.

5. Make a sentence telling why you think the United States ought to join the League of Nations or why you think it ought not to join. _____

6. On what pages can you find material about Henry Ford? _____
Where did you look? ___[*Index.*]___ Under which word did you look?
Henry [ ]   *Ford* [√]

Exercise in Organization. Each child outlines the first story independently. The class judges the outlines.

D

STORY 2. CONSTITUTIONAL CHANGES · STORY 3. POLAR EXPLORATION · OUR UNSOLVED PROBLEMS   [*1 Week*

Conversational Approach

[Stories 2 and 3 are treated separately for the reading periods and the discussion; for other activities, both together]

"While the World War was going on, and our people were in a serious mood, they began to think about some of our national problems. One was drunkenness. Why is drunkenness bad, not only for the person himself but for all his city?" Children give the reasons they can think of. "So a law was made that no liquor should be made or sold. Why is such a law hard to enforce?

"Another problem was that the United States had not been fair to its women. Why is it not fair to give the right to vote to men and not to women?

"Besides these hard problems, the United States was interested in other matters, about which we shall read later."

Reading and Study

The Reading Periods (First Story)

Independent Readers	**Lower Group**
TEXTS	The teacher explains the problems orally to this group, writing on the board the most important words as she mentions them. Children practice the pronunciations.
BARKER, DODD, WEBB, *Our Nation Grows Up*, 276–277.	
BEARD and BAGLEY, *First Book in American History*, 407–414.	
BURNHAM and JACK, *Growth of Our Country*, 300–306.	Then the teacher and this group read together the story as given in the text.

KELTY, *Growth of the American People and Nation*, 605–607.

EXTENSIVE READING

GORDY, *Leaders in Making America*, 449–454.
MOORE, *When They Were Girls*, 30–36, 155–162.
SANFORD and OWEN, *Modern Americans*, 177–185.

The teacher guides the silent reading, section by section, by such questions as "About which changes in the Constitution are we going to read?"

Children read silently and answer orally. When they have read the story through they test themselves by the questions at the end of the story.

READING FOR RECREATION

HORTON, *A Group of Famous Women.*
SHAW and JORDAN, *Story of a Pioneer.*

The Discussion (First Story)

Children answer the study-guide questions. The teacher is particularly on guard against verbalism. She writes on the board the words *prohibition, suffrage, woman suffrage.* Children discuss the meanings.

The Reading Periods (Second Story)

Independent Readers

TEXTS

BARKER, DODD, WEBB, *Our Nation Grows Up*, 307–314.
KELTY, *Growth of the American People and Nation*, 608–613.
SMALLIDGE and PAXSON, *Builders of Our Nation*, 586–602.
WOODBURN and MORAN, *Makers of America*, 340–344.

EXTENSIVE READING

FARIS, *Real Stories of the Geography Makers*, 289–302.
McLEAN, *Heroes of the Farthest North and Farthest South*, 154–173.
SANFORD and OWEN, *Modern Americans*, 109–116.
TAPPAN, *Heroes of Progress*, 245–253.
WADE, *The Light Bringers*, 1–63.

Lower Group

The teacher tells the story orally to this group, writing on the board the most important words as she mentions them. Children practice the pronunciations.

Then the teacher and this group read together the story as given in the text. The teacher directs the silent reading, section by section, by such questions as "Why is it very hard to travel to the regions about the north pole?"

Children read silently and answer orally. When the story has been completed they test their understanding by the questions at the end of the story.

OTHER BOOKS

BARROWS and PARKER, *Journeys in Distant Lands*, 122–123.
EGGLESTON, *Stories of Great Americans*, 132–140.
PEARY, *Snow Baby's Own Story.*

READING FOR RECREATION

BAYNES, *Polaris.*
CRUMP, *Boys' Book of Arctic Exploration.*
DUNCAN, *Billy Topsail with Dr. Luke of the Labrador.*
DUPLAIX, *Pee-Gloo.*
ELIAS, *Young Folks' Book of Polar Exploration.*
SPERRY, *One Day with Tuktu.*
STEFANSSON and SCHWARTZ, *Northward Ho!*
WADE, *Pilgrims of Today.*

The Discussion (Second Story)

Children answer the study-guide questions. The teacher writes on the board the expressions *north pole, south pole, polar exploration*. Children discuss the meanings.

Multisensory Aids

Children and teacher talk over together the pictures in the text, pointing out features of geographic and historical significance. They show the arctic and antarctic regions on a map; they point out the north pole and the south pole on the globe.

AUDIO-VISUAL MATERIALS OBTAINABLE

Compton's Pictured Teaching Materials: *Hot and Cold Lands,* Plates VIII–XII.
International Educational Pictures: Admiral Byrd at the South Pole, Amundsen's North Pole Explorations.
Keystone Views: 221, 222.
National Geographic Magazine, LVIII, 127–227 (August, 1930).

General Activities

Creative Activities: Group and Individual, Correlated with Other Subjects or Voluntary Projects

The girls in the class prepare an assembly program on "Famous Women of America." They include reports on Pocahontas, Abigail Adams, Anne Hutchinson, Harriet Beecher Stowe, Mary Lyon, Emma Willard, Clara Barton, Louisa M. Alcott, Jane Addams, Susan B. Anthony, Julia Ward Howe, Anna Howard Shaw, Helen Hunt Jackson, Lucretia Mott, Dorothy Dix, Elizabeth Cady Stanton, Lucy Stone, Frances E. Willard, Charlotte Cushman.

The teacher shows a copy of the Constitution and reads the Eighteenth, Nineteenth, and Twenty-first amendments.

Children draw scenes of arctic or antarctic travel based on their readings.[1]

Those who have seen polar pictures in the motion pictures describe incidents they remember.

A volunteer writes an imaginary diary of a polar expedition.

Application to Present-Day Conditions

What is the number of the last amendment to the Constitution? About what subject is it?

Do you think that the United States has now solved its problem of drunkenness? What do you think should be done to solve it?

Is it an easy matter to decide how one ought to vote? What things does a person have to do in order to get ready to vote wisely?

What did Admiral Byrd hope to accomplish by his studies in the Antarctic?

How does a scientist know when he reaches the pole?

[1] Suggestions for activities may be obtained from *The Byrd Antarctic Expedition,* Teachers' Lesson Unit Series, Teachers College, Columbia University.

Geographies used to speak of the "six continents and the seven seas." Now they speak of the "seven continents and the six seas" (Bowman). Why has this change come about?

Exercises in Reasoning

Do you think that a man should be allowed to drink whatever he wants to, although his family may suffer?

How has the use of the automobile made drunkenness more dangerous than it used to be?

Was the United States really a democracy before the Nineteenth Amendment was passed? Explain your answer.

Do you think it is a good thing to allow everyone to vote — criminals, uneducated persons, and everyone else? Explain your view.

Should people obey laws of which they do not approve? What will happen if they do not?

Compare the north polar region with the south polar region.

Do you think it is worth while to spend money for polar expeditions?

How many generations of Americans have made all these changes about which you have been reading? (Count thirty years to a generation.)

Drill Games

Place names are best drilled upon at the map: *Arctic Ocean, Antarctica.* Drill cards are made as follows:

Eighteenth Amendment	⇔	the amendment which brought about national prohibition
Nineteenth Amendment	⇔	the amendment which gave women the right to vote
Susan B. Anthony	⇔	a great leader in the movement for woman suffrage
Robert E. Peary	⇔	the first man to reach the north pole
Roald Amundsen	⇔	the first man to reach the south pole
polar exploration	⇔	traveling over new lands in the farthest north or south
prohibition	⇔	the forbidding of liquor
woman suffrage	⇔	women's right to vote

Drill games are held with all the cards of the unit.

Testing

Tests of Understanding are given in Kelty's *The Growth of the American People and Nation,* pp. 607, 613.

Tests of Reasoning and Skills

1. The amendment which has since been changed is the   Twenty-first.   Nineteenth.   √ Eighteenth.

2. The prohibition question taught us   to make a law first and then teach people to obey it.   √ to teach people how to solve a problem and then pass a law about it.

3. Mark this statement as true or false:

True   False

[   ]   [√] Giving women the right to vote solved all the problems of government in our country.

4. Write a sentence here, telling whether or not you think polar exploration is foolish, and why. _____

If the teacher feels capable, she may now give the children an oral story of the events leading up to the depression, the depression itself, and the attempts of the government to bring about recovery.

Our Unsolved Problems

The teacher and the entire class may read together the discussion given on pages 614–616 of Kelty's *The Growth of the American People and Nation*, different children reading the paragraphs orally in turn.

"Do you think that you are ready now to solve all these problems mentioned? By the time that you are grown up will you be any better prepared? What things will help to prepare you? Do you suppose that there may be some new problems by that time which today we know nothing about? Why is this likely? What can the school do to help you get ready to solve these new problems? What can you do for yourself?"

Tests on the Entire Unit

Test of Place Sense

I. Pass crayon and double-sized outline maps of North America. Give the following directions.

1. Place the letter *C* in Cuba.

2. Make a dot where Havana is.

3. Make a cross (X) in Puerto Rico.

4. Draw two lines (=) where the Canal Zone is.

5. Color Panama yellow.

6. Make a circle (O) around the Virgin Islands.

7. Trace the Mexican border in green.

8. Make a blue dot for Detroit.

9. Place a star (*) over the north pole.

II. Pass double-sized outline maps of the world. Give the following directions.

1. Make a dot where Honolulu is.

2. Color the Hawaiian Islands green.

3. Make a cross (X) where Manila is.

4. Color the Philippines yellow.

5. Put the letter *B* in Belgium.

6. Show the Marne by a wavy line (∿).

7. Make a circle (O) for Verdun.

8. Make a brown dot for Geneva.

9. Draw a little arrow (→) from Paris to Versailles.

Test of Time Sense. Pass mimeographed sheets with the following directions.

I. 1. Here is a list of names. Put the figure *1* before the name of the man who did his great work first, the figure *2* before the name of the man who came next, and so on.

> [__2__] William McKinley
> [__3__] General Pershing
> [__1__] President Monroe

2. Here is another list. Do the same.

> [__1__] General Sherman
> [__3__] General Hindenburg
> [__2__] George Dewey

3. Here is another list. Do the same.

> [__2__] Wright brothers
> [__1__] Alexander Graham Bell
> [__3__] Woodrow Wilson

4. Here is another list. Do the same.

> [__2__] Colonel Goethals
> [__3__] General Foch
> [__1__] John Ericsson

5. Here is another list. Do the same.

> [__2__] Theodore Roosevelt
> [__3__] Woodrow Wilson
> [__1__] William McKinley

6. Here is another list. Do the same.

> [__3__] General Hindenburg
> [__2__] Colonel Gorgas
> [__1__] General Grant

7. Here is another list. Do the same.

> [__1__] Commodore Perry
> [__2__] Robert Peary
> [__3__] Admiral Byrd

8. Here is another list. Do the same.

> [__1__] Eli Whitney
> [__2__] Andrew Carnegie
> [__3__] Henry Ford

II. 1. Here is a list of events. Put the figure *1* before that which happened first, the figure *2* before that which happened next, and so on.

> [__3__] the coming of the airplane
> [__1__] the Monroe Doctrine
> [__2__] the Spanish-American War
> [__4__] the armistice ending the World War

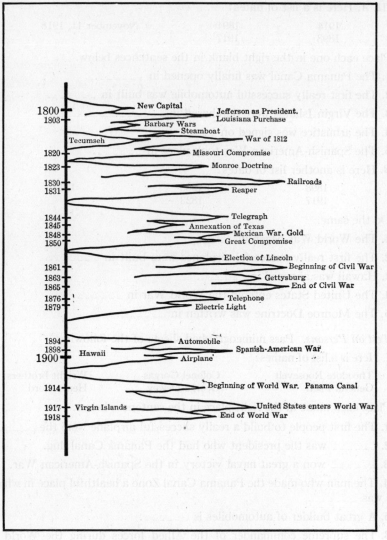

1800
1803
New Capital
Jefferson as President.
Louisiana Purchase
Barbary Wars
Steamboat
Tecumseh
War of 1812
1820
Missouri Compromise
1823
Monroe Doctrine
1830
1831
Railroads
Reaper
1844
1845
1848
1850
Telegraph
Annexation of Texas
Mexican War. Gold
Great Compromise
Election of Lincoln
1861
Beginning of Civil War
1863
Gettysburg
1865
End of Civil War
1876
1879
Telephone
Electric Light
1894
1898
1900
Automobile
Hawaii
Spanish-American War
Airplane
1914
Beginning of World War. Panama Canal
1917
1918
Virgin Islands
United States enters World War
End of World War

Time Chart — Unit Seven

2. Here is another list. Do the same.
  [--2--] annexation of Hawaii
  [--3--] the opening of the Panama Canal
  [--4--] United States enters the World War
  [--1--] coming of the automobile

3. Here is another list. Do the same.
  [--2--] beginning of the World War
  [--1--] the United States gets possession of the Philippines
  [--3--] purchase of the Virgin Islands

III. *A.* Here is a list of dates:

1914	1894	November 11, 1918
1898	1917	

Place each one in the right blank in the sentences below.

1. The Panama Canal was finally opened in _____.

2. The first really successful automobile was built in _____.

3. The Virgin Islands were purchased in _____.

4. The armistice was signed on _____.

5. The Spanish-American War took place in _____.

B. Here is another list of dates:

1898	1903	1914
1917	1823	

Do the same.

1. The World War began in _____.

2. The first really successful airplanes were built in _____.

3. Hawaii was annexed in _____.

4. The United States entered the World War in _____.

5. The Monroe Doctrine was written in _____.

Test on Persons. Pass mimeographed sheets of the following.

I. Here is a list of names:

Theodore Roosevelt	Colonel Gorgas	Wright brothers
General Foch	George Dewey	Henry Ford

Place each name in the right place in the sentences below.

1. The first people to build a really successful airplane were the _____.

2. _____ was the president who had the Panama Canal dug.

3. _____ won a great naval victory in the Spanish-American War.

4. The man who made the Panama Canal Zone a healthful place in which to live was _____.

5. A great builder of automobiles is _____.

6. The supreme commander of the Allied forces during the World War was _____.

II. Here is another list:

Colonel Goethals	General Pershing	General Hindenburg
Woodrow Wilson	William McKinley	Robert E. Peary

Do the same.

1. _____ discovered the north pole.

2. _____ was president during the Spanish-American War.

3. _____ was president during the World War.

4. _____ was commander of the American forces during the World War.

5. The man who dug the Panama Canal was _ _ _ _ _ _.

6. _ _ _ _ _ _ was a commander of the German forces during the World War.

Test on Historical Terms

I. Here is a list of terms:

Monroe Doctrine	prohibition	"Crossroads of the Pacific"
limitation of armaments	*Maine*	Spanish-American War
polar exploration	kaiser	airship

Place each in the right blank in the sentences below.

1. The German people's title for their emperor was _ _ _ _ _ _.

2. The _ _ _ _ _ _ was an American warship that was blown up.

3. Forbidding the manufacture or sale of liquor is _ _ _ _ _ _.

4. Cutting down land or naval forces is called _ _ _ _ _ _.

5. A large vessel sailing through the air and depending on gases to make it float is an _ _ _ _ _ _.

6. The war for the liberation of Cuba was the _ _ _ _ _ _.

7. Searching through unknown regions near the poles is _ _ _ _ _ _.

8. Hawaii is called the _ _ _ _ _ _.

9. The principle that European countries should not interfere in the affairs of the Western Hemisphere nor colonize there is the _ _ _ _ _ _.

II. Here is another list:

Washington Conference	good roads	airplane
woman suffrage	disarmament	"watchful waiting"
World War	submarine	Rough Riders
hundred days' war with Spain		

Do the same.

1. The recent war between the Central and Allied powers was the _ _ _ _ _ _.

2. A boat that can travel beneath the surface of the water is a _ _ _ _ _ _.

3. The act of greatly reducing land or naval forces is _ _ _ _ _ _.

4. Our policy of waiting to see what would happen in Mexico was _ _ _ _ _ _.

5. Roads which have been given a hard surface are _ _ _ _ _ _.

6. The Spanish-American War is sometimes called the _ _ _ _ _ _.

7. A flying machine supported by wings is an _ _ _ _ _ _.

8. The meeting to talk about limitation of armaments was the _ _ _ _ _ _.

9. A special troop of cavalry in the Spanish-American War was called the _ _ _ _ _ _.

10. Women's right to vote at election is _ _ _ _ _ _.

III. Here is another list:

League of Nations	Progressive party	allies
Danish West Indies	armistice	protectorate
Philippine independence	*Lusitania*	Central Powers
peace conference		

Do the same.

1. The meeting to talk over the terms by which the war should be ended was the _ _ _ _ _ _.

2. A great ship blown up by the Germans was the _ _ _ _ _ _.

3. Countries leagued with each other are _ _ _ _ _ _.

4. Before we bought the Virgin Islands they were the _ _ _ _ _ _.

5. An agreement to stop fighting for a little while is an _ _ _ _ _ _.

6. The political party organized by Theodore Roosevelt was the _ _ _ _ _ _.

7. The protection and part control which a stronger nation has over a weaker nation is a _ _ _ _ _ _.

8. The alliance which attempts to prevent war is the _ _ _ _ _ _.

9. Germany, Austria, Turkey, and Bulgaria were the _ _ _ _ _ _.

10. The problem of whether or not to allow the Philippines to become a nation was the problem of _ _ _ _ _ _.

IV. Here is another list:

Treaty of Versailles	Liberty Loans	submarine war zone
Western Front	island possessions	Panama Canal
blockade	alliances	tank
draft		

Do the same.

1. The shutting in of a line of coast by enemy ships is a _ _ _ _ _ _.

2. Compelling men to enroll for military or naval service is a _ _ _ _ _ _.

3. Connections formed between states to aid each other in war are _ _ _ _ _ _.

4. The great waterway dug between the Atlantic and the Pacific is the _ _ _ _ _ _.

5. The money raised by the United States to carry on the World War was raised largely by _ _ _ _ _ _.

6. An armored gasoline engine traveling on a caterpillar tread is a _ _ _ _ _ _.

7. The terms which ended the World War made up the _ _ _ _ _ _.

8. Our possessions in the oceans are often called our _ _ _ _ _ _.

9. Where the armies of the Allies and the armies of the Central Powers came together in western Europe was the _ _ _ _ _ _.

10. The part of the seas surrounding the British Isles was declared a _ _ _ _ _ by Germany.

Comprehension Test on Unit Seven

Check the best answer.

1. The United States   has solved all its problems.   √ still has many problems to solve.

2. The United States did not join the League of Nations because   √ it was afraid of being mixed up in the troubles of Europe.   it did not want to help any other nation.   President Washington had told us to stay at home.

3. When there was trouble on the Mexican border the United States √ waited to see what would happen.   thought this was a good chance to seize Mexico's land.   helped Mexico to settle the trouble.

4. During recent years the United States   has explored many new lands.   has kept all her explorers at home.   √ has discovered the north pole.

5. When Germany was quite worn out, and failed in the last westward drive, she   gave up all the land she had conquered.   √asked for an armistice.   got Russia to help her.

6. We bought the Virgin Islands because   √ they would help us to protect the Panama Canal.   they were valuable.   we wanted more territory.

7. The Monroe Doctrine stated that   European powers must not come to America at all.   √ European powers must not colonize in or interfere with the Western Hemisphere.   America would keep out of Asia and Europe.

8. The United States entered the World War because   she hated Germany.   she thought the Allies were going to lose.   √ Germany interfered with her shipping.

9. We wanted to build a canal at Panama   to be ahead of the other nations.   √ to save the long journey around South America.   to get Panama away from Colombia.

10. The World War was caused chiefly   √ by the struggle for markets.   by Germany's wickedness.   by the kaiser.

11. We secured Hawaii   by purchase.   √ by annexation.   by the Spanish-American War.

Check two answers.

12. The Spanish-American War was caused   by our desire to obtain Cuba.   √ by the fact that Americans had property in Cuba.   √ by our sympathy with Cuba.   by our hatred of Spain.

13. Two of the latest amendments to our Constitution were about   √ prohibition.   Negro votes.   the income tax.   √ woman suffrage.

14. Check three answers. Three great inventions during this period were
   the telegraph   √ the automobile   the railroad
  √ the submarine   the telephone   √ the airplane

15. What is the title of the unit which you have just completed? _ _ _ _ _ _

A test of the entire field of American history is now given to measure progress. Form B should be used of the same test as was administered in Form A before any study of history was attempted. (See page 39.)

A school fair may be planned, each story of this unit being allotted a booth, and an explanation given to visitors regarding the contents of each booth.

PART FOUR. LEARNING AND TEACHING THE BEGINNINGS OF CIVILIZATION

Unit One · *Man's Earliest Discoveries are Made*

STORY 1. THE OLD STONE AGE [2 Weeks

Conversational Approach

"How many of you have ever camped out in the woods? How was your life there different from your life at home? What things did you have to go without?

"Now suppose that you should be lost some day in the deep woods and could not find your way out. You probably would not live long because you would not know how to do things for yourself. Can you think of any possible way by which you might keep yourself warm? What could you find to eat? What should you do when winter came? What should you do for clothing when yours wore out? How should you protect yourself against wild animals?"

Children speculate as to various possibilities. The purpose of the exercise is to make them appreciate the difficulties under which man began his climb.

"There was a time, many thousands of years ago, when all people had to live in the way we have mentioned. They were much worse off, however, than anyone today who might be lost. Anyone today would at least have many *ideas* which he had learned at home. He would know that fire can be made, that meat can be cooked, that seeds put into the ground will grow, that animals can be killed with tools, — and many other such things. The people about whom we are going to read today did not know any of these things at first. They had to discover each one, slowly and painfully. It is because they found out how to solve these problems so long ago that we are able to live comfortably today. We could have solved very few of them for ourselves. Do you think that you would like to have lived at that time?"

Reading and Study

The Reading Periods (First Part of Story)

The class is now divided into two groups, the independent readers and the lower group. They remain in the same classroom and carry on their activities at the same time.

Independent Readers

This group reads the first part of the story through silently, as given in their text. They then test their comprehension by those of the study-guide questions furnished by the teacher or by the text which refer to this part of the story. Reading from several other texts may follow.

TEXTS

BEEBY, *America's Roots in the Past*, 2–7.
CHAPMAN, *Stories of the Ancient Peoples*, 58–62.
CLARK-GORDY, *Early Story of Mankind*, 31–40.
CLARK-GORDY, *Westward toward America*, 3–10.
CORKE, *A Book of Ancient Peoples*, 1–6 (hard).
KELTY, *How Our Civilization Began*, 5–10.

Lower Group

If these children are very much below grade in reading ability, the teacher should first tell them the story orally, writing on the board the most important of the new words as she mentions them.

Then the teacher and these children read together the story as given in the text. The teacher directs the silent reading, section by section, by such questions as "In what ways did the earth look different then from the way it looks now?"

Children read silently and answer orally. When the entire story has been read in this manner, they test themselves by the study-guide questions at the end of the story.

MORE DIFFICULT TEXTS

BARKER, DUNCALF, BACON, *Old Europe and Our Nation*, 11–15, 20–22.
BEARD and BAGLEY, *Our Old World Background*, 26–28, 31–34.
COULOMB, MCKINLEY, and WHITE, *What Europe Gave to America*, 1–9.
GORDY, *American Beginnings in Europe*, 5–10.
HALLECK and FRANTZ, *Our Nation's Heritage*, 4–7.
HARDING, *Old World Background to American History*, 2–3.
HAWLEY, *Adventures in Old World History*, 3–11.
MARSHALL, *Story of Human Progress*, 8–19, 75–83.
NIDA, *Dawn of American History*, 3–7.
SOUTHWORTH, *What the Old World Gave the New*, 1–3.
VOLLINTINE, *The American People and Their Old World Ancestors*, 12–19.
WICKHAM and PHILLIPS, *America's Heritage from the Long Ago*, 1–7.
WOODBURN and HILL, *Historic Background of Our United States*, 5–12, 15–16, 22–25.

The Discussion

Children answer the first study-guide questions as fully as possible. The exercise gives the opportunity to clear up half-comprehensions or misapprehensions. The teacher insists on the children's answering in their own words rather than in the words of the book.

The teacher writes on the board the words *fist hatchet, tool, flint, cave dwellers, civilization*. Children discuss the meanings.

The Reading Periods (Rest of Story)

Independent Readers

This group reads the rest of the story through silently as given in their text. They then test their comprehension by the rest of the study-guide questions. Reading from several other texts may follow.

TEXTS

BEEBY, *America's Roots in the Past*, 7–10.
CHAPMAN, *Stories of the Ancient Peoples*, 69–70.

Lower Group

The same procedure is continued. First the teacher tells the rest of the story orally, writing on the board the most important of the new words as she mentions them.

Then the teacher and this group read together the story as given in the text. The teacher guides the silent reading, section by section, by such questions as "Before man could have any clothes, what did he have to learn?"

CLARK-GORDY, *Early Story of Mankind*, 40–43, 48–52.

CLARK-GORDY, *Westward toward America*, 15–22.

KELTY, *How Our Civilization Began*, 11–17.

KNOWLTON and GERSON, *Our Beginnings in the Past*, 61–72.

Children read silently and answer orally. When the entire story has been completed in this manner, children test themselves by the other study-guide questions at the end of the story.

MORE DIFFICULT TEXTS

BARKER, DUNCALF, BACON, *Old Europe and Our Nation*, 15–17.

BEARD and BAGLEY, *Our Old World Background*, 37–38.

BURNHAM, *Our Beginnings in Europe and America*, 10.

HALLECK and FRANTZ, *Our Nation's Heritage*, 12–13.

HARDING, *Our Old World Background*, 2–3.

NIDA, *Dawn of American History*, 7–9.

WICKHAM and PHILLIPS, *America's Heritage from the Long Ago*, 11–14.

WOODBURN and HILL, *Historic Background of Our United States*, 18–22.

The Discussion

Children answer the rest of the study-guide questions as fully as possible. This exercise enables the teacher to set up adequate standards as to what constitutes understanding. During the first units she will show the children repeatedly that they were not ready to answer the questions when perhaps they thought that they were. By insisting that children's answers shall show a real grasp of the story, the teacher is furnishing excellent training in the "ability to follow a coherent cumulative train of thought." (See page 7.)

She writes on the board the words *dugout, Old Stone Age, 100,000 years.* Children discuss the meanings.

Easy Reading

EXTENSIVE READING

COFFMAN, *Child's Story of the Human Race*, 1–13, 15–19, 25–31.

CORKE, *The World's Family*, 15–21, 36–37.

ERLEIGH, *In the Beginning*, 1–22.

HILLYER, *Child's History of the World*, 3–19.

HOLBROOK, *Cave, Mound, and Lake Dwellers*, 9–12, 37–42, 47–52, 98–102.

KINER, *How the World Grew Up*, 1–42.

MOHR, WASHBURNE, BEATTY, *Days Before Houses*, 9–58.

SCHWARTZ, *From Then till Now*, 1–36.

WADDELL and BUSH, *How We Have Conquered Distance*, 6–9, 17–23, 157–167.

WELLS, *How the Present Came from the Past*, I: 1–16, 19–32, 35–67, 134–142.

READING FOR RECREATION

DITMARS and CARTER, *Book of Prehistoric Animals*.

DOPP, *The Early Cave Men*.

DOPP, *The Early Sea People*.

DOPP, *The Later Cave Men*.

DOPP, *The Tree Dwellers*.

EATON, *Story of Light*, 1–6.

HADER, *Picture Book of Travel*, 6–10.

NIDA, *Ab, the Cave Man*.

NIDA, *Fleetfoot, the Cave Boy*.

NIDA, *The Tree Boys*.

PERKINS, *The Cave Twins*.

PETERSHAM, *Story Book of Things We Use* (houses, clothes, food).

WATERLOO, *Story of Ab*.

More Difficult Reading

EXTENSIVE READING

BOYLE, *Man Before History*, 13–49.

CLODD, *Childhood of the World*, 17–22, 42–57.

FELLOWES, *Stories of the Stone Age*, 3–80.

HARTMAN, *The World We Live in*, 27–63.

HEAL, *How the World Began*.

KUMMER, *First Days of Knowledge*, 112–125.

READING FOR RECREATION

BUCHANAN, *How Man Made Music*.

CRUMP, *Og of the Cave People*.

CRUMP, *Og, Boy of Battle*.

CRUMP, *Og, Son of Fire*.

GARIS, *Tam of the Fire Cave*.

HAYES, *The Tongues of Man*.

KUMMER, *First Days of Man*, 19–28, 76–147.
LANSING, *Man's Long Climb*, 82–83.
MARSHALL, *Readings in the Story of Human Progress*, 8–23, 49–51, 169–173.
MILLER, *Picturesque Tale of Progress*, I: 11–39.
NIDA, *Man Conquers the World with Science*, 5–10, 79–84.
QUENNELL, *Everyday Life in the Old Stone Age* (pictures).
SMALL, *Boys' Book of the Earth*.
Story of Our Calendar (American Council on Education), 3–8.
Story of Numbers (American Council on Education), 5–10.
Telling Time (American Council on Education), 4–7.
VAN LOON, *Story of Mankind*, 3–16.
WASHBURNE, *The Story of the Earth*.
WEBSTER, *World's Messengers*, 4–12.

HOUGH, *The Story of Fire*.
KIPLING, *Jungle Book*.
KIPLING, *Just So Stories*.
KNIGHT, *Before the Dawn of History* (pictures).
LACEY, *Light Then and Now*.
LANGFORD, *Pic, the Weapon Maker*.
LANGFORD, *Kutnar, Son of Pic*.
MCINTYRE, *Cave Boy of the Age of Stone*.
MIX, *Mighty Animals*.
REED, *The Earth for Sam*.
ROLT-WHEELER, *The Finder of Fire*.
ROLT-WHEELER, *The Monster Hunters*.
SMITH, *The Cave Mystery*.
STEARNS, *Story of Music*, 2–5.
WALKER, *Tales of the First Animals*.
WYSS, *Swiss Family Robinson*.

Multisensory Aids

Children and teacher talk over together the pictures in the text, noting features of geographical or historical significance.

They turn to the time line and discuss the appropriateness of the symbols used. (See page 501.)

AUDIO-VISUAL MATERIALS OBTAINABLE

Compton's Pictured Teaching Materials: *Prehistoric Man*, Plate I, 1, 2, 3; Plates II, III, IV, V, VI, XII; *American Indians*, Plate IV, 2; Plate V, 6; *Water and Air Transportation*, Plate I, 1.

Copley Prints: The Cairn, Oral Tradition.

Keystone Views: Prehistoric Man, 1–15.

LEHMANN. Colored History Pictures: III, 1.

McKINLEY. Illustrated Topics for Ancient History: A 1.

MILLER. *Picturesque Tale of Progress*, I, 11–39.

National Geographic Magazine, XLIV, 52–69 (July, 1923); XLVI, 136–144 (August, 1924).

Society for Visual Education. University Museum (Philadelphia): Men of the Old Stone Age.

See also "Visualizing Prehistoric Life," *Educational Screen*, X, 39–41 (October, 1931).

Music. The teacher plays records of selections from Haydn's *Creation*; from Saint-Saëns's *The Deluge*; and the "Zuñi Sunrise Call."

General Activities

Creative Activities: Group and Individual, Correlated with Other Subjects or Voluntary Projects

A volunteer committee models in the sand table a typical scene from prehistoric times. Other committees draw pictures of prehistoric animals, based on their outside reading, and place the animals at appropriate spots.

Volunteers draw other scenes to place on their own time line.

The class makes a visit to the local museum to observe arrowheads and any other relics of prehistoric times.

The teacher reads to the class the description of arrow-making as given in Longfellow's *Hiawatha*.

The class makes a picture collection of tree dwellings.

A committee experiments with the class to find out how many ideas may be conveyed only by signs.

A volunteer demonstrates striking a spark from flint and steel.[1]

The class tries the experiment of burning out a tiny dugout from a piece of wood.

Children compare their own drawings of animals with those of primitive man.

The class may make from this story the drawings for Reel One of a moving picture to be entitled "Man's Earliest Discoveries."

A committee tries to dramatize the story of a hunt, as primitive man did by his fireside so many thousands of years ago.

Volunteers model in clay the home of the cave dwellers.

The class makes its own time line.

More Difficult Activities

The science teacher compares for the class the brains of animals and the brains of people.

If there is anyone in the community who can demonstrate the chipping of flint, he is invited to do so for the class.

A volunteer may show his collection of stones, pointing out the differences between flint and the others.

The class studies the legend of Prometheus the Fire-Bringer.

A volunteer demonstrates how skins are scraped and prepared for use.

Volunteers report on sign languages. (See the reading lists.)

A volunteer reports on the words which different languages employ to designate the same idea.

A volunteer Boy Scout demonstrates making fire by rubbing two pieces of rotten wood together.

The teacher reads to the class Charles Lamb's "Dissertation on Roast Pig," from his *Essays of Elia.*

Application to Present-Day Conditions

Children list the familiar articles in their environment which were unknown to prehistoric man.

Children list the articles of food which prehistoric man might have found in their own community; the wild animals which man might have had an opportunity to run down.

Is our language still growing by the addition of new words? (See an unabridged dictionary under "Supplement," "Addenda," or the like.)

Have any new tools been invented recently?

The class makes a visit to a furrier's shop to observe the elaborate equipment needed nowadays to sew skins together.

Are animals still afraid of fire?

Do people nowadays ever try to keep fires always burning? [*In some churches; in some countries before the tomb of the unknown soldier.*] Why? Compare with the Vestal Virgins of Rome.

[1] Send for *The Story of Lighting*, Teacher's Lesson Unit Series, Teachers College, Columbia University.

Compare the art of primitive men with modern tendencies in art.

Do people today ever tell time by the sun? [*Rude guesses of farmers and elaborate instruments of ships at sea.*] How is our month based on the moon's changes? Why are our group leaders still the older men?

Exercises in Reasoning

What possible preparations could prehistoric man make for winter?

Why could man have made little progress without language?

How did primitive man make fire work for him?

Why did women's work come to differ from men's work?

How do we know that primitive man must have believed in a life after death? [*Buried articles for use in the Hereafter.*]

Why is man sometimes called "a thinking animal"?

What did primitive women use for thread in their bone needles? [*Tendons.*]

More Difficult Exercises in Reasoning

Name the respects in which animals seem better adapted to life in a wilderness than man.

What is the difference between a tool and a machine?

How do people today know anything about how prehistoric men lived, since they left no records?

Make a list of words which may have been suggested by the sounds in nature that they represent; for example, *bang, ripple, murmur, bow-wow, hiss.*

Were clothes first used for protection or as ornaments?

Notice that early man made no distinction between the fine arts and the practical arts. Give examples from your reading.

Why is our number system today based on tens? [*Counting began by using fingers.*]

Is co-operation needed more today than in primitive times or less? Explain.

Why have many primitive peoples worshiped fire?

In what way does man have an advantage over the animals in that he walks erect? In what way is his thumb an advantage which no animal possesses?

Drill Games

Association cards may be made as follows:

ONE SIDE		THE OTHER SIDE
fist hatchet	⟷	the first tool ever made by man
flint	⟷	a kind of stone which chips very smoothly
tool	⟷	an implement to help man's work with his hands
Old Stone Age	⟷	the period of time during which men used tools of chipped stone
dugout canoe	⟷	a small boat made by burning out a large log

Children practice with both sides of the cards until they can give the correct descriptions.

Testing

Tests of Understanding are given in Kelty's *How Our Civilization Began*, p. 17.

Tests of Reasoning and Skills

1. In the following list draw a line through the things which primitive men never saw:

forests	~~fences~~	~~buildings~~	~~shops~~
~~roads~~	animals	plants	fire
plains	~~farms~~	~~ships~~	~~railroads~~

2. Draw a line under the right word:

a. Man was <u>weaker</u>   stronger   than the animals.

b. The first method used in crossing rivers was   dugout canoes.   <u>swimming.</u>   sailboats.

3. Put the right word in the blank: Man learned from the _ _ _[*animals*]_ _ _ that he would be safer in a cave.

4. Check the right answer: The making of language made progress possible because   people like to talk to one another.   √ each man could tell the others his ideas.   one man used better language than the others.

5. Check the right answer: The Old Stone Age was   a thousand years ago.   ten thousand years ago.   √ a hundred thousand years ago.

Exercise in Organization. Children copy the topic headings and prepare to give a few summary sentences about each.

More Difficult Tests

1. Complete this sentence: Man was able to conquer the animals because _ _ _[*he had a better brain*]_ _ _.

2. Put the figure *1* before the thing which man did first, and the figure *2* before that which he did later.

[_ _*1*_ _] Man used as a tool a stick or stone which he found.

[_ _*2*_ _] Man made a tool by chipping the edges of a flint.

3. Do the same.

[_ _*2*_ _] Man learned to make fire.

[_ _*1*_ _] Man learned to use fire.

4. Complete this sentence: Women's work came to be different from men's work because _ _ _[*she had to stay at home to tend the fire*]_ _ _.

5. Check the right words: Man first learned to tell time from   watches.   √ the sun.   the stars.

STORY 2. THE NEW STONE AGE   [*1 Week*

Conversational Approach

The teacher shows the class a chipped arrowhead and also a cutting tool with a smooth edge. "Which one will cut more easily and smoothly? Why? Can you think of any way in which these rough edges might be made smooth?"

Children may have seen grindstones or implements for grinding knives. "Our story today tells us who first made this discovery.

"Now we find that primitive man has an enormous amount of work to do. He must have help to carry his heavy loads. Where do you suppose he can get help?" Children offer suggestions.

"Also he finds that he cannot always find an animal to kill when he is hungry. And fruits are not always in season. What can he do to secure a more certain supply of food?" Children consider the problem. "Our story this week will tell us."

Reading and Study

The Reading Periods

Independent Readers

This group reads the entire story through silently, as given in their text. They then test their comprehension by the study-guide questions furnished by the teacher or by the text.

Lower Group

The teacher tells the story orally to this group, writing on the board the most important of the new words as she mentions them.

Then the teacher and these children read together the story as given in the text. The teacher directs the silent reading, section by section, by such questions as "When did the New Stone Age begin?"

Children read silently and answer orally. When the entire story has been read in this manner, they test themselves by the questions at the end of the story.

TEXTS

BEEBY, *America's Roots in the Past*, 10–12.
CHAPMAN, *Stories of the Ancient Peoples*, 62–64, 70–73.
CLARK-GORDY, *Early Story of Mankind*, 43–47.
CLARK-GORDY, *Westward toward America*, 10–14.
CORKE, *A Book of Ancient Peoples*, 6–12 (hard).
KELTY, *How Our Civilization Began*, 18–28.
KNOWLTON and GERSON, *Our Beginnings in the Past*, 75–84, 106–114.

MORE DIFFICULT TEXTS

BARKER, DUNCALF, BACON, *Old Europe and Our Nation*, 17–20, 22–24.
BEARD and BAGLEY, *Our Old World Background*, 28, 34–36, 38–40.
BURNHAM, *Our Beginnings in Europe and America*, 10–18, 21–24.
COULOMB, McKINLEY, and WHITE, *What Europe Gave to America*, 9–11.
GORDY, *American Beginnings in Europe*, 10–13.
HALLECK and FRANTZ, *Our Nation's Heritage*, 7–9, 11, 13–15.
HARDING, *Old World Background to American History*, 3.
MARSHALL, *Story of Human Progress*, 21–35.
NIDA, *Dawn of American History*, 9–15.
VOLLINTINE, *The American People and Their Old World Ancestors*, 19–22.
WICKHAM and PHILLIPS, *America's Heritage from the Long Ago*, 7–11.
WOODBURN and HILL, *Historic Background of Our United States*, 12–14, 16–18, 26–27.

Easy Reading

EXTENSIVE READING

COFFMAN, *Child's Story of the Human Race*, 19–24, 32–35, 37–39, 42–44.
CORKE, *The World's Family*, 21–26.
ERLEIGH, *In the Beginning*, 23–36.

READING FOR RECREATION

DOPP, *The Early Herdsmen*.
DOPP, *The Early Farmers*.
DOPP, *The Early Sea People*.
HADER, *Picture Book of Travel*. 20–37, 38–45.

HOLBROOK, *Cave, Mound, and Lake Dwellers*, 13–16, 17–24, 43–46, 72–76, 93–97.
KINER, *How the World Grew Up*, 43–72.
MOHR, WASHBURNE, BEATTY, *Days Before Houses*, 59–90.
WADDELL and BUSH, *How We Have Conquered Distance*, 24–27, 29–36.
WELLS, *How the Present Came from the Past*, I : 70–83, 143–150.

NIDA, *Dan-Hur and the First Farmers*.
NIDA, *Taming the Animals*.
O'HARA, *From Hunters to Herdsmen*.
PETERSHAM, *Story Book of Food*.
PETERSHAM, *Story Book of Things We Use* (houses, food, transportation).
PETERSHAM, *Story Book of Transportation*.
PETERSHAM, *Story Book of Wheels*.

More Difficult Reading

EXTENSIVE READING

BOYLE, *Man Before History*, 50–57, 81–100.
CLODD, *Childhood of the World*, 23–55.
HARTMAN, *The World We Live in*, 65–77.
KUMMER, *The First Days of Man*, 173–181, 209–224.
LANSING, *Man's Long Climb*, 3–21, 91–98.
MARSHALL, *Readings in the Story of Human Progress*, 24–29.
MILLER, *Picturesque Tale of Progress*, I : 40–48, 53–65.
NIDA, *Man Conquers the World with Science*, 85–98.
O'NEILL, *World's Story*, 1–9.
QUENNELL, *The New Stone, Bronze, and Early Iron Ages*, 1–101 (pictures).
Story of Weights and Measures (American Council on Education), 5–8.

READING FOR RECREATION

DEFOE, *Robinson Crusoe*.
HAWKS, *The Romance of Transport*.
LONDON, *Call of the Wild*.
SETON, *Wild Animals I Have Known*.

The Discussion

Children answer the study-guide questions as completely as possible. The teacher emphasizes the importance of the children's answering in their own words by commending those who do so.

The teacher writes on the board the expressions *New Stone Age, domestication of animals,* B.C., *domestication of plants, lake dwellers, private property, chief.* Children discuss the meanings.

Multisensory Aids

Children and teacher talk over together the pictures in the text, noting features of historical or geographical importance. They discuss the symbols used on the time line, p. 501.

AUDIO-VISUAL MATERIALS OBTAINABLE

Compton's Pictured Teaching Materials : *Prehistoric Man*, Plates VII–X. *American Indians*, Plates VII, 3, 4 ; VIII, 4. *Food*, Plate I. *Land Transportation*, Plates I, 1–4 ; II ; III ; IV, 1, 2, 4. *Trade*, Plate XI, 5.
International Educational Pictures : Grass.
LEHMANN. Colored History Pictures : I, 14.
MILLER. *Picturesque Tale of Progress*, I, 40–48, 53–65.
Society for Visual Education (SPENCER). Transportation — Beginnings, Animals.
Society for Visual Education. University Museum (Philadelphia) : Men of the New Stone Age in Europe, Primitive Tools.

General Activities

Creative Activities: Group and Individual, Correlated with Other Subjects or Voluntary Projects

Children draw figures to represent the advances of the New Stone Age and place them at appropriate points along the time line.

A volunteer graphs the comparative lengths of the Old Stone Age and the New Stone Age. (See the time line.)

The manual-training instructor demonstrates how to sharpen tools and explains the principle involved.

Children list all the animals which work for man. They make a picture collection of the animals at work.

The class devises a pantomimic dance illustrating the domestication of plants.

Volunteers draw scenes illustrating the life of lake dwellers.

A committee draws up a table of measures used today in measuring land.

The teacher reads to the children the Bible story of the separation of Abraham and Lot in the attempt to find pasturage for their herds.

The class continues the time line.

More Difficult Activities

A committee attempts to fasten a sharp stone to a handle with thongs of leather and thus make a primitive ax or club.

Children practice hitting a target, using bow and arrow.

A committee makes a map of the areas covered by prehistoric nomads in their wanderings.

A volunteer gives a special report on the evolution of the plow. (See a children's encyclopedia.)

A committee makes a list of local industries. Each member investigates to find out how his chosen industry depends on the use of the wheel.

Children study their geographies to determine where, in the world, the domestication of plants might have been the most easily begun. Why were the Mediterranean river valleys especially suitable?

A volunteer attempts to grind a rough stone on a grindstone.

Volunteers grind grain between two stones and show their "flour" to the class.

Application to Present-Day Conditions

Do people today ever use the bow and arrow for pleasure?

What does the word *horsepower* mean? Contrast it with *man power*.

Which of all our animals today is the most thoroughly domesticated?

Are there any people in the world today who live mainly on their herds of animals? (See your geography.)

Do people who own large herds of cattle today have to move their dwellings constantly? Why not?

Can you name any modern invention for getting work done which seems to you as important as the discovery of the use of the wheel?

Why are most wheels today made with spokes instead of solid pieces of wood?

Have any plants been domesticated near your home which were not native there?

Is there any property in your town which is not private property?

How is land measured today?

A volunteer reports how Venezuela received its name.

Exercises in Reasoning

In what way was the bow and arrow a great advance over the spear as a means of securing food? [*With it one could kill at a greater distance.*]

For what kind of work did primitive men use dogs? horses?

In what way did the domestication of the dog help in the domestication of cattle?

Why did moving about the country force men to build huts instead of living in caves?

Why was farming considered women's work when it was done with a hoe, but considered men's work after plows came to be used?

Why do hunting people, like the Indians, not need private ownership of land?

What kind of man was apt to be chosen as chief?

More Difficult Exercises in Reasoning

Why are fishhooks and fish spears curved or barbed?

Why is the power of an engine measured in horsepower?

Which of our great industries today are directly dependent on the domestication of animals?

How is a speedometer able to measure the distance traveled by a car?

Which has to work more regularly, a hunter or a farmer?

Why is the domestication of plants usually chosen as the dividing line between the period of savagery and the period of barbarism?

Why has private ownership of land brought about many wars in the world's history?

Why were all strangers regarded as enemies?

Can you explain that private property was really the gift of the group?

Drill Games

Drill cards are made as follows:

New Stone Age	↔	the period of time during which the edges of tools were ground or polished
domestication of animals	↔	the taming of animals to serve or please man
B.C.	↔	abbreviation meaning " before Christ "
domestication of plants	↔	planting seeds in chosen places in order to make crops grow there
lake dwellers	↔	people who built their houses over water in order to be safe
private property	↔	anything which a person is allowed to own
chief	↔	a person chosen to be leader

Testing

Tests of Understanding are given in Kelty's *How Our Civilization Began,*
p. 28.

Tests of Reasoning and Skills. In the following, underline the right answers:

1. The New Stone Age began about   1,000,000 B.C.   100,000 B.C.
10,000 B.C.

2. The period of time during which people used tools with edges of ground
or polished stone is called the   Old Stone Age.   New Stone Age.   Age
of Steel.

Put the right word in the blanks below:

3. The first invention which made it possible to kill animals at a distance
was the ___[*bow and arrow*]___.

4. Man first got help in doing his work by ___[*domesticating animals*]___.

5. "Domestication of plants" means ___[*planting seeds in places where
crops are wanted*]___.

6. Check the right answer: The thing that led men to want private property
in land was   √ the beginning of agriculture.   the practice of electing
chiefs of villages.   the use of the plow.

7. Which are the only pages in your book which tell about the lake dwellers?
_____ Where did you look to find out? ___[*In the index.*]___

Exercise in Organization. Children make one summary sentence for each of
the main discoveries of the New Stone Age.

More Difficult Tests

Finish these sentences:

1. Men who owned herds of cattle had to roam about the country because
___[*the cattle had to find grass*]___.

2. Farming came to be looked upon as men's work because ___[*plows were
very heavy*]___.

3. Men had to learn how to measure because ___[*they had to divide land*]___.

4. Houses or huts were first used by men   who hunted for a living.
√ who raised cattle for a living.   who farmed for a living.

5. The most important invention toward making transportation easy was
√ the wheel.   fire.   the bow and arrow.

6. The advance which has caused the greatest amount of trouble is   polished stone tools.   domestication of animals.   √ private property.

STORY 3. THE END OF THE STONE AGES   [1 Week

Conversational Approach

"Now that men are raising crops of grain for use during the winter, how
will they keep their grain?" Children speculate as to possible ways.

"What will they do if they have more grain than their families can eat?

"To understand the next great invention we must examine this cloth." The teacher shows here a piece of coarse linen. Children pull threads out of both warp and woof to discover the principle that cloth is made by threads going one way interlacing with threads going the other way.

They then untwist the threads to discover that thread is made of several fibers twisted together. They notice that this is true of rope, darning cotton, embroidery silk, etc.

"It may seem to us a very simple thing to twist fibers together into thread and to interlace the threads to make cloth. But it is not easy. Do you think you could do it yourself? Or could you make an implement to do it?"

Reading and Study

The Reading Periods

Independent Readers

This group reads the entire story through silently, as given in their text. They then test their comprehension by the study-guide questions furnished by the teacher or by the text.

Texts

CHAPMAN, *Stories of the Ancient Peoples*, 64–67, 78–81.

CLARK-GORDY, *Westward toward America*, 15–17.

CORKE, *A Book of Ancient Peoples*, 12–18 (hard).

KELTY, *How Our Civilization Began*, 29–39.

KNOWLTON and GERSON, *Our Beginnings in the Past*, 86–94.

Lower Group

The teacher tells the story orally to this group, writing on the board the most important words as she mentions them.

Then the teacher and these children read together the story as given in the text.

The teacher directs the silent reading, section by section, by such questions as "Why could baskets not keep grain well?"

Children read silently and answer orally. When the entire story has been read in this manner, they test themselves by the questions at the end of the story.

More Difficult Texts

BARKER, DUNCALF, BACON, *Old Europe and Our Nation*, 20–21, 24–27.

BEARD and BAGLEY, *Our Old World Background*, 28–31.

BURNHAM, *Our Beginnings in Europe and America*, 18–21.

COULOMB, McKINLEY, and WHITE, *What Europe Gave to America*, 11–12.

GORDY, *American Beginnings in Europe*, 13–14.

HALLECK and FRANTZ, *Our Nation's Heritage*, 9–10.

MARSHALL, *Story of Human Progress*, 35–40.

NIDA, *Dawn of American History*, 25–26.

Easy Reading

Extensive Reading

COFFMAN, *Child's Story of the Human Race*, 13–14, 35–37, 44–47.

HOLBROOK, *Cave, Mound, and Lake Dwellers*, 58–71.

KINER, *How the World Grew Up*, 93–98.

SCHWARTZ, *From Then till Now*, 39–81.

WADDELL and BUSH, *How We Have Conquered Distance*, 9–10.

WELLS, *How the Present Came from the Past*, I: 83–99, 102–117.

Reading for Recreation

PETERSHAM, *Story Book of Clothes*.

PETERSHAM, *Story Book of Ships*.

PETERSHAM, *Story Book of Things We Use* (clothes).

More Difficult Reading

EXTENSIVE READING

BOYLE, *Man Before History*, 107–127.
HARTMAN, *The World We Live in*, 63–64, 77–80.
ILIN, *What Time Is It?* 16–19.
KUMMER, *First Days of Knowledge*, 84–96.
KUMMER, *First Days of Man*, 148–172.
LANSING, *Man's Long Climb*, 38–42, 71–74, 77–80, 103–104.
MARSHALL, *Readings in the Story of Human Progress*, 30–39.
MILLER, *Picturesque Tale of Progress*, I: 48–52, 65–70.
NIDA, *Man Conquers the World with Science*, 113–119.
QUENNELL, *New Stone, Bronze, and Early Iron Ages*, 119–126 (pictures).

READING FOR RECREATION

CARTER, *Story of Money*.
HALL, *Days Before History*.
LAMPREY, *Long Ago People*.
PEAKE and FLEURE, *Peasants and Potters*.
TRUE, *The Iron Star*.

The Discussion

Children answer the study-guide questions as completely as possible. The teacher tries to show the value of saying the answers to themselves while studying and of rereading a part of the story when they come to a question which they cannot answer.

The teacher writes on the board the words *pottery, flax, spinning, weaving, loom, barter, division of labor, myth, primitive*. Children discuss the meanings.

Multisensory Aids

Children and teacher talk over the pictures in the text, pointing out features of geographic and historical significance.

AUDIO-VISUAL MATERIALS OBTAINABLE

Compton's Pictured Teaching Materials: *Prehistoric Man*, Plates I, 5–6; X; *American Indians*, Plate VI.
International Educational Pictures: *Pottery Maker*.
MILLER. *Picturesque Tale of Progress*, I, 48–52, 65–70.
Society for Visual Education. University Museum (Philadelphia): *History of Clothing*.

Music. The teacher plays selections from Stravinski's *The Rite of Spring*. She plays *Omphale's Spinning Wheel*, by Saint-Saëns, and "Her Blanket," arranged by Lieurance.

General Activities

Creative Activities: Group and Individual, Correlated with Other Subjects or Voluntary Projects

In the handicraft class, children weave baskets of reeds or raffia. They make small vessels of clay. They try to draw out and twist fibers of raw wool into a thread with their fingers.

A visit is made to the local museum to observe the pottery exhibit and the exhibit of Indian baskets.

Children show pictures of the flax plant.

Samples of famous pottery are shown; for example, Wedgwood.

If possible the children observe spinning on a spinning wheel and weaving on a hand loom.

Children give examples of barter from their own personal experience.

The high-school science teacher may show a committee of children some of the stars which change their positions.

Children draw from the last two stories materials for Reel Two of their moving picture "Man's Earliest Discoveries."

The class continues the time line.

More Difficult Activities

Children attempt to fire clay vessels. They make designs for decorations.

If there is a potter's wheel in the community, children make a visit to observe it.

A committee of boys attempts to tan a hide from which a committee of girls attempts to make a garment.

A volunteer explains the steps in the preparation of the flax plant.

The class goes to the museum or to a local store to see samples of cloisonné. They study its manufacture.

A committee lists woven articles used in the home.

Children give examples of division of labor in their own communities.

Volunteers demonstrate with a set of balances how the seeds of plants might be used as weights.

A volunteer explains the principles of the lever and the pulley.

Volunteers tell myths explaining the creation of the world or the seasons; for example, Greek myths, Roman myths, Norse myths.

Application to Present-Day Conditions

How is food prepared today for an old-fashioned clambake? Do you know any other kinds of food prepared with hot stones supplying the heat?

Does the United States produce flax? What countries in the world produce the most flax?

Why are our household dishes called "china"? (See the encyclopedia.)

In what way does the expression "going to town to do their trading" show that man once used barter?

Is barter ever used today?

What is the scientific study of the stars called?

Do any people still believe in spirits? Where did such beliefs come from?

Do any people in the world still live in tribes with tribal chiefs?

How has the problem of government been solved in your own schoolroom?

Exercises in Reasoning

Why did pottery change the ways of cooking food?

Why did man find that trading was better than taking articles by force?

Which plan of work demanded greater co-operation — the old plan of each man's doing all his own work or division of labor?

Why would man's language grow steadily as trade grew?

Why were shepherds the first persons who noticed that the stars change their positions at different seasons of the year?

Why did early man worship the sun?

Why did several villages find it necessary to join together under one leader?

Children put in one sentence the principles they have discovered about the making of cloth.

More Difficult Exercises

Why does firing render clay vessels watertight?

Why does the use of the potter's wheel make vessels more true in shape?

Why does trade increase with division of labor? Why did increase of trade lead to the use of sailboats instead of dugout canoes?

Why did trade make it necessary to begin to use money?

You often hear that man is learning to control nature. Can you give examples from the stories you have read so far?

Do you think it was a good thing or a bad thing that the villages found it necessary to band together into large groups?

In what way is pottery better than a skin to hold water? In what way is the skin better?

Why can people who believe in magic never advance very far in science?

Drill Games

Cards to emphasize correct associations are made as follows:

pottery	↔	dishes and jars
flax	↔	the plant from whose stalks linen is made
spinning	↔	drawing out and twisting into a thread
weaving	↔	making cloth ¦by interlacing up-and-down threads with crossway threads
barter	↔	direct exchange of one kind of goods for another kind
division of labor	↔	a system by which each man does only one kind of work and all exchange their surplus products
myths	↔	stories about the beginning of the world which are believed by people of a later time
primitive	↔	belonging to "the earliest times"
loom	↔	the frame used in weaving

Children drill especially on the items which they find difficult. Games are then played.

Testing

Tests of Understanding are given in Kelty's *How Our Civilization Began*, pp. 38–39.

Tests of Reasoning and Skills. Complete these sentences:

1. Pottery is better for some things than baskets of reeds because _ _ _[*it is watertight*]_ _ _ _.

2. After the use of fire was known, the boiling of food had to wait until the discovery of _ _ _[*pottery*]_ _ _.

3. Clothing made of cloth is more healthful than clothing made of skins because _ _ _[*it can be washed; it can cover all parts of the body*]_ _ _.

4. The myths of early men tried to explain such things as _ _ _[*where the earth came from and what made it run*]_ _ _.

Underline the right words:

5. Trading one kind of goods for another kind of goods is   money. barter.   division of labor.

6. Each man's doing only the kind of work at which he is most skillful is known as   domestication of plants.   private property.   division of labor.

7. Trading by barter   is not   is   the same as using money in trade.

Exercise in Organization. The teacher shows the class how the topic headings may be arranged in outline form. The class copies the outline and gives a brief topical recitation on each subhead.

More Difficult Tests

Write your answers:

1. What can bits of glazed pottery tell us about the state of civilization of the people who made it? _ _ _[*High development; use of fire; development of art in decorations.*]_ _ _

2. The process of spinning and weaving is very complicated. Primitive man learned it. What does that show about the brain power of primitive man? _ _ _[*He was highly intelligent.*]_ _ _

3. Why does barter increase greatly with division of labor?_ _ _[*More goods are produced.*]_ _ _

4. Barter is an awkward form of exchange because _ _ _[*you must keep goods till you find a buyer who wants that particular thing and who has something you want*]_ _ _.

5. Men from several primitive villages sometimes had to unite in order to _ _ _[*defend themselves; accomplish public works*]_ _ _.

STORY 4. THE DAWN OF CIVILIZATION   [1 Week

Conversational Approach

"What things do you think of when you hear it said that certain people live in a state of *civilization*?" Children suggest characteristics. "Do you notice how many of those things are dependent on the use of metals?" The children enumerate some which could not exist without metals. "Why do you suppose it took mankind so long to learn to use metals?

"Man's progress would also be very slow if there were no way of letting children know about the discoveries made by their fathers and grandfathers.

How do children today learn about the discoveries that mankind has already made?" Children tell of various means. "What do you suppose would be the result if writing or printing had never been invented?"

Reading and Study

The Reading Periods

Independent Readers

This group reads the entire story through silently as given in their text. They then test their comprehension by the study-guide questions furnished by the teacher or by the text.

Lower Group

The teacher tells the story orally to this group, writing on the board the most important words as she mentions them.

Then the teacher and these children read together the story as given in the text. The teacher directs the silent reading, section by section, by such questions as "What was the most serious fault of the tools of 5000 B.C.?"

Children read silently and answer orally. When the entire story has been read in this manner, they test themselves by the questions at the end of the story.

TEXTS

CHAPMAN, *Stories of the Ancient Peoples*, 73–76.

CLARK-GORDY, *Early Story of Mankind*, 53–54.

CLARK-GORDY, *Westward toward America*, 23–24.

KELTY, *How Our Civilization Began*, 40–47.

KNOWLTON and GERSON, *Our Beginnings in the Past*, 96–104.

MORE DIFFICULT TEXTS

BEARD and BAGLEY, *Our Old World Background*, 28–31, 86–87.

BURNHAM, *Our Beginnings in Europe and America*, 18–21.

COULOMB, McKINLEY, WHITE, *What Europe Gave to America*, 12–14.

HARDING, *Old World Background to American History*, 3–4.

MARSHALL, *Story of Human Progress*, 40–65, 85–91, 218–222.

NIDA, *Dawn of American History*, 25–27.

SOUTHWORTH, *What the Old World Gave the New*, 3.

VOLLINTINE, *The American People and Their Old World Ancestors*, 26–36.

WICKHAM and PHILLIPS, *America's Heritage from the Long Ago*, 34–35.

Easy Reading

EXTENSIVE READING

BEST, *Egypt and Her Neighbors*, 29–36.

COFFMAN, *Child's Story of the Human Race*, 39–41.

HOLBROOK, *Cave, Mound, and Lake Dwellers*, 108–115, 126–130.

KINER, *How the World Grew Up*, 73–92, 104–109.

WADDELL and BUSH, *How We Have Conquered Distance*, 169–184.

WELLS, *How the Present Came from the Past*, I : 117–132.

READING FOR RECREATION

MAXWELL, *The Story of Books*, 1–11.

WILEY and EDICK, *Lodrix*.

More Difficult Reading

EXTENSIVE READING

BARNES, *Man and His Records*.

BOYLE, *Man Before History*, 128–130.

READING FOR RECREATION

BEARD, *American Boys' Book of Signs, Signals, and Symbols*.

FELLOWES, *Stories of the Stone Age*, 93–98, 135–142.

HART, *How Our Grandfathers Lived*, 196–198 (Indian writing).

HARTMAN, *The World We Live in*, 54–55, 115–118.

ILIN, *Black on White*, 1–40.

KUMMER, *First Days of Knowledge*, 36–67.

KUMMER, *First Days of Man*, 259–293.

LANSING, *Man's Long Climb*, 84–87, 130–133, 138–142.

MILLER, *Picturesque Tale of Progress*, I: 79–81, 85.

NIDA, *Man Conquers the World with Science*, 10–13, 18–19.

QUENNELL, *The New Stone, Bronze, and Early Iron Ages*, 102–118 (pictures).

Story of Writing (American Council on Education), 3–8, 15–20.

WEBSTER, *The World's Messengers*, 13–21.

GRUENING, *Story of Mining*, 1–13.

MASON, *History of the Art of Writing.*

REASON, *Bran, the Bronze-Smith.*

The Discussion

Children answer the study-guide questions as fully as possible. If a child's answer leaves out important phases of the topic, the teacher questions him. She calls the attention of the class to what she is doing, and tells them that they may question one another for the same purpose as soon as they learn how it is done.

She writes on the board the words *bronze, Bronze Age, forge, Iron Age, Metal Age, prehistoric, picture-writing, ore.* Children discuss the meanings.

Multisensory Aids

Children and teacher talk over together the pictures in the text, noting features of geographical or historical importance. They discuss the symbols used on the time line. (See page 501.)

AUDIO-VISUAL MATERIALS OBTAINABLE

Compton's Pictured Teaching Materials: *Prehistoric Man*, Plates I, 6; XI. *American Indians*, Plate VIII, 8. *Communication*, Plate II, 1–4.

International Educational Pictures: Primitive Housekeeping.

Society for Visual Education. University Museum (Philadelphia): The Development of Writing.

Music. Play records of "The Armorer's Song"; "Oriental Temple Bells."

General Activities

Creative Activities: Group and Individual, Correlated with Other Subjects or Voluntary Projects

A volunteer graphs the relative lengths of the Metal Age, the New Stone Age, the Old Stone Age.

The teacher tells the story of Tubal-cain.

The class makes a trip to the museum to observe bits of free copper and tin and gold nuggets. They contrast these with iron ore.

Volunteers show the class some articles made of bronze.

A committee reports to the class the countries producing the largest quantities of each one of the metals. (See the World Almanac.)

Volunteers make symbolic drawings to add to the time line.

Children try to send a message by picture-writing. The class tries to read it.[1]

The teacher shows some of Theodore Roosevelt's picture-writing from *Theodore Roosevelt's Letters to His Children.*

A volunteer shows how a piece of birch bark may be used as writing material. The class adds to the time line.

More Difficult Activities

The class makes a visit to a local forge, foundry shop, or blacksmith shop to observe metal in its melted state.

The industrial-arts teacher may demonstrate the casting of bronze.

Volunteers report on the famous bronze bells of Japan and China.

Volunteers write messages by drawing syllables. The class tries to read them.

Volunteers show Chinese symbols and explain that they were originally pictures.

A volunteer reports on the Archives Building of the government in Washington.

Volunteers report on government among bees and ants. (See Persing and Thiele's *Elementary Science,* IV, chap. 1; V, chap. 31.)

Application to Present-Day Conditions

Is gold today used more in ornamental objects or as money?

For what is copper used chiefly today? (See the encyclopedia.) Why does its price rise when war breaks out?

Is bronze used much nowadays? For what?

How is bronze decorated today? How can decoration be applied to stone?

Can you mention a source of metals that has been fought over for many years? Locate it. [*Alsace-Lorraine.*]

Which is worth more today, our annual production of gold or our annual production of iron? (See the World Almanac.)

Why do we call a phonograph disk a record?

How many books are published each year in the United States? How many newspapers? (See the World Almanac.) Do these figures give us any indication of the importance of records in the modern world?

How do business firms of today keep their records safe? Why do they take such pains to keep them safe?

Exercises in Reasoning

Why was the discovery of smelting of great value to primitive man?

Why could a tribe with bronze weapons beat a tribe with stone weapons?

Why are metal supplies the causes of many wars?

Why did the use of iron come later than the use of gold, copper, or tin? When it was first discovered, why was it more valuable than gold?

[1] See *The Story of Records,* Teacher's Lesson Unit Series, Teachers College, Columbia University.

Why do we not know the names of any of the men who made the earliest inventions and discoveries? [*There was no way of keeping records; people forgot.*]

What kind of people first felt the need of keeping records? [*Businessmen.*] Why?

Why have no names of persons been given in our stories so far? [*There were no records.*]

More Difficult Exercises in Reasoning

Why is stone more apt to crack than metal?

Why did primitive men use gold as an ornament and not as money? [*They were still in the barter stage.*]

Compare the methods of cutting down trees by charring and chipping with stone axes and by cutting with metal axes. What effect will the improvement have on the building of houses?

Why were most of the early mines in hillsides? [*It was easier to follow seams.*]

How much could you remember of what took place last year, two years ago, five years ago, if there were no written records?

How did the invention of writing make it possible for people to avoid the mistakes of their ancestors?

What did Emerson mean when he said of the present day that we are still "in the cock-crowing and the morning-star"?

Why is it easier to write a history of the World War than to write a history of the wars between primitive tribes? [*More records are available.*]

Drill Games

Drill cards are made as follows:

bronze	⟷	a mixture of copper and tin
Bronze Age	⟷	period of time when bronze was the principal metal used
forge	⟷	a kind of fireplace where metal is heated for shaping with a hammer
Iron Age	⟷	period of time when iron is the principal metal used
Metal Ages	⟷	period of time when man's ways of living are largely dependent on his use of metals
prehistoric	⟷	before written records were used
picture-writing	⟷	keeping records by means of rude drawings
ore	⟷	rock which contains metal

Children drill by twos.

Testing

Tests of Understanding are given in Kelty's *How Our Civilization Began*, p. 47.

Tests of Reasoning and Skills

1. Put the figure *1* before that which came first, and the figure *2* before that which came later.   [__2__] Iron Age   [__1__] Bronze Age

Check the right answer:

2. Stone weapons were not so good as metal because   they were much heavier.   they were more difficult to make.   √ they cracked and fell to pieces.   they did not look so nice.

3. The tribe which could win in war was the tribe with   √ iron weapons.   stone weapons.   bronze weapons.   •

4. Write the correct word in this blank: A great industry which grew up after the use of metals was discovered, in order to supply the raw material, was _ _ _[*mining*]_ _ _.

Exercise in Organization. Children copy the topic headings and prepare an oral summary of each.

More Difficult Tests

1. Check the right answer: Iron was worth more than gold when it was first discovered because   people were not yet used to it.   √ it could perform more useful work.   it lasted longer than gold.   people thought it was prettier.

2. Write the correct word in this blank: Bronze was used for _ _ _[*money*]_ _ _ as well as for weapons.

3. Complete this sentence: We know very little of what was done during prehistoric times because _ _ _[*no written records were kept*]_ _ _.

4. Can you make a sentence telling why businessmen were the ones who began to keep written records? _ _ _[*They must know who owes money.*]_ _ _

5. Writing has been said to be the greatest gift to mankind since language and number. Why is it of such value? _ _ _[*It transmits the wisdom of each generation to the next.*]_ _ _

Tests on the Entire Unit

Tests of Time Sense. Pass mimeographed sheets of the following:

I. In each exercise put the figure *1* before that which took place first, and the figure *2* before that which took place later.

1. [_ _1_ _] New Stone Age
    [_ _2_ _] Bronze Age
2. [_ _1_ _] domestication of plants
    [_ _2_ _] Iron Age
3. [_ _2_ _] picture-writing
    [_ _1_ _] domestication of animals
4. [_ _2_ _] use of money
    [_ _1_ _] Old Stone Age

5. [_ _1_ _] use of fire
    [_ _2_ _] barter
6. [_ _2_ _] weaving
    [_ _1_ _] chipped-stone tools
7. [_ _1_ _] language
    [_ _2_ _] writing
8. [_ _2_ _] weighing
    [_ _1_ _] counting

II. Here is a list of dates. Put each one in the right blank below.

100,000 B.C.   5000 B.C.   10,000 B.C.

_ _[10,000 B.C.]_ _ beginning of the New Stone Age
_ _[100,000 B.C.]_ _ the Old Stone Age
_ _[5000 B.C.]_ _ beginning of the Metal Age

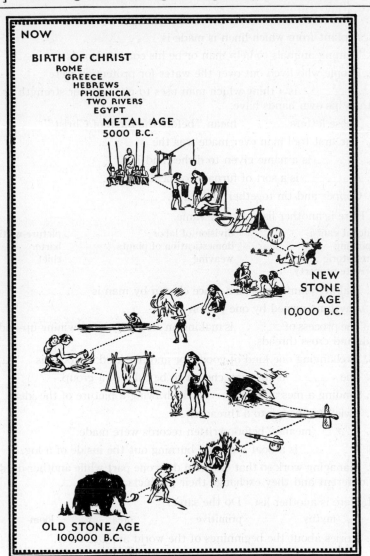

NOW

BIRTH OF CHRIST
ROME
GREECE
HEBREWS
PHOENICIA
TWO RIVERS
EGYPT
METAL AGE
5000 B.C.

NEW STONE AGE
10,000 B.C.

OLD STONE AGE
100,000 B.C.

From the Old Stone Age to Now
A time line

Tests of Historical Terms. Pass mimeographed sheets of the following.

I. Here is a list of terms. Put each one in the right blank in the sentences below :

fist hatchet   flint   forge
domestication of animals B.C.   tool
pottery   flax   lake dwellers
bronze

1. _____ is a kind of stone which cracks evenly and smoothly.

2. A plant from which linen is made is _____.

3. Taming animals to help man or be his companions is _____.

4. People who lived out over the water for protection were _____.

5. A _____ is a thing which man uses to give greater strength or sharpness than his own hands have.

6. These letters _____ mean "before the birth of Christ."

7. The first tool man ever made was the _____.

8. _____ is a name given to dishes and jars.

9. A _____ is a sort of furnace for heating iron.

10. Copper and tin together make _____.

II. Here is another list. Do the same.

dugout canoe	division of labor	picture-writing
spinning	domestication of plants	barter
prehistoric	weaving	chief
private property		

1. Making plants grow in a place chosen by man is _____.

2. Anything owned by one person is _____.

3. The process of _____ is making an article by intertwining up-and-down threads and cross threads.

4. Exchanging one kind of goods for another kind of goods is _____.

5. The _____ is the man chosen to be ruler of a group.

6. Sending a message by _____ is drawing a picture of the idea.

7. Twisting fibers into a thread is _____.

8. _____ means "before written records were made."

9. A _____ is a boat made by burning out the inside of a log.

10. Managing work so that one man does one part while another does something different and they exchange their products is _____.

III. Here is another list. Do the same.

myths   primitive   ore   loom

1. Stories about the beginnings of the world are _____.

2. _____ is rock that contains minerals.

3. The word _____ means "referring to earliest times or to people who have not made much progress."

4. A _____ is a rack made to hold weaving.

Test of Comprehension

Check the best answer:

1. Man was able to rise above the animals because   he was stronger than they were.   √ he had a better brain than they had.   they were afraid of him.   they were weaker than he.

2. Tools of the New Stone Age were better than those of the Old Stone Age because   they were made of different stone.   they were better-looking. they had handles tied to them.   √ their edges were ground or polished.

3. The use of pottery began in the   √ New Stone Age.   Old Stone Age.   Age of Bronze.   Age of Iron.

4. Man never had weapons he could depend on until he discovered how to   carve the handles.   work with other people in the village.   √ melt metals.   use gold as decoration.

5. The first objects man ever used as tools were   things he made by weaving.   things he made from melted metal.   things he made out of stone.   √ things he found lying on the ground.

6. When man first domesticated animals he used them   √ for food. for pets.   for carrying loads.   to ride on.

7. Our clothing today depends on which invention of primitive man? Barter.   √ Spinning and weaving.   Division of labor.   Domestication of animals.

8. Man's first manufactured tools were made by   melting metals. polishing stone.   √ chipping stone.   pounding metals.

9. The world's greatest industry today depends on which of these? Keeping of records.   Domestication of animals.   Spinning and weaving. √ Domestication of plants.

10. Primitive man exchanged most of his goods by   money.   √ barter. force.   checks.

11. We know little about the life of primitive men until they learned how to √ keep records.   make poems.   sing songs.   count.

12. Which came first?   The invention of writing.   √ The making of language.

13. Man could never have learned the use of metals if he had not first learned   to live in caves.   the use of spinning.   √ the use of fire. to domesticate animals.

14. Almost all our factories today use primitive man's discovery of the use of   √ the wheel.   the boat.   the loom.   the forge.

15. Which of the following are true? Check the right item in each exercise.

a. [√] Primitive man was an artist.
　[　] Primitive man was not an artist.

b. [　] Primitive man could not count.
　[√] Primitive man could count.

c. [√] Primitive man could tell time.
　[　] Primitive man could tell time by the clock.

d. [　] Primitive men never obeyed their leaders.
　[√] Primitive men learned to obey their leaders.

e. [√] Primitive men believed in a life after death.
　[　] Primitive men did not believe in a life after death.

f. [ ] From the beginning of time, men owned private property in land.

[✓] In the beginning, men did not own private property in land.

16. What is the title of the unit which you have been studying? _ _ _ _ _ _

Are any children now ready to be transferred from the lower group to the group of independent readers?

Unit Two · *Men learn to live in Great Cities and Nations*   [6 Weeks

STORY 1.   ANCIENT EGYPT   [2 Weeks

Conversational Approach

Teacher and children examine a map of Eurasia, paying special attention to the general region of the Mediterranean. They attempt to decide which places would be best for primitive man to grow his crops, on the bases of (1) temperature, (2) water supply, and (3) protection from attack.

For younger children a sand-table model is superior to a map.

"Let us now turn to our story for the week and find out whether or not we selected any of the right places."

Reading and Study

The Reading Periods (Life of the Egyptians)

Independent Readers

This group reads the first part of the story through, as given in their text. They then test their comprehension by the study-guide questions furnished by the teacher or by the text.

TEXTS

BEEBY, *America's Roots in the Past*, 14–17.

CHAPMAN, *Stories of the Ancient Peoples*, 83–88.

CLARK-GORDY, *Early Story of Mankind*, 63–64, 75–77.

CLARK-GORDY, *Westward toward America*, 31–42.

CORKE, *A Book of Ancient Peoples*, 28–38 (hard).

KELTY, *How Our Civilization Began*, 51–59.

KNOWLTON and GERSON, *Our Beginnings in the Past*, 117–126.

Lower Group

The teacher tells the story orally to this group, writing on the board the most important words as she mentions them. Children practice the pronunciations.

Then the teacher and this group read together the story as given in the text. The teacher directs the silent reading, section by section, by such questions as "What two things would primitive man look for in seeking a home?"

Children read silently and answer orally. When the entire story has been read in this manner, they test themselves by the questions at the end of the story.

MORE DIFFICULT TEXTS

BARKER, DUNCALF, BACON, *Old Europe and Our Nation*, 30–38.
BEARD and BAGLEY, *Our Old World Background*, 42–47, 56–64.
BURNHAM, *Our Beginnings in Europe and America*, 26–30.
COULOMB, MCKINLEY, WHITE, *What Europe Gave to America*, 14–20.
GORDY, *American Beginnings in Europe*, 17–22.
GREENWOOD, *Our Heritage from the Old World*, 10–15, 28–29.
HALLECK and FRANTZ, *Our Nation's Heritage*, 18–20.
HARDING, *Old World Background to American History*, 4–6.
HAWLEY, *Adventures in Old World History*, 15–22.
NIDA, *Dawn of American History*, 17–19, 23–25.
NIVER, *Old World Steps to American History*, 38–40.
SOUTHWORTH, *What the Old World Gave the New*, 5–8.
VOLLINTINE, *American People and Their Old World Ancestors*, 26–36.
WICKHAM and PHILLIPS, *America's Heritage from the Long Ago*, 19–20, 29–34, 35–40.
WOODBURN and HILL, *Historic Background of Our United States*, 30–33.

Easy Reading

EXTENSIVE READING

BEST, *Egypt and Her Neighbors*, 1–22.
COFFMAN, *Child's Story of the Human Race*, 48–66.
CORKE, *The World's Family*, 57–66.
ERLEIGH, *In the Beginning*, 43–49.
HILLYER, *Child's History of the World*, 24–35.
HODGDON, *The Enchanted Past*, 26–48.
HOLBROOK, *Cave, Mound, and Lake Dwellers*, 116–120.
MOHR, WASHBURNE, BEATTY, *Egyptians of Long Ago*, 11–86.
WADDELL and BUSH, *How We Have Conquered Distance*, 46–48.
WELLS, *How the Present Came from the Past*, II : 1–10.

READING FOR RECREATION

MCDONALD and DALRYMPLE, *Hassan in Egypt*.
MCNAB, *Picture Book of Rivers*, 18–21.
NIDA, *Inventions and Discoveries of Ancient Times*, 5–33.
PALMER, *Abdul, the Egyptian Boy*.
PETERSHAM, *Story Book of Ships*.

More Difficult Reading

EXTENSIVE READING

ARNOLD, *Stories of Ancient People*, 15–40.
BAIKIE, *Peeps at Many Lands: Egypt*.
HARTMAN, *The World We Live in*, 81–94.
KUMMER, *First Days of History*, 24–50.
KUMMER, *First Days of Knowledge*, 167–179, 245–255, 301–314.
LANSING, *Man's Long Climb*, 49–66.
MEYER and others, *A Trip to the Valley of the Nile*.
MILLER, *Picturesque Tale of Progress*, I : 71–109.
MILLS, *Book of the Ancient World*, 13–24, 33–46.
NIDA, *Man Conquers the World with Science*, 19–22.
RICHMOND, *Egypt, Greece, and Rome*, 1–4.
Story of Our Calendar (American Council on Education), 9–12.
VAN LOON, *Story of Mankind*, 17–26.
WEBSTER, *World's Messengers*, 21–24.

READING FOR RECREATION

HOWARD, *Sokar and the Crocodile*.
LAMPREY, *Long Ago in Egypt*.
PAKINGTON, *How the World Builds*.
PERRY, *With Azir Girges in Egypt*.
STUART, *The Boy through the Ages*.

The Discussion

Children answer the study-guide questions as fully as possible. Again the teacher questions them as to phases omitted, in preparation for their questioning one another. She points out that only the most important matters need be included,— not everything told in the text.

The teacher writes on the board the words *Pharaoh*, *"gift of the Nile,"* *canal*, *scribes*, *Upper Egypt*, *Lower Egypt*. Children discuss the meanings.

The Reading Periods (Egyptian Buildings and Science)

Independent Readers

This group reads the rest of the story through as given in their text. They then test their comprehension by the study-guide questions furnished by the teacher or by the text.

TEXTS

BEEBY, *America's Roots in the Past*, 17–36.
CHAPMAN, *Stories of the Ancient Peoples*, 88–99.
CLARK-GORDY, *Early Story of Mankind*, 64–75, 77–82.
CLARK-GORDY, *Westward toward America*, 42–50.
CORKE, *A Book of Ancient Peoples*, 39–51 (hard).
KELTY, *How Our Civilization Began*, 60–73.
KNOWLTON and GERSON, *Our Beginnings in the Past*, 126–133.

Lower Group

The teacher tells the rest of the story orally to this group, writing on the board the most important words as she mentions them. Children practice the pronunciations.

Then the teacher and these children read together the story as given in the text. The teacher directs the silent reading, section by section, by such questions as "What three things kept the Egyptians together as one people?"

Children read silently and answer orally. When the entire story has been read in this manner, they test themselves by the study-guide questions at the end of the story.

MORE DIFFICULT TEXTS

BARKER, DUNCALF, BACON, *Old Europe and Our Nation*, 38–44.
BEARD and BAGLEY, *Our Old World Background*, 77–79, 81.
BURNHAM, *Our Beginnings in Europe and America*, 38–46.
COULOMB, McKINLEY, WHITE, *What Europe Gave to America*, 21–24.
GORDY, *American Beginnings in Europe*, 22–30.
GREENWOOD, *Our Heritage from the Old World*, 15–27.
HALLECK and FRANTZ, *Our Nation's Heritage*, 20–32.
HAWLEY, *Adventures in Old World History*, 22–27.
NIDA, *Dawn of American History*, 19–23.
NIVER, *Old World Steps to American History*, 40–46.
WICKHAM and PHILLIPS, *America's Heritage from the Long Ago*, 20–29.
WOODBURN and HILL, *Historic Background of Our United States*, 33–41.

Easy Reading

EXTENSIVE READING

BEST, *Egypt and Her Neighbors*, 22–28, 39–66.
COFFMAN, *Child's Story of the Human Race*, 67–72.
HILLYER, *Child's History of the World*, 36–41.
HODGDON, *Enchanted Past*, 49–57.
MOHR, WASHBURNE, BEATTY, *Egyptians of Long Ago*, 87–154.
WELLS, *How the Present Came from the Past*, II : 10–41.

READING FOR RECREATION

FLEMING, *Stories from the Early World*.
MACMANUS, *Our Little Egyptian Cousin*.
MAXWELL, *Story of Books*, 13–14.
NIDA, *Inventions and Discoveries of Ancient Times*, 34–113.

More Difficult Reading

EXTENSIVE READING

ARNOLD, *Stories of Ancient People*, 40–81.
BARNES, *Man and His Records.*
HARTMAN, *The World We Live in*, 118–119.
ILIN, *Black on White*, 41–48, 83–95.
LANSING, *Man's Long Climb*, 68–70, 99–102.
MILLER, *Picturesque Tale of Progress*, I: 110–248.
MILLS, *Book of the Ancient World*, 24–32, 46–59.
POWER, *Great People of the Past*, 1–17.
RICHMOND, *Egypt, Greece, and Rome*, 5–23, 68–69, 84–88.
Story of Weights and Measures (American Council on Education), 24–25.
Story of Writing (American Council on Education), 8–13, 20–28.
Telling Time (American Council on Education), 7–8.
VAN LOON, *Story of Mankind*, 26–28.

READING FOR RECREATION

EBERS, *An Egyptian Princess.*
HENTY, *Cat of Bubastis.*
MULLER, *How They Carried the Goods*, 17–34.
ROLT-WHEELER, *The Pyramid Builder.*
SCALES, *Boys of the Ages*, 1–20.
SYRETT, *Rachel and the Seven Wonders.*

The Discussion

Children answer the study-guide questions as fully as possible. They question one another as to phases omitted.

The teacher writes on the board the words *mummy, pyramid, sphinx, obelisk, papyrus, hieroglyphics.* Children discuss the meanings.

Multisensory Aids

Children and teacher talk over together the pictures in the text, noting features of geographical and historical importance.

They turn to a map of Ancient Egypt and point out the Mediterranean Sea, the Red Sea, the Nile, Upper Egypt, Lower Egypt, the cities of Memphis and Thebes, the Sinai Peninsula. They explain why Upper Egypt is at the bottom of the map. They point out these places on a large wall map.

AUDIO-VISUAL MATERIALS OBTAINABLE

Compton's Pictured Teaching Materials: *Water and Air Transportation*, Plate I, 3; *Hot and Cold Lands*, Plate VII, 1–3; *Communication*, Plate II, 5.
Copley Prints: Egyptian Hieroglyphics.
EASTMAN. Educational Slides: Set 301.
GRANT. *Story of the Ship*, p. 5.
International Educational Pictures: Egypt, Ancient and Modern Aspects of Egypt, Ancient Customs of Egypt, Cairo to the Pyramids, Daily Life of the Egyptians, Egypt as it was in the Time of Moses, Egypt — Land of the Pyramids, Land of the Pharaohs, Pyramids and Temples of Ancient Egypt, Temples and Tombs of Ancient Egypt.
Keystone Views: Egypt, 1–10, 15–30, 33–40, 54–55, 57–61, 65–66, 77, 88, 100–103.
LANGL. Colored History Pictures: Egypt.
LEHMANN. Colored History Pictures: II, 1–2.
LEHMANN. Geographical Pictures: L. G. 21.
LEHMANN. Historical Pictures: L. H. 1, 2.

McKINLEY. Illustrated Topics for Ancient History: A 2.
MILLER. *Picturesque Tale of Progress*, I, 71–248.
National Geographic Society Series: Sahara Life.
Society for Visual Education. University Museum (Philadelphia): The Pyramids of
    Egypt, Excavating Seneferu's Pyramid, Egypt in the Time of the Exodus, The
    Egyptian Mummy, Life in Ancient Egypt, Egyptian Arts.
Society for Visual Education (BRIGGS). Ancient Egypt.
Society for Visual Education (BURTON HOLMES). Egypt.
Society for Visual Education. History in Architecture, I.
University of Chicago Oriental Institute. Motion Picture: The Human Adventure.

A cutout Egyptian house may be secured from the Educational Department, University Museum, Philadelphia.

Music. The teacher tells the children the story of Verdi's opera *Aïda* and plays a record of the "Triumphal March."

The teacher plays selections from Henry Hadley's opera *Cleopatra's Night*; "Lament of Isis for the Lost Osiris," from Granville Bantock's *Songs of Egypt*; Rossini's *Moses in Egypt*; Handel's oratorio *Israel in Egypt*.

General Activities

Creative Activities: Group and Individual, Correlated with Other Subjects or Voluntary Projects

A committee models Egypt in the sand table, and marks Upper Egypt, Thebes, Lower Egypt, and Memphis. The deserts on both sides are marked.

The class makes a picture collection of ancient Egypt and posts it on the bulletin board.[1]

Volunteers draw figures to represent the Pharaoh, a noble, a priest, a worker, a slave.

A volunteer makes a model of an Egyptian boat. A committee loads the boat with articles seen in the pictures.

A committee dramatizes the judgment of a soul before Osiris.

The class makes a trip to the local museum to observe the section on Egypt.

A volunteer carves copies of hieroglyphics on a cake of soap.

The art teacher shows the class two of the favorite Egyptian designs — the papyrus plant and the lotus.

Volunteers show samples of hieroglyphics from the *Book of Knowledge* and *Compton's Pictured Encyclopedia*.

A volunteer shows a picture of the Egyptian obelisk in Central Park, New York.

A volunteer writes a short poem on a roll like an Egyptian roll.

A visitor to Egypt describes both ancient Egypt and modern Egypt to the class.

Each pupil makes a map of Egypt, marking the places mentioned under "Map Study."

The class continues the time line.

---

[1] *Egypt*, Teacher's Lesson Unit Series, Teachers College, Columbia University.

More Difficult Activities

A volunteer makes a physical model of Egypt and paints the Nile in order to show that the Nile flows downward to Lower Egypt. He marks the site of the great Aswan dam and shows a picture of it.

Volunteers investigate how modern men learned to read hieroglyphics.

The teacher reads to the class Shelley's sonnet "Ozymandias of Egypt."

A volunteer draws a cartoon to illustrate Egyptian social classes, or castes.

One of the boys shows that the shadoof was the first application of the lever.

A volunteer carves a sphinx and pyramids from soap and places them on the sand-table model.

A committee explains the difference between a column and an obelisk.

A volunteer reports on other war leaders besides Thutmose III who have tried to conquer the world.

A committee reports on the story of the later Egyptian queen, Cleopatra.

The class lists distinguishing characteristics of Egyptian architecture and Egyptian art.

A volunteer finds a list of the "seven wonders of the world."

A volunteer explains how a delta received its name.

Application to Present-Day Conditions

Is Egypt an independent country today? (See encyclopedia.) What form of government does it have? Can you find a picture of the present ruler?

Does the soil in other lands ever "wear out"? What do people do about it?

In what way has the Suez Canal greatly increased the importance of Egypt?

What is the present-day name of Thebes? (See a modern map.)

Has the ruler of any other country ever been head of the church too? [Czar of Russia.] Is any head of a church today ruler of a country? [Pope — Vatican City; Dalai Lama.]

How did the city workers of ancient Egypt differ from the city workers of today? How did the farmers differ from the farmers of today?

What do rich men do today so that the world may remember them after they are dead?

How do scientists today study the hieroglyphics and the records left by the ancient Egyptians?

What is the origin of our word paper?

Did the ancient Egyptians have anything to do with Ethiopia?

The class traces the Blue Nile to its source and shows the Sudan. Does this explain one reason why Great Britain, owner of the Sudan, was interested in the war between Italy and Ethiopia in 1936?

Exercises in Reasoning

Where does the Nile get the mud which it spreads over Egypt?

In what article did Egypt trade with the Sinai Peninsula?

Ancient Egypt dug a canal to the Red Sea. Why?

Why did the priests not want the lower classes to learn to read and write? [The lower classes might not believe what they were told.]

Why did it take a special class of people to do the reading and writing in ancient Egypt?

Compare the Ten Commandments of the Jews and Christians with the things which an Egyptian thought were right.

Why did the Egyptians never become good doctors?

Why did the Egyptians learn to make paper? [*Owing to scarcity of wood and stone; difficulty of carving stone.*]

Where does the water of the Nile come from, since it seldom rains in Egypt?

What is meant by "going *up* a river"? by "going *down* a river"?

More Difficult Exercises in Reasoning

How were the Egyptians able to get the water of the Nile up from the river to water their fields during the time of year when there was no flood?

Why does a great city require an enormous back country to support it?

Why were the Egyptians organized into rigid social classes?

Where could such enormous numbers of slaves be found as were needed in building? [*As captives in war.*]

Why did the Egyptians take such great care of the bodies of their dead?

Why did the Egyptians have to begin the science of geometry?

How could the Egyptians ever have learned that the year has 365 days just by watching and counting?

Compare the story of Osiris with our story of Easter.

How could the Egyptians have handled such enormous blocks of stone without modern machinery?

Did the fact that Egyptians could get their food without working all the time have anything to do with their developing a high civilization?

Drill Games

Place names are best drilled upon at the map: *Upper Egypt, Lower Egypt, Nile River.*

Drill cards may be made as follows:

Thutmose III	↔	a great Pharaoh who tried to conquer the world
papyrus	↔	a Nile plant from which paper was made
hieroglyphics	↔	the Egyptian method of writing both syllables and single sounds
Karnak	↔	the largest temple of Egypt
Khufu	↔	the Pharaoh who built the largest pyramid
pyramids	↔	great four-sided buildings rising to a peak
mummies	↔	bodies dried and preserved in the Egyptian manner
Pharaoh	↔	the ruler of Egypt, who was also regarded as a god
" Gift of the Nile "	↔	a nickname given to Egypt
sphinx	↔	a figure with the head of a man and the body of a lion
scribes	↔	a class of writers in ancient Egypt
4000 B.C.	↔	date when civilization was well begun in Egypt

Testing

Tests of Understanding are given in Kelty's *How Our Civilization Began*, pp. 72–73.

Tests of Reasoning and Skills

1. Go through the story and make a list of the things which ancient Egypt taught us.

Fill in the blanks with the right words:

2. The Egyptians watered their fields by means of ___[canals]___.

3. Egypt was well settled by the year ___[4000 B.C.]___.

4. The different classes of people in Egypt were ___[Pharaoh, nobles, priests, workers, slaves]___.

5. The world's first brain workers were the ___[scribes]___ of Egypt.

6. The pyramids were built to serve as ___[tombs]___.

7. We know much more about the Egyptians than we know about primitive man because of their ___[records]___.

8. Turn to a map of ancient Egypt. Check the following: Upper Egypt is north of Lower Egypt.   Yes [ ]   No [√]

Exercise in Organization. The teacher outlines the story, and the children give a topical recitation on each part of the outline.

More Difficult Tests

Complete these sentences:

1. Ancient Egypt was a good place for the beginning of civilization because ___[it had fertile soil and was warm]___.

2. Upper Egypt is called "Upper" Egypt because ___[it is farther up the river]___.

3. The Egyptians got their thousands of slaves by ___[war]___.

4. The Egyptians took very good care of the bodies of their dead people because ___[they thought the soul needed the body after death]___.

5. The priests had to learn to count how many days there are in a year in order to ___[tell when the Nile would overflow]___.

Fill in these blanks with the right words:

6. The Sinai Peninsula was valuable to Egypt because of its supplies of ___[copper]___.

7. All the land in Egypt belonged to ___[Pharaoh]___.

8. The Egyptians could never become good doctors because they believed in curing sickness by ___[magic]___.

STORY 2. THE LAND OF THE TWO RIVERS   [2 Weeks

Conversational Approach

Teacher and children again turn to the map or the sand-table model and find another great river valley which has most of the characteristics of the Nile valley. [*The Tigris-Euphrates.*]

"Why might it be reasonable to expect that primitive men would choose to settle here as well as in Egypt? They did settle here as early or perhaps even earlier. Our story today tells us about this center of early civilization. There were many others also, about which we have not time to read,—some in India and some in China."

Reading and Study

The Reading Periods (Babylonia and Assyria)

Independent Readers

TEXTS

BEEBY, *America's Roots in the Past,* 38–41, 45–52.

CHAPMAN, *Stories of the Ancient Peoples,* 100–110.

CLARK-GORDY, *Early Story of Mankind,* 85–90.

CLARK-GORDY, *Westward toward America,* 61–64.

CORKE, *A Book of Ancient Peoples,* 18–27, 77–89 (hard).

KELTY, *How Our Civilization Began,* 74–84.

KNOWLTON and GERSON, *Our Beginnings in the Past,* 135–141.

Lower Group

The teacher tells the story orally to this group, writing on the board the names of the most important persons and places as she mentions them. Children practice the pronunciations.

Then the teacher and these children read together the story as given in the text. The teacher directs the silent reading, section by section, by such questions as "In what ways is this land like Egypt?"

Children read silently and answer orally. When they have completed the ten pages, they test themselves by the questions at the end of the story which pertain to this part of the material.

MORE DIFFICULT TEXTS

BARKER, DUNCALF, BACON, *Old Europe and Our Nation,* 49–56.
BURNHAM, *Our Beginnings in Europe and America,* 28–38.
COULOMB, McKINLEY, WHITE, *What Europe Gave to America,* 24–28.
GORDY, *American Beginnings in Europe,* 30–34.
GREENWOOD, *Our Heritage from the Old World,* 1–10.
HALLECK and FRANTZ, *Our Nation's Heritage,* 33–37.
HARDING, *Old World Background to American History,* 7–9.
HAWLEY, *Adventures in Old World History,* 30–50.
NIDA, *Dawn of American History,* 29–31.
NIVER, *Old World Steps to American History,* 47–52.
SOUTHWORTH, *What the Old World Gave the New,* 8–12.
VOLLINTINE, *The American People and Their Old World Ancestors,* 37–51.
WICKHAM and PHILLIPS, *America's Heritage from the Long Ago,* 43–49, 53–56, 60–67.
WOODBURN and HILL, *Historic Background of Our United States,* 43–47.

The Discussion

Children answer the study-guide questions as fully as possible. They question one another on important phases omitted.

The teacher writes on the board the words *city-kingdoms, empire, code.* Children discuss the meanings.

The Reading Periods (Chaldea and Babylonian Culture)

Independent Readers

TEXTS

BEEBY, *America's Roots in the Past*, 41–45.
CLARK-GORDY, *Early Story of Mankind*, 90–99.
CLARK-GORDY, *Westward toward America*, 53–61.
KELTY, *How Our Civilization Began*, 84–93.

Lower Group

The teacher tells the story orally to this group, writing on the board the most important words as she mentions them. Children practice the pronunciations.

Then the teacher and this group read together the rest of the story as given in the text. The teacher directs the silent reading, section by section, by such questions as "Where did the new conquerors of Babylon come from?"

Children read silently and answer orally. When they have completed the story in this manner, they test themselves by the other questions at the end of the story.

MORE DIFFICULT TEXTS

BURNHAM, *Our Beginnings in Europe and America*, 38–42.
COULOMB, MCKINLEY, WHITE, *What Europe Gave to America*, 28–30.
HALLECK and FRANTZ, *Our Nation's Heritage*, 37–45.
MARSHALL, *Story of Human Progress*, 158–163.
NIVER, *Old World Steps to American History*, 52–55, 63–66.
WICKHAM and PHILLIPS, *America's Heritage from the Long Ago*, 49–53, 56–58, 67–69.

Easy Reading

EXTENSIVE READING

COFFMAN, *Child's Story of the Human Race*, 73–88.
CORKE, *The World's Family*, 40–43, 48–56.
ERLEIGH, *In the Beginning*, 30–49, 62–69.
HILLYER, *Child's History of the World*, 42–48, 94–108.
HODGDON, *The Enchanted Past*, 85–109.
MOHR, WASHBURNE, BEATTY, *Babylonia and Assyria*, 9–92.
WELLS, *How the Present Came from the Past*, II : 44–94, 96–117.

READING FOR RECREATION

CARPENTER, *Our Little Friends of the Arabian Desert*.
HADER, *Picture Book of Travel*, 46–50.
LUTHER, *Trading and Exploring*, 9–27.
RATZESBERGER, *Camel Bells*.

More Difficult Reading

EXTENSIVE READING

ARNOLD, *Stories of Ancient People*, 91–105.
BAIKIE, *Peeps at Many Lands: Assyria*.
BARNES, *Man and His Records*.
ILIN, *Black on White*, 48–53.
ILIN, *What Time Is It?* 23–27.
KUMMER, *First Days of History*, 51–76, 200–215.
KUMMER, *First Days of Knowledge*, 147–166, 180–184.
LANSING, *Man's Long Climb*, 112–121.
MARSHALL, *Readings in the Story of Human Progress*, 114–116, 212–214.
MEYER-HAMER, *Babylonia*.
MILLER, *Picturesque Tale of Progress*, II, 11–86.
MILLS, *Book of the Ancient World*, 75–109, 177–192.
NIDA, *Man Conquers the World with Science*, 22–25.

O'NEILL, *World's Story*, 10–26.
RUSSELL, *The Shining East*, 79–125.
Story of Numbers (American Council on Education), 10–14.
Story of Weights and Measures (American Council on Education), 8–9.
Story of Writing (American Council on Education), 14–15, 28–30.
VAN LOON, *Story of Mankind*, 29–37.
VAUGHN, *Great Peoples of the Ancient World*, 11–26, 113–154.
WEBSTER, *The World's Messengers*, 24–27.

The Discussion

Children answer the study-guide questions as fully as possible. Those who have read widely are given an opportunity to add their contributions.

The teacher writes on the board *Hanging Gardens, cuneiform*. Children discuss the meanings.

Multisensory Aids

Children and teacher talk over together the pictures in the text, pointing out features of geographical and historical significance.

They turn to a map of the Land of the Two Rivers and find the Tigris, the Euphrates, Babylonia, Assyria, the cities of Babylon and Nineveh. They show the desert at one side and the hill country at the other. They point out these same places on a large wall map.

AUDIO-VISUAL MATERIALS OBTAINABLE

Compton's Pictured Teaching Materials: *Communication*, Plate II, 6.
Keystone Views: Mesopotamia, 5–8, 15, 18, 20–26, 28, 30, 41.
LANGL. Colored History Pictures: Assyria, 10.
McKINLEY. Illustrated Topics for Ancient History: A 3.
MILLER. *Picturesque Tale of Progress*, I, 253–326.
Society for Visual Education. University Museum (Philadelphia): Ur of the Chaldees, Ur in the Time of Abraham, Palaces and Temples of the Kings of Assyria, Babylonia in the Time of Nebuchadnezzar.
Society for Visual Education (BRIGGS). Assyria, Babylonia.
University of Chicago Oriental Institute. Motion Picture: The Human Adventure.

A cutout Babylonian house may be secured from the Educational Department, University Museum, Philadelphia.

Music. Play selections from Rossini's *Semiramide*.

General Activities

Creative Activities: Group and Individual, Correlated with Other Subjects or Voluntary Projects

A committee models in the sand table the area of the Land of the Two Rivers and marks all the places mentioned above.

A volunteer attempts to make a brick of mud dried in the sun. Why is it hard to do?

A committee makes caravans of camels and donkeys and loads them with articles in which Babylonia traded. The caravans are placed on the sand table.

Children design their individual seals and make them of clay or soap.

The class writes the date, using our system of numerals, the Egyptian system, and the Babylonian system. Which is the easiest to use?

Volunteers try to copy the Assyrian figures of animals.

The class visits the local museum to observe the Babylonian and Assyrian exhibits. Are colored tiles to be observed in any building in the community?

The teacher reads to the class some of the Bible descriptions of Babylon and Assyria. (See Concordance.)

Children make small tablets of clay and write on them with a sharp nail. They bake the tablets.

The class makes a visit to a brickyard to see how bricks are made today.

Each child makes a map of the area of the Two Rivers, marking on it all the places mentioned above. The class continues the time line.

More Difficult Activities

Can you suggest some of the chapter headings for Hammurapi's two hundred and eighty-two chapters of laws?

Children attempt to add columns of figures written in the Babylonian and Egyptian systems.

A volunteer makes a map of Assyria at the height of its power. (Shepherd's *Historical Atlas*, p. 5.)

A volunteer committee constructs some hanging gardens on the sand table.

A volunteer builds a Babylonian tower, and tells the Bible story of the Tower of Babel.

Volunteers draw and color designs for colored tiles.

A group of children, from their reading in *A Picturesque Tale of Progress*, I, represent a Babylonian school.

A volunteer reports on the value of a number system that counts by sixes instead of by tens.

A volunteer draws a sundial and explains how it is used.

Application to Present-Day Conditions

What country occupies the Land of the Two Rivers today? (See your geography.) Is it an independent country? What form of government has it? (See an encyclopedia.) Can you find a picture of the present ruler?

If we had city-kingdoms here, name some of the neighboring cities which would be independent kingdoms.

Are there any empires in the world today? Name them.

Do we have any codes of laws? (Ask a lawyer.)

Why do countries today still try to conquer land that will give them a sea-coast? Name some countries which do not have any seacoast.

Do any buildings in your community use ramps to lead from one story to another? Do we ever use seals in closing letters today?

Why are countries today so much interested in the Land of the Two Rivers? [*Because of oil.*]

Do some people today still believe in "lucky stars"? Do they believe that the arrangement of the stars at the time a person is born will tell his fortune? (See *Horoscope* in an encyclopedia.)

What is the scientific study of the stars called?[1]

[1] See *Astronomy*, Teacher's Lesson Unit Series, Teachers College, Columbia University.

Exercises in Reasoning

Where do the two rivers get the mud they spread over the land when in flood?

Why is the history of the Land of the Two Rivers a history of wars?

Why were most of the buildings made of sun-dried brick? Why is less left of them than of the buildings in Egypt?

How did the ordinary citizen of Babylon differ from the ordinary citizen of Egypt? How did their rulers differ from the Pharaohs?

Why did the Babylonians have to have metal bars as money instead of using barter?

Why was Assyria able to conquer Babylonia? Why would the people they conquered not be willing to fight for their Assyrian masters?

How would a Babylonian library differ from our libraries? Do you think ours will last as long as some of theirs have?

More Difficult Exercises in Reasoning

What lesson can you learn from the Land of the Two Rivers as to the dangers of a nation's settling down to an easy life of money-getting?

Can you name any way in which some of the laws of Babylon were better than our laws?

Is America ever called "the world of the business man"? Why?

Why was the Hall of Records in Babylon the next most important building after the king's palace and the temples?

How does the history of Babylon prove that the ruler of a state in great danger ought not to be chosen just because he is the son of a king?

How was civilization able to continue after so cruel a people as the Assyrians conquered the then known world?

In what ways were the Babylonian beliefs much like the Christian beliefs?

Why was the religion of Babylonia a gloomy religion?

Drill Games

Place names are best drilled upon at the map: *Babylonia, Babylon, Assyria, Nineveh, Tigris, Euphrates.*

Drill cards are made as follows:

city-kingdom	↔	an independent city under the rule of its own king
Hammurapi	↔	the great king of Babylon who collected the laws and divided them into classes
code	↔	a classified system of laws
Nebuchadnezzar	↔	the king of Babylonia who built the Hanging Gardens
cuneiform	↔	wedge-shaped writing
Sennacherib	↔	a great king of the Assyrians
empire	↔	a country which includes parts that have been conquered
2100 B.C.	↔	date when Hammurapi lived

These cards are added to those from the previous story, and the game includes them both.

Testing

Tests of Understanding are given in Kelty's *How Our Civilization Began*, p. 93.

Tests of Reasoning and Skills. Finish these sentences:

1. The chief danger to the early Babylonians came from _ _ _[*the hill peoples to the east*]_ _ _.

2. The Babylonians made their buildings of sun-dried bricks because _ _ _[*their country had no stone*]_ _ _.

3. Hammurapi collected his laws in about the year _ _ _[*2100 B.C.*]_ _ _.

Underline the right word:

4. The Babylonians and Assyrians lived in   city-kingdoms.   kingdoms.   republics.

5. The people who carved the best figures of animals were the   Egyptians.   Babylonians.   Assyrians.

6. Turn to a map of the Land of the Two Rivers. Check the right square: The Euphrates is west of the Tigris.   Yes [√]   No [ ]

7. Should you believe everything written about the Assyrians by a people they had conquered? _ _ _[*No.*]_ _ _. Explain why. _ _ _[*Because of prejudice.*]_ _ _.

Exercise in Organization. Teacher and children together make a co-operative outline of the story. Children tell an oral story about each part of the outline.

More Difficult Tests

Finish these sentences:

1. We know less about the Babylonians than about the Egyptians because _ _ _[*most of their buildings did not last*]_ _ _.

2. The difference between the Babylonian king and the Egyptian Pharaoh was that _ _ _[*the Babylonian king was not a god*]_ _ _.

3. Assyria sent its armies to the west because it wanted _ _ _[*to secure a seacoast*]_ _ _.

4. Check the best answer: The greatest thing which Hammurapi did was   to make good laws for business.   to force everyone to obey the laws.   √ to classify the laws in a code.

5. In the following list, check those things in which the Babylonians did better than the Egyptians:

√ banks	canals	√ counting
buildings	√ weights and measures	writing
√ trading		

6. Check the things which the Assyrians had which their neighbors did not have:

√ horses	boats	weapons
spears	√ chariots	√ iron weapons

STORY 3. PHOENICIA [1 Week

Conversational Approach

"You remember that Assyria had wanted a seacoast. Why? With what countries could she have traded if she had been able to keep it? What could she have got from Egypt? from Babylonia?

"What powerful Assyria could not keep, another smaller country kept for many years." Turn to a map of the ancient Mediterranean world. "What small country stretches along the eastern end of the Mediterranean? What business do you think its people would be likely to carry on? Our story this week is about these people."

Reading and Study

The Reading Periods

Independent Readers

TEXTS

BEEBY, *America's Roots in the Past*, 70–78, 83–84.

CHAPMAN, *Stories of the Ancient Peoples*, 117–119.

CLARK-GORDY, *Early Story of Mankind*, 111–119.

CLARK-GORDY, *Westward toward America*, 77–86.

KELTY, *How Our Civilization Began*, 94–103.

KNOWLTON and GERSON, *Our Beginnings in the Past*, 159–163.

Lower Group

The teacher tells the story orally to this group, writing on the board the most important new words as she mentions them. Children practice the pronunciations.

Then the teacher and these children together read the story as given in the text. The teacher directs the silent reading, section by section, by such questions as "Why was the half-moon-shaped country so important?"

Children read silently and answer orally. When they have read the entire story in this manner, they test themselves by the questions at the end of the story.

MORE DIFFICULT TEXTS

BARKER, DUNCALF, BACON, *Old Europe and Our Nation*, 56–59.

COULOMB, MCKINLEY, WHITE, *What Europe Gave to America*, 30–33.

GORDY, *American Beginnings in Europe*, 34–36.

GREENWOOD, *Our Heritage from the Old World*, 42–51.

HALLECK and FRANTZ, *Our Nation's Heritage*, 45–47.

HARDING, *Old World Background to American History*, 9–10.

HAWLEY, *Adventures in Old World History*, 62–68.

NIDA, *Dawn of American History*, 31–33.

NIVER, *Old World Steps to American History*, 56–58.

SOUTHWORTH, *What the Old World Gave the New*, 15.

VOLLINTINE, *The American People and Their Old World Ancestors*, 52–66.

WICKHAM and PHILLIPS, *America's Heritage from the Long Ago*, 71–81.

WOODBURN and HILL, *Historic Background of Our United States*, 51–55.

Easy Reading

EXTENSIVE READING

BEST, *Egypt and Her Neighbors*, 159–170.

COFFMAN, *Child's Story of the Human Race*, 93–95.

HILLYER, *Child's History of the World*, 74–78.

READING FOR RECREATION

CURTIS, *Boats*.

GIMMAGE, *Picture Book of Ships*.

GRAVATT, *Pioneers of the Deep*.

HADER, *Picture Book of Travel*.

MOHR, WASHBURNE, BEATTY, *Palestine and Syria.*
SCHWARTZ, *From Then till Now*, 85–93.
WADDELL and BUSH, *How We Have Conquered Distance*, 48–49, 184–187.
WELLS, *How the Present Came from the Past*, II, 161–187.

LUTHER, *Trading and Exploring*, 28–61.
MAXWELL, *Story of Books*, 11–13.
NIDA, *Inventions and Discoveries of Ancient Times*, 157–171.
PETERSHAM, *Story Book of Ships.*

More Difficult Reading

EXTENSIVE READING

BARNES, *Man and His Records.*
BEST, *Egypt and Her Neighbors*, 159–170.
CLODD, *Story of the Alphabet.*
HARTMAN, *The World We Live in*, 94–95, 120–124.
ILIN, *Black on White*, 54–69.
KUMMER, *First Days of History*, 142–159.
LANSING, *Man's Long Climb*, 145–149.
MEYER-HAMER, *Syria, Palestine, Phoenicia.*
MILLS, *Book of the Ancient World*, 195–212.
NIDA, *Man Conquers the World with Science*, 120–121.
Story of Writing (American Council on Education), 30–58.
TAPPAN, *Travelers and Traveling.*
VAN LOON, *Story of Mankind*, 42–43.
WEBSTER, *World's Messengers*, 27–29.

READING FOR RECREATION

ARNOLD, *Phra the Phoenician.*
KENT, *Two Children of Tyre.*
MULLER, *How They Carried the Goods*, 71–87.

The Discussion

Children answer the study-guide questions as fully as possible. The teacher checks firmly those children who read rapidly but inaccurately, and who have run through several books but still cannot answer the study-guide questions.

The teacher writes on the board the words *colony, Tyrian purple.* Children discuss the meanings.

Multisensory Aids

Children and teacher talk over together the pictures in the text, pointing out features of historical and geographical importance. They turn to a text map and find Phoenicia and the cities of Tyre and Sidon. They show them also on a large wall map.

AUDIO-VISUAL MATERIALS OBTAINABLE

Compton's Pictured Teaching Materials: *Water and Air Transportation*, Plate I, 4; *Trade*, Plate IV, 1; *Communication*, Plate III.
McKINLEY. Illustrated Topics for Ancient History: A 4.
Society for Visual Education. University Museum (Philadelphia): Four Canaanite Temples.

General Activities

Creative Activities: Group and Individual, Correlated with Other Subjects or Voluntary Projects

A committee models Phoenicia and its neighbors on the sand table and marks Tyre and Sidon.

Another committee places on the model a caravan coming from Egypt to Babylonia.

A third places a caravan going from the Land of the Two Rivers to Egypt.

A volunteer finds pictures of cedars of Lebanon.

A volunteer makes a model of a Phoenician boat.[1] A girl sews a sail for it. A committee loads it with Phoenician products.

A volunteer brings a piece of cloth of the color which was formerly called "Tyrian purple"; also a piece which we today call purple.

The children write the alphabet on the board and give the sound of each letter; they write opposite them some syllables and show how many more syllables could be used than there are letters.

· The teacher reads to the children Bible references to Tyre and Sidon; for example, Ezekiel xxvii, 3–25.

Each child adds Phoenicia to his map already made.

The class continues the time line.

More Difficult Activities

A volunteer reports the meaning of the word *Armageddon*.

A volunteer makes a graph comparing the area of ancient Phoenicia with the area of Delaware.

Volunteers copy designs borrowed from Assyrian, Babylonian, and Egyptian sources.

A volunteer draws a map of Phoenician trade routes on the slated map of the Eastern Hemisphere (both land routes and sea routes).

A committee dramatizes Phoenicians trading with a tribe in an unknown country.

Application to Present-Day Conditions

What country owns ancient Phoenicia today? (See a modern geography.) What form of government does it have? (See an encyclopedia.)

What places have been called "Armageddon" in modern times? [*Belgium.*]

What kind of work does a traveling salesman do today?

Do countries today still make colonies? Has the United States any colonies? Do we want more?

Do all the countries in the world today use the same alphabet?

Why were the Phoenicians called "the English of antiquity"?

Exercises in Reasoning

Why is a great trade highway between nations not a safe place to live? What advantages does such a place have?

Why were the Phoenicians called "the world's first traveling salesmen"?

Why did ancient peoples consider strangers as enemies?

Do you think a country deserves credit for spreading ideas if those ideas are not its own?

Why did trade lead to exploration?

Why were the Phoenicians called "the men who went down to the sea in ships"?

[1] See *Ships and Navigation*, the record of a fifth-grade unit by Baxter and Young, Bureau of Publications, Teachers College, Columbia University.

More Difficult Exercises in Reasoning

Find out what an oligarchy is and compare it with a monarchy. Phoenicia was an oligarchy.

Why did ancient sailors have to keep close to the shores?

Why could few people read among the Egyptians and Babylonians?

How did it happen that the invention of the alphabet took place in the Sinai Peninsula?

What is an invention? Is fire an invention? Is bread an invention? Have any inventions been made that use fire?

Why would the Phoenician sailors not tell sailors from other countries all that they had learned about winds and sea currents in far parts of the earth?

Drill Games

Place names are best drilled upon at the map: *Phoenicia, Tyre, Sidon.*
Association cards are made as follows:

colony	⟷	a group of people sent out by a country to live in a far country
Tyrian purple	⟷	a dye for which the ancient Phoenicians were famous
1000 B.C.	⟷	date of height of Phoenician power

These cards are added to those used previously in the unit.

Testing

Tests of Understanding are given in Kelty's *How Our Civilization Began,* p. 103.

Tests of Reasoning and Skills. Draw a line under the right words:

1. Phoenicia   was   <u>was not</u>   located in a peaceful place.

2. The geography of the country forced the people to become   farmers. <u>sailors.</u>   miners.   warriors.

3. Because the people of Phoenicia wanted to trade they were also obliged <u>to explore new lands.</u>   to fight their neighbors.   to irrigate their fields. to learn from the Egyptians.

4. The alphabet   <u>was not</u>   was   made by the Phoenicians themselves.

5. Turn to a map of the ancient world. Check the following: Phoenicia is at the western end of the Mediterranean Sea.   Yes [ ]   No [√]

6. On what pages in your book can material about Tyre be found? _ _ _ _ _ _ Where did you look to find out?   _ _ _[*In the index.*]_ _ _

Exercise in Organization. Children copy the topic headings and make a summary sentence for each topic.

More Difficult Tests

Check the best answer:

1. People lived in Phoenicia because   they wanted to keep Assyria from conquering any seacoast.   they wanted to be where war would break out between Egypt and Babylon.   √ it was one of a very few fertile spots between Egypt and the Two Rivers.   it was the best place from which to get cedar trees.

2. Phoenicia was governed by   kings.   √ wealthy families.   all the people.   the priests.

3. The Phoenicians spread the use of the alphabet because   their poems could be written in the alphabet.   histories could be written more easily with it.   their beliefs had to be written down.   √ accounts could be kept more easily by its use.

4. The Phoenicians did the world a service by spreading also the idea that   √ strangers need not be enemies.   strangers were people of another country.   strangers were always dangerous.   enemies need not be fought.

STORY 4. THE HEBREWS AND THEIR COUNTRY   [*1 Week*

Conversational Approach

"Are the religions about which we have so far read much like our own religions today? What are the chief differences?

"There was, however, one ancient people whose religion was much like ours. Does anyone know who they were? Our story this week is about those people."

Reading and Study

The Reading Periods

Independent Readers

TEXTS

BEEBY, *America's Roots in the Past,* 54–68.

CHAPMAN, *Stories of the Ancient Peoples,* 112–117.

CLARK-GORDY, *Early Story of Mankind,* 101–109.

CLARK-GORDY, *Westward toward America,* 67–75.

CORKE, *A Book of Ancient Peoples,* 51–57, 90–101 (hard).

KELTY, *How Our Civilization Began,* 104–110.

KNOWLTON and GERSON, *Our Beginnings in the Past,* 145–154.

Lower Group

The teacher tells the story orally to this group, writing on the board the most important words as she mentions them.

Then the teacher and these children read together the story as given in the text. The teacher directs the silent reading, section by section, by such questions as "In what kind of country did the Hebrews live?"

Children read silently and answer orally. When they have read the entire story in this manner, they test themselves by the questions at the end of the story.

OTHER BOOKS

WAYLAND, *History Stories for Primary Grades,* 72–78, 131–135.

More Difficult Texts

BARKER, DUNCALF BACON, *Old Europe and Our Nation*, 59–62.
BURNHAM, *Our Beginnings in Europe and America*, 46–48.
COULOMB, McKINLEY, WHITE, *What Europe Gave to America*, 33–35.
GORDY, *American Beginnings in Europe*, 36–38.
GREENWOOD, *Our Heritage from the Old World*, 52–70.
GUERBER, *Story of the Chosen People*, 27–63, 118–157, 157–202.
HALLECK and FRANTZ, *Our Nation's Heritage*, 47–48.
HARDING, *Old World Background to American History*, 9–10.
HAWLEY, *Adventures in Old World History*, 68–72.
NIDA, *Dawn of American History* 11–12.
NIVER, *Old World Steps to American History*, 59–62.
SOUTHWORTH, *What the Old World Gave the New*, 13–15.
VOLLINTINE, *The American People and Their Old World Ancestors*, 52–59.
WICKHAM and PHILLIPS, *America's Heritage from the Long Ago*, 98–114.
WOODBURN and HILL, *Historic Background of Our United States*, 48–51.

Easy Reading

Extensive Reading

BEST, *Egypt and Her Neighbors*, 67–158.
BONSER, *How the Early Hebrews Lived and Learned.*
COFFMAN, *Child's Story of the Human Race*, 89–93.
COLLINS and HALE, *Hero Stories for Children*, 3–74.
CORKE, *The World's Family*, 67–71.
HILLYER, *Child's History of the World*, 49–55, 70–73.
HODGDON, *Enchanted Past*, 135–154.
MOHR, WASHBURNE, BEATTY, *Palestine and Syria.*
WELLS, *How the Present Came from the Past*, II, 142–159.

Reading for Recreation

BALDWIN, *Old Stories from the East.*
GROVER, *Old Testament Stories.*
KING, *Amnon, a Lad of Palestine.*
WADE, *Our Little Jewish Cousin.*

More Difficult Reading

Extensive Reading

ARNOLD, *Stories of Ancient Peoples*, 152–166.
BURNHAM, *Hero Tales from History*, 1–10.
KUMMER, *First Days of History*, 160–180.
MEYER-HAMER, *Syria, Palestine, Phoenicia.*
MILLER, *Picturesque Tale of Progress*, I, 327–509.
MILLS, *Book of the Ancient World*, 113–156.
O'NEILL, *World's Story*, 13–26.
RICHMOND, *Egypt, Greece, Rome*, 25–34.
RUSSELL, *The Shining East*, 145–149.
VAN LOON, *Story of Mankind*, 38–41.

Reading for Recreation

ASCH, *In the Beginning.*
FINNEMORE, *Egypt and the Holy Land.*
FRIEDLANDER, *Jewish Fairy Book.*
HAGEDORN, *Book of Courage*, 10–21.
KALEEL, *When I Was a Boy in Palestine.*
LANGSTAFF, *From Now to Adam.*
LOBINGIER, *Hebrew Home Life.*
MULLER, *How They Carried the Goods*, 53–69.
OLCOTT, *Bible Stories to Read and Tell.*
RUBINSTEIN, *Adventuring in Palestine.*
SMITH, *Old, Old Tales from an Old, Old Book.*
STEARNS, *The Story of Music*, 5–8.
TAPPAN, *An Old, Old Story.*
UPJOHN, *Friends in Strange Garments*, 1–8.

The Discussion

Children answer the study-guide questions as fully as possible. The teacher makes a special attempt to draw the lower group into the discussion.

The teacher writes on the board the words *century, prophets, Old Testament.* Children discuss the meanings.

Multisensory Aids

Children and teacher talk over together the pictures in the text, pointing out features of historical and geographical importance. They turn to the map and locate Palestine and Jerusalem.

AUDIO-VISUAL MATERIALS OBTAINABLE

DENOYER-GEPPERT. Prints for Bible History.
International Educational Pictures: Wanderers of the Arabian Desert, City of David, Holy Land, Jerusalem, Kingdom of David, Palestine, Solomon's Temple.
LEHMANN. Colored History Pictures: II, 6, 7.
LEHMANN. Geography Pictures: L. G. 19.
LEHMANN. History Pictures: L. H. 6–7.
McKINLEY. Illustrated Topics for Ancient History: A 4.
MILLER. *Picturesque Tale of Progress*, II, 87–269.
Society for Visual Education. University Museum (Philadelphia): Ancient Biblical Cities of Palestine.
Copies of Sargent's frieze of "The Prophets."

Music. The teacher tells the story of Samson and Delilah and plays selections from Saint-Saëns's *Samson and Delilah.*

Selections may also be played from Gounod's *Queen of Sheba*; from Goldmark's *Queen of Sheba*; from Méhul's opera *Joseph*; from Handel's oratorios *Israel in Egypt, Samson, Saul, Esther*; from Mendelssohn's *Elijah*; from Rossini's *Moses in Egypt.*

Ancient Hebrew music may be played, such as the Kol Nidre. (See lists from phonograph companies.)

General Activities

Creative Activities: Group and Individual, Correlated with Other Subjects or Voluntary Projects

A committee models Palestine on the sand table and marks Jerusalem. It divides the kingdom of Israel from the kingdom of Judah.

Another committee dresses figures as shepherds and puts them on the model, together with their flocks of sheep.

A volunteer looks up the area of the state of Vermont and reports to the class. [*About the size of Palestine.*]

Volunteers tell the Bible story about how the Hebrews entered "the land of Canaan."

The class makes a picture collection of Jerusalem and the Holy Land.[1]

A committee constructs a walled-in well and shows how the water was raised.

A volunteer draws a picture of the Hebrews escaping from Egypt through the Red Sea while the sea drowns the pursuers.

A visitor to Jerusalem describes it to the children.

Each child adds Palestine to his map and marks the city of Jerusalem.

The class continues the time line.

---

[1] See *Life of the Early Hebrews*, Teacher's Lesson Unit Series, Teachers College, Columbia University.

More Difficult Activities

The teacher reads to the class some of the most beautiful passages from Amos and Isaiah, and the passage beginning "and what doth the Lord require of thee, but to do justly, to love mercy and to walk humbly with thy God?" (Micah vi, 8)

The teacher reads to the class Byron's poem "The Destruction of Sennacherib"; Moore's "Sound the Loud Timbrel"; Browning's "Saul"; Byron's "Song of Saul before His Last Battle"; Southey's "Triumph of Woman."

Volunteers write poems on the fate of the northern kingdom of Israel; on the captivity of the southern tribes.

A volunteer writes the document in which King Cyrus announces that the Jews are to be allowed to return to their homes.

The teacher reads to the class the description of the Temple as given in the Bible (2 Chronicles iii–iv). A volunteer shows how both Egypt and Phoenicia helped in the building of the Temple.

Application to Present-Day Conditions

How do we know anything today about the life of the ancient Hebrews? [*From the Bible.*]

What are the Hebrews usually called today? [*Jews.*]

Have you ever seen a Yiddish newspaper? (The Hebrew alphabet is shown in the World Book Encyclopedia.)

Does the country of Palestine exist today? (See a geography.) Under what government is it? (See encyclopedia.)

Have you ever heard the expression "the judgment of Solomon"? To what story does it refer?

Do city people and country people still have trouble in understanding one another? Are country people still likely to think that city people are wicked?

A volunteer explains why the former ruler of modern Ethiopia claims to be a descendant of Solomon.

Have you ever heard the expression *the lost tribes*? To what does it refer?

Has Jerusalem a port today? (See a geography.)

To what bad conditions in our own country today might a prophet very well call attention?

Can you name any of the "books" of the Old Testament?

Why do we today know more about the life of the ancient Hebrews than we do about the life of the Phoenicians?

Exercises in Reasoning

In what way was Palestine a "bridge between Asia and Africa"?

Why was the kingdom of the Hebrews less likely to last after it divided into two parts?

What did the Hebrews believe that a man had to do to serve God? How does this compare with the way the Egyptians and Babylonians had honored their gods?

Why were the Hebrews the first people in the world who tried to teach all their children to read?

More Difficult Exercises in Reasoning

What is the difference between a prophet and a fortune-teller?

Do nations at war today ever behave as if they still believed God to be a tribal God?

Were the Hebrews the only people of the time who believed in one God?

Drill Games

Place names are best drilled upon at the map: *Palestine, Jerusalem.*

Game cards are made as follows:

David	⟷	the ruler under whom the Hebrew kingdom was established
prophet	⟷	one who tells what will happen if people continue in the same evil ways
century	⟷	a period of one hundred years
Solomon	⟷	the Hebrew king who built the great Temple
Old Testament	⟷	the part of the Bible which tells the history of the ancient Hebrews
about 600 B.C.	⟷	the date when the southern Hebrew tribes were conquered by Babylonia

Children drill one another by twos.

Testing

Tests of Understanding are suggested in Kelty's *How Our Civilization Began,* p. 110.

Tests of Reasoning and Skills. Check the right answer:

1. The greatest gift of the Hebrew nation to the world was   their poems about captivity.   their prophets of the future.   √ their idea of one God. their invention of the alphabet.

Underline the right answer:

2. The leader under whom the Hebrews established their kingdom was named   Moses.   Abraham.   David.   Solomon.   Amos.

3. The kingdom reached its greatest power under the ruler   David. Jacob.   Isaiah.   Joseph.   Solomon.

Turn to a map of the ancient world. Check the following:

4. Palestine is south of Phoenicia.   Yes [√]   No [ ]

5. On what page is the table of contents for the unit which you have just completed? _ _ _ _ _ _

Exercise in Organization. The children who believe themselves able to do so may make an independent outline of the story. The rest of the class and the teacher make a co-operative outline.

More Difficult Tests

Complete the following sentences:

1. Parts of the Old Testament of the Bible are history because _ _ _[*they tell what happened to the Jews*]_ _ _.

2. The Hebrew kingdom was easily conquered because _ _ _[*it had divided into two parts*]_ _ _.

3. Many different nations wanted Palestine because _ _ _[*it was a highway of commerce*]_ _ _.

Match the following columns:

   a. Nebuchadnezzar   [*b*] conqueror of the northern kingdom
   b. Sennacherib   [*a*] conqueror of the southern kingdom

Tests on the Entire Unit

Test of Place Sense. Pass double-sized outline maps of the Mediterranean region. For smaller children, maps showing water bodies in color or land bodies in shading are preferable. Give the following directions:

        Write the word *Egypt* in the proper place.
        Put the letter *N* beside the river Nile.
        Put the letter *T* beside the river Tigris.
        Put the letter *E* beside the river Euphrates.
        Put the letter *B* in Babylonia.
        Put the letter *A* in Assyria.
        Put the letter *P* in Phoenicia.
        Put the letter *H* in the land of the Hebrews.

Test of Time Sense. Pass mimeographed sheets of the following.

Here is a list of dates. Put each in the right blank in the sentences below:

   4000 B.C.   2100 B.C.   1000 B.C.   600 B.C.

1. The date when Nebuchadnezzar carried the southern Hebrew tribes away into captivity was _ _ _ _ _ _.

2. The year _ _ _ _ _ _ saw civilization well begun in Egypt.

3. Hammurapi's code of laws was made in about the year _ _ _ _ _ _

4. In _ _ _ _ _ _ the Phoenicians had set up their city-kingdoms.

Test of Persons. Here is a list of persons. Put each name in the right blank in the sentences below:

   Nebuchadnezzar   Solomon   David
   Thutmose III   Khufu   Sennacherib

1. A great Assyrian king was _ _ _ _ _ _.

2. The Egyptian who tried to conquer the world was _ _ _ _ _ _.

3. King _ _ _ _ _ _ established the Hebrew kingdom.

4. A great king of Babylon was _ _ _ _ _ _.

5. The Pharaoh _ _ _ _ _ _ built the largest of the pyramids.

6. King _ _ _ _ _ _ built the Hebrew temple.

Tests of Historical Terms. **I.** Here is a list of terms. Put each one in the right blank in the sentences below.

papyrus	prophet	colony
code	hieroglyphic	century
Tyrian purple	city-kingdom	cuneiform

1. A man who forecasts what is to happen is a _ _ _ _ _ _.

2. One hundred years are a _ _ _ _ _ _.

3. Material which the Egyptians used as paper was _ _ _ _ _ _.

4. A city which is independent and has its own rulers is a _ _ _ _ _ _.

5. The system of writing in the Land of the Two Rivers was _ _ _ _ _ _.

6. A dye for which Phoenicia was famous was _ _ _ _ _ _.

7. A collection of laws is called a _ _ _ _ _ _.

8. A group of people sent to live in a far land is a _ _ _ _ _ _.

9. A system of writing used by the Egyptians was _ _ _ _ _ _.

II. Here is another list. Do the same.

empire	mummy	scribe
sphinx	Karnak	"gift of the Nile"
Pharaoh	Old Testament	pyramid

1. A great peaked building serving as the tomb of a Pharaoh is a _ _ _ _ _ _.

2. A dead body kept in the manner of the Egyptians is a _ _ _ _ _ _.

3. An Egyptian figure with the head of a man and the body of a lion is a _ _ _ _ _ _.

4. The part of the Bible which tells of the ancient Hebrew nation is the _ _ _ _ _ _.

5. A country made up partly of conquered lands is an _ _ _ _ _ _.

6. A man who wrote for other people for a living was a _ _ _ _ _ _.

7. A name often given to Egypt is the _ _ _ _ _ _.

8. The largest temple in the world is the temple of _ _ _ _ _ _.

9. The title of the king of Egypt was _ _ _ _ _ _.

Test of Comprehension

Check the best answer in each exercise below:

1. The country of Palestine was wanted by many nations because   √ it was on the road from Africa to Asia.   it had very rich soil.   it contained many copper mines.   it could send out ships to many places.

2. The people of the Two Rivers believed that   their ruler was a god.   their gods could die.   √ their ruler was only a man.   men became gods after death.

3. The people of Phoenicia turned to the sea for a living because   sailing is easier work than farming.   their wealthy rulers wanted more money.   sailing let them see many strange sights.   √ their country was too small to support them by farming.

4. After the death of Thutmose III Egypt   was greater than ever.
✓ fell to pieces.   conquered the world.   ruled Assyria.

5. The kingdom of the Hebrews divided into two parts because   one of
them was conquered by Assyria.   it was on the great trade highway.   David
and Solomon could not agree.   ✓ the people did not like the heavy taxes
that they had to pay.

6. The chief cities of Phoenicia were   ✓ Tyre and Sidon.   Babylon
and Nineveh.   Memphis and Thebes.   Jerusalem and Bethlehem.

7. The land of the Two Rivers was run mainly for the benefit of   nobles.
✓ business men.   warriors.   farmers.

8. The Egyptians took such great care of the bodies of their dead because   they knew how to do such fine work in making mummies.   bodies
would keep well in the dry air of their climate.   ✓ they thought the soul
needed a body in the next life.   their Pharaoh ordered that all bodies
should be cared for.

9. The reason why the world today remembers the ancient Hebrew nation
is that   ✓ they believed in only one God.   they built a great temple.
they taught their children to read.   they were carried away into captivity.

10. The ancient people who did the finest building were the   Hebrews.
Phoenicians.   Babylonians.   ✓ Egyptians.

11. The ancient people who did the finest carving of animals were the
✓ Assyrians.   Babylonians.   Phoenicians.   Egyptians.

12. In ancient Egypt all the land was owned by the   farmers.   nobles.
✓ Pharaoh.   priests.

13. In Babylonia the land was owned by the   priests.   ✓ citizens.
officials.   king.

14. The material used by the Egyptians in writing was   clay.   sun-
dried brick.   ✓ papyrus.   paper.

15. The material used by the Assyrians for writing was   ✓ clay.   sun-
dried brick.   papyrus.   paper.

16. Match the systems of writing used by the following:

a. Phoenicians   [*b*] hieroglyphics
b. Egyptians   [*c*] cuneiform
c. Babylonians   [*a*] alphabet

17. What is the title of the unit which you have just finished? _____

**Are any children now ready to be transferred from the lower group to the
group of independent readers?**

UNIT THREE · *The Greeks teach the World about Freedom* [6 Weeks

STORY 1. THE GREEK RACE AND RELIGION [1 Week

Conversational Approach

Teacher and class turn once more to a large physical map of the Mediterranean area or to a sand-table model. The children show the areas already studied.

"Do you see something that would make a very easy stepping-stone for the sailors of Egypt and Phoenicia sailing from their own country to the lands farther north? [*The island of Crete.*] They did sail north and found people already there. Do you suppose these people would be as highly civilized as the Egyptians? Why not? What is the name of their country?

"Our story today is about these Greeks — where they came from, what they believed about the world, and how they got along with their neighbors."

Reading and Study

The Reading Periods

Independent Readers

This group reads the entire story through as given in their text. They then test their understanding by the study-guide questions furnished by the teacher or by the text.

TEXTS

BEEBY, *America's Roots in the Past*, 78–83, 87–99.

CHAPMAN, *Stories of Ancient Peoples*, 1–47, 121–123.

CLARK-GORDY, *Early Story of Mankind*, 127–133.

CLARK-GORDY, *Westward toward America*, 95–102.

CORKE, *A Book of Ancient Peoples*, 65–71, 101–110 (hard).

KELTY, *How Our Civilization Began*, 113–121.

KNOWLTON and GERSON, *Our Beginnings in the Past*, 34–44, 47–57, 159–182.

Lower Group

The teacher tells the story orally to this group, writing on the board the most important names as she mentions them. Children practice the pronunciations.

Then the teacher and this group read together the story as given in the text. The teacher directs the silent reading, section by section, by such questions as "What steps toward civilization have already been taken?"

Children read silently and answer orally. When they have read the entire story in this manner, they test themselves by the questions at the end of the story.

OTHER BOOKS

BALDWIN, *Thirty More Famous Stories Retold*, 136–155.

TERRY, *History Stories of Other Lands*, I: 9–12.

MORE DIFFICULT TEXTS

BARKER, DUNCALF, BACON, *Old Europe and Our Nation,* 63–72.
BURNHAM, *Our Beginnings in Europe and America,* 50–54.
COULOMB, McKINLEY, WHITE, *What Europe Gave to America,* 38–39, 41–45.
GORDY, *American Beginnings in Europe,* 43–47.
GREENWOOD, *Our Heritage from the Old World,* 72–78, 103–104.
HALL, *Our Ancestors in Europe,* 1–11, 13–19.
HALLECK and FRANTZ, *Our Nation's Heritage,* 51–52, 72–74.
HARDING, *Old World Background to American History,* 13–19, 21–24.
HAWLEY, *Adventures in Old World History,* 84–89, 119–120.
NIVER, *Old World Steps to American History,* 69–76.
SHERWOOD, *Our Country's Beginnings,* 9–16.
SOUTHWORTH, *What the Old World Gave the New,* 18–24.
TAPPAN, *Our European Ancestors,* 10–17.
VOLLINTINE, *The American People and Their Old World Ancestors,* 82–102.
WICKHAM and PHILLIPS, *America's Heritage from the Long Ago,* 116–125, 148–150.
WOODBURN and HILL, *Historic Background of Our United States,* 63–71.

Easy Reading

EXTENSIVE READINGS

BAKER, *Stories of Old Greece and Rome,* 1–6, 317–323.
BEST, *Glorious Greece and Imperial Rome,* 1–77.
COFFMAN, *Child's Story of the Human Race,* 94–120.
HALL, *Four Old Greeks.*
HILLYER, *Child's History of the World,* 56–69.
HODGDON, *The Enchanted Past,* 160–165.

READING FOR RECREATION

BALDWIN, *Golden Fleece.*
BALDWIN, *Old Greek Stories.*
HALL, *Buried Cities,* 159–171 (pictures).
KUPFER, *Stories of Long Ago.*
MITCHELL, *Horses: Now and Long Ago.*
NIDA, *Inventions and Discoveries of Ancient Times,* 172–181.
PYLE, *Tales from Greek Mythology.*

More Difficult Reading

EXTENSIVE READINGS

BAIKIE, *Peeps at Many Lands: Ancient Crete.*
BURNHAM, *Hero Tales from History,* 10–15.
GUERBER, *Story of the Greeks,* 11–60.
HAAREN and POLAND, *Famous Men of Greece,* 1–109.
HARTMAN, *The World We Live in,* 96–103.
INGRAHAM, *Story of Democracy,* 23–39.
KUMMER, *First Days of History,* 181–199.
MACGREGOR, *Story of Greece,* 1–75.
MILLER, *Picturesque Tale of Progress,* II : 66–117.
O'NEILL, *World's Story,* 27–31.
POWER, *Great People of the Past,* 18–26.
QUENNELL, *Every Day Life in Homeric Greece.*
RICHMOND, *Egypt, Greece, and Rome,* 107–121, 134–151.
VAN LOON, *Story of Mankind,* 48–57.

READING FOR RECREATION

BURT, *Odysseus.*
CHURCH, *Story of the Iliad.*
CHURCH, *Story of the Odyssey.*
CHURCH, *Three Greek Children.*
COLUM, *Children's Homer.*
COLUM, *Golden Fleece.*
CREW, *The Lost King.*
CREW, *The Trojan Boy.*
HARDING, *Story of Greek Gods, Heroes, and Men.*
HARSHAW, *Council of the Gods.*
HAWTHORNE, *Tanglewood Tales.*
HAWTHORNE, *Wonder Book.*
KINGSLEY, *Greek Heroes.*
LAMPREY, *The Childhood of Greece.*
RENICK, *Star Myths of Many Lands.*
UPJOHN, *Friends in Strange Garments,* 14–21.

The Discussion

Children answer the study-guide questions as fully as possible. The teacher observes very carefully the performance of any children who may have been recently transferred from the lower group to the group of independent readers.

The teacher writes on the board the words *chiton, Iliad, Odyssey.* Children discuss the significance.

Multisensory Aids

Children and teacher talk over together the pictures in the text, pointing out features of geographical and historical significance. They turn to the map and locate Greece in reference to Egypt, Palestine, Phoenicia, and Crete. They point out the Aegean Sea and Troy. They tell why Greece is called a peninsula.

Audio-visual Materials Obtainable

CYBULSKI. Greek and Roman History Pictures: 1, 2, 3 A.
GALL-REBHANN. Charts: 18–20, 23.
GRANT. *Story of the Ship*, p. 6.
Keystone Views: Asia Minor, 22–24.
LANGL. Colored History Pictures: Greece.
LEHMANN. Colored History Pictures: L. H. 110.
McKINLEY. Illustrated Topics for Ancient History: A 5.
MILLER. *Picturesque Tale of Progress*, III, 67–141.
National Geographic Magazine, LX, 407–418 (October, 1931).
Society for Visual Education (MUIR). Ancient Greece, 900 B.C.–400 B.C.

Music. The teacher plays selections from operas: *Orpheus and Eurydice* (Gluck), *The Trojans* (Berlioz), *La Belle Hélène* (Offenbach), *Sappho* (Gounod), *Atalanta* (Handel); the Greek "Hymn to Apollo" and records of other ancient Greek music. (See lists from phonograph companies.)

General Activities

Creative Activities: Group and Individual, Correlated with Other Subjects or Voluntary Projects

A volunteer committee models the eastern end of the Mediterranean area in the sand table.

Volunteers draw pictures of the Greek valleys surrounded by high hills.

Committees make lists of the things the Greeks could learn from the Egyptians; the Babylonians; the Phoenicians.

The class divides into committees. Each committee chooses a Greek god about whom to read and to tell the rest of the group.

The class makes a dramatization of the story of the Trojan War.

A committee reports on the life of the Greeks while they were still wanderers.[1]

The class makes a picture collection of the Greek gods and goddesses and posts it on the bulletin board.

Volunteers report fables from Aesop. Committees read to the class the dramatizations from Aesop given in Stevenson's *Children's Classics in Dramatic Form* (II: 1–10, 19–25, 45–48, 63–68), and those given in Hofer's *Festival and Civic Plays from Greek and Roman Tales*.

Volunteers dress dolls in the clothing of a Greek man and a Greek woman.

The class divides into committees, and each tells of one of the labors of Hercules.

---

[1] See *When We Were Nomads*, Teacher's Lesson Unit Series, Teachers College Columbia University.

A committee reads to the class the dramatization of "Persephone" from Stevenson's *Children's Classics in Dramatic Form* (IV: 98–115).

The class dramatizes some of the incidents of the Odyssey.

A volunteer shows the class a book printed in the language of the ancient Greeks. (Perhaps the public library can help.) The class tries to copy some of the Greek letters.

The teacher reads to the class the burlesque on the story of Pyramus and Thisbe from Shakespeare's *Midsummer Night's Dream.*

A volunteer reports on the life work of Dr. Schliemann. (See an encyclopedia.)

Application to Present-Day Conditions

Do people today do their own thinking, or is their thinking done for them by the newspapers and the radio?

Are the Greeks today a nation of sailors? (See your geography.)

What do we mean today when we speak of someone's performing a Herculean feat?

Have you ever heard a very large or very strong woman called an Amazon? Why?

Do the Greeks of today look like the Greeks about whom you have been reading?

Have you ever heard anyone say that the future is "on the knees of the gods"? What did he mean?

Exercises in Reasoning

Why is a peninsula well suited to be the home of sailors?

Why is it better for people to do their own thinking than to be told by their rulers what to think?

Why are iron weapons better than bronze?

Why did it take the Greeks such a long time to conquer the Trojans? [*Because supplies had to be sent across the sea to the army.*]

More Difficult Exercises in Reasoning

Why did the early Greeks have most of their dealings with the people to the east of them?

Why did many cities claim the honor of being the birthplace of Homer?

Since the Greek gods had most of the faults of human beings, what effect should you expect them to have upon people's lives?

Can you find any other places on the map where islands serve as stepping-stones?

Do you know of any other people who believed that the forces of nature were gods? (For example, the *Northmen.*)

Why did it seem to the Greeks that there must be many gods?

In case of war between any nations using the Mediterranean Sea, why would the Greek peninsula be a place of great importance?

Why is Greece a place of importance in the airway lines from Europe to Africa and the East?

Drill Games

Place names are best drilled upon at the map: *Greece, Aegean Sea, Troy.*
Drill cards are made as follows:

chiton	⟷	the outer dress of the Greeks
Zeus	⟷	the chief of all the Greek gods
Hera	⟷	wife of the chief Greek god
Poseidon	⟷	the Greek god of the sea
Hades	⟷	god of the world of the dead
Aphrodite	⟷	the goddess of love
Apollo	⟷	the young god of the sun, music, poetry, and medicine
Athena	⟷	the goddess of wisdom
Mt. Olympus	⟷	the home of the gods
Hercules	⟷	the strong hero of the Greeks
Helen	⟷	the queen over whom the Trojan War was fought
Homer	⟷	the blind poet of ancient Greece
Iliad	⟷	the poem telling about the Trojan War
Odyssey	⟷	the poem telling of the wanderings of a Greek hero after the Trojan War

Children drill individually on the items which they find most difficult.

Testing

Tests of Understanding are given in Kelty's *How Our Civilization Began,*
p. 121.

Tests of Reasoning and Skills. Check the right answer:

1. The Greeks differed from the other people about whom we have read in
that they dared   to sail unknown seas.   ✓ to think for themselves.   to
fight against their king.   to make a new religion.

2. The Greek gods and goddesses were   ✓ much like ordinary men and
women.   better than the Hebrew God.   worse than the Babylonian
gods.   like the gods of the Egyptians.

Turn to a map of the ancient world. Mark the following: **Yes**   **No**

3. The Aegean Sea is west of Greece.   [ ]   [✓]
   The land of Greece is much broken up.   [✓]   [ ]
   Crete is south of Greece.   [✓]   [ ]
   Troy is west of Greece.   [ ]   [✓]

Exercise in Organization. Children make a list of the topic headings and
prepare to give a topical recitation on each heading.

More Difficult Test

It is often said that the geography of a country influences its history. Can
you give one example of this principle in the case of Greece? _____

STORY 2. THE CITY-STATES: ATHENS AND SPARTA [1 Week

Conversational Approach

"We have spoken of the Greeks so far as if they were one united nation. They were not. What have you already learned about their life in their mountain valleys? And since you have also learned that the Greeks liked to think for themselves, do you suppose they would like to have a king rule over them?

"Our story today is about the two greatest centers of Greek life. The title of the story tells you what they were. Name them."

Reading and Study

The Reading Periods

Independent Readers

TEXTS

BEEBY, *America's Roots in the Past,* 106–122.
CHAPMAN, *Stories of the Ancient Peoples,* 123–125, 132–136.
CLARK-GORDY, *Early Story of Mankind,* 133–157.
CLARK-GORDY, *Westward toward America,* 109–122.
KELTY, *How Our Civilization Began,* 122–134.
KNOWLTON and GERSON, *Our Beginnings in the Past,* 182–185.

Lower Group

The teacher tells the story orally to this group, writing on the board the most important words as she mentions them.

Then the teacher and these children read together the story as given in the text. The teacher directs the silent reading, section by section, by such questions as "Did the Greeks live as our farmers do?"

Children read silently and answer orally. When they have read the entire story in this manner, they test themselves by the questions at the end of the story.

MORE DIFFICULT TEXTS

BARKER, DUNCALF, BACON, *Old Europe and Our Nation,* 72–77.
BEARD and BAGLEY, *Our Old World Background,* 47–50, 84–86.
BOURNE and BENTON, *Introductory American History,* 30–42.
BURNHAM, *Our Beginnings in Europe and America,* 54–57.
COULOMB, McKINLEY, WHITE, *What Europe Gave to America* 47–50.
GORDY, *American Beginnings in Europe,* 53–56, 63–68.
GREENWOOD, *Our Heritage from the Old World,* 78–80, 83–89, 92–94.
HALL, *Our Ancestors in Europe,* 29–51.
HALLECK and FRANTZ, *Our Nation's Heritage,* 52–62.
HARDING, *Old World Background to American History,* 25–28.
HAWLEY, *Adventures in Old World History,* 110–116.
NIDA, *Dawn of American History,* 41–46.
NIVER, *Old World Steps to American History,* 76–84.
SHERWOOD, *Our Country's Beginnings,* 20–26, 52–55.
SOUTHWORTH, *What the Old World Gave the New,* 24–31.
TAPPAN, *Our European Ancestors,* 25–28.
VOLLINTINE, *The American People and Their Old World Ancestors,* 103–116.
WICKHAM and PHILLIPS, *America's Heritage from the Long Ago,* 128–148, 150–152.
WOODBURN and HILL, *Historic Background of Our United States,* 71–81.

Easy Reading

EXTENSIVE READING

BEST, *Glorious Greece and Imperial Rome,* 78–86.
CORKE, *The World's Family,* 79–88.

READING FOR RECREATION

ANDREWS, *Ten Boys Who Lived on the Road from Long Ago to Now,* 45–78.
BAKER, *Stories of Old Greece and Rome.*

HALL, *Four Old Greeks.*
HILLYER, *Child's History of the World,* 79–88, 114–118.
HODGDON, *The Enchanted Past,* 166–169.
SCHWARTZ, *From Then till Now,* 95–137.

BALDWIN, *Old Greek Stories.*
COWLES, *Our Little Athenian Cousin of Long Ago.*
COWLES, *Our Little Spartan Cousin of Long Ago.*
HALL, *Buried Cities,* 94–157 (pictures).
HALL, *Men of Old Greece,* 11–87.
NIDA, *Inventions and Discoveries of Ancient Times,* 182–192.
PERKINS, *Spartan Twins.*

More Difficult Reading

EXTENSIVE READING

GUERBER, *Story of the Greeks,* 61–70, 77–81.
HAAREN and POLAND, *Famous Men of Greece,* 110–116, 117–122.
HARTMAN, *The World We Live in,* 103–105.
INGRAHAM, *Story of Democracy,* 41–67.
MACGREGOR, *Story of Greece,* 76–118.
MILLER, *Picturesque Tale of Progress,* III: 118–164.
O'NEILL, *World's Story,* 31–32.
RICHMOND, *Egypt, Greece, and Rome,* 122–133.
VAN LOON, *Story of Mankind,* 58–70.

READING FOR RECREATION

DAVIS, *A Day in Old Athens.*
LAMPREY, *Children of Ancient Greece.*
SCALES, *Boys of the Ages,* 21–40.
SNEDEKER, *Theras and His Town.*
STEARNS, *The Story of Music,* 8–13.
UPJOHN, *Friends in Strange Garments,* 14–21.
WITHINGTON, *Book of Athletics.*

The Discussion

Children answer the study-guide questions as completely as possible. If certain children in the group of independent readers are still reading rapidly but inaccurately, it may be necessary to transfer them to the lower group for training in study habits.

The teacher writes on the board the words *democracy, city-state, Olympic games.* Children discuss the meanings.

Multisensory Aids

Children and teacher talk over together the pictures in the text, pointing out features of historical and geographical importance. They locate Athens and Sparta on the map. On a physical map they point out the difference in the country surrounding the two.

AUDIO-VISUAL MATERIALS OBTAINABLE

Compton's Pictured Teaching Materials: *Ancient Greece and Rome,* Plates I, II, III, IV, VI; *Trade,* Plate IX, 2.
CYBULSKI. Greek and Roman History Pictures: 10, 14a, 14b, 16–18.
GALL-REBHANN. Charts: 9, 11, 12, 14, 16–17.
HOFFMANN-SCHMIDT. Pictures: 16.
Keystone Views: Greece: 72–76.
LEHMANN. Colored History Pictures: II, 5.
LEHMANN. History Pictures: L. H. 4.
MCKINLEY. Illustrated Topics for Ancient History: A 7.
MILLER. *Picturesque Tale of Progress,* III, 142–164.
Society for Visual Education. University Museum (Philadelphia): Greek Life, Greek Games.

General Activities

Creative Activities: Group and Individual, Correlated with Other Subjects or Voluntary Projects

The sand-table committee marks Athens and Sparta on the model.

A committee draws on a slated map of the Mediterranean world a map of the Greek colonies. (See Shepherd's *Historical Atlas*, 12.)

The class dramatizes a day in the life of a Spartan child; a day in the life of an Athenian child.[1]

A committee loads ships with the articles of Athenian commerce and puts them on the sand-table model.

The art teacher helps the class to make and decorate clay vases and jars like those of the Greeks.

Olympia and Mt. Olympus are marked on the sand table, to show that they were not the same.

The teacher of athletics helps the class to hold a series of Olympic games like those of the Greeks.

Volunteers write the diary of a Spartan boy and of an Athenian boy.

More Difficult Activities

Volunteers compare the training of the Spartan youth with that of the youth of Russia, Italy, and Germany today. They compare the school work of the Athenian boys with our school work today.

Volunteers show how Greek art beautified the common articles of daily use.

A volunteer explains the system of ostracism, and shows how the same word is used today.

The class makes a picture collection of the most recent world Olympic games.

With the help of the index, the children make a list of all the articles which have been used as money, and answer these questions: Why are coins the best of those mentioned so far? Does the world of today use anything else not mentioned so far?

The class finds out the difference between a democracy and a republic.

Application to Present-Day Conditions

Are Athens and Sparta in existence today? (See a map in a geography.)

Is Greece a democracy today? (See the latest World Almanac.) Can you find a picture of its ruler?

Point out on the map of the world some of the colonies belonging to nations of the present day.

What nations today are democracies? What nations are monarchies?

What does the expression *a Spartan life* mean when used of people today?

Do countries today allow foreigners to become citizens? What do they have to do?

Do people today have nicknames for money? [*Bucks, berries,* etc.]

Do you know any fraternities or sororities with Greek names?

[1] See *Ancient Athens Rebuilt and Relived*, Teacher's Lesson Unit Series, Teachers College, Columbia University.

Where did we get our word *gymnasium*? (See an unabridged dictionary.) Have you ever heard the expression *won his laurels*? What does it mean? From what word does our word *citizen* come?

Exercises in Reasoning

Why did Greek ideas spread through the Mediterranean world?

Why was the city-state a weakness in Greek unity? Is it easy for a very small state to remain independent? Why not?

What does self-government mean? Do you have it in your home? in your school? Do grown people have it in the United States? Does it mean that a man may do exactly as he pleases?

In what ways was the Spartan life a poor life?

Why did Athens become a trading city, while Sparta did not?

Why were the Greeks satisfied with such simple homes? To what kind of climate were such houses suited?

Do you think that Athens was a real democracy? Explain your answer.

What did the Greeks mean by "a sound mind in a sound body"? by "everything in moderation — nothing to excess"?

More Difficult Exercises in Reasoning

Make a list of the steps by which the Greek cities attained democracy. Name each of the forms of government in the list. [For example, *monarchy, oligarchy, democracy.*]

Members of the class commit to memory the Athenian oath, taken by the youth upon his being admitted to full citizenship.

The Greeks believed that no state should be so large that the citizens could not all come together in one place and hear one man speak. If they had had the radio, might their states have been larger? Why?

The people who own slaves usually consider themselves fortunate. Do you think slavery is good for the owner or for the slave? Explain fully.

Why did the Greeks take so much interest in their government?

Compare the Olympiad with a presidential administration.

Compare the amount of time which American citizens spend on the public business with the amount of time which the Greeks spent on the public business.

How do we know anything about how the Greeks spent their time so many years ago?

Compare the Greek city-states with the city-kingdoms of the Land of the Two Rivers.

Drill Games

Place names are best drilled upon at the map: *Athens, Sparta.*

Drill cards may be made as follows:

city-state	⟷	a self-governing city and the land immediately surrounding it
Olympic games	⟷	great contests held throughout the Greek world once in four years
democracy	⟷	government directly by the people

Testing

Tests of Understanding are given in Kelty's *How Our Civilization Began,* p. 134.

Tests of Reasoning and Skills. All these statements are true. Check that which gives the most important reason.

1. Sparta gave the world little art or literature. The chief reason was that   she was on a plain far from the sea.   her people did no ordinary work.   √ she was interested chiefly in matters of war.   her people spent little time at home.

2. The citizens of Athens knew a great deal about their own government. The chief reason was that   most of the citizens were well educated.   most of the citizens were very proud of their city.   each citizen fought in the army when his services were needed.   √ each citizen helped to make the laws and served as a judge.

3. Turn to a map of Greece. Check the following: Sparta was on the seacoast.   Yes [ ]   No [√]

Exercise in Organization. The teacher supplies the main headings for an outline of the story, and the class chooses a few subheadings for each.

More Difficult Tests

Mark the following as true or false:

True False

[√] [ ] **1.** The Greeks sent out colonies because they could not feed all their own people.

[ ] [√] **2.** The "country" of a Greek was the whole Greek peninsula.

[ ] [√] **3.** Greece was always a democracy.

[√] [ ] **4.** Sparta and Athens were independent cities.

[ ] [√] **5.** The Spartans did no farm work because they were lazy.

[ ] [√] **6.** A Spartan boy was given no education.

[√] [ ] **7.** Athens was a great trade center.

[ ] [√] **8.** The Athenians were the first people to use coins.

[√] [ ] **9.** The homes of most Athenians were poor and dark.

[ ] [√] **10.** The women of Athens were as well educated as those of Sparta.

[√] [ ] **11.** The Athenians spent much time on public business.

[√] [ ] **12.** Any Greek citizen might make a speech in the assembly.

[ ] [√] **13.** At the Olympic games all the contests were athletic contests.

STORY 3. THE FIRST CONTEST OF THE WEST WITH THE EAST

[1 Week]

Conversational Approach

"The history of the world is much like a many-ringed circus. What is your difficulty when you attend a circus with more than one ring?

"While we have been watching to see what the Greeks were doing farther west, we have lost sight of the East. Another great empire has grown up there, called Persia." The teacher shows its extent on the map.

"You notice that Persia had extended clear to the shores of the Aegean Sea. The Greek cities had sent out many colonies to this same region. What will probably happen now? But how could Persia get at Greece since she was a land power?

"Which should you expect to win if war broke out, the Greeks or Persia? Why? Our story today tells us about their great struggle."

Reading and Study

The Reading Periods

Independent Readers

TEXTS

BEEBY, *America's Roots in the Past*, 99–103.
CHAPMAN, *Stories of the Ancient Peoples*, 125–127.
CLARK-GORDY, *Early Story of Mankind*, 122–126.
CLARK-GORDY, *Westward toward America*, 129.
CORKE, *A Book of Ancient Peoples*, 119–129, 137–148 (hard).
KELTY, *How Our Civilization Began*, 135–140.
KNOWLTON and GERSON, *Our Beginnings in the Past*, 185–187.

Lower Group

The teacher tells the story orally to this group, writing on the board the most important words as she mentions them. Children practice the pronunciations.

Then the teacher and these children read together the story as given in the text. The teacher directs the silent reading, section by section, by such questions as "What was it that the Greeks wanted to keep?"

Children read silently and answer orally. When they have finished the entire story in this manner, they test themselves by the questions at the end of the story.

MORE DIFFICULT TEXTS

BARKER, DUNCALF, BACON, *Old Europe and Our Nation*, 81–89.
BOURNE and BENTON, *Introductory American History*, 15–21.
BURNHAM, *Our Beginnings in Europe and America*, 57–62.
COULOMB, McKINLEY, WHITE, *What Europe Gave to America*, 50–52.
GORDY, *American Beginnings in Europe*, 38–40, 47–51.
GREENWOOD, *Our Heritage from the Old World*, 80–83.
HALL, *Our Ancestors in Europe*, 53–59.
HALLECK and FRANTZ, *Our Nation's Heritage*, 62–65.
HARDING, *Old World Background to American History*, 29–38.
HAWLEY, *Adventures in Old World History*, 89–97.
NIDA, *Dawn of American History*, 37–41.
NIVER, *Old World Steps to American History*, 66–68, 84–91.
SHERWOOD, *Our Country's Beginnings*, 16–19.
SOUTHWORTH, *What the Old World Gave the New*, 32–35.
TAPPAN, *Our European Ancestors*, 17–18.
VOLLINTINE, *The American People and Their Old World Ancestors*, 117–125.
WOODBURN and HILL, *Historic Background of Our United States*, 83–95.

Easy Reading

More Difficult Reading

The Discussion

Children answer the study-guide questions as fully as possible. Those who have read additional material are given an opportunity to present their contributions. They are encouraged to remember the name of the book in which they found it.

The teacher writes on the board the word *naval*. Children discuss the meaning.

Multisensory Aids

Children and teacher talk over together the pictures in the text, pointing out the features of geographical and historical importance. They turn to a map of the ancient world and show the Persian Empire. "What is Asia Minor? Why do you suppose it was given that name? Find one of the Persian cities. Read the key and explain it. Trace the route of Darius on this map; on a large wall map. Show Marathon. Trace the two routes of Xerxes — by sea and by land — on this map and on a large wall map. Show Thermopylae and Salamis."

AUDIO-VISUAL MATERIALS OBTAINABLE

CYBULSKI. Greek and Roman History Pictures : 4, 9.

HOFFMANN-SCHMIDT. Pictures : 1.

Keystone Views : Greece, 81–83, 139, 172–173.

LEHMANN. Colored History Pictures : L. H. 101.

LOHMEYER. History Pictures : 5.

McKINLEY. Illustrated Topics for Ancient History : A 6, 7.

MILLER. *Picturesque Tale of Progress*, III, 165–198.

University of Chicago Oriental Institute Motion Picture : The Human Adventure (part on Persia).

Music. Play the "Largo" from Handel's *Xerxes*; explain that it was written originally in praise of a tree in Xerxes' garden.

General Activities

Creative Activities: Group and Individual, Correlated with Other Subjects or Voluntary Projects

A volunteer committee models the theater of war in the sand table and stretches strings of colored yarn to trace all the routes mentioned. The scenes of battles are marked.

The class meets as the assembly of a Greek city and decides whether or not to oppose the Persian advance. Speeches are given on both sides.

The teacher reads to the class Browning's poem "Pheidippides."

Volunteers may wish to design a headpiece for the story.

Volunteers write poems on the defense at Thermopylae. Other volunteers may set the poems to music.

Each child makes a map of the Persian Wars.

The class continues the time line.

More Difficult Activities

A volunteer tells of "the law of the Medes and Persians which changeth not."

A volunteer draws on the slated map a map of the Persian Empire at its greatest extent. (See Shepherd's *Historical Atlas*, 8.)

A volunteer gives an imaginative speech describing the battle of Marathon.

The teacher reads to the class Tennyson's "Charge of the Light Brigade," which is about a battle that took place not far from Thermopylae. The class compares the two battles.

A volunteer looks up in a dictionary the derivation of *Thermopylae*.

A volunteer carves from soap a memorial of Thermopylae.

The teacher reads to the class selections from Webster's *Readings in Ancient History* (14–16, 17–18, 23–24, 72–73).

Application to Present-Day Conditions

Is there a country called Persia today? [*Iran.*] Under what form of government is it? (See World Almanac.) Can you find the name of the present ruler?

Does it make any difference to you personally whether the Greeks won or the Persians? How?

What other possible contest may there be between the East and the West in your lifetime? [*Japan versus United States or Great Britain.*]

Why is a long-distance race called a marathon?

Do we have any words today containing the root *therm*, meaning "heat"?

Have you ever heard the saying "Westward the star of empire takes its way"? Has history proved this to be true?

Exercises in Reasoning

Was the act of the Persian king Cyrus in freeing the Jews from their Babylonian captivity the act of a cruel tyrant?

Do you think the Greeks were right to wage the Persian Wars?

Can you describe how a bridge of boats could be built?

How did a naval battle of those days differ from a naval battle of today?

More Difficult Exercises in Reasoning

Why do the dates we have studied since the beginnings of Egypt seem to be going backward?

Do you think Themistocles was wise in telling the Athenians to give up their city to the Persians? Why?

Did Athens or Sparta do more to save Greece from the Persians?

Why has the battle of Marathon been called one of the fifteen decisive battles of the world?

Do you think the Spartans were foolish to remain at Thermopylae when they were hopelessly outnumbered?

Drill Games

Place names are best drilled upon at the map: *Persia, Asia Minor, Marathon, Thermopylae, Salamis.*

Drill cards may be made as follows:

naval	⟷	having to do with ships and the navy
Miltiades	⟷	the Athenian commander at the battle of Marathon
490 B.C.	⟷	date of the battle of Marathon
Darius	⟷	leader of the first Persian invasion of Greece
Pheidippides	⟷	the runner sent to ask help from Sparta before the battle of Marathon
480 B.C.	⟷	date of the battle of Salamis
Leonidas	⟷	leader of the little Spartan band at Thermopylae
Themistocles	⟷	leader of the Athenians who believed that the Persians could be beaten only on the sea
Xerxes	⟷	the Persian king who was beaten at Salamis

Children drill one another by twos.

Testing

Tests of Understanding are given in Kelty's *How Our Civilization Began,* p. 140.

Tests of Reasoning and Skills

1. Make a list of the battles of the Persian Wars in the order in which they occurred.

2. Put the letter *G* before the names of Greeks and the letter *P* before the names of Persians in the following list:

[G] Miltiades   [G] Pheidippides   [G] Themistocles
[P] Darius   [G] Leonidas   [P] Xerxes

3. Match these two columns:

a. 480 B.C.   [b] battle of Marathon
b. 490 B.C.   [a] battle of Salamis

4. Turn to a map of the Persian Wars. Which Persian king attacked Greece by the shortest route? _ _ _[*Darius*.]_ _ _

Exercise in Organization. Children attempt to make their own outline of the story. The class appraises the results.

More Difficult Tests

1. The battle of Salamis ended the Persian Wars because   the Persians found the Greeks were better fighters than they were.   √ the Persians could not bring food and supplies from home without their ships.   the Greeks had many more soldiers that they had not yet called upon.   the Greek ships had proved themselves better than the Persian ships.

2. Most of our histories of the Persian Wars have come down to us from the Greeks. Which people do they therefore tell us were the braver? The Greeks [√]   The Persians [ ]

3. Can you make a sentence telling why it was a good thing for the world that the Greeks won? _ _ _ _ _ _

STORY 4. ATHENS IN ITS DAYS OF GLORY   [*2 Weeks*

Conversational Approach

"What happened to the city of Athens in our last story? Now we must read about how it was built up again. What had been the chief business of Athens? [*Trading*.] Trading usually makes a city or country rich. Why do you suppose the rich people of Athens would be willing to spend great sums for their city?

"Our story today tells how Athens became probably the most beautiful city the world has ever seen."

Reading and Study

The Reading Periods (Greek Buildings)

Independent Readers

TEXTS

BEEBY, *America's Roots in the Past*, 124–125.
CHAPMAN, *Stories of the Ancient Peoples*, 136–141.
CLARK-GORDY, *Early Story of Mankind*, 157–163.
CLARK-GORDY, *Westward toward America*, 102–109.
CORKE, *A Book of Ancient Peoples*, 148–161 (hard).
KELTY, *How Our Civilization Began*, 141–146.
KNOWLTON and GERSON, *Our Beginnings in the Past*, 192–197.

Lower Group

The teacher and this group read together the story as given in the text. The teacher directs the silent reading, section by section, by such questions as "Who was the new leader in Athens?"

Children read silently and answer orally. When they have read the assigned pages in this manner, they test themselves by the study-guide questions at the end of the story.

The Discussion

Children answer the study-guide questions as completely as possible.

The teacher writes on the board the words *Acropolis, Parthenon*. Children discuss the significance.

The Reading Periods (Greek Culture)

Independent Readers

TEXTS

CLARK-GORDY, *Westward toward America,* 123–129.
KELTY, *How Our Civilization Began,* 146–150.
KNOWLTON and GERSON, *Our Beginnings in the Past,* 197–202.

Lower Group

The teacher and this group read together the rest of the story as given in the text. The teacher directs the silent reading, section by section, by such questions as "What history stories did Herodotus write?"

Children read silently and answer orally. When they have finished the entire story in this manner, they test themselves by the rest of the questions at the end of the story.

The Discussion

Children answer the remaining study-guide questions as fully as possible. The teacher writes on the board the words *the Father of History, the Hippocratic oath, water clock.* Children discuss the significance.

MORE DIFFICULT TEXTS

BARKER, DUNCALF, BACON, *Old Europe and Our Nation,* 99–112.
BEARD and BAGLEY, *Our Old World Background,* 79–80, 82–84, 89–90.
BOURNE and BENTON, *Introductory American History,* 22–30.
BURNHAM, *Our Beginnings in Europe and America,* 62–72.
COULOMB, McKINLEY, WHITE, *What Europe Gave to America,* 39–41, 45–47, 55–72.
GORDY, *American Beginnings in Europe,* 56–62, 68–71.
GREENWOOD, *Our Heritage from the Old World,* 104–117.
HALL, *Our Ancestors in Europe,* 21–29, 51–52, 59–61.
HALLECK and FRANTZ, *Our Nation's Heritage,* 75–89.
HARDING, *Old World Background to American History,* 39–46.
HAWLEY, *Adventures in Old World History,* 101–110, 116–118.
NIDA, *Dawn of American History,* 48–54, 56–67.
NIVER, *Old World Steps to American History,* 94–101.
SHERWOOD, *Our Country's Beginnings,* 20–50.
SOUTHWORTH, *What the Old World Gave the New,* 35–39.
TAPPAN, *Our European Ancestors,* 19–24, 29–34.
WICKHAM and PHILLIPS, *America's Heritage from the Long Ago,* 152–163.
WOODBURN and HILL, *Historic Background of Our United States,* 97–114.

Easy Reading

EXTENSIVE READING

BEST, *Glorious Greece and Imperial Rome,* 101–110.
COFFMAN, *Child's Story of the Human Race,* 121–130.
HALL, *Four Old Greeks.*
HILLYER, *Child's History of the World,* 143–155.
HODGDON, *The Enchanted Past,* 171–183.

READING FOR RECREATION

HALL, *Men of Old Greece,* 171–217, 221–263.
NIDA, *Inventions and Discoveries of Ancient Times,* 202–213.

More Difficult Reading

EXTENSIVE READING

BAIKIE, *Ancient Greece*, 23–39.
BURNHAM, *Hero Tales from History*, 15–19.
GUERBER, *Story of the Greeks*, 136–138, 146–150, 157–163, 173–180.
HAAREN and POLAND, *Famous Men of Greece*, 163–172, 186–195.
HARTMAN, *The World We Live in*, chap. vii.
ILIN, *What Time Is It?* 19–20, 27–39.
KUMMER, *First Days of History*.
KUMMER, *First Days of Knowledge*, 68–83, 185–188.
KUMMER, *First Days of Man*.
LANSING, *Man's Long Climb*, 121–127.
MACGREGOR, *Story of Greece*, 237–239.
MILLER, *Picturesque Tale of Progress*, III: 199–257.
POWER, *Great People of the Past*, 51–59.
RICHMOND, *Egypt, Greece, Rome*, 153–162.
Story of Our Calendar (American Council on Education), 12–13.
Story of Numbers (American Council on Education), 15.
Story of Weights and Measures (American Council on Education), 26.
Story of Writing (American Council on Education), 59–60.
Telling Time (American Council on Education), 8–11, 18–23.
VAN LOON, *Story of Mankind*, 71–73.

READING FOR RECREATION

CHURCH, *Crown of Pine*.
HAGEDORN, *Book of Courage*, 1–9.
LAMPREY, *Children of Ancient Greece*.
ROBINSON, *The Days of Alkibiades*.
SCALES, *Boys of the Ages*, 21–41.
STUART, *The Boy through the Ages*.
SYRETT, *Rachel and the Seven Wonders*, 146–172.

Multisensory Aids

Children and teacher talk over together the pictures in the text, pointing out features of geographical or historical importance.

AUDIO-VISUAL MATERIALS OBTAINABLE

Compton's Pictured Teaching Materials: *Ancient Greece and Rome*, Plates I, V.
CYBULSKI. Greek and Roman History Pictures: 10, 12–14, 16–18.
Denoyer-Geppert Company, Chicago. Plaster models illustrating the Greek orders of architecture.
GALL-REBHANN. Charts: 1–3, 5–7, 28, 32.
HOFFMANN-SCHMIDT. Pictures: 5, 14, 16, 17.
International Educational Pictures: Ancient Greece, Athens, Eternal Athens, Greece.
JÖNDL. Ancient History Charts: Greece.
LANGL. Colored History Pictures: Greece, 16–20.
LEHMANN. Colored History Pictures: II, 4, 5.
LEHMANN. Geography Pictures: L. G. 18.
LEHMANN. History Pictures: L. H. 3, 4, 105, 110, 114, 116, 117.
McKINLEY. Illustrated Topics for Ancient History: A 8–10, 14, 15.
MILLER. *Picturesque Tale of Progress*, III, 199–257.
Society for Visual Education. University Museum (Philadelphia): Development of Greek Sculpture; Development of Greek Vase-Painting.
Society for Visual Education (BRIGGS). Golden Age of Greece.
Society for Visual Education (MacHARG). Ancient Athens.

Music. Play selections from the opera *Alceste* (Gluck).

General Activities

Creative Activities: Group and Individual, Correlated with Other Subjects or Voluntary Projects

A committee models the Acropolis on the sand table.

The class divides into committees, each of which reads about one of the buildings on the Acropolis. They report to the class, showing pictures of their building. (See an encyclopedia.)

Children choose one of the orders of capitals about which to read — Doric, Ionic, Corinthian. They show pictures to the class and draw copies.

Volunteers report on Ictinus, Phidias, Praxiteles.

Volunteers carve Greek capitals or entire Greek buildings from soap.

The class makes a visit to the local museum to see the exhibits connected with Greek culture.

The teacher reads some of the most interesting selections from Herodotus.

A visitor to modern Athens describes it to the class.

More Difficult Activities

Volunteers construct models of the buildings to place on the sand table.

Volunteers make carvings for the pediment of the Parthenon.

Committees report to the class on the Elgin marbles. (Notice the pronunciation: hard g as in go.)

What is Pentelic marble? Find the names of some of the other fine marbles of the world.

A volunteer demonstrates to the class how to play the flute. Another demonstrates how to play the harp.

The science teacher gives a lesson on the pitch of musical notes, showing how the pitch is changed. If there is no science teacher, perhaps a local piano-tuner will perform this service.

The gymnasium teacher teaches the class a Greek dance.

The teacher shows the class some of the figures from a textbook in geometry and explains that the Greeks developed this science.

A volunteer demonstrates a water clock. Another draws the plan of a Greek house.

Application to Present-Day Conditions

The children make lists of buildings in the community which use Doric columns; Ionic columns; Corinthian columns.

Did the average Greek know more or less about music than the average American does?

Would the average American citizen be a good judge of a play written in poetry?

Can poor people attend the theater in America today? Could they attend in Greece? Why? [*The state gave the tickets.*]

Where did the modern world get its ideas about building stadiums?

Why do some older people today call geometry Euclid?

Do any places in the United States today have out-of-door Greek theaters?

Are there any places in your city which the Athenians would have beautified?

Exercises in Reasoning

Why was the Acropolis a good place for public buildings?

Where did the Greeks get splendid models for their statues of gods? (What is a model?)

Americans listen to music over the radio. The Greeks made their own music. Which requires more skill?

The Greeks believed that what was good for all the citizens was better than what was good for only a few. Contrast this idea with the ideas of the other people about whom you have read.

Was Columbus the first person who believed that the world is round?

More Difficult Exercises in Reasoning

Why were the artists and the craftsmen ready to work together in the building of the city? Do they work together today?

Why were the public buildings so beautiful when the private homes were so simple?

Why do we know little about Greek paintings?

Can you find out how the Greek scholars discovered the true size of the earth?

Why should you have expected the Greeks to make great advances in science? [*They thought for themselves.*] Why could they go no farther without telescopes and microscopes?

What did a great scientist [1] mean when he said that western Europe might never have become a great industrial and scientific civilization if it had not been given the ideas of the Greeks?

How did the climate and scenery help to make the Greeks lovers of beauty?

Drill Games

Association cards may be made as follows:

Acropolis	↔	the flat-topped hill on which were the most beautiful buildings of Athens
Parthenon	↔	the great temple of Athena
"the Father of History"	↔	a name given to Herodotus
Pericles	↔	the leader who rebuilt Athens
the Hippocratic oath	↔	a promise taken by doctors about their duty
Herodotus	↔	the first Greek historian
water clock	↔	an invention for telling time, used by the Greeks
Phidias	↔	one of the greatest Greek sculptors
Socrates	↔	the first of the great Greek "wise men"
Ictinus	↔	the architect who built the Parthenon

Children drill themselves on their own difficulties.

[1] Boas, *Mind of Primitive Man.*

Testing

Tests of Understanding are given in Kelty's *How Our Civilization Began*, p. 151.

Tests of Reasoning and Skills. Complete the following sentences:

1. Ictinus was the man who _ _ _ _ _ _.
2. Pericles was the man who _ _ _ _ _ _.
3. Herodotus was the man who _ _ _ _ _ _.
4. Phidias was the man who _ _ _ _ _ _.
5. The Parthenon was the _ _ _ _ _ _.
6. On what pages in your book can you find out about the science of the Greeks? _ _ _ _ _ _ Where did you look? _ _ _[*In the index, under* Science.] _ _ _.

Exercise in Organization. Children copy the topic headings and give an oral summary of each heading.

More Difficult Tests

Complete the following sentences:

1. The Greek temples were small because _ _ _ [*Greeks worshiped individually*]_ _ _.
2. The Greeks were good scientists because _ _ _[*their minds were free*]_ _ _.
3. The Greeks made the alphabet larger by _ _ _[*adding vowels*]_ _ _.

STORY 5. ALEXANDER AND THE DOWNFALL OF GREECE [*1 Week*

Conversational Approach

"Is Greece one of the great powers of the world today? What do you suppose could have happened to her, after she had had such a good beginning? Could the very independence of the small city-states have had anything to do with their downfall?

"After their downfall another great soldier tried to conquer the world. Name the men about whom we have already read who made the same attempt. Did they succeed? This man did not succeed, either, but he came nearer to success than any other one man has ever come. Does anyone know his name?"

Reading and Study

The Reading Periods

Independent Readers

TEXTS

BEEBY, *America's Roots in the Past*, 122–124.
CHAPMAN, *Stories of the Ancient Peoples*, 127–129.
CLARK-GORDY, *Early Story of Mankind*, 164–166.

Lower Group

The teacher tells the story orally to this group, writing on the board the most important words as she mentions them. Children practice the pronunciations.

Then the teacher and these children read together the story as given in the text.

CLARK-GORDY, *Westward toward America*, 130–132.

CORKE, *A Book of Ancient Peoples*, 163–178 (hard).

KELTY, *How Our Civilization Began*, 152–160.

The teacher directs the silent reading, section by section, by such questions as "What was one of the great evils of Greek life?"

Children read silently and answer orally. When they have read the entire story in this manner, they test themselves by the questions at the end of the story.

OTHER BOOKS

TERRY, *History Stories of Other Lands*, I: 31–34.

WAYLAND, *History Stories for Primary Grades*, 59–62.

MORE DIFFICULT TEXTS

BARKER, DUNCALF, BACON, *Old Europe and Our Nation*, 89–95.

BOURNE and BENTON, *Introductory American History*, 42–44.

BURNHAM, *Our Beginnings in Europe and America*, 72–73.

COULOMB, McKINLEY, WHITE, *What Europe Gave to America*, 52–54.

GORDY, *American Beginnings in Europe*, 72–78.

GREENWOOD, *Our Heritage from the Old World*, 94–103.

HALL, *Our Ancestors in Europe*, 59–73.

HALLECK and FRANTZ, *Our Nation's Heritage*, 66–70.

HARDING, *Old World Background to American History*, 47–56.

HAWLEY, *Adventures in Old World History*, 126–149.

NIDA, *Dawn of American History*, 69–72.

NIVER, *Old World Steps to American History*, 91–94, 98–106.

SHERWOOD, *Our Country's Beginnings*, 55–62.

TAPPAN, *Our European Ancestors*, 34–35.

VOLLINTINE, *The American People and their Old World Ancestors*, 125–132.

WOODBURN and HILL, *Historic Background of Our United States*, 114–121.

Easy Reading

EXTENSIVE READING

BEST, *Glorious Greece and Imperial Rome*, 111–123.

COFFMAN, *Child's Story of the Human Race*, 130–134.

COLLINS and HALE, *Hero Stories for Children*, 79–95.

HILLYER, *Child's History of the World*, 156–167.

HODGDON, *The Enchanted Past*, 184–185.

READING FOR RECREATION

COWLES, *Our Little Macedonian Cousin of Long Ago.*

More Difficult Reading

EXTENSIVE READING

BURNHAM, *Hero Tales from History*, 20–24.

GUERBER, *Story of the Greeks*, 217–255.

HAAREN and POLAND, *Famous Men of Greece*, 210–236.

MACGREGOR, *Story of Greece*, 300–348.

MARSHALL, *Readings in the Story of Human Progress*, 114–118.

MILLER, *Picturesque Tale of Progress*, III: 258–302.

POWER, *Great People of the Past*, 61–71.

TAPPAN, *Old World Hero Stories*, 67–75.

VAN LOON, *Story of Mankind*, 81–84.

READING FOR RECREATION

CHURCH, *A Young Macedonian in the Army of Alexander the Great.*

SNEDEKER, *Perilous Seat.*

SYRETT, *Rachel and the Seven Wonders*, 129–145.

The Discussion

Children answer the study-guide questions as completely as possible. The teacher continues to study their responses, to ascertain misapprehensions.

The teacher writes on the board the words *league, orator, citizen.* Children discuss the meanings.

Multisensory Aids

Children and teacher talk over together the pictures in the text, pointing out features of geographical and historical significance.

AUDIO-VISUAL MATERIALS OBTAINABLE

HOFFMANN-SCHMIDT. Pictures: 11.
JÖNDL. Ancient History Charts: 7.
LEHMANN. Colored History Pictures: II, 111.
LEHMANN. History Pictures: L. H. 111.
McKINLEY. Illustrated Topics for Ancient History: A 11, 12, 13.
MILLER. *Picturesque Tale of Progress,* III, 258–302.
Society for Visual Education. Picturol: Intimate Glimpses of Macedonia.
Society for Visual Education (BRIGGS). Graeco-Oriental World.
Society for Visual Education (MUIR). Ancient Greece — 400 B.C.–86 B.C.

Music. Play selections from Beethoven's *Ruins of Athens* and Massenet's opera *Thaïs.*

General Activities

Creative Activities: Group and Individual, Correlated with Other Subjects or Voluntary Projects

Volunteers give speeches before the Greek assembly denouncing the evils in Greek life.

The teacher reads to the children a short passage from Thucydides describing the Peloponnesian Wars.

A volunteer committee models Alexander's empire in the sand table. (Shepherd's *Historical Atlas,* 18–19.)

Volunteers report on the education of the youth Alexander by the scholar Aristotle.

A volunteer tells the story of Alexander's horse, Bucephalus.

A volunteer reports on the famous Alexandrian library.

The class continues the time line.

More Difficult Activities

The class dramatizes the process by which a foreigner becomes a citizen of the United States. (See *Naturalization* in a children's encyclopedia.)

Each child makes a map of Alexander's empire, tracing on it the routes of Alexander's army. A volunteer prints on his map the names of all the modern countries included.

Volunteers report on the empires of India and China at the time of Alexander. (See a children's encyclopedia.)

A volunteer gives one of Demosthenes' speeches warning the Greek cities against Philip.

A committee studies the organization of Alexander's army.

Committees construct the breakwaters and jetties of Pharos. (See Miller's *Picturesque Tale of Progress*, II, 12.)

Application to Present-Day Conditions

Do the different nations quarrel among themselves today much as the Greek city-states quarreled among themselves?

Is there slavery anywhere in the world today?

Are voters today likely to follow a man who can make a stirring speech? What is a demagogue? (See unabridged dictionary.) What can be done to lessen the influence of such men?

Have any of the attempts to conquer the world been successful in the past? Are such attempts more or less likely to succeed today?

Have you ever heard the expression "weeping for more worlds to conquer"? What does it mean?

Sometimes Greek coins are found nowadays in the heart of China. Can you account for this?

Can you name any orators of the present day?

What countries today include Macedon?

Exercises in Reasoning

Should foreigners be allowed to become citizens? Give reasons for and against.

Why is choosing officers by lot a poor method?

Do people have to give up some of their own independence if they wish to work with others? Why?

Did Alexander really "conquer the world"?

How did Alexander think that he was going to bring about a joining of Greek civilization with the civilization of the East?

Why do some of the ancient statues of India have Greek features?

Why is Alexander called a Greek, when he came from Macedon?

Did Alexander deserve his title ".the Great"?

More Difficult Exercises in Reasoning

Do you think that persons who are not citizens should have to pay taxes? Should they be forced to fight in the army?

Do the men in a country have to suffer when the women are poorly educated? [*Mothers cannot help educate their own sons.*]

People often say that choosing officers by lot is "democratic." What do they mean? Do you think this is a good argument?

What happened to Alexander's empire after his death? How does this go to show the fatal weakness of a dictatorship?

Do you think Alexander's life work accomplished any good results?

Why was Alexander able to conquer the Persians, whereas the Persians had not been able to conquer the Greeks?

Compare Jesus and Alexander, each of whom died at the age of thirty-three. Which one "conquered the world" to a greater degree? How?

Drill Games

Place names are best drilled upon at the map: *Macedon, Alexandria.*
Drill cards are made as follows:

league	↔	a union among countries
333 B.C.	↔	date when Alexander conquered the Persians
orator	↔	a great speechmaker
Alexander the Great	↔	the first man to conquer a large part of the then-known Western world
citizen	↔	a person who owes a country loyalty and is bound by its laws
Demosthenes	↔	one of the greatest of the ancient Greek orators
Thucydides	↔	the Greek historian who wrote about the wars between the city-states

Children drill one another in preparation for class games.

Testing

Tests of Understanding are suggested in Kelty's *How Our Civilization Began,*
p. 160.

Tests of Reasoning and Skills. Fill the blanks with the right words:

1. Athens thought that she could use the money of the other cities because
they were in the same ___[*league*]___ with her.

2. The Greek men did not have to do much work because they had
___[*slaves*]___.

3. The Macedonian army was the first to ___[*ride horses*]___ in battle.

4. Underline the right word or words: The foreigners who made their resi-
dence at Athens   were   were not   all allowed to become citizens.

5. List the titles of the stories in this unit. Where did you find them?
___[*In the table of contents.*]___

Exercise in Organization. Children copy the topic headings and give a brief
summary of each heading.

More Difficult Tests

Check the best answer:

1. The main reason why the king of Macedon was able to conquer the
Greek cities was that   his army was so much better than theirs.   his
navy was so much better than theirs.   √ the city-states would not work
together.   the city-states would not tax their people.

2. The best thing which Alexander did for the East was   to conquer the
Persians.   √ to bring in Greek ideas.   to have his soldiers marry Persians.
to march as far as India.

3. Fill in the blank with the right word: Most of our histories represent
Alexander as a very great man partly because they come down to us from
the ___[*Greeks*]___.

Tests on the Entire Unit

Test of Place Sense. Pass double-sized maps of the Mediterranean World, showing water bodies in color. Give the following directions:

Write a capital *A* in the Aegean Sea.
Put the initials *A. M.* in Asia Minor.
Write the word *Greece* in the proper place.
Put the letter *T* where Troy was.
Make a circle where Athens is.
Put a cross (**X**) where Sparta was.
Write the word *Persia* in the proper place.
Put the letter *M* in Macedon.
Put the letters *Al* where Alexandria is.

Tests of Time Sense. Pass mimeographed sheets of the following:

I. In the following exercises put the figure *1* before that which was first in time, and the figure *2* before that which was later:

1. [__*2*__] the war with Persia
[__*1*__] the war with Troy

2. [__*1*__] the writing of the Iliad
[__*2*__] the writings of Herodotus

3. [__*1*__] kings in Athens
[__*2*__] Athens a democracy

4. [__*2*__] Alexander invaded Persia
[__*1*__] Xerxes invaded Greece

5. [__*1*__] the building of Sparta
[__*2*__] the building of Alexandria

6. [__*2*__] the time of Pericles
[__*1*__] the time of Homer

II. Here is a list of dates. Put each one in the right blank in the sentences below: 333 B.C.   490 B.C.   480 B.C.

1. The battle of Marathon took place in _____.

2. Alexander conquered the Persians in _____.

3. The battle of Salamis took place in _____.

Tests on Persons. **I.** Here is a list of persons. Put each name in the right blank in the sentences below:

Zeus	Apollo	Demosthenes
Miltiades	Pheidippides	Athena
Pericles	Herodotus	Xerxes
Thucydides		

1. The man who wrote the history of the wars between the city-states was _____.

2. The goddess of wisdom was _____.

3. _____ was the man who ran from Athens to Sparta for help before the battle of Marathon.

4. _____ was a great orator who urged the Greeks to unite against the Macedonians.

5. The man who wrote the history of the Persian Wars was _____.

6. _____ was the great statesman who built up Athens after the Persian Wars.

7. The sun-god was _____.

8. _ _ _ _ _ _ was the Greek leader at Marathon.

9. The Persian king who was beaten at Salamis was _ _ _ _ _ _.

10. The chief of all the gods was _ _ _ _ _ _.

II. Here is another list. Do the same.

| Phidias | Homer | Socrates | Leonidas |
| Alexander | Themistocles | Ictinus | |

1. The leader who wanted the Athenians to fight a naval war against Xerxes was _ _ _ _ _ _.

2. _ _ _ _ _ _ was the architect who built the Parthenon.

3. The blind poet who is supposed to have written the Iliad and the Odyssey was _ _ _ _ _ _.

4. _ _ _ _ _ _ was the first of the great Greek "wise men."

5. One of the greatest of the Greek sculptors was _ _ _ _ _ _.

6. The man who came nearest to conquering the world was _ _ _ _ _ _.

7. The Spartan leader at Thermopylae was _ _ _ _ _ _.

Tests on Historical Terms. I. Here is a list of terms used. Put each one in the right blank in the sentences below:

chiton	Acropolis	Mt. Olympus	Odyssey
city-state	Hippocratic oath	Olympic games	orator
naval	league		

1. The _ _ _ _ _ _ was a hill in Athens on which the temples were built.

2. The outer robe of the Greeks was called the _ _ _ _ _ _.

3. The great contests held once in four years were the _ _ _ _ _ _.

4. _ _ _ _ _ _ was the home of the gods.

5. A man who can make moving speeches is an _ _ _ _ _ _.

6. The _ _ _ _ _ _ is a poem about the wanderings of a Greek hero after the fall of Troy.

7. Anything having to do with ships is called _ _ _ _ _ _.

8. A _ _ _ _ _ _ is a city which rules itself.

9. The _ _ _ _ _ _ was a promise taken by doctors.

10. A _ _ _ _ _ _ is a union of different countries or states.

II. Here is another list. Do the same.

Iliad	Hercules	citizen	Hera
democracy	Hades	Poseidon	water clock
Parthenon	Aphrodite	"Father of History"	Helen

1. The goddess of love and beauty was _ _ _ _ _ _.

2. A name given to Herodotus is _ _ _ _ _ _.

3. The _ _ _ _ _ _ was a Greek means of telling time.

4. A person who owes obedience and loyalty to a country is a _ _ _ _ _ _.

5. The _ _ _ _ _ _ is a poem describing the Trojan War.

6. _____ was the god of the world of the dead.

7. The strong man about whom the Greeks told many stories was _____.

8. The wife of the god Zeus was _____.

9. _____ was the god of the sea.

10. The woman whose beauty caused the Trojan War was _____.

11. _____ means "government of the people, by the people, for the people."

12. The _____ was the great temple of Athens.

Test on Comprehension

Check the best answer:

1. The Greeks differed from earlier people because they dared to   fight their enemies.   sail to far-away lands.   fight the Persians.   √ think for themselves.

2. The Greeks sent out colonies in order to   be able to take more lands.   √ be able to feed all their people.   spread the glory of Greece. get rid of troublesome young people.

3. The Greeks fought Persia in order to   √ keep their free ways of living.   keep their free trade in the Mediterranean.   win the lands of the Persians.   win glory for their armies.

4. The Greek cities could not stand against Macedon because they would not   tax their people.   raise an army.   √ stand together.   give everyone the right to vote.

5. The early Greeks sailed east instead of west because they   √ could go from one island to another.   could speak the language of the East. were afraid of Rome.   were afraid of the western seas.

6. The form of government of later Athens was   a kingdom.   an oligarchy.   √ a democracy.   a republic.

7. The Persians could not fight after their navy was beaten because   their armies could not fight on land.   their armies had learned to fear the Greeks. their ships were poorer than the Greek ships.   √ their ships could no longer bring them supplies.

8. We should know about the Greek temples because   they were the most beautiful in the world.   √ many of our buildings have been copied from them.   they were much larger than our buildings.   none of them are left today.

9. Citizens in Greek cities were   all persons living in the cities.   only those persons who were born in the cities.   √ only those people whose families had lived there for many years.   all persons who wanted to become citizens.

10. The Greek religion was not hard to live up to because   the gods were only images of stone.   the Greeks did not believe in their gods. they were religious only on Sundays.   √ the gods were much like ordinary people.

11. Athens did more for the world than Sparta because ✓ Athens gave the world more ideas. Athens traded with places far away. Sparta's soldiers were not so good. Sparta engaged mainly in farming.

12. Alexander's empire fell to pieces after his death because he had made no plans for it. ✓ it had depended on him alone. it was too large. he had left no son to rule it.

13. What is the title of the unit which you have just completed? _ _ _ _ _ _

Are any children now ready to be transferred from the lower group to the group of independent readers?

UNIT FOUR · *The Romans teach the World about Law*

[*6 Weeks*

STORY 1. THE BEGINNINGS OF ROME   [*1 Week*

Conversational Approach

"Again we must go back to our idea of a three-ringed circus. While we have been busy following 'the glory that was Greece,' another country has been growing strong."

Children examine a physical map of Italy to decide in what part the early settlements might be made. They notice the location of the mountain ranges, which make Greece and Italy stand "back to back" instead of facing each other. "Do you think these two will become acquainted very early? Why not?

"As in many other cases, there is a *story* about how the settlements began, and there are quite different *facts* about the beginning. Our new history lesson tells us both the facts and the tale."

Reading and Study

The Reading Periods

Independent Readers

This group reads the entire story through. They then test their understanding by the study-guide questions furnished by the teacher or by the text.

TEXTS

BEEBY, *America's Roots in the Past*, 127–133, 149–151.

Lower Group

The teacher tells the story orally to this group, writing on the board the most important new words as she mentions them. Children practice the pronunciations.

Then the teacher and these children read together the story as given in the text. The teacher directs the silent reading,

CHAPMAN, *Stories of the Ancient Peoples*, 143–147.

CLARK-GORDY, *Early Story of Mankind*, 169.

CLARK-GORDY, *Westward toward America*, 135–139.

CORKE, *A Book of Ancient Peoples*, 110–119 (hard).

KELTY, *How Our Civilization Began*, 163–170.

KNOWLTON and GERSON, *Our Beginnings in the Past*, 207–210.

section by section, by such questions as "From what direction did the first settlers come?"

Children read silently and answer orally. When they have read the entire story in this manner, they test themselves by the questions at the end of the story.

OTHER BOOKS

BALDWIN, *Fifty Famous Stories Retold*, 76–81.

BALDWIN, *Thirty More Famous Stories Retold*, 177–196.

TERRY, *History Stories of Other Lands*, I: 13–30; II: 9–32.

MORE DIFFICULT TEXTS

BARKER, DUNCALF, BACON, *Old Europe and Our Nation*, 115–120.

BEARD and BAGLEY, *Our Old World Background*, 51–56.

BOURNE and BENTON, *Introductory American History*, 46–54.

BURNHAM, *Our Beginnings in Europe and America*, 76–82.

COULOMB, McKINLEY, WHITE, *What Europe Gave to America*, 75–80.

GORDY, *American Beginnings in Europe*, 81–85.

GREENWOOD, *Our Heritage from the Old World*, 120–132.

HALL, *Our Ancestors in Europe*, 74–77.

HALLECK and FRANTZ, *Our Nation's Heritage*, 91–94.

HARDING, *Old World Background to American History*, 57–66.

HAWLEY, *Adventures in Old World History*, 153–163.

NIVER, *Old World Steps to American History*, 107–119.

SHERWOOD, *Our Country's Beginnings*, 63–68.

SOUTHWORTH, *What the Old World Gave the New*, 43–48.

TAPPAN, *Our European Ancestors*, 37–44.

VOLLINTINE, *The American People and Their Old World Ancestors*, 133–151.

WICKHAM and PHILLIPS, *America's Heritage from the Long Ago*, 167–173.

WOODBURN and HILL, *Historic Background of Our United States*, 129–136.

Easy Reading

EXTENSIVE READING

BEST, *Glorious Greece and Imperial Rome*, 127–144.

COFFMAN, *Child's Story of the Human Race*, 148–154.

HILLYER, *Child's History of the World*, 89–93, 119–123.

HODGDON, *The Enchanted Past*, 187–194.

READING FOR RECREATION

ANDREWS, *Ten Boys Who Lived on the Road from Long Ago to Now*.

HANCOCK, *Children of History*, 5–10.

PERKINS, *Italian Twins*.

More Difficult Reading

EXTENSIVE READING

BAIKIE, *Ancient Rome*.

GUERBER, *Story of the Romans*, 11–98.

HAAREN and POLAND, *Famous Men of Rome*, 9–24, 58–60, 76–81.

HARTMAN, *The World We Live in*, chap. vii.

KUMMER, *First Days of History*, 218–241.

MACGREGOR, *Story of Rome*, 1–84.

MILLER, *Picturesque Tale of Progress*, IV: 11–29.

VAN LOON, *Story of Mankind*, 105–108.

READING FOR RECREATION

CHURCH, *Stories from Vergil*.

LAMPREY, *Children of Ancient Rome*.

The Discussion

Children answer the study-guide questions as fully as possible. The teacher attempts to draw the members of the lower group into the discussion.

The teacher writes on the board the words *Aeneid, republic, patricians, plebeians.* Children discuss the meanings.

Multisensory Aids

Children and teacher talk over together the pictures in the text, pointing out features of historical and geographical importance. They turn to the map and locate Rome and the Tiber River. They notice the location of the mountain ranges of Italy and the direction in which the peninsula "faces." They tell why Italy is called a peninsula.

AUDIO-VISUAL MATERIALS OBTAINABLE

Compton's Pictured Teaching Materials: *Ancient Greece and Rome*, Plate IV, 3.
CYBULSKI. Pictures: 15a.
HOFFMANN-SCHMIDT. Pictures: 6, 9.
LANGL. Colored History Pictures: Roman Monuments.
LEHMANN. Colored History Pictures: II, 106, 109.
LEHMANN. History Pictures: L. H. 109.
McKINLEY. Illustrated Topics for Ancient History: A 16.
MILLER. *Picturesque Tale of Progress*, IV, 11–29.
Society for Visual Education (MACHARG). Roman Forum.
Society for Visual Education (MUIR). Ancient Rome, 775 B.C.–41 B.C.

Music. Purcell's opera *Dido and Aeneas.*

General Activities

Creative Activities: Group and Individual, Correlated with Other Subjects or Voluntary Projects

A committee models the area of the western Mediterranean in the sand table, using care to show the location of the mountain ranges and plains correctly.

A committee dramatizes the story of Aeneas.

A volunteer tells in detail the story of Romulus and Remus.

A committee dramatizes the story of Cincinnatus.

Volunteers carve the Roman wolf from soap.

The class discusses the difference between myth and legend on the one hand and fact on the other.

Each pupil begins to make a map of the Roman world by locating Rome, the Tiber River, and the Adriatic Sea.

More Difficult Activities

A volunteer models the seven hills of Rome in a small sand pan.

The teacher shows the class a copy of Vergil's Aeneid and reads selections from it.

Volunteers tell the class some stories from the period of the kings.

The class begins to plan a pageant to be given at the end of the unit. The following episodes are written: (1) The Story of Aeneas; (2) Romulus and Remus and the Founding of Rome; (3) A Meeting of the Senate; (4) Cincinnatus as Dictator.

A volunteer finds a city in the United States in the same latitude as Rome and explains the difference in climate.

Application to Present-Day Conditions

Is there a country called Rome today? How long has the modern country called Italy been in existence? (See the encyclopedia.)

Are there any wolves in the neighborhood of Rome today?

Do the Italians speak Latin today? Does anyone? [*In the services of the Roman Catholic Church.*]

What is the origin of our word *republic*?

Do we use the word *patrician* today? What does it mean? Do we use *plebeian*? What does it mean?

From what source did we get our words *senate* and *senator*? What did they mean originally?

Does the city of Cincinnati take its name in any way from the old Roman, Cincinnatus?

Have the Italians in recent times ever given power into the hands of one man? [*To Mussolini.*]

Exercises in Reasoning

Compare the peninsula of Italy with the peninsula of Greece. Why is it sometimes called a boot?

Why do the Romans especially honor the wolf? Why are there many statues of wolves in Rome?

Compare the length of time [*five hundred years*] that the Senate ruled Rome with the length of time that the United States has been a republic.

How did the Roman city-state differ from the Greek city-states?

Compare the plebeians with the poor people in Greece.

Why was George Washington called "the Cincinnatus of the West"?

More Difficult Exercises in Reasoning

Can you see any ways in which the geography of Italy has influenced the history of Italy?

Compare the Aeneid and the Odyssey.

Why should you expect the Romans to have great respect for government?

Would Cincinnatus have been a greater man if he had kept supreme power in his own hands?

Why did both primitive men and the early Romans choose old men to make their rules for them?

At the United States Naval Academy at Annapolis, why do they call the students just entering "plebs" [*plebeians*]?

Drill Games

Place names are best drilled upon at the map: *Italy, Rome, Tiber River, Adriatic Sea.*

Association cards are made as follows:

the Aeneid	↔	a great poem about the settlement of Aeneas in Italy
Romulus and Remus	↔	twin founders of the city of Rome
Senate	↔	the group that made the laws when Rome was a republic
plebeians	↔	the common citizens of Rome
Cincinnatus	↔	an old man who left his plow to save Rome
patricians	↔	the noble classes in Rome
republic	↔	a state in which the people rule themselves, not directly, but by their representatives

Children drill themselves individually in preparation for class games.

Testing

Tests of Understanding are given in Kelty's *How Our Civilization Began,* pp. 169–170.

Tests of Reasoning and Skills. Underline the right words:

1. The tale about Aeneas is   a story.   the truth.

2. The settling of Italy by shepherd tribes from the north is   a story. the truth.

3. Italy faced toward   the east.   the west.

4. The tale about Romulus and Remus is   a story.   the truth.

5. In the beginning Rome was ruled by   kings.   a republic.   a democracy.

6. The only persons who could be chosen as officers were   the plebeians. the patricians.

Turn to a map of the ancient world. Check the following:

	Yes	No
7. Italy is a peninsula.	[✓]	[ ]
8. Rome is in the eastern part of Italy.	[ ]	[✓]
9. Italy is west of Greece.	[✓]	[ ]
10. The Tiber River empties into the Adriatic Sea.	[ ]	[✓]

11. What is the name of the unit which you are now studying? ＿＿＿＿＿＿
Where did you look? ＿＿＿[*In the table of contents.*]＿＿＿

Exercise in Organization. Children copy the topic headings and give a topical recitation about each heading.

More Difficult Tests

Check the best answer:

1. A settlement grew up along the Tiber River because   the place was easy to defend.   √ the place was a natural trade center.   the place had natural beauty.

2. The patricians were the rulers of Rome because the Romans   thought the patricians could make better speeches than the common people.   knew they had more time than the common people.   √ believed they had higher ideas of duty than the common people.

3. In time of great danger the Romans gave all power to   the plebeians. √ one man as leader.   the patricians.

STORY 2. ROME CONQUERS ITALY   [1 Week

Conversational Approach

"Had Athens or Sparta ever been able to bring all Greece under its power? [*Not for long.*] We find that the Romans were able to do what the Greeks had never been able to do. The title of the story tells what they did. Why do you suppose they were able to do it?

"Should you have expected the patricians or the plebeians to take the lead in spreading Rome's power? Why?

"Our story today tells us also how the Romans of the Republic dressed, what they ate, and in what kind of houses they lived."

Reading and Study

The Reading Periods

Independent Readers

TEXTS

BEEBY, *America's Roots in the Past*, 133–138, 151–157.

CLARK-GORDY, *Westward toward America*, 139–141.

CORKE, *A Book of Ancient Peoples*, 179–185 (hard).

KELTY, *How Our Civilization Began*, 171–180.

KNOWLTON and GERSON, *Our Beginnings in the Past*, 210–217.

Lower Group

The teacher tells the story orally to this group, writing on the board the most important words as she mentions them. Children practice the pronunciations.

Then the teacher and these children read together the story as given in the text. The teacher directs the silent reading, section by section, by such questions as "When did the Romans begin to spread out along the Tiber River? Why?"

Children read silently and answer orally. When they have completed the entire story in this manner, they test themselves by the study-guide questions at the end of the story.

MORE DIFFICULT TEXTS

BARKER, DUNCALF, BACON, *Old Europe and Our Nation*, 122–129.

BEARD and BAGLEY, *Our Old World Background*, 70–77.

BOURNE and BENTON, *Introductory American History*, 47–54.

COULOMB, McKINLEY, WHITE, *What Europe Gave to America*, 80–82.
GORDY, *American Beginnings in Europe*, 84–88, 108–112.
HALL, *Our Ancestors in Europe*, 77–88.
HALLECK and FRANTZ, *Our Nation's Heritage*, 94–101, 103–109.
HAWLEY, *Adventures in Old World History*, 163–171.
NIDA, *Dawn of American History*, 24–27.
NIVER, *Old World Steps to American History*, 120–122, 130–134.
SHERWOOD, *Our Country's Beginnings*, 68–71.
TAPPAN, *Our European Ancestors*, 49.
VOLLINTINE, *The American People and Their Old World Ancestors*, 138–151.
WICKHAM and PHILLIPS, *America's Heritage from the Long Ago*, 173–181, 207–218.
WOODBURN and HILL, *Historic Background of Our United States*, 137–140.

Easy Reading

EXTENSIVE READING

BEST, *Glorious Greece and Imperial Rome*, 145–164.
COFFMAN, *Child's Story of the Human Race.*
CORKE, *The World's Family*, 88–92.
HILLYER, *Child's History of the World*, 177–190.
TERRY, *History Stories of Other Lands*, III: 12–36.

READING FOR RECREATION

ANDREWS, *Ten Boys Who Lived on the Road from Long Ago to Now*, 79–114.
COWLES, *Our Little Roman Cousin of Long Ago.*

More Difficult Reading

EXTENSIVE READING

BAIKIE, *Ancient Times*, 40–60.
BURNHAM, *Hero Tales from History*, 24–31.
GUERBER, *Story of the Romans*, 98–121, 146–152.
HAAREN and POLAND, *Famous Men of Rome*, 142–147.
HARTMAN, *The World We Live in*, 105–108.
ILIN, *Black on White*, 96–101.
MACGREGOR, *Story of Rome*, 84–154, 258–277.
MILLER, *Picturesque Tale of Progress*, IV: 50–64.
NIDA, *Man Conquers the World with Science*, 26–27.
O'NEILL, *World's Story*, 96–110.
VAN LOON, *Story of Mankind*, 109–118.

READING FOR RECREATION

SCALES, *Boys of the Ages*, 42–64.
STUART, *The Boy through the Ages.*

The Discussion

Children answer the study-guide questions as fully as possible. Has there been improvement among the children who read rapidly but inaccurately?

The teacher writes on the board the words *stylus, Forum, tunic, toga, Vestal Virgins, Twelve Tables.* Children discuss the meanings.

Multisensory Aids

Children and teacher talk over together the pictures in the text, pointing out features of geographical and historical significance.

AUDIO-VISUAL MATERIALS OBTAINABLE

Compton's Pictured Teaching Materials: *Ancient Greece and Rome*, Plate VIII; Plate XII, 3.
CYBULSKI. Greek and Roman History Pictures: 11, 19, 20.
GALL-REBHANN. Charts: 8, 21, 26, 29, 30.
GURLITT. Historical Pictures: G. H. 1.
LEHMANN. Colored History Pictures: II, 8–10.
LEHMANN. Historical Pictures: L. H. 8, 9, 10, 112.
MCKINLEY. Illustrated Topics for Ancient History: A 17, 18, 20.
MILLER. *Picturesque Tale of Progress*, IV, 50–64.
Society for Visual Education (BRIGGS). Rise of Rome.
Society for Visual Education. University Museum (Philadelphia): Roman Life.

A cutout Roman house may be secured from the Educational Department, University Museum, Philadelphia.

General Activities

Creative Activities: Group and Individual, Correlated with Other Subjects or Voluntary Projects

A committee draws a plan of a Roman house.

Volunteers dress dolls in the costume of a Roman man and a Roman woman.

A volunteer makes a tablet covered with beeswax and shows how to write on it with a stylus.

The class makes two columns of the gods, naming in one column the Roman gods and in the other the corresponding Greek gods. (See an encyclopedia.)

The teacher reads to the children selections from Macaulay's *Lays of Ancient Rome*, especially "Horatius at the Bridge."

Children color Italy on their maps of the Roman world.

The class continues the time line.

More Difficult Activities

A volunteer carves a wooden plow like that of the Romans.

A volunteer gives the speech which Tiberius Gracchus might have given to the Roman Senate asking for more rights for the plebeians.

The class makes a picture collection of the Roman Forum.

The following episodes are planned for the pageant: (5) Tableau of a Roman House; (6) A Roman School; (7) The Vestal Virgins; (8) A Speech of Tiberius Gracchus.

Application to Present-Day Conditions

Does the father of an American family teach his children citizenship? In what ways?

Do Americans ever hold meetings that they call forums? What is done there?

Would it be possible for an American father to train his son by having the son with him all day long?

Get a copy of the magazine called *The Forum*. Why does it have this name?

Compare the way the Romans learned citizenship with the way that you learn it today.

Do some people today still believe in signs, as the Romans did? What are some of the signs? Are these beliefs superstitions?

Do our lawmakers go through any religious ceremonies before beginning sessions?

In what way were the reforms of Tiberius Gracchus like the reforms that people are trying to work out today?

Did the Romans have the same problems of relief of the poor that we have today?

Why do we call a speaker's platform a rostrum? (See the dictionary.)

What do we mean today when we say a man wants the toga? [*To be elected as lawmaker*.]

Have you ever heard anyone called "an old Roman"?

Does the peninsula of Italy possess many minerals? (See your geography.) How does this lack help to account for Italy's great desire for more colonies?

Exercises in Reasoning

Why did Rome become "a nation in arms"?

Was it a good thing for the Romans that the Greeks had made many colonies? Why?

Compare Roman women in the days of the Republic with Greek women.

Compare the way that a Roman spent his day with the way that a Greek spent his.

Compare the rights of the plebeians as citizens with the rights of the patricians as citizens.

Why do the common people wish to have the laws written down?

Why was it a good thing that all free Italians were made citizens of Rome?

Why was it easier to unite Italy than to unite Greece?

Do you think American fathers should be more strict?

More Difficult Exercises in Reasoning

What was Rome's purpose in building roads through the parts of Italy that she conquered?

Would good roads make it easier for other people to invade the Roman territory, as well as for the Romans to attack their neighbors?

When did the Mediterranean world first begin to notice the Romans?

Why did the Romans think that the old and well-known families were "the best"?

Do all American citizens today have equal rights?

Why did not the people of Italy revolt against Rome the first chance that they got?

What did Rome do with the land she won in Italy?

How do you suppose we know anything about what the Romans talked about in their Senate meetings?

Drill Games

Association cards may be made as follows:

stylus	↔	a sharp-pointed instrument for writing on a wax tablet
toga	↔	a dress that could be worn only by a citizen
Twelve Tables	↔	the laws written down in 450 B.C.
Forum	↔	the meeting place of the Romans
Vesta	↔	the goddess of the home and the sacred fire
Tiberius Gracchus	↔	the patrician who fought for the rights of the plebeians
89 B.C.	↔	the date when free Italians were made Roman citizens
Jupiter	↔	the Roman Zeus
Juno	↔	the Roman Hera
Minerva	↔	the Roman Athena
Vestal Virgins	↔	maidens who spent their lives guarding the sacred fire
450 B.C.	↔	date when the laws known as the Twelve Tables were written
Caius Gracchus	↔	a patrician who started the plan of relief for the poor

Testing

Tests of Understanding are given in Kelty's *How Our Civilization Began*, p. 180.

Tests of Reasoning and Skills. Fill the following blanks with the right words:

1. Rome was able to unite all the people of _ _ _[*Italy*]_ _ _.
2. Rome learned much from the _ _ _[*Greek*]_ _ _ colonies.
3. Home life was important among the _ _ _[*Roman*]_ _ _ people.
4. A Roman boy became a citizen at the age of _ _ _[*fifteen or sixteen*]_ _ _.
5. The sacred fire was kept burning by the _ _ _[*Vestal Virgins*]_ _ _.
6. The Romans believed that the gods spoke to them by _ _ _[*signs*]_ _ _.
7. All free _ _ _[*Italians*]_ _ _ were made citizens of Rome in 89 B.C.

Exercise in Organization. Children make a summary sentence for each topic heading in the story.

More Difficult Tests

Fill the following blanks with the right words:

1. Rome wanted more land for _ _ _[*farming*]_ _ _ and for _ _ _[*pastures*]_ _ _.
2. In the days about which you are reading, the government of Rome was a _ _ _[*republic*]_ _ _.
3. The Roman gods were much like the _ _ _[*Greek*]_ _ _ gods.
4. The citizens who did not have full rights were the _ _ _[*plebeians*]_ _ _.
5. The writing down of the laws was a victory for the _ _ _[*plebeians*]_ _ _.
6. Two subjects about which the patricians and plebeians quarreled were [*land*]_ _ _ and _ _ _[*equal rights for citizens*]_ _ _.

STORY 3. ROME CONQUERS THE MEDITERRANEAN WORLD

[1 Week

Conversational Approach

"Now that Rome has united all Italy, do you expect that she will be satisfied? Where will she want to spread next?

"Turn to a map of the Roman world. Give the name of as many present-day countries as you can which became parts of the Roman Empire. Does this look as large to you as Alexander's empire?

"You may be very sure that Rome did not win all this land without many fierce struggles. Our story today tells how she won many victories."

Reading and Study

The Reading Periods

Independent Readers

TEXTS

BEEBY, *America's Roots in the Past*, 138–146.
CHAPMAN, *Stories of the Ancient Peoples*, 147–152.
CLARK-GORDY, *Early Story of Mankind*, 173–184, 198–202.
CLARK-GORDY, *Westward toward America*, 181–185, 235–237.
CORKE, *A Book of Ancient Peoples*, 182–212 (hard).
KELTY, *How Our Civilization Began*, 181–191.
KNOWLTON and GERSON, *Our Beginnings in the Past*, 217–219.

Lower Group

The teacher tells the story orally to this group, writing on the board the most important words as she mentions them. Children practice the pronunciations.

Then the teacher and these children read together the story as given in the text. The teacher directs the silent reading, section by section, by such questions as "Why did Romans first go out upon the Mediterranean?"

Children read silently and answer orally. When they have finished the entire story in this manner, they test themselves by the study-guide questions at the end of the story.

OTHER BOOKS

BALDWIN, *Fifty Famous Stories Retold*, 95–96.

MORE DIFFICULT TEXTS

BARKER, DUNCALF, BACON, *Old Europe and Our Nation*, 133–145.
BOURNE and BENTON, *Introductory American History*, 56–65, 70–76.
BURNHAM, *Our Beginnings in Europe and America*, 83–89.
COULOMB, McKINLEY, WHITE, *What Europe Gave to America*, 82–91.
GORDY, *American Beginnings in Europe*, 89–101.
GREENWOOD, *Our Heritage from the Old World*, 132–137, 143–154.
HALL, *Our Ancestors in Europe*, 90–110.
HALLECK and FRANTZ, *Our Nation's Heritage*, 101–103, 108–109.
HARDING, *Old World Background to American History*, 67–74, 81–90.
HAWLEY, *Adventures in Old World History*, 175–186, 196–197.
NIDA, *Dawn of American History*, 74–80.
NIVER, *Old World Steps to American History*, 123–130, 135–139.
SHERWOOD, *Our Country's Beginnings*, 72–103.
SOUTHWORTH, *What the Old World Gave the New*, 48–54, 55–59.
TAPPAN, *Our European Ancestors*, 44–49, 51–56.
VOLLINTINE, *The American People and Their Old World Ancestors*, 151–163.
WICKHAM and PHILLIPS, *America's Heritage from the Long Ago*, 186–200.
WOODBURN and HILL, *Historic Background of Our United States*, 142–158.

Easy Reading

EXTENSIVE READING

BEST, *Glorious Greece and Imperial Rome,* 165–182.
CORKE, *The World's Family,* 92–98.
HILLYER, *Child's History of the World,* 168–176.
HODGDON, *The Enchanted Past,* 194–197.
TERRY, *History Stories of Other Lands,* III: 12–36.

READING FOR RECREATION

FARJEON, *Mighty Men from Achilles to Caesar.*
NIDA, *Inventions and Discoveries of Ancient Times,* 214–220.
WINSLOW, *Our Little Carthaginian Cousin of Long Ago.*

More Difficult Reading

EXTENSIVE READING

BAIKIE, *Ancient Times,* 60–67.
BURNHAM, *Hero Tales from History,* 24–31.
GUERBER, *Story of the Romans,* 121–142, 176–187.
HAAREN and POLAND, *Famous Men of Rome,* 181–202.
INGRAHAM, *Story of Democracy,* 69–91.
MacGREGOR, *Story of Rome,* 155–257, 356–404.
MILLER, *Picturesque Tale of Progress,* IV: 30–49, 65–93.
NIDA, *Man Conquers the World with Science,* 121–124.
O'NEILL, *World's Story,* 111–128.
POWER, *Great People of the Past,* 72–79, 81–91.
RICHMOND, *Egypt, Greece, and Rome,* 78–81, 198–210, 226–235.
VAN LOON, *Story of Mankind,* 88–104.

READING FOR RECREATION

ANDERSON, *With the Eagles.*
HAGEDORN, *Book of Courage,* 22–37.
HENTY, *Beric the Briton.*
HENTY, *The Young Carthaginian.*
LAMPREY, *Children of Ancient Britain.*
LAMPREY, *Children of Ancient Gaul.*
LANG, *Red Book of Heroes,* 43–94.
WELLS, *On Land and Sea with Caesar.*
WELLS, *With Caesar's Legions.*
WHITEHEAD, *The Standard Bearer.*

The Discussion

Children answer the study-guide questions as fully as possible. The teacher attempts to help the children to understand that not every detail must be included, but only the most important points.

The teacher writes on the board the words *province, triumph, emperor, Roman peace, nation.* Children discuss the meanings.

Multisensory Aids

Children and teacher talk over the pictures in the text, pointing out features of historical and geographical significance. They turn to a map of the Roman world and point out which provinces were conquered first. They show Carthage, Sicily, Spain, Macedon, Egypt, Asia Minor, Gaul, and Britain.

AUDIO-VISUAL MATERIALS OBTAINABLE

Compton's Pictured Teaching Materials: *Ancient Greece and Rome,* Plate XI, 4.
CYBULSKI. Greek and Roman History Pictures: 5–8.
GALL-REBHANN. Charts: 21.
GRANT. *Story of the Ship,* p. 7.
GURLITT. History Pictures from Caesar's Gallic Wars: 1–7.

International Educational Pictures: Ancient Rome in Africa, Excavations at Carthage, Antony and Cleopatra, Julius Caesar.

LEHMANN. Colored History Pictures: L. H. 10.

LOHMEYER. History Pictures: 17–18.

McKINLEY. Illustrated Topics for Ancient History: A 6, 19.

MILLER. *Picturesque Tale of Progress*, IV, 30–49, 65–93.

Society for Visual Education (MUIR). Ancient Rome, 60 B.C.–70 A.D.

Music. Play selections from Massenet's opera *Cleopatra* and from Handel's *Julius Caesar*.

General Activities

Creative Activities: Group and Individual, Correlated with Other Subjects or Voluntary Projects

A volunteer draws a picture of a Roman trireme.

A committee dramatizes the tragic story of Hannibal.

The class makes a list of the bad conditions in the Roman world.

The class makes a visit to the local museum to see the Roman exhibit.

The teacher explains the meaning of the letters A.D. as used with dates. [*Anno Domini*, "in the year of our Lord"; or "after the birth of Christ."]

The following episodes are planned for the pageant: (9) The Story of Hannibal; (10) The Triumph of a Roman General; (11) Julius Caesar Seizes Power; (12) Farming the Taxes; (13) The Death of Cleopatra.

Each child completes his map of the Roman Empire at its greatest extent.

The class continues the time line.

More Difficult Activities

Volunteers report on the life of Julius Caesar.

The teacher shows the class a copy of Julius Caesar's *Commentaries*.

A volunteer reports on the use of paper money by the Carthaginians; he explains why paper money is good.

Volunteers draw pictures showing how Hannibal's elephants were carried across rivers.

A volunteer letters a scroll with Augustus's statement "I found Rome brick and I left it marble."

Application to Present-Day Conditions

Is Italy considered a poor country today? What products does she need to import? Does this explain why both ancient and modern Italians have wanted to own land outside Italy?

Is any country in the world today as large as the ancient Roman Empire? (See a map of modern Russia.)

Is northern Africa still a grain-growing region? (See a geography.)

Have the titles of any modern rulers been taken from the word *Caesar*? [*Czar, Kaiser.*]

Does Italy have an emperor today? (See periodicals of spring of 1936.)

Would it be strange if modern Italy should still dream of building up the old Roman Empire?

Does the city of Carthage exist today? In what country is the territory it occupied?

Do you think the Roman officials were worse than our officials today?

Has there ever been a period in modern times like that of the "Roman peace"?

Exercises in Reasoning

Why did not Italy grow grain for herself?

Why did Rome decide that she needed a navy?

How was Hannibal able to support his army during the fifteen years he spent in Italy?

Was too much prosperity good for the Romans? Explain your answer fully.

What did Augustus Caesar mean when he said that he found Rome brick and left it marble?

Compare what took place in 89 B.C. with what took place in 212 A.D.

Why did ancient peoples sow with salt the sites of ancient cities that they destroyed?

Most of our stories about the Punic Wars came down to us from the Romans. Should you expect them to appreciate fully Hannibal's bravery?

More Difficult Exercises in Reasoning

Why were the Punic Wars considered the second great struggle between the West and the East? (What was the first?)

Of what value were elephants in war?

What is the difference between a province and a state?

Was it a good thing for the Romans to make the other people pay all the taxes? Why not?

Why were few farmers left with small farms?

Modern France inherited many of the ideas of the Romans. Can you explain why?

When Roman citizenship was given to all the provinces in 212 A.D., why did that make the provinces part of the Roman *nation*? Had they been part of the Roman nation before? What is the difference between being part of a nation and being a possession of a nation?

Explain this sentence: "Greek civilization was brought into Asia in the chariot of a conqueror; it was brought into Italy in the chains of slaves."

Drill Games

Place names are best drilled upon at the map: *Carthage, Sicily, Alps Mountains, Gaul, Britain.*

Drill cards are made as follows:

Punic Wars	⟷	the wars between the Carthaginians and the Romans
a province	⟷	a large section of a country; in the Roman world, a conquered section
Hannibal	⟷	the world-famous general of the Carthaginians

146 B.C.	↔	date of the destruction of Carthage by Rome
"Our Sea"	↔	what the Romans called the Mediterranean
a triumph	↔	a great parade in Rome by a general who had won a famous victory
Julius Caesar	↔	a famous Roman who overthrew the Republic
49 B.C.	↔	the date when Julius Caesar became supreme leader in Rome
Augustus Caesar	↔	the first ruler who received the title of "Emperor" in Rome
212 A.D.	↔	the date when all the freemen in the provinces were made Roman citizens
emperor	↔	ruler of an empire
"the Roman peace"	↔	the long period of peace within the Roman Empire

Children drill one another by twos.

Testing

Tests of Understanding are given in Kelty's *How Our Civilization Began,* pp. 190–191.

Tests of Reasoning and Skills. Check the best answer:

1. Rome fought Carthage over the question of √ trade. mines. farming. lumbering.

2. Hannibal had to leave Italy after fifteen years because he had no money left. he could not find enough food. his soldiers were worn out. √ his home country was attacked.

3. The Roman ruler at last became emperor because the Romans liked to have a king. the Romans were not used to ruling themselves. √ one strong man could put matters in order. one man was wiser than the Senators.

Turn to a map of the Roman world. Mark the following:

	Yes	No
1. Rome won all of Africa.	[ ]	[√]
2. Rome won Egypt.	[√]	[ ]
3. Rome owned some land east of the Tigris River.	[√]	[ ]
4. Rome owned some land north of the Black Sea.	[ ]	[√]
5. Rome took the island of Britain.	[√]	[ ]
6. Carthage was in Phoenicia.	[ ]	[√]
7. Macedon was taken by Rome.	[√]	[ ]

Exercise in Organization. Teacher and pupils make a co-operative outline of the story. Children tell a brief story about each subheading.

More Difficult Tests

Check the best answer:

1. The provinces were the lands   owned by Roman soldiers.   √ conquered by Rome.   that joined Rome willingly.   inhabited only by Romans.

2. Rome conquered Macedon and Greece because   she never had liked Greeks.   she wanted to reach the Black Sea.   √ the Greeks had helped Carthage.   the Greeks had been cruel.

3. The Roman citizens lost the habit of paying taxes because   √ they made the provinces pay them all.   no tax money was needed.   they were too poor to pay.   the army paid all the taxes.

STORY 4. THE GRANDEUR OF ROME   [2 Weeks

Conversational Approach

"Do you suppose it makes any difference to us today whether or not any such people as the ancient Romans ever lived? What ideas have we already mentioned that we got from them?

"You have also already read about how the early Romans lived in the days of the Republic. Which of their ways of living seemed to you very good? Now you will want to know whether or not the later Romans changed those ways when they became rich and powerful. Do you think they naturally would?

"The story that we begin today tells us about these two matters: how the later Romans lived and what Rome gave to world civilization."

Reading and Study

The Reading Periods (Roman Buildings)

Independent Readers

TEXTS

BEEBY, *America's Roots in the Past*, 158–165, 167–173.

CHAPMAN, *Stories of the Ancient Peoples*, 154–158.

CLARK-GORDY, *Early Story of Mankind*, 184–197.

CLARK-GORDY, *Westward toward America*, 142–150.

CORKE, *A Book of Ancient Peoples*, 214–221 (hard).

KELTY, *How Our Civilization Began*, 192–200.

KNOWLTON and GERSON, *Our Beginnings in the Past*, 223, 229–231.

Lower Group

The teacher and this group read together the part of the story as given in the text. The teacher directs the silent reading, section by section, by such questions as "Why did Rome learn from the Greeks?"

Children read silently and answer orally. When they have finished this part of the story in this manner, they test themselves by the study-guide questions at the end of the story, which deal with the matters above.

MORE DIFFICULT TEXTS

BARKER, DUNCALF, BACON, *Old Europe and Our Nation*, 149–167.
BEARD and BAGLEY, *Our Old World Background*, 64–66, 80, 90.
BOURNE and BENTON, *Introductory American History*, 78–88.
BURNHAM, *Our Beginnings in Europe and America*, 89–93.
COULOMB, McKINLEY, WHITE, *What Europe Gave to America*, 91–98.
GORDY, *American Beginnings in Europe*, 102–108.

GREENWOOD, *Our Heritage from the Old World*, 137–143, 155–166.
HALL, *Our Ancestors in Europe*, 110–128, 135–139.
HALLECK and FRANTZ, *Our Nation's Heritage*, 110–129.
HARDING, *Old World Background to American History*, 75–80.
HAWLEY, *Adventures in Old World History*, 186–192.
NIVER, *Old World Steps to American History*, 140–148.
SHERWOOD, *Our Country's Beginnings*, 103–109.
SOUTHWORTH, *What the Old World Gave the New*, 59–65.
TAPPAN, *Our European Ancestors*, 56–61.
VOLLINTINE, *The American People and Their Old World Ancestors*, 164–168.
WICKHAM and PHILLIPS, *America's Heritage from the Long Ago*, 200–204.
WOODBURN and HILL, *Historic Background of Our United States*, 159–166.

The Discussion

Children answer the study-guide questions as fully as possible. Those who have read widely are encouraged to contribute additional material, giving the name and author of the book in which they found it.

The teacher writes on the board the words *mosaic, circus, gladiators, amphitheater, "bread and games," Pompeii.* Children discuss the meanings.

The Reading Periods (Roman Culture)

Independent Readers

TEXTS

CHAPMAN, *Stories of the Ancient Peoples*, 158–159, 161–162.
CLARK-GORDY, *Westward toward America*, 150–167.
KELTY, *How Our Civilization Began*, 200–213.
KNOWLTON and GERSON, *Our Beginnings in the Past*, 231–236.

Lower Group

The teacher and this group read together the rest of the story as given in the text. The teacher guides the silent reading, section by section, by such questions as "How did the gifts of the Romans to the world differ from the gifts of the Greeks?"

Children read silently and answer orally. When they have finished the story in this manner, they test themselves by the study-guide questions at the end of the story, which deal with the matters above.

MORE DIFFICULT TEXTS

BEARD and BAGLEY, *Our Old World Background*, 84, 90–92.
BURNHAM, *Our Beginnings in Europe and America*, 94–98.
COULOMB, McKINLEY, WHITE, *What Europe Gave to America*, 100–108.
GORDY, *American Beginnings in Europe*, 113–119.
GREENWOOD, *Our Heritage from the Old World*, 166–173.
HALLECK and FRANTZ, *Our Nation's Heritage*, 103–107.
HARDING, *Old World Background to American History*, 91–103.
HAWLEY, *Adventures in Old World History*, 198–208.
NIDA, *Dawn of American History*, 87–90.
VOLLINTINE, *The American People and Their Old World Ancestors*, 174–178.
WICKHAM and PHILLIPS, *America's Heritage from the Long Ago*, 219–233, 241–242.
WOODBURN and HILL, *Historic Background of Our United States*, 166–168.

The Discussion

Children answer the rest of the study-guide questions as fully as possible. Again those who have read widely are given an opportunity to contribute.

The teacher writes on the board the words *public buildings, dome, aqueduct, Eternal City, Latin, Justinian Code, Roman numerals, Colosseum.* Children discuss the meaning or significance.

Easy Reading

EXTENSIVE READING

BEST, *Glorious Greece and Imperial Rome,* 183–194.

COFFMAN, *Child's Story of the Human Race,* 155–164, 171–181.

HILLYER, *Child's History of the World,* 177–214.

HODGDON, *The Enchanted Past,* 197–222.

SCHWARTZ, *From Then till Now,* 141–185.

TERRY, *History Stories of Other Lands,* III: 36–45.

READING FOR RECREATION

HALL, *Buried Cities,* 193 (pictures).

NIDA, *Inventions and Discoveries of Ancient Times,* 221–243.

POWER, *Boys and Girls of History,* 1–14.

WELLS, *Beppo the Donkey.*

More Difficult Reading

EXTENSIVE READING

BAIKIE, *Ancient Times,* 67–85.

DALKEITH, *Stories of Roman History.*

DAVIS, *A Day in Old Rome.*

GUERBER, *Story of the Romans,* 197–221.

HAAREN and POLAND, *Famous Men of Rome,* 203–208.

MILLER, *Picturesque Tale of Progress,* IV: 94–120.

NIDA, *Man Conquers the World with Science,* 98–101.

O'NEILL, *World's Story,* 152–157.

PRESTON and DODGE, *Private Life of the Romans.*

Rules of the Road (American Council on Education), 4–6.

SHUMWAY, *A Day in Ancient Rome.*

Story of Our Calendar (American Council on Education), 13–18, 21–23.

Story of Numbers (American Council on Education), 3–5, 20–25.

Story of Weights and Measures (American Council on Education), 10–11.

Story of Writing (American Council on Education), 60–64.

Telling Time (American Council on Education), 11–13, 23–24.

VAN LOON, *Story of Mankind,* 117–118.

READING FOR RECREATION

CHURCH, *Lords of the World.*

CHURCH, *Roman Life in the Days of Cicero.*

CLARKE, *The Story of Caesar.*

GENN, Peeps at Great Cities: *Rome.*

LOVELL, *Stories in Stone from the Roman Forum.*

MULLER, *How They Carried the Goods,* 89–106.

Multisensory Aids

Children and teacher talk over together the pictures in the text, pointing out features of geographical and historical significance.

AUDIO-VISUAL MATERIALS OBTAINABLE

Compton's Pictured Teaching Materials: *Ancient Greece and Rome,* Plates VII, VIII, IX, X, XI, XII; *Prehistoric Man,* Plate I; *Transportation,* Plates V, 5; VII.

EASTMAN. Education Slides: Set 302.

GALL-REBHANN. History Charts: 4, 31.

HOFFMANN-SCHMIDT. History Pictures: 2, 3, 7, 8, 12, 13.

International Educational Pictures: Buried City — Pompeii; Roman Country; Rome; Rome — the Eternal City.

JÖNDL. Ancient History Charts: Rome.
Keystone Views: Rome.
LEHMANN. Geography Pictures: L. G. 14, 15, 58.
LEHMANN. History Pictures: L. H. 9, 10, 102, 103, 107, 112.
LOHMEYER. History Pictures: 1, 6.
Longman's Historical Wall Pictures: 1.
McKINLEY. Illustrated Topics for Ancient History: A 22–26.
MILLER. *Picturesque Tale of Progress*, IV, 94–120.
Society for Visual Education: (BRIGGS) Roman Empire; (BURTON HOLMES–BRAY) Immortal Rome; (MACHARG) Ancient Rome; (MUIR) Ancient Rome, Roman Life, Famous Roman Temples.

Music. Play selections from Rubenstein's opera *Nero*.

General Activities

Creative Activities: Group and Individual, Correlated with Other Subjects or Voluntary Projects

A committee dramatizes the life of the Romans.[1]

The class makes a picture collection of all the public buildings mentioned in the readings.

Volunteers report on the destruction of Pompeii and Herculaneum by Vesuvius.

A volunteer makes a cross section of a Roman road.

Children attempt to add columns written in Roman numerals. They then understand why the Romans could not advance far in arithmetic.

Children may wish to model in clay the Roman eagle; a triumphal arch; a column of victory.

Someone who has visited Rome and Pompeii describes them to the children.

The class plans additional episodes for the pageant: (14) A Day in Imperial Rome; (15) Gifts of Rome to the World.

The art teacher shows the children the color known as Pompeian red.

More Difficult Activities

A volunteer makes a trade map of Rome, drawing lines to her sources of supply and on each line naming both the imports and the exports.

The class divides into committees. Each committee chooses a public building to construct. These are placed on a sand-table plan of the city of Rome. (See *Rome* in the World Book Encyclopedia.)

Compare Roman methods of road-building with road-building today. (See the encyclopedia.)

Compare the Roman arch with the Gothic arch. (See the encyclopedia.)

A committee makes a list of English words taken from the Latin. (An unabridged dictionary will help.)

A volunteer draws a diagram illustrating the Roman plan of government.

The teacher reads to the class passages describing the eruption of Vesuvius from Bulwer-Lytton's *Last Days of Pompeii*.

[1] See *Rome from Legendary Kings to Great Emperors*, Teacher's Lesson Unit Series, Teachers College, Columbia University.

Application to Present-Day Conditions

Are mosaics ever used nowadays? Are there any in your city?

The class makes picture collections of the town houses and country houses of rich people today.

How long ago did Americans catch up with the Romans in their use of bathrooms?

Are houses built in the Spanish style of architecture today anything like the houses of the Romans?

Is false hair for women a modern idea? Is rouge? face powder? coloring the fingernails?

Do people today ever listen to cases in the law courts?

Compare the Roman circus with the circus of today.

Do we have some customs today which people later may think of as uncivilized? [For example, "*walkathons*," *marathon dances, prize fights, hunting for pleasure.*]

Children find names of cities of today which are about the size of imperial Rome. [*About one million people.*]

Were there any apartment houses in ancient Rome? (Kelty's *How Our Civilization Began*, p. 198.)

Is there any building in your city with a dome? with a vaulted roof?

Are there any milestones on your roads?

Where did we get our idea of using glass for windows?

What are the Romance languages? Why are they so called? (See the dictionary.)

Is American law based more on the Roman law or on the English law? (Ask a lawyer.)

From what words do the following words come: *January, June, July, August, October, November, December*? (See the dictionary.)

For what purposes are Roman numerals used today?

Exercises in Reasoning

Where did the Romans get water for their bathrooms?

How did the Romans find time enough to do so many things just for pleasure?

How did the public bathing places take the place of the newspaper?

Why is it a bad thing to have too much land taken up by rich men's large estates? Does this mean that there should not be any such estates?

How did Pompeii help us to learn many of the ways of living of the Romans?

Why were the Romans especially interested in public buildings?

Why did towns grow up where Roman roads crossed one another?

What customs were common throughout the Roman world?

Why is it better to be ruled by law rather than by the will of each individual ruler?

How long a time passed between the Code of Hammurapi and the Justinian Code?

More Difficult Exercises in Reasoning

You sometimes hear it said that "the conquerors become the conquered." Can you apply this saying in the case of the Greeks and the Romans?

How did it happen that our ancestors learned the ideas of the Greeks not directly from the Greeks themselves but through the Romans?

How did the Romans heat the water for their baths? (See the encyclopedia.)

Compare prize fights of today with gladiatorial contests.

Which do you think is better for people — the circus and the gladiatorial games or baseball, football, golf, tennis, etc. Why?

Is supporting a large number of people who do not work a danger to our government today? How? Does this mean that the government should let those people starve?

How does the rule of law differ from rule by the whim of a ruler?

Drill Games

Association cards may be made as follows:

mosaics	↔	small, flat pieces of stone joined together to make a pattern
circus	↔	a race track surrounded on three sides by rows of seats
gladiator	↔	a man who fought to kill, for the amusement of the public
amphitheater	↔	a building in which the gladiatorial contests were held
"bread and games"	↔	food and entertainment given free to the mobs in the city
Pompeii	↔	a small city, in Italy, destroyed by Vesuvius
public buildings	↔	buildings for the people's business or pleasure
dome	↔	a circular top of a building
aqueduct	↔	a channel for carrying water from a distance
"Eternal City"	↔	a name showing that Rome was expected to last forever
Latin	↔	the language spoken by the Romans
Justinian Code	↔	a collection of laws made by a great Roman emperor
Roman numerals	↔	the system of writing numbers used by the Romans
Colosseum	↔	the largest building in which the gladiators fought
Cicero	↔	a great orator before the Roman Senate

Children drill individually on their own difficulties.

Testing

Tests of Understanding are given in Kelty's *How Our Civilization Began*, p. 213.

Tests of Reasoning and Skills. Mark the following as true or false:

True False

[✓] [ ] 1. The Roman houses were built around an open space.

[ ] [✓] 2. The Roman men wore long beards.

True False

[✓]   [ ]   3. Some of the Roman houses had bathrooms.

[✓]   [ ]   4. The Romans were much interested in the law courts.

[ ]   [✓]   5. The Roman circus was where animals performed.

[✓]   [ ]   6. The gladiatorial games cost huge sums of money.

[✓]   [ ]   7. About a fourth of the Romans did no work.

[ ]   [✓]   8. Most of the gifts of the Romans to the world were ideas.

[✓]   [ ]   9. Slaves did the work that is now done by machinery.

[ ]   [✓] 10. The Colosseum was a public bathhouse.

[✓]   [ ] 11. Pompeii has shown us how the Romans lived.

[ ]   [✓] 12. The aqueducts were ornaments built to celebrate a famous victory.

[✓]   [ ] 13. The city streets in Rome were paved.

[ ]   [✓] 14. The Romans did not know how to bridge rivers.

[ ]   [✓] 15. The English language is more like Latin than the Spanish language is.

[✓]   [ ] 16. Rome spread her own civilization and Greek civilization all over the Mediterranean world.

[✓]   [ ] 17. Rome tried to find out what was right to do and then to make laws forcing people to do it.

[ ]   [✓] 18. Julius Caesar was the first person ever to arrange the calendar.

Exercises in Organization. Children copy the topic headings and give oral summaries of each.

More Difficult Tests

Mark the following as true or false:

True False

[ ]   [✓]   1. Rome was the teacher of the Greeks because she conquered them.

[✓]   [ ]   2. The Roman books were written on rolls.

[ ]   [✓]   3. Even the slaves could use the public baths.

[ ]   [✓]   4. The gladiatorial games were held in the Circus.

[✓]   [ ]   5. A great many Romans worked for the government.

[ ]   [✓]   6. Italy was a land of small farmers in the days of the Empire.

[✓]   [ ]   7. Rome had a million inhabitants.

[✓]   [ ]   8. Because Rome was so large, she had to carry on much trade.

[ ]   [✓]   9. The Romans did not use any ideas of their own in building.

[✓]   [ ] 10. We borrowed our use of the dome from the Romans.

[ ]   [✓] 11. The Circus Maximus was a theater.

[✓]   [ ] 12. The top of the aqueducts had to be kept level.

[ ]   [✓] 13. The Romans learned the use of concrete from the Greeks.

[✓]   [ ] 14. The Romans knew how to make windowpanes of glass.

[✓]   [ ] 15. Latin was the only language which all the Western world understood for hundreds of years.

[ ]   [✓] 16. In the Roman world what was right and what was lawful were two different things.

STORY 5. THE RISE OF CHRISTIANITY   [1 Week

Conversational Approach

"Where is the Latin language used today? [*In the services of the Roman Catholic Church.*] Why do you suppose this church today uses the language that the Romans spoke two thousand years ago? Did Christianity begin in Rome? Where was Jesus born?

"We have found that Rome had a religion of its own long before Christ was born. What was that religion? Why do you suppose Rome gave up its own religion and took up Christianity instead? Our story will tell us."

Reading and Study

The Reading Periods

Independent Readers

TEXTS

BEEBY, *America's Roots in the Past*, 174–177.

CHAPMAN, *Stories of the Ancient Peoples*, 160–161.

CLARK-GORDY, *Early Story of Mankind*, 202–205.

CLARK-GORDY, *Westward toward America*, 193–195.

CORKE, *A Book of Ancient Peoples*, 226–234 (hard).

KELTY, *How Our Civilization Began*, 214–221.

KNOWLTON and GERSON, *Our Beginnings in the Past*, 219–222, 236.

Lower Group

The teacher tells the story orally to this group, writing on the board the most important words as she mentions them.

Then the teacher and these children read together the story as given in the text. The teacher directs the silent reading, section by section, by such questions as "In what part of the Roman world was Jesus born?"

Children read silently and answer orally. When they have completed the reading of the story in this manner, they test themselves by the questions at the end of the story.

MORE DIFFICULT TEXTS

BARKER, DUNCALF, BACON, *Old Europe and Our Nation*, 190–202.
BEARD and BAGLEY, *Our Old World Background*, 100–106.
BOURNE and BENTON, *Introductory American History*, 89–94.
BURNHAM, *Our Beginnings in Europe and America*, 99–107.
COULOMB, McKINLEY, WHITE, *What Europe Gave to America*, 111–116.
GORDY, *American Beginnings in Europe*, 121–127.
GREENWOOD, *Our Heritage from the Old World*, 264–273.
HALL, *Our Ancestors in Europe*, 128–135.
HALLECK and FRANTZ, *Our Nation's Heritage*, 131–140.
HARDING, *Old World Background to American History*, 104–111.
HAWLEY, *Adventures in Old World History*, 212–220.
NIDA, *Dawn of American History*, 90–91, 93–102.
NIVER, *Old World Steps to American History*, 148–151.
SHERWOOD, *Our Country's Beginnings*, 113–119.
SOUTHWORTH, *What the Old World Gave the New*, 65–68.
TAPPAN, *Our European Ancestors*, 61–65.
VOLLINTINE, *The American People and Their Old World Ancestors*, 168–173.
WICKHAM and PHILLIPS, *America's Heritage from the Long Ago*, 233–234.
WOODBURN and HILL, *Historic Background of Our United States*, 169–175.

Easy Reading

EXTENSIVE READING

BEST, *Glorious Greece and Imperial Rome*, 194–200, 211–225.
COFFMAN, *Child's Story of the Human Race*, 165–171.
CORKE, *The World's Family*, 98–108.
HILLYER, *Child's History of the World*, 215–218.
HODGDON, *The Enchanted Past*, 222–224.
TERRY, *History Stories of Other Lands*, III: 73–80.

READING FOR RECREATION

HODGES, *When the King Came*.
SMITH, *Old Old Tales from an Old Old Book*.
TAPPAN, *The Old Old Story Book*.

More Difficult Reading

EXTENSIVE READING

GUERBER, *Story of the Romans*, 221–227, 269–271.
HAAREN and POLAND, *Famous Men of Rome*, 254–261.
HARTMAN, *The World We Live in*, 109–112.
MILLER, *Picturesque Tale of Progress*, IV: 121–217.
O'NEILL, *World's Story*, 157–165.
Story of Our Calendar (American Council on Education), 23–25.
VAN LOON, *Story of Mankind*, 119–123, 131–137.

READING FOR RECREATION

HAGEDORN, *The Book of Courage*, 38–52.
LANG, *The Book of Saints and Heroes*.
LETTS, *The Mighty Army*.
STEWART, *The Shepherd of Us All*.
STODDARD, *The Sword-Maker's Son*.

The Discussion

Children answer the study-guide questions as fully as possible. The teacher studies particularly the performance of any pupils who are soon to be transferred from the lower group to the group of independent readers.

The teacher writes on the board *the Twelve Apostles, catacombs, bishop, Pope*. Children discuss the meanings.

Multisensory Aids

Children and teacher talk over together the pictures in the text, pointing out features of geographical and historical significance.

AUDIO-VISUAL MATERIALS OBTAINABLE

ENGLEDER. History Pictures: 28.
International Educational Pictures: St. Paul the Apostle.
LANGL. Colored History Pictures: Early Christian Monuments.
LEHMANN. Colored History Pictures: II, 11.
LEHMANN. History Pictures: L. H. 6, 11.
McKINLEY. Illustrated Topics for Ancient History: A 28.
MILLER. *Picturesque Tale of Progress*, IV, 121–217.

Music. Play selections from Handel's *The Messiah*; Stainer's *The Crucifixion*; Schütz's *The Seven Last Words of Christ*; Mendelssohn's *Saint Paul*.

General Activities

Creative Activities: Group and Individual, Correlated with Other Subjects or Voluntary Projects

A volunteer makes a list of the Twelve Apostles.

From a book of Bible stories a volunteer tells how far Paul journeyed preaching about Christ.

Children tell incidents which they have seen in the motion pictures representing the suffering of the early Christians.

The class plans other episodes for the pageant: (16) A Meeting of the Early Christians; (17) Rome Accepts Christianity. The entire pageant is now given.

The teacher reads to the class some short selections from Paul's letters (the Epistles).

A visitor to Rome describes the catacombs to the children.

The class decides upon a symbol on the time line for the birth of Christ.

More Difficult Activities

A volunteer makes a map of Paul's missionary journeys.

Two volunteers represent officials of the Roman Empire talking together about the peculiarities of this new Christian religion.

A volunteer makes a diagram of the order of officials of the Roman Catholic Church and compares it with the order of officials in the Roman Empire.

Why are both *Jesus* and *Christ* used as names of the same person?

Why does the year 1936 belong to the *twentieth* century?

Application to Present-Day Conditions

Which of all the persons living today do you think may go down in history as great men and women?

Do all people today measure time from the birth of Christ? (For example, Mohammedans, Japanese, Chinese.)

Is Rome today the head of all the Christian churches?

Consult the map of the Roman Empire. Are all parts of that empire Christian today?

Are Christians persecuted anywhere in the world today?

Do you think the Western world of today is really Christian? Give reasons for your answer.

Can you name other religions of the world today besides Christianity?

Exercises in Reasoning

Why is Jesus today considered greater than Augustus Caesar?

Do you think the Roman nobles would be willing to believe that all men are brothers? Why not?

Why did the early Christian groups meeting in houses have a leader?

Why could Paul make more people understand his teachings if he wrote in Greek rather than in Hebrew?

Why did the poorer classes in the Roman Empire accept Christianity gladly?

Where did the Christian Church find a model for the government of its members?

How did it happen that Paul, a Jew, could be a Roman citizen?

More Difficult Exercises in Reasoning

Why is it very difficult to tell whether or not a living person will go down in history as a great man or woman?

Does the world today behave as if it believed really that all men are brothers? (For example, questions of colored people, or war.)

Why did Paul want to preach Christianity to other people besides Jews?

How did the Pope come to be considered more important than any other of the early bishops?

Why did the Romans persecute the Christians and the Jews when they did not persecute the religions of the other peoples they conquered?

Why did a Roman emperor finally allow Christianity to be recognized as one of the religions of the Empire?

What does the word *catholic* mean? (See the dictionary.) Was the Church universal throughout the Roman Empire after 312 A.D.?

Is persecuting any belief a good way to put a stop to it? What is the meaning of the expression "The blood of the martyrs is the seed of the Church"?

Drill Games

Review the place names *Palestine, Syria*.

Review the meaning of the initials B.C.; A.D.

Drill cards are made as follows:

Twelve Apostles	⟷	followers of Jesus who traveled about with him
catacombs	⟷	underground burial places used as meeting places by the Christians
312 A.D.	⟷	the date when Christianity became lawful in the Roman Empire
bishops	⟷	high officials of the Church
Constantine	⟷	the Roman emperor who made Christianity a lawful religion in the Empire
Paul	⟷	the great missionary of the early Christian Church
Pope	⟷	the head of the Roman Catholic Church

Children drill first on the items for this story and then on all the items of the entire unit.

Testing

Tests of Understanding are given in Kelty's *How Our Civilization Began,* pp. 220–221.

Tests of Reasoning and Skills. Finish these sentences:

1. The Christian world now measures time from ___[*the birth of Christ*]___.

2. Jesus taught that the principal rules of life were ___[*love, brotherhood of man*]___.

3. The bishop of Rome became more important than the other bishops because ___[*Rome was the world center*]___.

4. The Romans persecuted the Christians because ___[*they would not bow down and reverence the emperor*]___.

5. How many stories have been included in this unit? ___[*Five.*]___ Where did you look to find out? ___[*In the table of contents.*]___

Exercise in Organization. Children who feel able to do so make outlines of the story independently. The teacher and the other children make a co-operative outline.

More Difficult Tests

Finish these sentences:

1. Paul was a great help to the early Christian Church because ___[*he preached to others besides Jews; he was an educated man*]___.

2. Life in this world held little of joy for the poorer Romans; so they were glad to ___[*find hope for the next world in Christianity*]___.

3. The emperors allowed Christianity at last, hoping that it would ___[*help to hold the Empire together*]___.

4. The model for the government of the Roman Catholic Church was ___[*the Roman Empire*]___.

Tests on the Entire Unit

Test of Place Sense. Pass double-sized outline maps of the Mediterranean area which show the water bodies in color or the land bodies in shading. Give the following directions:

1. Write the word *Italy* in the proper place.

2. Trace the Tiber River in blue crayon.

3. Make a circle where Rome is.

4. Put the letter *A* in the Adriatic Sea.

5. Put a cross (X) where Carthage was.

6. Put the letter *S* in Sicily.

7. Make peaks (ʌʌʌ) where the Alps Mountains are.

8. Put the letter *G* in Gaul.

9. But the letter *B* in Britain.

10. Write the word *Syria* in the proper place.

Tests of Time Sense. Pass mimeographed sheets of the following:

I. In the following exercises put the figure *1* in each case before the event which happened first, and the figure *2* before that which happened later.

1. [__2__] Cicero made speeches.
   [__1__] Cincinnatus saved Rome.

2. [__2__] Rome conquered the Mediterranean world.
   [__1__] Rome conquered Italy.

3. [__1__] Tiberius Gracchus worked for the plebeians.
[__2__] Julius Caesar conquered Britain.

4. [__1__] Rome destroyed Carthage.
[__2__] Rome conquered the Greek cities.

5. [__2__] Christ was born.
[__1__] Julius Caesar seized power in Rome.

6. [__1__] Octavius became emperor.
[__2__] Christianity was allowed in the Roman Empire.

II. Here is a list of dates. Put each one in the right blank in the sentences below.

89 B.C.	212 A.D.	450 B.C.
146 B.C.	312 A.D.	49 B.C.

1. Christianity was allowed as one of the lawful religions of the Roman Empire in ___[312 A.D.]___.

2. All free Italians were made Roman citizens in ___[89 B.C.]___.

3. In ___[146 B.C.]___ Carthage was completely destroyed.

4. All free inhabitants of the Empire were made Roman citizens in ___[212 A.D.]___.

5. The Twelve Tables of the Law were written down in ___[450 B.C.]___.

6. In ___[49 B.C.]___ Julius Caesar took power into his own hands.

Tests on Persons. I. Here is a list of persons. Put each name in the right blank in the sentences below.

Romulus	Cicero	Tiberius Gracchus	Constantine
Vesta	Paul	Julius Caesar	Minerva
Hannibal	Cincinnatus		

1. The emperor who made Christianity one of the lawful religions of the Roman Empire was _____.

2. One of the greatest of the Roman orators was _____.

3. _____ was the Roman goddess of wisdom.

4. The man who made Rome an empire but did not take the title *emperor* was _____.

5. _____ was the brave Carthaginian who invaded Italy.

6. The greatest of the early Christian missionaries was _____.

7. _____ was an old man who left his plow to save Rome during the early days of the Republic.

8. The man who fought for the rights of the plebeians was _____.

9. The man who was supposed to have founded Rome was _____.

10. _____ was the Roman goddess of the home.

II. Here is another list. Do the same.

Jupiter	Caius Gracchus	Juno
Augustus Caesar	Remus	

1. The first ruler of Rome to receive the title *emperor* was _____.

2. _____ was the twin brother of Romulus.

3. The greatest of the Roman gods was _____.

4. The man who began the practice of giving food to the poor people from the state treasury was _____.

5. _____ was the wife of Jupiter.

Tests on Historical Terms. I. Here is a list of historical terms used. Put each in the right blank in the sentences below.

Aeneid	stylus	province	toga
Punic Wars	Twelve Apostles	Circus	catacombs
mosaic	Senate		

1. Romans wrote on their wax tablets with a _____.

2. A _____ was a part of the world conquered and governed by Rome.

3. The _____ was a dress that could be worn only by a full citizen of Rome.

4. The struggles between Rome and Carthage were known as the _____.

5. The _____ were the personal followers of Jesus.

6. A great poem telling the imaginary story of the beginning of settlement in Italy was the _____.

7. The laws in Rome during the time of the Republic were made by the _____.

8. The _____ was where horse races were held in Rome.

9. _____ were underground meeting places of the Christians.

10. A _____ is a design made with many small stones, some of them colored.

II. Here is another list. Do the same.

plebeians	gladiator	a triumph	"bread and games"
"Our Sea"	bishop	Forum	Pope
Twelve Tables	republic		

1. When the Senate made the laws for Rome, the government was a _____.

2. The written laws of the early Republic were the _____.

3. The Romans called the Mediterranean _____.

4. The _____ was a high official of the early Christian Church.

5. The _____ were the lower-class citizens of Rome, who for centuries did not have equal rights with the upper classes.

6. A parade celebrating the return to Rome of some soldier who had won great victories was _____.

7. The meeting place in which the Romans talked about the public business was the _____.

8. The _ _ _ _ _ _ is the head of the Roman Catholic Church.

9. A _ _ _ _ _ _ was a man who fought with deadly weapons for his living.

10. The city mobs in Rome expected to have free _ _ _ _ _ _.

III. Here is another list. Do the same.

patricians	public buildings	dome	"Roman peace"
emperor	aqueduct	Pompeii	"Eternal City"
amphitheater	Vestal Virgins		

1. A rounded roof over a circular hall is a _ _ _ _ _ _.

2. The place where the gladiators fought was an _ _ _ _ _ _.

3. An _ _ _ _ _ _ rules over countries which have been conquered.

4. Rome was called the _ _ _ _ _ _.

5. Buildings in which the people's business is carried on are _ _ _ _ _ _.

6. A channel or trough for bringing water from one place to another is an _ _ _ _ _ _.

7. The _ _ _ _ _ _ were women whose duty was to guard the sacred fire.

8. _ _ _ _ _ _ was a place destroyed by the volcano Vesuvius.

9. The _ _ _ _ _ _ were the upper-class citizens who had full rights.

10. The _ _ _ _ _ _ was the very long period of time in which there was no war in most of the Roman Empire.

IV. Here is another list. Do the same.

Latin	Roman numerals	Justinian Code	Colosseum

1. The language of the Romans was _ _ _ _ _ _.

2. The _ _ _ _ _ _ was the largest building in which gladiatorial games were held.

3. The figures that the Romans used to represent numbers were _ _ _ _ _ _.

4. The great collection of the Roman laws was the _ _ _ _ _ _.

Tests of Comprehension

Check the best answers:

1. The earliest Romans had little to do with the countries of the eastern Mediterranean because   they were enemies of the people of the East.   they did not have enough ships.   √ their country faced toward the west.   their country was a farming country.

2. It was easier to unite Italy than to unite Greece because   Italy was not such an independent country.   √ Italy was not cut up into small valleys.   Italy was farther away from the Eastern world.   Italy had more roads leading to all parts.

3. Rome and Carthage fought one another because they both   √ wanted the trade of the western Mediterranean.   had large navies and armies.   wanted to be the largest empire in the world.   had great captains as leaders.

4. The Romans borrowed many of the Greek ideas because   √ the Greek ideas were better than their own.   the Greeks conquered the Romans. the Romans had no ideas of their own.   the Romans were not as strong as the Greeks.

5. The Christian religion began among   √ the Jews.   the Romans. the Greeks.   the Phoenicians.

6. Rome was called a republic as long as its laws were made by   the emperor.   √ the Senate.   the Twelve Tables.   all the people.

7. Rome took a step the Greeks never had taken when she   kept citizenship only for the patricians.   took citizenship away from the plebeians. gave citizenship to the slaves.   √ gave citizenship to the people she conquered.

8. Many of the countries which Rome conquered accepted her rule gladly because   she did not make their people pay any taxes.   she did not make them serve in her armies.   √ she gave them better government than they had had before.   she gave them money to pay their debts.

9. In the Roman world the actions of the people were governed by whatever the king wanted.   √ what the law said was right.   whatever the people wanted to do.   what the Senators wanted.

10. The Romans wanted to drive out the Christians because   √ they thought the Christians would not be loyal to the emperor.   they thought the Christians lived wicked lives.   the Christians plotted against the emperor.   the Christians would not fight in the Roman army.

11. The patricians and the plebeians engaged in a long struggle because √ the patricians wanted to keep more rights for themselves than the plebeians had.   the plebeians wanted to keep more rights for themselves than the patricians had.   the plebeians did not want to give the patricians any rights at all.   the patricians did not want to give the plebeians any rights at all.

12. The problem which both Tiberius and Caius Gracchus were trying to solve was what to do about   the poor farmers who could not sell their crops.   the poor workmen who had little shops of their own.   the poor pay of the soldiers.   √ the poor people who had no work.

13. One of the greatest weaknesses of the Roman world was that   √ many rich people paid no taxes.   a few rich people paid all the taxes.   the people in the provinces paid no taxes.   the people engaged in trade paid no taxes.

14. Julius Caesar took away the power that had belonged to   the emperor.   √ the Senate.   the army.   the Vestal Virgins.

15. What is the title of the unit which you have just completed?   _ _ _ _ _ _

Are any children now ready to be transferred from the lower group to the group of independent readers?

UNIT FIVE · *A New Civilization takes Form during the Middle Ages*   [7 *Weeks*

STORY 1. THE END OF THE ROMAN WORLD · STORY 2. THE DARK AGES
[*1 Week*

Conversational Approach

"Why was Rome called 'the Eternal City'? And yet we know the Roman Empire did not last forever. Does the city of Rome today rule the Mediterranean world? Does it even rule over the rest of Italy? We must try to find out why the change came about.

"Have we already learned about weaknesses in the Roman world which were dangerous? What were they? Have you any idea who the people were who put an end to the Roman Empire?"

Reading and Study

The Reading Periods (First Story)

Independent Readers

This group reads the entire story through. They then test their understanding by the study-guide questions furnished by the teacher or by the text.

TEXTS

BEEBY, *America's Roots in the Past*, 178–185.
CHAPMAN, *Stories of Our European Forefathers*, 1–3.
CLARK-GORDY, *Westward toward America*, 185–191.
CORKE, *A Book of Ancient Peoples*, 221–226 (hard).
KELTY, *How Our Civilization Began*, 225–230.
KNOWLTON and GERSON, *Our Beginnings in the Past*, 223–225.
KNOWLTON and WHEELER, *Our Past in Western Europe*, 8–34 (hard).

Lower Group

The teacher tells the story orally to this group, writing on the board the most important words as she mentions them.

Then the teacher and these children read together the story as given in the text. The teacher guides the silent reading, section by section, by such questions as "How far did the later Roman Empire extend?"

Children read silently and answer orally. When they have read the entire story in this manner, they test themselves by the study-guide questions at the end of the story.

MORE DIFFICULT TEXTS

BARKER, DUNCALF, BACON, *Old Europe and Our Nation*, 173–186.
BEARD and BAGLEY, *Our Old World Background*, 112–115.
BOURNE and BENTON, *Introductory American History*, 67–70, 95–100.
BURNHAM, *Our Beginnings in Europe and America*, 110–113, 121–124.
COULOMB, MCKINLEY, WHITE, *What Europe Gave to America*, 98–99, 117–124.
GORDY, *American Beginnings in Europe*, 133–147.
GREENWOOD, *Our Heritage from the Old World*, 178–186.
HALL, *Our Ancestors in Europe*, 140–148.
HALLECK and FRANTZ, *Our Nation's Heritage*, 124–129, 140–154.
HARDING, *Old World Background to American History*, 108–110, 112–127.
HORNE and BUCKS, *Europe, the Mother of America*, 7–10.
NIDA, *Dawn of American History*, 80–82, 103–116.
NIVER, *Old World Steps to American History*, 148–154, 157–160.
SHERWOOD, *Our Country's Beginnings*, 121–128.
SOUTHWORTH, *What the Old World Gave the New*, 70.
TAPPAN, *Our European Ancestors*, 67–76.
VOLLINTINE, *The American People and Their Old World Ancestors*, 174–178, 182.
WICKHAM and PHILLIPS, *America's Heritage from the Long Ago*, 236–240, 245–249.
WOODBURN and HILL, *Historic Background of Our United States*, 181–186.

Easy Reading

EXTENSIVE READING

BEST, *Glorious Greece and Imperial Rome*, 201–210.
BEST, *Nations of Western Europe*, 1–65.
COFFMAN, *Child's Story of the Human Race*, 182–185.
CORKE, *The World's Family*, 108–114.
HILLYER, *Child's History of the World*, 219–230.
TERRY, *History Stories of Other Lands*, III: 81–106, 110–115.

READING FOR RECREATION

SCHWARTZ, *From Then till Now*, 139–185.

More Difficult Reading

EXTENSIVE READING

HAAREN and POLAND, *Famous Men of the Middle Ages*, 27–35.
HARDING, *Story of the Middle Ages*, 9–11.
HARTMAN, *The World We Live in*, 112–114, 127.
MILLER, *Picturesque Tale of Progress*, V: 11–60.
VAN LOON, *Story of Mankind*, 124–130.

READING FOR RECREATION

BALDWIN, *Story of Siegfried*.
LAMPREY, *Children of Ancient Gaul*.
ROLT-WHEELER, *In the Time of Attila*.

The Discussion

Children answer the study-guide questions as completely as possible. The teacher studies especially the performance of children who may have been recently transferred from the lower group to the group of independent readers.

The teacher writes on the board the words *Teutons, barbarian invasions*. Children discuss the meanings.

The Reading Periods (Second Story)

Independent Readers

TEXTS

CLARK-GORDY, *Westward toward America,* 177–181, 203, 237.

CORKE, *A Book of Ancient Peoples,* 234–244 (hard).

KELTY, *How Our Civilization Began,* 231–236.

Lower Group

The teacher tells the story orally to this group, writing on the board the most important words as she mentions them.

Then the teacher and these children read together the story as given in the text. The teacher guides the silent reading, section by section, by such questions as "What did the barbarians do to the country and the city?"

Children read silently and answer orally. When they have read the entire story in this manner, they test themselves by the questions at the end of the story.

MORE DIFFICULT TEXTS

BARKER, DUNCALF, BACON, *Old Europe and Our Nation,* 206–207.
BEARD and BAGLEY, *Our Old World Background,* 115–116.
BOURNE and BENTON, *Introductory American History,* 86–91.
BURNHAM, *Our Beginnings in Europe and America,* 113–118.
COULOMB, McKINLEY, WHITE, *What Europe Gave to America,* 128–132.
GORDY, *American Beginnings in Europe,* 147–148.
GREENWOOD, *Our Heritage from the Old World,* 179–186.
HALL, *Our Ancestors in Europe,* 144–148.
HALLECK and FRANTZ, *Our Nation's Heritage,* 149–154.
HAWLEY, *Adventures in Old World History,* 221–231.
HORNE and BUCKS, *Europe, the Mother of America,* 10–12.
NIDA, *Dawn of American History,* 116–141.
NIVER, *Old World Steps to American History,* 152–154.
SOUTHWORTH, *What the Old World Gave the New,* 80–83.
VOLLINTINE, *The American People and Their Old World Ancestors,* 183–203.

Easy Reading

EXTENSIVE READING

COFFMAN, *Child's Story of the Human Race,* 184–185.

HILLYER, *Child's History of the World,* 230–235.

More Difficult Reading

EXTENSIVE READING

HAAREN and POLAND, *Famous Men of Rome,* 262–269.

HARDING, *Story of the Middle Ages,* 10–51.

MILLER, *Picturesque Tale of Progress,* V: 61–89.

O'NEILL, *World's Story,* 166–188.

TAPPAN, *Heroes of the Middle Ages,* 17–31, 35–40.

VAN LOON, *Story of Mankind,* 126–130.

READING FOR RECREATION

LANSING, *Barbarian and Noble.*

The Discussion

Children answer the study-guide questions as fully as possible. The teacher writes on the board *Dark Ages, Middle Ages.* Children discuss the meanings.

Multisensory Aids

Children and teacher talk over together the pictures in the text, pointing out features of geographical and historical importance. They turn to a map of the Roman world and point out the boundaries. They show where the Teutons lived, and they locate Constantinople.

AUDIO-VISUAL MATERIALS OBTAINABLE

Compton's Pictured Teaching Materials: *Middle Ages*, I, Plate I.
International Educational Pictures: Sack of Rome, Siegfried.
LEHMANN. Colored History Pictures: I, 1, 21.
LEHMANN. Historical Pictures: I, L. H. 201.
LOHMEYER. History Pictures: 7.
MCKINLEY. Illustrated Topics for Ancient History: A 27.
MCKINLEY. Illustrated Topics for Medieval and Modern History: M M 1.
MEINHOLD. Colored History Pictures: 7.
MILLER. *Picturesque Tale of Progress*, V, 11–89.
Society for Visual Education (BRIGGS). Decline of Rome, Romano-Teutonic Europe.

Music. Play selections from Verdi's opera *Attila* and Liszt's *Battle of the Huns.*

General Activities

Creative Activities: Group and Individual, Correlated with Other Subjects or Voluntary Projects

The class draws headpiece designs for the first story.

Volunteers make symbolic drawings, symbolizing the weaknesses of the Roman Empire.

Volunteers dress dolls in the costumes of the Teutonic peoples.

A committee makes a graph comparing the length of time the United States has been settled [*beginning with 1607*] with the length of time that Rome lasted [*beginning with about 400 B.C. and extending to 476 A.D.*].

Volunteers compose poems on the barbarian invasions. Other children may wish to set the poems to music.

The class continues the time line.

More Difficult Activities

Children make picture maps of the Roman Empire, afterwards comparing their small drawings.

A volunteer committee constructs a German village to show how the Teutonic peoples lived.

The teacher reads to the children some of Tacitus's descriptions of the Germans. (The library may have a copy.)

Volunteers make maps showing the invasion of the different barbarian tribes. (Shepherd's *Historical Atlas*, 45, or a high-school text.)

Volunteers construct mosaic designs from small pieces of colored paper pasted on a heavy cardboard.

Three volunteers represent (1) the world of Greece and Rome, (2) the barbarians, and (3) the Christian Church. Each explains what he has to give to the world of the Middle Ages.

Volunteers make diagrams to illustrate the difference between the Middle Ages and the Dark Ages.

Application to Present-Day Conditions

Is our country today faced by any of the same weaknesses that were in the Roman Empire?

In what ways was the coming of barbarians into the Roman Empire different from the coming of immigrants into the United States?

Do soldiers at war today destroy buildings and works of art? Do you think they have more excuse or less than the medieval Teutons?

What is the "Roman fever"? [*Malaria.*] Why is it so called?

Does our civilization today owe anything to the classical world? the Teutons? the Christian Church?

Tell why the Great Wall, which is one of the most interesting sights in China, was built.

Exercises in Reasoning

What kept up the power of the later Roman emperors? How? Who made up these armies during the late Empire? Was it wise for the Romans to enlist barbarians in their armies?

Why is it more correct to speak about the "decay" of the Roman Empire than the "fall" of the Empire?

Did Roman civilization last longer in the West or in the East? Should you have expected this?

Did the barbarian invasions destroy Roman civilization completely?

Why did trade naturally fall off after the barbarian invasions?

Why did the falling down of the aqueducts spread disease?

Why did the barbarians borrow some of the Roman plans of government?

What do we mean when we speak of the great "middle class" of people? Who are the upper classes? Who are the lower classes?

Which lasted longer, the Middle Ages or the Dark Ages?

More Difficult Exercises in Reasoning

Do you think the emperors were wise to allow their armies to become so powerful that they alone kept the emperor on his throne? Explain your answer.

Why should every citizen pay some tax to the government, even if it is a very small one?

Why is it bad for a country to have many people who cannot find work?

Did the Roman Empire end because of attacks from without or because of decay within? Explain.

Compare the extent of the Italian possessions today with that of the Roman Empire at its greatest height.

Why were the Dark Ages so called?

In what ways were the Germans somewhat like the Spartans?

Drill Games

Association cards may be made as follows:

Dark Ages	↔	the period during which civilization seemed to have died
476	↔	date of the end of the Roman Empire in the West
barbarian invasions	↔	the pushing into the Roman Empire of great tribes of uncivilized people
400	↔	date of the beginning of the Dark Ages
Teutons	↔	the group that most of the barbarian tribes belonged to
Middle Ages	↔	the period of time between ancient and modern times
800	↔	date of the end of the Dark Ages
1500	↔	date of the end of the Middle Ages

Children drill one another by twos.

Testing

Tests of Understanding are given in Kelty's *How Our Civilization Began*, pp. 230, 236.

Tests of Reasoning and Skills. Underline the right words:

1. The chief reason why the Roman Empire came to an end was because it was attacked from without.   decayed from within.

2. The barbarians belonged to a large group of tribes called   Teutons. Carthaginians.   Macedonians.   Britons.

3. Many barbarians had been admitted to the Empire to serve as   farmers. soldiers.   traders.   missionaries.

4. The time when all civilization seemed to be destroyed was called the Middle Ages.   Dark Ages.

5. The Teutons liked best   city life.   country life.   village life.

Turn to a map of the Roman world. Check the following as true or false:

True False
[✓]   [ ] 1. The Roman Empire included England.
[✓]   [ ] 2. The Roman Empire included Turkey.
[ ]   [✓] 3. The Roman Empire included Germany.
[✓]   [ ] 4. The Roman Empire extended all around the Mediterranean.
[ ]   [✓] 5. The Roman Empire included all of Africa.
[ ]   [✓] 6. The Roman Empire included Arabia.

Where in your book can you find material about the Dark Ages? _ _ _ _ _ _. Where did you look to find out? _ _ _[*In the index.*]_ _ _ Under which word did you look?   Dark [✓]   Ages [ ]

Exercise in Organization. One half of the class copies the topic headings of the first story, and the other copies the topic headings of the second story. Each child prepares to give a topical recitation about his headings.

More Difficult Tests

Underline the right words:

1. The part of the Roman Empire that the barbarians were not able to take during the Dark Ages was   the west.   <u>the east.</u>   the north. the south.

2. The period which lasted the shorter time was   the Middle Ages. <u>the Dark Ages.</u>

3. Underline all the words which describe the Dark Ages truly:

<u>no ships built</u>	many policemen	much trade	<u>travel dangerous</u>
<u>no weapons made</u>	<u>much writing</u>	<u>aqueducts decayed</u>	property safe
<u>many pirates</u>	<u>runaway slaves</u>	<u>money not coined</u>	much wealth

STORY 3. CHARLEMAGNE AS A MAN OF WAR · STORY 4. CHARLEMAGNE AS A MAN OF PEACE   *[1 Week*

Conversational Approach

"What three things joined together to make up a new world during the Dark Ages? Do you suppose this could be done quickly? Why not? What are the dates for the beginning and end of the Dark Ages? What began about the year 400? Then something must have happened also about the year 800. Why? Do you think it was probably something good or something bad? Why? Our stories this week will tell what it was that brought the Dark Ages to an end."

Reading and Study

The Reading Periods (First Story)

Independent Readers

TEXTS

CHAPMAN, *Stories of Our European Forefathers*, 3–5.
CLARK-GORDY, *Westward toward America*, 195–198, 211–213, 237–239.
KELTY, *How Our Civilization Began*, 237–245.
KNOWLTON and WHEELER, *Our Past in Western Europe*, 34–42, 47–59 (hard).

Lower Group

The teacher tells the story orally to this group, writing on the board the most important words as she mentions them.

Then the teacher and this group read together the story as given in the text. The teacher directs the silent reading, section by section, by such questions as "What was the homeland of the Franks?"

Children read silently and answer orally. When they have completed the entire story in this manner, they test themselves by the study-guide questions at the end of the story.

MORE DIFFICULT TEXTS

BARKER, DUNCALF, BACON, *Old Europe and Our Nation*, 207–209, 212–215.
BEARD and BAGLEY, *Our Old World Background*, 163–167.
BOURNE and BENTON, *Introductory American History*, 108–110.
BURNHAM, *Our Beginnings in Europe and America*, 118–120.
COULOMB, McKINLEY, WHITE, *What Europe Gave to America*, 124–126.

GORDY, *American Beginnings in Europe*, 128–130.
GREENWOOD, *Our Heritage from the Old World*, 186–192, 273–290.
HALL, *Our Ancestors in Europe*, 148–154, 322–329.
HALLECK and FRANTZ, *Our Nation's Heritage*, 156–162.
HARDING, *Old World Background to American History*, 127–137.
HAWLEY, *Adventures in Old World History*, 235–246, 249–255.
HORNE and BUCKS, *Europe, the Mother of America*, 12–17.
NIDA, *Dawn of American History*, 191–195, 243–255.
NIVER, *Old World Steps to American History*, 161–164, 170–180.
SHERWOOD, *Our Country's Beginnings*, 128–129.
SOUTHWORTH, *What the Old World Gave the New*, 70–78.
TAPPAN, *Our European Ancestors*, 76–79.
VOLLINTINE, *The American People and Their Old World Ancestors* 203–218.
WICKHAM and PHILLIPS, *America's Heritage from the Long Ago*, 249–259.
WOODBURN and HILL, *Historic Background of Our United States*, 209–212.

The Discussion

Children answer the study-guide questions as fully as possible. The teacher continues to follow closely the work of children recently transferred from the lower group.

She writes on the board the words *Franks, kingdom, Lombards, count, coronation, Holy Roman Empire.* Children discuss the meanings.

The Reading Periods (Second Story)

Independent Readers

TEXTS

CHAPMAN, *Stories of Our European Fore-fathers*, 5–7.
CLARK-GORDY, *Westward toward America*, 213–220.
KELTY, *How Our Civilization Began*, 246–254.
KNOWLTON and WHEELER, *Our Past in Western Europe*, 59–68 (hard).

Lower Group

The teacher and these children read together the story as given in the text. The teacher directs the silent reading, section by section, by such questions as "Why did Charlemagne live simply?"

Children read silently and answer orally. When they have finished the entire story in this manner, they test themselves by the questions at the end of the story.

OTHER BOOKS

WAYLAND, *History Stories for Primary Grades*, 63–65.

MORE DIFFICULT TEXTS

BARKER, DUNCALF, BACON, *Old Europe and Our Nation*, 215–218, 250–263.
BEARD and BAGLEY, *Our Old World Background*, 163–167.
BOURNE and BENTON, *Introductory American History*, 110–111.
BURNHAM, *Our Beginnings in Europe and America*, 118–120.
HALL, *Our Ancestors in Europe*, 154–156, 161–163.
HALLECK and FRANTZ, *Our Nation's Heritage*, 162–164.
HARDING, *Old World Background to American History*, 137–141.
HAWLEY, *Adventures in Old World History*, 255–257.
HORNE and BUCKS, *Europe, the Mother of America*, 17–18, 20–22.
NIDA, *Dawn of American History*, 191–195, 220–222.
NIVER, *Old World Steps to American History*, 181–189.
SHERWOOD, *Our Country's Beginnings*, 128–129.
TAPPAN, *Our European Ancestors*, 76–78.
VOLLINTINE, *The American People and Their Old World Ancestors*, 218–222.
WICKHAM and PHILLIPS, *America's Heritage from the Long Ago*, 340–344.

Easy Reading

EXTENSIVE READING

BEST; *Nations of Western Europe*, 65–75, 85–124.

COFFMAN, *Child's Story of the Human Race*, 186–194.

COLLINS and HALE, *Hero Stories for Children*, 98–106.

CORKE, *The World's Family*, 114–119, 126–132.

HILLYER, *Child's History of the World*, 242–263.

TERRY, *History Stories of Other Lands*, III: 156–161, 170–177.

READING FOR RECREATION

Arabian Nights' Entertainments.

MITCHELL, *Horses: Now and Long Ago.*

NIDA, *Inventions and Discoveries of Ancient Times*, 244–256.

SCHWARTZ, *From Then till Now*, 189–232.

STEIN, *Our Little Frankish Cousin of Long Ago.*

More Difficult Reading

EXTENSIVE READING

BURNHAM, *Hero Tales from History*, 32–36.

HAAREN and POLAND, *Famous Men of the Middle Ages*, 61–70, 101–111.

HARDING, *Story of the Middle Ages*, 62–102.

HARTMAN, *The World We Live in*, 128.

MILLER, *Picturesque Tale of Progress*, V: 120–141, 142–176.

O'NEILL, *World's Story*, 195–200.

POWER, *Great People of the Past*, 103–111.

Story of Numbers (American Council on Education), 15–20.

TAPPAN, *Heroes of the Middle Ages*, 56–72.

Telling Time (American Council on Education), 24.

VAN LOON, *Story of Mankind*, 144–149.

READING FOR RECREATION

BALDWIN, *Story of Roland.*

BOYLAN, *The Piper of Clovis.*

CHURCH, *Stories of Charlemagne.*

SCALES, *Boys of the Ages*, 65–88.

SHERWOOD, *A Merry Pilgrimage.*

VAN DYKE, *The First Christmas Tree.*

The Discussion

Children answer the study-guide questions as completely as possible. The teacher writes on the board the words *medieval, reign, parchment, capitularies, missi, Palace School.* Children discuss the meanings.

Multisensory Aids

Children and teacher talk over together the pictures in the text, pointing out the features of historical and geographical significance. They turn to a map of Charlemagne's empire and show the three chief countries of today included in it.

AUDIO-VISUAL MATERIALS OBTAINABLE

International Educational Pictures: Adventures of Prince Achmed.

LEHMANN. Colored History Pictures: 5.

LEHMANN. Historical Pictures: I, L. H. 205.

LOHMEYER. History Pictures: 2.

McKINLEY. Illustrated Topics for Ancient History: A 28.

McKINLEY. Illustrated Topics for Medieval and Modern History: M M 2.

MILLER. *Picturesque Tale of Progress*, V, 120–176.

Secure a copy of Dürer's "Charlemagne."

Music. Play the following records: "Hymn of Charlemagne"; "Festival of Bagdad" (in connection with the story of Charlemagne's relations with the East).

General Activities

Creative Activities: Group and Individual, Correlated with Other Subjects or Voluntary Projects

A committee reports to the class who the Mohammedans were and why they were such a danger to the Christian world.

A volunteer dresses a doll as Charlemagne dressed.

The class finds pictures of the present church in Rome called St. Peter's.

A committee constructs one of Charlemagne's manors on the sand table.

The class makes a visit to the museum or the library to see books written on parchment.

The teacher reads to the class Longfellow's "Poet's Tale," from *Tales of a Wayside Inn*.

Children letter a motto of one of Charlemagne's favorite sayings: "He that ruleth his spirit is greater than he that taketh a city."

The class continues the time line.

More Difficult Activities

The teacher reads to the class passages from *The Song of Roland*.

Volunteers make a design for the "Iron Crown of the Lombards."

A volunteer committee constructs the great hall of one of Charlemagne's manors.

A volunteer tells the class one of the stories from the Arabian Nights and shows an attractive copy of the book.

A committee reports how the Christian world learned the system of Arabic notation from the Mohammedans.

The teacher reads to the class Longfellow's "Haroun Al Raschid."

Volunteers paint a long frieze representing a procession from one of Charlemagne's manors to the next.

Application to Present-Day Conditions

Were the Franks a Germanic people? How, then, does it happen that the French and the Germans are so different today?

The class finds out from the World Almanac how many people in the world today are Mohammedans. They compare this number with the number of Christians. Are all the Mohammedans under one ruler?

How do the Mohammedans measure time?

Are kings "chosen" by their people today, as Charlemagne was?

Are there any countries today in which every man must serve some time in the army? (See *conscription* in the encyclopedia.) Does he have to do so at his own expense?

Does the Pope own land in Italy today? (See *Vatican State* in the encyclopedia.)

What part of Germany today is known as Saxony?

What three countries of today were carved out of Charlemagne's empire after his death?

Using the scale of miles in your geography, estimate the shortest distance from the Rhine to the Danube. Does a canal connect these rivers today?

Are any bridges today half a mile long?

Has Ireland ever been the center of learning of the Western world since 800?

Exercises in Reasoning

Why did the Franks find it easier to mix with the Romans than the other Teutonic tribes did?

What kind of civilization might Europe have had today if the Mohammedans had won against the Franks?

Why did Charlemagne help the Pope?

Why were counts left in the forts in Saxony?

Why did Charlemagne take the title *Emperor of Rome*? Why was the word *holy* added, so that the new title became *Holy Roman Empire*?

What things does a workman's home have today which Charlemagne could not have?

Why did the manors have so little household linen?

Why is it hard to rule tribes which do not speak the same language?

Compare the expressions *reign* and *presidential administration*.

More Difficult Exercises in Reasoning

Why did the Franks give their name to France rather than to Germany?

Compare Clovis's conversion to Christianity with the conversion of the emperor Constantine.

Why can foreign trade usually not grow greatly during wartime?

Do you think that Charlemagne really made Christians of the Saxons?

How did Charlemagne help to introduce Roman art standards into his rude kingdom?

Why did learning live on in Ireland after it died out in most of the Western world?

Why must we always be careful to speak of the learning of the "Western world" at this time? Was there learning in the "Eastern world" too? [*China, Japan, India.*]

Drill Games

Place names are best drilled upon at the map: *Aix-la-Chapelle*.

Drill cards may be made as follows:

Franks	↔	a Teutonic tribe that spread over France
Charlemagne	↔	the man who brought order to western Europe at the end of the Dark Ages
kingdom	↔	a country ruled by a king
Lombards	↔	a Teutonic tribe that settled in northern Italy
count	↔	an official who ruled over a section recently taken from the barbarians

coronation	⟷	the crowning of a ruler
800	⟷	date when Charlemagne became emperor
Mohammedans	⟷	followers of a leader named Mohammed who became powerful in Asia and Africa
Saxons	⟷	the last Germanic tribe in Charlemagne's empire to become civilized
reign	⟷	the time during which a certain king rules
Palace School	⟷	Charlemagne's chief educational institution
medieval	⟷	belonging to the Middle Ages

Children drill themselves in preparation for the games in class.

Testing

Tests of Understanding are given in Kelty's *How Our Civilization Began,* pp. 245, 254.

Tests of Reasoning and Skills

1. With the help of your book make a list of the different peoples against whom Charlemagne fought. ___[*Lombards, Mohammedans, Saxons.*]___

2. Find out from your book what three modern countries were made from Charlemagne's empire. ___[*France, Germany, Italy.*]___

3. Charlemagne's capital city was ___[*Aachen, or Aix-la-Chapelle*]___.

4. Turn to a map of Charlemagne's empire. Check the following:

	Yes	No
a. Charlemagne's empire included all of Italy.	[ ]	[✓]
b. Charlemagne's empire went beyond the Elbe River.	[✓]	[ ]
c. Charlemagne's empire was as large as the old Roman Empire.	[ ]	[✓]
d. Charlemagne's empire included all of France.	[✓]	[ ]

5. What is the name of the unit which you are now studying? _____.
Where did you look to find out? ___[*In the table of contents.*]___

Exercise in Organization. Teacher and class make a co-operative outline of the first story.

More Difficult Tests

1. Can you make a sentence telling the chances for lasting success of an empire depending entirely on the strength of one person; for example, Alexander or Charlemagne? ___[*The empire is not apt to last after his lifetime.*]___

Fill the blanks with the right word.

2. Europe is Christian today because the Franks defeated the ___[*Mohammedans*]___.

3. Charlemagne united for the first time all the ___[*German, or Teutonic*]___ peoples of Europe.

4. Charlemagne became emperor of ___[*the Holy Roman Empire*]___.

STORY 5. THE NORTHMEN IN EUROPE · STORY 6. THE
NORSE DISCOVERY OF AMERICA   [1 Week

Conversational Approach

"There was one group of Teutonic people with whom Charlemagne had little to do. He had soldiers but few ships. They had ships but no regular army. They lived here" (showing at the map). "Because they lived in the North they were called Northmen or Norsemen. Have you ever heard of them?

"Our story today tells us of many adventures of the Northmen."

Reading and Study

The Reading Periods (First Story)

Independent Readers

TEXTS

CHAPMAN, *Stories of the Ancient Peoples*, 49–56.

CHAPMAN, *Stories of Our European Forefathers*, 9–10.

CLARK-GORDY, *Westward toward America*, 204–209.

KELTY, *How Our Civilization Began*, 255–260.

KNOWLTON and WHEELER, *Our Past in Western Europe*, 69–79 (hard).

Lower Group

The teacher tells the story orally to this group, writing on the board the most important words as she mentions them.

Then the teacher and these children read together the story as given in the text. The teacher directs the silent reading, section by section, by such questions as "Why could not Charlemagne conquer the Northmen?"

Children read silently and answer orally. When they have read the entire story in this manner, they test their understanding by the questions at the end of the story.

OTHER BOOKS

TERRY, *History Stories of Other Lands*, II: 33–41.

MORE DIFFICULT TEXTS

BARKER, DUNCALF, BACON, *Old Europe and Our Nation*, 232–235.
BOURNE and BENTON, *Introductory American History*, 93–99.
COULOMB, MCKINLEY, WHITE, *What Europe Gave to America*, 152–155.
GREENWOOD, *Our Heritage from the Old World*, 219–220.
HALL, *Our Ancestors in Europe*, 157–160.
HARDING, *Old World Background to American History*, 151.
HORNE and BUCKS, *Europe, the Mother of America*, 22–26.
NIVER, *Old World Steps to American History*, 157–160, 191–192, 198–200.
SOUTHWORTH, *What the Old World Gave the New*, 84–85.
TAPPAN, *Our European Ancestors*, 95–96.
VOLLINTINE, *The American People and Their Old World Ancestors*, 228–236.

The Discussion

Children answer the study-guide questions as fully as possible. Have they by this time acquired the habit of answering in their own words?

The teacher writes on the board the words *Vikings, raids, pirates*. Children discuss the meanings.

The Reading Periods (Second Story)

Independent Readers

TEXTS

CHAPMAN, *Stories of Our European Fore-fathers*, 10–12.

KELTY, *How Our Civilization Began*, 261–267.

KNOWLTON and WHEELER, *Our Past in Western Europe*, 79–80 (hard).

Lower Group

The teacher tells the story orally to this group, writing on the board the most important words as she mentions them.

Then the teacher and these children read together the story as given in the text. The teacher directs the silent reading, section by section, by such questions as "Why did many nobles leave Norway?"

Children read silently and answer orally. When they have read the entire story in this manner, they test themselves by the questions at the end of the story.

MORE DIFFICULT TEXTS

BOURNE and BENTON, *Introductory American History*, 104–106.

GREENWOOD, *Our Heritage from the Old World*, 220–222.

HORNE and BUCKS, *Europe, the Mother of America*, 26–29.

TAPPAN, *Our European Ancestors*, 147–149.

VOLLINTINE, *The American People and Their Old World Ancestors*, 235–236.

WICKHAM and PHILLIPS, *America's Heritage from the Long Ago*, 365–366.

WOODBURN and HILL, *Historic Background of Our United States*, 218–220.

Easy Reading

EXTENSIVE READING

BEST, *Nations of Western Europe*, 148–159.

BEST, *Steer for New Shores*, 33–37.

COFFMAN, *Child's Story of the Human Race*, 202–218.

CORKE, *The World's Family*, 132–135, 139–143.

HILLYER, *Child's History of the World*, 269–271.

LUTHER, *Trading and Exploring*, 88–147.

TERRY, *History Stories of Other Lands*, III: 177–181.

WADDELL and BUSH, *How We Have Conquered Distance*, 50–51.

READING FOR RECREATION

BAKER, *Out of the Northland*.

BROWN, *In the Days of Giants*.

COLE, *A B C Book of People*.

D'AULAIRE, *Conquest of the Atlantic*, 7–14.

EVERSON, *Coming of the Dragon Ships*.

HALL, *Viking Tales*.

HARSHAW, *My Viking Book*.

HOLBROOK, *Story of Fridthjof*.

JOHNSTON, *Our Little Viking Cousin of Long Ago*.

PETERSHAM, *Story Book of Ships*.

POWER, *Boys and Girls of History*, 15–27.

More Difficult Reading

EXTENSIVE READING

HAAREN and POLAND, *Famous Men of the Middle Ages*, 126–134.

HARDING, *Story of the Middle Ages*, 114–123.

INGRAHAM, *Story of Democracy*, 93–112.

MILLER, *Picturesque Tale of Progress*, V: 207–236.

NIDA, *Man Conquers the World with Science*, 124–134.

O'NEILL, *World's Story*, 200–209.

POWER, *Great People of the Past*, 112–123.

STUART, *The Boy through the Ages*, 95–110.

TERRY, *History Stories of Other Lands*, IV: 14–22.

VAN LOON, *Story of Mankind*, 150–154.

READING FOR RECREATION

ADAMS, *Swords of the Vikings*.

BOYESEN, *Modern Vikings*.

BRADISH, *Old Norse Stories*.

COLUM, *Children of Odin*.

CROSS, *Music Stories for Boys and Girls*.

DU CHAILLU, *Ivar the Viking*.

DU CHAILLU, *The Thrall of Leif the Lucky*.

FRENCH, *Story of Rolf and the Viking's Bow*.

GILBERT, *Boys' Book of Pirates*.

HYDE, *The Singing Sword*.

MABIE, *Norse Stories*.

PYLE, *Heroic Tales from the Norse*.

STEIN, *Our Little Norman Cousin of Long Ago*.

The Discussion

Children answer the study-guide questions as completely as possible. The teacher writes on the board the words *Vinland, voyage, to found a colony.* Children discuss the meanings.

Multisensory Aids

Children and teacher talk over together the pictures available in the text, pointing out features of geographical and historical significance. They turn to a map of Europe and show how the Vikings might reach the Black Sea, pointing out on a large wall map how they might return to their homes by way of the Mediterranean and the Atlantic. Children name all the rivers and water bodies they must pass in making the complete journey.

AUDIO-VISUAL MATERIALS OBTAINABLE

Compton's Pictured Teaching Materials: *Middle Ages,* I, Plate I, 4. *Water and Air Transportation,* Plate II, 1, 2.
GRANT. *Story of the Ship,* 8.
International Educational Pictures: Greenland, Land of the Vikings.
LEHMANN. History Pictures: I, L. H. 337, 340.
McKINLEY. Illustrated Topics for Medieval and Modern History: M M 2.
MILLER. *Picturesque Tale of Progress,* V, 207–236.
Society for Visual Education (MUIR). English History, 55 B.C.–1297 A.D.
Yale Pageant Educational Slides: 1, 2, 6.

The teacher finds a copy of Walter Sargent's "Tree of Life" to show the class.

Music. Play selections from the Wagnerian operas, such as *Parsifal, Rheingold,* and *Siegfried,* especially "The Ride of the Valkyries" and "The Magic-Fire Music," from *Brünnhilde;* Weber's opera *Der Freischütz;* Meyerbeer's opera *Robert le Diable;* Elgar's cantata *King Olaf;* and the following songs: Coleridge-Taylor's "Viking Song," Faning's "Song of the Vikings," Schubert's "Erlkönig," Grieg's "Land-Sighting."

General Activities

Creative Activities: Group and Individual, Correlated with Other Subjects or Voluntary Projects

A committee models in the sand table the home of the Northmen, showing the fjords, the seas, and the islands visited by them.

A volunteer carves a Norse ship. Other volunteers make the shields to place along its sides. Girls make the sail. Volunteers load it with Norse trading goods.

Girls dress dolls in the costumes of the Northmen.

Volunteers make lists of original names for Norse ships.

The class divides into committees. Each chooses one of the Norse gods about whom to read. The committees report to the class and show pictures.

Volunteers write letters describing their journeys "west overseas."

Committees make picture collections of Iceland; of Greenland.

Children draw designs for Norse shields.

The class continues the time line.

More Difficult Activities

Volunteers draw designs for Norse helmets.

A volunteer draws a map of Norse routes of trade and exploration, and colors the countries or sections taken over by them, such as Sicily and Normandy. (Shepherd's *Historical Atlas*, 45.)

The class takes an imaginary tour through Normandy.

The teacher reads to the class Longfellow's poem "The Skeleton in Armor"; Longfellow's "King Robert of Sicily"; and Sidney Lanier's "The Story of Vinland," from *Psalm of the West*.

A volunteer reports on the Norse sagas.

Application to Present-Day Conditions

Do Norway, Sweden, and Denmark still get much of their living from the sea? (See your geography.)

Does Russia still use the trade routes to the Black Sea followed by the Northmen? (See a trade map of Russia.)

Have you ever heard of raids' being made nowadays?

Are there pirates anywhere in the world today? [*In China.*]

What form of government have Norway, Sweden, and Denmark nowadays?

To whom does Iceland belong now? Greenland?

For which of the Norse gods are our days of the week named (except Saturday)?

Exercises in Reasoning

Compare the reasons why the Northmen were sailors with the reasons why the Greeks and Phoenicians were sailors.

Why would not Charlemagne sell weapons to the Northmen?

Which is the better place for a colony, Greenland or Iceland? Why? (See your geography.)

Why are the trees in Greenland and Iceland small?

Why is it difficult for people who do not understand one another's language to trade with one another?

What is the difference between "finding a colony" and "founding a colony"?

More Difficult Exercises in Reasoning

How could the Northmen steer their ships without a compass?

By what routes could traders from the Far East reach Constantinople with such goods as spices and silk?

Why was it very difficult for the Franks to guard their country against Viking raids?

Prove from the story that Norway had become a Christian country before the year 1000.

Why do people always say that Columbus discovered America, although Leif reached it almost five hundred years earlier?

How do people of today know whether or not Leif discovered Vinland?

Drill Games

Place names are best drilled upon at the map: *Greenland, Iceland, Vinland, Normandy.*

Drill cards may be made as follows:

voyage	⟷	a long journey over the sea
to found a colony	⟷	to begin a settlement in a place away from home
Eric the Red	⟷	the man who found Greenland
Vikings	⟷	another name for the Northmen
raid	⟷	a sudden breaking in by an enemy
pirate	⟷	a robber on the seas
Leif the Lucky	⟷	the first white man who touched the mainland of North America
1000	⟷	the year Leif discovered Vinland

Children drill on their own difficulties in preparation for the class games.

Testing

Tests of Understanding are given in Kelty's *How Our Civilization Began,* pp. 259–260, 267.

Tests of Reasoning and Skills. Check the best answer:

1. The Northmen first appeared in Europe as   √ traders.   explorers.   pirates.   colonists.

2. A modern country which the Northmen helped to found was   Italy.   Greece.   √ Russia.   Turkey.

3. The man who found Greenland was   Rollo, the Norman.   Harold Fairhair.   Leif the Lucky.   √ Eric the Red.

Finish these sentences:

4. The Northmen had to be sailors because _ _ _ [*their own country was too poor to feed them*] _ _ _.

5. The Northmen wanted to make colonies in some countries farther south because _ _ _ [*they sought a better climate and soil*] _ _ _.

Exercise in Organization. Children prepare oral summary paragraphs for every topic heading in the two stories.

More Difficult Tests

Check the best answer:

1. Charlemagne had never conquered the Northmen because   they were stronger than his soldiers.   they would not fight with him.   he was too busy conquering the Saxons.   √ he had no ships in which to reach them.

2. The Russian river down which the Northmen traveled was the   Volga.   Don.   √ Dnieper.   Dvina.

Finish these sentences:

3. The Northmen became pirates instead of traders because _ _ _[*it was easy to take from weaker people*]_ _ _.

4. Many Norse nobles left Norway for the West because _ _ _[*they wouldn't accept the rule of a strong king*]_ _ _.

5. Underline the right word or words: The Northmen   did   <u>did not</u> make permanent colonies on the mainland of North America.

STORY 7.   TEUTONIC TRIBES IN ENGLAND   [*1 Week*

Conversational Approach

Turn to a map of the Roman Empire. "Did the Roman Empire include the British Isles?" Compare with a wall map of Europe to determine whether the Empire had ever included all the British Isles.

"Does anyone remember any of the experiences Julius Caesar met with when he led his army into Britain?

"When the Roman Empire in the West decayed, what do you suppose happened to the Roman soldiers in Britain? Do you suppose Britain had a barbarian invasion too? Our story will tell us about it."

Reading and Study

The Reading Periods

Independent Readers

TEXTS

CHAPMAN, *Stories of Our European Forefathers*, 12–15.
CLARK-GORDY, *Westward toward America*, 223–227.
KELTY, *How Our Civilization Began*, 268–274.
KNOWLTON and WHEELER, *Our Past in Western Europe*, 80–86 (hard).

Lower Group

The teacher tells the story orally to this group, writing on the board the most important words as she mentions them.

Then the teacher and these children read together the story as given in the text. The teacher directs the silent reading, section by section, by such questions as "What product had the Romans been getting from Britain?"

Children read silently and answer orally. When they have read the entire story in this manner, they test themselves by the questions at the end of the story.

OTHER BOOKS

TERRY, *History Stories of Other Lands*, II: 35–48.

MORE DIFFICULT TEXTS

BARKER, DUNCALF, BACON, *Old Europe and Our Nation*, 210–212.
BEARD and BAGLEY, *Our Old World Background*, 171–172.
BOURNE and BENTON, *Introductory American History*, 100–102.
BURNHAM, *Our Beginnings in Europe and America*, 126–134.
COULOMB, McKINLEY, WHITE, *What Europe Gave to America*, 143–148.
GORDY, *American Beginnings in Europe*, 149–158.

GREENWOOD, *Our Heritage from the Past*, 202–208, 215–219.
HALL, *Our Ancestors in Europe*, 181–187.
HALLECK and FRANTZ, *Our Nation's Heritage*, 167–170.
HARDING, *Old World Background to American History*, 142–150.
HAWLEY, *Adventures in Old World History*, 259–263.
NIDA, *Dawn of American History*, 154–173.
NIVER, *Old World Steps to American History*, 166–169.
SHERWOOD, *Our Country's Beginnings*, 129–131.
SOUTHWORTH, *What the Old World Gave the New*, 80–84.
TAPPAN, *Our European Ancestors*, 81–86.
VOLLINTINE, *The American People and Their Old World Ancestors*, 223–228.
WICKHAM and PHILLIPS, *America's Heritage from the Long Ago*, 319–323, 334–335.
WOODBURN and HILL, *Historic Background of Our United States*, 186–188.

Easy Reading

EXTENSIVE READING

BEST, *Merry England*, 1–120.
COFFMAN, *Child's Story of the Human Race*, 195–201.
CORKE, *The World's Family*, 119–122.
DUTTON, *Little Stories of England*, 85–104.
HILLYER, *Child's History of the World*, 219.
TERRY, *History Stories of Other Lands*, II, 37–49; III, 1–12, 66–70, 116–146.

READING FOR RECREATION

ANDREWS, *Ten Boys Who Lived on the Road from Long Ago to Now* (Wulf, the Saxon Boy).
COLE, *A B C Book of People*.
COWLES, *Our Little Saxon Cousin of Long Ago*.
LANSING, *Life in the Greenwood*.
LUTHER, *Trading and Exploring*.

More Difficult Reading

EXTENSIVE READING

HARDING, *Story of the Middle Ages*, 58–61, 124–126.
KUMMER, *First Days of History*, 282–303.
MARSHALL, *Island Story*, 171.
MILLER, *Picturesque Tale of Progress*, VI, 133–148.
QUENNELL, *Everyday Life in Anglo-Saxon, Viking, and Norman Times*.
QUENNELL, *Everyday Life in Roman Britain*.

READING FOR RECREATION

CASE, *The Banner of the White Horse*.
CHURCH, *Stories from English History*, 8–48, 60–66.
HANSON, *Stories of the Days of King Arthur*.
HENTY, *Beric the Briton*.
KINGSLEY, *Hereward the Wake*.
KIPLING, *Puck of Pook's Hill*.
LAMPREY, *Children of Ancient Britain*.
LANIER, *The Boys' King Arthur*.
LETTS, *The Mighty Army*.
PYLE, *King Arthur and His Knights*.
SMITH, *Number Stories of Long Ago*.
STEIN, *Our Little Celtic Cousin of Long Ago*.
STUART, *The Boy through the Ages*.
WARREN, *King Arthur and His Knights*.

The Discussion

Children answer the study-guide questions as completely as possible. Are they by this time habitually questioning one another as to important phases omitted?

The teacher writes on the board the words *Angles, Saxons, heathen, Witan, Round Table*. Children discuss the meanings.

Multisensory Aids

Children and teacher talk over together the pictures in the text, pointing out features of geographical and historical significance.

ARNOLD. History Pictures: A. H. P. 1, 5.
BLACK. Wall Pictures: 1–3.
EASTMAN. Educational Slides: Set, 303.
LONGMANS. Historical Wall Pictures: The Roman Wall; St. Augustine.
MILLER. *Picturesque Tales of Progress*, VI, 133–148.
Viaduct History Pictures: 1.

Music. Play selections from Taylor's *King's Henchman.*

General Activities

Creative Activities: Group and Individual, Correlated with Other Subjects or Voluntary Projects

A volunteer makes a map showing the Roman wall in Britain.

Volunteers tell the class stories of King Arthur and his Round Table.

Volunteers dramatize the incident of the monk and the Angle slave boys in the market place.

A volunteer makes a sort of candle from dried reeds placed in melted fat.

Volunteers draw the Black Raven flag.

The class continues the time line.

More Difficult Exercises

The class chooses certain of the stories about King Arthur and the knights of his Round Table to dramatize.

Volunteers report on the lives of Saint Augustine and Saint Patrick.

A committee constructs on the sand table an Anglo-Saxon village in England. (See the model in the World Book Encyclopedia in the article on England under " History.")

The class dramatizes a meeting of the Witan.

The class meets as a group of Northmen and plans an attack on Britain.

Application to Present-Day Conditions

Are you an Anglo-Saxon? How can you tell? [*It depends on where your ancestors came from.*]

Do *Great Britain* and *England* mean the same thing today? How do they differ? (See the map.)

Where did we get our use of the mistletoe at Christmas time?

What parts of Great Britain today are inhabited by the ancient (Celtic) inhabitants? Why are very few left in England?

Do you think that the civilization of the United States is really an Anglo-Saxon civilization now, in view of the many immigrants from other parts of the world?

What is the origin of our expression *board* meaning meals?

How is your local community governed today? Is this an English idea?

How did St. Patrick's Day originate?

Exercises in Reasoning

Why did the ancient world so greatly desire tin?

Compare the difference in spelling and meaning between the words *Britain* and *Briton*.

Were the Saxons who invaded Britain the same people whom Charlemagne conquered?

Why did the early English help one another in their farming?

How did the early English govern their own villages? Compare this kind of government with the government of the Romans.

Why did the Northmen make raids upon the churches especially?

More Difficult Exercises in Reasoning

During the Roman period in Britain, why did the Romans remain in the cities and the Britons in the country?

Why is the climate of England more pleasant than the climate of Saxony?

Why was the conversion of Britain and Ireland of great importance in civilizing them?

In what way was the Witan much more democratic than the Roman Senate?

Compare the conquest of the Anglo-Saxons by the Northmen with the conquest of the Babylonians by the Assyrians.

Drill Games

Place names are best drilled upon at the map: *Britain, Wales, Scotland, Ireland.*

Drill cards may be made as follows:

Angles and Saxons	↔	the Teutonic people who conquered the Britons
heathen	↔	people who worship false gods
King Arthur	↔	the greatest hero of the Britons
Britons	↔	the native people of Britain
Round Table	↔	the meeting place of King Arthur's knights
Witan	↔	a meeting of chiefs and freemen in early England to give the king advice

Children drill on their own difficulties.

Testing

Tests of Understanding are suggested in Kelty's *How Our Civilization Began,* p. 274.

Tests of Reasoning and Skills. Fill the following blanks. Use your book if it will help you.

1. The English people were formed from a mixture of the _ _ _[Romans]_ _ _, the _ _ _[Britons]_ _ _, the _ _ _[Angles]_ _ _, and the _ _ _[Saxons]_ _ _.

2. Britain had been a _ _ _[province]_ _ _ of the Roman Empire.

3. Missionaries were sent to Britain from _ _ _[*Rome*]_ _ _.

4. Any _ _ _[*freeman*]_ _ _ who wished to do so might attend the Witan.

5. The _ _ _[*Britons*]_ _ _ in England were not Teutonic people.

6. The last danger to the English people in this story came from the _ _ _[*Northmen*]_ _ _.

7. Where in your book is King Arthur mentioned?   Where did you look to find out? _ _ _[*In the index.*]_ _ _ Under which word did you look?

King [   ]   Arthur [√]

Exercise in Organization. Children make summary sentences about the story.

More Difficult Tests

Fill the following blanks. Use your book if it will help you.

1. The first Teutonic peoples to invade Britain were the _ _ _[*Angles*]_ _ _ and the _ _ _[*Saxons*]_ _ _. Three hundred years later came the _ _ _[*Northmen*]_ _ _.

2. With Christianity _ _ _[*civilization*]_ _ _ once more came to Britain.

3. The king had to hear the advice of the _ _ _[*Witan*]_ _ _.

4. Our idea of self-government in local communities came down to us from the _ _ _[*early English*]_ _ _.

5. The native Britons were driven into _ _ _[*Wales*]_ _ _, _ _ _[*Scotland*]_ _ _, and _ _ _[*Ireland*]_ _ _.

STORY 8. KING ALFRED   [*1 Week*

Conversational Approach

"At the end of our last story we left the English facing what great danger? What do you suppose will happen? What had happened in France when the Northmen came? Do you suppose the English will have to give them another Normandy? Or will the Northmen mix with the English, as the Angles and Saxons had mixed with the Britons? Our story will tell us."

Reading and Study

The Reading Periods

Independent Readers

TEXTS

CHAPMAN, *Stories of Our European Fore-fathers*, 18–23.
CLARK-GORDY, *Westward toward America*, 227–230.
KELTY, *How Our Civilization Began*, 275–284.
KNOWLTON and WHEELER, *Our Past in Western Europe*, 86–92 (hard).

Lower Group

The teacher tells the story orally to this group, writing on the board the most important words as she mentions them.

Then the teacher and this group read together the story as given in the text. The teacher guides the silent reading, section by section, by such questions as "What was the English king doing during these years?"

Children read silently and answer orally. When they have completed the

entire story in this manner, they test themselves by the questions at the end of the
story.

OTHER BOOKS

BALDWIN, *Fifty Famous Stories Retold.*
TERRY, *History Stories of Other Lands*, I,
35–37, 38–41.
WAYLAND, *History Stories for Primary
Grades*, 66–68.

MORE DIFFICULT TEXTS

BEARD and BAGLEY, *Our Old World Background*, 172–174.
BOURNE and BENTON, *Introductory American History*, 111–114.
BURNHAM, *Our Beginnings in Europe and America*, 134–141.
COULOMB, McKINLEY, WHITE, *What Europe Gave to America*, 148–151.
GORDY, *American Beginnings in Europe*, 158–167.
GREENWOOD, *Our Heritage from the Old World*, 222–224.
HALL, *Our Ancestors in Europe*, 187–192.
HALLECK and FRANTZ, *Our Nation's Heritage*, 170–178.
HARDING, *Old World Background to American History*, 151–159.
HAWLEY, *Adventures in Old World History*, 263–264.
HORNE and BUCKS, *Europe, the Mother of America*, 34–39.
NIDA, *Dawn of American History*, 174–190.
NIVER, *Old World Steps to American History*, 192–198.
SHERWOOD, *Our Country's Beginnings*, 132–144.
SOUTHWORTH, *What the Old World Gave the New*, 86–88.
TAPPAN, *Our European Ancestors*, 86–93.
VOLLINTINE, *The American People and Their Old World Ancestors*, 273–276.
WICKHAM and PHILLIPS, *America's Heritage from the Long Ago*, 323–327.
WOODBURN and HILL, *Historic Background of Our United States*, 212–218.

Easy Reading

EXTENSIVE READING

BEST, *Merry England*, 121–133.
COLLINS and HALE, *Hero Stories for Children*, 110–118.
CORKE, *The World's Family*, 122–126.
HILLYER, *Child's History of the World*, 264–268.
TERRY, *History Stories of Other Lands*, III, 181–205.

READING FOR RECREATION

FARJEON, *Mighty Men from Beowulf to William the Conqueror.*
POWER, *Boys and Girls of History*, 15–27, 103–111.

More Difficult Reading

EXTENSIVE READING

BURNHAM, *Hero Tales from History*, 37–41.
DUTTON, *Little Stories of England.*
HAAREN and POLAND, *Famous Men of the Middle Ages*, 135–142.
HARDING, *Story of the Middle Ages*, 126–129.
MILLER, *Picturesque Tale of Progress*, VI, 148–153.
QUENNELL, *Everyday Life in Anglo-Saxon, Viking, and Norman Times.*

READING FOR RECREATION

CHURCH, *Stories from English History*, 82–92.
COMSTOCK, *A Boy of a Thousand Years Ago.*
HENTY, *The Dragon and the Raven.*
LANSING, *Barbarian and Noble*, 123–136.
LEIGHTON, *Olaf the Glorious.*
McKILLIAM, *Alfred the Great.*
MADISON, *A Maid at King Alfred's Court.*
TAPPAN, *In the Days of Alfred the Great.*

The Discussion

Children answer the study-guide questions as completely as possible. Are they by this time answering habitually in their own language rather than in the words of the book?

The teacher writes on the board the words *treaty, burg, sheriff, Anglo-Saxon Chronicle, Danes.*

Multisensory Aids

Children and teacher together talk over the pictures in the text, pointing out features of historical and geographical significance. They turn to a map of early England and show London, the Thames, the old Roman wall, the Danelaw.

AUDIO-VISUAL MATERIALS OBTAINABLE

Longmans Historical Wall Pictures: A Danish Raid.
MILLER. *Picturesque Tale of Progress*, VI, 148–153.
Viaduct History Pictures: 2.

General Activities

Creative Activities: Group and Individual, Correlated with Other Subjects or Voluntary Projects

The class dramatizes the story of King Alfred and the cakes.

Volunteers draw Alfred's flag "The Golden Dragon."

The class words and signs the treaty drawn up between Alfred and the Danes.

A volunteer divides a candle by lines, as Alfred did, and illustrates its use to tell time.

A committee reads to the class the dramatization from Stevenson's *Children's Classics in Dramatic Form*, II, 115–128.

More Difficult Activities

A committee reports on the Danish kings who ruled England later, giving special attention to Canute.

The class makes an *American Chronicle* for as many years back as they can remember.

Some child who knows a foreign language explains how books may be translated from one language into another. He illustrates by translating sentences.

Application to Present-Day Conditions

How long do pupils have to study today, even in the best modern schools, before they can read Latin easily?

Do you think that paying enemies or gangsters to let you alone works in the long run?

Is fear of a foreign enemy ever used to unite quarreling groups within a country nowadays?

Is London still a center of the wool trade?

Can you name any cities whose names end in the syllable *burg*, and which were once forts? [For example, *Pittsburgh, Edinburgh*.]

What are the duties of the sheriff of today?

Are chronicles kept nowadays?

Can we today learn any lessons from Alfred's willingness to learn from other people even though he was a king?

Is any nation today disunited, somewhat as England was in Alfred's time? [*China*.]

Exercises in Reasoning

Compare Alfred and Alexander. Which ruled more land? Which had the greater army? Which did more lasting good for his people?

About when was Alfred chosen king?

What finally made the little English kingdoms unite into one?

Why are the Northmen who came into England also called Danes?

Compare Alfred with Charlemagne.

Compare Alfred's written laws with the Twelve Tables of the Romans.

Why did Alfred send out judges to travel about the country?

More Difficult Exercises in Reasoning

A committee makes a list of all the rulers that it can find who have ever been called "the Great."

How did Alfred's visits to Rome influence his ideas?

Did the English have professional soldiers in Alfred's time? What incidents in the story answer this question for you?

Why was Alfred able to hold his own against the Danes after he built ships?

Why do you suppose that the part of the country given to the Danes was called the Danelaw?

Who served as officers in Alfred's army?

In what way do you suppose that the story which you just read depended on the *Anglo-Saxon Chronicle*?

In what sense is it true that the English *nation* begins with Alfred?

Drill Games

Place names are best drilled upon at the map: *London, Thames.*

Drill cards are made as follows:

Alfred the Great	↔	the king who united many small English kingdoms into one
treaty	↔	an agreement between two or more countries
Danelaw	↔	the part of England set aside for the Danes
burg	↔	a fort or a strong town
Danes	↔	Northmen from Denmark
sheriff	↔	the English officer at the head of each county
Anglo-Saxon Chronicle	↔	an early history of England kept year by year

Children drill by twos.

Testing

Tests of Understanding are given in Kelty's *How Our Civilization Began,* p. 284.

Tests of Reasoning and Skills. Check the right answer:

1. When Alfred was a child, England had   one united kingdom. ✓ many small kingdoms.

2. In the treaty between Alfred and the Danes   the English kept all of England for themselves.   the Danes kept all of England for themselves. ✓ each side took part of the country.   neither side had any of the country.

3. Complete this sentence: Alfred had the laws written down so that ___[*everyone might know what they were*]___.

Turn to a map of early England. Check the following:

	Yes	No
4. The Danelaw was in the eastern part of England.	[✓]	[ ]
5. The Danelaw included all of England.	[ ]	[✓]
6. London is on the river Thames.	[✓]	[ ]
7. The Roman wall was between England and Wales.	[ ]	[✓]

Exercise in Organization. The children who believe themselves able to do so make an independent outline of the story. The others work with the teacher on a co-operative outline.

More Difficult Tests

Check the best answers:

1. Alfred wanted his people to learn Latin because   the Romans spoke and wrote the Latin language.   ✓ most of the world's knowledge was written in Latin.   Charlemagne had had his nobles study Latin.

2. Alfred wanted foreigners to come to London because   ✓ foreigners knew things which the English did not.   foreigners were better than his own people.   there were not enough of his own people.

Complete these sentences:

3. The English at last united into one kingdom because ___ [*that was the only way to defend themselves against the Danes*] ___.

4. The *Anglo-Saxon Chronicle* is useful to us today because ___ [*our histories of the period are based on it*] ___.

STORY 9. THE NORMAN CONQUEST   [*1 Week*

Conversational Approach

"By how many different peoples has Britain been conquered by this time?" The teacher lists the names on the board as they are given: *Romans, Angles and Saxons, Danes.*

"Britain is conquered one more time. We shall have one more name to add to this list. And then there will be no more. Britain has never again been conquered, after this one time, from that day to the present. She has been beaten in battles, but her homeland has never since been conquered.

"This last conquest is by the Northmen who had settled in France. What were they called?"

Reading and Study

The Reading Periods

Independent Readers

TEXTS

CHAPMAN, *Stories of Our European Fore-fathers*, 23–29.
CLARK-GORDY, *Westward toward America*, 230–231.
KELTY, *How Our Civilization Began*, 285–294.
KNOWLTON and WHEELER, *Our Past in Western Europe*, 92–97, 99–102 (hard).

Lower Group

The teacher tells the story orally to this group, writing on the board the most important words as she mentions them.

Then the teacher and this group read together the story as given in the text. The teacher directs the silent reading, section by section, by such questions as "What changes had taken place among the Northmen in France?"

Children read silently and answer orally. When they have finished the entire story in this manner, they test themselves by the questions at the end of the story.

OTHER BOOKS

TERRY, *History Stories of Other Lands*, II, 42–49, 58–68.

MORE DIFFICULT TEXTS

BARKER, DUNCALF, BACON, *Old Europe and Our Nation*, 319–320.
BEARD and BAGLEY, *Our Old World Background*, 174–176.
BOURNE and BENTON, *Introductory American History*, 103–104, 114.
BURNHAM, *Our Beginnings in Europe and America*, 141–144, 184–186.
COULOMB, McKINLEY, WHITE, *What Europe Gave to America*, 155–158.
GORDY, *American Beginnings in Europe*, 168–170.
GREENWOOD, *Our Heritage from the Old World*, 226–237, 253–260.
HALL, *Our Ancestors in Europe*, 192–200.
HALLECK and FRANTZ, *Our Nation's Heritage*, 178–181, 193–204.
HARDING, *Old World Background to American History*, 160–164, 166.
HAWLEY, *Adventures in Old World History*, 264–268.
HORNE and BUCKS, *Europe, the Mother of America*, 39–45.
NIDA, *Dawn of American History*, 256–263.
NIVER, *Old World Steps to American History*, 201–204.
SOUTHWORTH, *What the Old World Gave the New*, 88–91.
WICKHAM and PHILLIPS, *America's Heritage from the Long Ago*, 328–330.
WOODBURN and HILL, *Historic Background of Our United States*, 235–239.

Easy Reading

EXTENSIVE READING

BEST, *Merry England*, 134–146.
COFFMAN, *Child's Story of the Human Race*, 219–226.
HILLYER, *Child's History of the World*, 286–291.
TERRY, *History Stories of Other Lands*, III, 205–207.

READING FOR RECREATION

LANSING, *Life in the Greenwood*.
POWER, *Boys and Girls of History*, 28–39.
STEIN, *Little Count of Normandy*.
STEIN, *Our Little Norman Cousin of Long Ago*.

More Difficult Reading

EXTENSIVE READING

BURNHAM, *Hero Tales from History*, 42–47.
DUTTON, *Little Stories of England.*
HAAREN and POLAND, *Famous Men of the Middle Ages*, 167–172.
HARDING, *Story of the Middle Ages*, 129–131.
MARSHALL, *An Island Story.*
MILLER, *Picturesque Tale of Progress*, VI, 154–163.
QUENNELL, *Everyday Life in Anglo-Saxon, Viking, and Norman Times.*
TERRY, *History Stories of Other Lands*, IV, 23–40.

READING FOR RECREATION

BULWER-LYTTON, *Harold, the Last of the Saxon Kings.*
CHURCH, *Stories from English History*, 107–142.
GILBERT, *Boys' Book of Pirates.*
LYNN, *For Land and Liberty.*
O'NEILL, *Stories That Words Tell Us.*
PYLE, *Merry Adventures of Robin Hood.*
STUART, *The Boy through the Ages.*
TAPPAN, *In the Days of William the Conqueror.*
TAPPAN, *Robin Hood: His Book.*

The Discussion

Children answer the study-guide questions as fully as possible. The teacher checks carefully to see that a few children do not do all the talking while others never participate.

She writes on the board the words *conqueror, Domesday Book, conquest, Tower of London.* Children discuss the meanings or significance.

Multisensory Aids

Children and teacher together talk over the pictures in the text, pointing out features of geographical or historical significance; for example, the characteristics of the Norman style of architecture.

AUDIO-VISUAL MATERIALS OBTAINABLE

ARNOLD. Historical Pictures: 7.
EASTMAN. Educational Slides: Ivanhoe.
International Educational Pictures: Apple-Blossom Time in Normandy, The Prince and the Pauper, Ivanhoe.
LONGMANS. Wall Pictures: Harold's Last Stand.
MILLER. *Picturesque Tale of Progress*, VI, 154–163.
Viaduct History Pictures: 3.
Pictures of the Bayeux tapestry are shown in the Encyclopædia Britannica, Fourteenth Edition.

Music. Play selections from De Koven's opera *Robin Hood* and Sullivan's opera *Ivanhoe.*

General Activities

Creative Activities: Group and Individual, Correlated with Other Subjects or Voluntary Projects

A volunteer draws a picture of the heavy English battle-ax.

Children draw their own designs for a tapestry representing the battle of Hastings.

The teacher shows the children a sample of tapestry with figures woven into it. Perhaps a local shop can help.

Children measure off thirty feet, to see the thickness of the Norman walls.

A committee constructs a Norman castle, from the description in the story.

More Difficult Activities

The girls in the sewing classes may make a wall tapestry of appliquéd figures, based upon their own drawings.

Volunteers report on the story of Robin Hood.

The class studies characteristics of the Norman style of architecture and makes a picture collection to illustrate the study. Does the Norman style use the Roman arch?

The teacher reads to the class passages from Scott's *Ivanhoe* to illustrate the differences between the English and the Normans.

A volunteer reports on the part which the Tower of London has played in English history. He shows a picture of the Tower.

A visitor to England describes Norman architecture to the class.

Volunteers make soap carvings of the Tower of London.

The teacher posts copies of the imaginative newspaper *The Contemporary World*: Medieval History, 1066 (McKinley Publishing Co.).

Application to Present-Day Conditions

Does the Witan still choose the king of England?

How do game preserves of today differ from "the king's forests"?

You often hear it said that French is today the "court language" of Europe. What does this mean?

Do we today have any plan, somewhat like the Domesday Book, for finding out the amount of taxes different people ought to pay? [*Assessment rolls.*] Is this the same as a census? How does it differ?

Exercises in Reasoning

Would William have conquered England just as easily if Alfred had been king at that time?

Was it necessary for William to be elected by the Witan? Why did he choose to be elected?

Did William take away the right of the people to govern their own home counties? Why not?

Why did the Englishmen hate the Norman castles?

Why was trade in English ports safer under William than it had been since the days of Alfred?

More Difficult Exercises in Reasoning

Why would it have been better if Harold could have waited several months after William's landing before fighting a battle? Why didn't he wait?

Why did William make every man in England who was given any land swear to be true to him directly, without any lords or counts or princes between the two? In what way did this make the king of England stronger than the kings on the continent of Europe?

Compare the final fate of the Normans in England with the fate of the Danes and the Angles and Saxons.

Drill Games

Drill cards may be made as follows:

conqueror	⟷	one who gets possession of a country by war
Domesday Book	⟷	a list, made by William I, of all goods and persons in England
battle of Hastings	⟷	the battle which decided that William was to rule England
conquest	⟷	obtaining by means of war
Tower of London	⟷	a fort in London later used as a prison for the nobles
William the Conqueror	⟷	the Norman who made himself king of England
1066	⟷	date of the battle of Hastings

Children drill themselves individually.

Testing

Tests of Understanding are given in Kelty's *How Our Civilization Began,* p. 294.

Tests of Reasoning and Skills

1. List three things the Normans had done in France.   *a.* _ _ _[*settled down*]_ _ _.   *b.* _ _ _[*learned the French language*]_ _ _.   *c.* _ _ _[*become Christians*]_ _ _.

Check the best answer:

2. William became king of England   √ by force.   by the free will of the Witan.

3. Every man who received any land in England had to promise to be true   to the lord next above him.   √ to William himself.

4. The king counted the amount of tax each man should pay from   the *Anglo-Saxon Chronicle.*   the Twelve Tables.   √ the Domesday Book.

5. How many stories have you now read in this unit, counting this story? _ _ _[*Nine.*]_ _ _   Where did you look to find out?   _ _ _[*At the table of contents.*]_ _ _

Exercise in Organization. Children copy the topic headings of the story and prepare a topical recitation on each heading.

More Difficult Tests

Check the right answer:

1. After Alfred's death in England until William's time   the king was strong and the nobles were weak.   the nobles were strong and the king was weak.   √ each kept the other weak.   both were strong.

2. The English   loved William because he was a just king.   √ did not like William because he had conquered them.

3. Write here William's excuse for attacking England.   _ _ _[*He said it had been promised that he should be next king. Now Harold was made king.*]_ _ _

4. Tell here how William won the battle of Hastings.   _ _ _[*He pretended to be running away. The English ran after him.*]_ _ _

STORY 10. ENGLISH KINGS AND THE ENGLISH LAW   [*1 Week*

Conversational Approach

"After the time of William the Conqueror there was no question but that the common people in England had to obey the law. Was that a good thing?

"So long as William was alive, the barons and other nobles had to obey the law too. Was that a good thing? In most of Europe at that time the nobles did not obey any laws, and there was little order or safety for anyone. Our story today tells us that England had one more lesson to learn in this matter of the nobles.

"And now we come to the question of the king himself. Should the king obey the laws? In Europe the kings would have felt insulted if anyone had said that they should *obey* the law. They *were* the law. But in England at this time a surprising new idea was brought forward. That idea was that the king too must obey the law. Our story will tell us how this surprising thing happened."

Reading and Study

The Reading Periods

Independent Readers

TEXTS

CHAPMAN, *Stories of Our European Fore-fathers*, 29–35.
KELTY, *How Our Civilization Began*, 295–300.
KNOWLTON and WHEELER, *Our Past in Western Europe*, 102–105 (hard).

Lower Group

The teacher tells the story orally to this group, writing on the board the most important words as she mentions them. Children practice the pronunciations.

Then the teacher and these children read together the story as given in the text. The teacher directs the silent reading, section by section, by such questions as "Who kept the nobles or barons in order in England?"

Children read silently and answer orally. When they have finished the entire story in this manner, they test themselves by the questions at the end of the story.

OTHER BOOKS

TERRY, *History Stories of Other Lands*, I, 49–59.

MORE DIFFICULT TEXTS

BARKER, DUNCALF, BACON, *Old Europe and Our Nation*, 321–326.
BEARD and BAGLEY, *Our Old World Background*, 177–179.
BOURNE and BENTON, *Introductory American History*, 122–128.
BURNHAM, *Our Beginnings in Europe and America*, 174–179.
COULOMB, McKINLEY, WHITE, *What Europe Gave to America*, 158–164.

GORDY, *American Beginnings in Europe*, 171–175.
GREENWOOD, *Our Heritage from the Old World*, 237–242.
HALL, *Our Ancestors in Europe*, 200–212.
HALLECK and FRANTZ, *Our Nation's Heritage*, 184–191.
HARDING, *Old World Background to American History*, **168–179.**
HAWLEY, *Adventures in Old World History*, 269–277.
HORNE and BUCKS, *Europe, the Mother of America*, 45–51.
NIDA, *Dawn of American History*, 265–271.
NIVER, *Old World Steps to American History*, 218–219.
SHERWOOD, *Our Country's Beginnings*, 146–154.
SOUTHWORTH, *What the Old World Gave the New*, 103–106.
TAPPAN, *Our European Ancestors*, 98–108.
WICKHAM and PHILLIPS, *America's Heritage from the Long Ago*, 330–334, 336.
WOODBURN and HILL, *Historic Background of Our United States*, 239–248.

Easy Reading

EXTENSIVE READING

BEST, *Merry England*, 173–182.
HILLYER, *Child's History of the World*, 311–315.

More Difficult Reading

EXTENSIVE READING

BURNHAM, *Hero Tales from History*, 47–51.
DUTTON, *Little Stories of England*.
GILMAN, *Magna Charta Stories*.
HAAREN and POLAND, *Famous Men of the Middle Ages*, 185–188.
HARTMAN, *The World We Live in*, 153–158.
INGRAHAM, *Story of Democracy*, 114–145.
MILLER, *Picturesque Tale of Progress*, VI, 164–182.
ROSS, *From Conquest to Charter*.
TERRY, *History Stories of Other Lands*, IV, 53–61, 101–110.
VAN LOON, *Story of Mankind*, 184–190.

READING FOR RECREATION

CHURCH, *Stories from English History*, 187–191.
FARJEON, *Kings and Queens*.
YONGE, *The Prince and the Page*.

The Discussion

Children answer the study-guide questions as fully as possible. Since these matters are somewhat abstract, the answers may be given by several different sets of children. The teacher makes an earnest attempt to ascertain whether their answers convey real concepts or are merely words.

The teacher writes on the board the words *charter, common law, jury, Magna Charta, representatives, Parliament*. Children discuss the meanings.

Multisensory Aids

Children and teacher talk over together the pictures in the text, pointing out features of geographical and historical significance.

AUDIO-VISUAL MATERIALS OBTAINABLE

ARNOLD. History Pictures: 5.
Compton's Pictured Teaching Materials: *Middle Ages*, II, Plate VIII, 1, 2.
MILLER. *Picturesque Tale of Progress*, VI, 164–182.
Viaduct History Pictures: 4, 5.

General Activities

Creative Activities: Group and Individual, Correlated with Other Subjects or Voluntary Projects

Volunteers draw scenes in England under the weak kings, illustrating the sufferings of the common people.

The class dramatizes the scene at Runnymede.

The class carries on some activity with other schools, ·which necessitates the election of representatives to plan the movement. The regular forms of election should be followed, and the persons chosen should be called *representatives*. Such an activity as this is needed if children are to grasp any real concept of representation. Without it their explanations are mere verbalism.

The class draws up a document entitled Magna Charta, very carefully letters it, signs it, and seals it with a seal designed for the purpose.

The class continues the time line.

More Difficult Activities

If possible, the class is taken to a courtroom to see the judges, jury, lawyers, etc. No attempt is made to follow the details of the case.

Volunteers report on the exploits of John's brother, Richard the Lion-hearted.

The class collects pictures of the English Parliament in session.

The teacher reads to the class Act IV, Scene I, of Shakespeare's *King John*.

Application to Present-Day Conditions

Are there any classes of people today who regularly do not obey the law? [*Gangsters and racketeers.*]

Have you ever seen a schoolroom in which the teacher could not keep order? Were the pupils well off and happy? Is it a good thing for a school to have such a teacher?

Is there such a thing as the common law in the United States? (Ask a lawyer.)

Does the jury system work as well in large cities as in places where the neighbors all know one another? Tell why.

Why is it a good thing for us that the English learned how to govern themselves during the Middle Ages?

Some countries do not have juries. Their cases at law are decided by trained judges. In what ways might this system be better than ours? In what ways worse?

Why should our citizens be willing to serve on juries when they are called upon to do so?

What documents form the "American Magna Charta"?

Do most kings today have to obey their country's laws? Do the kings themselves make the laws?

Is the title *baron* used today?

What body in the United States corresponds to the English Parliament? [*Congress.*]

Are the English people even yet noted for the fact that they obey their own laws? Do Americans do as well?

Exercises in Reasoning

Why would it be a bad thing for the nobles to be so strong that they would not obey the law?

Which did the country people trust more, the king or the nobles? Why?

Why was it a good thing that the English kings lost the lands they had held in France?

Was there any written law saying that the nobles did not have to follow the king to France? On what kind of law did the nobles depend, then?

Why would representatives of the people be likely to make better laws than the king alone could make?

More Difficult Exercises in Reasoning

Why was it a bad thing to allow the nobles to build strong castles for themselves?

Suppose that a new case came up and there had never been any law made about it. For example, suppose that one man's bull killed another man's calf. No law had ever been made saying what to do in a case like this. The judges would have to depend on what the custom of the country was. This was called the common law. Can you think of an example of your own, showing when the common law would be called upon?

Who made the common people form the habit of obeying the law? Who made the nobles form the habit of obeying the law? Who made the king promise to obey the law?

How did it come about that kings of England ever owned lands in France? [*William the Conqueror had been Duke of Normandy.*]

Most of our descriptions of King John have come down from his enemies. Do you suppose that their descriptions may not have been entirely fair to John? Why?

Drill Games

Drill cards may be made as follows:

jury	⇔	a group of men who have to decide whether a man is guilty or not
1215	⇔	the date of Magna Charta
representative	⇔	a person chosen to carry out the desires of his community
charter	⇔	a paper stating certain rights
Runnymede	⇔	the place where King John was forced to sign Magna Charta
common law	⇔	unwritten law based on custom
Magna Charta	⇔	the state paper in which King John promised to obey the law of the land
King John	⇔	the king who was forced to sign Magna Charta
Parliament	⇔	the group of men who make the laws for Great Britain

Children drill first on these items and then on all the cards in the unit. They practice in groups of twos.

Testing

Tests of Understanding are given in Kelty's *How Our Civilization Began,* p. 300.

Tests of Reasoning and Skill. Mark the following as true or false:

True False

[✓] [ ] 1. The Englishmen learned that their country needed a strong king.

[ ] [✓] 2. Henry II was a weak king.

[ ] [✓] 3. The common law is different in different parts of the country.

[✓] [ ] 4. A jury is made up of the people themselves.

[ ] [✓] 5. The nobles continued to refuse to obey the laws after the time of Henry II.

[✓] [ ] 6. John and his nobles quarreled because he asked them to fight for him in France.

[✓] [ ] 7. The barons were ready to make war against John.

[ ] [✓] 8. Magna Charta said that the nobles must obey the law.

Exercise in Organization. Children copy the two topic headings and make oral summaries of each.

More Difficult Tests

True False

[✓] [ ] 1. The sons of William the Conqueror were strong kings.

[ ] [✓] 2. The persons who suffered most under a weak king were the nobles.

[✓] [ ] 3. The common law was spread by the king's judges.

[ ] [✓] 4. All countries of Europe in the time of Henry II used juries.

[ ] [✓] 5. It was a great misfortune to England that her kings lost their possessions in France.

[✓] [ ] 6. King John was forced to promise to obey the law by the action of his own nobles.

[ ] [✓] 7. In all the other countries of Europe at the same time the king had to obey the law also.

[✓] [ ] 8. The system of representation began in England.

Why would you probably not believe all the bad things said about a man by his bitter enemies?

Tests on the Entire Unit

Test of Place Sense. Pass double-sized maps of Europe showing the water bodies in color or the land bodies by shading. Give the following directions:

1. Put the letter *A* where Aix-la-Chapelle should be.

2. Put the letter *G* in Greenland.

3. Put the letter *I* in Iceland.

4. Put the letter *N* in Normandy.

5. Put the letter *S* in Scotland.

6. Put the letter *W* in Wales.

7. Write *Ire* in Ireland.

8. Make a circle where London should be.

Tests of Time Sense. Pass mimeographed sheets of the following:

I. In each of the exercises below, place the figure *1* before that which happened first, and the figure *2* before that which happened later.

1. [___*1*___] End of Roman Empire in the West.
   [___*2*___] Northmen reach Iceland.

2. [___*2*___] Holy Roman Empire.
   [___*1*___] Dark Ages.

3. [___*2*___] Coronation of Charlemagne.
   [___*1*___] Barbarian invasions of the Empire.

4. [___*1*___] Northmen enter Normandy.
   [___*2*___] William conquers England.

5. [___*2*___] Vinland is found.
   [___*1*___] Iceland is settled.

6. [___*2*___] Danes enter England.
   [___*1*___] Saxons enter England.

7. [___*1*___] Romans conquer Britain.
   [___*2*___] Alfred saves Britain.

8. [___*1*___] Henry II spreads common law.
   [___*2*___] John signs Magna Charta.

9. [___*2*___] Parliament begins.
   [___*1*___] King agrees to obey the law.

II. Here is a list of dates. Put each one in the right blank in the sentences below.

476	1215	400	800
1500	1000	1066	

1. Leif Ericson reached Vinland in _____.

2. Charlemagne was crowned Emperor in _____.

3. The Roman Empire in the West ended in _____.

4. The battle of Hastings took place in _____.

5. The Middle Ages came to an end in about _____.

6. The Dark Ages began in about _____.

7. King John signed Magna Charta in _____.

Test on Persons. Here is a list of persons. Put each name in the right blank in the sentences below.

Charlemagne	King Arthur	Leif the Lucky
Eric the Red	Alfred the Great	William the Conqueror
King John		

1. The man who was forced to sign Magna Charta was _____.

2. The person who found Vinland was _____.

3. The man who united many small English kingdoms into one was _____.

4. The Briton who fought against the Angles and Saxons was _____.

5. The person who made a colony in Greenland was _____.

6. The man who became emperor in 800 was _____.

7. The Norman duke who made himself king of England was _____.

Tests on Historical Terms

I. Here is a list of historical terms. Put each one in the right blank in the sentences below:

Dark Ages	Angles and Saxons	barbarian invasions	kingdom
Franks	treaty	jury	to found a colony
voyage	conqueror		

1. A _____ is one who makes himself master of a country by fighting.

2. The time between the barbarian invasions and Charlemagne is known as the _____.

3. A _____ is a solemn agreement between countries.

4. A group of men who have to decide whether or not someone has done something against the law is a _____.

5. A _____ is a long journey over the sea.

6. The territory ruled by a king is a _____.

7. The _____ were attacks upon the Roman Empire.

8. The _____ were the barbarians who founded modern France.

9. The first Teutonic tribes to force their way into Britain were the _____.

10. To start a new settlement away from home is _____.

II. Here is another list. Do the same.

heathen	representatives	Vikings	burg
Danelaw	Teutons	Britons	battle of Hastings
Domesday Book	Lombards		

1. The Northmen were sometimes called _____.

2. The _____ was the part of England given to the Danes.

3. _____ are people who worship idols or believe in false gods.

4. The native inhabitants of Britain were _____.

5. The _____ were Germanic tribes who lived over all northern Europe.

6. The Normans conquered England at the _____.

7. _____ are persons chosen to carry out the wishes of the people who choose them.

8. A fort was called a _____ in Britain.

9. The _____ were Teutons who forced their way into Italy.

10. The list of all the people and property in England was the _____.

III. Here is another list. Do the same.

charter   raid   conquest   Mohammedans
Middle Ages   Round Table   Runnymede   pirate
coronation   Danes

1. Northmen who lived in Denmark were called _____.

2. The _____ was where King Arthur called his knights together.

3. King John and his barons met at _____.

4. The time between the end of the Roman Empire in the West and the year 1500 is known as the _____.

5. A paper giving certain rights or privileges is a _____.

6. A _____ is a sudden unexpected attack by a few people.

7. The crowning of a king is the _____.

8. A person who robs ships at sea is a _____.

9. The _____ were followers of a religious teacher called Mohammed.

10. The conquering of a land or people is called a _____.

IV. Here is another list. Do the same.

Witan   common law   Magna Charta   Palace School
sheriff   Saxons   reign   medieval
Tower of London   *Anglo-Saxon Chronicle*   Parliament

1. The _____ were at last conquered by Charlemagne.

2. The body of men who make the laws for Great Britain is the _____.

3. The word _____ is used to describe the Middle Ages.

4. The _____ was an old history kept year by year.

5. The chief officer in a British county was the _____.

6. A king's _____ is the period during which he rules.

7. Charlemagne's children and nobles were taught at the _____.

8. The _____ was a gathering of the chiefs and wise men in Britain.

9. The law which was based on custom and which was the same all over England was the _____.

10. The paper signed by King John was the _____.

11. The _____ was a fort built to protect London.

Test of Comprehension

Check the best answer:

1. The Roman Empire in the West came to an end because   there were so many more barbarians than Romans.   the Empire was too big to be governed.   √ there were so many bad customs in the Empire.   the Empire had no soldiers to defend it.

2. The Dark Ages were given that name because   √ it seemed as if civilization had died.   the houses no longer had lights in them.   it seemed as if large empires could not last.   the barbarians were a dark race of people.

3. During the Dark Ages   the mixture of different peoples got along well together.   greater progress was made than during the Empire.   absolutely no progress was made whatever.   √ a new mixture of people and ideas was being formed.

4. The Franks were the most successful of all the many barbarian peoples because   they wandered away from their own lands and became Romans. √ they kept their own lands and ideas, but took on Roman ways also.   they kept their old ways and refused to learn anything from the Romans.   they were the only barbarians who became Christians.

5. Charlemagne's greatest work was   √ to spread civilization throughout western Europe.   to spread Christianity throughout eastern Europe. to give back the lands taken from the Pope.   to carry on wars against the Saxons.

6. The Northmen were feared throughout Europe because   they traveled so far from home.   they were of such huge size.   they made many colonies.   √ they made raids upon peaceful people.

7. The discovery of America by the Northmen was not of great importance to the world because   we are not sure that they did discover it.   no trade with America was possible.   √ no use was made of the discovery. we are more interested in Columbus.

8. When the Roman soldiers had to leave Britain   the Britons were strong enough to defend it.   √ the Angles and Saxons conquered it.   the Franks added it to their empire.   the Danes were defeated there.

9. King Alfred's greatest work for Britain was   to make peace with the Danes.   to build up the city of London.   to write many books in Latin.   √ to unite many small kingdoms into one.

10. When William of Normandy conquered England   √ he made every landholder promise to be true to him.   he told the landholders to follow the nobles.   he gave no land to the nobles.   he left the people free to choose whom they would follow.

11. England learned that it was better for the country   to have a weak king.   √ to have a strong king.   to have no king at all.

12. William and Henry II together   made the king obey the laws. made the common people obey the nobles.   √ made the nobles obey the laws.   made the nobles obey the common people.

13. In 1215 at Runnymede   √ the barons made the king obey the law.   the king made the barons obey the law.   the barons made the common people obey the law.   the common people made the barons obey the law.

14. What is the title of the unit which you have just completed? _ _ _ _ _ _.

Are any children now ready to be transferred from the lower group to the group of independent readers?

UNIT SIX · *How People lived during the Middle Ages*

STORY 1. THE FEUDAL SYSTEM [1 Week

Conversational Approach

"Now we must go back to shortly after the time of Charlemagne to get a picture of how the people lived. What date do we remember for Charlemagne?

"Life during the Middle Ages was not nearly so safe as it is now. Our farmers, even those living far out in the country, are safe. What makes them so? Why are city people comparatively safe, also?

"But in the early Middle Ages there were no policemen, no sheriffs, no armies, no strong kings. Anybody who wanted something went out and got it, if he was strong enough. How do you suppose people could manage to protect themselves and their families?" Children try to devise plans.

"Our story this week will tell about a plan that was worked out almost everywhere."

Reading and Study

The Reading Periods

Independent Readers

This group reads the entire story through. They then test their understanding by the study-guide questions furnished by the teacher or by the text.

TEXTS

BEEBY, *America's Roots in the Past,* 188–194.
CHAPMAN, *Stories of Our European Forefathers,* 36–39.
KELTY, *How Our Civilization Began,* 303–308.
KNOWLTON and WHEELER, *Our Past in Western Europe,* 109–114 (hard).

Lower Group

The teacher tells the story orally to this group, writing on the board the most important words as she mentions them.

Then the teacher and these children read together the story as given in the text. The teacher directs the silent-reading, section by section, by such questions as "What happened after the death of Charlemagne?"

Children read silently and answer orally. When they have finished the story in this manner, they test themselves by the questions at the end of the story.

MORE DIFFICULT TEXTS

BARKER, DUNCALF, BACON, *Old Europe and Our Nation,* 226–231.
BEARD and BAGLEY, *Our Old World Background,* 116–118.
BOURNE and BENTON, *Introductory American History,* 130–132.
COULOMB, McKINLEY, WHITE, *What Europe Gave to America,* 132.
GORDY, *American Beginnings in Europe,* 179–182.

Easy Reading

EXTENSIVE READING

More Difficult Reading

EXTENSIVE READING

READING FOR RECREATION

The Discussion

Children answer the study-guide questions as completely as possible. The teacher makes an attempt to draw members of the lower group into the discussion.

She writes on the board the words *fief, feudalism, vassal, serf, overlord.* Children discuss the meanings.

Multisensory Aids

Children and teacher talk over together the pictures available in the text, pointing out features of geographical and historical significance.

AUDIO-VISUAL MATERIALS OBTAINABLE

Compton's Pictured Teaching Materials: *Middle Ages*, I; Plate II, 1.
Copley Prints: Oath of Knighthood.
Emery Prints: The Vigil.
LEHMANN. Colored History Pictures: I, 24.
LOHMEYER. History Pictures: 23.
McKINLEY. Illustrated Topics for Medieval and Modern History: MM 3.
MILLER. *Picturesque Tale of Progress*, V: 237–239.
Society for Visual Education (BRIGGS). Feudal Age.

General Activities

Creative Activities: Group and Individual, Correlated with Other Subjects or Voluntary Projects

The class writes out the terms of an agreement between a poor farmer and a nobleman at the beginning of the feudal system. The agreement should state what each one promises and what he secures in return. A similar agreement is worded between a lord and a common laborer.

A volunteer draws a diagram of fiefs which a lord might hold in different parts of a country.

Children draw on the blackboard a diagram showing a king with twenty great nobles; each great noble with thirty lesser nobles; and so on as far as board space will permit, down to knights who possess only one small fief.

The class dramatizes the ceremony of swearing fealty.[1]

The class explains the title of the story.

More Difficult Activities

Volunteers dramatize the ceremony of the swearing of fealty by a son upon the death of his father. The son then returns home and receives the homage of his vassals in turn.

The class lists the powers of the overlord, and the duties of the vassal.

The class lists the duties of a serf.

A volunteer committee reports on feudalism in Japan. (See the encyclopedia.)

Application to Present-Day Conditions

Make a list of all the agencies which we have today to keep us safe from enemies, fire, flood, and disease. What did people of the Middle Ages have in each case to protect themselves?

How did the use of titles such as *earl, duke, count, viscount, baron,* etc. originate? Did the titles remain even after the lands had been taken away? Can a citizen of the United States have a title?

Why was there never a feudal system in the United States?

When were the slaves freed in the United States? When were the serfs freed in Russia? (See the encyclopedia: *Alexander II of Russia.*)

How do poor people today get protection from persons who might injure them?

What title are Englishmen given when they are made knights today? [*Sir.*]

Exercises in Reasoning

Which do you think got the better of the bargain — the vassal or the overlord?

Were all fiefs the same size?

To whom did each vassal swear to be true, to his overlord or to the king?

Could the same man be both an overlord and a vassal? Explain.

---

[1] The teacher may find assistance in the series of articles on children's dramatics in *Progressive Education*, VIII: 3–98 (1931).

How did feudalism put a stop to so many people's wandering about the country?

Explain the difference between a serf and a slave.

Was a serf given land, as a vassal was?

More Difficult Exercises in Reasoning

Why did the small independent farmer disappear entirely under feudalism?

Did the feudal system tend to give the king great power? What was his greatest danger? How had William the Conqueror guarded himself against this very thing? Does this explain why feudalism was never so strong in England as it was on the Continent?

Why did a vassal often pay his overlord in goods instead of in money?

Was feudalism a good thing or a bad thing for the times?

You may have heard this statement, "A serf was as much a part of a fief as a tree was." Explain it.

What is a "private" war? Does the world have private wars nowadays?

Drill Games

Association cards may be made as follows:

fief	↔	an estate granted for use of a vassal by an overlord
feudalism	↔	a plan by which men held gifts of land on condition that they fight for and serve their lord
vassal	↔	a man who received land from his overlord
serf	↔	a person whose labor belonged to the estate
overlord	↔	the man who granted some of his land to his followers

Children choose partners with whom to practice.

Testing

Tests of Understanding are given in Kelty's *How Our Civilization Began,* p. 308.

Tests of Reasoning and Skills. Fill the following blanks with the right word or words:

1. Feudalism began after the death of _ _ _[*Charlemagne*]_ _ _.

2. Small farmers could protect themselves by giving up _ _ _[*their land*]_ _ _.

3. Common laborers could win protection by _ _ _[*giving themselves as serfs*]_ _ _.

4. An overlord had to give _ _ _[*protection*]_ _ _ to his people.

5. An estate granted by an overlord was a _ _ _[*fief*]_ _ _.

6. The man who was given land by his lord was a _ _ _[*vassal*]_ _ _.

7. The system of granting land from lord to vassal was called _ _ _[*feudalism*]_ _ _.

8. A man who worked on land which he did not own and who received part of the crop was a _ _ _[*serf*]_ _ _.

Exercise in Organization. Children copy the topic headings and give oral summaries of each topic.

More Difficult Tests

Use your book.

1. List the powers of a lord within his own fief:

    a. _ _ _[*He could lead in war.*]_ _ _

    b. _ _ _[*He could make his followers keep peace among themselves.*]_ _ _

    c. _ _ _[*He could judge cases at law.*]_ _ _

2. List the things a vassal had to do for his lord:

    a. _ _ _[*To fight a certain number of days a year.*]_ _ _

    b. _ _ _[*To furnish his own fighting equipment and supplies.*]_ _ _

    c. _ _ _[*To pay sums*

            when the lord's oldest son was made a knight,

            when his daughter was married,

            when the lord was captured.]_ _ _

3. How did a serf differ from a vassal? _ _ _[*He was not free to move.*]_ _ _

4. How did a serf differ from a slave? _ _ _[*He could not be sold.*]_ _ _

STORY 2. LIFE IN THE CASTLES   [1 Week

Conversational Approach

"Suppose one of these lords of the Middle Ages had been attacked by an enemy. How could he protect himself? How could he give the protection that he had promised to his vassals? What would happen to his serfs? How could so many people live in one castle? What would they have to eat? What would become of the cattle, pigs, sheep, geese, etc.? Our story will give us a picture of life in a medieval castle.

"What things about such a life should you like? What things about it should you not like? Perhaps the story will give you new ideas about these questions."

Reading and Study

The Reading Periods

Independent Readers

TEXTS

BEEBY, *America's Roots in the Past*, 196–203.

CHAPMAN, *Stories of Our European Forefathers*, 39–45, 48–57.

CLARK-GORDY, *Westward toward America*, 245–262, 296–298.

KELTY, *How Our Civilization Began*, 309–317.

KNOWLTON and WHEELER, *Our Past in Western Europe*, 97–99, 116–127, 136–142, 147–152 (hard).

Lower Group

The teacher and this group read together the story as given in the text. The teacher directs the silent reading, section by section, by such questions as "How large were the castles?"

Children read silently and answer orally. When they have finished the entire story in this manner, they test themselves by the questions at the end of the story.

MORE DIFFICULT TEXTS

BARKER, DUNCALF, BACON, *Old Europe and Our Nation*, 237–242.
BEARD and BAGLEY, *Our Old World Background*, 124–125.
BOURNE and BENTON, *Introductory American History*, 132–138.
BURNHAM, *Our Beginnings in Europe and America*, 149–155.
COULOMB, MCKINLEY, WHITE, *What Europe Gave to America*, 132–136.
GORDY, *American Beginnings in Europe*, 182–196.
GREENWOOD, *Our Heritage from the Old World*, 196–200.
HALL, *Our Ancestors in Europe*, 217–248.
HALLECK and FRANTZ, *Our Nation's Heritage*, 224–230.
HARDING, *Old World Background to American History*, 180–192.
HAWLEY, *Adventures in Old World History*, 284–289.
HORNE and BUCKS, *Europe, the Mother of America*, 56–65.
NIDA, *Dawn of American History*, 205–217.
SHERWOOD, *Our Country's Beginnings*, 158–162.
SOUTHWORTH, *What the Old World Gave the New*, 107–113.
TAPPAN, *Our European Ancestors*, 110–115.
VOLLINTINE, *The American People and Their Old World Ancestors*, 244–249.
WICKHAM and PHILLIPS, *America's Heritage from the Long Ago*, 267–276.
WOODBURN and HILL, *Historic Background of Our United States*, 192–196.

Easy Reading

EXTENSIVE READING

COFFMAN, *Child's Story of the Human Race*, 227–239, 248–255.
CORKE, *The World's Family*, 135–138.
HILLYER, *Child's History of the World*, 273–277, 278–283.

READING FOR RECREATION

ANDREWS, *Ten Boys Who Lived on the Road from Long Ago to Now* (Gilbert, the Page).
HALL, *Boy's Book of Chivalry*.
POWER, *Boys and Girls of History*, 40–51.
TANNER, *Yesterday's Children*.

More Difficult Reading

EXTENSIVE READING

HARDING, *Story of the Middle Ages*, 158–172.
HARTMAN, *The World We Live in*, 130–134.
MILLER, *Picturesque Tale of Progress*, V: 240–243.
TAPPAN, *When Knights Were Bold*, chaps. i–v.
VAN LOON, *Story of Mankind*, 159–161.

READING FOR RECREATION

FROST, *The Knights of the Round Table*.
LANSING, *Page, Knight, and Esquire*.
MABRY, *Castles in Spain*.
MABRY, *Over the Castle Walls*.
MARK TWAIN, *The Prince and the Pauper*.
MARK TWAIN, *Connecticut Yankee in King Arthur's Court*.
NEWBOLT, *The Book of the Happy Warrior*.
PYLE, *Men of Iron*.
PYLE, *Otto of the Silver Hand*.
ROBIDA, *Treasure of Carcassonne*.
SPYRI, *Jörli*.
STEIN, *Troubadour Tales*.
STEVENSON, *The Black Arrow*.
STODDARD, *Story of Youth*, chap. vi.

The Discussion

Children answer the study-guide questions as completely as possible, questioning one another as to important phases omitted.

The teacher writes on the board the words *moat, drawbridge, armor, falcon, tournament, jousting, chivalry, page, squire, knight.* Children discuss the meanings.

Multisensory Aids

Teacher and children talk over together the pictures in the text, pointing out features of geographical and historical significance.

Audio-visual Materials Obtainable

ARNOLD. Historical Pictures: A. H. P. 15.
Compton's Pictured Teaching Materials: *Middle Ages*, I, Plates II–IX.
International Educational Pictures: Carcassonne, Châteaux of France, Visit to Armor Galleries, Days of Chivalry.
JOHNSTON. Pictures of Social History: 4.
LEHMANN. Colored History Pictures: 2, 3, 4.
LEHMANN. History Pictures: I, L. H. 202, 203, 204, 206.
McKINLEY. Illustrated Topics for Medieval and Modern History: MM 3, 9, 10.
MEINHOLD. Colored History Pictures: 10.
MILLER. *Picturesque Tale of Progress*, V: 240–243.

Music. Glazunov's *Raymonda*; Handel's *Rinaldo*.
Selections from Wagner's *Lohengrin* (illustrating ordeal by battle).
Phonograph records of troubadours, minnesingers, or minstrel songs (see list from phonograph companies).

General Activities

Creative Activities: Group and Individual, Correlated with Other Subjects or Voluntary Projects

The class constructs on the playground, in the corridor, or on the sand table a large-scale model of a medieval castle, based on the picture study. This may serve as the background for a program on the entire unit to be presented before the Parent-Teachers' Association.

The class makes a picture collection of medieval castles and posts it on the bulletin board.

A visit is made to the local museum to observe relics of medieval life.

Boys construct drawbridges for the castle.

Children design decorations for shields.

Volunteers dress dolls in costumes of the Middle Ages.

More Difficult Activities

The class divides into committees to make a study of the weapons and the materials used for warfare in medieval times. See the following topics in the encyclopedia: *Battering-ram, Broadsword, Greek fire, Bow and arrow, Longbow, Crossbow.* If possible, each committee secures a picture to show the class.

The teacher reads to the class the description of an attack on a castle from Scott's *Ivanhoe.*

A committee of boys constructs a complete suit of armor. (See the encyclopedia.) They explain the use of each piece.

A committee reads to the class "Sir Percivale" from Stevenson's *Children's Classics in Dramatic Form* (IV: 163–178).

A committee studies heraldry in the encyclopedia and reports to the class, showing the pictures given.

Someone who understands the game of chess shows the class the boards and men.

The class plans a tournament.[1]

The teacher reads to the class the knight's vow as worded by Tennyson in his *Idylls of the King*, beginning "To break the heathen and uphold the Christ."

A volunteer investigates to find out whether armor was always made of steel. (See the encyclopedia.)

Committees report on the troubadours.

The teacher reads to the class the description of a tournament from Scott's *Ivanhoe*.

Application to Present-Day Conditions

Find out how much ground fifteen acres cover, in order to appreciate the size of a medieval castle.

Why are castles useless in warfare nowadays?

Make a list of some of the famous old castles still in existence. (See the encyclopedia: *Castle*.) If possible, secure a picture of each.

Do you know any family which has a right to use a coat of arms? Do Americans often use such symbols?

How did our custom of raising the hat in greeting originate? [*Knights opened the visors of their helmets to be recognized.*] Of shaking hands? [*This showed that no weapon was concealed in the hand.*]

What was the duty of the lord's steward? Does this explain the origin of our expression *stewardship*?

Do our tournaments today resemble medieval tournaments?

In what way was a knight's vow somewhat like the Boy Scout code?

Are there knights anywhere today?

What does the word *chivalry* mean as used today?

Is there any place near your home which would be a good place for a castle? If so, why?

Exercises in Reasoning

Why was a castle on a hill easier to defend than one on a plain?

Why did the Europeans of the Middle Ages wear wool rather than cotton or linen or silk?

Why was a special breed of horses required to carry knights?

Why did the lord's habits of hunting lead to hatred between lords and serfs?

Why were colors used by the lords who took part in the tournaments?

More Difficult Exercises in Reasoning

Why were the castles damp? Why were they full of bad smells?

Do you think it likely that a lord had a castle on each one of his many fiefs?

What invention made armor useless?

Why was the use of sugar unknown? How could food be kept in the summer when there was no ice?

Why did men of the Middle Ages drink little water?

What things helped to take the place of the newspaper?

[1] See *A Medieval Tournament*, Teacher's Lesson Unit Series, Teachers College, Columbia University.

Do you think medieval tournaments were a civilized form of entertainment? Explain.

Do you think it likely that the knights lived up to all their vows?

Drill Games

Drill cards may be made as follows:

moat	⟷	a ditch filled with water outside the wall of a fort or castle
drawbridge	⟷	a narrow bridge across the moat, to be pulled up when danger came
armor	⟷	a covering of steel to give protection to the body
falcon	⟷	a bird trained to hunt other birds
tournament	⟷	a sham battle between two groups of mounted knights
jousting	⟷	a contest between two knights on horseback
chivalry	⟷	the knightly system of bravery and courtesy
page	⟷	a medieval boy receiving training from the ladies of the court
squire	⟷	a medieval youth receiving training in the arts of war
knight	⟷	a man who has been admitted to the order of chivalry

Children keep a record of the number of mistakes they make in practice; of their mistakes in the class games.

Testing

Tests of Understanding are given in Kelty's *How Our Civilization Began,* p. 308.

Tests of Reasoning and Skills. Underline the best answer:

1. A medieval castle was   a single building.   a group of buildings. a city.

2. The only way to enter the castle was to let down   the drawbridge. the keep.   the moat.   the battlements.

3. To a child of today a medieval castle   would   would not   seem a comfortable place to live.

4. At night, light was supplied by   reeds in melted fat.   lamps. candles.

5. People of the Middle Ages   wrapped their clothing about them. fastened their clothing.   sewed their clothing upon them.

6. The styles of clothing in the Middle Ages   changed slowly.   changed very quickly.

7. People in the Middle Ages   saw many strangers.   saw few strangers. never saw strangers.

8. When a boy was learning the use of weapons, he was a   knight. page.   squire.

Exercise in Organization. Children write the topic headings in the form of an outline and write a few important subheadings under each.

More Difficult Tests

Finish these sentences:

1. The lord did not live all the time in his castle because _ _ _[*the food supply would be used up*]_ _ _ _.

2. The only way to tell who a knight was when he was in full armor was by _ _ _[*his decorations*]_ _ _ _.

3. The tournaments were thought to be very useful because _ _ _[*they gave training for war*]_ _ _ _.

STORY 3.   LIFE AMONG THE SERFS   [*1 Week*

Conversational Approach

"In what ways did we find that a serf differed from a vassal? from a slave? If the lord had not taken him as a serf, what would have become of him? Then, bad as his condition was as a serf, it might have been worse. Did he live in the lord's castle? How did he earn his living?

"Our story today tells us how the serf lived, what work he did, and whether or not he had any pleasures."

Reading and Study

The Reading Periods

Independent Readers

BEEBY, *America's Roots in the Past*, 194–196.
CHAPMAN, *Stories of Our European Forefathers*, 65–67.
CLARK-GORDY, *Westward toward America*, 263–266.
KNOWLTON and WHEELER, *Our Past in Western Europe*, 114–115, 127–135 (hard).

Lower Group

The teacher and this group read together the story as given in the text. The teacher directs the silent reading, section by section, by such questions as "Where did the serfs live?"

Children read silently and answer orally. When they have finished the entire story in this manner, they test themselves by the study-guide questions.

MORE DIFFICULT TEXTS

BARKER, DUNCALF, BACON, *Old Europe and Our Nation*, 287–295.
BEARD and BAGLEY, *Our Old World Background*, 118–123.
BOURNE and BENTON, *Introductory American History*, 115.
BURNHAM, *Our Beginnings in Europe and America*, 146–149, 168–170.
COULOMB, MCKINLEY, WHITE, *What Europe Gave to America*, 174–178.
GORDY, *American Beginnings in Europe*, 197–201.
HALL, *Our Ancestors in Europe*, 249–263.
HALLECK and FRANTZ, *Our Nation's Heritage*, 232–236.
HARDING, *Old World Background to American History*, 193–200.
HAWLEY, *Adventures in Old World History*, 289–297.
HORNE and BUCKS, *Europe, the Mother of America*, 65–72.
NIDA, *Dawn of American History*, 218–228.
SHERWOOD, *Our Country's Beginnings*, 162–166.
SOUTHWORTH, *What the Old World Gave the New*, 113.
TAPPAN, *Our European Ancestors*, 115–119.
VOLLINTINE, *The American People and Their Old World Ancestors*, 244.
WICKHAM and PHILLIPS, *America's Heritage from the Long Ago*, 280.
WOODBURN and HILL, *Historic Background of Our United States*, 196.

Easy Reading

EXTENSIVE READING

COFFMAN, *Child's Story of the Human Race,*
266–269.
HILLYER, *Child's History of the World,* 277.

More Difficult Reading

EXTENSIVE READING

HARDING, *Story of the Middle Ages,* 173–181.
HARTMAN, *The World We Live in,* 134–136.
Rules of the Road (American Council on
Education), 6–17.
TAPPAN, *When Knights Were Bold,* chap. vi.

READING FOR RECREATION

MARSHALL, *Cedric the Forester.*
STEIN, *Little Shepherd of Provence.*

The Discussion

Children answer the study-guide questions as completely as possible. Those who have read widely are given an opportunity to contribute.

The teacher writes on the board the words *manor, three-field system.* Children discuss the meanings.

Multisensory Aids

Children and teacher talk over together the pictures in the text, pointing out features of geographical and historical significance.

AUDIO-VISUAL MATERIALS OBTAINABLE

Compton's Pictured Teaching Material: *Middle Ages,* I, Plates X, XI.
JOHNSTON. Pictures of Social History: 1.
LEHMANN. Colored History Pictures: I, 10.
LEHMANN. Historical Pictures: L. H. 210, 211.

General Activities

Creative Activities: Group and Individual, Correlated with Other Subjects or Voluntary Projects

The class constructs a manor on the sand table.

The class secures very large sheets of wrapping paper. On them they mark hills and creeks, the castle, the church, the village. All the rest of the land they divide into fallow fields, fields for spring planting, fields for fall planting. Each kind is painted a different color. The spring-planting fields are then measured off into strips for the different serfs.

A volunteer committee constructs an interior scene in a serf's home.

The class decides which of the activities they are to use in their program for the Parent-Teachers' Association.

More Difficult Activities

Children interested in farming plan a rotation of crops for a manor, and explain why this system is better than the three-field system.

A volunteer reports on the medieval methods of grinding grain.

The class plans the dramatization of some Bible story which the Church might have used to teach the serfs.

A volunteer reports on the miracle plays.

A volunteer reports on the beginning of the use of chimneys.

A committee makes a picture collection of farm implements used during the Middle Ages.

Application to Present-Day Conditions

Do farmers today ever leave fields fallow? What other means do they use for fertilizing?

How does an American farm differ from the farming land on a manor?

Are cattle ever sheltered today under the same roof as farmers? Does this mean in the same room?

Are farm laborers today better or worse off than serfs in the Middle Ages? Present arguments on both sides.

Whose business is it today to repair the roads?

Exercises in Reasoning

Why is the lord's home on some of the manors called a castle and on others called only a manor house?

Did the serfs live as American farmers do? Explain the difference.

Did the serfs receive any pay for working on the lord's land? Did the lord receive any of the crops raised on the serf's strips?

Where were the cattle and pigs fed?

What kind of road do you suppose serfs would be able to build?

Why did the medieval Church have to teach religion to the serfs by means of dramatization?

Why did the clergymen and the nobles consider themselves much more important than the common people?

More Difficult Exercises in Reasoning

Why were not all the strips given to a serf in one part of the manor?

Since there were no fences, how were the cattle and the poultry kept from wandering about among the growing crops? Does this explain why stories of the Middle Ages had so many references to cowherds, swineherds, goose girls, etc.?

Why was it an advantage for the lord to have all the wheat on the manor ground at his mill, and all the bread baked in his ovens?

Compare tenant farmers of today with serfs.

Can you make a sentence, based on your knowledge of history, telling whether you think the world is growing better or worse than it was in the Middle Ages? Give your reasons why.

Drill Games

These cards are added to those of the preceding stories:

manor	↔	the land and buildings that made up a lord's estate
three-field system	↔	the system of farming used in the Middle Ages

Testing

Tests of Understanding are suggested in Kelty's *How Our Civilization Began*, p. 322.

Tests of Reasoning and Skills

1. All the farm land on a manor was divided into three main parts. These were (1) ___[fallow land]___, (2) ___[land for spring planting]___, (3) ___[land for fall planting]___.

2. Who were the slaves? ___[People who had been captured in war.]___

3. Where in your book can you find material about the three-field system? _____. Where did you look to find out? ___[In the index.]___ Under what word did you look?   *Three* [√]   *Field* [ ]   *System* [ ]

If you had not found it under any of these words, under what other words might you have looked? ___[Farming, Agriculture.]___

Exercise in Organization. Children give an oral summary paragraph of the entire story.

More Difficult Tests

Use your book. List the things a serf and his family had to do for the lord.

> *a.* ___[Work on lord's land.]___
> *b.* ___[Give him part of their crop.]___
> *c.* ___[Make roads.]___
> *d.* ___[Work in his kitchen.]___

STORY 4. THE MONASTERIES AND THEIR WORK   [1 Week

Conversational Approach

"We have learned that there was a priest on each manor. What were his duties?

"The manors and castles, however, were very few and far between. There were not nearly enough of them to take care of all the men who wanted to live a religious life. What do you suppose such people could do?

"Are there any men and women today who are not priests, nor ministers of churches, but who give up their entire lives to the service of religion? What are some such people called? [*Monks and nuns.*] Have you ever seen any of them? How do they dress? What do they do?

"Our stories today are about such people who lived in the Middle Ages."

Reading and Study

The Reading Periods

Independent Readers

TEXTS

BEEBY, *America's Roots in the Past*, 205–212.
CHAPMAN, *Stories of Our European Forefathers*, 58–64.

Lower Group

The teacher and this group read together the story as given in the text. The teacher directs the silent reading, section by section, by such questions as "What

CLARK-GORDY, *Westward toward America,* 268–275, 289–291.
KELTY, *How Our Civilization Began,* 323–328.
KNOWLTON and WHEELER, *Our Past in Western Europe,* 142–147 (hard).

two kinds of churchmen were there in the Middle Ages?"

Children read silently and answer orally. When they have finished the entire story in this manner, they test themselves by the study-guide questions at the end of the story.

MORE DIFFICULT TEXTS

BARKER, DUNCALF, BACON, *Old Europe and Our Nation,* 218–223.
BEARD and BAGLEY, *Our Old World Background,* 130–134.
BOURNE and BENTON, *Introductory American History,* 144–146.
BURNHAM, *Our Beginnings in Europe and America,* 107–108, 155–162.
COULOMB, McKINLEY, WHITE, *What Europe Gave to America,* 136–140.
GORDY, *American Beginnings in Europe,* 208–217.
GREENWOOD, *Our Heritage from the Old World,* 209–213.
HALL, *Our Ancestors in Europe,* 300–316.
HALLECK and FRANTZ, *Our Nation's Heritage,* 138–140, 212–215.
HARDING, *Old World Background to American History,* 213–224.
HAWLEY, *Adventures in Old World History,* 307–333.
HORNE and BUCKS, *Europe, the Mother of America,* 18–20, 77–82.
NIDA, *Dawn of American History,* 143–152.
SHERWOOD, *Our Country's Beginnings,* 170–181.
SOUTHWORTH, *What the Old World Gave the New,* 115–116.
TAPPAN, *Our European Ancestors,* 125–131.
WICKHAM and PHILLIPS, *America's Heritage from the Long Ago,* 296–301.

Easy Reading

EXTENSIVE READING

BEST, *Nations of Western Europe,* 174–183.
COFFMAN, *Child's Story of the Human Race,* 240–247.
HILLYER, *Child's History of the World,* 236–241.

READING FOR RECREATION

MAXWELL, *Story of Books,* 14–19.
POWER, *Boys and Girls of History,* 63–73, 89–111.

More Difficult Reading

EXTENSIVE READING

HARDING, *Story of the Middle Ages,* 195–206.
HARTMAN, *The World We Live in,* 162–166.
ILIN, *Black on White,* 102–114.
MILLER, *Picturesque Tale of Progress,* V: 188–206; VI: 97–103.
O'NEILL, *World's Story,* 209–217, 258–268.
POWER, *Great People of the Past,* 134–144.
TAPPAN, *When Knights Were Bold,* chaps. viii–ix.
VAN LOON, *Story of Mankind,* 219–223.

READING FOR RECREATION

ALDRICH, *Friar Jerome's Beautiful Book.*
HAGEDORN, *Book of Courage,* 53–67.
JEWETT, *God's Troubadour.*
STEARNS, *Story of Music,* 19–25.
STEIN, *Gabriel and the Hour Book.*
WHELDON, *A Little Brother to the Birds.*

The Discussion

Children answer the study-guide questions as completely as possible. Those who have additional material to contribute are reminded to be prepared to give the name of the book in which they found it.

The teacher writes on the board the words *monks, monasteries, abbot, manuscripts, parchment.* Children discuss the meanings.

Multisensory Aids

Children and teacher talk over together the pictures in the text, pointing out features of geographical and historical significance.

Audio-visual Materials Obtainable

Arnold. Historical Pictures: A. H. P. 22.

Compton's Pictured Teaching Materials: *Middle Ages*, I, Plate XII; *Communication*, Plate III, 5.

Copley Prints: The Manuscript Book.

Lehmann. Colored History Pictures: I, 9, 13, 18, 19.

Lehmann. Historical Pictures: L. H. 209, 213, 218, 219.

McKinley. Illustrated Topics for Medieval and Modern History, M M 4.

Miller. *Picturesque Tale of Progress*, V, 188–206; VI, 97–103.

Music. Play records of medieval church music. (See lists from phonograph companies.)

General Activities

Creative Activities: Group and Individual, Correlated with Other Subjects or Voluntary Projects

The class makes a picture collection of monasteries and mounts it on the bulletin board.

The class makes a time schedule of a monk's day.

A trip is made to the local museum or the library to observe handwritten books (manuscripts). Many beautiful pictures are included in some of the encyclopedias under the headings *Book, Manuscript, Book of Kells*, etc.

Children design decorated capital letters.

The class decides which of the activities of this story they will include in their program for the Parent-Teachers' Association.

More Difficult Activities

The class draws a plan of a monastery. (See Thompson's *Economic and Social History of the Middle Ages* for an example.)

Volunteers design title pages for books or for their own stories, decorated like medieval manuscripts.

The teacher may tell the class some stories from *The Canterbury Tales*.

A committee reports on Saint Francis of Assisi.

The teacher reads to the class Longfellow's "Legend Beautiful."

Application to Present-Day Conditions

How does the work of priests differ from that of monks today?

Children report on the present-day work of the Saint Bernard dogs and the monks of the hospice of Saint Bernard in the Swiss Alps. (See the encyclopedia.)

Do any present-day buildings have cloisters?

How are farmers of today taught the principles of better farming? [*Through study of rotation of crops, agricultural colleges, county agents.*]

How are the poor and the homeless cared for today? Where does the money come from?

Are any schools and colleges kept up by churches today?

Are there any monks or nuns in America today?

Were the California missions monasteries?

Exercises in Reasoning

Why did the monastery need a carpenter shop, a blacksmith shop, a brewery, etc.?

Why do you suppose the monks promised never to marry?

About what chronicle have we already read? [*The Anglo-Saxon Chronicle.*] Do you suppose it was written by monks?

Why did not the sons of the lords usually attend the monastery schools?

More Difficult Exercises in Reasoning

Why were most of the monasteries built far out in the country?

Why were there few hotels or inns during the early Middle Ages?

Why were not the unfortunate classes of society cared for by public taxation during the Middle Ages?

In what way are we indebted to the monks for our knowledge of Greek and Roman history?

Have you ever tried to copy a page from a book? Did you make any mistakes? Can you understand, then, how it was very easy for monks to make mistakes in copying Latin books? Do you suppose that they all understood Latin?

Drill Games

These cards are added to those used previously:

monks	⟷	men living under strict rules of religion in a monastery
monasteries	⟷	places where monks live and carry on their work
abbot	⟷	the head of a group of monks in a monastery
manuscript	⟷	material written by hand
parchment	⟷	sheepskin prepared for use in writing

Testing

Tests of Understanding are given in Kelty's *How Our Civilization Began,* pp. 327–328.

Tests of Reasoning and Skills. Fill these blanks with the right words:

1. Two kinds of churchmen in the Middle Ages were (1) ___[*priests in churches*]___ and (2) ___[*monks*]___.

Put a check in the right square:

	Yes	No
2. The monasteries contained only the building in which the monks lived.	[ ]	[√]

3. The monasteries owned thousands of acres of land.   [✓] [ ]

4. The monks were better farmers than the lords.   [✓] [ ]

5. How many stories are there in the unit which you are now reading? _ _ _[*Six.*]_ _ _ Where did you look to find out? _ _ _[*In the table of contents.*]_ _ _

Exercise in Organization. Children copy the topic headings in outline form. They then word a few subheadings for each topic.

More Difficult Tests

Finish these sentences:

1. It was necessary for the monasteries to serve as hotels and hospitals because _ _ _[*no other provision was made for travelers or the unfortunate*]_ _ _.

2. Books were written by hand because _ _ _[*there was no other means of duplicating them*]_ _ _.

3. (Use your books if necessary to make this list.) The monks had promised

a. _ _ _[*to remain poor*]_ _ _.

b. _ _ _[*not to marry*]_ _ _.

c. _ _ _[*to obey their officers*]_ _ _.

STORY 5. TOWN LIFE   [*1 Week*

Conversational Approach

"So far, all the people of the Middle Ages about whom we have read have lived in the country. Why did the Teutonic peoples prefer country life? As they learned Roman ways of living, perhaps they might learn to live in cities also.

"Why do cities grow up in certain places nowadays? Let us see whether any of these same reasons caused cities to grow up in the Middle Ages."

Reading and Study

The Reading Periods

Independent Readers

TEXTS

BEEBY, *America's Roots in the Past*, 212–215.

CHAPMAN, *Stories of Our European Forefathers*, 68–76.

CLARK-GORDY, *Westward toward America*, 276–289, 291–295.

KELTY, *How Our Civilization Began*, 329–339.

KNOWLTON and WHEELER, *Our Past in Western Europe*, 177–198 (hard).

Lower Group

The teacher and this group read together the story as given in the text. The teacher directs the silent reading, section by section, by such questions as "How long after the barbarian invasions were there still no towns?"

Children read silently and answer orally. When they have read the entire story in this manner, they test themselves by the questions at the end of the story.

MORE DIFFICULT TEXTS

BARKER, DUNCALF, BACON, *Old Europe and Our Nation*, 295–302.

BEARD and BAGLEY, *Our Old World Background*, 137–147, 151–158.

BOURNE and BENTON, *Introductory American History*, 138–144, 155–156.

BURNHAM, *Our Beginnings in Europe and America*, 148–149, 171.

GORDY, *American Beginnings in Europe*, 201–206.
GREENWOOD, *Our Heritage from the Old World*, 314–325, 336–350.
HALL, *Our Ancestors in Europe*, 263–295.
HALLECK and FRANTZ, *Our Nation's Heritage*, 208–212, 237–245.
HARDING, *Old World Background to American History*, 202–212.
HAWLEY, *Adventures in Old World History*, 297–304.
HORNE and BUCKS, *Europe, the Mother of America*, 72–77, 82–85.
NIDA, *Dawn of American History*, 230–242.
SHERWOOD, *Our Country's Beginnings*, 166–169.
SOUTHWORTH, *What the Old World Gave the New*, 113–114.
TAPPAN, *Our European Ancestors*, 119–123.
VOLLINTINE, *The American People and Their Old World Ancestors*, 249–256, 263–266.
WICKHAM and PHILLIPS, *America's Heritage from the Long Ago*, 282–293, 302–304.
WOODBURN and HILL, *Historic Background of Our United States*, 196–201.

Easy Reading

EXTENSIVE READING

COFFMAN, *Child's Story of the Human Race*, 269–282.
HILLYER, *Child's History of the World*, 304–310.

READING FOR RECREATION

BROWN, *John of the Woods*.
POWER, *Boys and Girls of History*, 74–88.
TANNER, *Yesterday's Children*.

More Difficult Reading

EXTENSIVE READING

HAPPOLD, *The Adventure of Man*.
HARDING, *Story of the Middle Ages*, 182–194.
HARTMAN, *The World We Live in*, 136–140, 148–150.
MILLER, *Picturesque Tale of Progress*, V: 244–249; VI: 76–95.
TAPPAN, *When Knights Were Bold*, chaps. x–xv.
VAN LOON, *Story of Mankind*, 174–183.

READING FOR RECREATION

GANDY, *In the Days of Lion-Heart*.
LAMPREY, *In the Days of the Guild*.
LAMPREY, *Masters of the Guild*.
LOUNSBERG, *Boy Knight of Rheims*.
MULLER, *How They Carried the Goods*, 125–140.
RAYNER, *Famous Cathedrals* (pictures).

The Discussion

Children answer the study-guide questions as completely as possible. Are they by this time answering habitually in their own words rather than in the language of the book?

The teacher writes on the board the words *burgher, cathedral, craft guild, merchant guild, apprentice, master craftsman, fair, Romanesque, Gothic*. Children discuss the meanings.

Multisensory Aids

Children and teacher talk over together the pictures in the text, pointing out the features of geographical and historical significance.

AUDIO-VISUAL MATERIALS OBTAINABLE

Compton's Pictured Teaching Materials: *Middle Ages*, II, Plates II–VI, IX; *Trade*, Plate IV, 2, 3, 4.
EASTMAN. Educational Slides: 402.
International Educational Pictures: Heidelberg and the Neckar Valley, Thousand-Year-Old Cities, Windows of Art.
LANGL. Colored History Pictures: Gothic Monuments.
LEHMANN. Colored History Pictures: I, 6, 7, 8, 22, 23.

LEHMANN. Historical Pictures: L. H. 207, 208, 217, 222, 223.
McKINLEY. Illustrated Topics for Medieval and Modern History: M M 6, 10, 19.
MEINHOLD. Colored History Pictures: 11.
MILLER. *Picturesque Tale of Progress*, V, 244–249; VI, 76–95.

A cutout medieval house may be secured from the Educational Department, University Museum, Philadelphia.

Music. The music of early folk dances, morris dances, etc.
Selections from Wagner's *Meistersinger.* (The teacher tells the story.)
Records of organ music written for cathedral use.

General Activities

Creative Activities: Group and Individual, Correlated with Other Subjects or Voluntary Projects

Volunteers draw pictures of walled towns.
If any industry in the city uses the apprentice system, the class makes a visit to observe it.
Volunteers write letters which a visitor to a market or fair may have written to his home in the country, describing the interesting sights he has seen.
A committee constructs a market scene on a miniature stage.
The class makes a picture collection of great cathedrals.
The art teacher gives a lesson on Rosa Bonheur's "Horse Fair."
A visitor to a European country describes market day to the class.
The class decides which of these activities they will use in their program for the meeting of the Parent-Teachers' Association.

More Difficult Activities

Volunteers report on the duties of watchmen in the Middle Ages.
The class dramatizes the meeting in which the burghers buy self-government for their city from the lord. The chief matters agreed upon are written down in a charter.
A committee reports on the Black Death.
Students who have studied American history may report on the cattle fairs of New Netherland.
Volunteers model small gargoyles in clay.
Committees make drawings comparing features of Romanesque architecture with Gothic architecture.
A visitor to Peiping describes the names of some of the streets: Jade Street, Embroidery Street, etc. The class compares these names with those of streets in medieval Europe.
Volunteers design signs or seals for different guilds.

Application to Present-Day Conditions

Are manufacture and trade still the main reasons why cities exist?
Why did your own city grow up just where it did?
Does your own city have self-government? Did it have to buy this right? What form of government has your city?
Does your city have a charter? If so, where did it get this charter?

Are craft guilds at all like labor unions? Are merchant guilds like our manufacturers' associations? Do labor unions today try to punish their members who do poor work?

How do boys and girls today prepare themselves for their lifework?

What does the word *masterpiece* mean as used today?

Why is Carpenter's Hall, Philadelphia, so called?

Are there any craftsmen in your city?

Are there any Gothic buildings in your city? any Gothic arches?

Is every large and beautiful church a cathedral?

Do any people's names today suggest the trade that their ancestors may have followed? [*Baker, Smith, Fuller, Weaver, Wright, Carpenter, Taylor.*]

Exercises in Reasoning

How were some serfs able to earn money enough to buy their freedom?

Why would peddlers rather settle down at a crossroads than to lead a wandering life?

Why were the lords always in need of money? Why was this a good thing for the burghers?

What health conditions must have resulted from the conditions of the streets?

Compare the period of apprenticeship of the craftsman with the period during which a lord's son was page and esquire.

Why were the merchants and craftsmen called the middle class?

More Difficult Exercises in Reasoning

Make a list of the influences, mentioned in your geography, which caused cities to grow up.

Where was all early manufacturing carried on? Does this explain why such a system is called domestic manufacture?

Why was it dangerous for a serf to run away?

Why did medieval cities not grow very large?

Do you think that men of the Middle Ages knew about germs? What makes you think so?

How did the medieval fairs differ from our county and state fairs?

Why did workmen of the Middle Ages take such great care of even the parts of their work that no one would ever see?

Should such great sums of money be spent for cathedrals? Give arguments on both sides.

Drill Games

Cards may be made as follows:

burgher	⟷	a well-to-do citizen of a medieval town
cathedral	⟷	a large church where a bishop holds his services
craft guild	⟷	a group of persons working in the same trade
merchant guild	⟷	a group of persons engaged in buying and selling
fair	⟷	a large market of the Middle Ages
Gothic	⟷	a style of building which uses the pointed arch

Testing

Tests of Understanding are given in Kelty's *How Our Civilization Began*, p. 339.

Tests of Reasoning and Skills. Mark the following as true or false:

True False

[√] [ ] 1. There were very few cities at the beginning of the Middle Ages.

[ ] [√] 2. There were no traders in the early Middle Ages.

[√] [ ] 3. Some serfs were able to buy their freedom.

[√] [ ] 4. Cities grew up where highways crossed.

[ ] [√] 5. Most of the lords gave the cities the right of self-government.

[ ] [√] 6. Serfs never ran away.

[√] [ ] 7. Disease was very common in the towns.

[ ] [√] 8. Medieval cities were very large.

[ ] [√] 9. Any man without training could enter any trade.

[√] [ ] 10. The goods at the fairs were for sale.

Exercise in Organization. Children make a list of the topic headings and give a topical recitation on each.

More Difficult Tests

Mark the following as true or false:

True False

[√] [ ] 1. The charter told what rights the citizens in the town had.

[√] [ ] 2. Citizens in the towns could elect their own officers.

[ ] [√] 3. Every freeman in the town could take part in the government.

[√] [ ] 4. The people who followed the same business lived in the same street.

[ ] [√] 5. The craft guilds were formed by men engaged in commerce.

[ ] [√] 6. The merchant guilds were formed by men engaged in skilled handwork.

[√] [ ] 7. The middle class did not have as many rights as the lords.

[ ] [√] 8. Townspeople bought their food supplies in stores as we do.

[√] [ ] 9. A fair was larger than a market.

[ ] [√] 10. The cathedrals were built by the government.

[√] [ ] 11. Gothic arches are pointed in shape.

STORY 6. THE RENAISSANCE   [1 Week

Conversational Approach

"As time went on, the matters about which we have been reading began to make great changes in men's thinking. Men were no longer satisfied to spend all their lives in one place, working hard and doing just as they were told.

"Why would trading in such goods as silk and spices naturally make the men of Europe begin to think and wonder? Why would governing some of their own towns make them depend more on themselves and less on their lords and churchmen?

"When a grown person tells you that you must not do a certain thing, would you rather have him say, 'You must not do it because I say so' or 'You must not do it because . . . ,' and then go on and give you the reason? Why?

"Men of the Middle Ages began at last to want to ask why in regard to the reasons for things in general. They had a hard time. The main reason why they did things was because they always had. No one knew the reasons.

"Of all the people that we have studied so far, which have been the clearest thinkers? Which have answered best their own questions about the world? The men of the Middle Ages now were so like the Greeks in their desire to learn reasons that it seemed as if the Greek spirit had been born again in the bodies of these men who lived so many hundreds of years later. Our story today is about how this spirit, or habit of thinking, was born again."

Reading and Study

The Reading Periods

Independent Readers

TEXTS

CHAPMAN, *Stories of Our European Fore-fathers*, 89–92.

CLARK-GORDY, *Westward toward America*, 332–339.

KELTY, *How Our Civilization Began*, 340–345.

KNOWLTON and WHEELER, *Our Past in Western Europe*, 198–212 (hard).

Lower Group

The teacher and this group read together the story as given in the text. The teacher directs the silent reading, section by section, by such questions as "What changes were taking place among the nobles? among the middle class? among the serfs? among the kings? When did these changes begin to appear clearly?"

Children read silently and answer orally. When they have finished the entire story in this manner, they test themselves by the questions at the end of the story.

OTHER BOOKS

TERRY, *History Stories of Other Lands*, I: 80–88.

MORE DIFFICULT TEXTS

BARKER, DUNCALF, BACON, *Old Europe and Our Nation*, 332–346.

BEARD and BAGLEY, *Our Old World Background*, 147–150, 182, 186–191, 199–202.

BOURNE and BENTON, *Introductory American History*, 146–152.

BURNHAM, *Our Beginnings in Europe and America*, 170–174, 196–207.

COULOMB, McKINLEY, WHITE, *What Europe Gave to America*, 181–190.

GREENWOOD, *Our Heritage from the Old World*, 314–325, 359–363.

HALL, *Our Ancestors in Europe*, 336–337.

HALLECK and FRANTZ, *Our Nation's Heritage*, 251–259.

HARDING, *Old World Background to American History*, 249–256.

HAWLEY, *Adventures in Old World History*, 351–363.

HORNE and BUCKS, *Europe, the Mother of America*, 105–116.

NIDA, *Dawn of American History*, 323–332, 343–383.

NIVER, *Old World Steps to American History*, 227–235.
VOLLINTINE, *The American People and Their Old World Ancestors*, 289–296, 302–304, 306–314.
WICKHAM and PHILLIPS, *America's Heritage from the Long Ago*, 344–348, 356–361.
WOODBURN and HILL, *Historic Background of Our United States*, 264–267.

Easy Reading

EXTENSIVE READING

COFFMAN, *Child's Story of the Human Race*, 294–301.
HILLYER, *Child's History of the World*, 322–326, 333–336, 359–364.
SCHWARTZ, *From Then till Now*, 237–271.

READING FOR RECREATION

MAXWELL, *Story of Books*, 24–43.
POWER, *Boys and Girls of History*.

More Difficult Reading

EXTENSIVE READING

CHANDLER, *Story Lives of Master Artists*, 56–93, 167–185.
HAAREN and POLAND, *Famous Men of the Middle Ages*.
HARDING, *Story of the Middle Ages*, 245–256.
HARTMAN, *The World We Live in*, 166–177.
HORNE and SCOBEY, *Stories of Great Artists*.
ILIN, *Black on White*, 115–129.
MILLER, *Picturesque Tale of Progress*, VI: 237–269.
NIDA, *Early Men of Science*.
O'NEILL, *World's Story*, 292–301.
POWER, *Great People of the Past*, 197–207.
STEEDMAN, *Knights of Art* (pictures).
VAN LOON, *Story of Mankind*, 191–218.
WHITCOMB, *Young People's Story of Art*.

READING FOR RECREATION

BRYANT, *Children's Book of Celebrated Buildings*.
CONWAY, *Children's Book of Art*.
GIBSON, *The Goldsmith of Florence*.
HAGEDORN, *Book of Courage*, 81–88.
LANSING, *Magic Gold*.
SCALES, *Boys of the Ages*, 116–138.
STEARNS, *Story of Music*, 25–36.
STUART, *The Boy through the Ages*.

The Discussion

Children answer the study-guide questions as fully as possible. The teacher studies the answers carefully, to detect misapprehensions and half-comprehensions.

The teacher writes on the board the words *Renaissance, modern*. Children discuss the meanings.

Multisensory Aids

Children and teacher talk over together the pictures in the text, pointing out the features of geographical and historical significance.

AUDIO-VISUAL MATERIALS OBTAINABLE

Compton's Pictured Teaching Materials: *Middle Ages*, II, Plate X.
International Educational Pictures: Historical Episode in the Life of Michael Angelo, Story of Raphael's Masterpiece, Making of a Stained Glass Window, Life of Dante.
LANGL. Colored History Pictures: Renaissance Monuments.
LEHMANN. Colored History Pictures: I, 16, 20, 28.
LEHMANN. Historical Pictures: L. H. 212.
McKINLEY. Illustrated Topics for Medieval and Modern History: M M 11.

MILLER. *Picturesque Tale of Progress*, VI, 237–269.
Society for Visual Education (BRIGGS). The Renaissance.
Society for Visual Education. Picturol: Artists of the Renaissance (2).

Music. Play compositions of Palestrina; Diaz's *Benvenuto Cellini*.

General Activities

Creative Activities: Group and Individual, Correlated with Other Subjects or Voluntary Projects

The art teacher helps to plan the study of Renaissance art. Some possibilities are the study of Raphael, Michelangelo, Titian. The lives of the painters and their masterpieces are studied.

The music teacher assists in the selection of materials appropriate to the study of Renaissance music.

The science teacher helps to plan the study of Renaissance science. Some possibilities are the study of the telescope and the microscope, the building of the first cannon, and gunpowder.

The class decides which of the activities it will include in the program to be given before the Parent-Teachers' Association.

More Difficult Activities

A committee studies and explains the main outlines of the Copernican theory.

The art teacher helps to plan the further study of Renaissance art; for example, the work of Benvenuto Cellini and Leonardo da Vinci.

Committees report on the history of the organ and the violin.

A committee studies the method of work proposed by Roger Bacon.

The art teacher demonstrates the use of oil paints.

Application to Present-Day Conditions

What were the most conspicuous and beautiful buildings in the towns of the Middle Ages? What buildings are the largest and most striking in the towns of today? What is the reason for the change?

Are some people today almost as much opposed to new ideas or to change as the people of the Middle Ages? Give examples.

Does the spirit of the Renaissance offer any explanation to you of why schools study history?

Exercises in Reasoning

In what ways was it true that the men of the Middle Ages thought more of the life to come in the next world than of life in this world? In what ways is it shown that modern men think more of life in this world?

Why did Renaissance people admire the Greeks so greatly?

More Difficult Exercises in Reasoning

The class makes a tabulation of changes occurring from the Middle Ages to the modern age in the various classes of society, as follows:

Class	During Middle Ages	During Modern Age
King	Weak	Strong
Nobles	In control	Less powerful
Clergy	Very powerful	Control of spiritual matters only
Middle class	Few rights	Very powerful
Serfs	In bondage	Freed

Why should you expect the spirit of the Renaissance to lead to great struggles in religion and government?

At what other periods besides the Renaissance have we read of a great flowering of art? [*The Age of Pericles in Greece; the Age of Augustus in Rome.*]

Drill Games

Cards may be made as follows:

modern history	↔	the period following the Middle Ages
Renaissance	↔	a new birth of the spirit of searching for truth

Games are played with all the cards used during the unit.

Testing

Tests of Understanding are suggested in Kelty's *How Our Civilization Began*, p. 344.

Tests of Reasoning and Skills. Check the best answer:

1. The spirit of the age began to change in about the year   √ 1200. 1300.   1500.

2. The Middle Ages had been most interested in   the life on this earth at present.   √ the life to come, beyond the grave.

3. The spirit of the Renaissance led to   keeping things as they were. going back to copy older peoples.   √ improvements along many lines.

Exercise in Organization. Children make their own summary sentences.

More Difficult Tests

Check the best answer:

1. During the Middle Ages men's thinking was done   by themselves. √ by those in power over them.   by the ancient Greeks.

2. Renaissance men were greatly interested in the Greeks because the Greeks   had taught the Romans who conquered them.   had produced better artists than any other people.   √ had tried to find out the reasons for things.

Tests on the Entire Unit

Tests on Historical Terms. Pass mimeographed sheets of the following:

I. Here is a list of historical terms. Put each in the right blank in the sentences below:

fief	monks	feudalism	three-field plan
drawbridge	burgher	moat	abbot
manor	modern		

1. Something that has happened in recent times is _____.

2. A well-to-do citizen of a town was a _____.

3. A _____ was land granted to a vassal by an overlord.

4. Men who lived and worked in monasteries were _____.

5. The _____ was let down to allow people to enter a castle.

6. Each of a lord's estates was a _____.

7. The chief officer of a monastery was the _____.

8. The plan by which two fields were planted at different times during the year while the third field rested was the _____.

9. The _____ was a ditch filled with water, around the walls of a castle.

10. The plan by which land was granted to a man if he would fight for the owner was _____.

II. Here is another list. Do the same.

squire	armor	serf	manuscript
Renaissance	monasteries	falcon	fair
vassal	craft guilds		

1. The unions of men in the same trade were _____.

2. The "new birth" of the desire to find out the reasons for things was the _____.

3. A _____ was a great meeting of buyers and sellers.

4. A man who had to work for some lord and who could not leave the estate was a _____.

5. Places where monks lived were _____.

6. Heavy covering to protect the body in fighting was _____.

7. A _____ was a bird taught to hunt.

8. Anything written by hand is a _____.

9. A _____ was a man who held land under someone else.

10. A young man being trained to use weapons was a _____.

III. Here is another list. Do the same.

overlord	merchant guild	chivalry	cathedral
tournament	jousting	page	knight
parchment	Gothic		

1. A trained man admitted to the order of chivalry was a _____.
2. A man who granted some of his land to a vassal was an _____.
3. The type of building which uses the pointed arch is _____.
4. A _____ was a contest between two groups of knights.
5. A _____ was a church where a bishop held his services.
6. Sheepskin carefully scraped and polished is _____.
7. The system, or order, to which knights were admitted was _____.
8. A _____ was an association of men who sold goods.
9. A young boy being trained by the ladies of his overlord was a _____.
10. _____ was exhibition fighting between two knights.

Test of Comprehension

Check the best answer:

1. Feudalism was a good thing during the early Middle Ages because it   ended the Roman Empire.   made the nobles strong.   kept the kings weak.   √ helped to bring about order.

2. The castles had to be built very strong because   the castles were to last for centuries.   the lord wanted to live in great style.   √ the lord had to protect all his vassals.   the castles were built on hilltops.

3. The best thing about the three-field system was that it   √ allowed part of the land to rest.   divided up the lord's land.   gave little work for the serfs to do.   allowed hunters to ride over the fields.

4. The monasteries were a great help during the Middle Ages because they   gave homes for the monks.   √ gave help to the poor and homeless.   did not have to pay any taxes.   were built far out in the country.

5. Some of the towns in the Middle Ages won the right of self-government by   asking for it from the churchmen.   declaring themselves independent.   fighting against the town's enemies.   √ buying it from the lord of the land.

6. The thing which brought the Renaissance was the new birth of the habit of   √ asking the reasons why things happened.   studying the ways of Greek living.   painting many beautiful pictures.   sailing on voyages of discovery.

7. Each vassal who received land from a lord had to agree   to give up some of his land.   to live in a castle.   √ to fight for the lord.   to have many serfs.

8. The order of chivalry was a good thing because it   made the knight proud of his sword.   √ made the knight promise to live right.   gave the knight an interesting life.   gave the knight lands and castle.

9. A serf was not a slave, because he   √ could not be sold away from the manor.   could not be made to work on the manor.   was a white man and not colored.   was allowed to work on the roads.

10. The monks copied many books by hand because   printed books cost too much.   handwritten books were beautiful.   there were many monks to keep busy.   √ there was no other way to get books.

11. Men in the same trade formed craft guilds to   control the boys who were being trained.   √ control the production of their kind of goods. furnish enough work for all workmen.   furnish supplies of all the goods needed.

12. Markets and fairs were needed during the Middle Ages because   the people had no other regular amusements.   there were no other ways of telling time.   √ there were no regular stores in which to buy goods.   the people did not raise any of their own food.

13. What is the title of the unit which you have just finished reading?

In order to test whether or not the objective "an interest in history" has been attained, the teacher may supply the children with a list of all the school subjects they are studying and ask them to rate the subjects by putting the figure *1* before that which they like best, the figure *2* before that which they like second-best, and so on. A tabulation of the results should give the teacher some indication of the success achieved.

Appendix

List of Names and Addresses of Firms Supplying the Illustrative Materials Mentioned under Audio-visual Materials Obtainable

Arnold History Pictures: A. J. Nystrom Co., Chicago, or Denoyer-Geppert Co., Chicago.
Black Wall Pictures: A. J. Nystrom Co., Chicago.
Compton's Pictured Teaching Materials: F. E. Compton Co., Chicago.
Copley Prints, Copley Co., 221 Columbus Ave., Boston.
Cybulski Pictures: A. J. Nystrom Co., Chicago.
Eastman Educational Slides, Iowa City, Iowa.
Engleder History Pictures: A. J. Nystrom Co., Chicago.
Gall-Rebhann Charts: A. J. Nystrom Co., Chicago.
GRANT, *Story of the Ship*: McLoughlin Bros., Springfield, Massachusetts.
Gurlitt History Pictures: A. J. Nystrom Co., Chicago.
Hoffmann-Schmidt Pictures: A. J. Nystrom Co., Chicago.
International Educational Pictures, 40 Mount Vernon St., Boston.
Johnston, Pictures of Social History: A. J. Nystrom Co., Chicago.
Jöndl Ancient History Charts: A. J. Nystrom Co., Chicago.
Keystone Views: Keystone View Co., Meadville, Pennsylvania.
Langl Colored History Pictures: A. J. Nystrom Co., Chicago.
Lehmann Colored History Pictures: A. J. Nystrom Co., Chicago.
Lehmann Geography Pictures: Denoyer-Geppert Co., Chicago.
Lehmann History Pictures: Denoyer-Geppert Co., Chicago.
Lohmeyer History Pictures: A. J. Nystrom Co., Chicago.
Longmans History Pictures: Longmans, Green & Co., New York, or A. J. Nystrom
    Co., Chicago.
McKinley Illustrated Topics: McKinley Publishing Co., Philadelphia.
Meinhold Colored History Pictures: A. J. Nystrom Co., Chicago.
MILLER, *Picturesque Tale of Progress*: Book House for Children, Chicago.
National Geographic Magazine, National Geographic Society, Washington, D.C.
Society for Visual Education, 327 South La Salle St., Chicago.
Viaduct History Pictures: A. J. Nystrom Co., Chicago.
Yale Pageant Educational Slides, 736 South Wabash Ave., Chicago.

INDEX